THE BIBLICAL RESOURCE SERIES

Published Volumes

Richard A. Burridge, *What Are the Gospels? A Comparison
with Graeco-Roman Biography,* Second Edition

John J. Collins, *The Apocalyptic Imagination,* Second Edition

John J. Collins, *Between Athens and Jerusalem:
Jewish Identity in the Hellenistic Diaspora,* Second Edition

Frank Moore Cross Jr. and David Noel Freedman,
Studies in Ancient Yahwistic Poetry

Roland de Vaux, *Ancient Israel: Its Life and Institutions*

S. R. Driver, *A Treatise on the Use of the Tenses in Hebrew
and Some Other Syntactical Questions*

Joseph A. Fitzmyer, *The Semitic Background of the New Testament*
Volume I: *Essays on the Semitic Background of the New Testament*
Volume II: *A Wandering Aramean: Collected Aramaic Essays*

Joseph A. Fitzmyer, *To Advance the Gospel,* Second Edition

Birger Gerhardsson, *Memory and Manuscript* and
Tradition and Transmission in Early Christianity

Hermann Gunkel, *Creation and Chaos in the Primeval Era and the Eschaton:
A Religio-Historical Study of Genesis 1 and Revelation 12*

Richard B. Hays, *The Faith of Jesus Christ:
The Narrative Substructure of Galatians 3:1–4:11,* Second Edition

Colin J. Hemer, *The Letters to the Seven Churches of Asia
in Their Local Setting*

Sigmund Mowinckel, *The Psalms in Israel's Worship*

Sigmund Mowinckel, *He That Cometh: The Messiah Concept
in the Old Testament and Later Judaism*

Anthony J. Saldarini, *Pharisees, Scribes, and Sadducees in Palestinian Society*

Mark S. Smith, *The Early History of God: Yahweh and the Other Deities
in Ancient Israel,* Second Edition

Samuel Terrien, *Till the Heart Sings: A Biblical Theology
of Manhood and Womanhood*

ἰδοὺ ποιῶ τὰ ἔσχατα ὡς τὰ πρῶτα
[*idou poiō ta eschata hōs ta prōta*
("Behold, I make the last things like the first things.")]

EPISTLE OF BARNABAS 6:13

CREATION AND CHAOS
IN THE PRIMEVAL ERA
AND THE ESCHATON

A Religio-Historical Study
of Genesis 1 and Revelation 12

Hermann Gunkel

with contributions by
Heinrich Zimmern

Translated by
K. William Whitney Jr.

WILLIAM B. EERDMANS PUBLISHING COMPANY
GRAND RAPIDS, MICHIGAN / CAMBRIDGE, U.K.

Originally published in German as *Schöpfung und Chaos in Urzeit und Endzeit: Eine religionsgeschichtliche Untersuchung über Gen. 1 und Ap. Jon 12;* © Vandenhoeck & Ruprecht, Göttingen, Germany, 1895 (1921).

English translation © 2006 K. William Whitney Jr.

Published 2006 by Wm. B. Eerdmans Publishing Co.
2140 Oak Industrial Drive N.E., Grand Rapids, Michigan 49505 /
P.O. Box 163, Cambridge CB3 9PU U.K.

Library of Congress Cataloging-in-Publication Data

Gunkel, Hermann, 1862-1932.
    [Schöpfung und Chaos in Urzeit und Endzeit. English]
    Creation and chaos in the primeval era and the eschaton: a religio-historical study
of Genesis 1 and Revelation 12 / Hermann Gunkel, with contributions by
Heinrich Zimmern; translated by K. William Whitney, Jr.
        p.   cm.
    Includes bibliographical references and index.
    ISBN-10: 0-8028-2804-3 / ISBN-13: 978-0-8028-2804-0
    1. Bible. O.T. Genesis I — Criticism, interpretation, etc. 2. Bible. N.T. Revelation XII —
Criticism, interpretation, etc.   I. Zimmern, Heinrich, 1862-1931.   II. Title.

BS1235.52.G8613   2006
222'.1106 — dc22

                                                          2006010896

www.eerdmans.com

Contents

REVELATION 12: CREATION IN THE END TIME

Foreword

The appearance of this English translation of Hermann Gunkel's *Schöpfung und Chaos in Urzeit und Endzeit* is an event in biblical studies. By common acknowledgment Gunkel's volume is one of the great classics of the modern critical study of the Bible, both Old Testament and New. First published in its German original in 1895, it was reprinted unchanged in 1921, yet unlike the rest of Gunkel's major works — and some minor as well — it was never translated into a foreign language. The rest all appeared in English and, in a few cases, in other languages over the course of the twentieth century,[1] but up to now there has been only a rather abridged rendering of the first part, dealing with Genesis 1 and its proposed Babylonian antecedent, in an anthology.[2]

William Whitney thus deserves our sincere thanks for his devoted labors in presenting Gunkel's classic, finally, in its full form. The task was a challenging one, and Whitney has succeeded not only in producing a careful translation but also in clarifying the many references to primary and secondary literature that Gunkel, in the convention of his time and place, cites in highly abbreviated fashion, without supplying a key to their complete form. Since a number of these references are to studies that are rarely noticed in contemporary discussions, Whitney's success in tracking down virtually all of them and providing for them a full bibliography is especially welcome, as is his effort to enlarge the rather parsimonious index in the original German volume so as to embrace all biblical and other texts to which Gunkel refers, all scholars mentioned, and the principal topics discussed. When these additions are joined to Whitney's long introduction, laying out the main arguments and contributions of Gunkel's volume, together with something of its background, it is plain that the present edition will be of value not simply to readers who cannot understand the original German, but even to those who can.

Creation and Chaos, as Whitney makes plain, is about the history of a particular mythological motif in some of the literatures of the ancient Near East, namely, the cosmic conflict between the forces, or, more precisely, the deities, of chaos and order. Taking as his central focus the treatment of this motif in the Old and New Testaments, preeminently in Genesis 1 and Revelation (Apocalypse) 12, Gunkel proposes that this treatment formed a single biblical tradition. Its matrix he finds in the ancient Babylonian myth of cosmic and human creation, represented most completely in the composition called Enuma Elish, which began to be edited and translated only in the two decades before Gunkel published his book. This myth, Gunkel argues, underlay the treatment of creation in Genesis 1 as well as in other Old Testament texts, whose authors considerably modified it to suit their views of their god, Yahweh, and his control of creation. In turn, the author of Revelation 12 and related chapters not only fastened onto this Old Testament usage and its extension in Second Temple Judaism but also in some way went back to the Babylonian mythic tradition itself in order to describe the final period of history that was to usher in the eschatological age. Central to this period, as Revelation lays it out, was the revival of the cosmic forces or monsters of chaos/evil, after their defeat in the primeval drama of creation, and then their renewed battle with the God of order/good, who this time brought upon them a final, irrevocable destruction, so allowing his eschatological kingdom to reign in perpetuity in the universe.

Gunkel's view of this combat tradition — or what he labels the chaos tradition — in the Bible and Babylonia was not entirely new. General interest in the Babylonian, and, more broadly, the Mesopotamian, background to biblical culture had been given a decisive boost in 1872-75, thus twenty years before Creation and Chaos was published, by George Smith's discovery and publication of a Babylonian account of the primeval flood, whose remarkable similarities to the biblical account in Genesis 6–8 Smith then discussed in a volume on the subject.[3] By the 1880s, when Gunkel became a university student, Assyriology was a going concern in the universities and academies of Europe and North America, though Gunkel himself did not pursue it at first, being focused on the New Testament for his doctorate at Göttingen, which entailed, of course, work in the Old Testament as well. But Gunkel's association at Göttingen with the "history of religions school" — see William Whitney's introduction to the present volume for an extensive discussion — sensitized him to the wider field of ancient religions and their impact on the biblical communities. And he made good on that wider vision when he left Göttingen in 1889, after the completion of his degree, to teach at the University of Halle, shifting in the process his focus from New to Old Testament. At Halle, Gunkel met as a faculty colleague the Assyriologist Heinrich Zimmern, one of the principal students of arguably the leading Assyriologist of the day, Friedrich Delitzsch. Zimmern, like virtually every Assyriologist of the period, was well acquainted with the Bible and biblical studies and particularly interested in its connections to Mesopotamia. He not only brought Gunkel into his field but also assisted him with the Babylonian portion of *Creation and Chaos*, and translated for inclusion in that volume *Enuma Elish* and other Mesopotamian mythic texts.[4]

Gunkel, it should be said, was not the only scholar of the period who was interested in the relevance of *Enuma Elish* to the Bible. W. G. Lambert[5] has drawn attention to two others who anticipated some of Gunkel's work, T. K. Cheyne and G. A. Barton. The latter is mentioned in *Creation and Chaos*, but his article is not fully engaged though at one point it is criticized for mixing "significant insights . . . with outlandish ideas."[6] Yet as J. Day has observed,[7] Gunkel probably started working on this combat tradition independently of Barton — Barton's article on the subject being published only in 1893, just a year before Gunkel concluded his *Creation and Chaos* (his preface to it is dated October 1894). More importantly, when one compares *Creation and Chaos* with Cheyne's and Barton's publications, it is easy to see that, in the depth, range, and subtlety of his examination, Gunkel goes well beyond them.[8]

The value of *Creation and Chaos*, indeed, is not only its treatment of the mythic combat motif. It is also that, with the combat motif as a case study, Gunkel was able to demonstrate the importance of myth as a fundamental category in the religions of the ancient Near East, including that of biblical Israel. More particularly, he showed that apocalyptic thought, whose core is the final battle of order and chaos ushering in the eschatological kingdom, was not a crazy, aberrant phenomenon in Second Temple Judaism and early Christianity. It was, rather, something with deep roots in ancient Near Eastern religions, more particularly in what Gunkel perceived as the cosmogonic conception basic to them; and it attempted, then, to resolve the theological challenges posed by this cosmogony.

Creation and Chaos is also significant as an exercise in comparative literary analysis: to construct the history of a particular literary theme or motif, as expressed in a particular narrative form, across several related cultures in time and space. This approach Gunkel called "tradition history" — he used the German term *Überlieferungsgeschichte* — and anticipated thereby, as Douglas Knight has noted,[9] the more fully developed usage of the term, for which he is largely responsible, in biblical studies. The heart of Gunkel's approach in *Creation and Chaos* is exegesis: coaxing out of a group of texts the language and motifs that connect them. The two parts of the volume are arranged in the same way, starting from a base text, Genesis 1 in the first part and Revelation 12 in the second, and seeking to understand by close reading what each says, that is, what its motifs mean. Gunkel demonstrates that in each text the motifs often appear as fragments, not fully expounded nor coherently integrated, and thus cannot really be understood within the contexts of these two texts alone. The motifs, and the texts themselves, must rather be linked up with related motifs elsewhere in the Old and the New Testaments. But even these Testaments, Gunkel argues, do not supply the full context for understanding the motifs; and so we are forced outside, to other Jewish and Christian texts, but ultimately behind them all to another culture, Mesopotamia, and to what Gunkel regards as the Mesopotamian base text for creation, *Enuma Elish*, where the motifs not only occur but occur in the full and connected context that he has been seeking. In the course of this exegetical sleuthing, it should be noted, Gunkel pays attention not only to the particularities of language and literary form in which the motifs are formulated; he also asks the question — though extensive examination would come only later in such publications as his commentary on Genesis — whether and when these formulations, in their compositional history, were in poetry or prose, in oral or written mode. The important point in all of this is clear: for Gunkel, internal analysis of an ancient text must be balanced by external comparison with analogues elsewhere in its environment. Such an approach is necessary because Gunkel believed, in concert with many of his contemporaries, that to understand the meaning of a text, its language and motifs, is to understand first where they came from. It is not enough, indeed it is misleading, to focus simply on the individual text alone, as though it were a completely independent, free creation of its author. The text must rather be seen as one link in a complex chain of tradition; and interpretation, therefore, must try to discover how its author worked within the tradition, what conditions in his community he was responding to, and why he adapted the tradition as he did in order to produce the text that he did.

Creation and Chaos was Gunkel's first substantial publication in Old Testament studies, and while it was greeted favorably, as by the noted ancient historian Eduard Meyer,[10] that reaction was not universal. A particularly outspoken critic was Julius Wellhausen, one of the greatest of biblicists, who wrote initially to a colleague: "'Schöpfung und Chaos' is a telling title for the writing of its newcomer; chaos, however, prevails."[11] In a later, published essay on apocalyptic literature, Wellhausen offered a more extended evaluation, conceding, against his first impression, that *Creation and Chaos* did contain "good observations" and that Babylonian influence was indeed to be recognized in biblical apocalyptic. Nevertheless, he went on, Gunkel had exaggerated the role of this influence in understanding what the biblical texts mean; even more, Gunkel had placed much too much emphasis on the origins and prehistory of a text as crucial to its understanding. The last point was, of course, a central one, but in making it Wellhausen does not appear entirely fair to the close analysis of the biblical texts and their meanings that Gunkel in fact provides. Gunkel himself was clearly wounded by the critique, and replied immediately in a sharply worded essay.[12] The whole controversy, as Werner Klatt has seen,[13] played into a growing alienation that Gunkel, together with some others of his generation, felt from the methods and conceptions of Wellhausen and his associates. Whether this controversy, or alienation, had a professional impact on Gunkel is difficult to assess, but the fact is that his academic career had more than its share of disappointments. It was, for example, not until 1907, when he was in his mid-forties — much later than would have been the case for a rising star in the German system of his day — that he finally achieved a full professorship, and then in Giessen, not one of the major German universities.[14]

Wellhausen probably overreached in his critique of *Creation and Chaos,* but in the hindsight now of more than a century since its publication, it is clear that Gunkel's volume is not without its problems. Most prominent, perhaps, is its too exclusive focus on Mesopotamia, and the Mesopotamian *Enuma Elish,* as the matrix of the biblical texts of cosmogony and apocalyptic. Discoveries made after the appearance of *Creation and Chaos,* which Gunkel could probably not have anticipated, demonstrate that the myth of cosmic combat had, in various forms, quite a wide distribution throughout the ancient Near East. Attestations from the Canaanite, or more precisely, West Semitic world have attracted particular attention, given the fact that it was in this world that Israel and the Bible emerged. The main evidence is the Baʻal and Anat cycle of texts excavated from the city of Ugarit in the 1930s and a more recent publication (1993) of a cuneiform letter from the city of Mari — both texts dating from the second millennium B.C.E., with the Mari earlier than the Ugaritic.[15] As William Whitney notes in his introduction to the present translation, this evidence has suggested to a number of scholars in the century after *Creation and Chaos* — and the work here has been abundant in quantity and often elaborate in execution[16] — that the West Semitic or Canaanite world was the immediate source for the biblical authors. Indeed, as Whitney adds, this West Semitic world has even been proposed as the origin of the combat motif in Mesopotamia, although that issue is hardly settled.

Creation and Chaos, thus, has not remained a definitive statement of the problem it has studied. But this is only to be expected in a dynamic field like the study of the Bible and the broader ancient Near East. The point is that the importance the combat myth has assumed in this field is largely due to the impe-

tus and commanding analysis offered by Gunkel's volume. And if certain particulars now require revision, still fundamental and challenging are the
questions Gunkel asked of his texts, and the method he formulated for answer-
ing them, with its rigorous and integrated balance between close internal analysis of the primary biblical sources and comparative assessment of analogues to
them. William Whitney's translation of *Creation and Chaos* now allows a new
audience to appreciate and appropriate Gunkel's great achievement.

PETER MACHINIST

Translator's Preface

I first looked at Hermann Gunkel's work *Schöpfung und Chaos* shortly after I began research on my doctoral dissertation at Harvard[1] in 1988. I had been asked to teach a course at Harvard Divinity School on the "Concept of God in the Hebrew Bible." Given that topic, I thought it logical to begin with a view of God as "Creator." Both Professor Paul D. Hanson and Professor Frank Moore Cross Jr. suggested that I take the time to look at Gunkel's work on the creation myth. So I checked *Schöpfung und Chaos* out of the library, took out my trusty *Cassell's German-English Dictionary*, and began to plow my way through Gunkel's work. It was a formidable task, but I did succeed in getting almost 125 pages of the work translated so that my students could have relatively easy access to Gunkel's thoughts, which I considered quite relevant, even if slightly out of date.

Out of date? Gunkel sought to show that the Hebrew creation account was derived from the one found in the Babylonian "creation epic" *Enuma Elish*. At the time that Gunkel wrote *Schöpfung und Chaos* (the early 1890s) this was certainly a powerful new idea. Since then, however, discoveries in the Canaanite area have shown that the Hebrew creation account probably arose from that milieu. Gunkel's argument (from slightly later in his career) that Canaanite myths were also derived from Babylonian sources now appears to be unlikely. Thorkild Jacobsen has argued, quite convincingly, that the West Semitic/Canaanite (i.e., from the Mediterranean eastern coastal areas) myths of the divine creative battle, rather, had a profound influence on the shape of the East Semitic (i.e., Mesopotamian/Babylonian) myth concerning the divine battle at the beginning of creation and that the process was not the other way around (i.e., east to west), as Gunkel presumed.[2]

Despite this, however, the methodology Gunkel devised and used in this work has had a profound and lasting significance on biblical scholarship in the time since *Schöpfung und Chaos* appeared. One thing you will often hear when Gunkel's name is mentioned in Hebrew Bible scholarly circles is the phrase "Old Testament form criticism." While Gunkel was a very important instigator of this way of examining Hebrew biblical texts (he spoke of it as *Gattungs-geschichte*),[3] that is not the primary significance of *Schöpfung und Chaos*. Rather, in this work we witness the first major movement away from the literary-critical approaches of the nineteenth century, approaches which were exemplified by the works of Julius Wellhausen and which are usually described under the designation "source criticism."

It is very important to understand that "source criticism," as practiced by Wellhausen and those who followed him, was more than anything else a *literary*-critical form of analysis. The "sources" Wellhausen sought out were viewed as written documents, written documents which, over history, were combined together by some sort of editorial activity into the form in which we now find them. Though later in his life Wellhausen would admit that some *oral* history probably lay behind these documents, the fact that the form in which we now have them is a written one meant that his primary interest was in the *written* history thereof.

One should not belittle the tremendous accomplishments of Wellhausen and his followers. By the latter part of the nineteenth century, however, biblical scholarship had, if you will, hit something of a snag. For both Wellhausen and many of those who followed him Israel's history was a history of Israel alone. It was as if Israel was a solo actor who came out onto an empty stage and developed as a character on that same empty stage, that development being affected only occasionally by the physical presence of a few others who would periodically wander across the stage, maybe say a word or two to the main character, maybe even do something to which the central actor just had to react, but who eventually would disappear from view. It was a very nice fantasy, but as the latter part of the nineteenth century progressed, archaeological discoveries throughout the area of the ancient Near East (including Egypt) made it very clear that it was a false view of historical reality. Even Wellhausen, later in his career, did have to concede this fact.

> The land of Palestine, the link between west Asia and Egypt, situated in the middle of those two ancient cultural centers, implicated the people in the vortex of world history, and even the religion was influenced by this vortex, although it was not eliminated thereby, but was successfully lifted up out of it.[4]

But even having conceded this, Wellhausen did not actually incorporate it into his ongoing theological or historical work. He still remained almost totally focused on Israel.

Part of the problem was the complexity of both Assyriology and Egyptology, a complexity which effectively put them beyond the reach of many late-nineteenth-century biblical scholars. Even those who could deal in scholarly terms with the materials being discovered found that their personal intellectual and religious interests made it very difficult to incorporate these other ancient Near Eastern materials into their theological/biblical scholarship.[5] One scholar of the period, Rudolf Kittel, noted well the frustrating situation within which those who attempted to deal with the biblical materials in light of these new discoveries found themselves. Kittel pointed out

> . . . that it was no longer possible to get by with the previous custom of nobly ignoring the ancient Near East. What was brought to the system by Wellhausen was, namely, that everything was right out in front of the Old Testament itself, and to some degree in Arabian antiquity, . . . everything, at the very least, which is necessary for the comprehension of Israel, which corresponds totally to the tradition into which I was raised.[6]

It was onto this scene that Hermann Gunkel gazed as he began to think about writing a commentary on the book of Genesis.

First a bit of background about Hermann Gunkel.[7] He was born May 23, 1862, at Springe (near Hannover) in Germany. He was the first son of Karl Wilhelm August Philipp Gunkel (1829-97), who dwelt there as the pastor of a local parish. His paternal grandfather was Johann August Kunkel (born ca. 1760), who had been an administrative official in the electoral district of Mainz. Originally a Roman Catholic, Kunkel had converted to evangelical Protestantism, an event which significantly changed his life since it cost him his job. On becoming a businessman in Heiligen-Stadt, Kunkel changed his name to Gunkel. His son, Johann Friedrich Gunkel, at first tutored in the Göttingen area, but later he became a pastor, first at Lutterberg and then at Landolfshausen, both near Göttingen.[8]

As a young man Hermann Gunkel attended the Johanneum in Lüneburg. Even at this early stage Gunkel exhibited a theological interest. Despite the weak light of his early morning Hebrew class (which eventually damaged his eyesight), he nevertheless pursued his study of the language resolutely. He graduated from the Johanneum on March 14, 1881. Shortly thereafter he went to the University of Göttingen. Very quickly he attained a high standing in the study of theology. In the course of his studies he worked with, among others, Adolf von Harnack (1851-1930) and Bernhard Stade (1848-1906). He continued his theological studies from the spring of 1885 to the fall of 1888 in Lüneburg, Göttingen, and Leipzig, supporting himself by working as a tutor.

On October 16, 1888, Gunkel received his Licentiate in Theology from the University of Göttingen. It was granted on the basis of an outstanding dissertation which is described in the university archives as testifying to ". . . learned dexterity, exegetical skill, and impressive discernment."[9] After a trial lecture on the eschatology of Jewish apocalypses, Gunkel was allowed to teach in the area of biblical theology and exegesis for a period of two years. At this point in his career Gunkel was fairly inconspicuous in the scholarly field. It took the agitation of his father, whose financial means were so decimated that he could offer no monetary support either to Hermann or to Hermann's younger brother Karl, . . . it fell to his father's agitation with the national Ministry of Culture to raise even the possibility that Hermann Gunkel might find longer-term employment in the academic sphere. After a protracted process, these parental inquiries paid off, as on October 19, 1888, Gunkel was offered a position on the theological faculty at Göttingen. Just before the new year he was given a modest but sufficient stipend for a two-year appointment beginning on April 1, 1889, with the possibility of an extension remaining dependent on his performance.[10]

During his days as a student, Gunkel had acquired a profoundly historical orientation. Historical methodology at that time was heavily influenced by the thought of Albrecht Ritschl. Ritschl had focused on the historical revelation of Jesus Christ as that which freed theology from philosophical development and which made it possible to perceive ongoing revelation within the text of the Bible.[11] For Ritschl this ongoing revelation required the concerted application of historical method to the text. Theology, acquired in this way, became for Ritschl the very basis for any authentic ecclesiastical community life.

This Ritschlian view did have its opponents. Ritschl attempted to construct a systematic theology based on the testimony of the New Testament. In the process, he tended to overlook things which did not easily conform to the systematization he was constructing. Later in his career Gunkel noted the problems he had had with the Ritschlian approach.[12]

> All those who have sat at the feet of Ritschl will recall the violence with which the old theologian dealt with the New Testament texts. It is, therefore, no accident, then, that the younger school has sincerely shown itself in opposition to this type of exegesis.

This "younger school" to which Gunkel alludes was known colloquially among theological students at Göttingen as "the little faculty." It included, among others, Albert Eichhorn (1856-1926), Wilhelm Wrede (1859-1906), Hermann Gunkel (1862-1932), Wilhelm Bousset (1865-1920), Ernst Troeltsch (1865-1923), Wilhelm Heitmüller (1869-1926), and, to some degree, Johannes Weiss (1863-1914). Clearly it was an impressive assemblage of minds.[13]

Under the strong influence of Adolf von Harnack and in critical dialogue with the theological thinking of Ritschl, Gunkel and his scholarly colleagues began to develop a religio-historical approach to the study of biblical religion. This religion could, to their way of thinking, be understood only in light of its historical development.[14] Writing later, Gunkel noted the ultimate goal which he and his colleagues pursued. "This then was our truest and ultimate endeavor: to comprehend the religion itself in all its depth and breadth."[15] Since this was an "historical" endeavor, an examination of the "developmental history" of the biblical religion was very necessary for Gunkel. He was not concerned with developing a theological or an ecclesiastical theory. What interested him was, rather, the history which lay behind the religion as it was expressed in the biblical text, or the manner in which various ancient traditions came together and interacted to form the "present tradition" as it was embodied in the biblical text. For Gunkel, though, that "present tradition" was a "given." It was a "given," however, only insofar as it embodied the end product of a formative process, a "traditioning" process. It was the developmental history of that process which Gunkel sought to uncover, and to understand. Gunkel was primarily concerned with "tradition history."

Of crucial importance to this shifting of focus from "sources" to "traditions" was the realization that the biblical text was itself the product not simply of *written* composition, but that even that *written* composition was the product of a long process of *oral* composition. In the larger sphere of scholarship the work of Jacob Grimm (1785-1863) and his brother Wilhelm Grimm (1786-1859) perhaps provided a theoretical stimulus for Gunkel's scholarly belief in the importance of *oral* tradition for understanding the biblical accounts. The Grimms devoted themselves to the study of the folklore of the Germanic peoples. In 1812 and 1814 they had published the product of their early work in *Kinder- und Hausmärchen,* a two-volume collection of Germanic folktales for children.[16] In 1816 and in 1818 they followed with another two-volume work entitled *Deutsche Sagen.*[17] This was more concerned with folktales in general and the various forms in which they appeared in German culture. Methodologically this was a very important work. Largely in response to these early works, in 1829-30 they became professors at Göttingen.[18]

Though the Grimms were no longer physically on the scene at Göttingen when Gunkel was there,[19] it seems likely that their work did have an effect on the way in which the study of narrative was pursued at that institution. Most important was their recognition of the crucial importance of orality for the understanding of narrative tradition. Whether Gunkel was directly affected by them or not, his focus on orally transmitted traditions within the biblical materials is at the very least indicative of a shift in scholarly interest from *textually* transmitted biblical materials (i.e. "sources") to *orally* transmitted biblical materials (i.e. "traditions"). In point of fact, he was a leading and groundbreaking proponent of such a shift.

Because of this, Gunkel was greatly concerned with the "here and now" of those who transmitted the tradition at each discernible stage along the way. In his first work, *Die Wirkungen des heiligen Geistes, nach der populären Anschauung der apostolischen Zeit und nach der Lehre des Apostels Paulus: Eine biblisch-theologische Studie* (Göttingen: Vandenhoeck & Ruprecht, 1888), among other things he attempted to explicate, as closely as possible, exactly what the meaning and significance of the Holy Spirit was to Paul when the apostle spoke of it.

> It must first be clear exactly what Paul meant by "Holy Spirit." Having worked this out, however, it was certainly not as clear whether the Pauline concept was identical to that of the nineteenth-century theologians. The Pauline comments had to be placed within the intellectual thought-world which was the environment of the apostle. In other words, without an awareness of the thought-world of the primal Christian community, Paul remains unidimensional![20]

In *Wirkungen* Gunkel began to work out the methodology by which he could discern the thought-world within which a biblical tradition arose and the ongoing thought-worlds within which it developed. It was in his next major work, *Schöpfung und Chaos,* that he actually put that methodology to the test, dealing in a very careful way with the manner in which the biblical traditions relating to creation arose, developed, and shifted in temporal focus (from primal to eschatological time) over the historical life of the Hebrew people, early Judaism, and early Christianity. Crucial to this study was the understanding that within an orally developed tradition vestiges of the developmental history of that tradition may be discerned and can allow the historian to understand something of the history of the communal consciousness out of which that tradition arose and within which that tradition developed. It is *that* understanding toward which the "tradition historian" strives.

Now, having placed Gunkel's work in some sort of historical and intellectual context, let us ask what exactly he does in *Schöpfung und Chaos.* The work is divided into two major units. The first (pp. 1-111 in our translation) deals with the manifestation of the creation myth in the Hebrew Bible/Old Testament. Starting with the Priestly creation account of Genesis 1, Gunkel carefully traces out the similarities of that account to the Babylonian creation account found in *Enuma Elish*. Though there are few direct connections, he does discern some, and from them he concludes that the tradition itself "could not have arisen in Israel."[21]

Unlike his scholarly contemporaries, Gunkel does not hesitate in his resolve to discern the origins of the biblical creation account outside of the immediate historical locus of Israel. Despite the pristine and methodical picture given of creation in the Priestly account of Genesis 1, Gunkel finds, even there, traces of a far more tumultuous and violent myth of creation, a myth which, he argues, undergirded ancient Near Eastern culture.[22] He also finds numerous other references to this mythic tradition, references of varying lengths and comprehensiveness, elsewhere in the Hebrew Bible and in the apocryphal and pseudepigraphical works connected to it.[23] Since this tradition begins with the idea that the world was once water, Gunkel sought the ultimate source of the tradition in "a land the character of which is defined by great rivers."[24] He identified this land as Mesopotamia (from Gk. Μεσοποτάμιος [*mesopotamios*], "between [the] rivers"), and it was there that he turned to look for a less fragmentary form of the myth than that found in the Bible. The Babylonian *Enuma Elish* creation account provided him with just such a fuller form of the myth, a form which, he argued, undergirds the primal Hebrew form, which is reflected only fragmentarily within the biblical account. That Babylonian account, which presents the story of a battle between the young warrior-god of Babylon *Marduk* and the olden goddess[25] *Ti'āmat*, has come to be described since Gunkel with the word *Chaoskampf* ("chaos battle" or "chaos struggle").[26]

Gunkel discerns this mythic motif as present in the background of a large number of texts from the Hebrew Bible. He divides these texts into two large groups: those dealing with the dragon ("Die Drachentraditionen," original German text, 29-90; my trans., pp. 21-61); and those dealing with the primal sea ("die Traditionen vom Urmeer," original German text, 81-111; my trans., pp. 61-75).

Having noted and carefully examined these two groups of texts, Gunkel raises the question as to when the Babylonian myth made its way into Israel. He rejects the logical assumption that it came into Israel during the period of the Babylonian exile (597-535 B.C.E.), though he does consider it.[27] He notes the presence of the myth in Isa 14:12-14 (preexilic),[28] and the presence of a distinctively Israelite form of the myth in exilic and early postexilic texts from Zechariah (4:1-6a, 10b-13),[29] Deutero-Isaiah, and, with Egyptian motifs, Ezekiel 29 and 32.[30] Most significantly, he discerns a clear reference to the myth in the undoubtedly preexilic Jer 4:23-26.[31]

All of this, however, raises the question whether the myth could have made its way into Israel only slightly earlier, i.e., during the period of Assyrian domination (ca. 721-621 B.C.E.).[32] Using techniques similar to those employed in relation to the time of Babylonian hegemony, Gunkel also rejects this possibility. Noting the importance of the myth in the prophetic corpus he concludes:[33]

> The acceptance of the creation myth into our prophetic tradition is explicable only if it had made its way into Israel at a much earlier time, so that its Babylonian origin had already been forgotten over several generations by the time of the prophets. This thesis, demanded by the course of religious history, would be supported by the observation that the other Babylonian myths concerning primordial history had also been received *en toto* at an earlier time.

In the second part of the work (pp. 115-250 of our translation) Gunkel turns to the examination of Revelation 12. Up to this point he has carefully laid the groundwork for this shift from a primeval mythic focus to an eschatological one. Throughout his examination of the Hebrew Bible and apocryphal and pseudepigraphical texts relating to it in the first part of this work, he has often discerned an eschatological dimension within the texts. At the conclusion of his examination of the dragon traditions he notes:[34]

> Furthermore, one should conclude from Isa 29:1; 30:7; 51:9; Ezekiel 29; 32; Pss 68:31; 74; 87:4; and *Psalms of Solomon* 2 that before its prophetic-apocalyptic expression, the myth was already being applied eschatologically, i.e. had become a prophecy: YHWH will vanquish the dragon in the future. *1 Enoch* 60:24f., *4 Ezra* 4:52, and *2 Apoc. Bar.* 29:4 have this form of the myth.

Gunkel discerns a similar eschatological shift in his examination of the later manifestations of the traditions dealing with the sea. "Just as the myth of the struggle against the dragon is to be interpreted eschatologically, so also are to be understood the applications of the defeat of the sea to the great judgment of the nations in the final days."[35] Again he carefully examines passages which exhibit this shift in temporal focus.[36]

Having noted all these things, Gunkel concludes the first half of his work, the portion in which he treats the Hebrew Bible and its early related Jewish texts, with these words:[37]

The creation myth had — so it appears — also come to Israel in an eschato-logical form, and had called forth from the prophets and the prophetic schools an impression of the coming judgment. We have, from the latest period, faint clues that it also began to be significant for the tenor of the eschatological final hope. Thereupon a new epoch of Babylonian influences began!

Going on, he states:[38]

As a result of our exposition of Revelation 12 up to now, we have gained a confirmation of the thesis of Vischer: the chapter is not of Christian origin since it could not be understood from the standpoint of a Christian composition and since the statement found therein about Jesus' birth and journey to heaven is totally untenable.

Here, as previously, Gunkel perceives the chapter as the literary deposit of a gradually developed oral tradition, the historical background of which he sets out to discern. He describes the crystallization of the whole of Revelation as "a complicated compilation of very many individual visions."[39] These visions, he argues, must be treated as originally independent. They must be treated in this way prior to the search for any insights into their present setting.[40]

First of all, the internal connection of the material is to be established. The boundaries of the material from independent individual visions are to be sought out. The detail within the vision, as far as it is possible, is to be explained from *these* contexts. And only after these questions are answered will it be permissible to investigate the present literary context. By this it is clearly to be thought that one will arrive at the present context only later in the process.

If Revelation 12 does not ultimately originate in Christian tradition, whence is its origin? In order to ascertain this, Gunkel moves to a closer examination of the chapter's text. To do this, however, he begins with a strong critique of contemporary biblical exegesis in relation to the Revelation of John. This exegetical methodology, he notes, focused on "the 'contemporaneous' explication"[41] of the text. He explains this in the following manner:[42]

According to the "contemporaneous" explanation the apocalyptist in his writing portrays the events of his time and the expectations which are the result of the current state of affairs. . . . The task of "contemporaneous" explanation would, consequently, be to rediscover from the varied forms of the revelation the historical *realia* artistically hidden within it.

Gunkel notes that this ideal is usually methodologically corrupted by his contemporary critics' zeal to find even within the most "fantastic" images the "proper" historical referent.[43]

> . . . even within the "contemporaneous" descriptions themselves a purely fantastic sequence must stand close to the actual "contemporary" feature which the features of other things frequently overshadow. So a reason has to be given for the vision of fabulous cavalry in chapter 9:13ff., a reason according to the customary explanation, i.e., the Parthian threat. But the vision itself, with its many remarkable individual themes, far surpasses this supposed reason.

Gunkel does admit that some of his contemporaries have exercised greater discretion in this regard. For them, however, ". . . only a small part of the Apocalypse is, all in all, understood 'contemporaneously,' . . . and the main body of it must . . . consist of fantasy images."[44]

This leads Gunkel to question whether the contemporary exegesis of the Revelation of John actually deserves the ideal designation of "contemporaneous exegesis" at all.[45] He goes on to argue that ". . . it is urgent that one adhere to a unified definition of the word 'contemporaneous.'" The definition he proposes is that which he has already put forward, i.e., that the "contemporaneous" interpretation should be concerned not simply with the "contemporary moment" of the person composing a passage, but also with the inherited "tradition" which shapes that person's vision of the moment. In short, Gunkel argues that "contemporaneous" exegesis cannot overlook the cultural, social, and communal tradition which has shaped the outlook which is embodied in a text composed within that culture, that society, that community. And, he goes on, that tradition bears within it marks of the cultural, societal, and communal history within which it developed, marks which may or may not be specifically relevant to the actual life situation (*Sitz im Leben*) of the one who composes a specific manifestation of the tradition at any point in time but marks which may remain nonetheless. Gunkel's goal is to discern those marks within the text, to examine them carefully, and to uncover something of the history by which the tradition which shaped the thinking which led to the text which is being examined . . . the history by which that tradition attained its "present" (i.e., "contemporary") form. In short, his view of his task dictates that he trace the history of the tradition as clearly as he possibly can. That, he argues, is the ultimate goal of "contemporaneous exegesis."

Having thus laid out his exegetical methodology Gunkel moves more directly to an examination of Revelation 12. He has already denied its ultimate Christian origin. He now argues that it is not ultimately of Jewish origin either. The problem is that certain features of the passage do appear totally consistent with a Jewish viewpoint:

- the birth of the Messiah after the seventh trumpet;
- the birth of the Messiah in heaven;
- the rescuing of the Messiah from the dragon, up to the throne of God, while the Messiah is still a child;
- the Messiah's appearance on earth as a grown man.

But even recognizing that all of this in no way renders a Jewish viewpoint out of the question, Gunkel goes on to note that these features themselves do not sufficiently explain the whole of the chapter. . . .[46]

> The problem which now arises is one of understanding the origin of the whole point of view, the point of view both of the messianic image and of the many quite remarkable details of the chapter, understanding the origin of these things as having been derived from Jewish assumptions.

Gunkel points to those contemporary critics who have attempted to understand Revelation 12 in this manner, and he demonstrates their failure to do so. In place of the usual "contemporaneous" treatments proposed by such critics, Gunkel puts forward a methodology for approaching this text which is much more consistent with his understanding of a correct "contemporaneous" approach.[47]

> Even though noncontemporaneous events could have been a factor, and even though the images of the Apocalypse certainly cannot easily be grasped, the force within the Hebrew Bible by which the imagination of the author was moved and set into motion . . . this force is to be sought out and discovered.

But there are other factors than simply the Hebrew Bible which influenced the thought of early Judaism.[48]

> The allusion to the Jewish faith in reference to the resurrection, to hell, to an eternal life in heaven — beliefs which are not Old Testament beliefs and have not even developed organically out of the Old Testament — . . . the al-

lusions to the Jewish faith in reference to these things is sufficient to demonstrate that in Jewish apocalyptic thought, in addition to that which is inherited from the Old Testament, there stand eschatological ideas which are of a greater originality than the Old Testament. It follows methodologically for apocalyptic exegesis, that it is not completely necessary to understand the details from the Old Testament alone, but that we have also to deal with the peculiarly Jewish possibility of traditions independent of the Old Testament.

Even having done this, however, Gunkel notes that where pieces of the tradition are ultimately derived from the Hebrew Bible, the Hebrew Bible itself may have only an indirect influence on the present tradition embodied in a specific passage. In this regard he suggests:[49]

> More direct or indirect dependence of these modalities on the Old Testament must be discerned in a clear manner in those cases in which the author writes down a tradition already present in the Old Testament, without, for some reason, that tradition necessarily being dependent on the Old Testament.

In light of this he suggests that two questions must guide the methodology used in approaching apocalyptic motifs where the motif is not clearly a literal reference to the Hebrew Bible:[50]

1. Does a striking, conceptually terminological correspondence within the Hebrew Bible actually exist?
2. Could such an apocalyptic form plausibly have developed from contemplation of the Hebrew Bible?

Gunkel then turns to a close examination of the current scholarly claims concerning the conceptual dependence of Revelation 12 on the Hebrew Bible. His discussion is *very* critical of those claims. He comes to the conclusion that, under critical examination, ". . . Almost all similarities which are believed to be found quietly disappear. . . ."[51] Gunkel sums up the results of his analysis.[52]

> We have raised up the need for a stronger methodology, and we have discovered that the usual explanations, judged according to that methodology, are altogether insufficient. So the result is that the details of the chapter cannot be understood in terms of the Old Testament.

Comparing Revelation 12 to Revelation 4 and 18 (which he sees as descriptive assemblages of individually received traditional pieces), Gunkel argues, instead, that the former is a conceptually unified narrative.[53] Though he does discern some originally independent pieces of traditional material within the chapter, for him the authorial intent was clearly one of unity. Materials drawn from the Hebrew Bible are used as "conceptual illustrations."[54]

Gunkel asserts that many of his contemporaries have treated chapter 12 as a statement of the apocalyptic writer that certain traumatic events would unfold prior to the final judgment, and that those difficulties would be overcome by the overpowering might of God's love.[55] He sharply assesses this judgment in light of the biblical account itself.[56]

> An exegesis, therefore, arises which, lacking the necessary care, gropes blindly about seeking the "concepts" of the apocalyptic writer, an exegesis in which the pressing danger is to deduce "ideas" from the writer's imagery, ideas which either stand conceptually pallid in very flagrant contradiction to the colorful richness of the apocalyptic forms, or, at the very least, are of such a different outlook that it becomes extremely difficult to comprehend exactly how the apocalyptic writer, working with such "ideas," could even have come up with such depictions.

The very impossibility of the imagery, Gunkel concludes, speaks against such an interpretation. Since the discrepancy of the chapter's imagery with the imagery of the Hebrew Bible is quite clear, he argues,[57]

> . . . the actual creative impetus which has produced this portrayal must have been the imagination of the author! He, in a totally individual fashion, a fashion in which he allows his imagination to break in quite freely, has created a completely refined innovation.

Even the attempts of certain of Gunkel's contemporaries to incorporate the authorial imagination into a view that the imagery ultimately stems from the Hebrew Bible . . . even these attempts he condemns. He notes that such a view, in effect, overthrows the clear reality of the text, i.e., that the author's faith, which "he had 'ardently' asserted with such visions, has been abdicated!"[58] In other words, in ultimate terms, the critics whose work Gunkel so strongly attacks here, say, in effect, that the words of Revelation 12 are nothing more than fanciful poetic imagery, i.e., that the author did not actually believe what he wrote.

In place of such a view, Gunkel points to the use in Revelation of the

Greek phrase ὁ μάρτυς ὁ πιστός [*ho martys ho pistos* — "the faithful witness"] at 1:15, 14:9, 21:5, and 22:6. This he sees as testimony which directly contradicts the so-called "nonbelief" of the author of the work. The writer of Revelation, he contends, seeks to impart truth. "It should not, therefore, contain, to any great extent, imaginary creations of its author!"[59]

Gunkel therefore asserts that critics have a choice: either Revelation reports that which was actually seen, or it does not! This choice has resulted, he argues, in uncertainty as to the truth of what is reported therein. "For this reason one must be on the lookout for another authority which affirms the 'meaning' of Revelation's depictions. That authority can be none other than — THE TRADITION!"[60] For Gunkel, then, Revelation 12 is a piece of Jewish apocalyptic tradition. And that tradition has a history, a history which can, to some degree, be uncovered by the discerning critical eye. At this point he puts forward what can only be described as a classic statement of traditio-historical methodology:[61]

It is in the very nature of oral tradition, when passing O so tenaciously from generation to generation, that it *is* subject to certain fluctuations. Such omissions, additions, displacements, which later generations have imposed on the ancient materials, are revealed in the present codification of the tradition. They are revealed by the fact that the continuity of the narrative, which had formerly been uninterrupted, currently exhibits some obscurities or peculiarities! Or they are revealed by the fact that certain features, features which had a proper meaning at the time of their origins, are neither intelligible from the present context, nor are they able to be considered as "generally" intelligible. They are, therefore, viewed as strangely brief and incomprehensible! Just as the age of a painting may be recognized by the degree of "darkening" which presently characterizes it, so too is the antiquity of a tradition recognized by such "darkenings." In any examination of a tradition this "darkening" *has* to be brought into play. The ultimate object of the investigation, however, is to reconstruct the original context and to indicate the basis of its alteration, i.e., to write the history of the tradition!

Gunkel's subsequent analysis of Revelation 12 follows this statement. He concludes that thorough analysis addresses the question of the original tradition which lies behind the text as it currently exists. He also deduces that, as he has already seen in the first half of his work, the original tradition which underlies this text is the Babylonian creation myth. And, he goes on to argue, that myth, imperfectly interpreted, to a large degree allegorically, by the Jewish community which transmitted it prior to its inclusion within Revelation, has been adopted and modified by Judaism.[62]

In the remainder of his work Gunkel examines this adoption and modification, looking first at the general presence of Babylonian mythic materials in later Judaism.[63] In doing this he first treats a variety of Hebrew biblical materials (and some postbiblical Jewish materials),[64] then he turns to chapters 13 and 17 of Revelation.[65] In the latter part of this treatment he comments upon the transference of the primal myth to the eschaton,[66] the Jewish interpretation of chaos as Rome,[67] and the mystery of the beast of chapter 17 and its number 666.[68] Gunkel concludes the work with a strongly argued assertion that Revelation 12 is of Babylonian origin and that it offers an interpretive reading of the Babylonian mythic materials, an interpretive reading of those materials by Judaism and Christianity. In short, Gunkel, in *Schöpfung und Chaos,* traces the Babylonian mythic tradition through the biblical materials into the very beginnings of Judaism and Christianity. He, at least by implication, also points toward the continuing influence of that myth within the symbolic and mythic structures of the Judeo-Christian worldview.

From a methodological standpoint alone, *Schöpfung und Chaos* marked a singularly significant turning point in the way in which biblical criticism *was* and *is* conducted in the scholarly world today. Though subsequent archaeological findings in the Canaanite area have raised significant critical doubts concerning Gunkel's assertion of a *Babylonian* origin for the Hebrew creation/new creation myth, it is the manner in which he argues his thesis, or, more specifically put, it is the traditio-historical methodology which he employs, which make the legacy of Gunkel's work in *Schöpfung und Chaos* to modern biblical scholarship a most profound and lasting one.

Acknowledgments

Several people have been instrumental in bringing this translation to completion, and I do wish to thank them. The translation itself is dedicated, with grateful thanks, to Frank Moore Cross Jr. (Hancock Professor of Hebrew and Other Oriental Languages, emeritus, of Harvard University), my scholarly mentor and friend, who first encouraged me to look seriously at the work of Hermann Gunkel. Professor Peter Machinist, who succeeded Cross as the Hancock Professor of Hebrew and Other Oriental Languages in the Department of Near Eastern Languages and Civilizations at Harvard, first seriously encouraged me to bring the translation to publication and actually has had much to do with getting it published, including taking the trouble to read and critique this Preface. For that and for his kind and always generous support I thank him greatly.

Thanks are also due to Professor François Bovon of Harvard Divinity School and to Professor-emeritus Helmut Koester, also of Harvard Divinity School. Both of them were especially helpful to me in translating some difficult passages and in finding certain difficult bibliographic references. I greatly appreciate their assistance and support.

I owe a special debt of gratitude to the Harvard University Library system and to other libraries around the world from which I received bibliographic assistance. Thanks especially to Gloria Korsman and Clifford Wunderlich (reference librarians at Harvard Divinity School Library), to Wojciech Zalewski (a reference librarian at Stanford University Libraries), to Roberta Schaafsma (a reference librarian at Duke University Divinity School Library), to Monika Kloos (a reference librarian at the Pfälzische Landesbibliothek in Germany), and to my spouse, Laura Whitney, who is Circulation Supervisor at Harvard Divinity School Library. Without these librarians' excellent and generously given support I would never have been able to complete the bibliographical work required as part of this translation project. Largely as a result of their assistance, I have been able to add a bibliography at the end of the work, something which Gunkel himself did not provide. That bibliography is based on the citations found in the footnotes.

I also owe gratitude to Professor Simon J. DeVries, with whom I corresponded for some time in an unfortunately unsuccessful search for the source of the statement of Abraham Kuenen to which Gunkel alludes on p. 96 of this translation. Great thanks also go to Allen C. Myers, Senior Editor at William B. Eerdmans Publishing Company, whose patience throughout the seemingly infinite period during which I completed this work has been most appreciated.

Finally, I am most thankful to God for the support I have received from my spouse Laura and my daughter Rachael during the long (and sometimes quite trying) period involved in the completion of this labor. Their confidence that, despite my sometimes difficult disposition and my overly high "focus" during the preparation of this translation, I really was someone worthy of their love and their support . . . that confidence, that love, that support has been my mainstay during the many years of this work. I thank them, and I give thanks to God for them.

K. WILLIAM WHITNEY JR.

Transliteration

Hebrew Transliteration Characters

א	ʾ	מ, ם	m	ְ	ě
בּ	b̲	נ, ן	n	ֱ	ě
בּ	b	ס	s	ֲ	ă
ג	g̲	ע	ʿ	ֳ	ŏ
ג	g	פ, ף	p̲	ִ	i
ד	d̲	פ	p	ֵ	ē
ד	d	צ, ץ	ṣ	ֶ	e
ה	h	ק	q	ַ	a
ו	w/w̄	ר	r	ָ	ā
ז	z	שׁ	š	ָ	o/ō
ח	ḥ	שׂ	ś	ֻ	u
ט	ṭ	ת	t̲	וּ	û
י	y	תּ	t	וֹ	ô
ך, כ	k̲			ִי	î
ך, פ	k	There is also the		ֵי	ē
ל	l	Semitic sound of a "hooked h" . . . . . ḫ		ֶי	ê

Greek Transliteration Characters

A α . . . . *A a*	Λ λ . . . . *L l*	Υ υ . . . . *Y y*
B β . . . . *B b*	M μ . . . . . . *M m*	(*u* in diphthongs only)
Γ γ . . . . . . *G g*	N ν . . . . *N n*	Φ φ . . . . . *Ph ph*
Δ δ . . . . . . *D d*	Ξ ξ . . . . *X x*	X χ . . . . . *Ch ch*
E ε . . . . *E e*	O o . . . . *O o*	Ψ ψ . . . . . . *Ps ps*
Z ζ . . . . *Z z*	Π π . . . . . . *P p*	Ω ω . . . . . . *Ō ō*
H η . . . . *Ē ē*	P ρ . . . . *R r*	' (smooth breathing before vowel)
Θ θ . . . . . *Th th*	Σ σ ς . . . . . . *S s*	ʿ (rough breathing before vowel) *h*
I ι . . . . *I i*	T τ . . . . *T t*	
K κ . . . . . . *K k*		

Introduction

([ ] = explanatory material inserted by the translator)

The reader finds on the following pages studies of a series of biblical texts from the first chapter of Genesis to the final chapter of Revelation. All these individual studies, however, have, in the last analysis, the same object in view. I have sought to order the individual discussions of which this work is composed into a unified whole. Thus the argument of the second part is a presupposition of the first.

Since I must sometimes oppose the prevailing view, I may be allowed to appeal to the impartiality of the reader. Since I do, here and there, journey untraveled paths, I have the responsibility to apologize should large or small errors creep in. I would be grateful for critical comment and reasonable contradiction.

I cannot totally avoid the above-mentioned comments on what follows. However, in the meantime, I ask that judgment concerning what follows be held in suspension. I promise to furnish proof concerning Hebrew verse shortly. The Babylonian verse[1] which we have discovered has now been reviewed by Heinrich Zimmern[2] and will shortly be treated by him. An exposition of the composition of Revelation in relationship to the history of apocalyptic should follow a short time later.

It is not customary in a historical study to reveal the controlling principles of the research. I have, however, the responsibility to discuss clearly a point which has opened up (as I shall later argue) an improper interpretation. I hold it to be methodologically objectionable to investigate only the beginning of a thing and to ignore the subsequent, often more important and more valuable, history of the same. Therefore, I have not limited myself to maintaining the Babylonian origin of biblical material, but rather, throughout, I have also explained the particular ways by which these materials were taken into Israel and re-formed. It is obvious, and is dealt with at great length in what follows, that the creation narrative, although of Babylonian origin, nevertheless first gained its particular meaning in Israel. Thus, I believe myself to be protected against misunderstanding, as if perhaps by proving that Israel did not lie outside the realm of world culture, I deny the particularity of Israelite religion and, in turn, lead to the destruction of the belief that in this history God has revealed himself in a special way.

I must be prepared for the opposition of another school to my position regarding the prevailing literary criticism and to my religio-historical method of investigation. Although not unknown to the normal practice of current biblical theology, this method of reconstruction is also not a customary part of that practice, at least to this degree of consequence. This will, I fear, cause some consternation. In the field of literary criticism everyone reconstructs. Should this be prohibited in the field of the history of religion? One notes that there are strict rules and norms for this task — which I have taken great pains to develop theoretically in what follows. Moreover, one notes that the series of results thus achieved will be confirmed by the documents. Furthermore, if the religio-historical method is applied with scholarly rigor, caution, and professionalism, then I can see no reason why, in this field, results cannot be obtained which are even more certain than those obtained through philology.

This book, however, is not written either for or against a given ecclesiastical or intellectual party. Indeed, I did not seek out the observations which it contains. Rather, they presented themselves to me. Others shall judge whether they are correct. This, however, I can sincerely guarantee: that I have taken great pains to apprehend its mystery in humble subordination to the object of my investigation, and to understand its peculiar nature. Indeed, I may be permitted to state the belief that the saying is true, "One understands as much as one has the ability to love and to revere."

I am most indebted to the man whose name adorns this book. Years ago, when I was beset by an unexpected conflict of conscience, his support bolstered me in these principles and this method of study. From the rich source, formed by *his* questions and answers, I have been able to sharpen my eyes and my ears. I have regularly communicated to him the results of this writing as soon as they were discovered. His counsel, his approval, and, at times, his disagreement were always valuable for me in terms of the completion of this work.

Heinrich Zimmern has appended the Babylonian texts to the book and has supplemented my exposition repeatedly by his remarks. These are marked by square brackets and numbers.[3] But Zimmern's intellectual contribution is still not circumscribed by these. For many long years we have engaged in daily intellectual discussion, so that now we no longer can, nor wish to, separate the common products of our labors. Therefore, I must note that I owe to him my first comment on salvation by means of an eagle in Revelation 12 in relation to the Etana legend.[4] The manner of our common work is generally characterized by the form of the following investigations: the theologian, starting with intra-theological observations, discerns the foreign character of a theme; postulates, for more general reasons, its Babylonian origin; seeks to reconstruct its original form; and then submits the results to the Assyriologist for confirmation. Thus one can also, perhaps, give credence to those results which have been discovered by a similar method, but which, at the present time, cannot be confirmed with the material preserved.

The international themes with which I have dealt have attempted to entice me into areas in which I am not at home. I have withstood these attempts and have satisfied myself with calling attention to such points. The fact that I am not an expert in the Talmud I have indicated by the form of my citations. There I have required the assistance of specialists. Professor Praetorius had the kindness to work through some passages of *1 Enoch* in the Ethiopic text with me. Professor Eduard Meyer has repeatedly supported me with kind counsel. Professor Petersen in Rome was so kind as to send me a photograph of the Titus reliefs and a description of the animals on the base of the menorah; his declarations that these creatures "manifest fully the imprint of Greco-Roman craftsmanship," I could not, unfortunately, exploit any more than I did.[5] I owe some notice also to *privat docents* Dr. Wernicke and Dr. Stübe.

As for the task of editing, Mr. Schüerl, cand. theol. from Marburg, and Mr. G. Schmidt, cand. theol., assisted me with the first reading. To the latter I also owe an excellent conjecture;[6] for the intermediate reading, my beloved father-in-law Dean Beelitz in Halle, who has helped me as well with his valuable counsel; the final reading was perused by the faithful eyes of my good father. In the case of citations, which I have collated once again as part of the editing (excepting quite a few which were not immediately accessible to me), someone else helped me. That person shall remain nameless. To all these, especially to my true and devoted friends, my heartfelt thanks.

I have expended considerable labor on the appended translations from the Babylonian and Hebrew. I have not only translated literally, but I wished also, as far as I was able, to reproduce the sense of the texts. I have accordingly allowed the poetic structure to stand out in the printed form; the reader can then satisfy himself through a close examination of the consistency of Hebrew and Babylonian poetry. Wherever a poetic form emerges in the German — or, I might more modestly say, a poetically similar form — I have not rejected it, although I have not deliberately sought it. The kindness of the publisher, whom I am also obliged to thank, has placed "cursive" typeface at our disposal for the main text, while conjectures and uncertain translations have been printed in "Antiqua" typeface. I especially call to the attention of the linguistically untrained reader this alternation of type. I have, moreover, exerted myself to demarcate as clearly as possible the differing levels of certainty by which the thesis might be advanced. The careful reader will not overlook these nuances.

I have endeavored to ascertain the particular assertions of my predecessors. Should I have failed to name one or another of them, as sometimes happens, it is because I did not know him. Sometimes I have had to contend with another point of view; though I totally disagreed with it, I have nevertheless striven herein for completeness. Certainly among the extensive literature which came to hand for this work I have overlooked many works from which I could have learned. For evidence of such, I would be most grateful.

I designate the following abbreviations.

Hw	[Eduard] Riehm's *Handwörterbuch des biblischen Altertums*
JRAS	*Journal of the Royal Asiatic Society*
KAT²	[Eberhard] Schrader's *Die Keilinschriften und das Alte Testament*
KB	[Eberhard] Schrader's *Keilinschriftliche Bibliothek* [*Sammlung von assyrischen und babylonischen Texten in Umschrift und übersetzung*]
Rawlinson, *CIWA*	*The Cuneiform Inscriptions of Western Asia,* ed. Sir H. Rawlinson [5 vols. London: R. E. Bowler, 1861-84]
SBAW	*Sitzungsberichte der Berliner Akademie der Wissenschaften*
ThT	*Theologisch Tijdschrift*
ZA	*Zeitschrift für Assyriologie* [*und verwandte Gebiete*]
ZDMG	*Zeitschrift der Deutschen Morgenländischen Gesellschaft*

The reader could, wrongfully, understand that the two series of planets put forward on pp. 85ff. are out of the Greek tradition.[7] On the contrary, however, they are a *conflation* of Babylonian, Hebrew, and Greek tradition.

So, I give over this work to the public. May the wind scatter that which is in error within it. However, whatever is true within it, so that it might not be totally worthless, may it, on its humble pages, help to promote the way of God and, thereby, build up his kingdom.

Halle, October 1894   HERMANN GUNKEL

GENESIS 1:
CREATION IN THE PRIMORDIAL AGE

1. Literature (Concerning the Babylonian Origin of Genesis 1)

Up to the present time, Old Testament study has concerned itself chiefly with literary problems and has dealt with the prevailing religio-historical questions in relation to literary criticism. Thus, in the study of Genesis the focus has fallen on the differentiation and dating of sources. To this point in time, the origin and tradition history of the narratives of Genesis have only been touched upon. The quest for the origin of the creation account of Genesis 1 lies, therefore, far from the main channel of contemporary research. This accounts for the fact that, with the exception of Genesis commentaries, only occasional remarks are put forward by certain theologians concerning this issue. On the other hand, given the current scholarly compartmentalization, it is understandable that the Assyriologists, to whom we owe the discovery and exposition of the cuneiform creation account, and the recognition of the relationship of the Babylonian tradition to Genesis 1, have likewise only recently touched upon the Old Testament issues which are broached here. Thus a true scholarly discussion of the origin of Genesis 1 has not yet taken place.

When scholars have considered the origin of Genesis 1, however, their opinions have been quite diverse. Sometimes one hears that the Babylonian creation myth lies behind Genesis 1. Of course, at the same time, there has been considerable dissension over the time of the adoption of the material. The time of the exile has been suggested,[1] or that of the Assyrian hegemony over Judah,[2] or, more commonly, in "the days of the kingdoms of Israel," when the high culture from Babylon would have been at home in Israel through the mediation of the Phoenicians,[3] or an earlier time, such as that of the Tell el-Amarna tablets.[4] Others, and by far the majority, argue that the Hebrews took up the myth from the Babylonians in their original home of Ur-Khasdim.[5] These estimated dates are in almost every case put forward not as secure pronouncements, but rather only as speculations. This accords with the current state of the question.[6] Riehm[7] acknowledges the tangencies of the biblical and Babylonian creation myth, but seems to want to explain the two myths as different manifestations of the same common-Semitic traditional material. On the other hand, Dillmann[8] has challenged the Babylonian origin of Genesis 1: "There are probably common backgrounds, but they already existed in ancient times."

In stark contrast to all these assertions is the view which advocates that Genesis 1 is a free "construction" of the exilic author.[9]

2. Genesis 1 Is *Not* a
Free Construction of the Author

It shall be my purpose in what follows to treat systematically the issue, sadly neglected to this point in time, of the relationship between the biblical and Babylonian creation accounts. In regard to this, however, it appears advisable first to establish what can be said concerning Genesis 1 without Assyriological comparison.

Wellhausen[1] has compared the two narratives, Genesis 1 and Genesis 2, with each other, in order to discover the manner and, thereby, the date of the account of the world's creation. In the paradise account, he recognized a marvelous myth for which the colorful tradition of the ancient Near Eastern world has provided material. "We find ourselves here in an enchanted garden made up of images of true antiquity, the fresh smell of ancient earth wafting toward us."[2] Genesis 1 is totally different. There is no attempt to describe the fantasy, the circumstances of the creation of the world, but rather it is a thoroughly circumspect consideration:

> ... a systematic construction, which can be checked with little difficulty. ...
> In reality only the unembellished framework of the creation remains. ...
> This then is the form of the whole: schema controls contents; instead of more concrete descriptions, we hear logical definitions.[3]

The whole is developed from images of chaos, which Wellhausen considers to be traditional.

In these observations is constituted the starting point — certainly only the starting point — for the historical analysis of Genesis 1. Genesis 1 is, therefore, as it presently exists, not ancient; it lacks the varied colors of primal my-thology; and the shades of grey which we also clearly know from elsewhere in the Priestly sources lead us to the time when judicious consideration was taking the place of ancient poetic contemplation on nature.

This still does not prove that Genesis 1 is anything other than the, admit-tedly, somewhat dispassionate fabrication of the author. By means of the study of legends one may rigorously distinguish between the present state of a narra-tive and its prehistory. In regard to all the narratives of Genesis, it is the task of scholarship, after the literary facts have been determined, to raise the question — often much more important — as to whether perhaps a statement can be made concerning the earlier history of the narrative. Thereby one will not in-frequently establish that a body of material which had been present in Israel long before the written record received by us, has been transmitted to us out of a later time, and in a more modern recension.

At the present time, moreover, strong grounds exist which demand the acceptance of such a prehistory for Genesis 1 as well. Cosmogonies, such as Genesis 1 offers, are generally not inventions of individuals, but rather are regu-larly based on tradition. Indeed, the first scholarly attempts to describe the world — attempts to which Wellhausen compares Genesis 1[4] — are developed from mythological traditions. The Priestly writer has generally not set down in Genesis his random discoveries, but has reshaped traditional material accord-ing to the sensibilities of his era. Fortunately, we still have, in many cases, the parallels from J and E, so that we can establish this. But indeed for this reason the teachings which the Priestly writer presents still should not be ignored. On the contrary, in many instances the Priestly writer harks back to a tradition par-alleling our Pentateuchal sources J and E.[5]

Now the investigator of legends knows of a sure sign on which it is possi-ble to determine whether a narrative flows from older accounts. It is the com-mon fate of older narratives which are preserved in later form that certain traces which first made sense in the earlier contexts are also transmitted in the newer account, in which they have, however, now lost their context. Such old traces, fragments of an earlier whole, without context in the present account, and hardly understandable from the standpoint of the one who finally reports it, disclose to the investigator the existence and the particular traces of an ear-lier form of the existing narrative.

The theme of chaos is just such an ancient trace. The corollary that the present world is derived from "separation" is properly joined with this. Indeed, Wellhausen recognized the theme of chaos as indicative of the narrator. In real-ity, an introduction such as this — darkness and water at the beginning of the world — belongs to mythology and should not be considered as a fabrication of a writer, much less of a person such as the author of the Priestly document. In addition, there are the manifold parallels from heathen creation myths which totally agree with this introduction, that the world was originally water and darkness.[6] One further notes the word בֹהוּ [*bōhû*], shown to be ancient by the Phoenician βάαυ [*baau*],[7] and תְהוֹם [*tĕhôm*] (also ancient because of the lack of an article). But even leaving this out of consideration, it is apparent to us from Jewish literature, above all from Deutero-Isaiah, that the idea of chaos is not consistent with the idea of God as an independently working creator.[8] If, however, a cosmogonic-mythological fragment is added to Genesis 1, the possibility that the whole chapter is a prosaically composed myth can no longer be denied.

Furthermore, there is the "brooding of the spirit over the waters." Indeed, Wellhausen figures this trace to be a part of the previously encountered starting point for the Priestly source. The רוח אלהים [*rûaḥ 'ĕlōhîm*] in this sense is a ἅπαξ λεγόμενον [*hapax legomenon*].[9] The Hebrews knew only the spirit which "falls" onto human beings and which, in them and through them, does all sorts of wonder. In addition, it is the spirit of God which works the secret of life in the body of human beings. The רוח [*rûaḥ*] of Genesis 1, the divine principle of order in the world, parallels of which are the Phoenician πνεῦμα[10] [*pneuma*] and the Greek ἔρως[11] [*erōs*] is a mythical conception. Nevertheless, the world "brooding" reverberates with the ancient mythological conception of a "world egg."[12] Indeed, Wellhausen established that the idea of the brooding spirit of God presupposes a totally cosmogonic conception: "From the brooding spirit, chaos moves on to self-development; however, in the Hebrew narrative, the immanent spirit gives way to the transcendent God and the evolutionary principle is suppressed by the peremptory word of the creator."[13]

What Genesis 1 says about the darkness is peculiar. It is not created by God, but rather it was there at the beginning. The light was created by God over and above the darkness, "which was there at the beginning." The author also avoids proclaiming the darkness as "good."[14] — Indeed, this is an echo of an older mythology, probably one which spoke of a divine light. The idea certainly does not stem from Jewish culture, of which the conception of God was much more consistent with the word of Deutero-Isa 45:7: יוצר אור ובורא חשך [*yôṣēr 'ôr û-bōrē' ḥōšek*].

One can also find an ancient clue in v. 12. God has not "made" the creatures and the animals of the earth, but rather the earth has allowed them to spring forth at the command of God. This expression is even more notable in that it has no apparent parallels among the other works of creation.[15] One must probably find here an echo of mythological speculation on the earth. It is easy to explain why only this trace has been preserved. It persisted because of the perception that the earth puts forth its plants anew every spring.

Moreover, the idea that the "luminaries" of the heavens were created for "dominion" over the day and the night sounds quite ancient. We know enough of the mind-set of ancient Israel and of Jewish culture to be able to place this expression in a larger context. The stars are mighty rulers[16] — the most noble image for the king is to compare him to a star[17] — who exercise dominion over the earth.[18] The peoples of the earth are assigned to them.[19] The constellations have a divine nature to the Hebrews. They are called כוכבי־אל [kôkĕbê-'ēl — "divine stars"].[20] They are אלהים ['ĕlōhîm — "gods"][21] or occasionally בני־אלהים [bĕnê 'ĕlōhîm — "children of gods"].[22] This idea is shown to be ancient in Israel by Judg 5:20.[23] This mythological reflection on the stars (not to mention, more distantly, star worship) clearly lies behind Gen 1:16f. The ancient idea that the constellations control the course of the year is replaced in v. 14 by another idea, i.e., that they only reflect it (אתת ['ōṭōṭ]). One must also note that the expression "the dominion" of the stars over the soil is not developed by Gen 1. Rather it lingers quietly here as a final reminiscence of a long-forgotten astral religion.

A whole series of ancient features are preserved in the narrative of the creation of humanity. God said, "Let us create humanity after our form, like us" (v. 26). The question is often asked what the plural indicates here.[24] It appears to me that the single most probable explanation is already championed by *Targum Jonathan* and by Philo,[25] i.e., that God is to be grouped with the rest of the אלהים ['ĕlōhîm]. Originally a divine council, a סוד קדשים [sôḏ qĕḏōšîm],[26] an עדת־אל ['ăḏaṭ-'ēl],[27] was presupposed here, just as it is described in 1 Kings 22:19-22, Isaiah 6, Dan 7:10, Job 1, *1 Enoch* 14:22ff., and Revelation 4. The plural at Gen 3:22; 11:7 and Isa 6:8, as well as here, is to be understood in this way.

Now, in an ancient and intact narrative it is simply a requirement that a comment should precede such a "we." That comment would concern the other beings with whom God associates himself in speaking the "we." Here, however, as well as in 3:22 and 11:7, this is lacking! This can only be explained in this way: that in all three instances this situation originally prevailed, or, more clearly, existed, but that it disappeared in the development of the traditions. The cause for such an omission is not difficult to discover. Narratives in which other אלהים ['ĕlōhîm] existed alongside YHWH, even as his servants, had a polytheistic ring in later times. Even the "assistance of the spirit at creation," of which the primitive form of Genesis 1 surely spoke, is a totally and completely non-Judaic concept (cf. Isa 44:24). Thus it is easily explained why the original situation is heavily clouded over at this spot. Now, if the parallel texts, Gen 3:22 and 11:7, which come to us in a very ancient setting, have already experienced the same fate, this means that we must assume a very high antiquity for the original recension of Genesis 1. Indeed, Job 38:7 (extremely archaic when compared to the present narrative of Genesis 1) knows the "sons of God" not as assisting in creation, but only as marveling onlookers. These considerations are strengthened by the observation that in the Priestly source any other mention of "angels" is missing,[28] from which it follows that the Priestly source on its own would never have come up with the introduction of other אלהים [*'ĕlōhîm*] besides YHWH.

The same result is achieved from the examination of the צלם [*ṣelem* — "image"] of God, according to which humanity is created. The account is also clouded here. We do not learn directly what the צלם [*ṣelem*] is. It is not the dominion of humanity over the animals, which is spoken of in v. 26b immediately following, and which Ps 8:6ff. and Sir 17:3ff. combine with the concept of the "divine likeness." This dominion was granted to humanity "by a special divine decree"[29] after it was created. On the other hand, when it says at Gen 5:1-3 that God created Adam according to his "likeness" and that Adam, in turn, gave birth to Seth according to his "likeness"; when further, at 9:5f. human beings and animals behold in humanity the divine image and must avoid injuring it, it is clear that behind the צלם [*ṣelem*] nothing other than that which is natural and concrete is to be understood: the likeness of the divinity, which is like the human body. By this, similarity in the spiritual sense was naturally not ruled out. This view was certainly not very apparent to the author of P, however. The primitive narrative, before P laid hands upon it, must have expressed it much more clearly.

That this idea is only slightly appropriate to P and its time can be gleaned from the interpretation of Ps 8:6ff. and Sir 17:3f. It cannot be argued that it was impossible for Hebrew antiquity. The ancient Hebrews always thought of YHWH in anthropomorphic terms. That the divinity could have a non-corporeal, spiritual existence is an idea which would have been totally inconceivable to them. The aversion to portraying YHWH graphically had a totally different basis. Besides, it was in the nature of the religion that, once it had reached a certain stage of development, it conceived of the divinity anthropomorphically; and the inverse view, that humanity bears the "likeness" of the divinity, is expressed not infrequently in antiquity.[30]

Wellhausen[31] maintains that the divine image of humanity according to Genesis 1 even stands in intentional opposition to Genesis 2f. What was granted to humanity from the beginning according to Genesis 1, he obtained by means of theft in Genesis 2f. But the two myths understand the similarity to God in different ways! In Genesis 1 it is the human body which is like God. In Genesis 2f. it is the "understanding" — i.e., that which differentiates children and adults, animals and human beings; not, as Wellhausen argues, "civilization" — which humanity has in common with God. Genesis 1 and 2f. also speak of different things. In turn, the respective terminology of each cannot stem from a polemic of one text against the other. Moreover, there is also the manner by which Genesis 1 speaks of humanity — the words sound almost like a hymn on humanity, the image of divinity, and the king of the animals — which must be understood as an ancient conception. Also ancient is the concept that the generative power of humanity and its dominion over the animals was granted by a blessing from God. Antiquity perceived in these things great mysteries which can be explained only by reference to primordial words of God which are vitally active, even up to the present moment. Wellhausen's judgment that Genesis 1 considers these conditions to be "physiological facts which cannot be questioned and give rise to thought"[32] is, thus, it appears to me, incorrect.

Likewise, in ancient times God considered each creation to be good. Indeed, here a stronger anthropomorphism lies in the background, i.e., the possibility of failure. God looked on each creation and questioned the nature of its existence. He found each to be "good," i.e., satisfactory. These are distinctions which P certainly does not draw and, perhaps, hardly understood, but which nevertheless lie behind his words.

The divine command which assigns only vegetables to human beings and animals (Gen 1:29f.), a command which is revoked after the flood (Gen 9:3f.), could reflect an ad hoc theory concerning the history of human nourishment. Yet this possibility recedes completely when one compares Isa 11:6-9.[33] Isaiah describes here the time of righteousness and joy as a time when the wolf dwells with the lamb, the panther lies down with the kid, and "the lion eats straw like the ox." Such a form certainly agrees with that which the creation narrative assumes. These descriptions cannot be deemed an invention of the prophet. This would be fantastic beyond belief and hardly understandable in the case of a person like Isaiah. It is conceivable only if it is recognized that the prophet is here adopting material which is transmitted by the tradition, and that he is using it for his own purposes.[34] He cites the well-known myth of the golden age. — The myth is much better preserved in Isaiah than in Genesis 1. In the former it is a poetic description with a deep meaning. In the latter it is compacted into a single command of God. — Every doubt vanishes, however, with the observation that similar descriptions appear in Greek and Persian myths.[35]

The distribution of the work of creation over six days and the narrative of the origin of the Sabbath which is joined with it are commonly understood to be late; it is even supposed that this distribution is only inserted into P by a second hand.[36] It is, indeed, correct that the special emphasis on the holiness of the Sabbath in our sources (which in the case of this text is very incomplete), emerged in a particularly strong way only after the exile, and that the division according to the specific works of creation (which belongs to the immediate level of the material) does not appear to be especially well suited to the schema of six days.[37] The description of the first day in which light is created raises a particular difficulty, for how then should one conceive of the regular alternation of evening and morning.[38] — Perhaps the situation is explained by the fact that in the present narrative the stars are created only after the plants of the earth. This peculiar order, which quite obviously contradicts the nature of things and which we can hardly understand in a unified narrative, is possibly clarified by the fact that with the introduction of the seven-day disposition, the plants, for which no special day remained, were assigned to the narrative concerning the earth, and therefore fell before that concerning the stars! — On the other hand, it is quite certain that the Sabbath was an ancient institution in Israel. The question concerning the origin of the holiness of this day could also quite possibly be ancient. And the conception that God rested himself after completing his work, which corresponds somewhat to the practice of Judaism, could hardly have been invented by P if it had not already existed in the tradition. Accordingly, there is no reason to hold that Exod 20:11, where the institution of the Sabbath is justified by the creation of the world, is postexilic.[39]

We thus recognize in Genesis 1 a series of mythologically resonant features. It follows from this that Genesis 1 is not the composition of an author, but rather the written deposit of a tradition; and at the same time, that this tradition stems from a period of high antiquity. We are in a position to detect a part of the history of this tradition inferred from Genesis 1. Two different cosmogonies are joined, the first of which considers the brooding spirit as the principle of cosmic origin, and the second of which views the divine command in the same way. At a later time the ordering of the narrative according to seven days, together with the Sabbath, was appended.

It now appears probable that this tradition could not have arisen in Israel. The parallels to Genesis 1 from the cosmogonies of other peoples lead to this conclusion. It could, however, also be derived from the concept that the world was once water. This concept apparently arose under the the imprint of a particular climate. The myth thus conceives the world's first origin according to the way in which the world comes forth, each new year, at the present time. First there is water and darkness; then, however, light rises and the water separates, going up to the clouds and down to the seas. This view is also apparent to a land the character of which is defined by great rivers. In the winter, rain streams from heaven and mixes with the waters below in a "chaos." But the spring of the year brings the separation of the waters above and those below. This is certain because of the similarity with that creation narrative which is currently joined to the paradise account. There the earth is originally without vegetation since it has no rain (Gen 2:5). A variant, from another tradition now joined with the first, reports that YHWH causes an אֵד [*'ēḏ*] ("a spring of water") to go forth from the earth (2:6). Both are Canaanite ideas. The water is not the enemy who must be expelled that the world might arise. Rather, it is the friend without which the field would not bring forth. It is the blessing of God.[40] Genesis 2, again characteristically, reflects this meditation on nature. In Genesis 1 the divinity overcomes the water. In Genesis 2 he creates it. The myth of Genesis 1 would, however, be completely understandable in Babylon.[41]

In connection with this, it is instructive to note how the Hebrews of antiquity and the Babylonians conceived of the New Year. According to ancient Hebrew tradition, the year begins in the fall. According to Babylonian tradition, it begins in the spring.[42] The time of rain is considered to be the beginning of the New Year in Israel. In Babylon it is considered to be the end of the old year. Now in nature the reality is that the world is created in the spring of the year. Because of this, in Israel water would be viewed as the first creation of God, but in Babylon, the first act of the god is to stop the rain. The application of this distinction to Genesis 1 and 2 is thus clear: the creation narrative of Genesis 2 arises from the Hebrew New Year, but Genesis 1 arises from the Babylonian view.

The few features which we have previously shown to be the remains of ancient tradition in Gen 1 also go back to Babylon: the view of light, and the "dominion" of the stars reflect a background in an astral cult, which is known to have been the religion of the Babylonians. Likewise, the myth of the golden age, a late echo of which is presently joined with the creation narrative, is hardly originally Hebrew. Because the slaughter of animals, offerings, and the joy of living were so totally identified by the ancient Hebrews and because the ancient Hebrew saga dates the slaughter of animals so unabashedly to the most ancient of times (Gen 3:21, 4:4, 7:2, and 8:20f.), we can hardly contend that the delicate feelings which appear to be professed in the myth are representative of ancient Hebrew thought.

The results at which our inquiry has arrived, without recourse to Babylonian cosmogonies, are thus: the creation narrative of Genesis 1, although late in its present form, is not a free construction of the author, but rather goes back to very ancient traditions, the *Sitz* of which we must seek with certain probability in Babylon.

3. The Babylonian Cosmogony

[handwritten annotations: Analysis of Gen 1 indicated that it also has roots in ancient Near East ... cultural appear[s] ... its Sitz im Leben - Babyl[on] (cultural ...)]

The Babylonian cosmogony is known from the Greek tradition through the reports of Damascius and Berossus. The Babylonian theogony of Damascius notes:[1]

> Among the barbarians, the Babylonians, it appears, pass over the singular primordial basis[2] of all things in silence; instead they put forward two principles: Ταυθέ [*tauthe*] and Ἀπασών [*apasōn*]; of these Ἀπασών is the husband of Ταυθέ; they also call her "mother of the Gods." From her is produced an only son, Μωυμῖς [*mōumis*], whom I take to be the intelligible world which comes forth from the two principles. From this one a second generation is produced, Λαχή [*lachē*] and Λαχός [*lachos*];[3] then a third from that pair: Κισσαρή [*kissarē*] and Ἀσσωρός [*assōros*]; from the latter stem the following three: Ἀνός [*anos*], Ἴλλινος [*hillinos*], and Ἀός [*aos*]. The son of Ἀός and Δαύκη [*daukē*] is βῆλος [*bēlos*], which, according to their contention, is the creator of the world.

In the cuneiform inscriptions the foregoing correspond to the following names: *Ti'āmat* and *Apsu*; the byform of *Ti'āmat's* name, *Mummu*, here depicted as the son of *Ti'āmat*; *Luḥmu* and *Laḥamu*; *Kishar* and *Anshar*; *Anu, Illil,* and *Ea*; *Marduk-Bel,* the son of *Ea* and *Damkina*.

The report of Berossus[4] is translated in the epitome prepared by Alexander Polyhistor[5] which Eusebius employed in *Chronicon* I. The text of Eusebius is contained in an Armenian translation and in Greek in the epitome of Syncellus.[6]

[handwritten: a priest in Babyl[on]]

13

Before time, so he narrates,[7] everything was darkness and water, and a wonderful being of singular form arose therein; there were men with two wings; some also had four wings and two eyes; some had one body but two heads, one male and one female, and, moreover, double sexual organs, male and female; other men with the legs and horns of goats or with feet of horses, thus having the form of centaurs. Steers with human heads were also produced at that time, as well as dogs with four bodies and hindquarters with the tails of fish; and there were even more beings with the forms of all sorts of animals, as well as fish, reptiles, snakes, and every kind of wonderful, oddly formed being. Their forms were to be seen in the Temple of Bel as votive offerings. Over them ruled a woman named 'Om 'Orqa[ye],[8] which is, in Chaldean *Thamte*,[9] translated into Greek by θάλασσα [*thalassa*] (of the same numerical value as σελήνη [*selēnē*]).[10] In this situation Bel[11] came into the world. He split the woman down the middle. He made from the one half of her the Earth, and from the other, the Heavens. And he annihilated the animals which belonged to her.[12] This narrative should now, so he[13] asserts, be understood as an allegorical description of natural occurrences. The "all" was originally fluid, and the beings described above[14] were produced in it;[15] Bel, however (Greek Ζεὺς [*zeus*]), split the darkness through the middle, differentiated the earth and the heavens from one another and established thereby the order of the cosmos. The beings, however, could not stand the power of the light, and they perished.[16]

When Bel saw the earth without inhabitants and fruit,[17] he commanded one of the gods to cut off his head and to mix the blood that flowed from it with earth, and thus to form humanity and animals, who would be able to hold up the sky. Bel also completed the stars, the sun, the moon, and the five planets. —

Berossus actually narrates this according to the witness of Alexander Polyhistor:[18] ["This god himself took off his head, and the other gods mixed the blood, which flowed forth, with earth, and from this humanity was formed; for this reason, they [human beings] are reasonable, partaking of the divine wisdom."]

This creation account, transmitted to us only at third hand, is in a terribly disorganized state. Only chaos and the creation of humanity are described in it. Concerning the rest of the motifs, the origin of light, of the gods, of the earth, and of plants . . . all have faded from view, though they certainly were not originally lacking. This conspicuous, and, for us, highly deplorable situation is explained by the *Tendenz*[19] of Eusebius, who has excerpted only the creation account of Berossus in order to prove the impiety of the Chaldean tradition.[20]

Eusebius has, therefore, chosen those two points which are in direct opposition to good common sense: the description of the extraordinary chaos animals and the peculiar narrative of the creation of humanity.

No matter against whom the anger and the indignation of the writer are addressed, the account is hardly objective. Eusebius may have rendered the description of the chaos animals properly. It is, however, less probable that that is true for the narrative concerning the creation of humanity.

According to the excerpts of Eusebius, that narrative contains a plethora of the foulest nonsense. The head is cut off by the god. There is no doubt that he is dead, yet then he creates the stars! This was probably not the sense of the source. The summary at the end, according to which the god himself cuts off his head, demonstrates how carelessly Eusebius has excerpted. In what went before, one of the other gods does it. Likewise, in the summary, only humanity is formed from the mixture of earth and divine blood. According to the narrative which precedes the summary, humanity and animals are formed from the mixture. Thus one could entertain doubts as to whether the Babylonian tradition actually told of the decapitation of *Bel!* It also appears very improbable that the head would be cut off the god who created the world!

It comes to this, then: We hear so much in the Babylonian creation narrative[21] and in the derivative recensions concerning the blood of *Ti'āmat*, which, as it appears, fertilized the previously unfruitful earth, that one could therefore surmise that originally *Bel* mixed the blood of *Ti'āmat* and the unfruitful earth. Perhaps Eusebius had already come across this corruption in the Babylonian account.

The accounts of Damascius and Berossus[22] concerning the Babylonian cosmogony are generally confirmed by the cuneiform discoveries as far as they presently exist. Even the notice of Berossus that images of the "beings" were to be seen in the Temple of *Bel* has found parallels in those cuneiform texts.[23]

We turn thankfully to the discoveries of George Smith for the cuneiform creation narrative. The account, of old Babylonian origin, transcribed by Assyrian scribes for the library of Assurbanipal was found in Kujundschik at the site of ancient Nineveh under the ruins of the palace of Assurbanipal. Further supplements have appeared since then, and still more are expected.[24]

In the beginning, before heaven and earth had names,[25] when the primal father *Apsu* (Ocean) and the primal mother *Ti'āmat*[26] still mingled their waters, when none of the gods was, as yet, created, no name given, no destiny established,[27] at that time the gods first came into being. *Luḫmu* and *Laḫamu* were named, then *Anšar* and *Kišar,* and finally *Anu.*

The rest of this tablet is fragmentary. According to what follows, what is probably described therein is how the "gods of the overworld" and the "gods of

War between Ti'amat + Ansar
+ gods + "horrible beings"

the deep" came to be. There also appears to be a speech concerning the origin of light. Then the myth describes further how *Ti'āmat*, the "mother of the gods," stirs up all the powers of the deep against the "higher gods." All that is preserved of the whole passage is a conversation between *Apsu* and *Ti'āmat* in which they discuss the plot against the gods. It appears that the occasion for the origin of light is found in this rebellion.

The ensuing war between *Ti'āmat* and the gods is described in what follows. On the one side *Anšar* appears as the commander. *Anu, Ea,* and his (*Ea's*) son *Marduk* are named. *Luḫmu* and *Laḫamu* stand in the background. On the other side stands *Ti'āmat*, with whom one party of the gods has joined ranks. Moreover, *Ti'āmat* has created eleven horrifying beings. Over all of them she has installed the god *Kingu* as commander. She has taken him as a husband and has placed the "Tablets of Lordship" upon his breast.[28]

Against this army, *Anšar* dispatches, first, *Anu,* and then, *Ea.* But *Anu* refuses, and *Ea* is terrified and comes running back. Finally, *Anšar* turns to *Marduk, Ea's* son. He is one of the most recent gods to arise and to be given power by "his fathers."

Here the narrative arrives at a new tablet. That the connection is so clearly recognizable we owe to the fact that the myth, like Homeric poetry, loves to recapitulate, in each speech, everything which has previously taken place.

Marduk declares himself to be ready to march out against *Apsu* and *Ti'āmat,* but he will be the "avenger of the gods" only if they, in a *puḫru,*[29] confer upon him the same right of dominion which they themselves have. *Anšar* dispatches his messenger *GA-GA*[30] to *Luḫmu* and *Laḫamu* with the report of *Ti'āmat's* rebellion and *Marduk's* demands. So the requested *puḫru* takes place. After the gods sate themselves on bread and wine,[31] they "establish the destiny" for *Marduk.* His power will be without equal. He shall have royal dominion over the totality of everything. "O Lord! Whoever relies on you, spare his life!" His word shall have miraculous power to call things into being and to cause them to vanish. A sign confirms their promise: a garment is placed in their midst which, at the command of *Marduk,* vanishes and reappears.[32] Thus *Marduk* becomes "king." He is now presented with royal insignia by "the gods, his fathers."

The narrative then describes how *Marduk* prepares for the battle. His armament is a bow and a quiver, a scimitar, and a weapon he receives from the gods as a present. On the basis of iconographic representations we infer that this was a thunderbolt depicted as a double triton.[33] *Marduk* also has a net, a gift of *Anu.* All manner of winds accompany him as allies. Equipped for battle, he mounts his chariot, which is drawn by terrifying creatures (horses?!), and thus he rides forth against *Ti'āmat.*

16

At his approach, *Kingu* "and the gods, his accomplices, who go at his side," were terrified. *Marduk*, however, summoned *Ti'āmat* to battle: "Come here! You and I shall fight!" Now, as the battle began, "the cleverest of the gods" [i.e., *Marduk* — trans.] caught *Ti'āmat* in his net, caused the arrow to fly into her gaping mouth, "and inflated her paunch with fearsome winds." He drew back the scimitar (?) and cut up her body. "He flung down her corpse. He stood over it!" Then *Marduk* overpowered "the gods, her accomplices." He smashed her weapons and he cast them into a net. Likewise, he put the eleven creatures into chains. *Kingu* had the same fate. *Marduk* seized "the tablets of lordship" from him, and he placed them upon his own breast. — Then the god turned back to *Ti'āmat*. He split (?) her head. He caused her blood to be conveyed by the north wind to obscure places.[34] The "gods his fathers" caused gifts to be brought to the victor.

The lord [i.e., *Marduk* — trans.] was appeased. He looked at her corpse and produced a work of art. He divided her body into two pieces. The one half he made into the arch of the heavens and he placed bars along with watchtowers in front of it, so that the waters would not flow forth from it. He set the arch of the heavens up against the primordial waters, and he constructed the heavens like a palace corresponding to the primordial waters, which were conceptualized as a palace. Then he created the stars, the sun, and the moon, and the remaining planets.[35] He established the zodiac and set up the pathways of the stars, and the twelve months. — The words which follow lack only a small fragment. They deal with the creation of animals, and they distinguish the three classes of land animals: the cattle of the field, the beasts of the field, and the vermin of the field. The end of the myth is preserved. In it honorific names are given to *Marduk* in a hymn. These names celebrate *Marduk* as lord of everything. "May he feed the gods like sheep, all of them!"

An explanation of the myth was first attempted by Jensen, *Kosmologie*, 307ff. I express the gratitude which I owe to this scholar by the fact that I am attempting to qualify his findings by means of the *religionsgeschichtliche* method.[36]

The narrative is apparently an aetiological myth, i.e., a myth which describes the origin of a contemporary situation, which seeks to give answer to a question. The myth of creation owes its existence to the question as to whence come the heavens, the earth, the deep, the gods, the plants, the animals, and humanity itself. This myth is thus related to many of the aetiological sagas and myths of Genesis, which explain the origin of names, mountains, springs, geographical features, or anthropological and ethnological distinctions.[37] It is characteristic of myth or saga that it should respond to such questions with an historical narrative.

The Babylonian creation myth describes the origin of the world by conceiving of the primal "arising" in the same way as, even now, the world rises up anew every spring. The time before the creation of the world is depicted as the harshest winter which the world has ever experienced. At that time the power of the Deep held sway — water and darkness were everywhere — until *Marduk,* the god of the emerging sun,[38] defeated *Ti'āmat* and divided the waters above and below.

The concept that there are waters above, half of *Ti'āmat,* arises from the contemplation of whence come the rains,[39] and also from the consideration that at the end of the rainy season, when everything is water, the sun breaks through and makes the waters part.[40]

It is totally understandable that the myth clarifies the rain-soaked impressions which winter and chaos leave, by the idea that that primeval sea swarmed with horrible creatures. This sort of idea is characteristic of myth. These beings are the constellations of the zodiac.[41] This may appear very remarkable at first glance. Nonetheless, the fact that these monstrosities are viewed as stars may be explained by the fact that the stars are children of the night. That they are specifically the stars of the zodiac may arise from the possibility that these stars correspond to the half which is below the horizon, i.e., which stands in the dark realm of the watery deep. At the same time, one should consider the distinction between the stars of the zodiac which remain permanently in their places, and the free wandering planets. The latter are the great, powerful gods. The former are "bound" by their service. The myth describes how *Marduk* "bound" the stars of the zodiac.[42]

When *Marduk* appears with the thunderbolt in the war with *Ti'āmat,* characteristics of the storm-god appear to have forced their way into the myth of the victory of light. This suggests that *Marduk,* the usual symbol of whom is the thunderbolt,[43] is none other than the storm god, who, even disregarding his battle with *Ti'āmat,* was known to the Greeks as *Zeus.*

At the same time, the myth answers the question of whence *Marduk's* present dominion over the world stems. Since *Marduk* is the god of the city of Babylon, this also means that the myth raises the question of the origin of the world dominion of Babylon.[44] Moreover, there is the assumption that *Marduk* is a relatively young god who only lately became equal to his father, indeed, who only lately became ruler of the world. Thus, in the myth the historical fact is reflected, the fact that the city of Babylon gained supremacy in Mesopotamia only in relatively later times.[45] Accordingly, in the myth we possess the specifically Babylonian narrative of the origin of the world. The Babylonians asserted with pride that their god *Marduk* was the ruler of the world, since he had defeated chaos and created the world. Then the gods granted him dominion in the *puḫru,* and he seized the "Tablets of Destiny" from *Kingu.* The privilege and the true right of Babylon to rule the world dates, therefore, from the origin of the world.

The determination of the age of the myth cannot be given with certainty from astronomical considerations.

[Jensen, *Kosmologie,* 315ff., beginning with the idea[46] that the monster *Ti'āmat* was only lately transplanted from the legend into the winter-half of the zodiac, comes to the conclusion that the framework of the Babylonian creation narrative must already have been on hand before 3000 B.C.E., since only in this early period (owing to the procession of the sun) did the vernal equinox fall in Taurus and the autumnal equinox in Scorpio.[47]

The problem is that the first of these ideas is probably so erroneous[48] that this astronomical argument in favor of the theory that the Babylonian epic of creation was already on hand in the fourth pre-Christian millennium simply cannot be pressed.] — Zimmern

We wrest more secure dates from certain notices in ancient royal inscriptions. Agum (ca. mid-second millennium B.C.E.) already reports his erection of a "Sea" *(tâmtu)* in the temple of *Marduk.*[49] In the same way, but even earlier, the ancient king Urninâ from Lagash (4th millennium B.C.E.) describes the erection of a "cosmic sea" *(Apsu).*[50] Accordingly, the myth of *Ti'āmat* is already being told in the 4th millennium B.C.E. — though not necessarily in the form which has been transmitted to us.

It may be inferred from many indications that the myth of *Marduk's* struggle was very popular. We possess numerous depictions of the struggle, especially on cylinder seals.[51] In the best known of these images, *Ti'āmat* appears as a dragon, the front half of which has the mouth and forequarters of a lion, and the rear half of which has the wings and the claws (i.e., on the hind feet) of an eagle. The human sexual organs either indicate a variant of the myth, or are to be understood as arising from the association of androgyny with monsters.[52]

Forms of the *Ti'āmat* monster are mentioned in the inscription of Agum[53] and by Berossus; depictions of the "Sea" in the inscriptions of Urninâ[54] and Agum;[55] cf. also the cultic description of "raging serpents" by Agum, Nebuchadnezzar, Neriglissar, etc.[56]

It may be surmised a priori that such a myth must have existed in many variant forms. We possess a fragment of such a variant.[57] It is interesting that here the myth is no longer set in primordial time, but rather has become a saga. *Ti'āmat* executes a regime of terror among human beings. The *Ti'āmat* myth is here — it appears — fused with a somewhat historical memory. The monster appears as the enemy of humanity and the gods. It is especially significant that in this narrative *Ti'āmat* appears to bear the name *ribbu* (= *rihbu* = Heb. רהב [*rahab*]), although this name cannot be established with complete certainty due to the nature of Babylonian writing.[58] One notes what is said in this text concerning the blood of *Ti'āmat*.[59]

Pinches has found a fragment of a third depiction of creation.[60] This one is characterized by the lack of a struggle with *Ti'āmat*. Indeed, it is here assumed that the whole of the dry land was once sea *(tâmtu)*, without the sea being personified as a monster. Here, as in the greater creation myth, the reed (here *qanû* = Heb. קנה [*qāneh*]) is named among the first creations. The narrative is chiefly concerned with the founding of the Babylonian cities.

4. Allusions to the Myth of the Struggle of *Marduk* against *Ti'āmat* in the Old Testament, apart from Genesis 1

The distinction between the Babylonian myth and Genesis 1 is so great in both religious outlook and aesthetic coloration that they appear, at first glance, to have nothing in common. One completely understands the reluctance of those who are hesitant even to mention the two narratives together. Therefore I consider it proper, before attempting a comparison of the myth to Genesis 1, to raise the question of whether, with the exception of Genesis 1 (which at this point shall remain totally out of the picture), other parallels to the Babylonian myth can be found in the Old Testament.

A number of texts which I wish to discuss have already been noted by certain Assyriologists and theologians.[1]

Rahab

Isa 51:9f.[2]

> 9   *Up! Up!*   *Arm yourself with strength,*
>   *O arm of YHWH!*
>   *Up as in days of old,*
>   *the generations of long ago!*
>   *Are you not the one who shattered Rahab,*[3]
>   *who disgraced the Dragon?*[4]
> 10 *Are you the one who dried up the Sea,*
>   *the water of the great flood?*

> *Who made the depths of the sea into a way,*
> *that the liberated might pass through?*[5]

This is a fervent prayer which desires that the mighty acts of YHWH, which he did once in primordial times, be done again for the liberation of Israel. That particular primordial action is that he once shattered Rahab, that he once violated the dragon (תנין [*tannîn*]). It alludes to a parallel situation, i.e., that he caused the Sea, the waters of the great deep, to dry up. — If this deed of YHWH opened a way through which the "liberated" might pass, it is apparently referring to the pathway through the Red Sea. This also appears as a precursor of the coming salvation; cf. Isa 43:16ff. — Meanwhile, the question remains as to how the destruction of Pharaoh could be depicted as the annihilation of a great monster. Such images are not randomly invented. Rather, they develop only as a later interpretation and appropriation of the tradition. One notes that Rahab is a name. This is even more certain here since the image of Rahab's shattering cannot be understood as a distinctive allegory invented by the poet. Then who might Rahab be? — Pharaoh and Egypt, or the Red Sea? — It is, thus, undeniable that the myth of the subduing of Rahab is presupposed here and that the destruction of Pharaoh has been painted in this text using the pigments of that myth. The peculiar play of colors, in which Rahab is first Rahab, and is then a symbol for Egypt, is characteristic of the style of Deutero-Isaiah.[6]

What this monster might be is apparent from the parallels. Rahab's "shattering" is the drying up of the water of the great "ocean." תהום רבה [*tĕhôm rabbāh* — "great flood"] is the primordial sea under the earth in Gen 7:11, Ps 36:7, and Amos 7:4. One must add that at Gen 1:2 תהום [*tĕhôm*] is the name of chaos. Thus the conclusion cannot be avoided that we are dealing here with the drying up of the primordial sea as part of the creation of the world. It is in this way that YHWH's arm has shattered Rahab. Rahab is, thus, the personification of תהום [*tĕhôm*], of chaos!

Because of the peculiarity of Hebrew style it is not clear to us from this text whether the prophet means a single monster, i.e., the dragon Rahab, or whether he means two creatures, i.e., Rahab *and* "the dragon." Likewise, it cannot be said, from the single allusion, what the "violation" means in concrete terms. What can be known from this one allusion, however, already coincides remarkably well, one must admit, with the Babylonian myth of the struggle of *Marduk* against *Ti'āmat*. One can also compare the fact that YHWH's arm was "girded with strength" in this text with the similar description of *Marduk's* "girding himself with arms" in the Babylonian myth.[7] One further notes that complete knowledge of the myth is assumed, as well as that the application of the miracle of the exodus is hardly being made here for the first time; and that the prophet sees here a recapitulation of every action of primordial time.

Ps 89:10-14[8]

10	*You remain as ruler*	*when the Sea rebels.*
	When[9] his waves rage,	*you quiet them.*
11	*You have violated*	*Rahab like a carcass,[10]*
	with a strong arm	*your enemies are dispersed.*
12	*Yours are the heavens,*	*yours the earth.*
	The world[11] and what fills it	*you have established.*
13	*Yours is the arm,*	*yours[12] the power.*
	Your hand is strong!	*Your right hand is raised!*
14	*On righteousness and justice*	*your throne is established.*
	Grace and fidelity	*go before you.*

The destruction of Rahab is celebrated in a hymn to YHWH. The parallel of "the Sea" is also found here. Since the relationship to creation is clearly indicated in this psalm at vv. 12f., the connection with Egypt is extremely improbable. Rahab is a monster who is killed at creation, or, more precisely, before the creation, since v. 11 stands before v. 12. Psalm 89 thus confirms our understanding of Rahab in Isaiah 51. — One notes the following features: YHWH has "violated" Rahab "like a carcass" at v. 11a; this stands in opposition to the "raging of the Sea," against which YHWH has applied his mighty rule.[13] The scene is to be conceived accordingly: Rahab has raged against YHWH with insolent bravado,[14] but YHWH has proven himself to be lord and has trod the presumptuous pride to the ground. It is also apparent from the parallels how Rahab's raging comes to pass. The roaring waves of the surf wish to take over the land, and YHWH contests their dominion over it. He, however, remains in control. Rahab's bravado, much more difficult to humiliate than that of the waves — thus an intensification from v. 10 to v. 11 — must have become even more arrogant. We conclude: the myth must, therefore, have told how Rahab once actually took possession of the land and in this possession asserted herself defiantly against YHWH.

The monster had confederates in the struggle against YHWH. V. 11b speaks in the plural of "enemies of YHWH." But these confederates are more easily handled than Rahab. Rahab is "violated." They are but put to flight.

The phrase "you have violated her like a carcass" gives a hint concerning the fate of Rahab after her death (cf. Isa 51:9). According to this, YHWH has done something horrible with her corpse. Thus he has dealt with Rahab in a manner similar to the special insults which one would inflict upon the body of a fallen foe.

The poet links praise of YHWH with the struggle against Rahab. There is no one like him among the children of YHWH, in the council of the heavens (vv. 7f.). The world which he has created belongs to him (vv. 12ff.). The description of the taming of the Sea and of Rahab is the centerpiece of the psalm: YHWH is the God of the world; he has proven it; it belongs to him for good reason! In addition to YHWH's power, however, the psalm praises his "grace and fidelity"; it is the good and graceful God who established the world and who has overcome the monster, the wicked, antagonistic being. So also Isa 51:9f. views the shattering of Rahab as a saving action.

The reader notes that all these features: the raging of Rahab, cosmic dominion and confederates, the unparalleled might of the divine conqueror, his right to rule over the world which he created, his character as a good God over against antagonistic Chaos . . . all of these features find their parallels in the Babylonian myth. It is now especially interesting to see from the parallels of vv. 10 and 11 that the myth is not only to be understood as one which is familiar, but, at the same time, that its original sense is conceptually still fully intact. Rahab is the monster of the primordial sea, defeated before the creation. At the same time, she is the Sea, which even now vainly rebels against the rule of YHWH.

Job 26:12f. and 9:13 confirm this understanding of Psalm 89.

Job 26:12f.[15]

  12 *With his might he calmed the Sea,*[16]
     with his understanding he has shattered Rahab.
  13 *The bolts of the heavens feel dread before him.*[17]
     His hand puts the twisted serpent to shame.[18]

That an allusion to a myth exists here is generally admitted. Psalm 89, Isaiah 51, and the context (which deals with YHWH's creative works), as well as the parallel "the Sea" make it indisputable that Rahab is also the Chaos Monster here. Indeed, Job considers Rahab to be the monster of the raging Sea which YHWH "calmed."[19] — A newer feature is that the slaying of Rahab proves not only the power of God but also his wisdom. In this regard one is reminded of how *Marduk*, the "cleverest among the gods," craftily captured *Ti'āmat* in a net. — Here we also hear of the "violating" of the monster. This characteristic, which comes up so very often (and thus is, apparently, a major feature of the tradition), stands here in a very conspicuous parallelism to the bolts of the heavens which shudder before God. We are able to determine the significance of the two expressions from the myth of *Ti'āmat*. *Marduk* cut the deceased monster into two pieces — antiquity perceived this as disgraceful treatment of a dead enemy. Half of *Ti'āmat* he placed above, and he secured it with a bolt so that the upper waters could not stream down. The sense of our text's allusions (which the poet considers to be familiar to his readers) is as follows: the bolts of the heavens, which God has set, are loath to overstep his order and to allow the water to flow down, except when *he* commands them to do so (cf. v. 8). It is he (God), however, who effects this arrangement, and who has so thoroughly disgraced the *hubris* of the serpent. — It is in this way, therefore, that we must understand the sense of "the one who is violated" of Job 26:13, Isa 51:9, and Ps 89:11. In the final colon, "the twisted serpent" apparently stands as a second being beside Rahab. The myth[20] also tells of two beings whom YHWH defeated. This juxtapositioning of Rahab and the twisted serpent recalls the pair "Rahab and the dragon" from Isaiah 51. In the Babylonian myth *Ti'āmat* and *Kingu* stand beside each other.

Job 9:13[21]

In a description of the creative power of God which nips every contradiction in the bud, we read the following.

> *God does not turn back his anger,*
> *Beneath him squirm*   *even the helpers of Rahab.*

"Rahab's helpers" are powerful beings in contrast to feeble humanity (v. 14); but even these must lie down at the feet of YHWH! The parallels describe the occasion for this: YHWH sits in unrelenting judgment over them. — Surely this is an allusion to a myth. One notes again that the poet does not describe this thing, but rather presumes. — This accords with the fact that in the Babylonian myth not only does *Ti'āmat* have helping assistants, assistants who are expressly called "Helpers of *Ti'āmat*," but that these beings also did not die. They were, rather, enchained. Indeed, Job 9:13 speaks of their subjugation, but not of their death; in the same way, Ps 89:11 speaks of the "scattering" of the enemies of YHWH. In the Babylonian account these are the eleven monsters of *Ti'āmat*'s gang. They stand in an extremely close relationship to the zodiac. When LXX translates κήτη τὰ ὑπ' οὐρανόν [*kētē ta hyp' ouranon*], it may, thereby, have in view a description of the figures of the zodiac.[22]

Ps 87:4

At Ps 87:4 Rahab is an apocalyptic code-name for Egypt,[23] which is placed beside the prosaic name בבל [bāḇel] without any explanation. It thus must have been a very common usage at that time. The reader is reminded of the fact that at Isa 51:9 the Rahab myth was also applied to Egypt. There the myth was employed to describe Egypt's fate at the time of the Exodus. The use of the name of the Chaos-Being as a designation for Egypt is very peculiar. Isa 30:7 informs us how such a tradition may have arisen.

Isa 30:7

At Isa 30:7 the early prophet, in an effort to prevent his contemporaries from entering into a pact with Egypt, summarizes, in a coded name, his conviction that this Egypt, despite its horses, its chariots, and its cavalry, will be of no help at all. Egypt is the silenced Rahab.[24] Here we can make out exactly the same Rahab of which Ps 89:10 and Job 26:12[25] speak when they tell of the sea and its waves. Accordingly, the presupposition of this saying is that Rahab, who was overcome by YHWH, was not discarded at that time, but still exists in the present, though "silenced," just as the sea still exists, though "calmed" (Job 26:12). The monster may also be attempting to rebel once again against YHWH as it did in ancient times, but he "silenced" it in primordial times, and he will hold it now in his mighty hand (cf. Ps 89:10). This is also the case with Egypt. It may be like Chaos in its great might, but it is only a conquered monster which rattles its chains, but which cannot break them. It will be no help and no salvation.

Thus we come upon a variant of the narrative, according to which Rahab was not killed by YHWH in primordial times, but rather has only been "silenced!"

The brief saying of Isaiah was meant to be very mysterious, but it would have been totally incomprehensible if the myth had not been commonly known at that time. Furthermore, the insertion of the myth into this text appears so abruptly that one must conclude with great probability that the application of the myth to Egypt was already customary before Isaiah, and that it was adopted by the prophet for his purposes.

Ps 40:5[26]

> Blessed is the man who makes
> YHWH his confidence;

> *And does not give himself up to [rĕhābim]*
> *who does not give in to falsehoods.*

The antithesis "to trust YHWH" ‖ "to give oneself up to רְהָבִים [rĕhābîm]"; the use of the technical term for divine worship (פנה אל [pānāh 'ēl]);[27] and finally the parallel "falsehoods" ‖ רְהָבִים [rĕhābîm], prove that רְהָבִים [rĕhābîm] is a divine name.[28] The psalmist calls the idols of the heathens Chaos Dragons, just as Deut 32:17 and Ps 106:37 call the idols שדים [šēdîm], "demons." In the very use of the name, the loathing of the pious poet for the worship of idols is expressed: the idols are wicked, demonic beings. At the same time, however — and this is the *real* point — this name expresses his conviction that only YHWH deserves trust, that these dragons, as awesome as they appear to be, are, in the last analysis, of no help. They are "falsehoods!"[29] Thus, the being of Chaos is portrayed here in an extremely similar way to that seen in Isa 30:7. The name רְהָבִים [rĕhābîm], which is formed according to analogy with בְּעָלִים [bĕ'ālîm], appears here as completely self-evident; it was, therefore, not uncommon at that time. The reproach, that heathen religion is the worship of Chaos, in this artlessly unjustified generalization, is, however, explicable only if Rahab was a god somewhere, in a religion known to Judaism, by the example of which Judaism could make clear the madness and the folly of idolatrous worship.

Leviathan

Ps 74:12-19[30]

12 *You,*[31] *YHWH, are*   *my*[32] *king from of old,*
   doing deeds of salvation   *in the midst of the earth.*
13 *You have divided*   *the sea mightily;*
   you have broken the heads   *of the dragon in the water.*[33]

14 *You have crushed*   *the heads of Leviathan;*
   you have given him as fodder,   *as food for*[34] *the jackals.*[35]
15 *You have split open*   *springs and brooks;*
   You have dried up   *primordial streams.*

16 *Yours is the day,*   *and yours the night;*
   you have established   *Moon*[36] *and Sun.*
17 *You have installed*   *all the powers*[37] *of the earth;*
   Summer and Winter,   *you have formed them.*

18 *Remember your possession.*[38]   *The enemy scoffs.*[39]
   The foolish people   *slander your name!*
19 *Do not surrender to the*   *the soul which acknowledges you.*
      underworld[40]
   The life of your poor   *do not forget forever!*

Traditional exegesis since the time of the Targum relates vv. 13-15 to the miracle of the Exodus; this is, however, contradicted by the fact that here, as in Psalm 89, the conquest of the dragon stands in the context of the creation of the world. The heroic deed of YHWH in vv. 13-15 takes place before the creation of the world in vv. 16f.[41]

In detail it is to be noted:

The defeat of the Sea and of the Dragon are also parallel here. It is interesting that the poet speaks of a "division" [פורר *[pôrar]*] of the Sea; the expression can be explained by recourse to our myth: the primordial sea was "divided" into the water above and the water below. V. 15 wishes to make clear how easily YHWH was able to deal with the "Sea." He made primordial streams[42] dry; springs and brooks he has "broken up," i.e. he has made moisture dry up and dryness become moist. This description thus says the same thing concerning the Sea that Isa 51:9, Ps 89:11, and Job 9:13 say concerning Rahab: YHWH has used violence on both at his discretion.

A series of new features are present in out text, however.

The name of the monster — clearly the most important — is given. It is Leviathan. One notes that he is conceived as many-headed. One Babylonian tradition[43] speaks of the seven heads of "the great serpent."

Other beings are associated here (as in Ps 89:11 and Job 9:13) with Leviathan. These are called רהבים [*rĕhābîm*] in Ps 40:5 and תנינים [*tannînîm*] here. We have already found the name תנין [*tannîn*] for the Chaos-Monster at Isa 51:9 and Job 26:13. It is characteristic of Psalm 74 that this monster is not only captured but also killed, a feature which differentiates the psalm from Job 9:13 and Ps 89:11.

It is likewise a new feature that Leviathan is cast down before the beasts of the wilderness as food (v. 14). We can perceive the nature of Leviathan from this. The wilderness, which is waterless, stands here in opposition to the element which is appropriate to the monster, i.e., water. Leviathan is, thus, a water monster which is expressly described as "the dragon" at v. 13. Accordingly, the myth tells the following: YHWH smashes the Sea Monster "on the heads" and casts it from the sea to the dry land, where the beasts of the wilderness devour it. This treatment of the body has been summarized by the word "disgraced" at Isa 51:9, Ps 89:11, and Job 26:13. — Moreover, there is the presupposition that the world existed in primordial times as Sea and Wilderness, a feature which recurs in the creation narrative of Berossus, but in another context. — On the other hand, the further assertion that the Deity cast the body of the dead beast into the wilderness is lacking, at present, in the Babylonian parallels. This cannot, however, be considered a reason for rejection of the Babylonian origin of the myth. The myth existed, by its nature, in many variants both in Babylon and in Israel.

The context of the whole psalm is especially important for the reconstruction of the myth. The devout poet looked upon the myth with sensibilities similar to those which are prominent in Isa 51:9f. Sighing under the severe affliction of his people, he created trust and hope from the ancient history. YHWH will, even now, carry out a saving action, an action which is like that which happened in ancient times. Thus the psalmist has seen a similarity between the primordial deed of YHWH and that deed for which he now hopes. Likewise he has seen a similarity between the affliction and the foe of the present and the affliction and the foe of the primordial age.

On the basis of this, the myth which is here presupposed may be reconstructed. The method for doing this is to inquire as to which features of the present situation may somehow be suited to the context of a Chaos Myth. Such a reconstruction can, of course, only lay out *probabilities or possibilities* which, however, become more certain *contentions* as soon as they receive confirmation from other places.

The opponent is called simply אויב [*'ôyēḇ* — "enemy"] in v. 3, צר [*ṣar* — "adversary"] in v. 10. He is "the foe, the antagonist" of God as well as of the world. He is God's foe, צרריך [*ṣirrêḵā*] קמיך [*qāmêḵā*]; he reviles, חרף [*ḥārāp*] (v. 10) and he slanders the name of YHWH, נאץ שמך [*ni'ēṣ šĕmekā*] (v. 10). He sends up an insolent roaring (to heaven) (v. 23). It would be a disgrace for YHWH to look on this any longer (v. 22).

What the context of this impious deed was emerges clearly from the individual expressions of the psalm: the enemy perpetrated upon the earth eternal devastation [משאות נצח [*maššu'ôt neṣaḥ*]] (v. 3), with roaring שאון [*šĕ'ôn*] (v. 23). His dominion on earth is a reign of terror — for YHWH's intervention is a moment of salvation, ישועה [*yĕšû'āh*]; and something which affects the whole world — YHWH defeats him before the watching eyes of the whole world, בקרב הארץ [*bĕ-qereḇ hā-'āreṣ*] (v. 12). Furthermore, one notes that the psalmist asserts with force that the world created after the extermination of Leviathan is the property of YHWH, אחזה [*'ăḥuzāh* — "possession"] (v. 18), that day and night, sun and moon belong to him, and, especially, that he is the one who has established the order of the world. The psalmist, who implores God to care for his own (v. 22), to consider his possession, and to attend to his creation

(v. 20), sees in the "violent deed" of the present (v. 20) a recurrence of primordial chaos. The enemies who oppress the people of God (v. 21), and who profane the holiness of YHWH (vv. 2-8), act as if they do not know that YHWH is the lord of the world. They launch a sacrilegious [נבל [*nābāl*]] assault against YHWH's ordinances (v. 22), as if they wish to unleash a new chaos into the world. "It shakes all the foundations of the earth" (Ps 82:5).

This is specified in how the existence and activities of Leviathan in primordial times are conceived. He has unleashed an immense confusion here below which defies any ordering; and he has disputed YHWH's right to rule. But YHWH has finally paid heed to his insult (vv. 1, 23) and has arisen (v. 22). YHWH has contested with him and imposed his (YHWH's) dominion upon the world.

This appears to be just about the complexion of the myth. We have already found the basic features of this myth, which ring through *this* passage in the form of an impious rebellion by Chaos against the reign of YHWH, . . . we have found them already in Psalm 89, and we have established that the myth is Babylonian. Indeed, in the Babylonian form, the Chaos Beast is named "the enemy."[44] The word "roaring"[שאה [*šāʾāh*] — "to make a noise"] is, in Ps 89:10, a technical term for the roaring of the surf.

The depiction of the foe of Israel as a recurrence of chaos also lies behind Isa 51:9, and thus, in this psalm, is not an independent creation of the poet, but rather it is drawn from the tradition. One notes the great similarity between Ps 74:16 and Ps 89:12, so much so that one may draw the conclusion that both are derived from the same, or better, form similar *Vorlagen*.[45] We must be dealing here with a whole literary *Gattung*[46] of creation hymns.

Isa 27:1[47]

> *On that day YHWH visits*
> *with his sword, the cruel, great, and strong sword,*
> *Leviathan, the twisting serpent,*
> *and Leviathan, the curving serpent,*
> *and he will kill the Dragon in the Sea.*

The apocalypse from which this verse stems has borrowed the code names of both Leviathan and the Dragon from circles of mythological thought. At the same time, it is clear that the mythological names are code words for the realm of the present, just as Rahab designates Egypt in Ps 87:4 and in Isa 30:7. One recognizes from these examples that Jewish apocalyptic thought, after the time of prophecy, was fully conversant with the use of ancient mythological material for its purposes.

On the basis of the foregoing there can be no question as to which myth allusion is being made here. We have established in regard to Ps 74:13f. that Leviathan is a Chaos Monster. To understand the same name here in another way has nothing to commend it, especially since the "Dragon of the Sea" is associated with him in our text, as well as in Isa 51:9 and Job 26:12f.

Accordingly, the attribute of Leviathan as a "curving serpent" can be understood. According to the Babylonian view,[48] which we also find in the Greek, the ocean flows as a ring around all lands. The same conception also exists in the Old Testament: the circle of the heavens, the boundary which separates light and darkness, stands on *tĕhôm* (Prov 8:22; Job 26:10; cf. also Ps 139:9). Thus in Hebrew poetry the primordial אפסי ארץ [*'apsê 'ereṣ*] — "ends of [the] earth"[49] — in Babylonian *apsû*, the primordial ocean — became an expression for the *utter* ends of the earth.[50] Because, consequently, the ocean is also circular, according to the Hebrew view, one can understand why, having the same shape, Leviathan is called "the curving serpent."

Indeed, the word לויתן [*liwyāṯān*] may originally mean the same thing. לויה [*liwyāh*] means "wreath"; לויתן [*liwyāṯān*], therefore, would mean "wreath-like," i.e., the ocean, "which winds its girdle of waves around the lands." Accordingly, the byword "the curving serpent" gives a clarification of the name of Leviathan which is etymologically correct.[51]

It is also probable that נחש בריח [*nāḥāš bārîaḥ* — often translated "fleeing serpent"] means the same thing. Jerome translates *tortuosus*, Symmachus συγκλείων *(synkleiōn);* perhaps this בָּרִיחַ [*bārîaḥ*] is to be connected with בְּרִיחַ [*bĕrîaḥ*] "bolt."[52]

It is now clear that this text enumerates not two (as in Isa 51:9 and Job 26:12f.) but rather three monsters, although only two names appear. Two Leviathans are distinguished, which can be differentiated only by their attributes — but which appear, indeed, by virtue of the names, to be practically identical. Concerning this remarkable situation a hypothesis comes to mind, a hypothesis that the myth spoke only of a single Leviathan, but that the apocalyptist, who had three worldly powers in mind, divided Leviathan, according to his two predications, into two beings. What is more, the author produced three code names. We could, thus, have an example of the way in which mythological material is transformed in the interest of its "contemporary" use in a given situation.

The weapon which YHWH employs in the battle is the sword. That it also receives three predicates, corresponding to the three monsters, is, thus, not an original feature.

The introduction of these three monsters into the apocalypse thus happens so far out of context that one recognizes clearly that the author did not *invent* this usage of the myth, but rather that, according to his customary technique, he *adopted* the prophetic-apocalyptic tradition.

Individual features from the text of Isaiah 24–27 cannot, as is the case with Psalm 74, be used for the reconstruction of the myth. Only this may be said from the text itself: Leviathan and the Dragon, who correspond to the empires of "the present," are conceived as powers, specifically as powers which are YHWH's foes. Leviathan and the Dragon have exercised an oppressive rule on earth, until the deadly sword of YHWH visits them. One may, therefore, see echoes of the Chaos Myth in the description of the final affliction in chapter 24.[53]

Furthermore, there is clearly something new in this text, something which the Jews wish to say to these mythological-apocalyptic code names. This is the idea which is summed up in one mysterious word in Ps 87:4. It is developed here as it is similarly in Psalm 74. The kingly empires of the present are viewed as recapitulations of those terrifying beings of primordial time; and the judgment of YHWH, which fell upon them before time, is desired to fall upon them again. Judaism has deposited its hatred and its scorn, together with its hope and its faith, on the names of these primordial creatures.

Job 40:25–41:26

This text is the well-known poetic description of Leviathan, which is, at present, commonly understood to refer to the crocodile. It is to be conceded that the poet wishes to describe a monster of the present, not one of primordial times. It is also to be conceded that Leviathan bears several features of the crocodile.[54] It needs to be asked, however, whether the text is intended only as a poetic description of the crocodile, or whether it has in view a legendary creature who shares with the Egyptian animal only certain features. This investigation must be undertaken with special caution because of the condition of our Hebrew text, which is considerably corrupted, as has been noted in the commentaries and in the translations.[55]

Leviathan is described in 41:10-13 as a *fire-breathing* monster. This feature is all the more notable since he, on the other hand, is a *water* monster. This can hardly be explained by the crocodile's "expulsion of water which is then illuminated by sunlight." The feature is, on the contrary, specifically mythological. It is known in the Old Testament from the theophanies of YHWH (e.g., Psalm 18). It is thus not simply the crocodile which is described here, but rather a mythological being.

We learn more from 40:25-29.

25 Can[56] you draw out Leviathan on a fishhook?
    Can you hold his tongue fast with a cord?[57]
26 Can you place hooks[58] in his mouth?[59]
    Can you pierce his cheek with a ring?
27 Will he beg you for mercy
    and speak gentle words to you?[60]
28 Will he enter into a covenant with you
    that you might have him forever as a servant?
29 Will you play with him like a sparrow,
    leash him like a pet for a child?[61]

The description, which forms a brief pericope in itself,[62] should indicate that Leviathan is totally insuperable for human beings. The poet is convinced that humans cannot capture him. It must be asked, however, whence the poet has drawn so concrete a picture of the capture of Leviathan? The answer: from the catching of fish. However, vv. 27-29 resist this interpretation. Hoffmann[63] is on the right track when he finds here a contrast between that which is impossible for humanity and that which is not beyond the reach of God's power. It is only a small step to comprehend the description in the same way as that of chapter 38: what humanity cannot do, God has done! Then, however, we theorize a minor mythological tradition as a probable presupposition of the text: God has fished out Leviathan with a hook and line. Yet he has not killed him. Rather, he has simply tied him up with a cheek ring. When the monster was captured, it whimpered very meekly for mercy and was keen to enter into a covenant with God,[64] and to be his servant forever. Now God plays with him as with a sparrow, like a child who holds a pet on a leash. Now God asks: "What person can do this thing which *I* have done?"

One might add that such a description of the capture of Leviathan should very probably be understood as an old Israelite myth. This text bears in abundance the characteristically grotesque complexion which we would expect of such a myth. Given that it is a myth, then is it a myth of chaos? Leviathan is, indeed, a creature of the water. He is fished for like a fish. The fact that Leviathan is not killed here, but rather is only bound, does not speak against the mythic understanding. Indeed, Isaiah also calls the monster of the primordial sea "the silenced Rahab" at Isa 30:7 (cf. p. 26 above).

The proof, however, that this is the correct view is furnished by the fact that the most peculiar element of the text, the playing of YHWH with the bound Leviathan, can only be understood in light of this view.

We already have had the mythological conception explained as a reflection on nature. The same conception of nature stands in the background here. The poet readily speaks of God's sovereign power over the sea, which manifests itself in the sea's overflowing and in its piling up.

> *He checks the waters so they dry up.*
> *He lets them loose, they surround the earth.*

Here the ebb and flow of the sea are both traced back to God.

Psalm 89 has something else. The primordial sea, which must have been vanquished by God, even now attempts, here and there, to seize the land. But "you remain Lord, though the sea rebels" (Ps 89:10). Here the tidal wave is interpreted as the rebellion of the sea, the subsequent ebb of that wave as the proof of divine dominion.

Or, according to mythological thought: the sea is guarded by a "spirit" which keeps it in check. If that spirit lets it go, the result is inundation.

> And the spirit of the sea is masculine and strong, and according to the power of its strength he drags it back with a bridle. And in this way it is driven out[65] and scattered to all the mountains (probably a confusion of ὅρος [*horos*] "boundary" and ὄρος [*oros*] "mountain" of the earth [1 Enoch 60:16].

Thus must one understand the "play" of God with Leviathan. God holds the monster of the sea fast by the ring which he has placed in his nose in primordial times. When he lets the chain loose a little, the monster surges onto the land; this yields an inundation. But then God pulls on it again, and the high and mighty Leviathan must return from the land. Thus, God has the sea in his power, not unlike the lad who allows his pet to run a little bit. This is a reflection on the *realia* of nature, which, though perhaps a bit naive by modern standards, is mediated according to the historical standards of native high-poetry.

The correspondence of Leviathan = Sea/Chaos, here inferred from the facts, is expressed by the poet himself at the end of the pericope. Job 41:23-26 describes Leviathan's sphere of influence.

> 23 *He makes the deep*[66] *boil like a pot.*
>   *the sea like a kettle of ointment.*[67]
> 24 *The foundation of the current is his track,*
>   *the ocean he considers to be a prize.*[68]
> 25 *In the mire*[69] *there is not his equal.*[70]
>   *He is created as the lord of the underworld.*[71]

26 *He is the one whom every "exalted one" fears.*[72]
   He is the one who is king over all the proud.[73]

Here the places of Leviathan are named: deep, sea, foundation of the current — which alternate with names of the underworld, as though underworld and sea normally coincide.[74] And, moreover, the word now appears which links the two conceptions and leaves its mark upon our view of Leviathan. That word is תהום [*těhôm*].[75]

Leviathan rules over the תהום [*těhôm*]. This means that he is the monster of the great depths of water which once covered the earth. He is the Chaos Monster. This also corresponds to what is said concerning him. He is the king of "those who are exalted," "the proud." These words are understood as names for the unruly beings of Chaos. One recalls that "pride" is also the characteristic quality of the sea and its monster at other places.[76]

The form of his rule and control in the water is described in v. 23. Rising and sinking he produces, with his monstrous body, a desolate confusion. "He makes the deep boil like a pot." This is the conception of chaos which we have already inferred from Psalm 74.[77] It happens, moreover, that the Manichean teachers, who also prove themselves to be dependent on ancient Babylonian tradition,[78] likewise described the rule of the devil in the primordial water:

> He "entwined and consumed (everything), spreading corruption to the right and to the left, and he rose up in the deep, bringing with all these movements destruction and annihilation from above."[79]

The tradition of Job 41 thus has in mind the rule of the dragon in the present, just as that rule existed in primordial times. He causes "chaos." Indeed, the oft-repeated theme of the Chaos Myth, that the dragon has arrogated his rule over that of God,[80] shines throughout, when it is reported that he "considers the ocean [תהום [*těhôm*]] as a prize."

Further mythological themes appear to lie behind 41:17 and 40:32–41:3.

41:17 *When he roars,*[81] *gods are afraid.*[82]
      they hide themselves away[83] *(high in the heavens).*[84]

40:32 *Lay your hands on him just one time,*
      then you will not think of battle a second time.[85]

41:1 *Then your*[86] *confidence will be fabricated as a lie!*
     His glance will cast down even a god.[87]

2 *(An angel is afraid)*[88] *to awaken him.*
  and who might venture to appear before him?[89]
3 *Who can do battle with him and come away from it?*[90]
  Under the whole heaven there is not one![91]

Such words are not empty phrases which can be explained only by recourse to the "imagination" of the poet, but rather they presuppose pre-existing narratives of a struggle with Leviathan. Gods have attempted to oppose him, but no one — nothing under the whole heaven — has ended up as a victor. A similar situation is described in the Babylonian Chaos Myth.

41:17 presumes another situation. There it is Leviathan himself who rises up against the upper world. When he roars in its direction, the heavenly beings tremble. Manichean reports also tell of such battles between heavenly beings and the dragon of the underworld.[92] Indeed, parallels may be brought to bear from the Mandaic tradition,[93] which itself draws from the Babylonian tradition.[94]

I do not believe that the mythological reminiscences of the fragments are exhausted with these things, but because of the lamentable condition of the text I think it is best to stop here for the time being.

The result is: Leviathan is indeed at Job 40f., no less than at Ps 74:14 and Isa 27:1, the monster of the תהום [tĕhôm]. According to the tradition reproduced by the poet, he still existed in the present time. All sorts of narratives concerning him are circulated among the people: how the gods once fought him in vain; how (finally) YHWH captured him and placed him in chains. — Therefore, the question emerges whether the poet himself understood the original meaning of these narratives, i.e., whether for him Leviathan was only an animal, or whether he was the embodied sea. The poet has picked up these reports because they were full of poetry and they wonderfully illustrated the almighty power of God. — The Chaos Monster here bears characteristics of the crocodile, an Egyptian animal. Thus, we again note the linking of the myth with Egypt: A *Babylonian* myth with certain *Egyptian* characteristics in the mouth of *Hebrew* poet!!

The understanding of Job 40:25-29 obtains an opportune confirmation at Ps 104:25f.[95]

25 *There is the sea, great and wide,*[96]
  in which there are innumerable swarms;
26 *In it live horrors,*[97]
  Leviathan, whom you have formed for yourself as a plaything.[98]

The psalm praises YHWH's great stature as a creator. All creatures are created by him, and in life and in death they are dependent on him.

27 *They all wait upon you,*
*   for you give them food at its appropriate time.*
28 *You hide your countenance, and they swoon;*
*   you withdraw[99] your breath, and they die.*

We thus understand what the poet wishes to say by the introduction of Leviathan. This powerful and wonderful being, whom God almighty loudly proclaims, should not be omitted from among the creations of God. We would not, however, be able to declare from the psalm alone how one arrives at the remarkable concept that Leviathan is a plaything of God. This is clear only from Job 40.

Thus Job 40 and Psalm 104 help to explain each other. Psalm 104 confirms our exegesis of Job 40. What we found presupposed in Job 40, i.e., that God really plays with Leviathan, Psalm 104 states explicitly. Conversely, Job 40 contains a whole series of ideas of which only the final member is contained in Psalm 104. In the latter it is said only that God plays with Leviathan. In the former, however, it is clear to us how the situation arrives at this play.

In Job it is already not terribly clear that Leviathan was originally the animal of Chaos in primordial times. In Psalm 104 this obscuring of the mythological significance is even more advanced. There Leviathan is simply one more great sea monster. He is created by YHWH, just as all the other animals on the earth and in the sea. That he was once the Chaos Dragon has been long forgotten. The verse is thus viewed as the last tiny residue of an already half-vanished myth.[100] Out of a mythological monster has developed a peculiar creature.

Job 3:8

Those who hold the sea[101] bewitched,[102] may they curse it,[103]
*   those who have power to awaken Leviathan.*

The two halves of the verse are complementary. Leviathan and the sea are parallel to one another. The "awakening"[104] stands in contrast to the "bewitching." "Bewitching" takes away power. "Awakening," which also takes place by conjurations, restores it. Accordingly אָרַר [*'ārar*] and עָרַר [*'ārar*] act as spell and counter spell. The supposition is, thus, that Leviathan and the sea lie in the

37

deep sleep of enchantment; that, however, the spell is occasionally broken and the sleepers awaken.

Who are these powers who exercise the "bewitching" and the "awakening"? They are commonly held to be human sorcerers . . . but incorrectly! The "bewitching" of Leviathan is not an impious interference in the divine order of nature, but rather is the mastering of a dark power opposed to God, . . . thus perpetrated in God's name and by his order. That the "awakening" also happens according to God's will is expressly stated through the use of the word העתידים [hā-'ătîḏîm, "the ones prepared"].[105]

That these powers are more than human is also proven by matching phrases in v. 4. Job calls upon these powers who rule the sea and Leviathan in order to curse the night of his conception, just as he has previously called upon God not to visit "from above" the day of his birth. Accordingly, these lower powers are angels commissioned by God.

The context further demonstrates that the lower powers are powerful in the night, while God has reserved for himself authority over the daylight. They free Leviathan, so darkening the stars of the dawn that the sunrise does not appear (v. 9).

All this evidence falls harmoniously into the picture which we have seen to this point, the picture of Leviathan as the monster of the tĕhôm. While darkness and water belong together in chaos,[106] the "deep" (תהום [tĕhôm]) is added as a third predicate.[107]

Job 41:1 also speaks of the awakening of Leviathan. The concept of Leviathan's enchanted sleep refers to one point already discussed, according to which God holds Leviathan with a ring and plays with him (Job 40:25-29; Ps 104:26; cf. 1 Enoch 60:16); or to another point, according to which God has "silenced" Rahab in the primordial age (Isa 30:7). These are distinct instances of the same concept, that the dark power of the primordial sea, although tamed by God, still resides in the deep.

That which Job 3 says concerning the "enchanting" of the sea is also related to the "calming" of the sea in Ps 89:10 and Job 26:12.

Accordingly, Leviathan is, in the concepts cited by Job 3:8, originally the Chaos Monster who undertakes occasional attempts against the creation of God. The waves of the sea break against the solid land. The darkness occasionally seeks to drive out the light.[108]

It is not, however, maintained that the poet still knew and knowingly cited the myth. Such mythological forms, originally pieces of a greater whole, could live on in the tradition by themselves for a long time, especially when they, as here, have a natural precedent as their basis.

What it is more accurate to say is this: Leviathan still clearly appears in

Job 3:8 as the personified sea, which was no longer the case at Job 40f. and Psalm 104. This means that Job 3 contains the myth in a more original form than the other two recensions. Probably, though not necessarily, the poet continued to think of a cosmic situation in which the sea and Leviathan were still not "enchanted," where Leviathan in the sea ruled over the world, i.e., where Leviathan was the Chaos Dragon!

Behemoth

Job 40:19-24

The description of Leviathan in Job 40 is joined with that of a monster called Behemoth, who likewise is for the poet a creature of the present and probably an animal.[109] Up to the present day it has been designated as the hippopotamus, and it has been thought that the name Behemoth was a hebraization of the Egyptian word *p-ehe-môu,*[110] "water ox." Now it must certainly be admitted here that Behemoth shares some traits of the hippopotamus,[111] just as Leviathan bears some of those of the crocodile. But, in the case of Behemoth (as that of Leviathan) the possibility must be held open that he was originally a mythological monster and only recently has he become a terrifying animal of the present, who is similar to the hippopotamus.[112]

In v. 19 mythic material lies in the background:

> *He is the first of the ways of God,*[113]
>   *created that he might rule the wilderness.*[114]

Behemoth is the first of God's creations. It is not possible, according to Prov 8:22, where the same is said of "wisdom," to interpret the word other than temporally. Behemoth is the first created being! Accordingly, one speaks of Behemoth as one speaks of the history of the creation. It follows, therefore, that Behemoth is more than an animal. He is a monster of the primordial age. This conclusion is further supported by the fact that the poet of Job 40f. describes Behemoth along with Leviathan, whom we have already recognized as a monster of the primordial age. This assumption is further supported by the fact that elsewhere two Chaos Animals stand beside each other (Isa 51:9; Job 26:12f.; cf. Isa 27:1). In the Babylonian account there are *Ti'āmat* and *Kingu.* The contention that Behemoth is the first creation of God is, accordingly, the echo of an older conception according to which he, at one time, existed *before* the creative acts of YHWH.

The second half-verse describes the commission of Behemoth. The brief passage is perfectly parallel to the sayings concerning Leviathan in 41:25b. Leviathan is created to rule the deep. Behemoth is created to rule the dry land. The Septuagint, which translates in both cases πεποιμένον ἐγκαταπαίζεσθαι ὑπὸ τῶν ἀγγέλων αὐτοῦ [pepoimenon enkatapaizesthai hypo tōn angelōn autou], still recognized that the two texts are parallel to one another, and inserted the same thing in both cases for the same reason.[115] Accordingly, before the creation of the world, Behemoth was originally the lord of the wilderness, Leviathan the lord of the watery deep.

1 Enoch 60:7-9

Thus we have here the conception that the most ancient world was not fertile soil, but was, instead, wilderness and water. We have already established this concept in the case of Ps 74:14f.[116] We hear the same thing concerning Leviathan and Behemoth at *1 Enoch* 60:7-9.[117]

> 7*And on that day two monsters*[118] *will be separated.*[119] *A female monster named Leviathan, in order to dwell in the abyss*[120] *of the sea over the sources of the waters.*[121] 8*The male, however, is called Behemoth, who with his breast*[122] *holds a desolate wilderness, called Dêndâin.*[123] . . . 9*I asked that other angel that he might show me the power*[124] *of these monsters, how they will be divorced on a day,*[125] *and how the one will be put into the depths of the sea, and the other onto the solid land of the wilderness.*

4 Ezra 6:49-52

> 49*et tunc* [on the fifth day] *concervasti duas animas. Nomen uni vocasti Behemoth* [Maz Vehemoth, Sg Enoch] *et nomen ecundi vocasti Leviathan,* 50*et separati ea ab alterutro; non enim poterate septima pars, ubi erat aqua congregata,*[126] *capera ea.* 51*Et dedisti Behemoth unam partem, quae siccata est tertion die, et habitet in ea, ubi sunt montes mille,*[127] 52*Leviathan autem dedisti septimam partem humidam, et servasti ea, ut fiant in devorationem, quibus et quando vis.*[128]

Here we hear again that Leviathan rules the deep and Behemoth the dry land. It is impossible for both texts to have concluded this from Job 40f. In addition, it happens that *4 Ezra* places the origin of these beings in the primordial age, and that *1 Enoch* even knows that Leviathan was a female monster and Behemoth a male.[129] Likewise in the Babylonian materials *Kingu* and *Ti'āmat* are husband and wife. Therefore we have in *4 Ezra* and in *1 Enoch* two traditions which are independent of Job 40f., and which give us a very favorable confirmation of our understanding of Job 40f.

In addition to this, there is also the probability that בהמות = *p-ehe-môu* = "water ox" could be impossible. Indeed, there is no basis whatsoever for viewing the word as non-Semitic.

The remaining verses provide us with only a slight yield:

Vv. 15-18 deal with Behemoth's food and his shape.

V. 20 appears to describe his kingdom. The beasts of the field view him with astonishment.[130] The verse is the parallel of 41:26.

Vv. 21ff. speak of the place where he dwells:

21 *In the wasteland*[131] *he lies down beneath lotus trees,*
   in a hiding place of reed and rush.
22 *Oaks*[132] *cover, overshadow him,*[133]
   the babbling of the brook surrounds him.
23 *If the stream ebbs,*[134] *he does not quiver,*
   he remains undaunted even if the flood[135] *breaks out.*

V. 24[136] deals with the capture of Behemoth by God. The passage is parallel to the subsequent description of the capture of Leviathan.

Accordingly the whole text has the following contents: All the animals of the dry land revere their master in Behemoth. He lies among the reeds, and although not a water animal, he is not afraid before its ebb and flow. Only God himself is able to overcome him.

Something Egyptian clearly echoes through such words: the "stream," the inundation of the Nile, the lotus trees, the Nile reeds. But although something Egyptian may have stood before the eyes of the poet, so too one should note that in the Babylonian recension the reed is also the oldest plant[137] — it thrives in the chaotic world of the swamp; that although יאור [*yĕ'ôr*] is certainly a name for the Nile, the domain of Leviathan is similarly designated in Job 41:24; and finally that inundation is also characteristic of the primordial sea (cf. Ps 89:10f., etc.).

The picture which vv. 20-24 paint allows us to conceive of it, as far as the text is clear, as a pallid description of an originally mythological monster. At any rate, these verses do not overturn the previous conclusion that Behemoth was originally a Chaos Animal.

These results are upheld by lines of support which are drawn from two other points.

Isa 30:6ff.

Isa 30:6ff. bears the superscription (by a later hand) משא בהמות נגב [*maśśā' bahămôt neḡeḇ*]. By analogy to other משא [*maśśā'*] superscriptions in the book of Isaiah, this refers to the saying which occurs in the verses which follow. In this regard it refers, in v. 7, to רהב המשבת [*rahaḇ ham-mošbat*], which we have already explained.[138] This very unusual formation will, at the very least, draw the attention of the reader to itself. Accordingly the superscription should be translated: "An Oracle concerning the Monster of Egypt."[139] We thus are able to perceive a similarity between רהב [*rahaḇ*] and בהמות [*bĕhēmôt*]. רהב [*rahaḇ*] is the proper name from the myth. In the case of בהמות [*bĕhēmôt*], however, which is used like a proper name, the Hebrew ear was still able to pick up the appellation "monster."

Ps 68:31

We draw another correspondence from Ps 68:31.[140]

[YHWH][141] has reproached[142]	the beasts[143] of the reeds,
the assembly of the gods,[144]	the princes of the people.[145]
The stirred-up sea[146]	he has made cleaner than silver;[147]
he has scattered the peoples	who took their delight in war.

The verse describes God's judgment upon the peoples of the world. According to v. 32, the poet focuses especially on Egypt and Ethiopia. He compares the war-loving nations, whom YHWH scatters, with a silty, stirred-up sea, which YHWH "makes cleaner-by-far than silver." — Likewise, however, the judgment of the peoples issues in the judgment of their gods. These are, according to Jewish teaching, the angels whom God has assigned to be the "princes of the peoples" but who have misused their divine commission for the oppression of the pure ones.[148] These rulers of the peoples, however, are also called "animals of the reeds." We are dealing here, therefore, with "reed beasts" who are also gods, who rule over the peoples, and who stand in parallel with "the sea."

These seemingly disparate predicates are, therefore, if the results obtained thus far are understood, arrayed together in a single unified form. The animals of the reeds stand in parallel to the sea, just as elsewhere the Chaos Beings Rahab (Isa 51:9f., Ps 18:10f., and Job 20:12) and Leviathan (Ps 74:12f., and Job 3:8) alternate with the sea. Ps 68 designates these beings as "reed animals." The reeds[149] are, according to Job 40:21, the dwelling place of Behemoth. This has already appeared in the Babylonian Chaos Myth. Psalm 68 speaks — as the context shows — of many "animals of the reeds," Job 40 of only a single Behemoth. Likewise, in Ps 40:5 the רהבים [rĕhābîm] stand beside רהב [rahaḇ].

Accordingly, the "animals of the reeds" should be viewed as beings of chaos. The proof of the correctness of this designation is found in the fact that by this designation the whole text becomes understandable. We will show later that the word גער [gā'ar], "to rebuke," is a technical term in this context.[150] The rule which the "animals of the reeds" exercise is depicted as a "stirred-up" sea; compare this to Job 41:23. This is the form of chaos; cf. also Ps 89:10.

The sea which is stirred up with silt will, in the latter days, be "clarified" by YHWH. "To calm" (Ps 89:10), "to still" (Job 26:12), and "to silence" (Isa 30:7) are all words which are used of the sea. They are completely parallel to this divine "clarifying." The Chaos Myth is here described eschatologically and applied to the peoples who are enemies of Israel. The same happens at Isa 30:7, Ps 87:4, Isa 27:1; cf. Isa 51:9f. and Ps 74:2ff.

It has been shown in the foregoing[151] which concepts are included in this interpretation: the rule of the "war-loving" (i.e., the murdering and thieving enemies of Israel) is designated as an inversion of all the ordinances of God, as a new chaos. The Jews could have found no more characteristic expression for the horror which they felt before the powers of the world, or for the faith that their God would indeed prevail over those powers. In regard to the judgment of the peoples, there is the word פזר [pāzar], "to scatter," as at Ps 89:11. The enemy who is symbolized by chaos is Egypt, as at Isa 30:7. Isa 51:9f. and Job 40f. also mention Egypt. The distinctive feature of this text (Ps 68:31) is that the Chaos Monsters are actually gods. Thus in all three of the texts in which Behemoth and the animals of the reeds are mentioned, the Chaos Myth lies in the background.[152]

The Dragon in the Sea

In our investigation to this point we have found creatures, "the dragons in the sea" (Ps 74:12f.), in the company of Leviathan. These dragons should be combined with בני שחץ [bĕnê-šāḥaṣ] ("children of pride") of Job 41:26, the "helpers of Rahab" in Job 9:12, the "enemies of YHWH" in Ps 89:11, and the "terrifying things" of Ps 104:25. In other places in the Old Testament such תננים

[*tannīnîm*] also appear. The dragons are snakelike beings with horrible venom. Sometimes they appear as land animals (Exod 7:9ff., Deut 32:33, and Ps 91:13). At other places they are residents of the waters. They are "the great *tannīnîm*," in distinction to the schools of fish (Gen 1:21). As Rahab or Leviathan stands in parallel to the *Tĕhôm*, the sea, at Isa 51:9f., Ps 89:10f., Job 26:12, and Ps 74:13f., so the "dragons" and the "floods" (תהמות — [*tĕhōmôt*]) stand beside each other in Ps 148:7. Thus, if Rahab and Leviathan are mythic personifications of the תהום [*tĕhôm*], we have to regard the dragons as the personifications of תהמות [*tĕhōmôt*], the ways of the sea at Ps 89:10.

The religious imagination also conceived of the "springs" as the dwelling place of the dragons. The name of a spring near Jerusalem, the "dragon spring" (עין התנין — [*'ên hat-tannîn*]) of Neh 2:13, is the only residue of the concept which has been transmitted to us. This idea also brings the dragon together with "water" and "deep."

Apart from these תנינים [*tannīnîm*], a certain תנין [*tannîn*] is mentioned in Isa 27:1 and 51:9, a תנין [*tannîn*] who is placed on a par with Rahab or Leviathan. Other texts also designate the chief monster himself as תנין [*tannîn*].

Job 7:12

*Am I the sea or the dragon
that you have set guards against me?*

The parallels make clear that the dragon here is the monster of the sea.[153] The setting of guards presumes that this monster is still alive and, perhaps, could be dangerous. A concept thus appears here which is similar to that which we postulated for Job 40:25-29 and for Job 3:8 (cf. pp. 33f. and 38f.). There Leviathan was shackled by a ring or bound by a spell. Here the dragon is placed under guard. In all three places he is still existent in the present as an antagonistic and sinister being, although a being who is under YHWH's control. The same mythical view of nature is the basis of all these texts, one in which the sea is seen as opposed to YHWH's creation but also kept within bounds by YHWH.

Ps 44:20

One notes that תנין [*tannîn*] is used as a proper name without an article. This has already been seen at Isa 51:9. Ps 44:20[154] is quite similar.

> *For you have violated us, instead of the dragon.*[155]
> *Darkness covers us over.*

In the same way that Job bemoans the harrowing judgment imposed upon him — "Am I the dragon that you must constantly guard me?" — so here the people wail, "You dealt with us as though we were *the dragon*," for whom, to be sure, "violation" and darkness are appropriate.

We should, therefore, infer from the text that "dragon" and "violated" go together. We have already seen this connection at Isa 51:9, Ps 89:11, and Job 26:12 — cf. Ps 89:11, which even has the word דכא [*dikkā'*] — and we have discussed its original significance in Job 26:13 (p. 25 — cf. Ps 74:14 on p. 28).

When he is "violated" by YHWH, the dragon is also covered with darkness, i.e., he is cast into the gloomy deep. This agrees with the picture which has been wrested from the materials to this point. In that picture darkness and the watery deep repeatedly appear together.

תנין [*tannîn*] is also a proper name here, the same as it is at Job 7:12, and just as at that location, knowledge of the story of תנין [*tannîn*] is a presumption of this text.

Ezek 29:3-6a[156]

3 *Thus says YHWH: Behold, I am against you,*
Pharaoh, you great dragon,[157]
  who lies in the midst of your stream,
who says, "Mine are the streams.[158]
  I have made them."
4 *I will place hooks in your jaws,*
  and make the fish of your streams stick to your scales.
I will haul you from the midst of your streams,
  and all the fish of your streams.[159]
5 *I will cast you into the wilderness,*
  and all the fish of your streams;
onto the open field you shall fall,
  you shall not be buried or entombed.
To the animals of the ground and the birds of the heavens
  I will give you as food.
6 *That all the dwellers of Egypt might recognize*
  that I am YHWH.

Ezek 32:2-7[160]

> 2 *Son of man, lift up a lamentation*[161] *over Pharaoh, the King of Egypt,*
> *and say to him:*
> *You are a young lion,*[162]
>
> . . . .
>
> *You were like the dragon*[163] *in the sea,*
> *you broke forth with your streams;*[164]
> *you muddied the waters with your feet*
> *and plowed up its streams.*
> 3 *Thus says YHWH:*
> *So I shall spread my net over you,*
> *drag you out in my share;*
> 4 *I shall cast you onto the land,*
> *onto the open field shall I toss you.*[165]
> *The birds of the heavens shall light upon you,*
> *the beasts of the whole earth shall sate themselves upon you.*
> 5 *Your flesh shall I cast onto the mountains*
> *to fill the valleys with your carcass.*[166]
> 6 *The lowlands shall drink your pus.*[167]
> *The watercourse shall be full of your blood.*
> 7 *I shall cover the heavens at your destruction,*[168]
> *and shall clothe its stars in darkness.*
> *The sun I shall cover with clouds,*
> *the moon will not be able to shine its light.*

These depictions of the destruction of Pharaoh are described as allegories. The prophet has selected the crocodile as a convenient image of the Pharaoh and has depicted Pharaoh's defeat as the capture of a crocodile.[169] It is correct that the תנין [*tannîn*] here has the form of a crocodile. Ezek 29:4 speaks of his scales. One should, however, question whether this תנין [*tannîn*] might be a particular crocodile.

In the mouth of the crocodile the speech "Mine are the streams, . . ." is probably appropriate. But the "I have made them . . ." is certainly not (29:3, 9). The crocodile can, perhaps, be lord of the Nile, but not its creator. In fact, the whole passage has many points which go far beyond even a poetic account of the capture of a crocodile. Especially noteworthy is the grandiose description of how the body of the dragon fills mountains and valleys, and how the brooks flow with his blood (35:5f.); or how sun and moon are darkened by his destruction (32:7f.).

One must distinguish clearly, by exegetical means, between the allegories which the author has poetically created, and such materials as he has found before him and in their turn allegorized. The primary feature of the first is the concept which existed in the mind of the writer, while that of the second is the depiction itself. Both stylistic *Gattungen* should recognize that since unity is given to the poetic allegory by the larger concept, the picture may, here and there, have unnatural characteristics. The controlling thread which runs through the depictions should be sought within the allegorized material. Therefore, certain things may not become immediately apparent in the interpretation.[170]

Now the above depictions contain much which cannot be descriptive of Pharaoh. It cannot be said that Pharaoh was the creator of the Nile (29:3). — Likewise, the description of the dragon mucking up the streams with his feet (32:2) makes a mockery of that designation. And then the prophet immediately repeats this: if humans and animals are rooted out from Egypt, the streams will again become as smooth as oil (32:13f.). Whence this peculiar interest on the part of Ezekiel in the clarity of the waters of the Nile? — This argument is especially enlightening if one, perchance, compares these "allegories" with Psalm 80, where all the main characteristics are clear, while here the form completely stifles the interpretation.

Therefore the conclusion is unavoidable that the material of Ezekiel 29 and 32 was not invented ad hoc by the writer, but rather was taken over by him. We do not have here a poetic allegory. What we have is, rather, an allegorized narrative.

Who "the dragon in the sea" originally was is clear from the context. He is the lord and creator of the "streams" (29:3). Each text elucidates its counterpart. He maintains himself to be the creator of the "streams," but he has only arisen with the stream. Indeed, in a positive sense he is himself the "stream." Ezek 32:2 "You break forth into his (the sea's) streams," uses the same word which appears elsewhere for the first breaking loose of the sea (Job 38:8) and for the assaults of the flooding Nile (Job 40:23). — From this the judgment upon the dragon and the judgment upon the stream (29:10) also issue. The dragon will be captured; the stream will be dried up (30:12). Accordingly, the text states that the earth will drink the blood of the dragon and the brooks will be full of it (32:5f.)!

Thus the Ezekiel texts prove that the dragon is a mythical monster, the personification of the "sea" or the "streams." This finding is confirmed by Isa 27:1, Isa 51:9, Job 7:12, and Ps 44:20, where *Tannîn* means exactly the same thing. Indeed, the name "Great Dragon" of Ezek 29:3 has a counterpart in the Babylonian "great serpent."[171] The task remains of reconstructing, according to the method developed in regard to Psalm 74 (cf. pp. 27ff.), the myth which Ezekiel had before him.

The dragon's element is water, in which he "lies spread out" [רבץ [*rābaṣ*]; cf. Gen 49:25] in Ezek 29:3, and with which he "bursts forth" (Ezek 32:2). This water appears to be the "sea" in 32:2. On the other hand, it is clearly the Nile, [with the dragon depicted] as the crocodile, as seen in 29:4. The Nile plays such a major role in the whole myth that one can hardly accept that the prophet was the first to bring it into the narrative. The dragon surely already had the form of the scale-covered crocodile before Ezekiel received the tradition. — We thus notice clear Egyptian characteristics in the myth. One could understand the myth as a description of the inundation of the Nile. We have also established Egyptian features in the descriptions of Leviathan and Behemoth in Job 40 and elsewhere.[172]

Besides the dragon, only water creatures, "the piscine race of his streams" (Ps 29:4), appear allegorized as the allies of Egypt, סמכי מצרים [*sōmkê miṣrayim*] (30:6); עזריה [*'ōzrêhā*] (30:8). These beings thus correspond to the עזרי רהב ['*ōzrê rāhab*] of Job 9:13, the תנינים [*tannînîm*] of Ps 74:13, the "foes" of YHWH of Ps 89:11, and the "arrogant ones" of Job 41:26, etc.

The characteristic attribute of the dragon is its pride. This feature is a major theme of the depictions of both the dragon and the Pharaoh. An arrogant word is placed in the mouth of the dragon in 29:3. It is so important to the prophet that he repeats it in 29:9. And in the interpretation, it is echoed by the impious arrogance of Pharaoh in almost every line. Indeed, the type of pride is similar in both cases. Egypt has lifted itself up over the peoples and has sought to rule over the peoples (29:15), but YHWH has "humbled" the "arrogant pride" of the ruler of the world. The idea is, therefore, that such might in human hands is a threat against YHWH.[173]

The dragon says: "The streams are mine. I have made them" (29:3, 9). This word is blasphemy against YHWH. The dragon "behaves in his pride as if there was no longer any divine power over him."[174] He contests with YHWH for dominion, so that God must prove "that he is YHWH." — The rule of Egypt is a rule of terror. "It has spread terror in the land of the living" (32:32).

The dragon stirs up the sea with his feet (32:2). YHWH is concerned that the stream again become smooth (32:13f.). Apparently the terrorization and antagonism of the reign of the dragon are depicted under these forms. — The capture of the dragon is variously depicted. YHWH places hooks in his jaw (29:4), or spreads out a net and a snare over him (32:2). Through all of this, fish of the sea remain hanging stuck to his [the dragon's] scales (29:4).

It is very interesting, accordingly, to be able to find two variants of the myth in Ezekiel. The narrative must have been extremely popular to have had such diverse forms. The capture by hooks recalls the description in Job 40. — This is a confirmation of what was noted there. — The capture by the net has its parallel in the Babylonian myth of *Marduk*.

It is striking that the dragon is not buried or entombed (39:5). This feature is so important to the prophet that he returns to it in the case of Pharaoh at 32:18ff. The attention which is given to the corpse of the dragon appears as the ultimate insult, the proper punishment for his earlier arrogance. Thus the dragon is violated even in his death. — Here once again is that which Isa 51:9, Ps 89:11, Job 26:13, and Ps 44:20 meant when they used the roots √דכא [√dk'] and √חלל [√ḥll]. The myth, in which the dragon was originally a divine being, considers it natural that the dragon should have an honorable funeral after his death. But, the prophet observes with great emphasis, he shall *not* be buried! Rather, he shall be cast onto the land, into the wilderness, where the beasts of the field and the birds [of the air] will eat him. This is such an important feature that both recensions contain it (29:4 *and* 32:4). The same is true at Ps 74:14. When this verse describes how the earth drinks up the blood of the dragon and the brooks fill up with it (32:6), a mythic view of nature emerges: The water is the vanquished enemy. The earth cannot bring forth fruit until the water is driven away, but the water is also the reason for the fertility of the dry land. The stream which covers the land is not only an image of destruction but also an image of the grace of God.

> *His grace is like an overflowing stream,*
> *like a flood which the dry land drinks.* (Sir 39:22 [27f.])

Thus we recognize the reason why the myth so emphatically expresses the feature of the non-burial of the dragon. The reason is the etiological explanation of the natural cycle, an explanation which the myth provides.

On the day when the dragon is overthrown the heavens are darkened and the stars do not shine. Darkness lies over the land (32:7-8). Indeed, other "days of YHWH" are described in similar ways (Amos 5:20 and 8:9; Zeph 1:15; Joel 3:3f., etc.). Nevertheless, it is because of the position of vv. 7-8 in unmediated proximity to features of a clear mythical origin, and because of the recapitulation of 30:3 and 30:18, that one must postulate that these also originally belonged to the myth. It must be postulated that YHWH appears in the darkness of the storm cloud for the judgment of the dragon.[175]

Jer 51:34, 36, 42

The descriptions of Jer 51:34ff. and *Pss. Sol.* 2:28-34 are similar. In Jer 51:34, the king (or *Bel*, v. 44) of Babylon is compared with a dragon who has filled his belly with the riches of Israel, until YHWH himself takes up Zion's cause against Babylon (v. 26) and rips the food out of *Bel's* mouth (v. 44). Beside these images of the dragon stands an extended "sea" image — of which, however, nothing more will be spoken in chapters 50f. — And that extended "sea" image is the judgment of Babylon by the drying up of its streams.

> I dry up its sea.   I cause its sources to run dry.

The same occurs at 51:43 and 50:38. We have seen a similar feature already at Ezek 30:12 (cf. above, p. 47).

The destruction of Babylon depicted as an "inundation" is described with another phrase.

> The sea has overrun Babylon.
> She is covered with the spray of its waves. (Jer 51:42)

At v. 55 the destruction of Babylon appears to be compared to raging waters.

Now the concept of water is already quite closely connected with Babylon. We recall, among everything which concerns Babylon, the "great waters" on which it lies (51:13). If we had only Jeremiah 51, therefore, we could conclude nothing concerning the dragon from it. Since, however, we have heard so much previously about a relationship between the dragon and the water, we cannot view the identification of these two as a coincidence here. The prophetic writer adopted the image of heathen power as a dragon. The water was also received by him, with the dragon. This was especially appropriate of Babylon. What he says about the food of the dragon can very probably be identified as an allegory established ad hoc. On the other hand, perhaps it is a feature of the "dragon myth" which is, as yet, unsubstantiated for us.

Pss. Sol. 2:28b-34[176]

28b Do not hesitate, O God
to pay them back,
29 to turn[177] the pride
of the Dragon[178] into shame!
30 He did not delay,[179]
for God showed me
his pride put to shame[180]
on the mountains of Egypt,[181]
he was abused, dishonored[182]
on water and on land.
31 With his corpse
the waves arrogantly played,
and no one buried him;
32 he was shamefully violated.
He had forgotten[183] that
forgotten at the end;
he was a man

33 *He had uttered, "I will be lord*   *of land and of sea.*
   He had not known   *that God is greater,*
   mightier in his great power,
34 *who alone is King in heaven*   *and judges kings and kingdoms.*

One recognizes in the psalm a description of the Jewish campaigns and lamentable end of Pompey.[184] Clearly the shameful death of the Roman general is described in the cited verse. Yet we do not have here a simply "realistic" description. The corpse of the slain enemy which lies upon the mountains, and with which the waves also play, has gigantic dimensions. If one compares Ezek 32:5f. with *Pss. Sol.* 2:30 one realizes that the image of the fate of the corpse of the dragon, which had already existed in the tradition for a long time, has also come down to the poet of this work. The pious Jew who knew the traditional material was moved when he recognized the striking similarity between the fate of the heathen and the fate of the dragon. He painted the death of Pompey with the colors of the dragon from Egypt.

In this regard he has the prophecies of Ezekiel in mind, but not them alone. The psalm contains a number of features which cannot stem from Ezekiel. The "pride" of the dragon is described at length. In Ezekiel, however, this is only hinted at in a single word (Ezek 29:3, 9). It consists, however, in the fact that the "impious one" (*Pss. Sol.* 2:1), the "arrogant one" (2:35), demands dominion over the world for himself. "He wishes to be ruler of the land and of the sea" (2:33). He has not honored God. God's great might he has not acknowledged (2:33). God, however, has proven his rule over the earth against this human arrogance (2:34ff.). With great emphasis the psalm describes how the most "shameful violation" has trampled the "insolent pride." God's judgment is righteous (2:16)!

All of this fits in with Ezekiel, but is not found there. We hold these features not to be arbitrary elaborations by the psalmist. We recall that the pride of the dragon, which places God's world dominion in doubt, was already encountered in other texts (cf. Psalms 89 and 74), and that throughout all of the texts the violation (shaming) of the monster stands in a special relationship to it (cf. Ezekiel 29 and 32). We thus recognize that mythical materials still existed as a living tradition within Judaism at this time. Moreover it explains the way in which the poet introduces the dragon in chapter 29 as a universally known quantity.

We have already repeatedly established the reference of the myth to the destiny of the world power and to an Egyptian event. One notes further that the myth, both here and in Psalm 74, refers to an "enemy" who arrogantly desecrates the Temple (v. 2), who tramples Jerusalem, and who deals badly with the people (24f.). One cannot help but think that in the myth itself there was an occasion for such an interpretation. Perhaps the myth itself already described how a monster once oppressed humanity, impiously inverting the divine and the human on earth, until God's judgement overcame him. We possess a Babylonian variant of the *Marduk* myth with similar contents (cf. above, pp. 19f.). We will find in that which allows broad support for the theory that a similar interpretation was known among the Jews.

Nothing more of the original sense of the myth is immediately called to mind in the psalm. Since the "impious one" wished to be the ruler of land and sea (v. 33), this could be looked upon as a reminiscence of that being who was not content with dominion within his own realm, the sea, but also strove to rule over the land!

The Serpent

Amos 9:2f.[185]

> 2   *If they force themselves*[186] *into the underworld,*
>   *my arm will draw them up from there;*
>   *And if they climb up to heaven,*
>   *I will hurl them down from there;*
> 3   *If they hide themselves on the summit of Carmel,*
>   *I will track them there and catch them!*
>   *If they hide before my eyes on the bed of the sea,*
>   *there I will direct the snake to bite them.*

The prophet assumes as an acknowledged fact that a נחש [*nāḥāš*] dwells on the bed of the sea. He uses the word נחש [*nāḥāš*]. As an example of the infinite power of YHWH Amos argues that YHWH himself has power at a place where his eyes do not appear to reach. The נחש [*nāḥāš*] on the bed of the sea is at his disposal.

We should recognize with certainty from this reference alone that this "serpent" is a mythological monster, the personified sea. In addition to the parallels, נחש בריח [*nāḥāš bārîaḥ*] (Isa 27:1; Job 26:13); נחש עקלתן [*nāḥāš ʿaqallāṭōn*] (Isa 27:1), in which Leviathan is called a נחש [*nāḥāš*] (Isa 27:1), or רהב [*rahab*] and נחש [*nāḥāš*] are juxtaposed (Job 26:13), there is also the Babylonian "great serpent."[187]

The idea that this monster is still currently in existence, but is under the control of YHWH we have established as present in Ps 104:26, Job 40f., Job 7:12, and Job 3:8. He lies on the bed of the sea. Ezek 32:2 is parallel: he lies in his streams. According to this, the tradition of the dragon of the sea was known in very ancient times in Israel. It is found in the oldest datable writer of Israel.

The allusion to our myth described to this point leads us to the very threshold of the New Testament. I will temporarily break off the investigation of the subject in later Judaism at this point in order to take it up later in another context.[188]

Let me then sum up the material which we have discovered:

- The mythological beings חיות [*ḥayyôṯ*] in Ps 68:31, the *animae* in 4 Ezra 6:49, are called:

  רהב [*rahaḇ*] in Isa 51:9, Ps 89:11, Job 26:12, Job 9:13, Ps 87:4, and Isa 30:7; רהבים [*rĕhāḇîm*] in Ps 40:5;

  לויתן [*liwyāṯān*] in Ps 74:14, Isa 27:1, Job 40f., Job 3:8, Ps 104:26; and בהמות [*bĕhēmôṯ*] in Job 40 and Isa 30:6.

- The following appear as names:

  תנין [*tannîn*] (without the article) in Isa 51:9, Jer 51:24, Ps 44:20, Job 7:12; ὁ δράκων [*ho drakōn*] in Pss. Sol. 2:25;

  התנין אשר בים [*hat-tannîn 'ăšer bay-yām*] in Isa 27:1;

  התנין בימים [*hat-tannîn bay-yammîm*] in Ezek 32:2;

  התנין הגדול הרבץ בתוך יאריו [*hat-tannîn hag-gāḏôl hā-rōḇēs bĕ-ṯôḵ yĕ'ōrâw*] in Ezek 29:3;

  חיות הקנה [*ḥayyôṯ haq-qāneh*] in Ps 68:31;

  הנחש [*han-nāḥāš*] — according to the context בקרקע הים [*bĕ-qarqaʿ hay-yām*] — in Amos 9:3; and

  נחש בריח [*nāḥāš bārîaḥ*] in Job 26:13; cf. Isa 27:1.

- The following are juxtaposed:

  רהב [*rahaḇ*] and תנין [*tannîn*] in Isa 51:9;

  רהב [*rahaḇ*] and נחש בריח [*nāḥāš bārîaḥ*] in Job 26:12f.

  לויתן [*liwyāṯān*] and התנין [*hat-tannîn*] in Isa 27:1; and

  לויתן [*liwyāṯān*] and בהמות [*bĕhēmôṯ*] in Job 40f., 1 Enoch 60:7-9, and 4 Ezra 6:49-52, where Leviathan is king of the creatures of the water, and Behemoth is lord of the dry land. According to 1 Enoch 60:7-9, Leviathan is a female monster and Behemoth is a male monster.

- Close beings subordinated to these are:

  עזרי רהב [*'ōzrê rahaḇ*] in Job 9:13;

  "Enemies of YHWH" (איבים [*'ōyēḇîm*] beside Rahab in Ps 89:11);

  תנינים [*tannînîm*] beside לויתן [*liwyāṯān*] in Ps 74:13f.;

  אניות [*'ŏnîyôṯ*] beside לויתן [*liwyāṯān*] in Ps 104:26;

  כל־גבה [*kol-gāḇōah*] ‖ כל־בני־שחץ [*kol-bĕnê-šaḥaṣ*], over whom לויתן [*liwyāṯān*] is king in Job 41:26; and

"Fish" of the streams in Ezek 29:4, as סמכי מצרים [*sōmkê miṣrayîm*] of תנין [*tannîn*] in Ezek 30:6, 8.

- Leviathan is described as:
  many-headed in Ps 74:14;
  a type of נחש [*nāḥāš*] in Isa 27:1;
  בריח [*bārîaḥ*] ‖ עקלתון [*'ăqallāṯôn*] "twisted" in Isa 27:1;
  a fire-breathing crocodile in Job 41:9-12;
  likewise the תנין [*tannîn*] is described as "scaly" in Ezek 29:4; as a Nile crocodile in Ezekiel 29 and 32.

- The relationship with the sea is especially clear:
  תנין [*tannîn*] ‖ רהב [*rahaḇ*] ‖ מי תהום רבה [*mê tĕhôm rabbāh*] ‖ ים [*yām*] in Isa 51:9f.
  הים [*hay-yām*] and its ways ‖ רהב [*rahaḇ*] and the enemies of YHWH in Ps 89:10f.;
  ים [*yām*] ‖ תנינים [*tannînîm*] ‖ לויתן [*liwyāṯān*] in Ps 74:13f.;
  רהב [*rahaḇ*] ‖ הים [*hay-yām*] in Job 26:12;
  לויתן [*liwyāṯān*] ‖ ים [*yām*] in Job 3:8;
  חיות הקנה [*ḥayyôṯ haq-qāneh*] ‖ ים [*yām*] in Ps 68:31;
  ים [*yām*] ‖ תנין [*tannîn*] in Job 7:12;
  תנינים [*tannînîm*] ‖ תהמות [*tĕhōmôṯ*] in Ps 148:7; and
  עין התנין [*'ên hat-tannîn*] in Neh 2:13.

- Throughout, the being appears as a water monster:
  In the sea, in Isa 27:1, Ezek 29:3, Ezek 32:2, and *4 Ezra* 6:52;
  On the waters, in Ps 74:13;
  On the bed of the sea, in Amos 9:3;
  In the abyss of the sea, in *1 Enoch* 60:7-9;
  In the deep, in Job 3:8; cf. v. 14.
  Leviathan as lord of the תהום [*tĕhôm*], in Job 41:25;
  As a being of the darkness, mighty in the night, in Job 3:8;
  Covered with darkness, in Ps 44:20.

- Only Behemoth is lord of the dry land:
  Job 40:19, *1 Enoch* 60:7-9, and *4 Ezra* 6:49-52.
  Thereby a co-existence of Sea and Wilderness is presumed for the era before the creation of the world; this is also so in Ezek 29:5, Ps 74:14f., and *Pss. Sol.* 2:30f.

- The following are linked with the Nile:
  The תנין [*tannîn*] in Ezekiel 29 and 32;
  לויתן [*liwyāṯān*] and בהמות [*běhēmôṯ*] in Job 40f.

- A relationship to the creation of the world appears throughout:
  Ps 89:12f. and Ps 74:15ff.; the conquest of the dragon is accomplished "in the days of primordial time, the generations of prehistory" in Isa 51:9;
  מקדם [*miq-qeḏem*] in Ps 74:12;
  The dragon is proud of himself: "I have created the streams" in Ezek 29:3; cf. 32:2;
  Yahwism fervently declares that the dragon is a creation of YHWH, in Ps 104:26ff.; Behemoth is the first of God's creations, in Job 40:19.

- The characteristic attribute of the dragon is pride:
  Ezek 29:3, Ps 89:10f., *Pss. Sol.* 2:28-29; cf. Job 41:26;
  He slanders (חרף [*ḥērēp*]) God in Ps 74:18;
  The roar (שאון [*šĕ'ôn*]) ascends to heaven in Ps 74:23; cf. שאת [*šĕ'ēṯ*] in Job 41:17.
  He demands dominion for himself over all the streams which he has created in Ezek 29:3; over the תהום [*tĕhôm*] in Job 41:24; over sea and land in *Pss. Sol.* 2:33.
  In his realm he does terrible things, Ezek 32:32:
    He produces "eternal devastation" in Ps 74:3;
    He mucks up the water with his feet and stirs up the streams in Ezek 32:3;
    He causes the תהום [*tĕhôm*] to boil like a kettle in Job 41:23.
  Jer 51:34 and 44 (if they belong to the myth) speak of a food with which he fills his belly and which he must restore later;
  He is the "enemy" pure and simple, אויב ['*ôyēḇ*], צר [*ṣar*] of Ps 74:3, 10, and 18; especially the enemy of YHWH in Ps 74:4, 23;
  His helpers are YHWH's "enemies" in Ps 89:11; he is called the "impious one" in *Pss. Sol.* 2:1, the "arrogant one" in *Pss. Sol.* 2:35.
  Parallel to these features stands the roaring (שאון [*šĕ'ôn*]) of the sea which charges against the land in arrogant pride (גאות [*gē'ûṯ*]) in Ps 89:10, stirring up the mire in Ps 68:31.

- YHWH subdues the monsters.
  An allusion allows us to conclude that other אלים ['*ēlîm*] made a vain attempt at battle before YHWH did so (Job 41:17; cf. v. 3).
  YHWH could no longer look upon the "outrage" (Ps 74:22) and the ac-

companying affliction. He acted in "anger" (Job 9:13), but at the same
time he carried out a "saving deed in the midst of the earth" (Ps 74:12).

He is the good and graceful God, who has vanquished the wicked, hostile
being (Ps 89:2f., 15). By this he has revealed his "might" (Isa 51:9; Ps
74:14; 89:10; Job 9:13; 26:12); also his "wisdom" (Job 26:12).

His "arm" (Ps 89:14) is "equipped . . . with might" (Isa 51:9). He has
proven himself to be מֹשֵׁל [mōšēl] (Ps 89:10), to be "king" (Ps 74:12;
Pss. Sol. 2:30).

The world which he has created fears him (Ps 74:15ff.; Job 26:13); the
world, to which he gave standards and laws (Ps 74:17); the world, which
belongs to him by right (Pss 74:16; 89:12).

There is no one like him in the assembly of the heavens (Ps 89:7).

· The battle with the dragon is described in the following:

One text alludes to the "arming" of YHWH (Isa 51:9); another describes
how the heavens were darkened by the conflict (Ezek 32:7).

Ps 68:31 alludes, perhaps, to an angry word, a גְעַר [gĕʿar], "a rebuke" —
which surely preceded the battle.

YHWH's armament is the sword (Isa 27:1), or hook and line (Job
40:25), or fishhooks (Ezek 29:4), or net and snare (Ezek 32:2).

Behemoth is captured with the snare (Job 40:25).

YHWH "dashes" Rahab "to pieces" (מָחַץ [māḥaṣ] — Isa 51:9; Job 26:12),
"smashes" (רִצַּץ [riṣṣaṣ]) Leviathan on the "heads" (Ps 74:14). He hauls
the dragon from the floods and tosses him onto the dry land (Ezek
29:5; 32:4; Ps 74:14), where the water monster is helpless.

The "helpers" of the dragon are "scattered" (פִזַּר [pizzar] — Ps 89:11; the
phrase occurs also at Ps 68:31), fall at YHWH's feet (שָׁחֲחוּ [šāḥăḥû] —
Job 9:13); or their heads are "shattered" as well (Ps 74:13). Hanging on
the scales of the dragon, they are hauled out with him and are flung to
the earth (Ezek 39:5).

The fate which the corpse of the dragon will suffer is given especially detailed treatment.

As a hideous punishment for his arrogance (Pss. Sol. 2:30ff.), he will be
"humiliated" (√חלל [√ḥll] — Isa 51:9; Job 26:12; Pss. Sol. 2:31), דכא
כחלל [dikkēʾ ke-ḥālāl] — Ps 89:11; דכא [dikkēʾ] — Ps 44:20), even
in death.

He will not be buried (Ezek 29:5; Pss. Sol. 2:31), but his body will rather
be cast into the wilderness (Ps 74:14; Ezek 29:5; 32:4).

There (in the wilderness) he will be eaten by the animals (Ezek 29:5;
32:4; Ps 74:14).

His flesh fills the mountains, his blood the brooks (Ezek 32:6).

- The extinction of the dragon appears in parallel to that which YHWH has done to the sea.

    He dried up the sea, the waters of the great תהום [tĕhôm] (Isa 51:10);

    He calmed (רגע [rāgaʿ] the sea (Job 26:12);

    He "split" it (פורר [pôrār] — Ps 74:15).

    He dried up the streams (Ezek 30:12; cf. Jer 51:26), made them run as smooth as oil (Ezek 32:13f.).

    He made the sea brighter than silver (Ps 68:31).

- According to another recension the dragon is not dead, but rather only subdued.

    He is "brought to quietness" (רהב המשבת [rahaḇ ham-mošbāṯ] — Isa 30:7).

    When God captured him, he acted very gentle and became God's servant. Now God holds him fast on rings (Job 40:26). God occasionally plays with him (Ps 104:2; Job 40:296).

    He lies at the bottom of the sea, but must hearken to God (Amos 9:3).

    He can still be dangerous, so that God places a watch over him (Job 7:12).

    According to another view, a magic spell took away his power (ארר ['ārar]), but the beings who cursed him — at YHWH's behest — are also capable of "awakening" (ערר ['ōrēr]) him (Job 3:8; 41:2).

- Such authority on the part of YHWH over the monster of the sea is parallel to YHWH's power over the waves of the raging sea.

    YHWH calms (שבח [šibbaḥ]) them in Ps 89:10.

    The spirit of the sea hold the sea fast on reins.

    The bolt of the heavens frightens him (Job 26:13).

Variants

This summary shows in how many different forms the myth was told — a circumstance which proves the richness of the material. This is not surprising when one realizes that the period from which we know our myth in Israel, i.e., from Amos up to the time of the *Psalms of Solomon*, encompasses more than seven hundred years, and that the time from which the sources for this myth flow most richly, i.e., the period from Ezekiel on, encompasses more than five hundred years. At that time, moreover, various influences from foreign sources appear to have flowed together.

The most important variants are:

1. Whether the dragon is dead or is allowed by the deity to live — the distinction is explained by different views of nature, i.e., whether or not one sees in the sea of the present a continuation of the primordial sea.

2. Whether the element of the dragon is the sea or the Nile (the latter clearly at Ezekiel 29 and 32). Clearly Egyptian materials have been completely woven into the latter recension.

3. From the application of the myth to the kingdoms of the world we are able to conclude that the dragon myth became a saga told about a terrible monster who oppressed humanity, blasphemed against the deity, and finally was overthrown. This postulated form of the myth, lying not so far behind *Psalms of Solomon* 2 and Psalm 74, is supported by a Babylonian variant of the myth (above, pp. 19f.) which has the theorized contents.

4. Furthermore, one should conclude from Isa 27:1; 30:7; 51:9; Ezekiel 29; 32; Pss 68:31; 74; 87:4, and *Psalms of Solomon* 2 that before its prophetic-apocalyptic expression, the myth was already being applied eschatologically, i.e., had become a prophecy: YHWH will vanquish the dragon in the future. *1 Enoch* 60:24f., *4 Ezra* 6:52, and *2 Apoc. Bar.* 29:4 have this form of the myth.

It cannot be explained from Israelite religious history how this transference of the myth from primordial time to the end time took place. It should, therefore, be postulated that the myth already possessed each form in pre-Israelite times. A parallel is found in the myth of a "golden age" which we similarly find as a prophecy in Isa 11:6-9 (cf. above, pp. 10f.). Because this myth is also transmitted in (unfortunately late) Greek and Roman sources, transmitted with the same eschatological twist, it should thus be concluded that the myth was also narrated in Israel before Isaiah narrated it as a prophecy.

From these and similar[189] considerations, the conclusion is — put forward provisionally with some caution — that pre-prophetic Israel already possessed an eschatology. It was told that just as was the case *at the beginning,* so also there will be a *future* destruction of the world and a blessed time which will follow. It can be maintained, without risk of contradiction, that this eschatology was not very important in the living religion of ancient Israel. But the existence of a pre-prophetic eschatology certainly is *not unimportant* for the origin of the prophetic future-expectation.

We know recensions in which not only the originally divine nature of the

Chaos Beings has been totally forgotten (it is attested only at Pss 68:31 and 40:5), but the very idea that they were personifications of the sea also has retreated more or less into the background; i.e., in these recensions the grandiose mythological forms of these Chaos Monsters have begun to become fabulous beings, remarkable animals. The process has begun for Leviathan in Job 40f. It is already in full swing for Behemoth in the same text. It has been concluded by the time of Ps 104:26.

Application

Nowhere in the literature which we have received is the myth of YHWH's struggle with the dragon narrated. The Judaism which assembled the canon over time did not adopt such myths which reflected paganism so strongly. Nevertheless, the way in which the myth is not described, but rather is presumed in every text which speaks of the dragon, proves that it was quite probably known and accepted among the people. The absence of the myth from the canon, which we, in the interest of the Christian reader, certainly do not regret, clearly appears as a striking example of the fact that we in our Old Testament possess only a fragment of the ancient religious literature of Israel.

From the very beginning, the myth was a hymn to YHWH. The YHWH-hymn was, therefore, the peculiar place where the dragon myth was customarily cited. A perfect example is Psalm 89. The poet, who describes the divinity of YHWH which overwhelms humanity (Job 40f.; 9:13; 28:13; cf. Psalm 104); the prophet, who frightens sinful people with God's omnipotence (Amos 9), or who points out the shameful dominion of foreigners (Isa 51:9) — both of these make reference to YHWH's power over the dragon.

"Bound Chaos" is the image of obstinacy which raises itself up against God, but which is unable to do anything against him (Isa 30:7). Generally, Judaism dealt with Chaos, which was revered as a god in certain religions known to the Jews, by making clear the powerlessness of *all* pagan gods (Ps 40:5). The poet draws the images of "humiliation" (Ps 44:20) and of the "fixed guard" (Job 7:12) from the myth. Both are characteristic of Chaos, and, at the same time, as allusions to the fantastic myth, are centerpieces of the texts which contain them.

The eschatologically shaped myth very often refers to the appearances of the present. In this regard Chaos, to which this recension of the myth ascribes a future reign of terror and a final defeat by YHWH, is understood as the earthly empire of the present. This earthly empire is a prophetically predicted, recurrent Chaos. In its arrogant desire for the world dominion of YHWH it grasps at the crown, it oppresses the pious, and it overthrows all the ordinances of YHWH. It is the enemy of God and of humanity. It will, however, surely be defeated by YHWH when the time comes. Thus Ezekiel represents the overthrowing of Pharaoh, Isaiah 27 represents the overthrowing of the three world empires, Ps 68:31 represents the overthrowing of Egypt and Ethiopia, Psalm 74 represents the overthrowing of Antiochus Epiphanes, and *Psalms of Solomon* 2 represents the overthrowing of Pompey — all of these are using features of the myth. Such application of the myth to Egypt — apparently in the Palestine of Ptolemaic times — was so common that Rahab has become a proper name for Egypt in Ps 87:4.

The individual uses of the ancient myth are differentiated from one another insofar as Ezekiel, Psalm 74, and *Psalms of Solomon* 2 use the ancient material, with a certain artistic freedom, as a marvelous image of the expected judgment of YHWH. Nevertheless, in the mysterious name "Rahab" (Ps 87:4) and at Isaiah 27, as well as at Ps 68:31, we witness the beginnings of another spirit quietly drawing near. The myth, in this interpretation of the world empire, becomes a fragment of eschatological dogma. Now it appears as secret knowledge. Judaism draws from it esoteric apocalyptic names. The individual features of the myth are pondered, and an attempt is made to interpret them. At the same time, the relationship of Chaos and the world empires is so apparent that the Chaos Creatures of the divine sphere become the people who rule the world (Ps 68:31). What is sought in them is information concerning the future. They are, thus, altered slightly in their detail in order to make the interpretive context of contemporary history even more evident. Isa 27:1 offers a good example of this. Thus the prophetic use of myth begins to become an apocalyptic interpretation.

Further development could lead to the fact that the myth, now become fully apocalyptic, taken over with all of its features, is allegorized and transmitted as a great mystery. If indeed this stage of Judaism is to be substantiated, we will have to investigate other texts.

It is of singular notice for us that once, at Isa 51:9, the myth is connected to an event of the past, the history of the Exodus, which, in the third reference, is described as the drying up of the sea (Isa 51:10a).

The fact that the myth is so often applied directly to Egypt still deserves special consideration.[190] The explanation of this fact must not deal only with Israelite circumstances, for we possess coins minted under Augustus in celebration of the conquest of Egypt, coins which depict Egypt as a crocodile. Even today, among the Arabs, *el-par'un* is still a comic nickname for the crocodile.[191]

We would note concerning this theory that the creation myth, which the sources named above presume, is not of purely Babylonian origin. Rather, an Egyptian myth has been added to the Babylonian one.[192]

We have to this point repeatedly shown that the description of the shattering of the dragon of which we have spoken is one which parallels what YHWH did to the sea in primordial times, what he still presently does. We still possess a series of poetic sayings which speak of the sea in exactly the same way, but without the mythological concepts of monsters of the deep.

The Conquest of the Sea in Primeval Times

Ps 104:5-9[193]

> 5 . . . Who[194] has established the earth on its foundations,[195]
>   *that it might not tremble, always and forever.*
> 6 *Long ago ocean constrained it, like a garment it covered it;*[196]
>   *waters*[197] *stood upon the mountains;*
> 7 *before your rebuke*[198] *they fled,*
>   *before the clap of your thunder they were driven off,*
> 8 *from the mountains down to the valley,*
>   *to the place which you have ordained.*[199]
> 9 *You have set a bound which they may not pass,*
>   *that they may never again cover the earth.*

Job 38:8-11[200]

> 8 . . . *who assisted at the birth of the Sea,*[201]
>   *as it burst forth, as it escaped from the womb;*
> 9 *when I gave him clouds*[202] *as a garment,*
>   *dark clouds as a diaper;*
> 10 *when I limited*[203] *him with my rule,*
>   *set a bar for him and a door,*
> 11 *and said: "You may come only up to this point.*[204]
>   *Here the insolence of your waves shall be stilled."*[205]

Prov 8:22-31[206]

> 22 *YHWH has prepared me as the firstling of his works,*[207]
>   *as the beginning of his creation in primordial time.*
> 23 *I was active*[208] *before eternity, in times of old,*
>   *before the beginnings of the earth. . . .*[209]

24 *When the torrents had not yet come to be, I was brought forth,*
    when the springs did not yet gush[210] water.
25 *Before the mountains had subsided,*
    before the hills, I was born.[211]
26 *When the earth had still not brought forth grass,[212]*
    and the fertile lands had not brought forth an herb of the earth;
27 *When he laid out the heavens, I was beside him,*
    when he described the upper circle upon the flood.
28 *When he fastened the clouds above,*
    designated the sources of the flood;[213]
29 *When he gave to the sea its boundaries,*
    that the water might not transgress his command;[214]
30 *Then I was beside him as a coddled child,[215]*
    I played before him all the time;
31 *I played with the fertile lands[216] of the earth,*
    joked with the children of humanity.

Jer 5:22b[217]

I placed the sand[218]	*at the boundary of the sea,*
an eternal statute	*which it cannot transgress;*
Yes, it surges up upon it,	*but it[219] has no power against it,*
Yes, its waves roar,	*but they do not overrun it.*

Jer 31:35[220]

Thus says YHWH,	
who created the sun	*as a light for the day,[221]*
the moon and the stars	*as lights in the night,*
who threatens the sea	*so that its waves are terrified,[222]*
YHWH Ṣ̌ĕḇā'ôṯ is his name.	

Ps 33:6-8[223]

6 *Through YHWH's word are the heavens created,*
    through the breath of his mouth all their host;
7 *who joined together the water of the seas like sheaves,[224]*

> who placed the floods in storerooms.
> 8 Before YHWH the whole earth is afraid,
>   all the inhabitants of the world tremble before him.

Ps 65:7f.[225]

> 7 Who in his strength laid out the mountains,
>   girded with power,
> 8 Who has quieted the raging of the sea,
>   the spraying[226] of its waves.

Sir 43:(25)23[227]

> Through his wisdom he has brought the deep[228] to peace,
> and islands[229] he has planted therein.

Prayer of Manasseh 2–4[230]

> 2 Who has created heaven and earth
>   together with all their host;[231]
> 3 who has fettered the sea
>   with his commanding word;
>   who has locked up and vanquished the abyss
>   with his terrifying[232] name;
> 4 so that[233] all might tremble and quake
>   before his majesty.

All these descriptions more or less clearly suppose that the creation was preceded by a subjection of the sea by YHWH. And they presume that YHWH still maintains the ordinance which he established at that time, as, e.g., against the sea which is disposed to rebellion. In our time when literary-critical questions are of dominant interest and when one is prone to determine the antiquity of the ideas, without further ado, according to the chronological assessment of the sources, the notion suggests itself that these descriptions, which probably all fall historically after P, should be understood as further elaborations of Genesis 1. Alone this stands completely improbable. Job 38, Psalm 104, and Proverbs 8 especially have an extremely independent stance over against

63

Genesis 1. All three texts speak of works of creation which Genesis 1 does not contain. And the common material of these works is often disposed quite differently. Thus, according to Job 38:6, the morning stars are in existence before the earth. In Genesis 1 they are created only after the plants. In addition, these descriptions are by far older and more mythological than Genesis 1 with its pale supernaturalism. What matters most for our theme, however, is the creation of the sea. Genesis 1 says simply that God divided the sea and the land by his creative word. Here, however, we hear of "the birth of the sea" (?), of the "calming" of the raging flood, of its "chasing back" by YHWH's "thunderclap," of the bolt and of the door by which it is held, even now, within boundaries. Moreover, it is more important to note that in the latest text, the Prayer of Manasseh, even such ancient concepts as the fettering, incarceration, and conquest of the ocean are mentioned. — In addition, it happens that the mythical concepts which are found in Genesis 1, the brooding of the spirit over the abyss and its division into an upper and a lower deep, occur in none of these descriptions. Thus it follows that other, and far more ancient, myths of creation were known to Judaism besides that of Genesis 1.

Now these statements concerning the overthrow of the sea are quite similar to those in Isa 51:10; Ezek 30:12; 32:13f.; Pss 68:31; 74:13; 89:10; Job 26:12; etc., which we have found to be parallels to the struggle of YHWH with the dragon. On the other hand, there is much which we hear in our descriptions of the sea which is related to that which was said above concerning the monsters of the deep. The words are, in part, repeated:

תהום [těhôm] is the residence of Leviathan (Job 41:24); in the parallel, the residence of Rahab (Isa 51:9f.); it also occurs in the present materials (Ps 104:6; Prov 8:24, 28; Sir 43:23; and Prayer of Manasseh 3).

גיח [gîaḥ] is used concerning the dragon (Ezek 32:28); concerning the "birth" of the sea (Job 38:8).

There is the dominion of the dragon over the sea and the land (*Pss. Sol.* 2:33, etc.); תהום [těhôm] once held the earth covered (Ps 104:6).

The offense of the dragon is pride (Ezek 29:3); the arrogant sea was a parallel of this (Ps 89:10); likewise at Jer 5:22, Ps 65:8, and Job 38:11.

גאות [gēʾût] [= "lifting up, majesty, pride"] of the Sea (Ps 89:10); likewise גאון [gāʾôn] [= "exaltation, majesty"] (Job 38:11).

The "silencing" of the dragon, רהב המשבת [rahab ham-mošbāt] (Isa 30:7), stands in parallel to the "calming" (רגע [rāgaʿ] (Job 26:12); שבח [šibbaḥ] (Ps 89:10) of the sea; likewise השביח [hišbîaḥ] (Ps 65:8); and ἐκόπασεν [ekopasen] (Sir 42:23).

"He has reprimanded [גער (gāʿar)] the animals of the reeds" (Ps 68:31);

the same word occurs in the following: the water flees before YHWH's "reprimand," גערה [gĕʿārāh] (Ps 104:7); גער [gāʿar] (Jer 31:35); the contents of one such "reprimand" (Job 38:11).

YHWH proved by the defeat of the enemy not only his (YHWH's) strength (Isa 51:9; Ps 74:12; etc.; likewise Ps 65:7 and Prayer of Manasseh 4), but also his (YHWH's) wisdom (Job 26:12f.; likewise Sir 43:23).

The rebellious sea is held in check by YHWH. It must respect the eternal boundaries (Jer 5:22, Ps 104:9, Job 38:10f., and Prov 8:29). It is held fast by bolt and door (Job 38:10, by fetters, prison, and seal (Prayer of Manasseh 3), in storerooms (Ps 33:7), and by a bridle (1 Enoch 60:16; cf. p. 34). These concepts correspond with what was said above concerning the dragon: God holds him on rings (Job 40:26; cf. Job 7:12, etc.).

These parallels prove that in the above testimonies concerning the creation of the sea we have before us our myth, from which only the specifically mythological feature, the defeat of the monsters, has been stripped away. The parallels are important because they provide a desired corroboration for a complete understanding of the struggle with the dragon and for individual features of that struggle. Above all, these texts, all of which speak of a creation, once again make clear that the defeat of Rahab — as we have recognized — originally belonged to the myth of creation. Likewise, it follows from Ps 104:7 and Jer 31:34 that YHWH's "reprimand" (Ps 68:31; cf. pp. 42f.) should be reckoned to the myth. And the "fettering" of the defeated Leviathan (which we have inferred from Job 40:26) receives new support in Prayer of Manasseh 3, where the *sea* is "fettered."

This narrative, like the myth of the battle with the dragon, was originally a hymn. It glories in YHWH's greatness. It is also applied in a way similar to that myth — e.g., Job 38:8-11 is like Job 40f.; Jer 5:22; 31:35 are like Amos 9:3; etc. Inspired poets like Deutero-Isaiah repeat the story when they want to describe YHWH's omnipotence:

Isa 50:2b, 3[234]

2b *By my reproof I dried up the sea,*
  turned streams into wilderness,
 so that its fish languished[235] without water,
  and its animals on thirsty ground.[236]
3 *I clothed the heavens in darkness*
  and made sackcloth its covering.

It is not clear that this is done by YHWH at the creation. Nevertheless, it should be supposed that the prophet had our myth in mind. According to the context, his intention was to express the magnificence of YHWH. There must be a special reason for his grasping immediately at *this* concrete thing, the drying up of the sea. He adopts common hymnic motifs, just as he has used hymnic literature elsewhere, e.g., at 41:10ff. and 43:16ff.; cf. also 63:7, etc. — The parallels prove, however, that these motifs are taken from the creation myth:

The drying up of the sea: Isa 51:10; Ps 74:15;
cf. Jer 51:36, whereby "the streams become wilderness,"
and Ezek 30:12;
by YHWH's "reproof" גערה [gĕʾārāh], Jer 31:35; Ps 68:31; 104:7.
The fish die on the dry land, Ezek 29:5.
The heavens are dark, Ezek 32:7f.

Without these assumptions the prophetic text would be more than peculiar. How could these descriptions be thought up unless they are generally common; that is, such natural events can also be interpreted otherwise, and, in any event, do not instill an unmediated conviction! Why is it said that the fish die on the dry land? "Is this a special consolation for the despondent ones?" This view of Duhm[237] is totally dismissed by our view: the poet alludes not to *arbitrary* events of nature, but rather to the great deeds of YHWH at the creation; and the death of the fish was a known feature of this fundamental deed of YHWH. It should be granted that the prophetic text receives both a context *and* a significant power by this assumption.

In fact, this allusion does not explicitly cite the history of the creation, but rather only points to it from afar. It has its parallel in Isa 43:16f., where the miracle at the Reed Sea is also mentioned indistinctly. The same thing happens not uncommonly in Job and in the Psalms. It appears to be a feature of hymnic style.[238]

Our text supplies further corroboration for certain features of the myth which have not, until now, been fully substantiated, especially the darkening of the heavens by the struggle against Chaos. Just as the myth of the struggle against the dragon is to be interpreted eschatologically, so also are to be understood the applications of the defeat of the sea to the great judgment of the nations in the final days.

Psalm 46

Psalm 46[239] describes the last judgment in the following manner: peoples and
kingdoms rage (המה [*hāmāh*]) (v. 7) against Zion, like an arrogant (גאוה
[*ga'ăwāh*]) (v. 4) sea, so that the mountain itself shakes (v. 3). However, in this
final difficulty, YHWH protects his holy city (v. 5). At the crack of dawn (לפנות
בקר [*lipnôt bōqer*]) he takes drastic measures (v. 6). He brings the war to an end
(משבית [*mašbît*]) (v. 10). He demonstrates his majesty among the peoples
(v. 11).

The theory can hardly be denied that, in this case, the myth, eschatologically applied, provides, in the final analysis, the basis for the poems. All the concrete features of the poems are in agreement with the myth: the arrogant, raging sea, which finally takes drastic action against YHWH's holiness, and which
YHWH brings to peace while he proves his unique majesty. The new feature,
i.e., that the moment of decision occurs "toward morning," agrees closely with
the myth in which the sea is associated with the power of darkeness.

Certainly this application of the myth is not original in Psalm 46. The
psalmist repeats common eschatological views of long-standing views which
were part of the faith of his time. One should speak here not of an intentional
interpretation of the myth. Rather, one should speak of a late adaptation of a
myth which has long been used eschatologically.

Isa 17:12-14

Isa 17:12-14[240] sounds much more original.

12 *Ah, the thundering of many peoples*
   like the thundering of seas they thunder.
Ah, the raging of powerful[241] nations,
   like raging of waters they rage.[242]
. . . .[243]
13   *and threatened it, so that it fled away;*
banished, like chaff on the mountains before the gale,
   like dust devils before the whirlwind.

14 *At evening time there was still terror;*
   before morning came it was no more.
This is the portion of our despoiler,
   the lot of our plunderer.

Surely in this case, were we are dealing with a man who is indeed the greatest of poets, we could understand each individual feature as a free prophetic conception. That nations should be compared with overflowing waters could be an independent idea of Isaiah, just as well as the fact that God does his work, which no human eye can observe, in the night! But, on the other hand, the correspondence of certain individual features with those of the myth is quite remarkable: the thundering (הָמוֹן [hāmôn], שָׁאוֹן [šā'ôn]) water which "flees" (נָס [nās] <√נוס [√nws]) before YHWH's word of rebuke (גער [gā'ar]); cf. Ps 104:7: מִן־גַּעֲרָתְךָ יְנוּסוּן [min-ga'ărātkā yĕnûsûn], "before his reprimand they flee," etc.). Likewise this happens at the dawning of the light; cf. Ps 46:6. In the same way as Isa 50:2f., our text in many ways gains a conceptual unity if the myth is understood to stand in the background. If the myth is not presupposed, the image of the thundering water, alluded to in vv. 12 and 13f., immediately falls away. But if the myth stands behind it, then the image of the extinction of the primordial sea is adhered to from beginning to end!

No objection may be raised against the use of myth by Isaiah himself, since in Isa 11:6ff. a clear reference to the myth of the "golden age" is found; cf. also pp. 94ff. on Jer 4:23-26. One recalls that we have already established a secure citation of the Chaos Myth in the "bound Rahab" text of Isa 30:7. This sort of application is in every way worthy of the great prophets. Isaiah, in complete control of his material, has extracted from it the features which are to be communicated and has conformed them to a powerful prophetic vision. This sort of application is similar to those of Ezekiel 29 and 32, although Isaiah demonstrates greater authority in his selection of material. What are allegories in Ezekiel are for Isaiah images which appear to be freely formulated in every way.

Hab 3:8

The eschatological psalms of Habakkuk 3, Nahum 1, and Psalm 18 are closely related to one another in terms of their attitude toward our myth. Habakkuk 3 tells how YHWH comes from Sinai for the judgment. In vv. 3-12 YHWH's terrifying theophany in the storm is described at length. In only a few words, words which remain totally insubstantial insofar as they are even recognizable given the condition of the text, . . . only in those few words does the poet add (at vv. 13f.) that YHWH has come to his people for salvation and to the godless oppressor for punishment. The theophany, which is described in detail, hardly bears any intrinsic relationship to the brief political prophecy which follows upon it. It is simply an extraordinary introduction. One thus recognizes that the themes of the theophany of YHWH lay before the poet as fully prepared poetic materials. He *adopted* them. He did not *invent* them!

Nah 1:4

This is even clearer at Nahum 1.[244] Here also there is first a theophany and then the judgment upon the oppressive people. And between the two parts there generally is no connection.

Ps 18:16-18

In Ps 18[245] a link between the two sets of material is found by the poet. YHWH appears in all his authority:

> 16 *Then were the beds of the sea[246] visible,*
>   *the foundations of the earth appeared*
> *before your rebuke,[247] O YHWH,*
>   *before the blast of the breath of your nostrils.*
> 17 *He stretched from on high and grasped me,*
>   *he drew me out from great waters.*
> 18 *He rescued me from before my fiercest[248] enemies.*
>   *from before those who hate me, who are too strong for me.*

The "I" of the psalm, who is about to be drowned in the rivers of disaster, is rescued by YHWH, who stirs up the sea and draws out of it the one who has almost sunk down to the underworld. — But this linkage of the two bodies of material is very artificial. The powerful apparatus of a theophany and the modest result, the rescue of a drowning person, stand in sharp contrast. This observation is not too disturbing if one also sees in the "I" the people of Israel — an idea which does not appear to be very improbable in the case of Psalm 18. This explains how the poet came to begin the rescue of the "I" with a theophany. However, as before, it remains remarkable that he can allow such a modest image to follow upon this monumental one. Accordingly, there are two conceptual fields which are totally distinct in their origin but which the poet has brought together here: an unwilling descent into subterranean waters as an image of extreme peril of death (cf., e.g., Jonah 2; Psalm 59) and the theophany.

Thus for all three texts we arrive at the conclusion that a theophany with fairly well-established features lay before the Jewish poets as a piece of inherited tradition material. Whence did this material come?

Descriptions of YHWH appearing in the storm cloud are not at all uncommon in the Old Testament. They are an apparently original expression of an ancient religious faith which perceived its God as near in the terrifying splendor of the storm cloud. The proper place of these storm theophanies is the ancient songs which deal with the appearance of God to Moses on Sinai. We have echoes of such songs at Deut 33:2f. and in prose at Exodus 19 and 34. The motif recurs at Judg 5:4f. and 1 Kings 19:11ff., then from the prophets at Isa 29:6; 30:27f.; Joel 2:2f.; Mic 1:3f.; and finally from the psalmists at Pss 50:1ff.; 97, etc. It is characteristic of these descriptions that since the connection with Sinai is more or less clearly retained, the . . .

> *Rushing and roaring*   *and powerful noise,*
> *the wind and the storm*   *and the blazing flames* (Isa 29:6),

. . . the quaking of the earth, the cracking of rocks, the melting of mountains . . . all are mentioned, but nowhere the effects of a storm on the sea. This is, of course, in the nature of the case: in the wilderness of Sinai,[249] just as infrequently as in the part of Palestine where Israel lived, the sea is seldom in the immediate vicinity.

All the more reason why the words of Nahum 1, Habakkuk 3, and Psalm 18 concerning the sea are so striking.

It is true that the sea appears only occasionally in Nahum 1.

> 4   *He rebuked the sea, so that it dried up,*
>   *every stream he made dry.*[250]

However, it plays a greater role in Habakkuk 3.[251]

> 8   *Is your wrath aroused against the rivers,*
>   *or your fury against the sea, O YHWH,*[252]
>   *that you cause your chargers to tread on the sea,*
>   *your chariot on the flood of water?*[253]

Whence stems this feature, i.e., the presence of the sea in these texts? The question is at first quite puzzling. The feature does not belong in the ancient Sinai theophany. It is in no way characteristic of the situation. If YHWH comes from Paran to Palestine for the judgment (v. 3), he does not encounter the sea at all. The question of the poet, i.e., "What does YHWH have to do with the sea?"

already appears to express the fact that this feature was known, but was not understood.

The sea comes to the fore even more strongly in Psalm 18. The whole theophany has as its purpose the stirring up of the sea and the exposure of its bed. The poet has used this climactic point from the appearance to YHWH to attach to it that which he is actually pursuing, i.e., the rescue of the drowning person. He could hardly have arrived at this rather remarkable concept if the theophany had not already possessed this conclusion.

We thus postulate, as an explanation for Habakkuk 3, Nahum 1, and Psalm 18, the existence of an ancient storm theophany in which the anger of YHWH was aroused against the sea. YHWH drives his steeds up over the great flood, and he lays bare its bed. "He rebuked the sea, so that it dried up!"

There is only one ancient narrative in which these features could have found a place, the myth of creation. One notes that the expression "to rebuke" (גער [gā'ar]) recurs at Nah 1:4 and at Ps 18:16. We have already recognized it at Ps 104:7, Ps 68:31, Isa 50:2, and Isa 17:13. Likewise, in Babylonian myth *Marduk* appears in the storm cloud. His weapon is the thunderbolt. His chargers and his chariot are also expressly mentioned, as they are in the case of YHWH at Hab 3:8.

One can also appropriately consider it a reflex of the myth when the roaring of the sea plays a role in the descriptions of the dominion of YHWH.

Ps 93:3f.[254]

> 3 *The streams have lifted up, O YHWH,*
> *the streams have lifted up their voice,*
> *the streams have lifted up their roaring.*
> 4 *More than the sound of a great water,*
> *more than the dominion[255] of the breakers of the sea,*
> *YHWH is glorious in the heights.*

Ps 96:11 *(The sea and that which fills it thunder)* and Ps 98:7 should be compared to the text of this psalm. The same motif is already found at Isa 42:10. One also notes Psalm 29 *(YHWH's voice over the waters).*

One must explain such words by recourse to a people who dwell by the sea and whose imagination is occupied with the sea. They would derive naturally from the perception of the storm clouds which stand above the sea. This situation, however, is not available to Israel. Moreover, there are only certain

motifs, first the drying up of the sea, and then the contrast between the dominion of YHWH and the billowing sea, which recur again and again.

Certainly one would err greatly if he sought here a conscious application
of the creation myth. We are dealing here only with individual features which
once existed as part of the myth, but which long ago lost this connection and
presently exist only as motifs of the poetic tradition. The establishment of such
a fact is not without value for the evaluation of our psalm. Though indeed one
may date the psalm which we have received as late, it is, on the other hand, quite
certain that the poetry of the psalm itself is ancient. One need only think of the
Babylonian hymns and the so-called "Penitential Psalms." In many cases the
history of individual psalm-motifs can be reconstructed from internal evidence
as well as from similarity with the prophets, who themselves often worked from
the poetic literature of their time.

Psalm 77:17

Psalm 77 is characteristic of this sort of psalm, binding at a later time received-
motifs which were not organically related. The psalm has, at 17ff., a storm theophany in imitation of Ps 18. Here it also focuses upon the sea:

> 17 *The waters saw you, O YHWH,*[256]
>   *the waters saw you. They trembled,*
> *indeed, the deeps were terrified!*

Again the object of the theophany is the division of the Red Sea so that Israel may be led through it. Thus an echo of the account of the creation of the
world and the account of the Red Sea come together. We observe the same flowing together of traditions at Ps 106:9.

> *He split the Red Sea so that it was afraid;*
>   *he let them go through the deep, as though it were dry land.*

וגער בים־סוף ויחרב [*w̄ay-yigʿar bĕ-yam-sûp w̄ay-yeḥĕrāb*], the same as at Nah
1:4: גוער בים ויבשהו [*gôʿēr bay-yām w̄ay-yabbĕšēhû*].

We have already found a linkage between the creation myth and the narrative of the Red Sea event at Isa 51:9f. (cf. p. 22 above).

Isa 59:15-20

Finally, a new feature perhaps is still to be wrested from Isa 59:15ff. YHWH sees that all faith and righteousness have vanished from the world. Ultimately he arises to create order.

> 15b *YHWH[257] looked down with his eyes.*
>> *He recognized[258] that there was no justice any more.*
> 16 *He looked! There was no one!*
>> *He was astonished that no one stepped into the breach!*
> *There his own power helped him,*
>> *his righteousness alone stood beside him.*
> 17 *He put on righteousness like armor,*
>> *placed the helmet of salvation upon his head.*
> *He put on the garment of vengeance,[259]*
>> *and arrayed himself with anger as a mantle.*
> 18 *He doled out the proper recompense,[260]*
>> *violence upon those who oppose him, abuse upon his foes;[261]*
> 19 *so that from the west they will perceive[262] the name of YHWH,*
>> *from the east, his glory;*
> *For the enemy will come like a stream,*
>> *which YHWH's breath puts to flight.[263]*
> 20 *Thus the deliverer for Zion will come,*
>> *the one who will remove the sin from Jacob.[264]*

This description of the future is already of a completely apocalyptic nature. It speaks not of a specific, hostile people, drawn perhaps from a historical situation, but rather of an enemy who is to come "once upon a time." In addition, there is the unusually laconic way in which these things are discussed. We could not understand the text if we did not possess parallels from other places — one thinks of God and Magog. So it follows that they should be understood as an allusion to the teaching concerning the "enemy" of the final days.

Now one notes that this enemy is compared to a stream in this text, a stream which "YHWH's breath puts to flight." We thus conclude that the image of the stream which is driven back belonged to the apocalyptic tradition of that time. We can infer the same thing in the case of Isa 17:12-14, Psalm 46, and Ps 65:8, especially since we have encountered the word "foe" (צר [ṣar]) many times already as a technical term for chaos (cf. p. 55), although some other things, perhaps Isa 8:7f., have had an influence here.

The previous description of the armies of YHWH for war, which has come into such great renown because of the imitation of it in the New Testament at Eph 6:14-17 and 1 Thess 5:8, is quite striking. One does not understand how the poet could have chanced upon this image on his own. YHWH arms himself. Afterward, however he does nothing with the weapons. The act of arming is therefore a feature which vanishes just as quickly as it appears. Indeed, one would not want to maintain that the view of the prophet, in which the theophany of YHWH brought both salvation and destruction at the same time, could have led directly to this image. The known qualities of YHWH have almost nothing in common with the particular weapons described. One could arbitrarily transpose the words. — All of this indicates that the arming of YHWH was also an established feature which the poet adopted because of its poetic beauty and which he has interpreted allegorically for his own purpose. Therefore, we will draw attention to an ancient poem which dealt with a war of YHWH and with the arming of God which preceded it. If what follows can now be understood as an allusion to our myth, then the assumption may be permitted that the whole prophetic text of the myth, which accordingly also dealt with the arming of YHWH, lies in the background. This assumption receives support, on the one hand, from the fact that Isa 51:9 also refers to the arming of YHWH, and, on the other, from the fact that the Babylonian myth speaks, at length, about the arming of *Marduk*.

We have attempted to track down all the branches of the eschatological application of our narrative concerning the overthrow of the sea. These allusion are certainly much less clear than the eschatological versions of the myth of the Chaos Monster. This is in the nature of the case. What *is* missing here, above all, are the names of the Chaos Monsters, names which appear so clearly in the myth itself. Also missing are the images of the sea, images which appear to be drawn from the myth and which are not so original that they would be simply inexplicable without the myth.

Compilation

I compile the above observations, then, with only some reservations, and draw on them as follows.

- The Chaos Myth existed in Israel in a form in which the mythological images of the dragon had vanished and which spoke simply of the sea.
- Indeed, in this form the myth had the character of a hymn. Besides a series of detailed descriptions we possess a number of hymnic allusions in which the myth is quietly echoed.

• In addition, we have observed how an eschatological twist was given to the narrative of the Chaos Monsters. There is mention of the "fact" that the sea, in the final days, rages against YHWH's creation and that then, however, the rebuke of YHWH puts it to flight. This prophecy may be described as a formulaic image of the final attack of the heathen and the great judgment of the peoples in the future. A great prophet appears to have led the way to this application of the myth. The latter prophets followed. In the earliest apocalyptic literature the image of the raging sea is an established one. Adopted details are carried along with it as poetic embellishments or they are allegorized as much as possible. Even in the New Testament the following is given, among other signs of the end: on the earth the peoples will be mortally afraid of the roaring of the sea (Luke 21:25). There are individual texts, by the way, in which the roaring sea of the future is not allegorized.

All of this is an historical trend which was probable in and of itself. There is, however, a further parallel in the tradition history which we have reconstructed for Rahab and his relatives. But we have achieved as new data in regard to this myth the following:

The rebuke of YHWH (גער [gā'ar])
The action of YHWH before the crack of dawn
YHWH's coming on the rain cloud . . .
. . . with chariots and steeds.

Moreover, the arming of YHWH has been described in detail. In regard to this last point, the idea suggests itself of imagining the manner of this arming according to the features it holds in parallel to the myth of *Marduk:* YHWH arms himself as he puts on the weapons of the storm cloud ‖ the myth of *Marduk* describes the arming of the god in exactly the same way.

*   *   *

We have found a vast and rich history of the "Creation of the World/Chaos Myth" in Israel. Certain parallels to the Babylonian *Marduk-Ti'āmat* myth have already been established by the study. I shall now draw together the main points at which the two myths overlap.

In both myths it is said that everything was water in primordial times. The primordial ocean is personified as a fertile being. The Babylonian form of the monster, *Ti'āmat,* actually corresponds in the Hebrew to the technical term for the primordial sea, תהום [*tĕhôm*]. The invariable use of this term *without* the definite article allows us to conclude that it was once a proper name and hence designated a mythical figure. The common name of the monster in Hebrew (רהב [*rahab*]) probably also appears in Babylonian sources, although this is still not established with complete certainty. Both myths present the monster in the form of a dragon with many heads.

There are other beings besides the dragon but similar to him, the "helpers" of the dragon. They also play a major role. In Babylonian mythology *Kingu* stands beside *Ti'āmat*. In the Hebrew myth *Rahab* and *Tannîn*, Leviathan and *Tannîn*, Leviathan and Behemoth, *Rahab* and *Nāḥāš Bārîah* appear beside each other. *Kingu* and *Ti'āmat* are man and wife, just as Behemoth and Leviathan are at 1 *Enoch* 60.

These mighty ones of the deep are arrayed against the gods of the heavens in the Babylonian myth. Among the latter is *Marduk*. In Israel also other divine beings appear over against YHWH (Job 41:17; 38:7 and Ps 89:7). These, naturally, withdraw completely before YHWH.

The Chaos Monsters of the Babylonian myth have rebelled against the power of the higher gods. They demand world hegemony for themselves. This arrogant and impious rebellion is also a standard feature of the YHWH myth.

Before the intervention of *Marduk,* individual gods have already attempted to do battle against *Ti'āmat*. Perhaps Job 41:3 and 41:17 are allusions to similar incidents in the Hebrew myth.

Finally, *Marduk*-YHWH appears. His arming is then described. He comes on a chariot drawn by chargers, with sword and net, or with the terrifying weaponry of the storm god. — The correspondence of the two myths in the last feature is all the more remarkable since it is not drawn from the contemplation of nature — the winter is not overthrown by the storm — but rather it is drawn from foreign influences in the myth (cf. pp. 18f. above).

An angry rebuke precedes the battle. In the battle itself God proves not only his strength but also his wisdom. The net plays a role in this. Indeed, it subjugates the "helpers" of the monster. They "writhe about under it." In the Babylonian account he deals with them without difficulty. A Hebrew recension (Ps 89:13 and Job 9:13) also alludes to this.

The corpse of the defeated monster is not buried — in the Hebrew versions this is often clearly emphasized — but rather the world is formed from it by the god. Hebrew recensions appear to derive the fertility of the land, which previously was a wilderness, from the blood and the decomposing body of the dragon. — The Babylonian myth reports that *Ti'āmat* was split into two pieces, into the waters above and the waters below. A Hebrew recension which clearly states this last point does not exist among the texts cited above. Ps 74:12, however, does speak of the "splitting" of the sea, and Job 26:12 also knows of the "bolt of the heavens." In any event, the creation of the world follows the defeat of the monster in the Hebrew as well as in the Babylonian sources.

Both myths conclude the narrative with the main theme, the climax of the whole *Marduk*-YHWH hymn, that the god who broke the destructive power of the deadly monster and who created this beautiful world is Lord and God from this point on, a Lord and God whom *all* praise rejoicing, the *greatest* among the gods!!!

In the Babylonian accounts we know of a variant in which *Ti'āmat* instigates a reign of terror among humanity (thus in the course of history). We have also found Hebrew parallels to this.

A similar sequence of arguments can be adduced from later Near Eastern traditions. On the one hand, these are dependent on the Babylonian accounts. On the other hand, they are often consistent with those accounts of the Hebrews. These are mentioned individually in the preceding on pp. 25, 26, and 61 (cf. 312, n. 201). Further elaboration concerning them is not appropriate here.

Both myths, the Hebrew and the Babylonian, have all their major points in common. Therefore, in the end it is no longer even a matter of two similar myths but rather of the same myth received in two distinct recensional families. When one considers the great difference between the two religions, one cannot marvel enough at the great similarity of the two recensions of the myth.

For the experts there is hardly any need for a demonstration of how to assess which side is dependent on the other. The Babylonian myth corresponds to the features of the Mesopotamian climate[265] and thereby proves itself to be genuinely Babylonian, while the Hebrew myth should be judged as specifically *non-Palestinian*.[265] The myth of *Marduk,* the mythic expression of Babylonian pride in their own world dominion, is much more ancient than even the Hebrew people themselves!

It is, therefore, our conclusion that the Babylonian *Ti'âmat-Marduk* myth was taken up by Israel and there became a myth of YHWH.

5. The Babylonian Origin of the Creation Account of Genesis 1; Its Character and the Time of Its Introduction into Israel

We return, after this digression, to Genesis 1, and we endeavor to ascertain at this point the relationship of this creation narrative to the established Babylonian-Israelite creation myth.

It has certainly been apparent from Genesis 1[1] that this narrative is simply the Jewish adaptation of a much older thing, which originally must have been more mythological. Some echoes suggest a polytheistic origin. One feature points to astral religion. Many themes accord with Phoenician, Greek, and Indian parallels as well. The Palestinian climate and the ancient Hebrew beginning of the year also speak against a local Israelite origin for the narrative. On the other hand, climate, the beginning of the year, and the lingering astral religion point to a Babylonian background. This conjecture will now be amply confirmed by a comparison of Genesis 1 side by side with the Babylonian myth.

This myth bears those features which we have postulated for the pattern of Genesis 1. And it agrees in characteristic details with Genesis 1. True, it does not have the Sabbath feature, but this arrangement did not even belong originally to the material of Genesis 1. Furthermore, the parallels between the two are relevant only to the introduction. They do demonstrate, however, that of the actual Babylonian creation myth we possess only minor fragments.[2] — The tangencies at the beginning are even stronger.

In both myths the world consists at first of water and darkness. In addition to these elements there is the name תהום [těhôm] — Ti'âmat. The name בהו [bōhû] is possibly Babylonian.[3] The world then comes into existence because God separates the primal waters into two parts by the division of the heavens. The reader recalls what role this sequence plays in the Babylonian myth. For Genesis 1 we already saw that it is specifically Babylonian and non-Palestinian. The agreement on these points is even more striking since the same is not found again in this regard in any Old Testament texts.[4]

The creation originates, in Genesis 1, through God's almighty word. In the *Marduk* myth the efficacy of the divine word is strongly emphasized (cf. p. 16). In the creation of the land animals both narratives have the same classifications: cattle, wild animals, and reptiles.[5] A series of features from Genesis 1 can be correctly understood only from the Babylonian parallels.

In terms of the creation of the heavenly bodies, their designated role, i.e., to rule over the times, is strongly emphasized in the narratives. This emphasis[6] is quite striking in Jewish tradition. It may be explained in terms of Babylonian astral religion.

It is quite noteworthy that in Genesis 1 light is created before the stars. In Babylonian myth as well light is considered as already existent before the appearance of *Marduk,* but he has created the stars. The feature is quite explicable from the Babylonian polytheistic outlook, according to which light belongs to the essence of the high gods. *Marduk,* however, emerged as a youthful deity when light already existed.

Furthermore, the idea that God has judged every creation to be good becomes a characteristic modality comparable to the Babylonian account. In a similar way the Babylonian hymn[7] proves the grace of the god who has slain the evil monster and has created the good world. Consequently, the predicate adjective "good" originally stood in apposition to the abomination of the primordial *tĕhôm.* That this predicate adjective is not applied to the darkness even in Genesis 1 is, thus, to be understood as a remnant of this outlook.

From these correspondences alone the conclusion that Genesis 1 goes back, fundamentally, to the Babylonian myth would have a strong likelihood. This conclusion attains even greater certainty, however, if we recall the rich abundance of allusions to the Babylonian Chaos Myth which we have established above. Thereby the situation will be decidedly altered. Now Genesis 1 is no longer an isolated piece of which a commonality with the *Marduk* narrative might look very strange. Rather, now it is one link in a great chain, a revision comparable to many others, for which we have already identified the Babylonian origin.

The theologian may advance — consciously or unconsciously — dogmatic objections against this historical thesis. He may point to the unmistakably vast difference between the Babylonian and the biblical creation reports. As far as he is, generally, willing to acknowledge the partial correspondence of both narratives, he may lean toward the thesis that here two peoples have put forward, jointly, a primordial tradition, received among the Hebrews in unadulterated form but received among the Babylonians in mythologically corrupted form.

This thesis is, however, clearly refuted by the character of both traditions. Genesis 1 is, as is shown above,[8] by its nature, a faded myth. Furthermore, strong internal reasons compel us, as we have seen,[9] to seek the origin of the tradition among the Babylonians. The remaining Hebrew Bible recensions are especially instructive to one who is generally willing to lend an ear to the religio-historical examples. Since these represent, in many respects, the connecting links between Genesis 1 and the Babylonian myth, they show the way in which the *Marduk* myth has become Genesis 1.

Hereinafter the statement should be understood as certain that even Genesis 1 is ultimately of Babylonian origin. In order to grasp the larger history out of which Genesis 1 must be understood, it is, first of all, necessary to ascertain the peculiarity of this recension of the myth.

The difference between the Babylonian creation account and that of Genesis 1 is quite great. It could hardly be conceptually greater! In the former there is totally wild and grotesquely titanic barbaric poetry. In the later there is the solemn, elevated tranquility of a spacious and at times rather temperate prose.[10] In the former, the gods arise in the course of things. In the latter, God is the same from the very beginning. In the Babylonian myth it is the god who, in the heat of battle, slays the monster and from its body forms the world. In the Hebrew account it is a God "who spoke and it was so."[11] — The poetry of the myth is certainly a bit attenuated in the Hebrew account. We don't regret it, though, since in return it is filled with the thinking of a higher religion.

The theologian would do well to treat even the *Marduk* myth with piety. One does not honor one's elders unless one gives thought to one's ancestors. Nevertheless, however, do *we* have the right to value Genesis 1 totally differently than we value any other ancient myth? Might our scientific views themselves have been assumed by Genesis 1? Might even the Judaistic-supernaturalistic understanding of God which is assumed in Genesis 1[12] appear to our piety not to be the highest thing? Notwithstanding that, it does continue to exist! In Genesis 1 we are able to discover again the God in whom *we* believe! All other cosmogonies are, to us, only interesting antiquities.

Historical examination cannot regard Genesis 1 as our ancestors did, as the remnant of a special revelation which was, perhaps, for the *first* human beings. The conviction remains unshakeable that in the development of the Israelite religion the hand of the living God manifested itself. The undeniable authority and responsibility of historians of religion is strongly to express this conviction at every high point of the history, where the opportunity arises on every side. Genesis 1 *is* such a high point, a milestone in the history of the world, a monument of God's revelation in Israel.

How does Genesis 1 stand in relation to the "poetic recensions"?

Genesis 1 is the only complete recension of the myth which we possess from Israel. All others are allusions, echoes, or applications. The reason why no other creation myth is preserved . . . that reason is clear. Genesis 1, which conforms to the Jewish imagination and to the Jewish mind, has superseded the remaining recensions.

Given this "fullness" of Genesis 1, it will be clear that it preserves many ancient things that are lacking in other recensions: the darkness at the beginning; the names תהו ובהו [*tōhû wā-bōhû*]; the dividing of the primordial sea; the naming of the created things; the assignment of the stars to the dominions;[13] the "we" during the creation of humanity; the benediction over the animals and humanity such that God "saw that it was good"; the Sabbath. There is also a feature which, it appears, entered into the Babylonian material through Phoenician influence: the brooding of the spirit. And there is the continuous reminder of a narrative development αὐτομάτως [*automatōs*] preceding it. Furthermore, there is one feature from another, probably also Babylonian, myth: the primordial diet of plants.

If then, even in Genesis 1, where, arguing from the remaining analogous features of P^c, Jewish editorial activity has certainly been fairly strongly active . . . if, given this, so many ancient materials are preserved, then we should conclude that similar ancient materials were even more definitely prominent in the base model for Genesis 1. The older narrative conceining the creation of the world must have breathed the ancient spirit through and through, if even as energetic an editor as P^c could not totally eliminate it. Many ancient individual features must have been attached to it.

On the other hand, Genesis 1 produces a modern impression which is opposed, in many ways, to the other recensions of the creation myth. Genesis 1 is prose — poetic language may echo only in vv. 2, 26, and 27. All other recensions are poetry. Here Genesis 1 has the later material since the creation myth is, by its nature, hymnic. Because of this, it is not maintained that the immediate predecessor of Genesis 1 could still have been written in verse. If I see it correctly, many tales by J and E can already be understood as prosaic reminiscences of early songs.

Comparing further, as the relationship of God to Chaos is described in the parallel recensions, a line of development clearly emerges. The Babylonian idea that Chaos could be older than the deity itself is not substantiated on Hebrew ground. On the contrary, the old Babylonian representation of Chaos Monsters and of the battle of the deity against them *is* preserved in a portion of the poetic recensions. Another portion possibly "took note" of the personification of Chaos. It has, however, at the very least, retained the battle of YHWH against the sea, which once even ruled over the land.

In Genesis 1 even this lingering residue has disappeared. It is something to which nothing more than allusion is made. God separates the waters under the firmament from the waters above the firmament. Out of the primordial monsters, however, a curious type of fish has come to be, which is among the other created figures (Gen 1:21). Thus we are able to study, step by step, the background of the mythology.

Similar results are attained if the remaining features of Genesis 1 are compared with old creation accounts like Prov 8:22-31, Job 38, Job 26, etc. In Genesis 1 we hear nothing at all of "the pillars of the heavens," of "the sources of the sea," of the "foundations of the mountains," etc. Accordingly, Genesis 1 is related to the poetic recensions in somewhat the same way that P^c is related, though distinctively, to the parallel traditions of J or E in the very strongly Judaizing revision: dispassionate prose in place of more ancient poetry, but along with that a higher concept of God in place of a more ancient naiveté. Notwithstanding, however, some very *ancient* features are preserved.

Accordingly, we have established the following religio-historical sequence concerning the creation myth:

1. *Marduk* myth . . .	1. The Babylonian myth is transferred to Israel;
2. Poetic recension of the YHWH myth; . . .	2. There it loses many of its mythological elements and nearly all of its polytheistic elements;
3. Genesis 1 . . .	3. In Genesis 1 it is, as far as it was possible, completely Judaized.

I observe distinctly that, having said this, still nothing about the age of the distinctive sources has been expressed. We do have very ancient descriptions several centuries after P^c. Accordingly, we should set out on an attempt to determine the time and nature of the adoption of the Babylonian material. The absolutely secure datum is the *terminus ad quem*, the time of P^c, thus around 500 B.C.E.[14] The question is whether the material was taken over by P^c directly from Babylon, or whether it stems from Israelite products which, in their turn, had come back in some way from Babylon.

We should, first of all, investigate whether the influence of the myth was possible in the Babylonian exile. The deported Jews came into Babylon under the immediate influence of the Babylonian-Aramaic culture. In a foreign land, among a foreign people, under new social circumstances, through the powerful impression of the catastrophe, their own states having been broken, or at least disturbed, there were also those who, for all that, remained true to the God of their ancestors, those whom the powerful influence of the foreign culture was not quite able to silence. The Babylonian-Aramaic influence did remain powerful, however, in the period that followed, even among the Jewish community which again arose in Palestine at a later time.

At that time a calendar other than the old ancestral Palestinian one made its way into Judaism. From this point on the year began with the spring. The Babylonian month-names were also adopted. Additionally there were different units of linear and weight measurement, and a new writing script.[15] Finally, Hebrew speech was superseded, even in Palestine, by Aramaic.

The influence of the Babylonian religion was also powerful at that time — its magnificent temples, its pompous feasts, its opulently adorned divine idols. And right into the innermost chambers of the heart went the thorn of the ideas themselves, since the gods of Babylon appeared to have triumphed over YHWH. — The polemic of Deutero-Isaiah illustrates this influence of the Babylonian religion. It was a central object of his prophecy to compare the gods of Babylon with Israel's God, to establish YHWH's superiority! Even in later times,[16] there remained a temptation to fall away to astral worship (Job 31:26ff.). And the prophets admonish, "Don't be afraid before the signs of the heavens!" (Jer 10:2). Since the stars have power in the world, the pious may often also act unfaithfully (Deut 4:19, Isa 24:21-23). But instead of this, YHWH's overarching power and his veneration in Israel should *not* be impugned. It was then that for the Jews the "religion of the *gôyīm*" became Babylonian religion. Heathen religion became star worship (Jer 10:2).

Accordingly, the possibility that at that time particular aspects of Babylonian religion crept into Judaism should not be pushed aside. One relic of such influences is the first part of the book of Zechariah. The night vision of Zechariah characteristically differs from those of the older prophets.[17] In it an abundance of remarkable forms of extraordinarily fiery coloration confronts us on several sides: four horns — to signify the peoples; four smiths — to sharpen the plowshares;[18] the horns are to be cut off (ch. 2); an angel, on a brightly colored steed, who brings a report to another mounted angel "in the glen, among the myrtles" (ch. 1); four chariots, hitched to brightly colored horses, which appear "between the two mountains, which are brazen mountains," to roam about around the earth — these are the four winds[19] of the heavens (ch. 6); a flying scroll twenty ells long and ten ells wide — "this is the curse which goes out over the whole land"; a woman in an *'êpāh*[20] closed with a lead cover, an *'êpāh* which was carried off by two women with the wings of a stork, between earth and heaven — "this is wickedness" (ch. 5); angels who have to debate with each other; and the prophets making their speeches to the witnesses (chs. 1, 2, and 3).

An explanation for the majority of these images is appended by the prophet himself. This is truly characteristic of Zechariah. The older prophets produced plenty of representations, but seldom any which required an explanation. Now it does not seem probable that Zechariah has invented all these representations. This is indicated, here and there, by the incongruity of the forms and the interpretation. In the vision of the women in the *'êpāh* the removal of wickedness must be represented. But why are they *women* who carry off the *'êpāh?* And why do these women have the wings of a stork?

Furthermore, the interpretation already reveals here and there that we are dealing with strongly defined ideas which the prophet presumes to be well known. Thus we have "the myrtles in the glen" (1:8) and "the pair of bronze mountains"[21] (6:1). Whence do these concepts arise?

"The myrtles in the glen" and "the pair of bronze mountains" are, naturally, from originally mythological conceptions. According to the same conceptual context, the divine throne is in the same place. To that place the couriers, who had been sent forth, return again. From there their servants will be sent forth into the whole world. — In the same way these couriers and servants are themselves originally mythological figures. The four colors of their steeds should be characterized, just as 6:5 will emphatically add, as the four winds of the heavens.

We know enough about the notions of ancient Israel concerning the divine throne to be able to say that the mythological concepts appearing here are *not* indigenously Israelite. Accordingly, the conclusion is this: Zechariah 1–8 shows us how the human imagination of that time was full of all sorts of weird images. An alien mythology had taken control of the mind. One who is so possessed is brought into a relationship with the peculiar way of thinking and attempts to expound it. It should not be argued that the religious concepts of Zechariah were essentially changed in this way. *His* imagination appears even more strongly when it is approached thus.

Whence this mythology comes can be concluded from Zechariah 4.

Zechariah 4:1-6a, 10b-14

1 *Again the angel who spoke with me awoke me, as one will be roused from sleep;*

2 *And he spoke to me: "What do you see?" I[22] said, "I see there a candlestick, totally of gold. Over the top of it is a candelabra.[23] It has seven*

lamps.²⁴ And the lamps are seven branches.²⁵ ₃Next to it, indeed, stand two olive trees, to the right and to the left.²⁶

4 *Then I spoke again to the angel who had spoken with me: "What does this mean, sir? ₅The angel who had spoken with me then answered me: "Don't you know what this means?" I said, "No, sir." ₆ₐThen he answered me: 10b²⁷"These seven signify the eyes of YHWH which range over the whole world."*

11 *I spoke to him again: "So what do the two olive trees to the right and the left of the candlestick signify? [. . . . .]²⁸*

12 *I began again and said to him: "What then do the two groves of olive trees to the side of the pairs of golden tubes which carry the oil from the trees to the golden branches signify?²⁹ ₁₃And he spoke to me: "You don't know what these signify?" I said, "No, sir!" ₁₄He answered, "They are the two 'anointed sons' who stand before the Lord of the whole earth."*

The explanation of the vision which v. 10b gives, "These seven [lamps] signify the eyes of YHWH," presumes "the eyes of YHWH" to be a commonly known thing. For us, however, to whom this concept is not completely known, the explanation itself requires a further explanation. — According to the context, the "eyes of YHWH" are a known designation for something which can be represented as seven lamps. These can be nothing other than stars. The fact that stars are represented as lamps lies in the very nature of the thing! It is represented thus because it is viewed thus: the stars are the "lamps of the heavens" (Gen 1:16, etc.). That one sees the eyes of God in the stars is attested often enough in ancient mythology and is even quite readily comprehensible to us modern folks.

Now the question turns to the specific stars of which it is characteristic (a) that there are seven of them; and (b) that they "roam [מְשׁוֹטְטִים [měšôṭěṭîm]] across the whole world." By such a description the seven planets would be characterized.³⁰

Accordingly, cosmic immensities will be represented here in a mythological form no differently than at 6:1ff. and 1:8ff., where "the four winds" appear. The religious concepts which the parallel texts express are also similar to each other. The four winds, represented as horsemen, are agents of God, "sent out over the earth to roam about" and to bring back intelligence to God. The omniscience of God is visualized thus: God's knowledge extends everywhere that the four winds³¹ blow. The four winds represent God's omnipotence with a similar image, as chariots dispatched in order to carry out God's commands *everywhere!*

In the same way a profound and thoughtful investigation of nature has sought to understand the significance of the planetary movements: they are the eyes of God! These eyes of God, however, do not stand still, so that they might be able to observe only a specific part of the earth. Rather they "range over the whole world" and perceive everything. "Before YHWH the deeds of the children of humanity in the whole world are apparent."[32]

Now it is clear that the prophet has not invented these representations of the seven planets as the seven lamps of a candelabra without assistance. This is simply the nature of the thing. Such a representation is produced in the form of a cultic symbol, just as the seven planets must have served the artist in regard to the temple of the supreme God of heaven. At the same time the fact is that the prophet interprets only the seven lamps; he cannot interpret the seven branches and the candelabra because he himself had not formulated the pattern on his own. He drew it from elsewhere!

The same thing is to be concluded from the parallels with the known seven-branched candelabra of the Second Temple.[33] Since we have a cultic symbol there, we must also postulate it to be present in Zechariah 4.[34] On the other hand, that Second Temple candelabra actually differs in character from the one described in Zechariah 4, for while the one in Zechariah possesses *seven* arms, the candelabra in P^c has only *six*. The seventh light is mounted at the center. It may be presumed that this discrepancy is not accidental, i.e., that the differing representations also express a differing meaning. The light in the center, which is specifically distinguished, must signify the most prominent of the "planets," i.e., the sun. I thus conclude concerning the two variants in the enumeration of the planets that, in the one case, the sun stands in the center,[35] and in the other case, it stands — according to the usual style, which is known especially from the sequence of the weekdays — in the first place. It follows, therefore, that Zechariah did not have the temple candlestick itself before his eyes, but rather had one related to it, a cultic symbol slightly divergent from it.

Both candlesticks had the following things in common: the fact that they simulated in their form a tree, with either six or seven branches.[36] This has also been noted, for example, by Riehm.[37] The intention of the craftsman to represent a tree symbolically would be totally apparent to the people of that time since the candlestick was adorned with tree sap, more precisely with the sap of the almond tree.

How did a lighting device develop into the form of the almond tree? Because of the appearance of an ancient cultic symbol, one could do pretty well in ascribing practically anything to the mere caprice of the craftsman. But the appearance is more likely to be explained by the idea that the characteristic form of an ancient symbol truly renders the characteristic form of the thing represented. It is, accordingly, to be concluded that the lights of the planets, in the same way as in the image depicted here, could indeed be carried by a tree. We thus arrive at a mystical concept of a heavenly tree, the leafy canopy of which is the heavens, and on which, perhaps, the "fruit" of the stars appears. The fact that this tree is, precisely, an almond tree appears to be motivated by an interpretation of the stars as almonds.

A further proof for the adoption of the concept by Zechariah is to be drawn from the second part of the account. Next to the candlestick, to the right and to the left, stand two olive trees, two olive clusters of which are linked with the reservoir of the candlestick by tubes. Apparently these two olive trees have the purpose of supplying the candlestick with oil.

This feature is also allegorized by the prophet. To be sure, the interpretation of the two olive trees has been omitted in the current text. On the other hand, that which the two clusters of olives should signify is preserved. "It is the two clusters of olives which stand before the Lord of the whole earth." In other words, they are the two anointed ones, Joshua and Zerubbabel. The third thing is similar: just as the two clusters of olives are in immediate proximity to the seven-branched candlestick, so also the two anointed ones stand before the seven eyes of God![38] Do not think that God's eyes would have turned away from them, that before God their fate would be hidden! God gazes at them constantly.[39]

Accordingly, it is permissible to conclude from the context that the two olive trees must represent the two anointed families which stand perpetually before God, i.e., the houses of David and of Aaron. Now it is, however, very striking that this interpretation of the form, an interpretation intended by the prophet, harmonizes only slightly with the form itself. The function of the olive trees and the bunches of olives, i.e., to supply the lamps with oil, cannot be explained. And indeed, it should, perhaps, not be explained. In fact, how could human beings pour oil into the lamp of YHWH?[40]

This difficulty points out that the apocalyptic writer had already encountered even this feature. We receive, therefore, a mythological image presented as his production. It is imagined that a seven-armed lampstand stands in the earthly sanctuary, as in the heavenly one. It may have been asked: "Why does the light of the seven heavenly lamps burn forever?" And in regard to this, the answer may have been given: "It is explained by the two heavenly olive trees to the right and the left of the lampstand. *They* supply the lampstand with *their* oil!"

Accordingly, the seven-branched lampstand of Zechariah is a cultic-mythological symbol. Could we perhaps speculate, with greater probability, whence this symbol arose?

First of all, it is clear that it did not grow up in the soil of Judaism! Judaism, especially that of a prophet like Zechariah, has certainly developed no mythological forms. The reason why the seven lamps are portrayed as fruit of a tree can hardly be known either. Moreover, it has already been reported to us from a much earlier time using similar symbols. The ten lamps of the Solomonic Temple possessed a similar form. This is to be deduced from the description recounted by P^c. And it is confirmed by 1 Kings 7:49, where it is mentioned in connection with the lamps of "floral workmanship."[41]

Accordingly, the lampstand is to be seen in the same way as the other symbols of the Solomonic Temple — the pillars, the sea, the *Fahrstühle*, the cherubim — which were, or at least quite possibly were, foreign influences which had settled into it.[42] We seek, therefore, a foreign religion which, in the earliest times and later, even up to the time of Zechariah, had an effect on the Israelites.

The Babylonian religion is the only one which is, generally, a possibility. In the Babylonian religion the seven great gods are the seven planets. There is preserved for us a series of distinct planetary listings. In some,[43] the sun stands at the head. In another,[44] it stands in the middle, so that the sequence Moon, Mercury, Venus, I Sun I, Mars, Jupiter, Saturn emerges. Thereby the planets are arranged according to their distances from the earth — as those distances were assumed by the Babylonians.

On the other hand, the image of the world tree (inferred by us), its depiction as a lampstand, and the introduction of the two olive trees have, to this point, still not been proven to be of Babylonian origin. Accordingly, we should give our opinion on the mythological material which we, by means of Zechariah 1–8, see as flowing into the picture. It is most probably of Babylonian origin. In this regard, at present, Zechariah 1–8 stands all by itself. These chapters give us a flash of light, flaring up in the blink of an eye and then immediately disappearing, a light which shines onto an extremely striking religio-historical situation. They illuminate for us the incursion of a foreign, probably Babylonian, mythology into Judaism.

Indeed, we may deduce the pathway along which these mythological conceptions have come to Zechariah. The prophet more than once presumes the matter to be well known (cf. p. 84). It follows that he was not the first who had spoken of them among the Jews, but that he was entering into an already existent Judean tradition. Prophecy did not bring in this material. Rather, it was the people. Prophecy has been known to employ, for its own purposes, material which has only just become tradition. This, certainly, lies in the very nature of the thing: the prophets and their adherents had the sense to be in possession of Babylonian religion over against the higher one, adapting it *just slightly* so as to take on elements of the foreign mythology. Most folk circles stood even more open to foreign influences. Those circles, without falling away from YHWH, nevertheless allowed themselves to be dazzled by the Babylonian mythology and by its fantastic images. — Zechariah was written in Palestine. Even in Palestine, we see, in postexilic times, the Babylonian influence working in this way. All sorts of things might have come together to produce this effect: the infectious Babylonian concept of "the return"; the well-defined Babylonian culture, in which those in Palestine lived as well; the influence of the Samaritans, certain elements of which were of Babylonian origin; not in the least, perhaps, the influence by which there remained in Babylon a quite spiritually active Judaism, a Judaism which continued to have relations with the motherland.

In regard to these developing materials from Zechariah 1-8 further particulars from other exilic prophets also come into view. Certainly the "dragon"-chapter of Ezekiel is ultimately of Babylonian descent. This is probably also the case in the description of the cherubim[45] in the "chariot vision" and the myth of the expulsion from paradise in chapter 28; finally, in chapter 21 the image of the world tree may lie in the background. Notwithstanding all these things, a mythological provenance is still open to the question of whether the myth was itself adapted in Babylon or whether it had already been accepted in the homeland. The first possibility is hardly the probable one, since the possibility that the Yahwistic prophet has consciously adopted foreign materials would be difficult to accept, given what has already been noted.

— Lilith [לילית [*lîlît*]; Isa 34:14] is an originally Babylonian figure;[46] likewise also the *šēdîm*[47] (Deut 32:17; Ps 106:32). Both appear only in the writings of the "Jews" and could have been adopted in Babylon.

The same might be applicable to the myth of הילל בן שחר [*Hêlal ben Šāhar*].

Isa 14:12-14[48]

12 *How you have fallen from the heavens,*
O Hêlal, son of Šāhar.
How[49] you are beaten down to the underworld![50]
You lie rigid among corpses![51]
13 *You thought, however, in your mind,*
"I want to go up to heaven,
high above the divine star,
to lift up the throne;
to sit myself upon the mountain of the gods,[52]
in the furthest north.

> *I want to go up above clouds,*
>> *to make myself equal to the highest ones!"*
> 14 *Rather, you must go down to the underworld,*
>> *unto the deepest abyss.*[53]

We know from the traditions of the versions that *Hêlal* is the morning star. Until now the radiant power had been understood as the fourth form of this comparison of the king of Babylon with the morning star. But the prophet himself says quite plainly that the point of the comparison is not only this but also its fall from heaven. Isaiah 14 alludes to an account according to which the morning star had fallen from the heavens. This account, however, can be nothing other than a myth. Accordingly we will have to understand *Hêlal* and *Šāḥar* as proper names. What follows is, then, a shortened narration of the *Hêlal* myth.

Hêlal, Šāḥar's son, was a mighty warrior who, in his arrogance, was presumptuous enough to act like עליון [*'Elyôn*]. He wished to ascend to the clouds to heaven, higher than all the other divine stars, to the mountain of assembly, to the furthest north, wishing there to reign as king of everything! But the end of the malicious plan was this: he had to descend deep into שאול [*šě'ôl*], a carcass on top of carcasses! — We must, however, add that it comes down to a battle. In opposition to him is, quite possibly, the one whose majesty he dared to impugn, i.e., *'Elyôn.* Since he, in שאול [*šě'ôl*] — if the above conjecture is correct — lies upon corpses, it will be quite clear that he had confederates who would have been thrown down before him and on whom he has, thus, to lie!

In the name הילל בן שחר [*Hêlal ben Šāḥar*] it is even more definitely certain that we are dealing with a native myth! The morning star, son of the dawn, has a singular fate. Brightly shining, it rushes up toward the heavens, but it does not arrive at the highest point. The beams of the sun make it turn pale. The myth portrays this natural process as a battle of עליון [*'Elyôn*] against הילל [*Hêlal*], who once wished to ascend to the heights of the heavens, but has descended to the underworld. The Greek myth of the early death of Phaethon, son of Eos, speaks quite similarly, Phaethon is also the moving star.[54] Φαεθον [*Phaethon*], his preferred designation, is identical to הילל [*Hêlal*] (= "gleaming").

That the myth cannot be of Israelite origin lies again in the nature of the thing. The divine name עליון [*'Elyôn*] demonstrates this especially clearly. In Babylonian the name *Hêlal* and the *Hêlal* myth are not attested at present.[55] The Babylonian origin is certainly not out of the question because of this.[56] If Babylonian, the myth itself would probably have made reference to Mercury. On the other hand, one might, perhaps, settle upon a Phoenician origin.

Indeed, what is found at Job 38:31f.,[57] just in passing, by allusions to stellar myths,[58] might be traced back to a Babylonian origin. Even then, however, there is, unfortunately, still no proof to be produced. The "poetic recension" of the creation myth which we have considered in the foregoing materials also comes to mind. A great number of those materials are younger, e.g., much younger than P^c; nevertheless, they contain the myth in a more archaic form than Genesis 1. One would best account for the state of affairs by asserting that the Babylonian myth had emigrated to Israel on various occasions, and finally in postexilic times.

Accordingly, by separate pathways, some of which may be quite *uncertain*, others of which — especially לילית [*Lilith*] — are *quite certain* . . . by all of this we recognize that the Jews, already in the century after their deportation, had not quite been able to resist Babylonian influence. So the question appears to be justified as to whether the narrative of the creation of the world found in Genesis 1 might not also have been received.

Many modern researchers would consider the question, even given the evidence above, to be little more than a question. The material is Babylonian. P^c wrote in Babylon. What could be more obvious than to infer *and* to conclude that the author of P^c translated and reworked the Babylonian myth? Then we arrive at a state of affairs like that which our "literary-critical times" also adopts quite willingly, . . . nothing other than an author who copied another author. And the material in which he clearly makes his first appearance in our sources had, by that time, become native to Israel.

In reality, to be sure, things often don't proceed quite so naturally. We have to deal, in the interpretation of myths and legends, not only with written texts and with literary works, but far more often with oral tradition. It is extremely important to distinguish throughout between the time of the ancients, the documentary evidence accessible to us for consideration, and the antiquity of the conceptual idea itself.

Indeed, in our case the "natural" assumption is in no way adequate for the state of affairs. We have been able to perceive in the case of Zechariah in what ways the Babylonian mythological material has made its way into Judaism. The prophets and the prophetic schools had not acquired it directly themselves. Rather, they adopted it from the Babylonian-infected traditions of their people.

This is indeed clearly the case with Genesis 1 in P^c. One person, such as the author of P^c, with such a pronounced and self-consciously Jewish individuality, would never have translated and reworked such a strongly mythological and polytheistic narrative, which this Gentile origin acknowledged by him. Nor would he have advanced his work as the first phase [of creation]. This very elementary (according to modern literary-critical views) conjecture is, hence, an unthinkable thing in terms of religious history!

Against such an assumption, however, Genesis 1 itself testifies! The chapter in its own way is something quite different from such an adaptation. The contiguities do not affect the wording, rather only the individual concepts. Additionally, there stands in the background of Genesis 1, another tradition, a tradition quite close to the Babylonian one, but more likely a Phoenician one. We have seen, furthermore, that Genesis 1 is itself not even a single uniform piece. The gathering of primordial and modern features, as well as the disposition of the Sabbath, something which was not linked to the material from the beginning of the tradition, . . . all of this permits us to infer a long history for the tradition in Israel. Above all, however, the remarkable distance between the Babylonian and the Hebrew reports necessitates a very considerable interval in which the old Babylonian myth could, in the course of a greater history, finally have become Genesis 1.

There is, therefore, every reason to believe that we should consider Genesis 1 no differently than we consider P^c generally, namely, as the Jewish adaptation of old Israelite tradition. It comes down to this very certain conclusion, a conclusion found by reference to Deutero-Isaiah's allusions to the narrative features in Genesis 1. The old cosmogony, in which not the darkness but only the light is God's creation, is outdone by the prophet.[59]

He formed the light,	and created darkness.
He produced the good,	and created the "not good."
I, YHWH, am the One	who brought forth all these things. Isa 45:7

Isa 45:18b recalls the Chaos Myth.[60]

He formed and made the earth.
He established it!
Not as chaos has he created it.
As a dwelling he has formed it!

We have here a linking of תהו [tōhû — "chaos, wilderness"] and creation. In the creation account of Genesis 1, תהו [tōhû] is a *terminus technicus* for chaos. On the other hand, what the prophet says of chaos here is not simply a reiteration of the tradition from Genesis 1.[61] The prophet gives no statement about whether the world had been a תהו [tōhû] before the creation, but he retains only the positive things because it is, since the divine creation, not a chaos but rather the designated home of humanity. He himself would, if he had sung a complete creation poem, doubtless have no longer spoken about a chaos previously established by God. Nevertheless, the thinking and the expression of the prophet is understandable only as an expansion of the tradition of Genesis 1.

Since Deutero-Isaiah quite frequently concerns himself with Babylonian gods, it shouldn't attract any attention if, in a few places, it sounds like an intentional polemic against the Babylonian theogony. According to Babylonian teaching, the world-dominating god, *Marduk,* arose relatively late. He is in possession of the dominion through the word of the "gods, his fathers." He has created the world with the help of the others. Not so YHWH.

Before me, no god has been created!
  After me there will be none!
As for me, I am YHWH.
  Other than me there is no helper. Isa 43:10b-11[62]

I, YHWH, am the first,
  and at the last I am the same. Isa 41:4; cf. 44:6; 45:5; 48:12, etc.[63]

Who alone stretched out the heavens,
  who spread out the earth besides me! Isa 44:24b[64]

We should imagine the religio-historical situation thus according to these references. Deutero-Isaiah appears familiar with the Israelite tradition. On the other hand, he knows, since he lives in Babylon, the main characteristics of the Babylonian theogony. He idealizes the former. He despises the latter from the ground up. The Israelite creation account is, however, by no means something new to him. Rather, it is a tradition from a primordial age.

Don't you know?[65] Don't you hear?
Has it not been made known to you from the beginning?
Have you not understood since the establishment[66] of the earth?

Isa 40:21

Indeed, here the possibility that we are dealing with simply a first reception of heathen material is completely impossible!

Likewise, at Ezek 29 and 32 we have met with the myth (here mixed with Egyptian motifs applied to the Pharaoh) in a form already quite extensively withdrawn from the old Chaos Myth, so that the inference of a long narrative prehistory seems to be imperative.

Then we will have no reservations about seeing an allusion to the myth in Jer 4:23-26.[67]

23 *I saw the earth;*	*it was a chaos.*[68]
The[69] *heavens,*	*which had no light.*
24 *I saw the mountains;*	*they trembled,*
every hill convulsed!	
25 *I saw that no humans were*	
there any more.	*Every bird was chased*
	from the mountains.
26 *I saw Mount Carmel as a*	
wilderness.[70]	*All its forests*[71] *burned up!*[72]
before [the scorching heat][73]	
of YHWH,	*before the fire of his wrath.*

The prophet describes with gruesome detail the horrible devastation of the land which the enemy has produced. There comes a time, such as that at the beginning of all things, when the earth is בהו [*bōhû*], when the heavens are without light, when no more living beings will be present on the land.

There are unmistakable allusions to the material of Genesis 1: "The earth was תהו ובהו [*tōhû wā-bōhû*] and darkness was upon the surface of the תהום [*tĕhôm*]." At the same time it is clear that to the prophet as well as to his hearers the myth was quite familiar. That the prophets have also adopted mythic materials for the depiction of their visions we have already established.[74] Furthermore, we again observe here an *eschatological* shifting of the myth. According to the above points, the possibility must be considered that the translation of the myth to the eschaton had taken place already before the prophets. We are, thus, referred to preexilic times.

One first turns to the time of Assyrian domination, i.e., the century from 730 to 630 B.C.E.[75] The influences of a culture upon a culture, and of a religion upon a religion, are binding upon such individual political events only in exceptional cases. Normally it comes to pass not in a moment but rather in a whole epoch. So great was the impression of Babylonian religion on the Judeans, however, that the Babylonian deities were not only officially venerated by the loyal vassal kings (2 Kings 21:5 and 23:5) but also the worship of them was revived among the people. And the Deuteronomic reform could only just, itself, survive the national catastrophe (Zeph 1:5; Jer 7:18; 8:2; 14:17-19; 19:13).[76]

One seems, therefore, to have good reason for assigning the adoption of the creation account to that time. Thus, it is maintained, the flood narrative, the Babylonian origin of which has been generally accepted, would have come to Israel. — These religio-historical assessments are presently linked with literary-critical allegations. Budde[77] has established an older layer in J, layer J^1, in which the flood narrative is lacking. He has, in addition, established a later source, J^2, which contains that narrative. Budde surmises that these two sources, for which "the dependence on the saga of Mesopotamia" is characteristic, stem from the time "of amicable relationships with the Assyrians," i.e., from the time of Ahaz.[78]

It is to be conceded that in the present Yahwistic Noah tradition two forms of the legend have flowed together: the Noah of J^1 (the ancestor of humanity and the originator of Palestinian culture with his three sons, Shem, Japhet, and Canaan), and the Noah of J^2 (the hero of the flood and the ancestor of renewed humanity, through his three sons, Shem, Ham, and Japhet). Now it follows from the nature of the thing that the saga of the Palestinian Noah was earlier than the immigrating Babylonian one. Furthermore, it is apparent from 9:20ff., where Ham is first inserted by way of addition, that in our Genesis the narrative of J^1 precedes that of J^2.

It certainly does not follow from this, however, that the flood account would have been unknown in Israel at the time of J^1. How many ancient legends did the later E have, legends which the older J did not present?!? Indeed, we ourselves discover from P^c even more ancient items, e.g., the sign of the rainbow (9:8ff.). Because the authors of J and E did not invent their materials but have only collected and, at most only slightly, edited them,[79] there is generally not much to be gained from literary-critical observations concerning the history of the materials themselves. The sagas, even before their formal literary establishment, had a history in the oral tradition, and this quite singularly important prehistory is not to be attained by literary criticism.

Accordingly, there is generally nothing to be concluded about the time of the influx of the Babylonian materials from the observation of the differences between J^1 and J^2. And otherwise J^1 is also in no way free of Babylonian materials. This source spoke, according to Budde, of Nimrod. The original place of humanity is, in J^1 chapter 11, שִׁנְעָר [*Šin'ar*], and both for its paradise account as well as for its ancestral list[80] one may surmise a Babylonian origin. We have, therefore, assigned the determination of the antiquity of the flood narrative once more to religio-historical considerations alone!

Because we possess the Babylonian flood narrative, we are in the happy situation of being able to compare it with the biblical one. The result of this comparison is that, for all the similarity in terms of specific points, there does exist an infinite discrepancy between the two accounts. Despite many ancient traces, such as 8:21, it is clearly visible that the Babylonian *Atraḫasis* legend and the *Marduk* myth belong together in regard to their style. They belong together in the same way that the Noah legend and Genesis 1 belong together stylistically. Here, too, the thought of a direct appropriation, in the same way as in Genesis 1, is quite remote.[81] On the contrary, a history must be established between them, a history in which the polytheistic things so totally disappeared, and in which the *poetry* has become a *prosaic* narrative.[82]

It comes then to this: We possess our "legend" tradition from the hand of prophetic schools. These people had written it down at a time[83] when the prophetic movement was strong and self-assured, and when the prominence of YHWH above the gods of the peoples was clearly recognized. Now would these people have accepted a Babylonian myth which had only just found its way into Hebrew thinking? Is it very comprehensible that they could not earnestly draw upon the magnificent old narratives of their own people, since the same probably corresponded, at times, with the great prophetic ideals? That they would have applied the same piety to foreign myths would be totally incomprehensible. And to myths which had arrived together with idolatrous rites?!? It was, take note, the very moment when the prophetic party was waging a life-or-death battle against the invading Babylonian religion. — It may not be argued that the Babylonian origin of such myths was very quickly forgotten. Could the prophetic circles, supposedly undecided about the Babylonians, have possessed, at the same time, a truly robust Yahwistic religion, if the foreign material was, in such a brief time, so dramatically amalgamated? Furthermore, there is every reason to think quite highly of the sensitivity with which the originally non-Yahwistic material was understood in prophetic circles.[84]

Accordingly, it follows that the tenet of Kuenen, "the later we designate such a borrowing to be, the more comprehensible it will be,"[85] may, according to literary-critical methodology, have an air of authority — only Ezek 14:14, 20 and Isa 54:9 speak of Noah — but religio-historical research must assert the opposite.

Similar considerations apply to the account of the flood, to the sagas of Nimrod, of Paradise, and of the Tower of Babel. For all of these accounts the adoption of a Babylonian provenance is very possible. Nimrod, the mighty hunter and the mythical first king of Babel and Nineveh, is, in the nature of things, a Babylonian figure. He has,[86] not without reason,[87] been identified with the Babylonian national hero Gilgamesh (ideographically *Gišdubar*). The Paradise account also exhibits a few motifs of Babylonian origin.[88] The Garden of Eden in the distant east, a residence of the deity and a source point for mighty rivers, among which are the Tigris and the Euphrates . . . surely this account is not an originally Hebrew compilation. The tradition that the Garden lies in the east and the concurrence with Iranian myths[89] make the Babylonian origin of the myth probable.[90]

The cherubim are probably Babylonian figures.[91] A mythic tree is often seen depicted on Babylonian memorials. It is probably the tree of life.[92] The building of the tower took place in Babylon and has numerous features of Babylonian life in mind: the land-type; the distinctive building materials; the multilinguistic nature of international trade (Jer 13:14; 50:37); the collaborative efforts of whole nations on a single building (Jer 51:50); above all, a primordial Babylonian building, the origin of which the tale seeks to explain. On the other hand, the explanation of the name "Babel," which is an essential feature of the whole narrative, and the interpretation of the edifice, which actually was a temple, as a tower for the eternal glorification of humanity, and therefore for the blaspheming of God, . . . these things indicate that the account could not have originated among the Babylonians. It is assumed that it stems from the barbarians, who, however, were not unaware of Babylonian things. From the Semitic etymology it is to be concluded that they were Semites. Accordingly, we conjecture them to be the Arameans who encamped in the vicinity of Babylon.[93]

When did these accounts[94] come to Israel? From the foregoing it appears quite impossible to place their reception in the prophetic period. At the same time, the accounts themselves speak in favor of the thesis that they had entered Israel at a very early time. These stories have come to us complete, in a more or less obscure form.

Of the saga of Nimrod we possess, in Genesis, only a single final echo, remnants of an earlier richness. The paradise narrative, however, actually contains certain obscure traces: the garden, which has become the locale of the deity and, at the same time, of the serpent, which has simultaneously become a demon; the "protevangelium" exists almost incomprehensibly in the present situation. In addition, we also have, elsewhere, two allusions to an older recension of the paradise account. There is, first of all, Job 15:7f.

7 *Are you the firstborn of humanity?*
  And were you brought forth before the hills?
8 *Should you attend to God's counsel,*
  and then steal[95] wisdom for yourself?

Here the primal human is still a hero, a hero who had been born before the hills, whom God had deemed worthy of being a member of the divine council, and who, not content with the great things which were granted him, had "stolen" for himself an even "deeper" wisdom.[96] In the same way, there is also Ezek 28:12ff., which speaks of a semidivine being who had lived in paradise among precious stones. He was unblemished on the day of his birth, splendid in beauty and wisdom, until his misdeed was visited upon him and God expelled him from paradise.

These are traces of an older recension of the paradise myth, traces which are more broadly mythological than those contained in Genesis 2f. We may, accordingly, conclude that, as ancient as Genesis 2f. sounds to us, the biblical narrative stands at an immense distance from the original, probably Babylonian, myth.[97] A similar distance, as we have established it in the cases of the creation and flood narratives, exists between the original and the biblical recensions.

Indeed, the story of the erection of the tower exhibits multiple obscurities: in 11:7 YHWH speaks to other divine beings, without it having been said "to whom" that may be; v. 5 reports that YHWH has descended to earth; v. 6 reports that YHWH is once again in heaven without in the meantime having reported that he again went up thither; the way that YHWH puts an end to the tree has also not been reported. Thus it follows that the primal legends, all together, present us with traces of a long tradition. They must have been narrated orally for a long time before their having been written down in Israel.

We now apply these results to the creation account. The acceptance of the creation myth into our prophetic tradition is explicable only if it had made its way into Israel at a much earlier time, so that its Babylonian origin had already been forgotten over several generations by the time of the prophets. This thesis, demanded by the course of religious history, would be supported by the observation that the other Babylonian myths concerning primordial history had also been received *en toto* at an earlier time.

From this point on, we will be dealing with the era after the immigration of Israel into Canaan, the early kingship. We have to ask whether the adoption of Babylonian influences was possible at that time. Then we have to ask, further, whether the "creation concepts" should be assigned such a high antiquity in Israel.

If a Babylonian influence on Old Testament religion has been mentioned up to this point, one should consider the nature of things in regard to the eras in which we have established a direct contact of Israel with Babylon, i.e., in regard to the exilic and postexilic periods and to the period of Assyrian hegemony. Dilettantes will readily launch themselves into musing about the religio-historical differences from that primal period, when Abraham dwelt in *Ur-Kasdîm*.

Now our horizon is considerably broadened by a fortunate discovery. Six years ago the archive of Amenophis III was discovered in Egypt. We have come to know, since then, certain letters which the kings of Babylon, Aššur, and Mitanni exchanged with the Pharaoh, and of reports of the Palestinian governors to their Egyptian overlords. All of these literary pieces are on clay tablets, in cuneiform, in the Babylonian language.[98]

We have, therefore, taken a look at the circumstances of Palestine around 1400 B.C.E., i.e., at a time before there were Hebrews in Canaan. At that time the hegemony of the Babylonian cult in Canaan was already quite pronounced. The Babylonian language, not the Canaanite or the Egyptian language, is even used in relations with the Pharaoh, the official language of the inhabitants of Canaan.

[This means, however, nothing other than the fact that around this time in Palestine, at least to a certain extent, there must have been knowledge of the Babylonian literature. Then in order to understand such a Babylonian document, as we possess it in quantity from Palestine, a not insignificant concern with the Babylonian writing method and language must be surmised. The possession of several hundred cuneiform signs together with their pronunciation and meaning would have saved even a devoted Palestinian cuneiform user just as little time as it does a present-day Assyriologist!

We have, then, begun to learn something in relation to each period about how an "outsider" learned "Assyrian." We know this as well from the Tell el-Amarna discoveries since, in addition to the Babylonian vocabularies, the compilations of signs, and the "cheat sheets" (which were useful for the acquisition of Babylonian), . . . in addition to these things, two of the more significant Babylonian mythological texts were found there. In these texts, which obviously served as a sort of "Assyriological Chrestomathy," the Egyptian scribes have indicated word divisions by red and black dots. By the discovery of these two mythological texts, it is documented that, at that time, mythological traditions had migrated into the west. In regard to its contents, one of the two myths, the narrative of Adapa,[99] the primal man (as it appears), is particularly interesting. The point of the myth is that Adapa, at the critical moment when the highest god of heaven held out to him the bread of life and the water of life, did *not* take them, and thereby — we can probably understand: "for himself and for his species" — forfeited immortality forever. The Adapa myth is, therefore, similar to the myth of "the fall."] — Zimmern

Through the Tell el-Amarna discoveries we have gained an impression of the prodigious power of the Babylonian culture in those lands so very distant from Babylon. We may assume that the Syro-Phoenician culture was completely saturated by the Babylonian.[100] Details from the history of Canaanite religion and its close environs are sufficient, however, to make this clear. The *Aštarte* of the Canaanites and the Philistines (in Sabean, ʿ*Attar*) is identical to the Babylonian goddess and "perhaps came from a Babylonian source."[101] And the name "Mount Nebo" suggests that this mountain was once holy to the Babylonian god *Nabu* (= Mercury).[102]

Much of the ancient Canaanite culture had been "buried," since the Hebrew "barbarians" took over the land. Much, but not all! Religious history shows clearly that the Hebrews in Canaan had been very strongly "Canaanized." They had taken over not only the agricultural and the ornithological, the rural and the urban lifestyles, but also the sanctuaries and the cultus. We may assume that a good portion of the Genesis legends, particularly those which originally belonged to certain holy places, are of Canaanite origin. Through this coalescence with the earlier population of the land, however, the Israelites came, indirectly, under Babylonian influence. And in consequent times the Babylonian materials, especially through Phoenician and Aramaic mediation, time and again had an influence, especially in times of prosperity when the Palestinians traded the fruits of their land in the Phoenician commercial centers and in Damascus traded the fruits of their land for the products of world culture. So, under Solomon, under Ahab, in the early periods of written prophecy, this was the case!

We can still establish a few things from our scanty sources. The ancient Israelite measured his grain and his wine with Babylonian measurements. He weighed objects with Babylonian weights.[103] He calculated the height and the breadth of his residence according to the Babylonian "rod."[104] Like the Babylonian,[105] he used the "mace" and the "signet ring." The characteristically Babylonian practice of "sealing" each contract at the bottom had come to Israel from the Babylonians by way of the Arameans and the Canaanites.[106] Products of Babylonian craftsmanship were also not unknown in Israel. King Ahaz had allowed a sundial to be installed. Sundials are a Babylonian invention.[107] The narrative tells of a "magnificent mantel from Shinar" which stimulated the avarice of the Israelites (Josh 7:21). The prophet zealously campaigns against the new fashion of sitting on the corner of the couch.[108] We know this practice from Babylonian images.[109]

We can also establish Babylonian influence on the sphere of religion. The Israelites who fell away to Astarte took up, thereby, the worship of, as it appears, an originally Babylonian goddess. But Babylonian features also penetrated into Yahwism at that time. The Solomonic Temple had been built by Phoenician master builders. Its construction and its furnishings had been done according to the Phoenician models of that time. Thus, standing before the Temple of YHWH were none other than two pillars, as in the temple of Melqart of Tyre,[110] or, at the very least, having a cosmological significance.[111] In the same way, the various ornaments with which the building was decorated, originally emblems of the nature religion, stemmed from heathen religious practice.

Among these Phoenician symbols are now a whole series which are not even at home in Phoenicia, but which were introduced there from Babylon. Kosters[112] has surmised that the bronze "Sea" was originally a Babylonian depiction of *Tĕhôm*.[113] This supposition has, of late, been corroborated by Babylonian inscriptions,[114] according to which *Urninā,* king of *Lagaš,* erected a large and a small "World Sea" *(apsū),* and *Agum* had set up a "Dragon" image beside a "Sea" *(tâmtu).* The form of the "Sea" can also be traced back to Babylonian models and was motivated by the nature of the mythological outlook which it represents. The twelve oxen, which — as is expressly added — were laid out according to the points of the compass, must have some relationship to the twelve constellations of the zodiac.

The ten candelabra of the Temple are to be treated just like the "Sea." These also are a cultic representation of a cosmological perception. A Babylonian origin is also very probable for them.[115] Finally, the cherubim of the Temple are probably Babylonian figures.[116]

We perceive, therefore, at the only places where ancient Hebrew cultic symbols were described in detail, just how strong the influence of the Babylonian ideas had been upon ancient Israel. Therefore, it is to be noted that among the imported representations many cosmological symbols appear. The Babylonian cosmology must, therefore, have made a great impression upon the Near Eastern world.

This is even apparent in a detailed way: ancient Israel knows of the great ocean which encircles the lands[117] and lies under the earth;[118] in Israel one speaks of the reservoir above the heavens, and of the dark land of the dead, שׁאול [šĕʾôl]. These are Babylonian concepts.[119] In Israel, these concepts belong to the most ancient traditions.[120] We would consider them, according to what precedes, to be borrowed.

A Babylonian origin can also be maintained for a Hebrew cultic institution, for the seven-day week, and for the Sabbath.[121] The seven-day week[122] had its locus in Babylon. And the name "Sabbath" as a holy day was established by the Babylonians.[123]

In that time a whole series of Babylonian myths were accepted: the narratives of paradise, of the flood, of the building of a tower, and of Nimrod. Likewise, the myth of the golden ages, which we have found in Isaiah, and the Babylonian origin of which we may surmise, had come to Israel at that time.

Accordingly, the result is this: Israel had existed under Babylonian influence in the earliest times. We can also establish the influence of Babylonian religion. And, up to a point, the adoption of primal myths is established in each period. From here on, therefore, nothing stands in the way of the assumption that the creation myth was adopted at the earliest period.

The question of when the creation myth was adopted is strongly connected with the antiquity of the creation faith in Israel. While earlier it was held to be obvious that this faith belonged to the oldest fundamental tenets of Old

Testament religion, lately one is inclined to question its actual antiquity. Indeed, it is quite possible to hold it as exilic.[124] Strong grounds certainly appear to speak in favor of the latter assumption, since Deutero-Isaiah is the first expression of this concept in the Jewish religion. The postexilic books articulate it on every side. Whoever moves now from Judaism to the preexilic writings is startled to discern so little about the creation. In the ancient tales — naturally without regard to Gen 1:2ff. — the idea of creation plays no role. It is, in any event, not a leading idea among the prophets. It is not even mentioned by first Isaiah!

What is even more aggravating is that a series of prophetic passages, passages which do contain the creation myth, are to be taken, with greater or lesser certainty, as pretentious glosses![125] These glosses show, then, that the later interpretive period had become aware of the absence of the creation idea within the ancient prophets and had endeavored to correct it!

Furthermore, it is quite comprehensible that the modern study of "creation faith" by no means considers it to be a self-evident tenet of the popular religion. On account of the God who dwells in the tree, or in the spring, as well as the God who directs Israel's general levy preceding the holy war, and the God who created the heavens and the earth, a broader measure is needed. Nevertheless, the conclusion that only the exile called forth a "creation faith" would be too rapidly attained!

Our sources teach us that it had once been a major theme of the religion. But no more!! Nevertheless, it could quite possibly have existed earlier. One would do well to work through such complicated matters thoroughly in dealing with so complex a religious history as that of Israel, so little of which is actually put forward explicitly. This is also the case with the idea that God dwells in heaven. The idea first became prominent in Judaism as a symbolic representation of the transcendence of the deity. It is, however, documented from the earliest periods (Gen 11:5; 28:12; 1 Kings 22:19; cf. Gen 19:24, etc.). At that time, however, it was of lesser influence, because of the even more impressive fact that YHWH had established a dwelling quite close by, right there in the land, within its holy symbols. Though the literary remains, from which we first hear of the creation frequently, are from the exile and later, the probability is that this faith had already been professed in a much earlier Israel, without being dissipated.

Furthermore, it is certain that the concept of the Creator-God stands in contrast, to a certain degree, to the popular god and to the god of natural symbolism. But this would only be an insurmountable obstacle, then, if the religion of Israel was a singular religion which had developed totally on its own. In actuality it was, in the earliest period of which we know, the product of an historical process. It had adopted pronounced motifs from the religion of Canaan. It was, therefore, at the time when our sources arose, a complex phenomenon. The YHWHs of the stones of Bethel, and of the thunderstorm, and of the battle are not easily set aside.

If, then, a new feature, [that of a creator-God], is added here, a feature which stands, to some degree, in contrast to the rest [of the divine features], it should not seem strange. To be precise, it has been added secondarily. Or was the concept of creation unattainable for ancient Israel? I am hardly concerned that this assertion might be put forward successfully. We find the idea of creation among the Babylonians, the Egyptians, the Phoenicians, and the Greeks. Should we envisage ancient Israel around the time of Elijah as so unrefined that it *could not* have apprehended such a concept?!

On the contrary, we are even in a position to designate the point at which the concept of creation could have attached itself to the ancient religion. Many aetiological legends indicate to us that even in ancient times they loved to seek after the origins of things! Whence comes that tree, this spring, these striking rocks? Whence the longing of the man for the woman? Whence the current fortunes of the peoples? And much more!! Cosmological concerns also creep about beneath such questions. "Whence come the springs?" is a question which is also asked. It is answered by the idea of a great sea thereunder. "Whence the rain?" Mighty waters above the heavens, heavenly windows and floodgates, are asserted! Or the question is asked, "Whither go the dead?" It is answered thus: "Into Sheol." Or it is asked, "Why is heaven so firmly established?" And it is answered by stories being told of the pillars of the heavens. Or, "What might the thunderstorm be?" The thunder is the battle cry of God, the lightning his arrow, the rainbow his battle bow, which he puts aside after the thunderstorm. It cannot accordingly be maintained that the ultimate question, "Whence does 'everything,' and especially 'we ourselves,' come?" would be unlikely in Israel.

No other response could have been given to such a question than this: "YHWH has formed all of it!" Indeed, this response certainly does not lie far from the other concepts of ancient Israel. It was YHWH who ruled "over sun, moon, and stars. He has caused the winds to blow. He has caused the heavens to thunder, to lightning, to rain. And he has sealed them up whenever it is agreeable to him."[126] Who else could have made "everything" other than YHWH? "If not YHWH, then who?"[127]

So it follows that the concept of creation in ancient Israel was the obvious answer to an obvious question. And it follows that the myth which reported the creation of the heavens and the earth by the deity must have been intelligible and plausible to ancient Israel. The sentiment with which such a myth might have been told can still be discerned from the Babylonian myth as well as from the "poetic recensions" of the myth in the Old Testament. According to its form, it was a hymn to YHWH. It is cited in admiration of YHWH's great power and wisdom, as well as in thankful worship of the good God who created from the starkness and terror of chaos this pleasant and beautiful world. At the same time, however, not only in the Babylonian myth but also in the "poetic recensions," the conquest of the terrible and mighty Chaos Storm stands in the foreground. It may be accepted that it was already the case in ancient times in Israel. The description of YHWH's battle with the monster was considerably more vivid, and therefore also more enthusiastic than the abstract concept that YHWH was the creator.

That God created the world is, according to the modern viewpoint, the most important thing which the ancient religion of YHWH was capable of saying. Nevertheless, one would do well not to endow the concepts of creation with too great a solemnity for ancient times. The ancient people, the interest of which was totally on Canaan and which was limited to its immediate environs, when they heard of the creation of "heaven and land," thought, first of all, of the land of Canaan and of Canaan's heaven. The sun, which YHWH has placed in the heavens, is the sun which illumines *our* pastures. And the thought that YHWH had formed everything in primordial time stands not so far from the thought that it is YHWH who sends forth the fructifying rain upon the fields, and who, with his heavenly hosts, the stars, comes to the help of Israel's fighting armies. That YHWH, the creator of the heavens and of the earth, is ultimately much more than YHWH, the God of Israel. . . . this was not evident to the ancients!

Furthermore, the importance of the creation faith within the ancient religion should not be overestimated. It was, at any rate, not a concept by which the ancient religion lived; otherwise its absence in the ancient sagas would be quite inexplicable. The religion generally focused a good bit more on the realm of the primordial accounts than it did on the realm of the present reality: the joyful harvest festival, the great wars of YHWH . . . these are motifs from the ancient religion. This creation myth, however, was an ancient account, an account close to the other one which was told.

From this point on, the religio-historical significance of the creation myth is judged to be similar to that of the paradise account. The significance of the latter, i.e., the paradise account, for ancient times has also been highly overrated, while, following the practice of the church, the whole Old Testament "anthropology" has been treated in connection with it. Currently it is known that the paradise myth was by no means a foundational concept of Old Testament piety. It is first cited by Ezekiel. Nevertheless, this account *is* primitive, although it did not possess, in ancient times, the significance which it came to receive only in considerably later Judaism, because of a later revival of speculation on Adam.

So, the creation concept was quite probably introduced in the early period, without the form of the Israelite religion (as Wellhausen has delineated it) having been altered thereby. At the same time, however, we do not rule out the possibility of holding onto the antiquity of the creation concept, even though it is found so rarely in the preexilic prophets.

First it must be established that it would be methodologically improper to compile, working from the prophetic writings, a compendium of the religious materials of their time. Their concern was with their people, whose transgressions they rebuked, whose valor they revived. They spoke of the events which YHWH had resolved for the *immediate* future. They might occasionally speak of the historical events of the past, insofar as they could draw from them a teaching for the present. However, *ex professo,* they did not deal with such materials. Even though we hear from the early prophetic writings so little of the patriarchal narratives, of the flood account, of paradise, and even of the creation, it cannot thus be shown that they did not know of these narratives.

And what should the creation teach? — The idea of creation was part of the contemplation of nature. The vocation of the prophets, however, was to interpret not the manifestations of nature, but rather the experiences of their people. It was, therefore, not by chance that so few cosmological materials are preserved by the prophets. And, in addition to this reality, we also need to comprehend better the dearth of creation concepts within their writings.

Nevertheless, there was a linkage of cosmology to the examination of history in the prophets of later times. In these later periods there is even the primary religious dogma that the God of Israel is the same as the God of the creation. Accordingly, it is comprehended, from the infrequent attestation of the idea of creation in the earlier prophets, that this linkage was missing. We might, perhaps, be surprised about it if a person like Isaiah, to whom the vastness of the world was quite apparent, who believed, with every aspect of his being, in YHWH as the sovereign of the strongest and mightiest peoples. . . . we might perhaps be astonished if such a person had, as a cornerstone of his own conceptual structure, the concept of creation according to our understandings thereof. Nevertheless, he lacks such a concept.

One can learn from all of this that the linkage of the two themes, cosmology and the contemplation of history, being, as it were, from different spheres, is not as self-evident as it may seem to us. To the earlier prophets the creation was a very distinctive thought: the power of YHWH over Israel would be established from the past, so that it might suggest, a bit more closely, something about the Exodus account, i.e., about the creation *of Israel;* and, for the same purpose, YHWH's power over nature would be recalled. So many more comprehensible and impressive examples would have come into existence, many more than simply the ancient narrative of the creation of the world.

One highly instructive example of this type of ancient prophecy is Jer 5:20ff. The prophet threatens that YHWH will send no rain. "Israel is a foolish people, without understanding, if it will not fear God, who has power over early- and late-rains, and over the time of the harvest." Such a reprimand was sufficiently impressive. So, if no rain was given, one must hunger.[128] Only the later prophets have deemed such a demonstration of divine power as insufficient and placed the reference to the creation of the sea beside it.[129] Ancient times would have understood what YHWH's power over the sea in such a situation actually signified: What did Israel have to fear or to expect from the sea?

The early prophet speaks of the creation of the world most often when he wishes to preach to foreign people in the name of YHWH, to whom world dominion belongs. Then it is tantamount to: "I have created earth, humanity, and animals, and, by virtue of the authority which I have over my creation, it has fallen to me to grant all lands to the king of Babylon. So listen to him, you peoples, for the world belongs to him."[130] Thus are the heathen addressed. Israel, on the other hand, can be addressed much more emphatically since it is involved quite differently with God and is in God's hand in a different manner.

Finally, it is still to be noted that the concept of creation at that time had its locus in primeval hymns to YHWH, hymns which we must consider in the same way that we consider "poetic recensions," only perhaps as slightly more archaic. These hymns would have been quite strongly blended, at that time, with mythology, and their pagan origin would have been present right there on the surface. One need only take note of the "we" of Genesis 1. The prophets were great enough also, at one point, to infer such a concept from a poetic contemplation of the significance of what was represented in a vision. Furthermore, they would have had a certain aversion in the face of such pagan accounts. This situation was altered only when these myths were produced in strongly Hebraized forms by the people and by the prophetic schools.

In the exile the creation concept, then, had obtained the strong significance which characterized it from that time on. We are able to divine the reason for this: the world had become visibly open to the people of that time. They then placed themselves in a land which had appeared, until then, as the end of the earth. Israel's destiny was now inseparably linked with the fate of the whole world. Israel's deliverance must, at the same time, be the downfall of Babylon, a shock for the peoples of the world. It is no longer sufficient to think about YHWH above all as the lord over Israel and Canaan. He must be more, if hope in him is not to be abandoned. In addition, it happened that the Jews in Babylonia confronted a religion which, as the religion of culture and of the empire, must have made a strong impression on them. And that religion appeared with the claim that *Marduk,* the god of Babylon, is the creator of the world.

At that time a certain Deutero-Isaiah — I have no intention of ascribing these heroic concepts to a hero — had discovered anew the ancient creation concepts. In effervescent hymns he celebrated the God who had made "all these things," and therefore rules over all these things. Since YHWH is the creator, he is also the almighty one. One should believe in him if he now promises gloriously to transfigure his people before the eyes of the whole world. "YHWH the Creator" is the sure anchor for all of Israel's hopes, the glorious comfort for its every sorrow, the secure point in the shifting fortunes of humanity! And from that point on this resounds across the centuries: "I believe in God, the Almighty, Creator of heaven and earth."

Accordingly, we have acquired this result: Even in the earliest Palestinian period of Israel there had been effective Babylonian influence. There are no grounds for denying the early age of the creation concept in Israel. In line with this, the apparently contradictory instances being removed, the way is now cleared for a positive line of reasoning. The existence of creation concepts is demonstrated for the prophetic period by Jeremiah 27.[131] For the pre-prophetic period it is proved by the creation myth of J, by Genesis 2, and by the Temple consecration prayer of 1 Kings 8:12:[132]

> *He has placed the sun in the heavens,*[133]
> *YHWH himself had wished to dwell in darkness.*

Whether the verse stems from Solomon is of no consequence for us. In any event, the words, according to the LXX, stem from the ספר השיר [*sēper haš-šîr*], and, according to them, YHWH dwells in the darkness of the *Adyton*[134] in primordial times.

The antiquity of the Babylonian Chaos-Creation myth in Israel ensues from Isa 17:12-14 and Jer 4:23-26, where the myth already appears in eschatological expression. Then there is the allusion to the myth in Isa 30:7, where the prophet designates Egypt as "Rahab who sits still." Furthermore, there is the existence of a series of mythological and cosmological ideas which originally belonged together with the Chaos Myth. Indeed, Amos 9:2 speaks of the sea serpent over whom YHWH himself has power. To ancient Israel the waters above the firmament[135] and the waters under the earth[136] were quite familiar. If it is called by the name of *Tĕhôm* since it "lies spread out" below,[137] it thus echoes the concept that *Tĕhôm* is a stormy one. The same expression will be used of the "dragon" of Ezek 29:2.

We obtain a chronological date for the antiquity of the myth from the report that Solomon had installed a "Sea" in the Temple. In the foregoing,[138] it has been demonstrated that this cultural symbol is of Babylonian origin. The Babylonian name shows that it was a representation of the primordial sea. In Babylon such a "Sea" was placed in the shrine of *Marduk*.[139] Thus was symbolized the power of *Marduk* over *Ti'âmat*. The artist therefore represents with this symbol the very concept which the creation myth expresses in words. Accordingly, the cultic symbol of the "Sea" in the Temple is classified together with the concept of the "World Sea" and the Chaos Myth.

Now a cultic symbol can quite probably be possessed or be taken over without the original sense of the symbol being understood.[140] So it would still not be possible to infer the existence of the Chaos Myth in Israel from the "Sea" of Solomon alone. The fact remains in this case, however, as we have already established from other sources, that the idea of the "World Sea" had been accepted by ancient Israel. Additionally, there is also the fact that a religious contemplation of the "Sea" must have been intelligible for a people who were in the habit of worshiping the deity at the springs and who also saw in these springs "the blessings of *Tĕhôm* which lies thereunder" (Gen 49:25). Furthermore, we have seen that ancient Israel had also known the account of the defeat of the sea by YHWH. Finally, the technical name "Sea"[141] shows that Israelite tradition quite specifically knew what the great reservoir, available for no practical use, should signify. Accordingly, we should assume that the answer to the question of why there would be a "Sea" erected in the Temple of YHWH would be: Because YHWH had overcome the "Sea" in primordial time. We therefore conclude that the Chaos Myth would have been professed in Israel at the time of Solomon.

Corroboration, even though not completely certain, comes from one other side. On the Triumphal Arch of Titus in Rome — as is well known — there is depicted the seven-branched candlestick.[142] In the six obvious fields on the arch's base all sorts of beings are to be seen. On the middle fields above, as it appears, there are two eagles. On the remaining fields there are seven monsters with twisting bodies which end with fish tails. It has been maintained that these animal forms were the particular fabrication of the Roman craftsman.[143] This is not, in itself, probable. The craftsman would have reproduced these important pieces of booty in a generally true fashion. And the whole form of the מנורה [*mĕnôrāh*] speaks loudly, at the same time, for the accuracy of the craftsman. That form, to a layman's eye like mine, is perceived as characteristically oriental and non-Greek.

Now we still have one feature about which we can verify the accuracy of the figure. The "floral decorations," of which we have already heard in regard to the lampstands of the Solomonic Temple,[144] and P[c],[145] and Josephus,[146] are also depicted on the lampstands of the Triumphal Arch. Thus we are gazing, here, upon an example of how this cultic symbol passed through a millennium totally unchanged. — If, moreover, small differences in detail are found — just as the description of the "floral decorations" in P[c] is not exactly comparable to the Titus depiction — so it has to be recalled that three craftsmen stand between the later candlesticks and those of the Solomonic Temple: two of them, who had reproduced the candlesticks according to the description — after the exile and during the Maccabean restoration — and the Roman craftsman of the arch who had depicted the candlesticks by order of Caesar. Such discrepancies, which are attributable to the craftsman, are, however, insignificant, perhaps because of the prevailing stylistic sentiments.

Thus it may be assumed that the craftsman of the Titus relief did not himself invent the monsters on the pedestal, but rather had composed them just a bit more stylistically, according to Roman sentiments. It is, however, to be further concluded that these creatures would have first appeared on the candlestick neither in Maccabean times nor after the exile. Above all, the Jewish abhorrence of images, which perceived a divine form even if only slightly similar, makes the idea that the actual candlestick was decorated with these kinds of figures from the time of its first fabrication particularly unlikely. Such figures could, at best, have been tolerated at the time *if* they were consecrated by the antiquity and the sanctity of the object itself, in the same way as the cherubim, the lions, and the bulls of the Temple, the Ark, and the "Sea" were tolerated. So it follows that these figures would already have been acceptable on the lamps of the Solomonic Temple.[147]

In addition, it appears that these ornaments are comprehensible from the Old Testament concepts known to us. These figures depict "dragons," i.e., Chaos Beings. They bear fish tails since the dragon beings are from the waters. The Manichean tradition[148] knows of a fish tail of the devil. And Berossus knows of Chaos Beings with fish tails.[149]

Furthermore, the remarkable coiling of their bodies is characteristic of these beings. We think, thereby, of "Leviathan, the twisted serpent"[150] and of the "coils" of the dragons in the Babylonian Ribbu myth.[151]

That these beings are depicted, as well, on the pediment of the seven-branched candlestick has a special significance. The great "Planet Tree," which this candlestick represents, has arisen from the great deep.

> *Water lifted it high,*　　　*Deep raised it up,*
> *caused its streams to flow*　*winding around its roots.*[152]

This candlestick is, therefore, all at the same time, an image of the κόσμος (kosmos), the tree stretching forth from the deep, where the turbulence of Chaos abides, unto the heavens where the stars shine. It *is* questionable whether the candlestick was already an institution of Solomon.[153] Nevertheless, it does belong to the earlier part of the royal period.

We come, therefore, to the depictions of the Chaos Monster from the pre-prophetic period. And we are in the position ourselves to put together an approximate picture of how ancient Israel itself represented this dragon. I must add, to be sure, that this conclusion should, for the time being, not be understood as certain. Among the Babylonian depictions of *Ti'âmat,* none is transmitted which is similar to the monster on the candlestick.[154] Dr. [Konrad] Wernicke has been so kind as to make me aware of a Pompeian mural portraying a dragon.[155] He called my attention to the very great similarity of this dragon to that of the lower middle panel [of the Titus arch]. How this similarity is to be explained I cannot say. I do hope that this question will soon be re-opened by a more competent person.

Even disregarding the monsters on the candlestick, we do have a whole series of indirect and direct lines of argumentation which all concur in the idea that the Babylonian creation myth was taken over in ancient times by Israel. Should we, perhaps, go back to an even earlier time and recall Abraham's residence in Ur-Cestum? I do not believe that the late appearance of this tradition is a reason to doubt its antiquity, for P[c] has certainly not concocted this feature himself. Even if no reason exists, however, the tradition itself is to be considered as unhistorical. It appears, nevertheless, not to be advisable to abandon the certain historical foundation and to make our way back into a more remote time, a time from which the Hebrew tradition, at the very best, has transmitted only an isolated memorandum. It is historically verified that Israel, by its migration into Canaan, took possession of a land which had, for centuries, been standing under Babylonian influence. Nothing compels us to fix the adoption of the creation myth to an earlier time than this. Even if the religion of the ancestors of Israel had been around for very many centuries before the time of Moses,[156] and if these "ancestors" had been susceptible to the influence of Babylon, who might believe them capable of retaining anything about it?[157]

Hereinafter we are in the position to delineate a history of the Babylonian-Israelite creation myth, even if only in outline form, while we, at the same time place that history into the context of the broader history of Babylonian influences on Israelite religion. Israel, at all times, had been standing under the influence of Babylonian culture, although in terms of religious history only two periods have real significance: the preprophetic period, since Israel's individuality in the religious sphere had not yet been consolidated; and the postprophetic period, as the religion began to languish and the Jews, at the same time, fell under the direct influence of the Babylonians. In the intermediate stage, between the two periods, lay prophecy, which is preeminent as well after the actual midpoint of the Old Testament. Prophecy also shows, here and there, a Babylonian influence, in its conceptual framework, though nowhere — or almost nowhere — in its true concerns. The time of prophecy is also the period in which the Babylonian religion was the state religion. The "Assyrian period" was, in contrast, only an episode for Israelite religious history. At that time, in a great reaction following the Assyrian period, i.e., Josiah's reform, the Babylonian influence had been eradicated.

The creation myth of Genesis 1 had come to Israel in preprophetic times. The "poetic" recensions teach that it had made its way anew into Judaism after the exile. The adopted material consisted, in the earlier period, of cosmological concepts and symbols, of an institution linked to moon worship, and of a primal myth. That precisely these things had been worked into the religion is shown by the attention which the Israelites gave to the surpassing "wisdom" of Babylon (Isa 47:10).[158] They learned from the Babylonians how the world was formed and came to be, and what its most ancient history had been. All of this was nothing more than "scholarship." It did not affect the core of the religion. For Israel's religious history, and thereby for us, this material is significant only because it would find its way into Israel with Israelite religious thought. This is the case for the Sabbath. This is the case for the myth of paradise, a myth which, until the latest time, was of little importance, but in the latest era of Judaism was newly revised. So also the creation account. That which was adopted of it was the knowledge, the knowledge which supposed the ancient time to have possessed a great, secret revelation, for which the present "better" knowledge of nature must make way. The religious concepts, however, which were added to this material in Israel, first made the myth what it has come to signify for us. The Babylonian comprehension of things is understood to be mistaken. Our faith rests on that of Israel.

In postprophetic times, as Babylonian ideas flowed in anew, had the religion been, nevertheless, stable enough, then the discourse would not have been affected by a substantial influence from the Babylonian ideology. The things that were accepted in that period were the fantastic forms. It was then that the Jews began, anew, to tell of Rahab and Leviathan.

The creation myth had — so it appears — also come to Israel in an eschatological form, and had called forth from the prophets and the prophetic schools an impression of the coming judgment. We have, from the latest period, faint clues that it also began to be significant for the tenor of the eschatological final hope. Thereupon a new epoch of Babylonian influences began!

REVELATION 12:
CREATION IN THE END TIME

1. Revelation 12 Is Not of Christian Origin

Eberhard Vischer[1] has recognized that Revelation 12 is of non-Christian origin. This observation, Vischer's starting point for his clarification of sources in Revelation ,[2] in addition to many diverse concurrences in other scholarly treatments,[3] has found a series of dissenting views as well,[4] and can, therefore, still not be viewed as a truly scientific judgement. It is for this reason that the renewed consideration of the various instances is not uncalled for.

The chapter tells of the persecutions which the Christ, while he was being born in heaven, endured at the hands of an immense Dragon; and it tells of the deliverance of the newborn child to the throne of God. It tells, thereafter, of the persecution and the fortunate flight of its mother.

In regard to this material, in which the exegetical tradition is not expressed, the question can hardly be answered as to which events from the story of Jesus this narrative could, generally, have been related. Therefore, it would be quite astonishing if it was discovered that the chapter actually referred to Jesus' birth and ascent.[5]

But Jesus was, according to the Gospel narrative, not born in heaven but on earth, in Bethlehem of Judea. And he was not carried off as a newborn child, but only after he had lived on earth approximately thirty years did he ascend to God. What this chapter, therefore, says about Christ is in no way concerned with the history of Jesus. — What is passed over in silence is even more significant! Not a single clear reference to the history of Jesus is found therein! Of his utilization of his divine power and of his crucifixion we hear *absolutely nothing!* It follows, therefore, that the chapter simply *does not* refer to Jesus, and, accordingly, it cannot be of Christian origin.[6] It is not easy to comprehend that such a singular and impressive consideration could find a contradiction; and yet, even now, the idea that it is a Christian interpretation of Jesus' birth and ascension is still held fast by many.

One seeks to overcome the immense difficulty which stands in the way of this exegesis, first of all, by the contention that in Revelation 12 the birth of the Christ does not take place in heaven, but rather takes place on earth.[7] This assertion, however, is incorrect. Concerning all events[8] up to the downfall of the Dragon (v. 9), it is expressly said (or tacitly assumed) that they took place *in* or *on*[9] the heavens:[10] the woman appears on the heavens, decorated with heavenly insignia; the Dragon also appears on the heavens; enraged, he flings a third of the stars of the heavens to the ground; the child will, as soon as he is born, be taken away to God's throne, which naturally is thought to be in heaven. Then a war breaks out in heaven between Michael and the Dragon. The context thus also demands that the birth of Christ be shifted into heaven. In this regard, however, neither possibility is able to place the account in a relationship to the historical Jesus.[11]

Further, it will be maintained that Revelation 12 would pass over Jesus' preaching, activity, and death as insignificant. An account of these thing should not be expected in a writing which has to do with the future and in which the essential point is seen only as having been realized by the return of Christ.[12] In such an apocalyptic meditation, the teaching life of Jesus remains the preferred path. Jesus' death will have no place here, since to the apocalyptist it is simply a station along the way to the ascension of the Lord.[13] — It is not recognized, however, that here the resurrection of Jesus is passed over along with the death! This most important word of all known early Christian preaching must have here alone been passed over silently! Indeed, the influence of Jesus on God's spirit could quite possibly be used in apocalyptic reflection as a sign of the times! Chapter 11, in which the two witnesses testify, do wonders, die, and rise up, . . . chapter 11 proves, unnecessarily, that all of it can also be uttered in an apocalyptic vision.

On the other hand, some say,[14] as regards the relationships of the chapters, absolutely no emphasis should be placed on these features. It is, however, hardly possible to think of a context in which, next to a description of the fate of Jesus, only the birth and ascension are described. Such a troublesome and generally established traditional matter as the death of Jesus might have been totally sublimated. — The context, however, which is commonly[14] given as a reason for this highly conspicuous feature, by no means furnishes the explanation for it! The account of the fate of the Messiah — it is said — should be just an introduction to that which follows. The birth and ascent of the Christ will be reported only as a prototype for the fate of Israel. Since the Roman empire could not be successful in eliminating the Messiah, the community as well will be saved. — In such a context, however, the account of Jesus' death would not be treated indifferently, but rather it would be absolutely necessary. Jesus' crucifixion is surely the actual attempt of the empire against the Christ of God. And Jesus' resurrection is the actual demonstration of the power of God, who would not let the spiritual one perish! The community found comfort and security in its own need from nothing so much as in reference to the worst thing which Christ had endured and to the divine action of the resurrection.[15]

Even disregarding these things, however, Jesus' preaching and death must have been mentioned distinctly here. How else can the reader know that he has to interpolate thirty years between [the] birth and [the] removal [of Jesus]; and that the one who enters into heaven is not a child, but rather a grown man? In other words, how else can the reader refer to the one who was, as a human being, slain and to the resurrected Jesus without explicit reference to the intervening period?

Or does one start the investigation by considering the mention of Jesus' preaching and death to have been inserted into our chapter?[16] The whole context would then have been directly imposed upon another, subsequent event. — The Dragon stands before the pregnant woman to gobble up the child at the moment of birth. When it has been born, the child will be "snatched away" to God immediately after its birth, before the Dragon can even open its mouth. It is, therefore, in the very nature of the narrative that no great time can elapse between birth and removal. Furthermore, the same thing is said by the expression ἡρπάσθη [*hērpasthē*], which signifies the haste with which the child has been given security before the persecutions.[17]

That the Christ had been taken up into heaven as a child is, moreover, by no means a passing theme. Chapter 12 is, by its nature, not independent, but rather points to a sequel in which more will be told about how the Christ, still a boy in chapter 12, is delivered *from* trouble *to* God, prior to the assault of the Dragon; how later he appears as the Christ and, in the newly developing struggle, overcomes the Dragon. Rev 19:11 provides this sequel. The correlation of the two pieces is clearly marked by 12:5 and 19:15. This child, as we hear in 12:5, shall lead the heathen with a rod of iron. 19:15 speaks of the appearing Christ. It is he who will lead the heathen with a rod of iron. The time between chapter 12 and chapter 19 is, thus, occupied by the development of the lad into a mighty, divine hero.[18] If, accordingly, the Christ appears as a child in chapter 12, it is in no way a deceptive pretense which, only though certain omissions, would have been evoked by nonessential themes from the life of Jesus. Rather, it is an *essential* moment, a moment evoked by the demands of the *whole* story.

It therefore follows that the teaching and death of Jesus are here not passed over as something of no consequence, but rather that the context simply does not tolerate their inclusion. Otherwise, should the escape of the Christ child to God be an insignificant allegory of the story of Jesus, "who, having just appeared, even before he could take in hand a proper messianic role," was killed, but raised to God?[19] But how can it be maintained that a child who captivates the world could be a possible allegory for a man who surrenders without having performed his work! Near to the prematurely dead youth lay the hopeful plans which died with him. However, no one expects work from a child, and no one mourns if he dies immediately after his birth, since he has not performed his task! Therefore it is improbable that the assumption of the Christ child is a symbol of the Jesus who was crucified before accomplishing his task.[20] The exegetes, in their passion to explain the principle here, have not considered that an allegory, which is intended as an allegory by the author, must convey its significance clearly right on the surface.

Even apart from this, however, the taking up of the child to God and the exaltation of Jesus are in no way very similar to one another. Jesus' resurrection is everywhere in the New Testament. Superhuman power is in mind every time a truly glorious triumph is considered: Jesus is a divine hero who victoriously overcomes all power and authorities, and rises over all of them to the very highest level.[21] What a contrast to the image of the newborn Christ of chapter 12, a completely helpless child who will be saved by God's intervention before the Dragon, and then is defended by Michael and his angels, but does not himself take part in the battle! — And once again this theme of the helplessness of the child is not an accident, but rather is essential in the context. It stands in contrast to the future coming of the Christ in divine power and splendor, and it substantiates why the Dragon, in the interim period, could exercise his terrifying power on earth unhindered. The Savior is still a frail child. He defends himself with difficulty against the Dragon. Only in the future will he be a man, and only then will he be king in the world. — This form of the enfeebled boy of chapter 12 is nothing other than an allegory on the ascending Jesus as a triumphantly conquering hero.

Nevertheless, this allegorical interpretation appears at least worth considering, as long as it is believed the Messiah was born on earth in chapter 12 and then was rescued by God, i.e., into heaven. Here indeed there exists at least a certain similarity with the ascension of Jesus. But we have seen[22] that the Messiah of chapter 12 was born in heaven, in the very place where he remains until his appearance at the eschaton (19:11ff.). So every similarity collapses with Jesus' ascension. The escape of the child, which takes place in heaven — from one heavenly place to another — and the taking up of Jesus from the earth have no significant relationship to each other. So, the thesis of Vischer must remain, namely, that Jesus cannot possibly be understood to lie hidden beneath the Christ of Revelation 12.

In the same way, interpreting the woman, the mother of the Christ, in a Christian manner, raises great difficulties. This woman is, in any event, none other than the heavenly Zion, "the (ideal) community."[23] Her persecution by the Dragon in vv. 13-16 cannot, if a Christian interpretation is generally allowed, possibly be anything other than an allegory for the persecution of Christians. Then it is a common conviction of the New Testament that those who believe in Jesus are the true children and heirs of heavenly Jerusalem.[24] Now, however, the same form, which appears in the second part of the chapter as a personification of the Christian community, is, in the first part, the mother of the Messiah. Thus arises a not insignificant complication: Has the Christian community, then, not really given birth to the Lord all by itself? This complication is not eradicated by the assertion that the woman is not just the faithful messianic community, but rather is, at the same time, also the Old Testament theocracy.[25] The impossibility still exists that the breadth of the aforesaid allegory can designate Christendom *and* the mother of the Lord.[26]

The confusion becomes even greater if "those who remain of their descendants," against whom the Dragon turns when he must abandon the persecution of the woman,[27] are interpreted as Christians. Since up to this point it was a question only of a child of the woman, namely, of the Christ, "those who remain" can only be the other sons of Zion, in contrast to the Messiah who dwells in heaven. In other words, they can only be the earthly people of God.[28] In a Christian writing, the people of God are the Christian community. So it comes to this: first there are vv. 13-16, in which the flight of the woman is depicted allegorically as the Dragon persecutes the Christian community. Then, as the Dragon sees that he can do nothing, he turns again, at v. 17 — here a new figure appears in the allegory — against the Christ! This totally overpowering repetition is not moderated since the woman is generally understood as Christianity, and "those who remain" as the individual Christians.[29] The woman is then, finally, none other than the aggregate of her children. Normally the two figures are distinguished in this way: behind the woman is the primal Christian community; behind "those who remain, who keep God's law, and have the testimony of Jesus" are understood to be the Gentile[30] and Diaspora Christians.[31] But this particular formulation of "those who remain" is indicated by nothing in the text, where the words simply indicate the children of Zion who believe in Jesus! If one is resolved to take the text in this way, one cannot escape the conclusion that this thing cannot be explained by a *Christian* viewpoint!

It is, moreover, quite impossible to understand the very characteristic details in the description of the flight of the woman as Christian! This description is commonly explained[32] as referring to the flight of the Christian community of Jerusalem into Pella[33] in the Jewish War. The third comparative point would be that the report of a flight is, in both, a report in which a river plays a role. — Pella lies beyond the Jordan. This similarity is, certainly, very striking, though the flight over the Jordan has occurred repeatedly in the history of Israel.[34] All the rest, however, is quite different. When Revelation reports that the woman is given "the two wings of a great eagle," that the Dragon, seeking to flush the woman away, spews a stream of water from his mouth, and that the earth comes to the woman's aid and swallows up that torrent . . . all these peculiar features are no longer allegorical, are no longer pointing to "contemporary" history![35] In an interpretation put forward by others,[36] about the flight of the Christians to Lydian Asia,[37] or about the persecution of Stephen, or about the conquest of Titus, the stream still is not to be taken allegorically.

One asks, quite astonished since such fantastic themes appear in the middle of a contemporary historical allegory, how it could be designated precisely as the characteristic "metaphorical language"[38] of Revelation. In the apocalyptic vision the historical material appears not simply to have been appropriated, but also to have been poetically transformed.[39] Such verse, imitating Old Testament models, has been accessed as poetry, but it is not to be degraded into prose by a fanciful detail-oriented interpretation! — It is, in any event, a singular form of poetry which seems to be found here in Revelation. The poetic art-form which is in question here, where the fate of the community in the Jewish War of 70 c.e. is described in the form of a woman fleeing before the Dragon, . . . the poetic art form is allegory. If now the ideal form of an allegory is found therein, since every single expression points to the represented object, that object, in which an abundance of incomparable forms stands beside the few points of comparison . . . , that object must be declared to be almost an accident! The fantasy seduces the reader by an almost incomprehensible overt development. The artist has completely corrupted the thing. Nevertheless, admiration for such "poetry" will have to be given up! It should no longer be termed "poetry," but, rather, a confused and desolate half-breed!

For such allegories one should not look to Judaism! We have enough Jewish allegories[40] to be able to know how Judaism usually formed them. There, we never become aware that the form has rankly grown, in its abundance, beyond the bounds of the explanation. Rather, we become aware of exactly the opposite, i.e., that features of the explanation force their way into the form, often in what is, in our view, an intolerable manner.[41] The Jewish allegories, on the main, do not permit fantasy; the mind, however, does!

If, however, despite this fantastic type of allegory, one attributes it to the apocalyptist, one must then at least give up the comprehension of such an incoherent "poetry." But if here appearance and fantasy actually stand side by side, how far does the historical extend, and how far the fabricated? One group maintains:[42] "The stream is historical. It is the Jordan. The remaining themes are, however, fabricated." Another group says:[43] "Even the stream means nothing more!" The third view:[44] "It is totally fantastic. Who can commit himself to determine it? And who can know the historical event by the description from Revelation which alludes to it, especially if this document is our only source for it?" — Suppose the difficulty in explanation is produced by the antiquity of the material. Would the earliest readers, contemporaries of each event, have understood it better than we do? Even those early reader, who possibly actually witnessed the flight to Pella, or the persecution of Stephen, or the Jewish War, . . . even those early readers could hardly have come to these images, images which contain an account so radically different, in order to explain those events. Indeed, for these images to be comprehensible the author would have had to speak a bit more clearly!

So the result is as follows: The apocalyptic writer has in mind, perhaps, the flight to Pella, or the destruction of Jerusalem, or the persecution of Stephen, or the flight of the Christians to Lydian Asia . . . or almost anything else! He has, however, blended contemporary history so fully with fabricated thematic images that it is impossible to discover the historical reality again. In other words, to secure the historical reckoning is quite unlikely! Thus, the usual Christian interpretation of these themes is to be considered as more prudent!

In the end it comes down to the fact that the object of the whole chapter cannot be understood in terms of an absolutely Christian composition. The thing which will be described here would have fallen, according to common assumptions, in the prophet's past. This is obvious in the case of Jesus' birth and his ascension. In the persecution of the woman is seen a major piece of an allegorical representation of a past event.[45]

Indeed, what is a description of things that have gone before supposed to do in an apocalypse, the purpose of which is to reveal the future? One recalls analogies in other apocalypses[46] where such descriptions are not extraordinary. It is questionable whether these analogies are actually correct. Accounts of past events in the Jewish apocalypses have an almost consistently similar, quite understandable purpose. An ancient man of God has prophecies placed into his mouth by the author, . . . prophecies which, at first, render a mystery, but, for the well informed, give a lucid, elaborated description of the time which lies between the "seer" and the actual author of the text, only then concluding with a brief delineation of the author's hopes. So the reader is able to gain some control by means of the history of the prophecies of the early prophets. He discerns, the more extensively he has read, with increasing admiration, that they all are pointing to more exact things. And he develops from this verificatory reading of the ancient "men of God" the secure belief that it may present him, even today, with unfulfilled prophetic beliefs.[47]

These representations of the past are, thus, in reality not even exceptions from the common themes, since the apocalypse contains only "future" events. This is so because, according to the fiction of the writer, all these events would have been, at the time the book supposedly was written, future events. But, nevertheless, they have a place in the apocalypse only because they attest to the actual prophecies, on which alone the writer ultimately depends.

Nevertheless, there does appear to be another instance which actually represents an exception to this general rule. In his dream Nebuchadnezzar beholds his current authority and that of God hanging over it! In the form of a great tree which is cut down he sees a temporary expulsion from the throne.[48] And 1 Enoch describes, at the beginning of an allegory on world history, the time of the first human couple.[49] Are we, therefore, standing, within the apocalyptic vision at this point, adjacent to future things . . . things which are, however, actually, from the standpoint of the visionary, current, or even past, events?[50]

Indeed, two totally different cases are to be distinguished here. A vision which deals generally with the future could quite possibly be, at the beginning, a vision of the present of the seer. But only insofar as it is absolutely necessary to the proper understanding of the subsequent future forms do those forms appear in a few features of the account of the seer's present. Such a description of current situations is sometimes necessary because of the subject, the future fate of which should properly be expressed clearly! Should, for example, anything whatsoever be expressed concerning Nebuchadnezzar, the vision must first give a description of him, since clearly that which follows will deal with him and with no other person. Furthermore, the present circumstances of the so-designated subjects must be quite broadly described, since without this the prophecy would be incomprehensible! If, for example, regarding Nebuchadnezzar it should be prophesied that the kingdom will be taken from him, a description of his current dominion must come first.[51] Or, should it be made known to the king that three lesser kingdoms would follow the Babylonian one, the vision must present a picture which makes this difference apparent, a picture in which, therefore, the present Babylonian kingdom also is depicted.[52] It lies in the very nature of the thing that such contemporarily described things will be as slightly smoothed-over as is possible, since the essential thing is that which follows, i.e., the revelation of that which the future will bring.

In the last analysis, these instances are, therefore, not exceptions. It does remain true, however, that the proper content of the vision is the *future,* and that the present has a place therein only so long as a picture of the future cannot be given without it!

Texts such as Daniel 7 and *1 Enoch* 85ff. are to be viewed quite differently, however. In such historical prophecies two preoccupations flow together: on the one hand, that discussed above, i.e., to authenticate the seer through a striking fulfillment of his "prophecy"; on the other hand, then, there is the preoccupation, through a sweeping review of the periods of world history, of allowing the reader an opportunity to calculate in which era he presently lives, and, accordingly, to determine the proximity of the end.[53] Both preoccupations are in agreement that the writer was permitted to see such a vision through a person who had lived immediately before the historical period in question. We do, however, repeatedly run up against the "moment" (since a difficulty arises at that point) when that beginning stage of the world's end time and the time of the seer do not quite coincide. In such a conflict, the apocalyptic writer has placed the preoccupations side-by-side, on the whole, and more or less strongly has violated that which was prophesied to a quite different period. It might have been pardonable if Daniel, living under a Babylonian king, in the vision of the four world empires[54] also dealt with the Babylonian empire, which was his contemporary. It is, however, a very coarse, and almost laughable, blunder when *1 Enoch*,[55] in the prelude of an historical vision, prophesies the history from Adam up to his own time, and even prophesies himself! Such a blemish might not be noted, since the ancient seer stands apart from the present, if the slight difference between his time and the appointed starting point of his vision can be overlooked. Such cases as these, where an ancient seer prophesies about current or perhaps bygone things, are a weakness of the literary form. It is not an insignificant misunderstanding when one, from such violations of the rule, infers a new rule. The apocalyptic seer might also behold in his visions any present or future. As long as Judaism still preserved the slightest glimmer of what prophecy meant, the self-evident principle could never be darkened, i.e., the principle that the prophet prophesies only about the future, since anyone can prophesy about the present or the past and since the vision contains only things which could *not* be known *without* a vision. Otherwise the wonder of the vision would be superfluous![56]

We apply this perception to Revelation 12. In an apocalyptic text the portrayal of the past has the goal of being an attestation of the actual prophetic saying. It fulfills this end only when it appears as a prediction from an ancient time, thus under the pseudonym of an ancient prophet. If, therefore, Revelation would maintain that an ancient man of God had this vision about Jesus' birth and ascension[57] and beheld the early fate of the Christian community, then the piece would have a very comprehensible purpose: The reader, filled with admiration that this ancient prophecy had come to fruition so very precisely, would given willing credence to the remaining words of the same person. — However, the chapter does not make such a claim. It claims — so the champion of its Christian heritage asserts — to have been written by a Christian.[58] The earliest reader should have known, then, that a Christian was speaking to him. But what would the purpose of this chapter then be? That a Christian could, by Jesus, describe destinies which filled no one with excited expectation is quite evident. A vision concerning this would say, once more, to the seer and to the reader the very thing which he, on supernatural grounds, already knew. It would be no "revelation." And since the author could expect belief in his assertion that he had seen all of this in a vision, then everyone would know! Just as he knew this thing, so he knew every contemporary thing.

The allegorical form of such descriptions has, in the apocalypses, a positive significance. It is the residue of the sense that it is proper for the prophet to forecast the future, to forecast it not with a more prosaic clarity, but rather to forecast it in dark "enigmas." What reason, however, would there be to depict Jesus' fate, which was known to everybody, so mysteriously, . . . what reason would there be if the author was not even pretending to prophesy about it? The manner in which the definitively Christian pieces of Revelation speak about Jesus could be likened to this. His fate is designated there either by simply using a nominative form or by using the commonly used metaphors of Christian edifying speech.[59] Nowhere, however, is it as skillfully adumbrated as it is here.

Is it permissible to regard the chapter, by analogy to Daniel 2:32 and 4:7-9, as an introduction to the vision of the future which follows? We have seen that the vision usually portrays totally undesirable events of the past, but only those without which it would be impossible to portray the future. Chapter 12, however, does not in any way bear such a character. In that which follows immediately, completely new images emerge. The "woman" generally no longer appears in what follows. If the chapter has the desire to refer to Jesus, about whom the vision of the future will prophesy, it must, naturally, speak of him as clearly as possible. This, however, doesn't quite take place. As regards the nature of the thing, such preliminary features in a prophecy are tolerable only when they depict present things or things of the immediate past. This description from chapter 12, however, does not cover, in the traditional view, more than the previous seventy years. The chapter, therefore, should not be interpreted by analogy to Dan 2:32; 4:7-9.

Is it ultimately possible to compare the description of the life of Jesus with texts such as 1 Enoch 85–87? In 1 Enoch it was a blunder of the writer, who transgresses his own fictions and because of an error allows his seer to prophesy things that have, contextually, already occurred. This is comprehensible where the issue is that of pseudonymity. But that is not the case here! Could the author of Revelation 12 perhaps have forgotten for a moment that he actually lived *after* Jesus?[60]

The result is this: Only by a superficial examination can the historical narrative, which Revelation will give in a Christian formulation, appear to be similar to certain parts of Jewish apocalypses. As soon as one looks a little more carefully, and also asks about the sense and the purpose of these pieces, . . . as soon as one does that, one recognizes that chapter 12 ought to be interpreted as a narrative without any analogy in apocalyptic literature. One reaches this conclusion on solid grounds since such a vision of bygone things would, in itself, certainly be impossible. Thereby it is once again established that chapter 12 does not deal with Jesus!

In chapter 12 only v. 11 and the words καὶ ἐχόντων τὴν μαρτυρὰν ᾽Ιησοῦ [*kai echontōn tēn martyrian Iēsou*] (or ᾽Ιησοῦ [*Iēsou*] alone) in v. 17 are quite certainly Christian.[61] These pieces certainly point quite clearly, however, to the *non*-Christian origin of the remaining pieces.

A heavenly hymn, vv. 10-12, celebrates the overthrow of the Dragon by Michael. Now has God won the victory (v. 10). Because of this, the heavens, which the Dragon must relinquish, are called to joy, but unto the earth, to which he now descends, woes are summoned (v. 12). In these hymns the words are interpolated, they — our (from the standpoint of the angel) brothers, i.e., the faithful of the earth — however, have been victorious through the blood of the Lamb and the word of his testimony, and did not cling to their lives right up to the moment of death (v. 11).

Vischer[62] has correctly seen that the words interrupt the context: διὰ τοῦτο [*dia touto*] in v. 12 points back past v. 11 to v. 10. And because they emanate from totally different presuppositions from that which precedes and follows them, the Christ, who is a child *there*, taken away to God, after his birth, is *here* "the Lamb who was slain." *There* woes are summoned upon the earth, into which the Dragon now descends, only then to begin a persecution of the pious (v. 17). *Here*, however, the report is surely of a victory which the faithful on the earth have sustained over him. *There* the Dragon will be overthrown by Michael. *Here* the pious are the victorious ones. *There* the downfall of the Dragon is an outward "mythologically"[63] similar event. *Here* the conquest of the devil, even in the deaths of the martyrs, is an even more splendid expression of the inner experiences of the Christian life.

The remark in v. 17 about this, that the pious have the testimony of Jesus, disturbs the context in just the same manner. In the preceding materials the Christ was still a child. Now, while the Dragon gives vent to his fury here below, the Christ grows up in the seclusion of heaven. Only at the end of things will he tread on earth. How can this report exist, given the "testimony" which has already been rendered. Again there is a great difference between the world-sovereign/Dragon killer — who is the Christ in chapter 12 in relation to chapter 19 — and the witnesses, i.e., the prophets of Jesus (v. 17).

The great attitudinal differences between these two Christian pieces "give evidence most obviously, not merely of the authorial diversity, but also of the essential dissimilarity of their religious standpoints."[64] The two pieces, most clearly v. 11, show how a Christian reader of the narrative, when he came upon it prepared, if all went well, would have come to understand it. He understood the material as an allegory and explained this or that feature, fairly unconcerned about the cohesion of the whole. But his Christian ideas stand at a distance from the foreign materials in order that he — no less than his present successor — would have been able to be a complete master of it.

I have, so far, presumed to make something of an argument from the place of this chapter in the arrangement of Revelation, and have limited myself simply to the context given by the nature of the material. This caution is urgently demanded by the present position of the literary-critical investigation of the book of Revelation. Even now the composition of the book is an open question, a question which — as I believe — has not, up to the present, had its answer found. There also exist manifold opinions concerning the context of our chapter.[65] It is debatable whether it was, generally speaking, the continuation of something which preceded it, or whether it was originally conceived as an independent thing.[66]

Furthermore, such circumspection is called for urgently by an investigation of the type of apocalypse. Revelation offers, as it presently exists, no coherent form developed in a continuous context, but rather a complicated compilation of very many individual visions.[67] At a great many points it is clearly discernible that these individual visions have their character in accordance with individual features and were not originally attached to one another.[68] Thereupon the methodology for this investigation of Revelation is established. First of all, the internal connection of the material is to be established. The boundaries of the material from independent individual visions are to be sought out. The detail within the vision, as far as it is possible, is to be explained from these contexts. And only after these questions are answered will it be permissible to investigate the present literary context. By this it is clearly to be thought that one will arrive at the present context only later in the process.[69]

In observance of this methodology[70] we have, from the beginning, interpreted chapter 12 as the first part of a vision, the conclusion of which is represented by those units from 19:11–20:8, which speak of the defeat of the Dragon. In addition, in the vision of the sixth bowl, the Dragon's preparation for war appears in 16:12-16, a fitting transition to the battle of 19:11ff. In the latter two passages two beasts are named in addition to the Dragon. They were described in detail in chapter 13. Since they have not even appeared in chapter 12, the possibility exists that they originally did not belong to the account of the Dragon. This question still cannot really be answered at this point.[71]

That which, in the present literary context, immediately precedes, the hymn of praise of the πρεσβύτεροι [*presbyteroi*] (11:15-18), which announces the beginning of the divine dominion and of the judgment upon the peoples, is clearly an introduction for the following narrative of the birth and of the Dragon battle of the Christ.[72] But, on the other hand, 11:15ff. and chapter 12 by no means belong so closely together since chapter 12 conveys, perhaps, a preliminary section of 11:15ff., and 11:15ff. could, given its nature, be in conformity with the introduction to that description of the final judgment upon the peoples. Furthermore, chapter 12 also conveys the foregoing in the face of highly original themes: the theme of a heavenly woman; of a Messiah who, being born, is, until now, still not the Word; also the Dragon may be described as a freshly appearing celebrity! The whole narrative starts out anew. Chapter 12 differs especially strongly from the preceding materials through its totally "fantastic" mythologically reminiscent posture.

Accordingly, it comes to pass that the noted material begins a new thing[73] with chapter 12, and that the introduction, 11:15ff., is added only later. If I, therefore, argue in the following from the literary context of chapter 12, I am emphatically drawing attention to the possibility that the sense of the vision, as it was properly placed in this context, could have been removed.[74]

Currently chapter 12 stands in the context of the trumpet vision. The birth of the Christ is reported after the seventh trumpet, of which 10:7 expressly reports that it brings in the final consummation. Indeed, in what precedes, future events are described even more clearly. Accordingly, the one who incorporated chapter 12 into this context also thought the birth of Christ was an event which the future would bring.

Nevertheless, the usual pretense does not help the author complete his hitherto "proleptic" description by a "conclusion." Since it is suggested by nothing in the text that the author will conclude the natural sequence of the successive events and jump back at once from the last signs into the past, those who have placed this vision *after* the seventh trumpet could not have considered, at any rate, the birth of Christ as an event in the future. If that was so, for them it could not have been the Christ!

From the standpoint of Judaism, however, it is completely understandable that the birth of the Christ would be reported in a description of the last things. So we come to the conclusion that the organization of the chapter in the context of Revelation indicates a Jewish hand.

One objection raised against the Jewish origin of our piece is that Judaism does not speak of a twofold appearance of the Messiah. This probably existed only in the Christian community, which looked retrospectively toward the earthly life of its Lord and awaited his second coming.[75] This argumentation, thinking of the birth of Christ as his first appearance on earth, is, then, untenable as soon as it is recognized that the Christ of Revelation 12 is not born on earth, but rather in heaven.[76] On the contrary, chapter 12 and the pieces connected with it, which know only one appearance of the Christ, that by which he overcame the Dragon, intimate by that singular knowledge that they are based on the viewpoints of Judaism and not on those of Christianity.[77]

Or, it is maintained, the coming of the Messiah *by birth* indicates a Christian origin for the chapter.[78] It is not necessary here to investigate the precondition of this conclusion, i.e., that the birth of the Messiah in Revelation 12 was an event of the past, since even if this hypothesis should be correct there is no way to establish the Christian origin of the piece. Then the chapter would say: "The Messiah has, to be sure, already been born, but until now has not yet appeared. Presently he lingers somewhere in seclusion." This conception of the Christ clashes with the Christian one, according to which Jesus had already been revealed. It is, however, abundantly manifested in Judaism.[79]

Among these Jewish parallels is one of especially great value, one which brings to a definitive end any doubt about whether it would be possible in Judaism. Vischer has already pointed out *y. Bĕrākôt*, fol. 5, chap. 1:[80] The Messiah will be born on the day on which the Temple will be destroyed, but sometime later his mother will be carried off by a storm wind. This text is strikingly similar to Revelation 12. The most peculiar element in the account of chapter 12 is that the Christ will be taken away to God after his birth. This finds a counterpart in the rabbinic passage just noted. Both are also parallel in terms of date. In the Talmudic text the Messiah will be born on the day of the destruction of the Temple. Similarly, in Revelation 12, immediately after the birth of the Christ follows the time when the Dragon has dominion on earth. This situation is even more significant since in the conjunction of the two events a concept was originally set forth: the day when the evil of the Dragon's dominion begins is likened to the day when the Good One is born. "If then the hostile power here below appears to be victorious, be of good cheer! The one who shall bring you help is already at hand!"[81]

The Talmudic text in its singularly abrupt way conveys the themes of a half-forgotten tradition. Whither and why the Messiah will be carried off is not said. We can fill it in from the context and from Revelation: The enemy who destroyed the Temple would also have liked, best of all, to slay the little Christ child, who would bring an end to his hegemony in days to come, if the child would not have been carried off to a place where the enemy's hand did not reach.

A series of themes which distinguish the Talmudic text from Revelation 12 demonstrates that we are dealing, in the Talmud, with an independent tradition. The main difference is that in Revelation the Messiah is born in heaven from a divine woman, while in the Talmud he is born from a human woman on earth. Thereupon, if the tradition lying at the base of the Talmudic text would have been completely preserved, a more drastic distinction in terms of the whole outline of the two accounts would be present. It appears strange to us that this material has existed in two so very different recensions since we know that the messianic image of Judaism had fluctuated between an earthly king and a form which comes on the clouds of the heavens.

A series of more concrete individual themes appears as well. In the Talmud the child is carried off from its mother by a storm wind. This is, in any case, more original than the colorless ἡρπάσθη [*herpásthē*] of Revelation. Only in the Talmud is there mention of the destruction of the Temple. This feature proves that someone had been comforted by this narrative after the catastrophe of 70 C.E. If, finally, the Talmud named Bethlehem as the earthly birthplace of the Christ, one could, hence, certainly not prove from that a dependence on Christian tradition. This assertion is well known in the Jewish thought of Mic 5:1, a piece of messianic dogmatism.

It is consistent with the literary-critical disposition of the time that one sought to place both the Talmudic text and Revelation in a literarily dependent relationship.[82] A valid proof of this has not been produced.

I summarize the result: The Talmudic text represents the remains of a tradition, a tradition connected to Revelation 12, a tradition already fading away in the Talmud. This proves that the underlying tradition in Revelation had once existed in Judaism.

Additionally, there is a more linguistic proof. That chapter 12 is very strongly Hebraized has long been recognized. It is, however, also possible that it was translated from a Semitic original.[83] Therefore, the place of composition was Palestine.

As a result of our exposition of Revelation 12 up to now, we have gained a confirmation of the thesis of Vischer: the chapter is not of Christian origin since it could not be understood from the standpoint of a Christian composition and since the statement found therein about Jesus' birth and journey to heaven is totally untenable.

2. The Interpretation of Revelation 12 according to "Contemporaneous Exegesis"

One's opinion concerning this exposition will be essentially moderated if one considers it in the context in which it belongs: It is an example of "contemporaneous" exegesis.[1] On the other hand, it would be impossible for any explanation of this to strike at the root of the matter if it did not, at the same time, refute the methodology of which it is a legitimate product. Because contemporary exegetical methodology, however, currently is considered to be an incontrovertible achievement of modern research[2] and appears to reign supreme in the scholarly world, I am obliged to range a little bit more broadly here. I intend to explain in detail *my* understanding of Revelation, which I can only outline in this context, at another place.

According to the "contemporaneous" explanation,[3] the apocalypticist in his writing portrays the events of his time and the expectations which are the result of the current state of affairs. He portrays them in a variety of images. Accordingly, the actual content of Revelation should be the then-contemporary history. This understanding, therefore, is in agreement with the remaining interpretive methods, i.e., with ecclesiastical-historical exegesis and its modern attenuations, since a history is depicted allegorically in Revelation. "Since a history must, at any rate, correspond to the image-cycle of Revelation, one actually has a choice only between a past (in the author's eyes), or a present and a history which (for him) lies in the future."[4] The former is the idea of "contemporaneous" exegesis, the latter the idea of ecclesiastical-historical exegesis. The task of "contemporaneous" explanation would, consequently, be to rediscover from the varied forms of the revelation the historical *realia* artistically hidden within it. This explanation finds its support particularly in certain passages of

Jewish apocalypses. Pieces like Daniel 7f., *1 Enoch* 85ff., *4 Ezra* 11f., and *2 Apoc. Bar.* 53ff. are clearly "contemporaneous" allegories. Indeed, in Revelation there are a few more securely contemporary points to be explained. The beast in chapter 13 should be an allegory for the Roman empire. The woman on the beast in chapter 17 symbolizes the city of Rome.[5] There is a question, however, as to whether the whole book of Revelation or, possibly, only a large part of it might be so explained.

Looking more carefully, one realizes that even in the present "contemporaneous" exegesis is not the exclusive approach. Not all pieces of Revelation will, at present, point to historical events. Very many are to be understood as "ideal" forms, i.e., as products — in other respects not quite fully invented, but rather inspired by prophetic and apocalyptic models — of fantasy. Thus are to be explained, for example, the heavenly scene of chapters 4f. and the new Jerusalem of 21:9ff., as well as the locusts of 9:1ff., the seven bowls of chapter 16, etc. — However, even within the "contemporaneous" descriptions themselves, a purely fantastic sequence must stand close to the actual "contemporary" feature which the other things' features frequently overshadow.[6] So a reason should have been given for the vision of fabulous cavalry of 9:13ff., a reason according to the customary explanation,[7] i.e., the Parthian threat. But the vision itself, with its many remarkable individual themes, far surpasses this supposed reason.

So "contemporaneous" exegesis offers a variegated picture to an individual researcher, since contemporaneous allegories or ideal images are found, rarely in pure form but more frequently in combinations: contemporaneous materials more or less fantastically embellished, or ideal images with more or less numerous contemporaneous themes. All of this is mixed together, without any recognizable rule. The form will be even more polychromatic when the explanations of different exegetes are put together, since even if all are in agreement as to the supposition that both of these types of material are present, they do differ on many points, specifically on what should be described as an image of fantasy which points to a "contemporary" phenomenon. What one interprets as poetry, another explains as a "contemporaneous" allusion, and vice versa. Despite this, there has hardly been a real controversy up to this point in time,[8] much less the debate which is so necessary in principle, the debate as to how the "contemporaneous" material and the vision are to be properly perceived.

While, therefore, the usual "scientific" method has, until now, still not itself been brought to clarity, in principle it has been so challenged that, up to a certain point, something is interpreted as "contemporaneous" and what seems to oppose this explanation is declared to be "fantastic." Of course, it can hardly be said where the "edge" of "contemporaneity" is no longer conceivable. The "perimeter" of the "contemporaneous things" in Revelation is, in that regard, quite uncertain. While the founders of the contemporary, dominant methodology, Lücke,[9] Bleek, de Wette, and slightly less Ewald, have striven for greater discretion in the interpretation of particulars — a tradition which is still maintained, up to the present, by scholars like Weizsäcker, Holtzmann,[10] B. Weiss,[11] and Jülicher.[12] The "contemporaneous" explanation stands in full blossom among modern source critics Völter, Spitta, and Erbes, who have, once again, reverted to the rationalistic exegesis which ruled at the beginning of the century. Nevertheless, only a small part of Revelation is, all in all, understood "contemporaneously," even by the latter critics, and the main body of it must, according to them, consist of fantasy images.

Accordingly, there may appear to be a question, a question which will probably be asked, a question as to whether the present exegesis of Revelation actually even deserves the designation "contemporaneous exegesis." That this question has not yet been sufficiently answered is explained at once by the fact that special emphasis has fallen on the material to be "contemporaneously" interpreted, material from which the chronological dating of the text might be attained. "Contemporaneous exegesis" even now discloses, through the designations of those things which it accepts, its one-sided interest in literary-critical questions. It certainly stands out even more strongly in terms of the rest of Revelation, about the contents of which modern research has concerned itself only insofar as they have become suitable for literary criticism.

Because of this, then, the many different definitions of the word "contemporaneous" get all mixed up among modern scholars. In addition to the view discussed above,[13] according to which contemporary events are skillfully concealed in the images of Revelation, there is another view: that the "prophecy" of Revelation — like all biblical prophecy — is determined by the circumstances of the time and by the author's view of those circumstances.[14] In addition, there is a third explanation for the word, according to which Revelation — like any book — is to be explained according to the concepts of its own time.[15] These definitions are, certainly, not necessarily precluded. They *do* all concur in opposition to the ecclesiastical-historical explanation. On the other hand, they clearly differ from one another. The second is more universalistic than the first, the third than the second. By the very nature of things we will not necessarily be led from the third to the second, or from the second to the first. It is, therefore, not proper to alternate among these different definitions *ad libitum.*

If one wishes to overcome the presently prevailing bewilderment afflicting the interpretation of Revelation, it is urgent that one adhere to a unified definition of the word. Even names are not insignificant to science since they frequently perpetuate the misunderstandings of earlier generations.[16] That definition can only be the first definition which I put forward at the apex of this discussion, since it alone could testify anything about Revelation and the characteristics of the apocalyptic genre.

It is now clear that the most substantial part of Revelation, which contains the "ideal forms," will not, in that sense of the word, be "contemporaneously" understood. The improperly common term should not confuse when it deals, in actuality, with two totally distinct methodologies, methodologies between which the current "scientific" explanation wavers without any discernible standard. The one methodology seeks after hidden contemporaneous events. The other describes the material as a completely fanciful imitation of an Old Testament original. In adherence to these two methodologies all scholars are "in agreement," to such a degree that they even differ in the definition of "contemporaneous"! The two methodologies shall, subsequently, be discussed, at some length, in regard to an example.

In addition to these two methodologies, traces of yet a third type of explanation appear. From the beginning it has been seen that the Old Testament has delivered not only an abundance of images and "symbols," but also positive expectations to the New Testament seer.[17] Recently Jewish apocalyptic literature has been drawn on in greater quantities for the interpretive enterprise. The influence of literature in Revelation "is never to be denied."[18] Now one might be inclined, even more so when one discovers a clear correspondence between the New Testament apocalyptic materials and the Jewish apocalypses, immediately to assume a literary dependence.[19] Certainly the better assessment has already been expressed, i.e., that there existed a "common body of apocalyptic material" in which even Revelation had shared.[20] Spitta has offered proof for the correctness of this viewpoint at several places.[21] A series of irregularities and incomprehensibilities in Revelation will be apparent if it is recognized that here "an original product of apocalyptic material exists only in a limited way" and "that our author, on the contrary, has produced his writings from well-established materials."[22]

Thereupon a new method for the exegesis of Revelation has been produced, a method which itself, until now, had to be skillfully distinguished from the other two since the essential conception of the materials which are basic to it is, in both cases, quite difficult. The first two explanations agree that the author (or authors) of Revelation is (are) to be considered creator (creators) of its materials. Accordingly, such an apocalyptic writing would have been the work of a particular person, would have originated from the situation of a particular time, and would have been an utterly literary totality. Of a totally different kind, however, are writings which appear in the fundamental codification of a tradition. The particular creator of the material deposited in them is not the writer, but rather a whole series of lineages; and the material in the form in which it currently exists presumes a centuries-old history[23] in which oral tradition also might have played a role. Consequently the interpretation must be different. According to the first two methodologies, the point of reference would be to understand the coherent work of an author from the standpoint of *his* "present." Exegesis encounters therein a codified tradition. Given that, exegesis is, perhaps, to investigate the extremely complex and chronologically long prehistory of the material and, from that investigation, is to explain the present condition of the tradition. Between the two types of explanation transitional forms are conceivable, for though it is possible that the final editor of the material wrote it down just as he received it, there is, on the other hand, the possibility as well that he was not a *servant,* but rather a *master* of his material, and, with greater or lesser spiritual freedom, worked that which he encountered into a new thing. Spitta mentions cases in which the former has occurred.[24]

This is still not the place to demonstrate how extensively this "tradition-historical" method may be employed in the study of Revelation, but the challenge, according to the foregoing, is already justified, the challenge that this method has to be thoroughly tested. It might not be considered obvious that the apocalyptist freely fabricated his material, nor even that he has dealt with the materials he encountered *ad libitum.* Rather, to each new body of material the question is to be raised as to whether it is not better explained by the history of tradition than by the human imagination. At the same time, one has to pay attention, above all, to the obscurities of the present text. One has to investigate whether oral apocalyptic tradition is to be assumed[25] and in which form the apocalyptic material had existed, in terms of its nature. "Contemporaneous" interpretation, however, is justified only when it is a question of a piece of material freely composed by the author, or, at least, revised by him.

One is, perhaps, inclined to be surprised concerning the fact that this methodology, up to this point attentive to tradition history, has now pulled back so greatly, . . . surprised, at least until the consistency of this manifestation is discerned. One is concerned, predominately, with literary questions, since "the problem of Revelation"[26] is currently seen as a literary-critical issue: "the biblical prehistory" is the title of a work which leads to investigation concerning the primordial sources. Moreover, there has been less preoccupation with the history of the oral tradition than there has been with the writings which preserve that tradition. We have just as complex inquiries concerning the synoptic problem as those concerning the written sources of Genesis, but only initial steps have been taken toward a history of the early Christian tradition about Jesus, and not as yet any toward a history of the origin and the tradition of the patriarchal sage. So also, in the case of Revelation, we have an abundance of source hypotheses but no history of the apocalyptic tradition![27]

For the founders of the scientific exegesis of Revelation there was the added problem that they would be misled by the prototype of Old Testament prophecy.[28] They overlook the fact that prophets and apocalyptic practitioners occupy very different places in oral tradition. The prophets are powerful, totally individual persons who speak for their own people and for their contemporaries. Completely different are the apocalyptic practitioners, who know nothing of the high originality of the prophets and do not venture, even once, to mention their own names. It is, therefore, very risky, because of the great difference of the two phenomena, to combine them under a classificatory name "biblical prophecy," and to explain the one by analogy to the other.

As we now turn to the actual "contemporaneous" interpretations, an extremely complicated phenomenon again comes before us. Not only shall the "contemporaneously" explained material — as we saw above — exist in many combinations with "fantastic" creations, but it shall likewise be itself of a highly multifarious nature. Sometimes its form:

- . . . is believed to be found in allegories of the book of Revelation;
- . . . is explained, in the proper sense, in those oh-so-common cases when more universalistic descriptions are linked with concrete historical situations.

In the same way, the "contemporaneous" material is distinct as regards its content. Sometimes it may be narratives of past events, sometimes descriptions of the present, sometimes images of the future which are consequences of the historical circumstances. The individual "contemporaneous" explanations represent the most diverse combinations among these interpretive styles. Often the contemporaneous exegetes disagree among themselves as to whether the individual piece should be interpreted according to one or another interpretive method. The demonic locusts (9:1-11) are explained allegorically as the Parthians by one scholar.[29] Another asserts that it must actually be locusts, sometime around the year 63 c.e.[30] Or the flight of the woman of chapter 12, by early-Christian exegesis understood allegorically, now will be understood by one critic as an event of the past[31] and by another as an image of the future.[32] Even though, up to this point, there has not been a debate on principle about what is an allegorical way of speaking within Revelation and what is a "realistic" way of speaking within Revelation, about how to distinguish an image of the future and a narrative, . . . one *does* feel reassured by the collective designation of a "contemporaneous" methodology which appears to cover all these highly diverse explanatory types. — But even when the explanatory type is the same or at least similar, a great difference in meaning still exists as to which concrete historical facts are intended. The locust vision of chapter 9, according to Spitta,[33] is to be explained by the unusual barrenness of 40 C.E.; according to Erbes,[34] is to be explained by the locust plague of 62 C.E., etc. The terrifying army (9:13ff.) is, according to most exegetes, the Parthians. The vision is linked to the fear of a Parthian invasion, since Caligula commanded half of the Euphrates division of the army to withdraw;[35] or to the cavalry victory of the Parthians in 62 C.E.;[36] or to the expectation of a Parthian attack in the final days of Vespasian.[37] The serpentine tails of these armies are to be explained by the waving of the tails of the Parthian horses, or by the rider's shooting of arrows during the retreat, or by the custom of braiding the hair of the tail of the horse toward the end,[38] etc. Or if the martyrs of 6:9-11 are interpreted historically, one thinks of the victims of the Neronic persecution,[39] or of the earlier persecution of the Christians by the Jews,[40] or some other persecution. Jews and Gentiles,[41] or Jews[42] or Gentiles[43] alone, may be viewed as the persecutors. As the persecuted, Jews and Christians,[44] or Jews alone,[45] or Christians alone.[46]

The great variation in results indicates that there is a need for a methodological revision. We, therefore, will examine the methodology in regard to certain significant examples.

First, there is the classification of certain historical features which ought to stand in the midst of fantastic representations.

The two witnesses, the life, death, and resurrection of whom will be described (11:3ff.) even before a conquest of Jerusalem has come into view, cannot be contemporary figures.[47] Only one feature, that their bodies lie still unburied, Völter[48] explains as an allusion to the two high priests, Ananus and Yeshua, who perished in the final days of Jerusalem and whose bodies would, similarly, not have been buried. Now a certain resemblance does surely exist between the historical events and the apocalyptic features. Much greater than the similarity, however, is the difference: the "witnesses" are not high priests, and furthermore what chapter 11 reports about them, that they lay on the street for three-and-a-half days, that all the people saw them, that there was rejoicing over their deaths since they had been struck in their earthly lives with all sorts of calamities, that they finally arose from the dead after three-and-a-half days and went to heaven . . . all of these things have no analogy to the actual history of these high priests. But there is even more: "contemporaneous" persons are not generally linked to the images of the two witnesses against whom the beast of the abyss wages war, who arise after their deaths. They represent expectations which, according to their nature, perhaps have nothing to do with contemporaneous events.[49] In history Rome waged war against *peoples*, not against two *prophets*. It is, however, exceedingly arbitrary to remove a particular feature from the whole image and to interpret it "contemporaneously." Rather there is reason to infer from this, as from everything in this context, a truly quite remarkable apocalyptic tradition.

It is even less acceptable to trace back the idea of the infernal pit from which the locusts of 9:1ff. come . . . to trace that idea back, with Erbes,[50] to a pit near Hieropolis, a pit from which poisonous mists gushed forth. Above all, it is very arbitrary to think directly about that pit of Hieropolis. Why not about any one of a number of others?[51] Furthermore, the context of the vision is not completely evident since a definite geographically fixed pit is in mind here. From the pit near Hieropolis come foul fumes (which might perhaps be considered as the cause of a plague), but not locusts with human faces, women's hair, and lions' teeth. The opening to hell, from which such beings emerge, is not sought in the vicinity. Likewise, the dreadful force of 9:14ff. comes from afar, from the Euphrates. And further, it was totally unnecessary to seek an historical explanation for this "well of the abyss." We do know that both in the Old Testament and in Judaism Hades bore the designation of "pit," and thus it was visualized as a pit.[52] The idea, however, that fumes come forth from the openings of hell is also attested among the rabbis.[53] Thus, again, the error, that something explained on the basis of random contemporary situations should, rather, be understood as a religious tradition of the Jews, even when it comes down to a point where the former case is clearly attested to us.

Likewise, it is rather high-handed to see in the designation Ἀπολλύων [*Apollyōn*] at Rev 9:11 "ein Stich auf den Kleinasian viel verehrten Apollo."[54] אבדון ['*Abaddôn*] is a name for שאול [*Šĕ'ôl*] in the Old Testament, and Ἀπολλύων [*Apollyōn*] is none other than the literal translation of these names. A theoretical allusion to Apollo may only be adopted, then, if it clearly stands out in a very different manner than simply through this word, and if it — considering the reputation of the writer — would make any sense whatsoever.

Christ gave to the faithful conqueror a white stone upon which is standing a top-secret new name (2:17). Erbes[55] compares this to the tokens of food and clothing which Titus Caesar tossed out among the people at the ceremonial opening of the Colosseum! Should it now really be believed that this event made such a powerful impression and provoked such an unlimited admiration, even among the Christians, that the desire was felt to speak of something similar in reference to Christ?!? On the contrary, it is required of those who have no proof that religious ideas be carefully constructed, not built on such insignificant inducements! The religio-historical explanation for the "new name" does not lie at such a great distance. Compare the similar statement about Christ at 19:12, and recall that the faithful will, in the end time, be transfigured into the likeness of Christ![56]

It is less methodically problematic when Holtzmann[57] describes the serpentine tiles of the horses in 9:13ff. according to the depiction of the reliefs on the altar of Zeus at Pergamum, wherein the giants instead have the bones of a snake. Both cases present either mythological or myth-like motifs. It is, of course, not improbable that apocalyptic accounts were dependent upon artistic representations. But that Greek art had an influence upon Revelation 6 is without analogy, and, within itself, is quite improbable. It is completely undemonstrable that the snakelike bones of the giants would have been selected by the apocalyptic writer so as to give his horses *serpentine tails*.[58] In that case, the assumption of the "contemporaneous" explanation, that the author had conceived of the motif independently, is also a complete misunderstanding. Rather, the thing which is obvious is to explain Revelation at this point on the basis of a tradition adopted by it. The origin of that tradition having been investigated, the relief mentioned above ought to be explained as well!

Since from this special approach some possibly more ingenious but arbitrary formulations might be preferable to secure results, the demands of a more stringent methodology must be put forward! It is not enough to have shown a greater or lesser similarity to a completely disparate contemporary manifestation. Rather, one has to consider, before one thinks generally about the possibility of a "contemporaneous" interpretation of a particular feature, whether that feature is not to be explained according to the context in which it stands, i.e., in terms of the history of the tradition. At that point, and only then, may allusions to contemporary events be assumed, where not only a striking conformity to an apocalyptic theme appears, but where, at the same time, it can be understood psychologically exactly how this specific event made so great an impression that a reflex of that event could have been projected onto an apocalyptic vision. Finally, a contemporary theme which stands in the midst of a fantastic image must clearly be lifted out of the remaining materials. The latter requirement not having been acted upon, one comes to a "confusion"[59] of historical events and ideal images, a confusion which one might, perhaps, believe to be the "fantasy" of the apocalyptic writer because of which, at any rate, one must totally give up any claim to an historical understanding.

This methodological requirement is — as has been demonstrated in the examples cited above — consistent with none of the interpretations put forward to this point in time.

A second class of "contemporaneous" interpretations considers fantastic explanations of the future which are said to have arisen from particular historical causes. The incredible cavalry of Rev 9:13-21, since it comes from the Euphrates, is generally linked to the Parthians. But what then is the fantastic description of the horses supposed to mean? Could Parthians actually be in view here . . . Parthians who would ride on such steeds, steeds which bob their lion heads, which spew forth fire, smoke, and brimstone, and which sting the human beings with their serpentine-tails?!? Such beliefs are ascribed to the seer, i.e., a rather dramatic amplification of the fantasy on his part, far beyond the even most judicious consideration of it by him. — The vision thus by no means bears features of a fantastic portrayal of a Parthian invasion. In such a portrayal the dreadful things which the Parthians had done in historical reality . . . such things should have reappeared, to a certain degree, . . . reappeared in intensified form! The prophetic parallels, e.g., Isa 5:20-30; 13:11-18; Jer 5:15-17, and the description of the Parthian march in *1 Enoch* 56:5ff., all are comparable to the physical evidence of this Parthian invasion. The apocalyptic vision, however, is quite different from such descriptions. There we hear nothing of murder, of robbery, and of devastation . . . nothing of that which the cavalrymen actually did! Rather, we hear only of the frightfulness of the steeds! — This army of fire-spouting monsters is not an historical quantity, but rather is a piece of mythological-apocalyptic tradition!

Accordingly, not only is the "Parthian" interpretation completely wrong, but *any* "contemporaneous" interpretation is impossible! It is quite arbitrary to interpret the vision as even pointing to an historical Parthian movement or to a definite Parthian threat. The text gives not even the shadow of a clue as to any historical situation![60]

The appearance of the terrifying locusts (9:1-11), according to Spitta,[61] stems from the year 40 C.E., which places the fear of a great locust plague adjacent to an extraordinary drought. But the locusts which might be feared in such times are quite different from those described in Revelation 9. The latter do not crawl out of their eggs in warm weather, but rather emerge from the hazes of the open chasms of hell. They do not eat that which is green, but rather they torment people with bites and with stings. They are monsters with human heads, hair like a woman, teeth of a lion, and tails of a scorpion. These demonic beings, over whom אבדון [*'Abaddôn*] himself is king, have, therefore, nothing more in common with the locusts of natural-historical-reality than their name! The fear that such hellish creatures could come upon the earth did not, therefore, arise in a definite historical situation, in a conspicuously barren year. Rather, we have here a tradition which is to be explained from mythology and not by means of a spell of dry weather![62]

When at 16:13ff. the Dragon and the two Beasts send forth froglike demons from their mouths in order to call together the kings of the whole world, Spitta[63] has explained this as the three "armies" which are known to have been anticipated in the year 49 C.E., i.e., the army of Petronius, half the army of the Euphrates, and the entourage of Caesar Caligula. But would the writer of Revelation really have believed that these three armies would be called together by frogs?!? On the contrary, armies which are gathered by frogs are *not* historical armies but rather are mythological ones. This view would have necessarily made any "contemporaneous" explanation quite impossible.

Even here, therefore, the "contemporaneous" exegesis will not attempt to place the facts in context. It must allow the fantasy of the seer, aroused by Old Testament and apocalyptic prototypes, a great amount of latitude in order to explicate the great discrepancy between the assumed historical event and the existing future forms of it.[64] But precisely by means of this form of "contemporaneous" interpretation it will become clear that thus arises an unbearable, or at least confusing, entanglement of the historical and the fantastic features. What sort of opinion should one have about a person who, in all seriousness, could believe that the Parthians, who were coming shortly, would ride on fire-breathing horses; that the locusts of the following year would have male heads and female hair; that the three Roman armies would be brought together by frogs?!? But might the apocalyptic writer, accordingly, also be interpreted as a confused dreamer — and this would actually be a rather mild judgment under these circumstances! — so that, in any case, the passage, by means of a trustworthy methodological interpretation, might no longer be such a mess. Insofar as the "contemporaneous" interpretation has been involved in these insuperable difficulties, it may only just now be the time to attempt to draw a proper interpretation (near at hand from the very beginning) from the tradition.

In a third *Gattung* of contemporaneous interpretations, there will be hypothetical situations and the expectations which are associated with them. These will generally be portrayed in Revelation in relation to concrete historical situations and expectations. So, for example, the souls of the martyrs, who cry for vengeance (6:9ff.), are described as a sacrifice of a particular historical persecution. We know, from 4 *Ezra* 4:35, that this vision also belonged to the apocalyptic tradition. The description of the vision itself reveals to us simply that these souls will be sacrificed, but it does not reveal a somewhat more tangible feature which would allow a specific historical situation to emerge. That it is concerned precisely with those Christians massacred after the burning of Rome in 64 C.E. — as the common interpretation[65] claims — is stated clearly by nothing. Any other explanation put forth has proven just as little.

The vision of 11:12 is not to be looked upon differently. The seer takes the dimensions of the Temple according to the prototype of Ezekiel. The Temple should, as a holy asylum, remain untouched in the dreadful turn of events in which the heathen trample down Jerusalem. The expectation which stands out here, the expectation that an eschatological heathen assault will certainly be leveled against Jerusalem, though God will cause an asylum to endure. . . . this expectation belongs to the eschatological dogma which was inherited from the prophets.[66] The verse is thus thoroughly explained as an expression of a Jewish belief. On the other hand, the setting of the vision does not point to an historical situation. The enemy is called, quite generally, "the heathen." Concerning the nature of that enemy's siege and conquest of Jerusalem, nothing concrete is reported, with the exception of two features, i.e., that the temple will be adorned by them, and that they will trample down the city for forty-two months. Both features, nevertheless, have surely arisen from religious faith, and not from political deliberations. It is, accordingly, rather arbitrary to link the vision to Titus's siege,[67] or to fearfulness of a Roman movement against Jerusalem sometime in the year 62 C.E.[68] The interpretation based on the conquest of Jerusalem by Pompey,[69] who had indeed trampled down the Temple and the city (*Pss. Sol.* 2:1-5), . . . this interpretation is certainly *completely impossible!*

The "great multitude" from all peoples, the multitude which stands before the throne and the Lamb in white garments and with palms in hand (7:9-17), this multitude has been linked by Weizsäcker[70] to the martyrs of the Neronic persecution. Because of this Weizsäcker wishes to fix the vision chronologically. The text, however, neither describes them as "martyrs," nor does it speak in any clearer manner of an historical persecution. "The great affliction" from which they come forth (v. 14) is none other than the generally known final great affliction, which, according to Judeo-Christian belief, the final Transfiguration (described here) precedes (Mark 13:19).[71]

In these cases we are dealing not with a vision of a particular situation which the seer had freely fabricated, but rather with ideas which were already present long before him in the religious tradition. Now it is not, in itself, unlikely that such traditions existed with a view toward the elucidation of an historical event. Nevertheless, this assumption is permitted only when either the material itself contains clear allusions to an historical situation — which, as we saw in the examples above, is not the case — or when a secure chronological assessment is given. This argument can, at present, not be employed at all, or can be employed only with the greatest care, as long as so many inconsistencies predominate the composition of Revelation.

Likewise, the ἄνομος [anomos] and the κατέχων [katechōn] of 2 Thess 2:3ff. also customarily point to definite historical persons. In actuality the references from both Thessalonian epistles must be understood as allusions to Judeo-Christian apocalyptic tradition. It is generally known that Judaism expected a great universal revolt at the end time. Since Daniel[72] it is reported that this consummation of wickedness will be embodied in a person, a person who insolently will cast aspersions on every holy thing, even the Temple of God in Jerusalem.[73] We know that Judaism was still employing such concepts after the beginning of the common era.[74] Even the remaining features of the form of the ἄνομος [anomos], which does not confront us in our extremely meager Jewish sources, are, quite possibly, to be considered as further confirmations of this tradition.[75] If the ἄνομος [anomos] is proclaimed, even in the Temple, as a god/ God, this deification of a human is the ultimate offense of which the Jews believed the Gentile kings capable. Furthermore, since the ἄνομος (anomos) hardly ever appears as a political king, but more often as the embodied power of evil and of temptation, a spiritualization of the political comes to the fore therein, a spiritualization which we also observe quite often in the Judaism of the time. I am reminded, for example, of the parallel development of the messianic form.[76]

The ἄνομος [anomos]-expectation of 2 Thessalonians is, therefore, not the arbitrary fabrication of an individual, but only the expression of a faith which came into existence over a long history and then circulated widely. The two parallels from early Christian literature give a very pleasing corroboration. In the Johannine letters[77] we find allusions to the same tradition. There the concepts ἀντίχριστος [antichristos], πλάνος [planos], πνεῦμα τοῦ ἀντιχρίστου [pneuma tou antichristou] will be mentioned as familiar things. The description of the two beasts of Revelation 13 is also similar. There we hear of the deification of the first beast and the satanically seductive power of the second. These three New Testament passages about the Antichrist are, however, quite characteristically distinguished from one another,[78] and show so little tangency in wording that it would be totally unmethodical to consider a literary dependence. We have to look upon the three expressions rather as variants of the same tradition. — It happens, as well, that these texts are not completely unusual, ad hoc–fabricated forms, but rather usually bear the established tradition. One notes, above all, that 2 Thessalonians, as well as 1 John, has already been strongly marked by these extremely great sacrilegious concepts, and, as has been assumed, employs commonly comprehensible names. — And to put an end to all uncertainty, 2 Thess 2:5 and 1 John 4:3 say explicitly that the tradition of the ἀντίχριστος [antichristos] was a piece of Christian teaching.

So it is, therefore, quite certain that political situations have had a part in the emergence and the later history of this expectation — the judgment on the Gentile empire reverberates through Judaism in the form of the ἄνομος [anomos]. — And it is also quite clear that these expectations were consciously held in Roman times by the impression of the Roman empire, in which the beginning of the fulfillment of this prophecy might be encountered with fear and trembling. So the ἄνομος [anomos] expectation is older than the Roman empire. None of the features in these visions calls the Roman empire to mind specifically. The deification of the ruler was at home in the east long before the

Caesar cultus. In addition, we see, right in 2 Thessalonians, a form of the Antichrist tradition which clearly deviates from the political issues of this eschatological form.

Now clearly the possibility that such a tradition would be revived anew by each great contemporary event and would be altered in form . . . this possibility is clearly to be retained. This hypothesis is still methodologically permissible only when clear allusions to specific events or persons actually come to the fore in the existing text. We are not, however, able to do this in this case. Reasonably certain allusions either to Caligula,[79] who intended to set up his own image in the Temple[80] (but not to seat himself therein), or to the "returned" Nero[81] are not to be found. Accordingly, the contemporaneous interpretations[82] of ἄνομος [*anomos*] have failed totally.

We have here a Judeo-Christian article of faith which is to be understood from the history of religious reflection and quite indirectly from the history of the Caesars.

The news which the Thessalonians learn now through a letter by no means also makes a contemporaneous interpretation necessary. The concepts of κατέχων [*katechōn*] and κατέχον [*katechon*] are not especially well attested for us. We do possess, however, some closer or more distant parallels. The heavenly or infernal powers, which shall make their appearance at the eschaton, are, according to Jewish faith, already in existence now. To the question why they did not then "reveal themselves" in the present, careful thought replies, "Something which suppressed them for a while must have been there."

The terrifying locusts of אבדון [*'Abaddôn)* are even now at hand *in* the abyss. But they are not known *outside* the abyss since the passageway to the abyss is sealed. Only when it is opened do they come upon the earth (Rev 9:1f.). Or the four angels who shall kill a third of humanity are already "prepared" at the great stream of the Euphrates. They are, however, *bound*. When, however, the time is fulfilled, their bonds will be *loosed* (Rev 9:13ff.). Likewise, the four winds, which shall, in the final days, blow calamity over land and sea, are "held" by four angels (Rev 7:1ff.). "In the *Pistis Sophia* angels, with which the Dragon of the Darkness interferes with the order of creation, are placed at the gates of Hell."[83] Reference should also be made to the dark and incoherent tradition of the two witnesses of Revelation 11: the Beast — which appears to be the sense of v. 7 — can come out of the pit only if they have completed their testimony.

The same concept is looked upon as the final "1,000 years." The Dragon will be bound in the abyss, locked up, and sealed until he is again let loose after the passage of 1,000 years (Rev 20:3). Furthermore, the answers to the often wistfully raised questions are parallel: "Why has the Messiah not yet come?"[84] Different explanations are given for the retardation in the progress of the dramatic action: God's forbearance; or his anger about the transgression of Israel; or his anger about the transgression of another. The great villain is at hand, but he has still not been fully revealed. Why? A power has been placed in his way! Only when this power is removed can "the rebellion" come. It is indicated by the appellation that this power appears as the wickedness which is in a person. Furthermore, we do not discover in this text that which speaks of the great secrets of the end time, as would be expected. Of course, the author knows quite well who this κατέχων [katechōn] was. The natural assumption, that he had received this knowledge through a tradition concerning κατέχων [katechōn], will be secure if it is noted that ὁ κατέχων [ho katechōn] also appears as an engraved name. Furthermore we may suppose that since the ἄνομος [anomos] has just appeared as a *human* being, so also the κατέχων [katechōn] will probably be a *heavenly* being. We are able to reflect on κατέχειν [katechein] in terms of the struggle of Michael with the angel of Persia (cf. Dan 10:13). Finally, it is to be recalled that the two witnesses of Revelation 11 occupy, in many ways, a position similar to that of the κατέχων [katechōn]. They precede the appearance of Christ and they carry out war against the Beast, a war in which they are defeated and killed. Also, in the context of Revelation 11 a period of time follows their death, a period when the Beast rules over the earth, until God puts it to an end. In Revelation 11 we have, therefore, a very closely related tradition. Accordingly, we now call the κατέχων [katechōn] "Elijah."[85]

At any rate, the κατέχων [katechōn] is not an historical person. Neither Aristobolus, brother of King Agrippa I, nor Agrippa I himself, who would protest to Caligula against the erection of his (Caligula's) image in the temple,[86] nor the Roman state, nor Galba Caesar,[87] who sought to put an end to rumors of Nero's return. Aristobolus and Herod Agrippa are just a little too insignificant to be able to obstruct the Antichrist whom Christ later annihilates! And Galba does not obstruct the "return," the "reappearance," of Nero. He, at best, struggles with him after Nero has appeared again. These "contemporaneous" exegeses, which are so arbitrary that they nearly elude refutation, can be justified only on the condition that a "contemporaneous" interpretation appears to be the only possible explanatory recourse.[88] They immediately fall by the wayside when a different way of explicating the text is demonstrated. Then all literary-critical results[89] which have been, or can be, drawn from such interpretations are easily refuted!

I come to a new *Gattung:* events of the immediate past in commonly held, or fantastically embellished, visions.

So the four apocalyptic horsemen of chapter 6 are commonly linked[90] to *definite* wars, *definite* famines, and *definite* pestilences[91] which had already occurred. Now the source of the vision is clear. It is the four horsemen of Zechariah,[92] who are understood eschatologically here. They are, certainly, to bring the final horrible afflictions upon the earth. The color of their steeds is, as far as possible, combined with the particular plagues, which another tradition[93] furnished. So the vision is to be understood as a combination of two apocalyptic materials.

If, at the same time, details remain somewhat unclear for us, e.g., v. 2 in its present form and the specific testimony of v. 6c, there is to be inferred a pre-history of the vision, a prehistory out of which the present discontinuity and incomprehensibility are explained.[94] — The "contemporaneous" exegesis has acted quite correctly at this point: the description of the plagues is sufficiently general, and hardly any specific time exists in which a war, a pestilence, or a famine would not have been taking place somewhere in the Roman empire. Thus, perhaps, one wishes the vision to refer to the time of Claudius,[95] or perhaps to that of Nero,[96] or to the time of almost anyone else, as if by means of some searching in the historical data the necessary war, pestilence, and plague will be found for sure. There was, for example, between the years 40 and 50 C.E. a bad harvest,[97] as well as a famine in the second half of the reign of Nero[98] ("extraordinarily great" was the famine in the year 68[99]). One could also consider the fact that a famine reigned in Britannia in 61/62, or the fact that the Parthian cavalry, because of an earlier locust plague, suffered a shortage of food, or the fact that the Jewish priests, of whom the ten most powerful were removed by the high priest Ananus, must have hungered.[100] There was a pestilence in Asia in 50/61 C.E.,[101] in Rome in 65 C.E.[102] It would be wonderful if the vision referred to the time of Claudius, thereby making the pestilence less of a problem.[103] — Wars were, indeed, really waged all the time: the Parthian conflicts, or the great Britannic revolution of 61 C.E., or the Jewish uprising,[104] or a terrifying Gallic or Asian rebellion, or whatever else one desires! Finally, there were also men in Palestine who, siding with the Zealot movement, were slain by the sword.[105] Such explanations do not really cancel each other out! On the contrary, they commonly appear in combination with each other!

Only the wild animals (v. 8) present any difficulty. Völter[106] connects them to the beast of the arena. Erbes[107] considers an allegorical explanation as possible: four hundred innocent slaves of Pedanius Secundus were slaughtered in Rome in 62 C.E.; Italy no longer raised humans, but rather wild animals! — All these explanations differ from one another only in the degree of choice.[108] A more substantial argument, which must rely on a distinct and characteristic similarity between certain contemporary events and the description of the vision, is furnished by no one, and, quite probably, by none of the explanations. Accordingly, the "contemporaneous" explanation of the four horsemen is to be considered as having failed.

Though the weakness in these explanations lies in the fact that, without proof, there has been an attempt to connect *indefinite* representations to *definite* events, a different weakness arises when such powerfully fantastic, yet totally realistic pieces as the description of the seven seals are "contemporaneously" understood. Then the darkening of the kingdom of the Beast (16:12) is said to be related to the darkening of the sun by the ashen rain from the eruption of Vesuvius in 79 C.E.[109] But though the text does speak of a darkening in the whole Roman empire, it nevertheless says nothing, of a volcano or of an ashen rain. Or the death of the fishes of the sea (16:3) could indicate the same event. In 16:3, however, the fishes die because the sea turns to blood, etc. Even if one does not really believe in the exacting accuracy of specific "contemporaneous" exegeses, one must be amazed that such interpretations are actually possible!

Within these interpretations there is the unspoken assumption (which, as far as I can see, is shared by all researchers) that in Revelation general facts about the immediate past and present not only *can* be found, but, by analogy to Daniel, *must* be found! In response to this assumption there are observations with which we must deal, observations which have been used above[110] in place of a concrete event and which must be generalized here. The vision obtains its nature from that which is simply strange: the prophecy of that which is yet to come. It obtains its nature from the present only insofar as the present is absolutely essential to the understanding of its depiction of the future!

If the seer, as he is generally conceived,[111] links the design of the work with these descriptions to demonstrate, by means of the signs of the times, the proximity of the end, then he must allude to older, well-known prophecies and then, for his own part, add the argumentation. So he recognizes, then, that the first part of each prophecy has been fulfilled. "You, indeed, who see all this, lift up your heads and understand. Your redemption stands near at hand."[112] The apocalyptist, however, has not written it in this way. — Or, if he once again would declare that which has already taken place to be a prophecy, then he must pretend that it had been written in an earlier period, before all these things were fulfilled, i.e., he must give his writing the name of an ancient holy man. That he [the apocalyptic writer] would prophesy a contemporary "past" would be just as shocking as it would be totally pointless: in what manner might faith anticipate, the thing speculates, that which everyone already knows!

Therefore, the scholar who accepts such descriptions of the past in Revelation, has, at the same time, to advance the claim that these "sayings" were originally written under an ancient pseudonym. No one has undertaken this investigation. The extremely superficial example of Daniel has been accepted as satisfactory, without considering the fact that Daniel and Revelation do diverge in regard to exactly one point. In Daniel a "more ancient" seer is the speaker, while in Revelation a Christian "contemporary" speaks! The result of this, then, is that in Revelation there can generally be no descriptions of the past, insofar as it cannot be assumed from the pieces in question that they have come into our New Testament book from an apocalypse written, in its turn, under an old pseudonym.

A fifth category, which interprets the apocalyptic account or a particular feature thereof allegorically, is represented quite sparsely in the "contemporaneous" explanation. The scarcity of allegorical interpretations is explained by the prevailing themes of evangelical-historical scholarship, which even in the Old Testament has reduced the allegorical interpretation to a few weak and almost invisible remnants — the so-called "standard" interpretation — and has appeared from the very start, especially in reference to Revelation, in conscious opposition to the former "religious," allegorically interpreted exegesis.[113] In reality clarity has not yet even been achieved for Revelation. Certain allegorical interpretations which still appear do demonstrate this!

So, for example, the signs of the sixth seal — the earth quaking, the sun and the moon losing their light, the stars falling from the heavens, the heavens rolling up — these signs will be regarded as an allegorical description of a "seemingly deadly crisis which set upon the Roman empire in the year 68 with Nero's downfall."[114] Such an explanation contravenes the commonly accepted axiom of historical exegesis (even beyond Revelation), the axiom that only that document may be allegorically interpreted which very clearly demands such an interpretation. Since now the famine, the war, and the pestilence of the first seal have to be understood in the proper way and should be taken in this way by all modern interpreters, it is improper to shift suddenly to using the allegorical interpretation in regard to the sixth seal.[115] In addition, we clearly know that such heavenly signs, according to Judeo-Christian eschatology, precede the end, e.g., Luke 21:25. Finally, the interpretation is not exactly compelled to focus on the death of Nero by anything in the text.

It is, of course, even more arbitrary if one removes just one particular feature from a whole description and understands that feature allegorically. This is the case in the interpretation (given above)[116] of the wild animals as pointing to the animalistic nature of the Roman people. And it is the case when the first of the four horsemen is interpreted as the Parthian king Vologases.[117]

Within Revelation, chapters 13 and 17 (in addition to their material contexts) hold a special place. They fulfill the condition put forward above because they will give allegories, namely, allegories (to the present) and to the future, allegories of historical importance. The first Beast of chapter 12 is the Roman empire. The spouse of the Beast of chapter 17 is the city of Rome itself. Here, then, the contemporaneous, that is the allegorical, interpretation is necessarily required just as in Daniel 7f., *1 Enoch* 85ff., *4 Ezra* 11f., etc.

These chapters, which for the context of these investigations are valuable, not only methodologically but similarly by reason of their content . . . these chapter will be dealt with in detail at a later time. I speak here, accordingly, only about their character, in order to interpret them. Thereupon, since allegorical-contemporaneous interpretation will be applied to them, the option which can discover the "all-in-all" may not be given full license. Rather, the task of historical exegesis here is, indeed, none other than this: to do justice to the original intentions of the author! If he did not express his thinking with clear words, but rather has concealed it in allegories, the exegete has to take very great care in interpretation. Now it is indisputable, e.g., for chapter 13, that a component of it — for the author, naturally, the main component — deals with the future, and that it is strongly dependent on apocalyptic tradition. Thereby it is acknowledged that not the whole chapter, but only a few themes of it, may point to actual events.

The ascent of the first Beast from the sea is a theme which also appears in the book of Daniel.[118] Contemporaneous interpretation is not necessary for the explanation of the origin of the theme here, but is only permissible when a striking similarity can actually be established. Völter[119] saw in the Beast that comes forth from the sea an allegory for Hadrian Caesar. In the name Hadrian a link has been found to the Adriatic Sea (*Sib. Or.* 5:47; 8:52; 10:163ff.) — but there is, here, absolutely no question of such a play on words; furthermore, the Caesar was traveling, in 129, by sea to Asia Minor — but Revelation says not a word about the Beast being on a journey. If the Beast really is to be explained by a Roman emperor and not by the Roman empire, then one might see in its ascent from the sea simply the manner of that specific emperor's accession to the throne, and not an arbitrary event illustrative of his reign!

Spitta[120] saw in the Beast an allegory for Caligula, and he commented thus on the image described in 13:2a: "[T]hat grotesque coalescence of animals, ranging from the leopard, the bear, and the lion, into a monster fits, in reality, none of the rulers in question better than Caligula," whom Suetonius also called a *monstrum*. But if the insane eccentricity of a ruler were to be described allegorically, is it then also just to a certain degree intelligible if it is said of him: "he had the paws of a bear and the maw of a lion and was, in other respects, similar to a leopard"? Spitta, naturally, also knows that these themes have an analogy in Daniel. But why assume, then, that they represent anything more than a piece of apocalyptic tradition?

A motive may have been to get the feelings of the pious aroused at the description of the mark of the Beast placed on the hand and the brow, which was something offensive in those days. But how can one assert that a Jewish head tax is implied and that the oracle is to be placed under Domitian since he, at one time, exacted such a tax severely and cruelly?[121] Is it, then, really a clear representation of the payment of a tax, since that is consistent with a stamp on the hand and the brow? And, furthermore, the head tax on Jews had actually been imposed by Vespasian!

As long as the interpretation of this chapter does not follow stronger methodology, the current state of affairs (i.e., that the chapter hints at the period sometimes of Caligula, sometimes of Nero, sometimes of Galba, sometimes of Vespasian, sometimes of Domitian, sometimes of Trajan, sometimes of Hadrian, sometimes of Antoninus Pius)[122] . . . this state of affairs will continue, a situation in which all explanations actually utilize approximately the same methodology and, therefore, have approximately the same value!

Let's put the whole thing together. In comparison to the polymorphic, but thoroughly arbitrary and inaccurate, immutably traditional type of explication . . . in contrast to this, the demand for greater precision and stronger methodology must urgently be asserted! This demand having been met, the result will be as follows: disregarding individual pieces in chapters 13 and 17 (and their contextual linkages), no single contemporaneous exegesis proves effective. This means: the contemporaneous exegesis is bankrupt which regards a widely predominant number of passive verbs as active only in certain passages of chapters 13 and 17. Thereupon it is acknowledged that all chronological estimates and source hypotheses which rely upon such "contemporaneous" explanations, even though they do not decay any further because of the above-mentioned models, nevertheless stand in need of a new methodological examination. The distinguishing and the chronological dating of sources can, properly, be asserted only when the method of understanding the writing being investigated is, to some degree, secure. At many points our investigation has yielded for us, as an incidental result, the realization that the traditio-historical explanation seeks to compensate for the contemporary reality in a future time. The application of this new interpretation to Revelation I, myself, reserve for another time and another place.

On the other hand, it seems to me, as a pious obligation, explicitly to add that contemporaneous exegesis has great merit since the ecclesiastical explanations which have prevailed until now have broken down, thereby preparing the way for a future historical understanding of Revelation. This exegesis actually had the right, at one time, to designate itself as "the scientific" exegesis of Revelation, and will maintain a significant place in the history of Gospel research even if it should not prove to be that research's last word.

While "contemporaneous" exegesis has, in regard to the materials which are found in Revelation, strongly differed from the heretofore prevailing ecclesial-historical exegesis, it has not, on the other hand, clearly extricated itself from the same in terms of the explanatory model. On the contrary, one has the impression, here as there, that Revelation is speaking figuratively, and that its visions must not be taken just as they sound but must be interpreted, somehow or other! In this connection the "contemporaneous" method is to be understood as a final consequence of the ecclesial-allegorical explanatory method. There is, even to the present day, an uninterrupted chain of exegetical tradition. This consideration is useful for understanding not just the existence of such an old-fashioned method, but also the impossibility of the same for proving itself useful for current historical research.

Into this context of "contemporaneous" exegesis, the Christian exegesis of Revelation discussed above must be placed so as to understand it, and then so as to refute it more definitively. It is a "contemporaneous" exegesis. It connects the chapter to events from the time of the seer, the birth and ascent of Christ, and the flight to Pella. More precisely, it is a contemporaneous-allegorical explanation, thus belonging to an infrequently represented form of this exegesis.

All of the errors established above, errors committed by use of this exegesis, have received a profusion of parallels in the methodological discussion. The bias which understands Revelation — not pseudonymous — to contain descriptions of the past, determines the exegesis not only of chapter 12 but also of other sections. The fact that the vision itself and the contemporary events, which should stand in something of a relationship, actually do not tally well by any means, but rather, at the most, have only an outward similarity . . . this fact has likewise been demonstrated at chapter 12 as well as in all other examples.

Likewise, that which is completely inadmissible since it is quite unverifiable, a blending of that which is contemporary and that which is "fantastic" (which stood out in chapter 12 especially with the flight of the woman) . . . such an inadmissible thing as this is nearly *the rule of contemporary exegesis*.

All these singular flaws are derived from the fundamental error of that explanatory methodology since what has been comprehended as the work of an individual author is, in reality, to be understood out of a history of the tradition. This is also the case at Revelation 12. Material which the Christian author has taken from the Jewish literature, and to which he has added only a few words, . . . this material has been dealt with as *his* original work.

In detail I do not find the Christian interpretation of Revelation 12 methodologically more objectionable than anything else which has been discussed above, or which has been put forward elsewhere. On the contrary, this Christian periodization has, at least, the excuse that it — as long as Christian composition of the chapter is looked upon as obvious — appears to be the only possible interpretation, and is believed to have legitimacy in the allegorizing additions of the Christians who worked on the text.

3. Revelation 12 Is Not of Jewish Origin

Another explanation for the fact that even now a Christian interpretation of the chapter is still possible lies in the fact that it cannot be understood under the assumption of a Jewish origin. A number of the difficulties discussed above, difficulties which make the assumption of a Christian origin for the chapter improbable, those difficulties fall away in the face of this fact without further comment. Yes, from the standpoint of Judaism it is completely comprehensible that the birth of the Messiah would be anticipated after the seven trumpets.[1] And this is also the remaining material which is simply inconceivable on Christian grounds: that the Christ is born in heaven; that as a child he was rescued from the Dragon to the divine throne so as to appear at first on earth as a mature person.[2] All of this is, at least, not impossible from the Jewish standpoint. But the chapter is still not, by any means, explained by that. The problem which now arises is one of understanding the origin of the whole point of view, the point of view both of the messianic image and of the many quite remarkable details of the chapter, understanding the origin of these things as having been derived from Jewish assumptions.[3]

The advocates of Jewish composition have attempted, moreover less completely, to adhere to the purpose. Vischer and Pfleiderer give an explanation of certain principal points. Spitta provides a systematic exegesis. In addition, Vischer states, with dispassionate calm (which brings special honor to his successful investigation of the *Jewish* components in Revelation) that particular themes of the chapter still, even now, escape explanation,[4] while Spitta and Pfleiderer, with the assumption of a Jewish origin, believe that they have overcome all difficulties.[5]

All three interpreters agree, however, in the assertion that the section cannot be understood "contemporaneously."[6] Naturally! This chapter deals with purely heavenly and extrahuman quantities and proceedings — a situation which, from the very beginning, any "contemporaneous" explanation would have to have ruled out. But there *is* the persecution of the "remnant" (v. 17), which could possibly suggest an historical event or situation.

Now the individual exegeses which are put forward by the three persons mentioned above are, for the most part, the same. They proceed on the theoretical basis of a Christian composition, even though the same method of explication rules on both sides. It is, therefore, permissible to regard their explanations as indicative of how one currently applies oneself to the explanation of units which are not "contemporaneously" understandable! I am guided by a more general interest, however, and will fill out the methodological discussion begun above only if I first discuss in more detail certain of these interpretations and particularly their methodologies.

The chapter will be interpreted as a free composition of the author — which appears to be the natural outcome of current research. Even though noncontemporaneous events could have been a factor, and even though the forms of Revelation certainly cannot easily be grasped, the force within the Hebrew Bible by which the imagination of the author was moved and set into motion . . . this force is to be sought out and discovered. Accordingly, the antecedent of such passages of Revelation is encountered in the fact that the Hebrew Bible passages onto which the apocalyptist "has fixed his vision" are, in each case, identifiable. At the same time it remains unclear whether the author has applied such received, visionary material to the "illumination" of concepts which he attempts to "read out from their multifarious contexts." All noncontemporaneously interpreted passages will be understood by modern exegesis according to this "referential" methodology. The same methodology surely also applies to a much broader realm. In the exposition of Revelation there is also common reference to the "ecclesiastical" standpoint.[7] Indeed, in the rest of the New Testament there will be multiple references to the interpretation of particular passages and broader conceptual frameworks.

Accordingly, the beginning of Revelation 12 presents itself thus: The author has encountered in the Hebrew Bible an abundance of individual forms. His own task in that context is, however, to extend the adopted visionary concepts and to bring his own ideas together into an illustrative image which is similar to a "mosaic."[8]

Now the deep significance of the Old Testament for postcanonical Judaism, as well as for earliest Christianity, especially for apocalyptic texts, requires no investigation. Apocalyptic thought can, generally, be comprehended only under the assumption that prophecy came first, and also, in greater detail, the assumption that the prophetic peculiarities in very many apocalyptic forms quite clearly reflect, throughout, the original prophetic models according to which they were designed. Additionally, it is frequently the case that a profusion of Old Testament recollections appear woven together in an apocalyptic vision. Revelation 4 (the heavenly scene) and 18 (the report concerning the great harlot) are instructive examples of passages put together in this way.

As certain as the influence of the Old Testament is on Revelation, it nevertheless still has to asked how broadly that influence extends into individual parts of the same, and how that influence is to be envisioned psychologically.

One is often inclined to explain everything in Revelation as an Old Testament echo, and to seek out an "originating" Old Testament passage for each apocalyptic expression, especially since the influence of the Old Testament on Judaism and on primal Christianity is generally — as far as I can tell — quite overrated. This erroneous idea, which cannot disavow its Protestant origin, is to be answered by the fact that both earliest Christianity and Judaism are *living* religions with independent religious needs, religions in which a book is certainly very, but not absolutely, important. Undoubtedly the essential historical events, i.e., the important features within them, may be nourished, to a great degree, by the reading of "the scriptures," or may, at the very least, be influenced by that reading. The final basis of these religions, however, never resides in the book, but rather in the persons, their observations and practical experiences, and in the history in which they are rooted. So also, Judeo-Christian apocalyptic thought is more than simply a consanguineous movement descended from the Old Testament. The allusion to the Jewish faith in reference to the resurrection, to hell, to an eternal life in heaven — beliefs which are not Old Testamental and have not even developed organically out of the Old Testament[9] — . . . the allusion to the Jewish faith in reference to these things is sufficient to demonstrate that in Jewish apocalyptic thought, in addition to that which is inherited from the Old Testament, there stand eschatological ideas which are of a greater originality than the Old Testament. It follows, methodologically for apocalyptic exegesis, that it is not completely necessary to understand the details from the Old Testament alone, but that we have also to deal with the peculiarly Jewish possibility of traditions independent of the Old Testament.

Even at a place where Old Testament influence exists, it is necessary to see clearly, in regard to the manner of that influence, just *how* the Old Testament has been used. To the scholars of our time it appears, perhaps, to be a natural thing to present the writer of Revelation according to his own models, since he had the Bible lying right beside his manuscript so that he could glance at it here and there whenever necessary. The possibility may, however, be conceded that

that writer, perchance, appealed to the Old Testament by means of memory. Even in the case of direct dependence on the Old Testament, one must discriminate among a diversity of types: the verbatim citation, the assumption of concepts, the use of motifs, allusion, the exegetical element, the expansive remark, the combination with other texts, and many other things. In addition, the possibility does arise that the Old Testament has had only an indirect effect. The writer could be dependent on a tradition which, in its turn, was developed from the Old Testament. The customary exegesis — even beyond Revelation — quite commonly speaks, in such cases, of "dependence" or "reference,"[10] i.e., it is content with the observation of Old Testament influence without the character of the same being examined more precisely. — More direct *or* indirect dependence of these modalities on the Old Testament must be discerned in a clear manner in those cases in which the author writes down a tradition already present in the Old Testament, without, for some reason, that tradition necessarily being dependent on the Old Testament.

However, even where the provenance of an apocalyptic motif is maintained to be from a particular Old Testament passage, if it is not clearly a literal reference, then two questions must be settled. The first would be whether a striking correspondence in conceptual terminology does actually exist! The second is whether such a development of the apocalyptic form out of a contemplation on the Old Testament actually appears plausible.[11]

According to these rules, we now look at the exegesis of Revelation 12 put forward by Spitta, Pfleiderer, and Vischer. The words of v. 2, the woman crying out in the pain of childbirth, should, according to Spitta,[12] be an "allusion to the expression of Mic. 4:10,"[13] where in actuality the outcry of Israel in labor is uttered.[14] But the labor pains of Israel are meant figuratively in the Micah passage: "Like a woman in labor" shall Israel cry out! The wailing of the woman giving birth is a metaphor for the anguished cries uttered by people who have been afflicted by a sudden misfortune. Accordingly, there is a great distinction between the Micah passage, a passage which compares the anguish of Zion with labor pains, and Revelation according to which the woman actually is in labor. So how does one come to the proposition that this passage from Micah lies at the root of the passage in Revelation? Is the metaphor of labor pains so very unusual that because of it the two passages appear profoundly related? By no means! This metaphor is extremely common in the Old Testament. — Or is the application of this metaphor to Israel perhaps characteristic of Micah? The Septuagintal versions of Jer 4:31 and 22:23 also speak, metaphorically of course, of Israel's labor pains. — Or is the expression similarly striking in both passages? Somehow a characteristic similarity does not come to the fore. — So the reference to Mic 4:10 is lacking in any foundation!

Apart from Mic 4:10, "reference" should be made to passages like Isa 54:1ff.,[15] where there is mention of the labor pains and the birthing of Israel. The passage has been chosen quite impropitiously since here the people of Israel will obtain numerous children, even though they have *not* given birth and have *not* been in labor! In other respects, the concept of lands and cities as mothers of their inhabitants — so that poetry might symbolically impute labor and child-birth to them — appears in the Old Testament as though it is a self-evident fact, and is, even in later times, so common[16] that it would be a labor vainly expended to seek out the particular Old Testament passage from which the apocalyptic writer has fashioned this image. Finally, however, it comes down to the fact that in Revelation there is a completely different concept: the heavenly Zion appears in Rev 12:2 not as mother of the Israelites, but as mother of the Christ.[17]

It is possible to acknowledge that the passages cited do have a certain similarity to Rev 12:2. They have no greater similarity than the many other passages which the different exegetes have noted. Certainly Isa 66:7-9[18] speaks of Zion's labor pains and parturition, though not of the birth of the Christ. Or Mic 5:1ff.[19] and — though this is not the place to contest it — Isa 7:14[20] might deal with the birth of the promised king. These latter passages, however, do not, in any case, mention Zion as his mother. Or Jer 4:51; 30:6; 49:24; Hos 13:13,[21] and Isa 26:17[22] employ the image of labor pains, while in Revelation 12 parturitive labor appears not as the image, but as an actual fact. The greatest similarity is presented further by the Protevangelium (cited by Völter), Gen 3:14-16, where "the woman's birth pains, increased by her offspring, but, in particular, by the serpent, and the deadly enmity which shall endure between it (the serpent) and the woman (and her offspring)" is "the report."[23] But who might venture to assert that the author actually had the Genesis passage right before his eyes, especially since the differences are greater than the similarities?[24] In all the passages, a list which, in many ways, could easily be augmented, there is the characteristic juxtapositioning (characteristic of Revelation) of the heavenly Zion and the Christ, as the mother and child without analogy. And the question as to why, particularly in this context, excruciating labor pains are ascribed to the woman . . . , this question cannot be answered in reference to the Old Testament. Should any of the passages mentioned by the author of Revelation 12 have been in mind, then his vision would have been interpreted so differently in terms of its character that it would be a totally insoluble problem for us to determine the point from which the totally irrepressible flight of his visionary experience actually began. A difficulty arises here, therefore, a difficulty closely linked to those which we have encountered in reference to the actual contemporaneous explanation. By means of this difficulty even the chief emphasis on the vision of the writer must fall.[25]

The dragon, who stands before the pregnant woman, casts down by means of his tail a third of the stars from the heavens. He casts them down onto the earth. This motif, both as a whole and in its particulars, is so unique within biblical literature that it does require special consideration. Spitta brings forth a whole slew of Old Testament passages to exposit it.[26] The downcast stars also appear, especially beside other heavenly portents, as signs of the end (Isa 34:4; Joel 2:10, 3:4; Amos 8:9).[27] However, "signs of the immediately forthcoming parousia" are out of the question. The Christ has not yet even been born. Rev 12:4, accordingly, has meant nothing by such σημεῖα τοῦ αἰῶνος [*sēmeia tou aiōnos* — "signs of the age"]. — Spitta adds that that "casting down of the stars from heaven possibly had its nearest basis in Dan 8:10, where the small horn extends right into the heavens and casts down stars."[28] The relationship of the two passages is clear. However, the portrayal is so much more vivid than the almost-static portrayal of Daniel, that, methodologically, it appears very precarious to look upon Revelation as secondary in this matter.[29] — Finally, Spitta supplies yet a third notion, one which "certainly has contributed, additionally, to the realization of the visionary form." It is Leviathan, the dragon, who, according to Spitta, brings about the darkness of the sun and of the moon (Job 3:8; 26:13; Isa 27:1), who is called the δράκων [*drakōn* — "dragon"] and ὄφις [*ophis* — "snake, serpent"], and to whom Ps 74:14 even ascribes several heads.[30] On the one hand, the relationship of the apocalyptic dragon to such an entity of popular religion[31] is to be acknowledged. Even then, however, it is in no way established that the author of Revelation has recorded a popular image and has used it for his own purposes, since it is transmitted in the book of Job alone — Spitta himself appears to surmise the circumstances in this very way.[32] Then neither can the details of the verses actually be explained as further fulfillment of any Old Testament idea.

How did the author come to such a remarkable conclusion as that the dragon had cast down a third of the stars with his tail? Nor is the mention of the idea from the Old Testament at all conceivable in this context — the idea that the devil will swallow up the Christ is indeed understood. But what does that have to do with the stars?[33] And was it, then, such an easy thing for the apocalyptist to equate the Satan and the old "eclipse-dragon"? Concerning these questions there is, as above, no other recourse than to resort to the incalculable visionary imagination[34] of the apocalyptist. It must be admitted that although related notions can be produced, no adequate explanation of the verse can be rendered.

The fact that the Messiah's birth and his immediate flight up to God precede his appearance must, according to Vischer,[35] be explained by a learned combination of different literary themes: according to one of these, the Messiah from David's lineage will, then, be born on earth; according to the other of these, his arrival will be presented as an unexpected thing. According to Daniel, the Son of Man, who was related to the Messiah, appeared on the clouds of the heavens and, therefore, came forth from heaven. All these concepts are brought together here into a total image, an image according to which the Messiah was, first born on earth, then was carried off into seclusion (i.e., to heaven), until finally he emerged, unexpectedly, from heaven.

This formulation presumes the birth of the Christ on earth for Revelation. It collapses, then, after this presumption is proven to be false.[36] But even disregarding the misunderstanding, the whole formulation is flawed methodologically. This is so because, on the one hand, the contention that this portion of the chapter is based on an amalgam of biblical passages would be justifiable only if the text contained identifiable references to such passages. There is, however, no evidence of such allusions. Rather, the text is altogether at variance with the sense of the assumed biblical passages: the birth of Christ out of Davidic lineage is neither explicitly indicated nor even tacitly presumed; the mother of the Christ is not an earthly, but a heavenly woman. On the other hand, the text, if it really were to have arisen in the manner indicated, must bear traces of learned contemplation. But this basic expectation is not in any way met! The text, so extremely rich in characteristic peculiarities, is certainly not the product of contemplative scribal practice. And the objective of the section under examination is not to bring together the theoretically distinct Christological dogmas, but rather to exhort the practical-minded to hope and to patience.[37] — Accordingly, Vischer's conjecture is totally unfounded. And the question as to how such a singular faith would have arisen, since the Christ, immediately after his birth and before the persecution of the dragon, would have been carried off to God, . . . this question remains, the same as ever, *without an answer!*

The struggle of Michael with the dragon (Rev 12:7) should, according to Spitta,[38] have "a starting point" in popular ideas. As proof, passages are cited where as indications of great events as well as of the end of the world, among other portents, squads of military men appear in the clouds.[39] But with such omens the battle of Michael has only the one meaning. That is, it really concerns a heavenly struggle by him. Everything else has passed away. Accordingly, one could establish, just about as easily, that the apocalyptist had such portents in mind that he alluded to the battle of Michael occurring in Dan 12:1;[40] or to the struggle of Satan and Michael over the corpse of Moses;[41] or perhaps to Zechariah 3;[42] or he was thinking of the downfall of the angel.[43]

The remarkable description of the flight of the woman (Rev 12:13-16) also produces no difficulties for this "dependency" methodology. According to

Spitta,[44] the author employed themes "which were apparently derived from the account of Israel's escape from Egypt."[45]

Just as the wings of the great eagle are given to the woman for the flight into the wilderness, so also was Israel (according to Exod 19:4 and Deut 32:11) borne through the wilderness on eagles' wings.[46] But the phrase "the two wings of the great eagle were given to the woman" is certainly not an allusion to an Old Testament passage in which, hypothetically, YHWH would have been compared to an eagle. Rather, it presumes a concept most definitely known to the reader, a concept of the "great eagle,"[47] a concept which perhaps reappears in Rev 8:13, but certainly appears in none of the cited Old Testament passages.

Furthermore, in the same way that Israel had been provided with heavenly bread according to Pss 78:24 and 105:40, so also has the woman been fed in the wilderness, apparently by angels.[48] Still, since nothing edible grows in the wilderness, any narrator who allows his heroes to go into the wilderness has the obligation to include a way in which food has been provided, e.g., Matt 3:4 in regard to John the Baptist; 2 Sam 16:2; 17:27ff. in regard to David (cf. also Matt 4:11 — Jesus' temptation — and Matt 15:33 — a feeding miracle). The tales often tell of miraculous eating and drinking in the wilderness — Gen 21 (Ishmael), 1 Kings 17:2ff.; 19:6 (Elijah). To the Israelite peasants the most wonderful thing in regard to the wilderness journey was that YHWH had preserved such a great people in the barren steppe; cf., for example, Jer 2:6. Hence there was the old Israelite interest in the narratives of the quails and of the manna. If, accordingly, the nourishment of the woman is reported here, it is a theme which the competent reader expects to encounter, and which is explained by the nature of the thing, and not by the use of certain biblical passages.

Furthermore, just as, in regard to Israel's flight, the hindrance of the Red Sea has been placed in the way, so similarly the serpent spews forth a flood of water in order to drown the woman. And just as in the earlier case the sea was miraculously dried up, so here the compassionate earth swallows up the dragon's flood of water.[49] But a little determination is necessary to see this resemblance. In the Exodus account we are dealing with a *sea*. In Revelation we are dealing with a *storm*. *There* the sea will be split. *Here* the storm will be swallowed up by the earth. The characteristic feature of the Exodus account, the idea that the children of Israel passed through with dry feet, but Pharaoh and his army were killed in the sea . . . , that characteristic is lacking in Revelation. On the other hand, the extreme peculiarity of Revelation, what gives the whole description the remarkable coloration which is similar to that of myth, i.e., that the dragon has sent forth a stream from his mouth, while the earth has come to the aid of the woman, . . . this extreme peculiarity has nothing corresponding to it in the Exodus account. Accordingly, what remains is only that water, by a flood in the wilderness, advances over the track but without blocking it indefinitely. This similarity, however, is hardly characteristic enough to enable us to build upon it the conclusion that the writer of Revelation has imitated the Exodus account.

So almost all similarities which are believed to be found quietly disappear. And even where an internal relationship with Old Testament passages can, possibly, be made, that relationship is *not* of such a nature that a literary dependency of the apocalyptist upon those passages can definitely be proven. The thorough discussion, however, in which we ourselves considered the mentioned passages side-by-side has its ultimate origin in an explanatory dialectic concerning the method to be employed. While it would hold the traditional exegesis to be legitimate, every more-or-less similar Old Testament parallel of an apocalyptic feature is to be comprehended, without further ado, as the basis of those things according to which any particular oriental text (e.g., any synoptic narrative) could be explained as an elaboration of an Old Testament motif. We have raised up the need for a stronger methodology,[50] and have discovered that the usual explanations, judged according to that methodology, are altogether insufficient. So the result is that the details of the chapter cannot be understood in terms of the Old Testament.

In the same way, the character of the whole section takes exception to such an explanation in terms of the Old Testament. Such a chapter, assembled out of allusions and reminiscences, bears the nature of the thing right out in front, in accordance with its mosaiclike character! It is comparable to the examples of chapters 4 and 18. In both those chapters the individually received pieces stand side-by-side with one another. It is, therefore, also not by chance that the two chapters are not narratives, but rather are descriptions! The narrative style needs to be more tightly uniform than the descriptive style. To construct a description out of adopted individual pieces is not difficult. To fashion a narrative from this is quite impossible, or at least very difficult!

Chapter 12 is, however, quite a different matter than chapters 4 and 18. Here we have, on the whole, a very unified narrative. It is a narrative which, therefore, appears much more like a unified conceptualization than like an assemblage of many individual pieces brought together from here and there.

Now, indeed, it is conceivably possible to detect in the chapter organizational influences through which originally independent pieces are brought together into a unified whole. It is maintained here, and in similar cases, that the author has employed the materials drawn from the Old Testament as *conceptual illustrations*. It is indeed striking how seldom the exegetes of the present time make mention of such "ideas," "ideas" which one could read with representatives of the earlier generations, e.g., Bleek, Düsterdieck, and Beyschlag, among others. The most recent schools of thought are commonly content to seek out Old Testament parallels. They believe, thereby, to have done all that is necessary! This is the case with Spitta in reference to the chapter we are considering (Revelation 12). Pfleiderer has, at least, found in the flight of the woman the representation of a conceptual idea: "the magnificence of the everlasting theocracy will surely vanish for a little while, but will actually only be hidden, so as to emerge again shortly with a victorious appearance."[51] Granted that it *is* possible to conceive of a Jewish point of view in regard to the former narrative, to this narrative, or to a similar narrative. It is possible to be thinking of this and, thereby, to be thinking correctly.

But there is a totally different issue here, namely, whether the narrative was intended, from the beginning, as an illustration of the idea which Pfleiderer has suggested. If we could comprehend the details of the narrative, without any difficulty, as an allegory for a specific concept, then this question would be answered affirmatively in this type of case, or in a similar one. But that is certainly *NOT* the case here! Had the apocalyptic writer actually wanted to depict that idea, he would have been able, perhaps, to call upon the form of a woman fleeing into the wilderness. But the other so characteristically isolated features have absolutely no connection to this concept, a concept which should be expressed by the *whole* thing rather than just by a *part!*[52]

The methodological weakness, which once again lies in the background here, . . . that weakness is not all that rare. It means no less than what Bleek[53] suggests concerning the plagues of chapters 6–11 and 16, i.e., that they were altogether "intended to be announcements of particular events which were presented in this sequence only as communal images used to designate traumatic times for the world,"[54] traumatic times preceding the return of the Lord. Nevertheless, if the apocalyptic writer had nothing more to say than a statement that even before the final judgement certain painful, nonspecific plagues would take place, . . . if he had nothing more than this to say, he would, perhaps, have been able to express it just a little bit more clearly. In the same way, Beyschlag[55] sees in the victory over the dragon the overcoming of evil by means of "the overpowering might of eternal love, as it has been revealed in the blood of Christ."[56] But Michael is actually the specific personification of the "everlasting, overpowering might." Why does the author remain silent concerning that which certainly far better represents the power of love, i.e., concerning the cross of Christ? An exegesis, therefore, arises which, lacking the necessary care, gropes blindly about seeking the "concepts" of the apocalyptic writer, an exegesis in which the pressing danger is to deduce "ideas" from the writer's imagery, ideas which either stand conceptually pallid in very flagrant contradiction to the colorful richness of the apocalyptic forms, or, at the very least, are of such a different outlook that it becomes extremely difficult to comprehend exactly how the apocalyptic writer, working with such "ideas," could even have come up with such depictions.

The intrinsic impossibility of the images, however, speaks against such an interpretation of the chapter. Those images themselves must have been fleshed out more fully by the literary activity of the author. For if the apocalyptic author actually had composed a piece like chapter 12 out of Old Testament "recollections" for the illustration, perhaps, of particular "truths" — which requires no proof, considering the great discrepancy which exists between the Old Testament passages and the ideas of the chapter itself — , . . . if this be the case, then the actual creative impetus which has produced this portrayal must have been the imagination of the author! He, in a totally individual fashion, a fashion in which he allows his imagination to break in quite freely, has created a completely refined innovation. We have already repeatedly come to the same conclusion in regard to the "contemporaneous" passages,[57] a result which will be accepted by modern exegesis without even giving it a second thought. A good many exegetes are heard to speak of the "imagination" of the "poet,"[58] of his "spiritual freedom,"[59] of the "great independence"[60] with which he has reflected about the Old Testament passages and the then-contemporary circumstances. One compares the "visionary imagination" of the apocalyptic writer with a mirror in which the "realities given" by the Old Testament and by history reappear peculiarly altered.[61] One longs for an aesthetic appreciation of the "poetic beauty"[62] of the book which can be called an "epic of the primitive Christian hope";[63] this book must be read with "poetic rhythm," so that the 'poetic speech of the prophet" may not be understood as "dispassionate prose."[64] Even researchers join in such judgments, which — against the flow of modern exegesis — assume actual visions and experiences by the apocalyptic writer. Indeed, Düsterdieck (in regard to the locus of 9:1ff.!) speaks of the "lovely dalliances of his sacred imagination";[65] and despite his acceptance of these assumptions, Spitta's exegesis in no way differs from the commonly prevailing one!

It has, however, apparently been overlooked exactly how dangerous is the foundation on the basis of which this strong emphasis on the power of the poetic imagination has been erected. As soon as the possibility has been conceded that the apocalyptic writer "improvised"[66] in a "very poetic"[67] fashion, then the faith he had so "ardently" asserted with such visions has been abdicated. So how shall it be made psychologically comprehensible that a person who has composed such a text as chapter 12 could ever have convinced himself that the Messiah would be born in this way and no other, and that his mother would be delivered in this way and no other.

It would follow, therefore, as a totally unavoidable conclusion that the apocalyptic writer had, strictly speaking, not believed in the truth of his own words. Actually, people like Bleek, de Wette, Düsterdieck, and Beyschlag have demonstrated more or less clearly this result: Large parts of Revelation, so we hear from them, are generally not intended as announcements of particular events,[68] "as prophetic utterances actually to be fulfilled."[69] They are, rather, "mere products of the poetic imagination,"[70] presented "in unrestrained imagery,"[71] by which nothing has been fundamentally affected.[72]

Therefore, the comprehension of Revelation has — I'm afraid — gone astray at a decisive point. In Revelation it is, indeed, the truest of truths that a "revelation" is given and it will be a proper witness to the truth: "these words are reliable and true."[73] An understanding of the apocalypse which interprets those words as "visionary, phantasmagorias,"[74] as "an imaginative illusion,"[75] those words which, for their own part, depict themselves as a "fact" . . . such an understanding has judged itself thereby. Thus we come to this conclusion: Revelation wishes to impart truth. It should not, therefore, contain, to any great extent, imaginary creations of its author!

It is not the intention of this discussion to dismiss every independent thought of the apocalyptist. The apocalyptic writer might have expanded and altered[76] the traditional material in a multitude of ways through interpretation, through further commentary, through combination and rearrangement. But such spontaneity is always to be considered in those contexts within which the belief of the author concerning the truth of his words cannot be considered as unlikely. The actual substance of the future expectation, to which the faithful reader should cling in any time of trouble, with hope and patience, could not have been conjured up arbitrarily by the apocalyptist.

One could, perhaps, raise as an objection to this argument the example of the prophet,[77] who was also at the same time a "poet." Now it seems to me that this comparison of apocalyptic writing with prophetic writing and the interweaving of the two under the name of "biblical prophecy" is not innocuous at all[78] since in each of the two we are dealing, fundamentally, with a very different thing. — Why is it that that which, for example, finds a chapter at the very core of Isaiah, or even at the core of Ezekiel, has been encountered similarly only at a distance in Revelation? On this point, however, both apocalyptist and prophet agree, namely, that they both make the claim to present *THE TRUTH*. Their words should be believed, and they should be believed *without proof!* Even though the form of prophetic speech may be a poetic one, never would a prophet have approved of an interpretation of his words that would have eliminated a part of them as "poetry," poetry which might not even deal with religious issues,[79] much less since such a restraint of the imaginative impulse as is found by the exegetes of Revelation 12 may very well have analogies among the prophets.

Finally, the above discussion also has significance for those who are somewhat suspicious of the depictions which the New Testament apocalypse contains, those who consider the style of the future images to be visionary, and who, therefore, oppose conclusions which begin with the unconditional truthfulness of the apocalyptist. The issue here is not the truthfulness of the author, but rather the deliberated desire to understand his composition. It may be that the supposed designation and form of the vision are fictions, fictions which appeared for the author as self-evident and relatively harmless. But these fictions can be psychologically interpreted. He wanted to give these images, in which he believed, authority as well in the eyes of his reader. Even more incisive, however, is this question: Whence would he have drawn this belief in the content of his "poetry" if he himself had independently invented the same?! To this question there is no answer!

Consequently, only two possibilities exist. Either Revelation's depictions of the future are a reported description of that which was actually seen and heard, or they are not.[80] Uncertainty has arisen from this realization, uncertainty as to whether to believe in the truth of such visions or not.[81] (By and large the majority of modern researchers would share such misgivings.) For this reason one must be on the lookout for another authority which affirms the "meaning" of Revelation's depictions. That authority can be none other than — THE TRADITION!

Thus we obtain this result: The explanations put together until now, explanations which would interpret Revelation 12 from the Jewish standpoint based on Old Testament echoes . . . those explanations are to be considered as having run aground. Having come to that realization, however, at the same time a more positive sense arises. The assumption of former exegetes was that the chapter was a free composition of the author.[82] We have seen, however, that it *cannot* be understood on the basis of such an assumption. The result, therefore, is that this assumption has to be abandoned. Revelation 12 is, then, a piece of *Jewish* apocalyptic tradition. This conclusion applies similarly to a great number of the other passages in Revelation.

Another line of argumentation leads to the same conclusion. There are certain features on the basis of which the systemic code of a tradition and the obvious editorial work of an author may be distinguished.[83] The history which has already been seen in more traditional material before it is encountered by us in this text . . . that history has quite commonly bequeathed clues which reveal its prehistory to the trained eye. It is in the very nature of oral tradition, when passing oh-so-tenaciously from generation to generation, that it is subject to certain fluctuations. Such omissions, additions, displacements, which later generations have impose on the ancient materials, are revealed in the present codification of the tradition. They are revealed by the fact that the continuity of the narrative, which had formerly been uninterrupted, currently exhibits some obscurities or peculiarities! Or they are revealed by the fact that certain features, features which had a proper meaning at the time of their origins, are neither intelligible from the present context nor are they able to be considered as "generally" intelligible. They are, therefore, viewed as strangely brief and incomprehensible! Just as the age of a painting may be recognized by the degree of "darkening" which presently characterizes it, so too is the antiquity of a tradition recognized by such "darkenings." In any examination of a tradition this "darkening" has to be brought into play. The ultimate object of the investigation, however, is to reconstruct the original context and to indicate the basis of its alteration, i.e., to write the history of the tradition!

Genesis offers examples in rich abundance. In the traditional paradise narratives, the serpent is an animal from which the contemporary generation of serpents are descended. But its hostility against God and its secret knowledge leads to the conclusion that it was, at one time, more than an animal,[84] and — because of the monotheistically rooted aversion of Israelite religion to mythological themes — it was degraded from a demon or an evil deity to a simple animal. The manner in which YHWH relates to the Garden of Eden is not declared to us by the present narrative. The way in which YHWH's appearance is described in the present narrative, however, practically infers that this garden had, in an earlier recension, been YHWH's dwelling, an idea at which a later period must have taken offense.

Or there is the narrative of Abraham's journey down into Egypt in Gen 12:10ff., which does not inform us by what means Pharaoh had actually heard what offenses he [Pharaoh] had committed. Perhaps there was an oracle by the Egyptian magicians,[85] an oracle which a later period, seeing only imposters in the heathen sacerdotal functionaries, had chosen to omit. Genesis 1 is rich in examples of such "obfuscations."

On the strength of this, let us examine Revelation 12. First of all, there are certain cases in which the context has been disturbed. After the Christ child was taken back to God, "a war arose in heaven as they fought against the dragon" (12:7). The context which these two events have is not mentioned in the text. Nevertheless it is practically indispensable, even if no great demands are placed on such a narrative by the larger account, that there would, at one time, have been a real relationship between these two features. Similarly, it would have to be thought that the dragon rushed at the child and that, however, a heavenly lord, in order to shelter the lad, must have confronted the dragon. The outcome of the battle is, then, not only that the lad is saved, but that the dragon is cast out of the heavens, the heavens in which he had hitherto been powerful! A plot development, therefore, is clearly present. — This whole context can still be very well inferred from the text, but only inferred!

So, the dragon has been cast down! Despite that, he now begins his terrifying reign on earth. Why did his defeat, even on earth, not take place immediately through the action of the heavenly "lord" who had cast him down, but rather take place only *after* a more considerable time — after three-and-a-half "times" — through the actions of the Christ? These questions, not necessarily to be raised in the context of the narrative, are all-the-more important since the faithful, languishing under the dominion of the dragon, certainly are on the look-out longingly for heavenly deliverance! Even here the text does not clearly give an answer. Again, however, the solution does not lie far away. The heavenly "lord" is able to cast down the dragon, but not to overcome him on earth. Only the Christ is strong enough to overcome him here at last!

Why, however, the interval of three and a half? Why doesn't the Christ come immediately? Something must have happened between chapters 12 and 19, something through which the Christ obtained the power for the battle with the dragon. Though chapter 12 now describes the Christ as a little child, chapter 19 describes him as a victorious hero! It is, therefore, presumed that he has grown up to adulthood in the interval. The world's deliverance from the dragon can occur only when the Christ has come of age. — It is noteworthy that these interwoven concepts, though they originally were certainly lying at the fundamental base of the narrative, are now neither explicitly articulated nor are they even simply implied!

The woman flees into the wilderness before the dragon (vv. 6, 13). Why into the wilderness? The text allows nothing to be said concerning that! Nevertheless it *is* possible for us to interpret the feature: it is characteristic of the wilderness that it is waterless. The woman, therefore, fled naturally to that place where she felt herself to be safe from her pursuer. We, therefore, conclude that the element proper to the dragon, the element in which he has power, . . . that element is water!

This conceptual association is totally confirmed by the striking narrative which follows, a narrative in which the dragon has spewed forth a river from his mouth, a river which, however, the earth, at just the right moment, has swallowed up! — This ultimately conforms to the fact that the dragon, at Rev 20:3, is bound up in the abyss (i.e., the primordial ocean — תהום [tĕhôm]) and will be sealed up there. The theme must have described how he would be taken back to the place where he belongs. His hegemony over the earth, not to mention in the heavens, was improperly arrogated. — In the background of this theme lies, therefore, the idea that the dragon was a water monster! But this idea no longer is contained in Revelation itself.

A second explanation concerning the nature of the dragon can be inferred from the fact that he cast stars down from the heavens (v. 4). Since his fury is directed only against the stars it must have been based in his very being! He must have been a monster of the darkness, a monster who is hostile to the light! Accordingly, it is only fitting that, according to 20:3, he belongs to the ἄβυσσος [*abyssos*, "abyss"], with which, as is commonly recognized, the very idea of darkness is linked. On the other hand, it is also fitting that the Lord of the heavens, having conquered him, appears on *white* chargers in *white* clothing (19:13f.). *White* is the color of light.

Accordingly, the dragon had originally been a being of the deep, dark waters. This nature of his, however, is not very evident in any clear way from our texts!

The context at the beginning of the chapter is full of holes. The first section of the chapter tells of the futile attempt of the dragon to gobble up the child of the woman. The reason why the dragon makes an attempt on the life of exactly *this* child, however, will neither be explicitly indicated nor clearly presumed. The context, however, can still be reconstructed with security even here. It can be reconstructed from the scattered fragments which are still here. The boy is destined to be, in days to come, *king* of the world (12:5; 16:14; 19:12, 15, 16). Presently, however, the dragon rules far beyond the abyss. He has control over the kings of the whole earth (16:14; 19:19; 20:3). When the child is born, he [the dragon] even has power in the heavens. Accordingly, the dragon does battle with the child, who shall one day thrust him aside from the throne and from the kingdom. This motif is, therefore, required by the context. In the text, however, it is no longer explicitly articulated!

Absolutely no clue is given as to whence the dragon came to know of the significance of the child even before his birth. Such awareness is in no way obvious. Would it not, at least, have been possible for the heavenly ones to conceal their secret intentions? Cf. 1 Cor 2:6-8. There is, therefore, a lacuna here. We lack the introduction which must have told how the dragon happened upon this knowledge!

In the same way, as it appears, the especially painful and extremely protracted labor pains of the woman (v. 2) have no clear impetus within the context. To be sure, their purpose may be divined from what follows. The cries of the child-bearing woman would lure the dragon to come around during her long period of labor. Even given that, however, the reason for this especially painful labor is not explained!

Regardless, if the reader of the narrative is concerned about the fact that the heavenly Lord protects his future king so lightly, that mother and child are abandoned to the murderous designs of the dragon . . . if the reader is concerned about such things, no answer can be found from this text!

The casting down of the stars appears to portray the rule of the dragon in the heavenly sphere. It is, therefore, parallel to the subsequent descriptions of this reign on earth (vv. 13ff.). But even this theme lacks any apparent motivation! Why this assault upon the stars just after the birth of the Christ child? It looks as if this feature originally belonged to another scene in the narrative!

Accordingly, our chapter inserts the following generally quite abruptly: a dragon stands before a parturient woman in order to gobble up her offspring at the very instant of its birth. We discern, incorrectly, who this woman might be! It can be surmised only by a combination of vv. 5 and 17 that the Jewish redaction in this regard had the image of Zion in mind! We hear just as little about who the dragon is. Only at v. 9 does the redactor give any explicit explanation concerning it. The woman is pregnant. We do not hear by whom! The dragon attacks her child. It is not stated why! He then tears the stars from the heavens. We do not learn exactly why this occurs *here!* Mother and child are at that moment in extreme danger. We do not hear how they could have arrived at that state!

This is not the exposition of a well-planned, artfully executed, reasonable narrative! Rather, the present chapter begins with a scene which could not originally have been the first scene in the totality of this narrative. The actual original beginning of the narrative is lost.[86]

Accordingly, we observe in the chapter, almost without exception, that the context of the narrative, although still discernible to a great degree for us, is, however, largely obscured. The one who wrote down this chapter was not able to have a completely clear perception of the whole "living structure" of the narrative himself.

Having made these observations, we notice two further, apparently contradictory, things which appear quite insignificant within the chapter, but which stand adjacent to more highly concrete themes. The child will be snatched away in v. 5. By whom? Or by what means? In what way? The ambiguous use of the passive here is especially noteworthy.

"There arose a battle in heaven that was fought with the dragon" (v 7).[87]

Who was it who took the field against the dragon?
The woman will be nourished "at her place" for three-and-a-half years. By whom? In what way? Again there is the passive (v. 14)! The context does not require the place where the woman would be sheltered in the wilderness to be

designated more specifically. Though this place is mentioned once, it is in a slipshod manner, since hardly anything is known concerning it! What, then, might the obscure "at her place" mean?

There is considerable uncertainty when it is said that the lad has been delivered up to God and to his throne (v. 5). — Is the place a royal throne to which the child will be lifted up? — Or when it says the woman will be given the two wings of the great eagle (v. 14). There is also uncertainty here. Again there is the passive! How should this be conceived? The idea that would adhere most closely to the image, i.e., the idea that the "great eagle" had borne her on its wings . . . that idea has been precluded by the text itself! That text appears, rather, to say that the woman has suddenly been whisked away. That depiction, however, is hardly a more likely one! What is left is some uncertainty.

We have, then, encountered a whole series of passages in which the narrative speaks in a singularly obscure manner! The impression appears to be unavoidable, therefore. . . . the impression that the instances in question were, at one time more *tangible,* and that through the same process by which the whole context came to be obscured, the once bright colors of that context's details also become more pallid!

This impression becomes more certain when it is noted that other highly tangible passages stand closely adjacent to these passages. Those other passages contrast quite remarkably with these obscured ones.

So the appearance of the woman is described. She is clothed with sunshine. She has the moon at her feet. And on her head she has a crown of twelve stars (12:1). This image is not explained by reference to the dream of Joseph (Gen 37:9f.),[88] in which, of course, the sun, the moon, and the twelve stars (i.e., the zodiac) appear as a representation of the family of the patriarch. In point of fact, however, the characteristic feature of our passage, that the stars are the raiment and the adornment of the "woman" . . . that characteristic feature is completely missing from Joseph's dream. We, therefore, acknowledge that this theme [i.e., the way the woman looks] can be interpreted neither from the context nor from the tradition of Israel.

There is, likewise, the red color of the dragon (v. 8), a theme which reappears in a kindred tradition at 17:3. It is not interpreted, however, as just about anything which is red, perhaps blood,[89] or the imperial robe,[90] or the fire,[91] or any similar thing! Since the dragon is the embodiment of the evil disposition, a comparison with Isa 1:18 should be made, Isa 1:18 where red is the color of wickedness. This is a piece of evidence, however, which for its part remains unclear to us!

The dragon pulls down a third of the stars (v. 4). Why a third? The allusion is, perhaps, to an incomprehensible preference of the author for the fraction "one-third." . . . But this is no real explanation. For that, one should focus, however, on this chapter, this chapter in which there is *so* very much of what we do not understand. One should focus on this since its evidence did originally have a positive meaning, and since the present form of the tradition is flawed at those points where the theme appears to make no sense.

Likewise the significance of "the great eagle" (v. 14) is otherwise unknown to us and is not apparent from the chapter itself. And regarding the frogs which, as messengers to the kings of the earth, come forth from the mouth of the dragon (Rev 16:13). . . . the significance of these frogs is similarly unknown to us. That significance is, likewise, not apparent from the chapter itself.

The Christ, when he comes down from heaven for the battle with the dragon, bears the name of the Lord of the world,[92] not on his brow nor on his diadem, but rather on his garment and on his hip (19:16),[93] a highly unusual and, to us above all, a very mysterious image.

All these features have in common the fact that they need clarification since they have few or even *no* parallels through their context! One can explain this phenomenon only in the following manner: we are dealing here with the last remnants of a primordially highly original, but currently partially forgotten, tradition. There is, therefore, a very important question as to whether the author of chapter 12 considered the tradition which he wrote down actually to be valuable, comprehending, therefore, more about its essential nature than we, as twenty-first-century readers, do. Two examples might substantiate this seemingly peculiar assertion.

The place where the dragon assembles his "beings" and where, therefore, the battle also probably takes place . . . that place is called Ἁρμεγεδών [*Harmegedōn*] (16:16). Customary exegesis, as usual, stands here with explanations right at hand. The word, it is said, means "Mount Megiddo."[94] The name is an allusion to the battles of Deborah and of Josiah. Nevertheless, it is debatable whether a "Mount Megiddo" is actually specified. Elsewhere a body of water and a plain are named "Megiddo." The aforesaid battles actually occurred on the *plain* of Megiddo, lying next to the great Mount Carmel. But why is this name not mentioned if it was actually meant? Even if a Mount Megiddo did exist, that would be no reason to disregard the question why the most "highly decisive" battle concerning world dominion should occur specifically at that place. It should, therefore, be assumed that this name is not just an insignificant trifle, but does have a certain significance. What kind of internal relationships can be discerned between those two conflicts from Israel's past and this eschatological battle?[95]

Before turning hastily to just any old explanation, the nature of such a name should first be understood, in order that we might have a basis and a direction for our further investigation. This name — having a Hebrew derivation — was virtually incomprehensible to a Greek reader. It would, therefore, be passed on, in a Greek document, without any interpretation being appended. Let us consider, then, exactly what it signifies. The name, as such, even though its significance was not really understood, was, nevertheless, considered to be a valuable thing worthy of transmission and worthy of awareness. In this example alone one can perceive quite well the characteristic tonalities with which Judaism has narrated its apocalyptic tradition. The impression, reached by means of these revelations of the future, is that we are dealing with infinitely deep "secrets" (cf. 13:18; 17:6f., 9). In these books flow "the springs of understanding, the fountains of wisdom, and the river of knowledge" (4 Ezra 14:47). A "delightful one" (Dan 9:29, 10:11), "more blessed than many" (4 Ezra 10:57), is one to whom these things have been revealed (4 Ezra 10:59). But indeed, whoever receives this revelation is alarmed (2 Bar. 53:12), is greatly amazed (Rev 17:6). It will not be revealed to just anyone, but only to "the wise" (4 Ezra 14:45f.); not to the young, but only to the mature (1 Cor 2:6f.); since only the "knowledgeable" (Dan 12:10), "who have understanding" (Rev 13:18), who have "eyes to see and ears to hear" (Rev 3:13), . . . only these can truly understand it. In this sense, here, standing before exceedingly wonderful mysteries, one does not normally ask that such mysterious wisdom should be prosaically easy to understand! On the contrary, "mysteries are at home in the darkness!" Indeed, for that which the apocalyptic author could have said with clear words, he instead willingly chose the allegorical diction in order to give the materials the form of mysteries. So even things which were not actually understood can be passed on with additional material. It is not to be considered insignificant because of its obscurity. On the contrary, one is inclined for just that reason to suspect the presence within it of a profound divine secret. And one may be otherwise consoled that God, in his time, in the days when all these things have occurred, will reveal their meaning. The knowledge of this particularly dreadful impression in relation to the tradition is most important for the comprehension of a major portion of apocalyptic literature, especially of Revelation.

Consequently it must be considered whether or not Rev 16:16 is communicating the secret and, for the Greeks, totally incomprehensible name *Armageddon*. In line with this the question must be asked whether the writer who put this tradition into a book actually understood the name at all himself! There is reason, on the basis of these questions, to give some consideration to the similar secret apocalyptic names, which remain within the text as quite phantasmal. If the writer knew the meaning of the word, why didn't he communicate it? In those other cases the "interpretation" is included, e.g., in the case of Ἀββαδών ['*Abaddōn*] at Rev 9:11.[96]

As a result, we come to the realization that "Armageddon" is a piece of apocalyptic secret tradition which was *probably* incomprehensible to the apocalyptic writer, and which was *certainly* incomprehensible to the Greek readership of the work. The modern investigator, therefore, has a right, on his part, to attempt an interpretation if he knows the provenance of the tradition, and if, from the context of the original tradition, he can produce an explanation. Should one speculate a priori, one would perhaps adopt a view that the name is connected in some way to the nature of the dragon. The monster assembles his army at the place where it feels most powerful and where Christ, descending from heaven, encounters it, and, having finally defeated it, comes into his kingdom. Even if, however, no explanation can finally be any more than probable for us, it appears best to me to state that fact right at the outset, and then to examine this baffling enigma more closely, under the assumption that a totally unsubstantiated "explanation" can be made more secure with just about anything at all.

The result produced by an investigation of the mysterious number "three and a half" (Rev 12:14, 16) is quite similar. Whence does it come? The chorus of exegetes replies, "From Daniel!"[97] And what does it mean? The New Testament scholar replies: "'Three and a half' would, as 'the broken seven,' be the unlucky number!" The chilling tone of the designation "broken seven" appears to have hypnotized scholars to such a degree that they have not recognized that this designation actually symbolizes a very common thing — "broken" means "divided." The word "fraction" comes to mind. Is it quite harmless? Or is it actually a very terrifying thing to divide the number "seven" in half?[98]

In Old Testament study it is customary to interpret this number, which in Daniel designates the sacrilegious hegemony of the eleventh horn, . . . to interpret it "contemporaneously," i.e., that the religious persecution under Antiochus lasted this long (three-and-a-half years). A great number of estimates have been advanced. None of them, however, has been successful in actually detecting, in an historical context, the number three and a half![99] — All these attempts have been frustrated because they started in the wrong place!

The assumption of these calculations, i.e., that this number is a "contemporaneous" one, is, according to the context itself, clearly in error! It is the "number" for the oppression of the community and for the attacks against the religion. When these have run their course, the judgment follows immediately, the judgment in which the hegemony of Antiochus and the kingdom of *Yāwān* (מַלְכוּת יָוָן], *malkût yāwān*]; Dan 11:2) will be destroyed. And their power over the earth will come unto the holy ones (Dan 7:25ff.). Accordingly, only the starting point of this number is to be fixed historically. It is the beginning of the religious distress under Antiochus. The end point, however, still lies in the future, which is the beginning of the final, blessed time (Dan 9:26; 10:14), when the deceased arise from the dead (Dan 12:1f.). The number three and a half was, therefore, held out as a consolation for those who were contemporary with the book of Daniel. The final affliction will not endure after God's countermeasures. Since the beginning had already been specified, the reader would calculate how much longer the end would be delayed. The modern scholar, however, who would work out this number "contemporaneously," has not understood the nature of the number itself and the singular pathos with which it has been expressed in Daniel (cf. Dan 12:5ff.).

Another explanation of the mysterious number is not to be seen in its entirety, perhaps, from the context of Daniel. From Daniel it would not be proper to say that this number expresses the duration of the final rule of the wicked, a rule which would immediately precede the kingdom of God.[100] Why the "evil one" should endure for three-and-a-half "times"[101] is totally inexplicable from Daniel.

Even though the author of Daniel himself had faith in this number, it is not to be assumed that he has arbitrarily invented it. The number three and a half would have already been a tradition even for him. Somewhere, in some context, the number must have had a positive sense. It is important to seek out that context.

In Rev 12:14 the number occurs in a particular context. The woman will be preserved for just that long. On the other hand, the dragon rules for just that long (Rev 13:5). The length of this rule, however — as we have seen[102] — is, at the same time, the period in which the Christ grows up to adulthood. At the birth of the Christ the terrifying rule of the dragon on earth had already begun (Rev 12:12). On the day he attains adulthood, i.e., on the first day on which he can help, . . . on that day the dragon is annihilated. We may, then, expect that God wanted, even a little bit, to provide help, just as humanity wanted to receive it. According to the explanation appended in the hymn at 12:12, this "brief time" is even acknowledged by the dragon. Now it is, at first, unclear to us from the context why this period of Christ's maturation is exactly "three and a half." But remember just how many dark, obscure and, therefore, certainly ancient features we have already found in the tradition. We have, therefore, no reason to disregard in any way that which we see, and to assume that a theme has been arbitrarily inserted from Daniel into this altogether remarkably well-preserved tradition. It must be added that the calculation of twelve-hundred-sixty days put forward in Rev 12:6 is in agreement with none of the Danielic calculations. It therefore could not have been copied from Daniel.

In line with this it is to be assumed that this mysterious number, as well as the name *Armageddon,* originally belonged to the tradition of Revelation 12, and, in that very tradition, originally stood in a substantial, but presently obscured, context. Again it is highly improbable that the writer of Revelation would have understood the original meaning of these features. A resolution of the mystery can be revealed only if the origin of the whole tradition is known, and if it is understood for which heavenly form it is characteristic that it "matures" in three-and-a-half years.

So the chapter itself bears all the traces on the basis of which the tradition is to be discerned in a way which is distinct from the work which is specifically attributable to the author.

A demonstration that Revelation 12 contains tradition must move beyond the allusions to that traditional material and the materials borrowed from it. Such allusions are:

- In Daniel, the number three and a half. The tradition is communicated in the book of Daniel without context. Revelation 12, however, transmits it within a specific context. It follows, therefore, that Daniel had employed a tradition to which our chapter is connected.
- Furthermore, it has been demonstrated above[103] that the casting down of the stars (Dan 8:10) is extremely incredible. Revelation 12:2, however, is related quite vividly. Daniel, therefore, is dependent at this point as well on the tradition of Revelation.

If the Christ of Revelation 12 were to be given a name he would be called "son of the woman." The Christ bears that name at *1 Enoch* 62:5. It is a name which, in any event, is not borrowed from Gen 3:15 — according to which he should be called "seed of a woman."

Jewish eschatology calls the tribulations which precede the end "messianic woes." The representation of woes as sorrows (sorrows which will change into joy; John 16:20f.) is clear. With the expression "messianic woes," however, it remains unclear who is being presented as the "child bearer." It must be assumed, therefore, that the end was not depicted ad hoc, but rather was taken from another context and only later was applied to the eschatological afflictions. Revelation 12, where the woes into which the Christ will be born play a significant role, . . . Revelation 12 offers a context, a context which has there been applied to the explication of the expression "messianic woes."

Eph 4:13 is looked upon as a goal for the Christian, i.e., to attain εἰς ἄνδρα τέλειον, εἰς μέτρον ἡλικίας τοῦ τεληρώματως τοῦ Χριστοῦ [*eis andra teleion, eis metron hēlikias tou telērōmatos tou Christou*, "to human maturity, to the measure of the full humanity of the Christ"]. This is parallel to the sayings "when the Christian rises from the dead with Christ and ascends with Christ" (Eph

2:5f.); when they "are circumcised with him, buried with him" (Gal 2:11f.). Such expressions about Christians consider Christ's resurrection, ascension, circumcision, and burial as starting points for speculation. We would conclude from such passages that such things had been explained by Christ himself, even if we have no further report concerning them. Likewise, a saying like Eph 4:13 would have been considered only if a teaching about the ἡλικία [hēlikia, "maturity"] of Christ himself had already been given. The ἡλικία [hēlikia, "maturity"] of Christ must have played a major role in the foundational tradition of Revelation 12.

Accordingly, one perceives, by many clues, that the tradition of Revelation 12 had at one time been "popular." Apocalyptic terminology like "messianic woes," "woman's son," . . . such terminology arose out of this popularity. Eschatological speculations concerning when the end of the world would come have been encouraged by that popular terminology. The answer to such questions has been drawn from our tradition. When the "three and a half" have come to pass, the number will be calculated according to that reality. Even the speculation of Eph 4:13, as totally distinctive as it is, has this eschatological interest in the ἡλικία [hēlikia, "maturity"] of Christ as its starting point.

Saying this, however, the chapter is still by no means explained. Rather, its exegesis is only pushed back a bit. From the contention that a portion of it is tradition, it only follows, in regard to its exegesis, that it is not to be understood from the author's conceptual framework, but rather from the conceptual framework of a period which preceded him. So the question now comes to this: "Out of which period is Revelation 12 to be interpreted?" To answer this question it is first necessary, insofar as it is still possible, to reconstruct the original form of the tradition!

We have observed in the preceding investigation the juxtaposition of highly tangible and quite-pallid features. We have perceived in the former the well-preserved remains of the ancient tradition. We may assume as a given the fact that the original recension — like all primitive things — had a unified style. It follows, therefore, that we ourselves have to think about this by way of the concrete (i.e., tangible) features.

Of what kind are these tangible features? For all of them there is, characteristically, a definite fiery coloration, the symptom of a passionately agitated imagination. Submitting ourselves to these aesthetic impressions and asking, further, whence analogies to these features are to be sought, the answer must be, "In the mythology."

The dragon who wants to gobble up the divine child, who casts down stars from the heavens with his tail, who spews forth a river from his craw, a river which the mouth of the earth then guzzles down; the frogs which come forth from the craw of the monster in order to proclaim a message; the great eagle; the heavenly army on white chargers; the name "Lord of the world" on the hip and robe of the divine hero; the sealing of the dragon in the abyss . . . and everything else which is depicted in this narrative. . . . all of this bears an unequivocally mythological character. Even the woman, in accordance with her remarkable insignias, appears as a heavenly goddess. We must seek out parallels to these forms in cultic depictions of such goddesses.[104]

Now if we have reason to consider the original form of the features which are no longer clear to us in regard to type, we must assert that the narrative was originally even more colorfully mythological than it presently is. The currently obscured relationships and faded individual features were originally of a more mythological nature. It is precisely in this, their nature, that we now also detect the reason why they are preserved for us in such attenuated states.

We come to the same conclusion when we observe every feature preserved, or even only half-preserved, in the tradition before us. First of all, there are those features which, as we have seen in the preceding discussion, are currently omitted, or — with a greater or lesser degree of probability — have to be restored because of the context.

Though the dragon is a monster of the darkness, a light-sensitive water animal, he does have claims to supremacy on earth as well as supremacy in heaven. This idea is well known to us from Near Eastern mythology. It is totally mythological when the heavenly figures are in no way powerful against him. At the beginning of the narrative they are not even secure against the dragon when they are in heaven. They abandon their future king to the attacks of the enemy, and he will be rescued only through a mediation. The dragon can even attempt to trail the lad right up to the point of his rescue. And even after they have successfully cast the dragon down from heaven, the heavenly beings are unable to break his dominion on the earth.

The tradition of Christ speaks in the same timbre: He is merely born — no differently than any other child — weak and helpless! He requires a certain time for growth, a time which must simply be awaited in patience, just as in the case of all other children, human or divine. The account of the flight of the woman was expressed through an oracular saying. The birth of the child is especially painful — perhaps because of a curse which lay upon the mother. It might even be supposed that the original recension of the tradition spoke not only of his divine mother but also of his divine father.[105]

Likewise, the presently obscured features are to be considered mythological. The child will be saved, then defended. The dragon will be cast down. The child's mother will be cared for by heavenly beings.[106] One of them is named. This is "the great eagle." The places where the Christ is born and to which the woman flees are, likewise, mythological places, as in the only named place, *Armageddon.*

All of these features are of a mythological nature. The basis of their elimination or adumbration is quite clear. That reason is the timidity of monotheistic Judaism in the face of mythology.

We see the same motif at work in another situation. The flight and the rescue of the woman is reported twice in chapter 12. It is reported, in all brevity, in v. 6, before the fall of the dragon. Then in vv. 13-16, after the fall of the dragon, it is reported in greater breadth. Now it is at least possible, from the beginning, that the same event was narrated twice in a unified report. The placing of a feature in a context is not completely insignificant, though the most appealing thing about a good ancient narrative is that it shows just how one thing has been derived from the other.

The context, however, makes clear that the second account was the more original one. The battle with the dragon in v. 7 — as we have seen above — had, in the presumed mythic tradition, become the direct continuation of the narrative about the escape of the lad. We therefore clearly recover for the whole an intensification of the rage of the dragon. His real adversary is the lad who will, someday, be dangerous to him. He [the dragon] wishes to gobble the lad at his birth. Accordingly, he attacks him as he arrives (Rev 12:4). Since, moreover, the lad is at that moment snatched out of the dragon's control, the dragon, in a blind rage, turns against the mother, even though *she* does not pose any real threat to him. When this woman is also rescued, however, he simply battles those who remain, the children of the woman, children who are perfectly harmless to him.

Accordingly, the second report is the more original one. Consideration of its stylistic nature testifies in favor of this conclusion. The first report, v. 6, is more detailed and has many more mythological features.

Comprehension of the reason for this remarkable repetition is thereby produced. Whoever added v. 6 would have culminated the whole piece with it. In the total narrative v. 6 arrives at the same point as v. 16. The one who added it, therefore, abridged not only the mythological narrative of the woman's flight, but at the same time left out the whole narrative concerning the fall of the dragon, a narrative which, similarly, bears a mythological character. For him it seemed to be enough simply to have told about the rescue of the child and of his mother. That was all he believed was necessary.

We have in our present text, therefore, two variants: v. 6 and vv. 7-16.[107] Of these the first has considerably abridged the narrative by reason of anxiety in the face of mythological features. That two variants are transmitted side-by-side in the text is not a remarkable occurrence at all. In the Old Testament, finding two versions of the same saying in close proximity to each other is not all that rare. In the LXX finding two or more translations of the same Hebrew text is also not uncommon. Of greater scope, for example, are the narrative variants in Genesis, the double tradition concerning Saul's selection as king, and the like.

Therefore Revelation 12 is a tradition of mythological style. Judaism, however, has definitely received and recast all sorts of mythological traditions from other peoples. It has not, however, produced independent myths. Furthermore, as we have seen,[108] the chapter itself does not bear the marks of an originally produced piece of work, but rather those of very faded tradition. Accordingly, as soon as the mythological character of the tradition is established, the extra-Judaic origin of the same becomes a "given."

Now there is, certainly, a series of details in the chapter which are of definite Jewish origin. Let's investigate which ones they are, and, having done that, let's figure out where they stand in relation to the mythological tradition.

There are certain characters in the account who are indicative of the Jewish myth. The divine child is the Christ, [the Messiah]. This is said clearly by a citation of Psalm 29 at Rev 12:5 and 19:15. Details from the description of the vision at 19:11ff. stem from the christological dogma of Judaism, e.g., the blood-stained robe of v. 13.[109]

At Rev 12:9 and 20:2, the dragon is designated as the so-called "Devil and Satan" (cf. Rev 12:12). Rev 12:10b designates him with another name, κατήγωρ [*katēgōr*], "the one who accuses the pious ones of God."

Judaism's interpretation definitely comes to the fore when seven heads (with seven crowns on them) and ten horns are ascribed to the dragon. This feature is to be understood according to Dan 7:6ff. and Rev 13:1, where the heads[110] or the horns[111] signify kings. That the seven heads here stand for seven kings is explicitly indicated by the fact that the seven heads bear seven crowns.[112] Accordingly, the dragon is understood here as a personification of the empire over which seven kings shall rule.[113]

The celestial army which defends the heavenly lad is said to be "Michael and his angels" (Rev 12:7). The "remaining ones of her seed" will be explained as the pious Jews by means of the inserted notation "who keep God's law" (Rev 12:17).

The binding of the dragon at the conclusion of the narrative is accomplished by an angel who comes down[114] from heaven.[115]

The Jewish comprehension of particular features of the chapter is also revealed by this interpretation of the characters. Accordingly, the conquest of the dragon by the young heavenly hero is understood as the conquest of the devil by the Christ. The continuation of the mythological tradition takes the form, in

Judaism, of the thousand-year hegemony of the Christ, the final attack by Gog and Magog, and so on, features which are eschatological traditions originally independent of the myth. The first verses of chapter 12 describe, according to a Jewish understanding of course, the birth of the Christ, a birth which precedes the persecution of the Jews by the empire (Rev 12:17). Apparently the Jewish explanation for the downfall of the dragon was expressed both as the defeat of the devil, who had disputed with God for power in heaven (v. 10a), and as the casting away of the accuser from the divine presence (v. 10b). It was also, however, described as the beginning of the woes of those who dwell on earth (v. 12).

With this, however, the totality of the material has not yet been totally absorbed into a Jewish interpretation. Above all, explicit explanations of the woman and of those things which are told about her flight are both lacking. The woman is usually interpreted as the heavenly Zion. It is, however, not even considered how Judaism, if it actually explained this entity at all, might have understood it differently. Even recognizing this interpretive lacuna, the explanation is afflicted with still more major difficulties.

Judaism has believed in the city of Zion in the heavens as an actual fact. As "a woman," however, Zion is presented allegorically.[116] This allegorical form, however, has a son, which must represent the Christ, therefore an actual person. So, specifically in that which follows, where the fates of the mother and the child are blurred together, a peculiar intermingling of allegory and realism occurs . . . an intermingling which, insofar as it might be generally accepted, can, in any case, no longer be understood as the original viewpoint of the author.[117] Harnack[118] has seen this difficulty for the interpretation of a *Christian* origin for the book of Revelation, though he has not recognized that it is, likewise, negatively applicable to his own viewpoint of its *Jewish* origin.

In the same way, the difficulty which is totally insurmountable for the "Christian" interpretation,[119] the problem of what the persecution of the "remnant" after the flight of the woman portends . . . this difficulty points to the Jewish background of the tradition as well.[120] If this flight would be more than an empty phantasmagoria — which may quite truly be anticipated — it could indicate nothing other than the heavenly image of a persecution of Israel. On the other hand, the "remnant" must also be the Jews. It then, however, would clearly be speaking twice — although under different forms — of the persecution of God's people.

One finds oneself entangled in just such difficulties when one does not adhere strongly to the methodology,[121] when one gives interpretations only at those points where either they exist in the very nature of the thing or they have been expressly indicated by the author. Against this, however, it must be said that the author has probably not explicated the woman, and certainly not her flight. Why? Because he could not explain it! It is hardly possible to say what he was thinking in regard to the persecution and rescue of the child. A passage which is intended allegorically from the beginning must quite clearly present the interpretation for which it is intended. It must present it in all its major features. That is not the case here. It follows, therefore, that the "Jewish allegorical explication," by which the entire thing *cannot* be understood, does not really originally belong to our tradition but has only come into it at a later time.

We come to the same conclusion when attention is paid to the relationship of the traditional interpretations to one another and to the context of the tradition. The exacting qualification, "who shall lead all people with a rod of iron" (Rev 12:5), like the other qualification, "who keep the laws of God" (Rev 12:17), does not belong to the context of the whole thing. Because of this, however, the dragon persecutes the child so that it might cast him down. And it harasses his kindred because of uncontrollable anger at the fact that they are the child's brethren. "Michael and his angels" (Rev 12:7), considered literarily, turn out to be a later addition as well.[122]

The two explanations which are given for the dragon — Satan and κατήγωρ [*katēgōr*, "accuser"], on the one hand; and the empire, Rome,[123] on the other — certainly do not so preclude each other that they, perhaps, must stem from different hands. It is not quite impossible, from the Jewish point of view, to identify the "angel of the abyss" with the angel of Rome.[124] On the contrary, however, the Jewish interpreter with this association believed himself to have identified the actual essence of Rome. On the other hand, the interpreter was able to apply this dual interpretation not to the general details, but rather to a diversity of individual features, here to the devil, there to Rome. The war of the dragon against the "remnant" is, thus, understood as the war of Rome against the Jews. The being whose fall Rev 12:10-12 celebrates, however, is certainly not Rome.

Two explanations have been put forward for the fall of the dragon as well. In Rev 12:10a and 12:12 the dragon is the mighty adversary of God, . . . the adversary who has, until now, brought the power of God itself into question in heaven. The consequence of his fall is that now God becomes *THE* power! In comparison, in Rev 12:10b the dragon is the κατήγωρ [*katēgōr*, "accuser"] who stands accused before the throne of God and whose fall has the consequence that God now is no longer angry. It is possible that v. 10b is a Jewish gloss by a second hand, but this is not really necessary. Just a tiny bit of intricacy may surely be credited to the person who elsewhere has identified Rome and the devil!

This is, however, no longer an organic interpretation, as we would expect in an allegory fabricated by the author, . . . an interpretation in which, of course, the same elements always designate exactly the same things. It is quite clear that the single major passage which the Jewish redactor has inserted into the tradition is to be perceived as an addition. This is the hymn concerning the downfall of the dragon (Rev 12:10-12). This hymn speaks of the power which the Christ has now received. The Christ, however, is still a lad at this point in the narrative, a lad who still cannot exercise any power, and a lad whose kingdom, which he will assume in the future as an adult, will be established not at the downfall of the dragon, but rather at his own victory over the monster. The hymn further interprets the fall of the dragon as the departure of the κατήγωρ [*katēgōr,* "accuser"]. But thereby two concepts are compared to each other, concepts which are quite dissimilar in regard to their actual natures:[125] the dragon was mighty in heaven because of the power of his immense body. — It was as an example of such power that he cast down the stars from the heavens with his tail. The κατήγωρ [*katēgōr,* "accuser"], however, was mighty since he denounced the pious before God with virulent speech. Accordingly κατήγωρ [*katēgōr,* "accuser"] and dragon are two completely different figures: the former is a monster with jaws and a tail, with horns and heads; the latter, however, is a malicious spirit who stands beside other angels before the throne of God.[126]

So the result is that the Jewish interpretive materials do not belong to the original context, but have only been added later on. At the same time we see the manner in which Judaism had taken hold of such materials. The modern effort to interpret every conceivable thing within such material in an identical way[127] . . . such an effort is therefore ignorant! One interprets what one understands. The remainder, which for that reason alone cannot be held as valueless, one allows to stand quietly just as it is.[128] And one interprets on a case-by-case basis, fairly unconcerned about the context of the interpretation and of the material.

Accordingly, the result is this: Revelation 12 is a myth which originated outside of Judaism, but which was accepted by Judaism.

4. Babylonian Materials in Later Judaism

At this point, then, the question presses itself upon us: Among which people was this myth originally at home?

In regard to such an investigation the greatest of prudence is necessary. It would not be enough to pick out any old myth, from any old mythology which is known to us . . . a myth which had somewhat greater or lesser similarities to Revelation 12, . . . to pick out such a myth and then to declare it to be the original of Revelation 12. Rather, a methodical inquiry into the acceptance of a traditional piece from a foreign religion may be successfully accomplished only if it can, possibly, produce the same results for traditions similar to Judaism, and especially to apocalyptic Judaism. Furthermore, such an inquiry may be carried through successfully only if it is in the position to understand the influence of that foreign religion on Judaism historically.

Dieterich[1] has drawn attention to the similarity of Revelation 12 to the Greek myth of Apollo's birth.[2] This myth had been demonstrably well known in Asia Minor and most definitely in Ephesus in the second century C.E. The contention of Dieterich is based on the idea that the Hellenistic-Christian author, writing in Ephesus, knew the Leto-Apollo myth, and that he explicated the wonderful lad from Bethlehem in a manner which was consistent with that myth.

The similarity which was established by Dieterich is undoubtedly quite striking. It had even been noted by the author of these lines prior to his reading of *Abraxas*. To me as well it appears unquestionable that the congruity of the two myths cannot be accidental, but is, rather, clearly established in an *historical* context. Nevertheless, I would consider the explanation produced by Dieterich to be a not insignificant mistake!

The basic assumptions from which Dieterich proceeds are erroneous. One may not speak of a "Hellenistic-Christian"[3] as the author of the passage [Revelation 12]. That chapter is rather, as we have seen, of Jewish, not Christian,[4] origin. It does not stem from the Diaspora, but from Palestine. And finally, it is not the work of a single man, but is the codification of a tradition. Accordingly, one should not imagine that an individual person in second-century-C.E. Asia Minor was responsible for the myth. Rather, the idea must be accepted that the Greek myth, in approximately the last century B.C.E., had made its way into Palestine.

Perhaps Dieterich would consider this hypothesis. He does find Greek influence even in the book of 1 Enoch.[5] Such speculation, however, stands in the face of the most significant misgivings. It is improbable to the highest degree that Palestinian apocalyptic Judaism accepted a Greek myth. Palestinian Judaism would have been much less open to Greek attitudes than the Judaism of the Diaspora. It therefore must have defended its religion to the death! Even then, however, when it was influenced by Greek culture, it was not the religion but rather the philosophy of the Greeks which it could not quite resist. Palestinian Judaism disdained the gods of יָוָן [yāwān, Ionia/Greece] even more than it had accepted its myths.[6] It was, at the very least, however, a tendency of Palestinian Judaism (which had produced books like 1 Enoch, and from which the matrix of Revelation arose) to imitate in form the Greek divine narratives. Read the words of these apocalypses concerning idolatry. The heathen gods are nothing but gold and silver, wood and stone; or they are evil demons (Rev 9:20; 1 Enoch 99:7). Woe to those who despise the eternal heritage of the ancestors and affix their souls onto idols! They have no part in the coming "peace" (1 Enoch 99:14). The dogs, the poisoners, the fornicators, the murderers, the idolaters, and all those who love falsehood and act out of it, . . . all of them will remain outside (Rev 22:15; cf. 21:8). Woe to those who either eat from the meat sacrificed to idols or who entice people to do so (Rev 2:20). — This Judaism is, consequently, quite unsyncretistically disposed. On the contrary, the warning goes forth even to the heathens themselves: "Fear God alone!" (Rev 14:7-11). — That the very people who speak of the idols in this way were willing, at the same time, to take on heathen myths, myths of which they knew the heathen origin — such a thing must be held as totally unthinkable![7]

Dieterich[8] has attempted to defend himself against the accusation that his identification of Revelation 12 and the Apollo myth is "methodically wild."[9] He will not, however, be absolved from the accusation of being, to some degree, religio-historically unsystematic. Theologians who repeat Dieterich's theory, however, should first reflect more carefully on the character of Revelation.

Even in detail Dieterich has frequently fallen far short of understanding

Revelation 12. He had sought to bring atmosphere and life into the "mystical confusion"[10] of the chapter. He has, however, arranged it according to the model of the Leto myth. Accordingly, he has gone to work quite energetically by means of transpositions,[11] omissions,[12] and new interpretations.[13] This investigation, which in reality is a mishandling of Revelation, teaches us that Revelation 12 and the Apollo myth have major differences, differences which should not be overlooked. They are distinct mythic recensions.

The similarity of the two things cannot be denied by these observations, and Dieterich's merit for having pointed out this concurrence for the first time is not to be diminished. The question which he has raised, but which he has answered far too readily, continues to persist. This is not the place to resolve the problem, which can be discussed only in another context. Wheresoever I choose to work out a solution thereto, experts will easily recognize it.[14]

We would like to avoid such erroneous methods. It is, therefore, necessary for us to look for similar materials in the apocalyptic literature. We have found a peculiarly fantastic, grotesque attitude to be characteristic of Revelation 12. A similar, common coloration confronts us in a not insignificant number of passages of that total work. In those passages the heavens and the earth are filled with fantastic forms. The gateway to the abyss is opened, and from its vapors come forth strange locusts. There are steeds having human faces and women's hair, as well as the fangs of lions and the tails of scorpions (Rev 9:1-12). Or a terrifying force of cavalry storms forth against humanity from the Euphrates River! The horses have fire-breathing lion heads, and their tails run out to serpent heads (Rev 9:13-21). From the heavens falls a fiery mountain which changes a third of the sea — changes it into blood; . . . or what falls is a burning star, a burning star which changes a third of the rivers — changes them into gall (Rev 8:8-9 and 8:10-11).

An eagle flies in the middle of the heavens and cries out with a voice, saying "Woe" over humanity! From the depths of the sea arises a being of wonderful form and wonderful destiny. One of its heads is smitten, but the mortal wound has been healed (Rev 13:1-3). There is another being with the horns of a lamb and which speaks like a dragon. This being entices the whole world, by powerful signs, to worship an image of the first beast and to be marked with his seal on their hands and brows (Rev 13:11-17). Two remarkable witnesses are at war with the beast [Rev 13:3-7]. They are killed, but after three-and-a-half days they ascend "on the cloud" into the heavens [Rev 11:8-12].

The beast, by means of the frogs which he sends out as messengers, assembles the kings of the world (Rev 16:12-16). They end up in the "lake of fire" (Rev 19:20), in which the impious, including death and the devil, perish (Rev 20:14f.). Heaven, however, opens up, and a wonderful city descends to the earth.

This city is shaped like — a cube. Its walls are made of jasper. The city itself is made of pure gold. The foundations of the walls are precious gemstones. The gates are pearls. A river of the water of life is in the middle of its main street. Here and there throughout it are trees of life (Rev 21:9–22:5).

The appearance of God in heaven is described in much the same style. He himself resembles jasper and chalcedony. Before his throne are seven flaming torches, twenty-four attendants, and wonderful winged beings (Revelation 4). So it goes throughout the whole of the book of Revelation.

Truly to grasp the vivid impact of this material one need compare it to other products of late Judaism, perhaps Jesus ben Sirach or the *Psalms of Solomon*. While everything in those texts, despite their poetic form, is actually simply prosaic, here the fiery spirit of an almost overheated imagination is wafting toward us. And while there we comprehend the major portion of the text without great effort, here we encounter a wealth of things which are comprehensible to us neither from the context nor from the Old Testament. This peculiar material is that which grants the book of Revelation its peculiarly unique colors. Exegetes have, here and there, taken great pains to interpret this. The comprehension of the material and the explanation of its development are the real "problems" of the book of Revelation, problems which, until now, have not been solved. Indeed — in spite of all the scholarly labor — the book has still not really been scrutinized methodically!

Chapter 12 also belongs to these materials, not just because of its whole outlook. Parallels are encountered between this chapter and certain others.[15] An answer to the question of the origin of chapter 12 can be found only in its relationship with the whole of this apocalyptic material. If we move back a bit from the Revelation of John in order to survey similar material, *1 Enoch* immediately comes into view. *There* the great mysteries of the creation are described. The gateway to the underworld is in the distant West, where the great rivers flow into the deep (*1 Enoch* 17). *There* lies the place of the dead, where righteous ones and sinners are kept separate as they await the universal judgment (*1 Enoch* 22:1-14). The seven mountains (made of precious stones) are in the south, where stands the throne of God, a throne which is made out of sapphire (*1 Enoch* 18:6-8). Or in the South there is also the deep chasm beyond the heavens and the earth, where the seven disobedient stars are bound, until the year of mystery, the year when their offense will be expiated (*1 Enoch* 18:11-16). In the South there is also the horrible place full of blazing fire, the prison of the rebellious angels (*1 Enoch* 21:7-10). Elsewhere the paradise lies near seven magnificent mountains. In that very place stands the tree of life, the fragrance of which makes its way into the very bones (*1 Enoch* 24–25 and 32). The secrets of the stars will be further disclosed, how they come out of the heavenly gates and enter into those which lie opposite to them (*1 Enoch* 33–36). Then there are the secrets of the hail, the frost, the rain, the dew, the snow, and the wind (*1 Enoch* 34–35 and 41). The dwelling place of God in heaven is described similarly to the description found in Revelation 14. Events from primal time are narrated, especially that of Genesis 6, but in a much more elaborate and highly fantastic form (*1 Enoch* 6ff.). Also, we hear how at one time the evil *Kasb'el* had stolen from the holy Michael the ineffable name of God, the name through which the heavens and the earth were created (*1 Enoch* 69:13-23). In addition, there are numerous wonderful revelations concerning the future when the son of the woman will be sitting on the throne of his authority and all will be right with the world (*1 Enoch* 62). On top of that, there is an abundance of angelic names, and much more. Whoever peruses this book for the first time regards everything herein as so remarkably incomprehensible that it is as if he has just entered into a new world!

Enoch may, in many things, be quite different from Revelation. In terms of content, in *1 Enoch* cosmological things predominate, while in Revelation, eschatological things. In terms of form, in *1 Enoch* an ultimately organized layout is lacking. The work is a total pandemonium of heterogeneous traditions. With all the differences, however, the two books do belong together. Why? Because of their coloration. Even in details they agree: Leviathan appears at the end time in *1 Enoch* 60, just as in Revelation 11, 12, and 13 the evil animals of the deep appear. The lake of fire in Revelation 19–20 is like the place of judgment in *1 Enoch* 21, and so on.

How is the emergence of such a remarkable vision to be understood? The explanation which up to this point has encountered us in regard to Revelation, according to which imaginatively expansive reconstructions of biblical traditions are put forward . . . such an explanation must also be attempted in regard to *1 Enoch*.[16] Such an attempt might have encountered "the accurate facts" in detail, but, as in the case of Revelation, the attempt is not really comprehensive enough to comprehend the whole.[17] At a great many points it is apparent, from the peculiar fragments and mysterious style in which these things are discussed, that in *1 Enoch* (as in Revelation) it is a question of traditions which the author himself no longer actually understood.[18]

Going even further back, we come to Daniel, a book in which similar dream images, though even less clearly and thoroughly allegorized, present themselves: an immense figure of gold, silver, iron, bronze, and clay, which will be dashed to pieces by a stone (without human hands) (Daniel 2); a tree which grows up from the center of the earth, even as far as heaven (Daniel 4); a holy one cuts it down and scatters its fruit, but its root remains firmly in the earth in bands of iron and bronze (Daniel 4); then the wonderful animals of the waters, who rule on earth and also slander God (Daniel 7); a ram and a billy goat, who battle each other for world dominion (Daniel 8).

Even here, despite the allegory which was attached later, it is quite clear that this material formerly had an independent existence.[19] Because of its nature, it is related to 1 Enoch and Revelation. To some degree the same things may be traced through all three books. As examples I take, in turn, the "blazing fire" as a place of torment (Dan 7:11), and the beings which ascend from the sea as well.

We have also become aware of a large group of similar materials from an even earlier period in the book of the prophet Zechariah, materials with which we have already dealt above.[20]

We find, then, a relationship among Zechariah, Daniel, 1 Enoch, and Revelation. The kinship of these writings has long been recognized, and they are, therefore, designated by the common named "apocalypse." We cannot rightly be said, however, to know exactly what an "apocalyptic" writing was. The peculiarity of these "apocalypses"[21] lies in the fact that they all share in a very distinctive essence. Characteristic of the essence is patterning according to an imaginative viewpoint which is quite different from other viewpoints in the Old Testament. As regards the content, it consists of cosmological and eschatological materials. Especially noteworthy in this regard are the angelological speculations. The literary framework in which this material is transmitted is laid out in the vision. — This is not the place to assess the importance of this material for the history of Judaism or for primitive Christianity.[22] The time for that has also probably not yet arrived. The admonition, however, is now certainly warranted . . . the admonition not to assess this material too insignificantly, no matter how peculiar it may seem to us, no matter in how intricate a form it may have come down to us. Both the belief in heaven and hell as places of reward and punishment after death, and the belief in the resurrection, therefore, belong to this material.[23]

Whence do these remarkable traditions arise? The answer to this question is the most important thing incumbent upon Old Testament, as well as New Testament, research! We can confidently say that these traditions do not arise from Judaism! That which we have already seen in regard to Zechariah and Revelation 12 may be generalized for the other comparable materials. We are able to see a few of the ways of Judaism out of which the Old Testament arose: The Psalms of Solomon offer the sequel to the canonical Psalms poetry. Jesus ben Sirach is linked to Proverbs. The legalistic orientation is along the lines of the priestly composition ["P"]. But the apocalyptic material is the continuation of prophecy only in part. Traditions such as those of the two witnesses, of the cavalry force, of the locusts (all from Revelation), and the cosmological theories (of *1 Enoch*) do not come from the Old Testament. On the other hand, however, Judaism certainly did not fabricate it on its own. This is also demonstrated by something which, in such an eventuality, can generally be trusted: the abrupt form in which these traditions frequently appear, a form which points to a pre-history of the material.

It comes down to this: A mythological background frequently shines through the accounts. We have already seen this in the case of Revelation 12, in the case of certain other traditions of Revelation,[24] and in the case of Zecha-riah.[25] In *1 Enoch* even the untrained eye will discern the mythological material at many places.[26]

We then obtain the following historical picture. We, having generalized from the impression given by P^c, often consider this Judaism as completely iso-lated from all "paganism." After the exile (the longer thereafter the more the following is the case) we see this Judaism giving way to a foreign religion. The foreign material had poured in without stopping, at first allegorized and inter-preted, but then received *just as it was!*

This foreign religion must have been extremely idiosyncratic. It possessed a wonderfully imaginative cosmology and eschatology, material which else-where appears as "secret knowledge." Given that it is remarkable that this self-assured Judaism could actually have taken over so much from a heathen reli-gion, we might, for the explication of this surprising thing, refer to the fact that, as far as I can see, absolutely no divine names are found among the received materials. The Judaism which appropriated all of this, in any case, did not, at the same time, have the desire to fall away from the protection of God. It is, therefore, to be concluded either that in the foreign traditions, even before they were appropriated, no other divine names appeared, or that at least these names were not stripped off when the traditions were appropriated.

Which religion might this have been? We are in no position to answer that question directly. This shows us most clearly how very little we actually know of the spiritual life of the Near East from that period. One would do well to call this depressing fact to mind on occasion.[27]

It is certain, right at the start, that we must not think of anything Greek. It is by now clear that that which is "apocalyptic" was already in evidence by the time of Zechariah, and in certain rudimentary forms even earlier.[28] In addition, there are the many names belonging to the material, names which, in any event, are clearly not of *Greek* origin. In the tradition of Revelation, for example, there is the name *Armageddon!*

There remains, therefore, only something which is Babylonian, or Persian, or both slightly mixed. For both religions the question, because of the condition of our sources,[29] is extremely difficult. It is not the purpose of these lines to settle the question of the collected material with which we are dealing here. This question is, as far as I can see, by no means still under investigation. For our purpose, which is to determine the origin of Revelation 12, it is sufficient simply to establish that a Babylonian origin is probable for some "apocalyptic" traditions.[30]

First there is the question of whether Babylonian influence may be assumed for so late a period. "Is it then generally possible that Babylonian writings and Babylonian culture would have penetrated so strongly at that time?"[31] We may answer this question positively with some confidence! The more Babylonian material has become known to us in the present the more clearly do we, at the same time, see that it was at work right into the very late post-Christian era. Babylonian elements are even found in the Hellenism of the Hellenistic period. Gnosticism, and later Manicheism and Mandaeism, have preserved, to some extent, originally Babylonian materials in rich abundance.[32] Accordingly, if Babylonian material were to be found in late Judaism, it would not be an exceptional and therefore unexpected thing. Instead, it would simply be one link in the great historical chain of Babylonian influence in the ancient Near Eastern world.

Let us begin with speculative ideas concerning the fixed stars and numbers. Let us begin there because those ideas are to be understood most clearly when viewed in relation to the Babylonian sphere. First of all, there are certain major features of the book of Revelation for which the number *seven* is characteristic. There are *seven* spirits before the throne of God (Rev 1:4). *Seven* angels stand before God (Rev 8:2). *Seven* flames of fire burn before the throne. These are the *seven* spirits of God (Rev 4:5). The lamb has *seven* eyes which are the *seven* spirits of God, which are sent out into the whole world (Rev 5:6). The Christ appears in the midst of *seven* golden candles and has *seven* stars in ("on" — Rev 1:20) his hand (Rev 1:16).

It would, then, be desirable, proceeding on the assumption that these things were inventions of the author,[33] to look for individual models from the Old Testament. In regard to the seven spirits the original passage was Isa 11:2.[34] There it is reported: On the root of Jesse shall rest

> the spirit of YHWH
>> a spirit of wisdom and understanding
>> a spirit of counsel and heroism
>> a spirit of knowledge and fear of YHWH.

Here, therefore, the light of the one spirit is depicted in a threefold[35] — if need be, one could say in a sixfold — radiance. It is, however, most certainly not proper to fuse the "radiant beams" together with the "light" itself. Accordingly, there is no report here of *a* sevenfold spirit.[36] *Pss. Sol.* 17:42 and *1 Enoch* 49:3,[37] which use Isaiah 11, have the sevenfold division just as infrequently. Accordingly, the seven spirits are a representation unrelated to Isaiah 11. If, then, this passage has become the *locus classicus* for the "sevenfold spirit of God," it has, for that very reason, been molded by a later significance, in much the same way that Isaiah 7 has become a *locus classicus* for the virgin birth. It is even less likely that Zech 4:10 could be the basis for "the seven spirits."[38] This is so because here "seven lamps" and "seven eyes" of YHWH are mentioned, but not "seven spirits." It is, therefore, apparently more precise to understand the "seven lamps" as a copy of the Old Testament "lamp."[39] If the author, however, had this old symbol in his mind, why then has he altered it and made the originally seven-branched shaft into seven lamps standing next to one another? The possibility must at least be admitted, therefore, that this is not an imitation, but is rather a related tradition!

Only a few Old Testament models are suitable for the whole complex of these related apocalyptic concepts. They are models, however, which are more or less questionable, and are certainly inadequate, in terms of explicating the whole complex. The attempt to explain it from the Old Testament has, therefore, run aground. We conclude that here that again a tradition is to be detected. The apocalyptic writer speaks of "the seven spirits of God" (Rev 1:4; 3:1; 4:5; and 5:6). He speaks of them as something well known to his readers. In the same way he speaks of "the seven angels who stand before God" (Rev 8:2). We hear of these "seven angels" — normally called "archangels" — at other places as well.[40] The "seven lamps" and the "seven stars" are indicative, for the apocalyptist, of the seven communities and their angels. If the seven communities are depicted by the "lamps," it would be possible to represent their angels by the "lights" which are part of those "lamps." These two symbols, however, correspond to each other so little that one must conclude that they predate the Christian interpretation.[41] Another interpretation — of the lampstand, so it seems — is seen when "the seven spirits of God and the seven stars" are dedicated to the Christ (Rev 3:1).

Furthermore, the peculiar relation in which the apocalyptic statements discussed above stand in regard to one another suggests a tradition. The "seven spirits" and the "seven angels" bear the characteristic attribute that "they (are) standing before God."[42] The sense of the word is, according to Luke 1:19 and Tob 12:15, that they have the privilege of being allowed to go directly before the throne of God. All other beings can visit only through the intercession of these angels with the Most High. This is a privilege (modeled after the pattern of earthly kings, by which model only they have the highest official access) . . . a privilege which, by its very nature, is given only to the highest class of angels.[43] These seven "stand before God!" This means that they are the highest class of angels. This interpretation of the attribute is confirmed by the positioning of the seven spirits even before Christ (Rev 1:4) and by the name ἀρχάγγελοι [archangeloi] ("archangels") = שָׂרִים הָרִאשֹׁנִים [śārîm hā-rī'šōnîm = "the head commanders"]. In the rabbinic tradition as well, the seven angels who stand before the countenance of God are the "princes of the angels."[44] The designation "standing before God" is, consequently, of a more limited nature.[45] It therefore follows that the "seven spirits" and the "seven angels" were originally the same thing. The difference in name signifies nothing. The same beings could originally have been called "spirits" because of the "spiritual nature";[46] "angels" because of their subservient status in relation to God. On the other hand, the seven angels appear in Rev 8:2, even after the "seven spirits" have been mentioned, several times, as a *new* (!) feature. The apocalyptist, therefore, had taken no notice of the original identity of the two names. This indicates that we have here two distinct traditions, traditions which are derived from a common stock but which have been split apart in the course of history.

The situation is quite similar in regard to the symbols themselves: the "seven torches," the "seven stars," the "seven lampstands," these originally symbolized collectively the same things: "seven spirits" or "seven angels." This is expressed explicitly in regard to the "seven torches." Even the Christian apocalyptist knew that the "seven lampstands" and the "seven stars" ought to portray the seven angels, that they are a mystery, i.e., that they have a secret (allegorized) meaning (Rev 1:20).[47] According to Rev 3:1, it is to be concluded that the lampstand represents the "seven spirits." As for the "stars," the apocalyptist knows that they must depict the "seven angels" (Rev 1:20). All these symbols are also related by type: luminous bodies must be illustrative of spiritual beings. — Even the equation "seven eyes" ↔ "seven spirits" (Rev 4:5), so peculiar at first glance, can be comprehended by an arrangement of these symbols in relation to other features: *eyes* are mythological forms of stars,[48] and, in what has gone before, *stars* appear to be linked together with spirits. All of these symbols are, therefore, related to one another both in content and in form. Although they take no notice of one another in our apocalypse, it is not precluded, even in the slightest way, that the same ultimate referent can be designated by both *lampstand* and *stars* in the same verse (Rev 1[:20]), or even by *torches* (Rev 4[:5]) and by *eyes* of the lamb (Rev 5[:6]). The *torches* of Rev 4[:5] and the *seven angels* of Rev 8:2 are mentioned in the same way. — It is, consequently, more than probable that the same concept lies behind all the symbols, a concept which has been quite badly obscured, however, in the book of Revelation.

This concept, in order to be sufficient for all these symbols, can be none other than that of the "seven stars." Stars, in antiquity considered to be endowed with a spirit, by some peoples even considered to be deities, are, in Judaism, simply "spirits" or "angels."[49] Their representation through torches or lampstands would be comprehensible as a cultic image. The imagination transfers such symbols, since they are visually observed in the earthly heavens, into the ἄδυτος [*adytos*], "innermost shrine, innermost sanctuary," of the heavens. The mythological viewpoint thinks of stars as the eyes of the deity.[50]

We could have here, then, a fundamental concept from which the origin of the individual names and symbols within Revelation could be understood in the best possible way. A whole series of other considerations speaks to the veracity of this conjecture. The concept of "stars" lies very near to the context of these traditions. One tradition has clearly clung to that ancient concept in its use of the word *stars* (Rev 1:16 and 3:1). The seven lampstands are apparently related to the menorah, the significance of which — as we have seen above (p. 85) — is the depiction of stars. The difference between the Old Testament cultic symbols and those presupposed in the book of Revelation is that in the former, the powers of heaven are understood as a unity, as a structure. In Revelation, however, they are understood as independent entities. At Rev 5:6, the spirits are represented by the eyes of the lamb. An interpretation other than that based generally on the equation "stars = spirits" is really not feasible. Zech 4:10, which Revelation recalls here, clearly speaks of seven "star-spirits" (cf. above, pp. 189f.). It can hardly be believed, however, that the apocalyptist actually still understood the original significance of the equation "eyes = spirits" and the original significance of the Old Testament passage (Zech 1:10).

Concerning the origin of "the seven spirits," then, we must ask whether that origin is actually to be sought in Judaism. That the stars are endowed with life, that they are mighty spirits, that they are the eyes of the deity . . . all of these are concepts which Judaism did not produce but which it accepted. Moreover, we see cultic symbols at work here, cultic symbols which had no place in Jewish worship.

From which religion did Judaism take "the seven astral deities?" In order to answer this question, we must first bring together the material which can be gained by inference from Revelation. The number *seven* is characteristic of these astral deities. This number is maintained in all traditions, apparently because it had a particular significance. At the same time, the context in which these beings are mentioned proves that they must have been gods of the first order in the religion being investigated by us. Judaism, which places them in close proximity to God, thereby confers upon them the highest authority among the angels, and at the same time extols the power of those who are, themselves, at the service of these mighty astral deities. The same idea is conveyed when seven torches burn before the throne, and when Christ appears among the lampstands. It resembles the time when Christ holds the seven stars in his hand (Rev 1:16). This must indicate that he is lord and master even of these seven (Rev 3:1).[51] The repetition of these concepts in the many symbols proves their importance. Once upon a time it was a great thing to maintain the power of God over the seven astral spirits. In the salutation of the document (Rev 1:4) the seven spirits are named even before Christ.

The worship of the stars is characteristic of Babylonian religion. Among the astral deities the planets were the "great gods" of the Chaldeans. The proposed identification of the seven gods with the seven planets is supported by a series of observations. Where Babylonian ideas have generally exercised an influence, we also hear of "Chaldean" astrology, quite often even of the seven stars. This is the case with Orphism, with Gnosticism, with Sabeanism, with Mandaeism, and many others.[52] For Judaism, however, it is expressly reported that the names of the angels had come from בבל [Bābel].[53] The influence of Babylonian astrology can also certainly be discerned in 1 Enoch. The twelve constellations of the zodiac even appear as angels in 1 Enoch 82:11-20. The significance of these twelve for the division of the year is also acknowledged. And 1 Enoch also knows that the "sinner" holds these stars to be "gods" (1 Enoch 80:7). Therefore, the Babylonian "twelve stars" have taken a place in Judaism. We should, therefore, not be surprised when we encounter the same "seven stars" in a later time.

In addition, the parallel of the seven-branched lampstand occurs here as well. This is the lampstand which is related to the symbol of the "seven lamps,"[54] and which, for its part, originally represented the seven planets. Finally, there is the tradition[55] that the control of a weekday is handled by each of the seven archangels. As far as this final point is concerned, it is well known that Babylonian astronomy had named the seven days of the week after the seven planets — names which endure even to the present day.[56] The Jews, so we discern at this point, have named the week after the seven archangels. We thus obtain here, once again, the equation "Archangels = Planets."[57]

Accordingly, we perceive the following religio-historical context. Judaism has come to terms with the Babylonian astral religion. It cannot deny the influence of the seven Babylonian planet-spirits, but it ardently maintains that these spirits are subject to a God of heaven and earth. For the expression of these concepts, so it appears, symbols from the Babylonian cultus are employed. We shall imagine the adoption of these symbols in the following manner: Such representations of the seven planets stood in the temple of the highest Babylonian deity. The Jews conceptually inserted their own God in place of that deity!

In the book of Revelation there is no further evidence of this emulation of Babylonian religion. Only its product, the tradition, is preserved, since it presents the seven highest spirits standing before God. The images, which had formerly been the identifying expression of the high Babylonian god, and had become that of the God of Israel . . . these images are now images of the superiority of both God and Christ.[58]

In the great introductory vision of Revelation 4, twenty-four πρεσβύτεροι [*presbyteroi*, "elders"] appear sitting on thrones in a ring around the divine throne. They are in white garments with golden crowns on their heads (Rev 4:4). In the same vision it is reported that they worship before "the Enthroned One," throw down their crowns before his throne, and give honor to him, to the Creator of the World (Rev 4:9-11). — In what follows in Revelation, as in the case of the four beings, they throw themselves at the feet of the Lamb, with a harp and golden bowls of incense in their hands. Then they sing a new song of praise for the Lamb (Rev 5:8f.). They are involved in the worship of God several times (Rev 5:14; 11:16; 19:4). One of the πρεσβύτεροι [*presbyteroi*] serves the seer as an angelic interpreter at one time (Rev 7:13).

The starting point is significant for the outcome of an investigation concerning these much-interpreted forms. Since it may be assumed (concerning that which precedes) that the πρεσβύτεροι [*presbyteroi*], as well as the thrones, those who are enthroned, the vitreous sea, the seven torches, and the four beasts all represent an apocalyptic tradition,[59] and since, on the other hand, this tradition is certainly to be sought in the names and in the basic description of the πρεσβύτεροι [*presbyteroi*] of chapter 4, as well as in the way in which the apocalyptic writer occasionally employs these forms for his own purpose . . . for both these reasons one has to situate the starting point of the investigation in chapter 4. Moreover, there is the fact that the statements concerning them in the next chapter (Revelation 5) (i.e., that they worship [having harps and incense bowls in hand — Rev 5:8]; and that one of them at one time interprets the vision to the seer [Rev 5:5]). . . . these statements about them are not peculiarly characteristic of them — the former statement they have in common with the four "living creatures" (Rev 5:8f.); and the assistance with interpretation is certainly not the actual distinctive office of those who wear crowns.

Accordingly, the essence of the πρεσβύτεροι [*presbýteroi*] will be defined by us on the basis of

> their thrones before God;
>> their name πρεσβύτεροι [*presbyteroi*];
>>> the number twenty-four.

The first feature is to be understood from the larger context. Just as the earthly king is encircled by major figures of his realm, so God in heaven, in much earlier and even later Jewish periods, is considered to be conferring about his plans, and reaching decisions concerning them together with other similar heavenly figures.[60]

The later period speaks of a דינא [dînā'] of God, a heavenly judicial collegium which sits before God on thrones.[61] Even in later Judaism much would be said concerning this בית דין [bêṭ dîn, "house of judgment"] without which nothing takes place.[62] According to the model of the heavenly judicial collegium, Judeo-Christian apocalyptic thought has presented participation in the divine world-administration, participation which is promised to the pious for the end time,[63] . . . has presented this participation as enthronement before the countenance of God.

This idea is also to be sought in the πρεσβύτεροι [presbyteroi] of Revelation 4. This is all the more advisable since this concept is exceptionally suitable for the introductory vision of a writing depicting a heavenly judicial convocation. That which follows such a vision must depict the judgment of God upon the world. Thus the title πρεσβύτεροι [presbyteroi] is explicated. The assessor of the divine law-court is led close to other names,[64] even that of the זקנים [zĕqēnîm, "elders"] of Isa 24:23,[65] which may be translated "senators," "judges."[66]

This heavenly collegium sits on thrones and wears diadems. One feature is quite striking: that πρεσβύτεροι [presbyteroi] should be wearing crowns is in no way a natural image. Ancient Israel also thought of the סוד אלהים [sôḏ 'ĕlōhîm], the council of the gods, in another form: YHWH sits upon his throne. The heavenly host stands before him.[67] This notion agrees with the picture which could be visibly seen in the conciliar gatherings of the earthly kings of Israel.[68] This gathering, based on such a singular image as that of the πρεσβύτεροι [presbyteroi] wearing crowns and sitting on thrones, is interpreted out of the context of the earthly imperial model, the sovereigns of which are called "kings," and the supreme ruler of which is called "king of kings."[69] If, accordingly, God's πρεσβύτεροι [presbyteroi] are also crowned and enthroned, i.e., are similar to earthly kings, then this feature portrays the "great ones" of the divine realm, who are royal counselors.

The same idea is expressed even more clearly at the end of the scene, where these kings rise from their thrones and lay themselves and their crowns at the feet of the enthroned one, since he is the creator of the world! This is a noble expression of the idea that the "creator-God" is the "king of kings."

It is noteworthy that here God's βασιλεία [basileia, "kingdom"] is presented in the form of the βασιλεία τοῦ κόσμου [basileia tou kosmou, "kingdom of the cosmos"], quite naturally making it a more *expansive* concept — an example from which a whole series of aspects in the New Testament view of God's kingdom are explicable.

It may *not* be raised as an objection against this explanation of the πρεσβύτεροι [*presbyteroi*, "presbyters, elders"] that these entities do not appear in the following materials in their capacity as judges, but rather in totally different roles, roles connected with the singing of hymns, the offering of incense, the playing of harps, and the interpretation of things. Exactly the same thing, however, is to be noted in regard to the rest of the material related to the divine throne, material which appears in the subsequent narrative neither in a general way[70] nor even in a way somewhat further removed from the original sense of these forms.[71] On the contrary, it should be inferred from this vision that the actual significance of the πρεσβύτεροι [*presbyteroi*] was no longer clear to the apocalyptist since, for example, the four "living creatures" were certainly quite obscure to him, even though these images were usually a piece of such apocalyptic introductory visions.

We may also hold the number twenty-four to be a tradition, something which is all the more certain since that number receives absolutely no illumination from the context. Previous interpretations understand the number as a "reduplication of the number twelve, the numerical appellation of the people of God."[72] In line with this, those interpretations explain the twenty-four presbyters as twelve representatives of the Gentile converts to Christianity, in addition to just as many representatives from Israel.[73] Or they explain it as twelve representatives of the New Testament community, beside which both the twelve patriarchs and the twelve apostles are brought to mind.[74]

These explications assume that the twenty-four presbyters were a free invention of the Christian author — an assumption made improbable by the background of these forms, which have a long prehistory in regard to every individual feature within the tradition. These explications even interpret these figures as transfigured human beings. That would have had to be "explicitly "stated in the text, however, since one would normally expect an angel and not a human being to be the highest enthroned one next to God.[75] Those other explications acquire the number *twenty-four* by reduplication of the number *twelve*, i.e., they presume a doubled "people of God." But early Christianity knew of only one people of God — in twelve tribes (Jas 1:1) — into which even the early Gentiles were implanted.[76] These same explications are finally proven to be totally capricious when the text itself characterizes the "twenty-four" neither as Judeo- and Gentile-Christians, nor as patriarchs and apostles, at least not in any discernible way.

Another interpretation[77] focuses on the twenty-four priestly classes, the heavenly agents of which would be the πρεσβύτεροι [*presbyteroi*]. This interpretation founders on the fact that the fundamental description of chapter 4 does not interpret them as priests, but rather as kings and judges. We, therefore, admit that the number *twenty-four* is not explicable from Old Testament models, nor is it explicable from New Testament concepts.

A methodical explanation of the number must emanate from the observation that the apocalyptic tradition has held fast to that number, even though it is no longer understood, e.g., in the book of Revelation. This would hardly have been the case if there had not been the impression that this number was somehow characteristic of the πρεσβύτεροι [*presbyteroi*]. Therefore, the number itself can be interpreted only if we know the original meaning of these forms. Where are we to seek out the origin of this tradition? Not in Christianity, where the number cannot be explained. The Christian author took possession of the πρεσβύτεροι [*presbyteroi*] from the Jewish tradition, just as he did all the other details of this chapter.

But we cannot seek out the origin of this tradition in Judaism either, for in Judaism, similarly, there does not exist any explanation for the number *twenty-four*. The same conclusion arises from consideration of the thrones of those living creatures who stand before God, a feature which, as we have seen, is not explicable from the circumstance of Palestine, but rather only from those of the empire.[78] Since this feature is now linked to the beings of the πρεσβύτεροι [*presbyteroi*], it is to be assumed that the whole concept has made its way into Judaism from the religion of an imperial people. This is even more remarkable since a series of other features (the four beasts,[79] the seven torches, etc.) is imported, ultimately, from abroad.

One now notes that these foreign features belong to the Babylonian tradition; and, since we expressly hear that the names of the angels have come from Babylon, we might conjecture that the twenty-four πρεσβύτεροι [*presbyteroi*] originally were twenty-four Babylonian deities. This conclusion is supported by the majestic splendor of the πρεσβύτεροι [*presbyteroi*] and the inference drawn from it. The origin of the idea should be considered in light of the fact that the Babylonians and Assyrians transferred the title of their king onto the heavenly king and thought about the divine assembly of the heavens according to the model of the earthly royal council. Since Judaism identified its own god with this highest Babylonian god, the Jews also could have associated a similar council with him.[80]

Diodorus Siculus[81] reports concerning the Babylonians:

Apart from the constellations, they classify twenty-four further stars (= star forms?), of which half stand on the northern heavens, and half on the southern heavens. Of these they [sometimes] reckon the visible to be living, the invisible to be dead, and they designate the judge of the universe.

Here we have, therefore, the tradition which has been sought: The divine beings and the judge are mentioned. And the number *twenty-four* is likewise a characteristic, like the number *seven* for the planets and the number *twelve* for the constellations.[82] According to the outlook of Babylonian astronomy, the twelve of them which are visible at any given time, i.e., are above the horizon, . . . those twelve linger in the upper world. The other twelve, which stand below the horizon, . . . they are with the dead. If here, then, the twenty-four are assembled together before the highest deity, we are, then, dealing with a report that deals with both the living and the dead. The appearance of the twenty-four as a judicial colloquium is, accordingly, the inherited preliminary for the judgment of the "cosmos."

In addition to the *twelve* constellations of *1 Enoch*, the seven spirits and the twenty-four elders of the book of Revelation, the seven hells of the rabbinic tradition[83] also appear. This tradition certainly does provide evidence for a fairly late Judaism, but from the seven *viae* [ways] of torment in *4 Ezra* [6:55ff.] the antiquity of the tradition can be inferred.[84] The Mandaeans[85] also knew of seven hells. The Babylonian origin of this idea is unquestionable.[86]

Therefore, a series of cosmological concepts of later Judaism are surely to be identified as being of Babylonian origin. I am not investigating at this point whether anything else from the cosmological materials referred to above is of Babylonian origin. I do take the liberty, however, of drawing the attention of the Assyriologists to this material, especially to *1 Enoch*.

I cannot completely ignore a late Judaic legend to which, in recent times, the eyes of scholarship have been drawn. I cannot completely ignore that legend, although it does not belong to the "apocalyptic" materials which concern us here; and although I am only in a position here to include observations made by certain other persons, remarks from the religio-historical point of view.

The book of Esther is the legend of the feast of Purim. That feast had entered into Judaism from a foreign source sometime in the second century B.C.E. Its non-Jewish origin follows, above all, from its name פור [*pûr*], which is interpreted in Esth 3:7 by the Hebrew word גורל [*gôrāl*] = "lot." The fact that such an interpretation was even necessary shows that the Jews did not, by nature, understand the word. Therefore the name and the feast itself were of foreign origin. The home of the feast and of the legend is to be sought out in the East. We have, therefore, in "Purim" and in "Esther" a new example of our observation that Judaism in pre-Christian times had remained open to foreign influences.

Until now, scholars have attempted to infer from the word פור [*pûr*] the soil out of which the feast arose. Lagarde[87] has put Purim together with the Persian *farwadîgān;* Zimmern[88] has put it together with the Babylonian word *puḫru* and the Babylonian New Year festival. A satisfactory explanation of the name — so far as I can see — has not yet been given.[89]

Jensen, however, has attempted to answer the question from another point of view. He[90] has shown proof that *"Haman"* is the name of the Elamite high god *(Humba = Humban = Humman)* and that *"Vashti,"* the deceased queen in the Esther narrative, was also the name of an Elamite goddess. Furthermore, he links the goddess *Kiriša*, the deity *Humman*'s consort, with זרש [*zereš*], *Haman*'s wife. Likewise he links Mordecai[91] with *Marduk* and Esther with *Ištar*.[92] The latter comparison is supported by the observation that even Esther's by-name *Hăḏassāh*, i.e., "the (one bedecked with) myrtle," probably has its origin, according to Jensen, in a Babylonian word for "bride" — *ḫadaššatum*. Accordingly, Jensen has asserted that the story of Esther is a Babylonian myth!

This assertion appears, according to the evidence presented above, quite plausible from a religio-historical standpoint. For the correct assessment of the myth the following is to be noted: Since the story of Esther appears as a legend of the feast of "Purim," it is probable that in Babylon as well, the *Ištar* myth would have been the legend of the Babylonian feast corresponding to the feast of Purim. The original *Ištar* narrative is a myth. The story of Esther is a saga. In other words, the gods have become human and the dimensions of their actions have to be projected into the human sphere. The story of Esther plays on the hope of a Persian king. Accordingly, the original Babylonian tradition has been blended with a Persian one. It had come to the Jews in this syncretistic form![93]

The purpose of this investigation is to examine which form the original Babylonian myth had. It is, perhaps, not superfluous to stress that there are guidelines for such an investigation. The reconstruction of this ancient myth can be successful only if it has sought out, in a profusion of examples, the way in which myths are regularly transmitted from generation to generation, how they migrate from nation to nation, and finally how they become mythic sagas. This is a methodology for the study of myths against which one may transgress just as little as one may transgress against the basic methodology of philology!

For the comprehension of the Babylonian myth, Jensen has astutely perceived that within that myth there is evidence of a primeval Babylonian liberation from the yoke of the Elamites. On the other hand, however, Jensen's remaining formulations are unsuccessful. He has lumped together this myth with the Babylonian twelve-tablet epic [*Enuma Eliš*], the hero of which is the dead and revivified son of *Ea* (= *Marduk*). The fasting of Esther is the funerary mourning over the son of *Ea*. The feast of the myth is the Babylonian New Year's celebration, which was received by Judaism and was shifted forward about a month by reason of a conflict with Passover.

The material as it is presently known does not allow such conclusions. The comparison with the "son of *Ea*" myth gets hung up because of the lack of striking similarities. That myth, on the contrary, has a totally different character than the account of Esther which is transmitted to us. The chief character of the *Ištar* myth is *Ištar*, not *Marduk*. Likewise, our material little supports the conclusion that the legend originally had belonged to the New Year's feast. The myth of the Babylonian New Year's feast is known to us. It was the creation myth. It is expressly reported concerning the Esther account, however, that it belonged to the feast of the 14th/15th of אדר ['*Ădar*],[94] thus not to the feast of the New Year. To me it seems methodologically incorrect to invalidate a traditional piece of data on the basis of such a questionable conjecture.

The weakness of these comparative views is that they have been put forward prematurely. First of all, the question must be asked exactly what the Esther narrative itself teaches. It may, then, be time to examine exactly how the Babylonian material at our disposal actually looks. One can seek to reconstruct — naturally only presumably — the original form of the myth, while attempting to remove the deeper Persian elements, and thereby to come to the "original" Babylonian subsoil. By doing that one at the same time brings the "human" element back into the divine.

The Jewish addition to the story is clear. Judaism has shifted the focus of the account, which originally reported on a defeat of the enemies of the Babylonians or Persians, to its own enemies, i.e., to the "heathen." And its hatred against those "heathen," as well as its desire to be admired and honored by them, . . . both of these things found their way into the narrative right along with Jewish monotheism.

The working of the material into a court history is of Persian provenance. The character of the king, who is a nonentity in the legend, may also be a Persian addition.[95]

The myth tells of the victory of the Babylonian gods over the Elamite gods. Furthermore, there is the peculiarity that the saving deed is not done by *Marduk* but by *Ištar*;[96] not by a man's valor and energy, but by a woman's beauty and cunning. *Ištar*, at a banquet, has given *Haman*[97] into the hands of his foes. After that the "people of *Marduk*" attack those who oppress them. Jensen has, moreover, pointed out the parallel to the Judith narrative: the death of the oppressor through the cunning of a woman at a banquet and the subsequent defeat of the enemy are narrated in both accounts.

Although not the liberator, however, *Marduk* still has come to royal honor through the death of *Haman*. The myth may well have narrated how *Ištar*, after the death of *Haman*, handed over the hegemony to *Marduk*.

Jensen has seen that historical *realia* reverberate in this myth:[98] an ancient subjugation of Babylon by Elam and then the subsequent expulsion of that "foreign" lord. Servitude and liberation are, therefore, historically attested. In the myth *Marduk* will become king through *Haman's* downfall. The fact that, since the war for independence from the Elamites, Babylon, *Marduk's* city, has become the queen . . . this conclusion is also confirmed by history!

It is indicated that the same great event which stands at the historical beginning of Babylonian history echoes both in the creation myth and in this *Ištar* myth. It is possible, therefore, to surmise that the "other" of that story (i.e., *Haman*) is also historical, that the Elamites (those who worship *Haman*) had been expelled by the city of *Ištar*, not the city of *Marduk*, although through that liberation the latter god does obtain a royal grandeur! The day of the festival would, therefore, have been motivated by the fact that though *Haman* would have annihilated the people of *Marduk* on a particular day, that very same day has now actually become the day of his annihilation! To the myth still belong, in the book of Esther, therefore, the designation "the evil Haman"[99] (Esth 7:6), and the designation "the people of *Marduk*" (Esth 3:6).

So perhaps the original Babylonian *Ištar* myth is to be considered. Once again I emphasize, however, that in regard to such a reconstruction we are dealing with speculations. And even the basis of the reconstruction lacks final confirmation as long as the word פור [*pûr*] is not satisfactorily explained!

In the preceding discussion we have established a few cosmological elements in apocalyptic literature to be Babylonian. We now have drawn a little closer to our focal topic, the investigation of Revelation 12, as we raise the same questions in regard to the eschatology of Judaism. We have already shown, in the first part of this book, a few vestiges of the Babylonian chaos myth in the latest forms of Judaism. In the Prayer of Manasseh the shackling of the sea in primal time is described with very archaic features.[100] Just as ancient is 1 *Enoch* 60:16, which speaks of the bridle by which the spirit of the sea is held fast like a monster.[101] The eschatological turning of the myth, often established by us, we have also found in Isa 27:1 and *Psalms of Solomon* 2. In both passages the myth, following prophetic custom, refers to a political foe of Israel.[102] The characteristic originality of all these texts makes it clear to us that the Babylonian chaos myth was well known to Judaism even into a much later period.[103]

Other passages exhibit to us the chaos myth turned to prophecy without political interpretation. 4 *Ezra* 6:52[104] mysteriously intimates that Leviathan and Behemoth have a divinely intended purpose: *servasti ea, ut fiant devorationem, quibus et quando eis*.[105] Thus these monsters shall one day die and then be transformed! When? By whom? God, who has issued a decree concerning them . . . God knows the answers.

1 *Enoch* 60:9ff.[106] speaks just as mysteriously of these monsters. When

Enoch asks the angel about the power of each monster,[107] the angel answers, v. 10: "You, O son of man, you now desire to know that which is hidden!"

One sees, therefore, that Judaism viewed the information about the appearance of Leviathan and Behemoth in the final days as deep secret knowledge. We still have in our sources, however, certain indications which give us evidence concerning these mysteries. *Second Apocalypse of Baruch* reports on the events of the end time, of the revelation of the Messiah, and then continues:

> *And Behemoth will be revealed from its place, and Leviathan will ascend from the sea, those two great monsters whom I created on the fifth day of creation and whom I will reserve until that time; and at that time they will be tasty treats for all who are left.*[108]

This passage comments on 4 *Ezra* 6:52. The time when Leviathan and Behemoth shall be "revealed" is the end time, when the Messiah comes. Then they shall be eaten by the ones who remain, who will be allowed to see salvation.[109] *Second Apocalypse of Baruch* speaks of the partaking of the flesh of these monsters as the first among the delights which those who are left will experience.[110] In addition, it is noteworthy that this passage says nothing about the way in which Leviathan and Behemoth will be killed. That mystery is so very deep that one is hesitant to reveal it to those who are profane. The expert did know it, however!

We are told something more by the answer which Enoch receives from the angel (1 *Enoch* 60:24f.).[111]

> 24 *These two monsters are prepared, in accordance with the greatness of God, to be consumed, so that the punishment of God will not be for nothing.*[112] *The sons with their mothers and the children with their fathers will be slain.*
>
> 25 *When, however, the punishment of the Lord of the Spirits upon them is at an end, then it will (generally) be at an end.*[113] *Then the judgment will take place according to his compassion and forbearance.*

The sense of this passage appears to be: The two monsters will be nourished, temporarily. Then God plans a portentous criminal tribunal. Since the tribunal will not come upon them gratuitously (i.e., without grounds), they must have committed a terrifying offense (against humanity). Sons together with mothers, children together with fathers will be murdered (by them). So then, it is totally understandable that a terrifying divine judgment takes place upon the two monsters. This passionate tribunal, however, is the last which God will hold concerning the world. When, then, his authority has been inflamed, God's compassion and his patience can be revealed even more.

The time when Leviathan and Behemoth appear is, according to 1 *Enoch* 60:25, the time immediately prior to the end of the world.[114] The expectation of the apocalyptist, consequently, appears to be as follows: There will be a time preceding the end of the world when Leviathan and Behemoth will dwell, horribly, on the earth. The judgment of God upon them, however, will follow upon that time. After these things have happened, then God's salvation will also appear!

The characteristic obscurity of our text may have been brought about by the multiple translations through which it has been transmitted.[115] It is also brought about in part, however, by the nature of the tradition. Only ἐν μυστηρίῳ[116] [*en mystērio*] can one speak of such things. One notes, above all, that even here the destruction of Leviathan and Behemoth is not described.

Among the rabbis, as well, the tradition of Leviathan and Behemoth appears. Various accounts exist. The two monsters must battle against one another. Or Gabriel undertakes, with God's support, a hunt for Leviathan. Then their bodies provide the blessed ones the exquisite meal of which a great many passages speak. Even the fact that Leviathan is a monster of the primal period is not completely forgotten. One tradition maintains that the (female) Leviathan had been slain at the beginning of time. This is combined with the meal which imports her body into the עולם הבא [*ʿôlām hab-baʾ*].[117] The body of the dead animal had been salted away in the primal era and is, therefore, stored for use at the end time.[118]

It has already been demonstrated on the preceding pages that these traditions, at base, stem from Babylon. Many things within them may be additions from later periods, additions which have augmented primitive material by contemplative combinations and by imaginative embellishments. It is not possible to explain the whole of late-Judaic Leviathan tradition in this way. The tradition, however, does preserve a whole series of more original features!

It is especially significant that the Leviathan myth here certainly exists in an eschatological form, but without a political interpretation. We have here, therefore, a form of the myth as it must have already been presented to the prophets.[119] On the other hand, however, the myth is not contained in the Old Testament in this configuration. It is only surmised from the Old Testament. It therefore cannot really be concluded from the Old Testament.

There is one further set of details: the tradition that Leviathan has dominion over the sea, Behemoth over the wilderness; the tradition that Leviathan is female, Behemoth male.[120] The original significance of Leviathan had not been totally unknown in Judaism.[121] It follows, therefore, that Judaism must have possessed a tradition concerning Leviathan, a tradition which was independent of the Old Testament. The Babylonian creation account has, then, been drawn anew into later Judaism as a prophecy of the end time.

Few misgivings can be held against this interpretation, since, as we have already indicated in the preceding discussion, in Manicheism[122] as well as in Mandaeism[123] the Babylonian chaos myth has survived![124]

A series of further testimonies is added to the dream of Mordecai in the Septuagintal additions to the book of Esther.

LXX Additions to the Book of Esther 1:4-10

4*And this was his dream:*[125]

Behold, noise and uproar, thunder and an earthquake, and terrors[126] *upon earth.* 5*And behold, two great dragons appeared, both ready to fight, and they made vehement noise.* 6*At their roaring all nations prepared themselves for war, to fight the righteous people.* 7*It was a day of darkness and gloom, affliction and distress, tribulation and great terror upon earth.* 8*So the whole righteous people were terrified and surely feared their destruction. And they made themselves ready for death,* 9*and cried out to God. Out of their tears,*[127] *however, there arose, as from a small spring, a mighty stream of abundant water,* 10*and light,*[128] *and the sun arose. The stream,*[129] *however, went ever higher,*[130] *until it entangled*[131] *the proud ones.*

The interpretation of the dream which is appended to LXX Esth 10:6-9 explains the stream (v. 8) as Esther and the two dragons as Mordecai and Haman.

As for those who have assembled (in the vision) to destroy the Jewish people, they are the heathens. Those, however, (in the vision) who cry out to God and are saved, they are my people.[132]

The derivation of the vision from the chaos myth[133] is quite obvious:

- התנין הגדול [*hat-tannîn hag-gāḏôl*] (Ezek 29:3) corresponds to the name "great dragons," δράκοντες μεγάλοι [*drakontes megaloi*];
- They make noise and spread terror abroad, as at Ezek. 32:32, etc.; Pss 65:8; 74:23; 89:10; Job 41:17; cf. above, pp. 55-56, 64.
- They appear on the day of darkness; cf. Isa 17:14; Ezek 32:7; Ps 46:6; Job 3:8.
- The fact that a great stream ὕδωρ πολύ [*hydōr poly*] is a parallel; cf. Hab 3:15; Pss 18:17; 93:4 (מים רבים [*mayim rabbîm*, "many waters"]) and Isa 51:9f. (תהום רבה [*tĕhôm rabbāh*, "great deep"]).

- The end of the terrifying vision comes when it becomes light and the sun rises; cf. Isa 17:14 and Ps 46:6.
- The whole thing points to a struggle of the heathen against Israel, as at Isa 17:12-14 and Psalm 46.
- As a date for the vision the first of ניסן [Nîsān][134] (i.e., New Year's day and the day of creation) is named.

So a few features of the ancient myth are quite well preserved. They have, however, lost much of their ancient context. For example, the idea that the dragons will do battle with each other, and that the stream is salvation, not, as originally, that which brings destruction, . . . these ideas are late. These changes have, as is clearly discerned, been carried out by the author, who wished to interpret the one dragon as Mordecai and the stream as Esther. Because of this, the ancient significance has been substantially lost. For that reason some strange things have found their way into the story: the description of the day of gloom and darkness goes back to prophetic passages;[135] the great stream from of small spring, of which 2 Bar. 36:3f. speaks, certainly does not belong to the chaos myth.[136] The vision of Mordecai has greatest affinity to Isa 17:12-14 and Psalm 46. While these passages have lost the "dragon" and have preserved only the overflowing waters, here the original connection of the dragon and water is preserved. It follows, therefore, that even though this vision has been created from the Old Testament, it does go back to an independent tradition.

The myth is preserved in a totally different form in the account of the "dragon in Babylon." This legend, stemming from the prophecy of Habakkuk and added to the book of Daniel in the LXX, relates the following: There was in Babylon a dragon[137] whom the Babylonians revered. Daniel had slain this monster, with no sword and with no staff, when he cooked together thirty minas of pitch, fat, and hair, formed cakes from the mixture, and threw them into the mouth of the dragon. When the beast had eaten them he was split asunder![138]

Such narratives were not snatched right out of the air! Furthermore, the legend bears a Babylonian pigmentation. We know well that dragon figures did stand in certain Babylonian holy places.[139] Accordingly we postulate a prototype of the legend, a prototype which reported the death of the dragon. If the narrative is ancient, then one who vanquished the dragon must have been a god. We infer, therefore, a Babylonian myth of the death of a dragon by the hand of a god!

That myth is none other than the Babylonian myth of the conquest of the great dragon *Ti'āmat* by *Marduk*.[140] The characteristic motif of the legend is that Daniel kills the dragon "without sword or staff." This feature is the central point of the narrative even in the account of the killing of *Ti'āmat* by

Marduk.[141] The original sense of the feature was this: the dragon is shielded by armor against any attack from outside:

> *He considers iron to be straw,*
> *bronze to be rotten wood.*[142]

But "the gifted one among the gods" knows a way to go against it. Because it is impossible to do that from outside, he kills the dragon from within![143]

The way of death is obscured in the legend: how cakes of pitch, fat, and hair, even if they have been eaten in such monstrous quantities, could blow a dragon apart is very difficult to say! Other recensions[144] of the legend have the more original feature here. According to one of them, Daniel cast straw in front of the dragon, straw in which nails were hidden. According to another version there were, hidden in pieces of meat, iron spikes the still-visible portions of which were coated with pitch and brimstone. The second recension is, so it appears, the prototype of the Δράκων [*drakōn*] legend.[145] The Mandaean tradition has preserved this mode of death: *Hibil-Ziwâ,* in the belief that he is about to be swallowed by *Krun,* surrounds himself with a sheath of swords, sabers, spears, knives, and daggers, which cut up the monster's belly.[146]

The Jewish tradition, therefore, has taken over the Babylonian myth and made from it a prophetic legend.[147] The Jewish prophet [Daniel] is playing out the role of a mythic deity! The Jewish community, to the injury of the Babylonians, says that the dragon was the deity of the Babylonians and had been slain by the Jewish prophet Daniel.[148] "See then what you worship!" (LXX Dan 14:27). Here is the attitude of the Jewish community toward the gods of the Gentiles, an attitude with which we are quite familiar from the preceding materials. The Gentiles worship — so the Jewish community maintains — malevolent, evil monsters who, however, in the end have no power![149]

Nothing in the legend indicates that the dragon is actually the chaos dragon. The story is not set in the time before creation. It may not be assumed that the Babylonian narrative which lay behind this legend already had this form, however. We come, therefore, to a form of the myth which is attested to us from Babylonian tradition[150] and which is to be reclaimed by inference from the Old Testament prophets.[151]

It is not possible that the legend was created out of the Old Testament. Rather it has been received directly from the Babylonians.[152] We have, therefore, once again established that Judaism has received Babylonian materials, and once again we see that this received material is, specifically, the chaos myth!

We can, now, apply ourselves to the task of explaining this seventh chapter of Daniel, a text just as important as it is difficult.[153] The seer, in a dream, perceives the four winds of the heavens which cause "the great sea" to be "in labor,"[154] so that four mighty beasts rise up out of it. The first is a lion with eagle's wings, which rises up from the earth[155] and like a human being is placed on its feet. It even receives a human mind! The second beast is a bear who already has three ribs in its mouth, when (once again) the decree is issued to him: "Go, eat a lot of flesh." The third is a panther with four wings and four heads. The fourth is especially dreadful, terrifying, and strong. With its remarkable teeth of iron, it eats and it crushes, and with its feet it tramples whatever it leaves behind! It is different from all the former creatures. Its exact form is, however, not described. It does have ten horns, though. Between these horns grows, at first small, but then extending beyond all the others, a new (therefore an eleventh) horn. That horn has human eyes and a mouth, a mouth which speaks powerful things.

Then the scene changes. The seer perceives how thrones will be put in place. A person of great antiquity with white robes and white hair is seated upon a fiery throne. A river of fire goes forth from him. Before him stand his attendants, a myriad of myriads. He passes judgment upon the fourth beast.[156] Its body will be given over to the fire. Dominion over the world, however, is received by someone "like a son of man," who comes with the clouds of heaven. His dominion is eternal. It will not — like that of the four beasts — be terminated after a season and a time.[157]

The second half of the chapter appends, in the form of an angelic speech, the proper interpretation[158] of the vision. The four beasts are four kingdoms.[159] Finally, however, the holy ones of the Most High receive a dominion for all eternity. — The seer requests special information about the fourth beast and its eleventh horn. He receives that special information. The fourth beast is an especially fearsome and mighty kingdom. The ten horns symbolize ten kings of that kingdom. An eleventh king, "different" from those who went before, will do away with three of his predecessors. He will make utterances against the Most High, wage war against the holy ones, and will wear them down. And he will seek to alter their religion. For a time, two times,[160] and a half-time the holy ones will be given into his hands. Then, however, the judgment will come upon the king and upon the whole kingdom generally. Dominion over the whole world will be given to the people of the holy ones of the Most High.

After a labor of many generations it now ranks among the secure possessions[161] of theological inquiry that this chapter understands to lay behind its symbol of the fourth beast the historical rule of the Greeks in the era after Alexander. Behind the symbol of the eleventh horn it understands Antiochus Epiphanes. Behind the symbol of that which is told about that horn it understands the religious persecution under Antiochus. Also ranking among the secure possessions of theological inquiry is the fact that the author of the book wrote under that very king! This is the starting point for our comprehension of this chapter. The goal of the vision is to comfort those who live during the time of the persecution of Antiochus Epiphanes.

> You who despair, whose religion the tyrant wants to take away, upon whom the empire treads unmercifully, who are alarmed about the blasphemous words of the impious . . . you who glance longingly toward heaven and ask "How long, O Lord?" . . . O you, hear now the vision of Daniel! This ancient prophet predicted the kingdom which would arise over the whole world, even over you. Daniel predicted, as closely as possible, exactly that which has now come down upon you.
>
> So hear then, first, that you are correct in your sighing. It is now truly "a time of hardship such as has never been seen on earth before";[162] the final terrifying revelation of evil!
>
> Know, however, that what you now experience *is* God's will. He has ordained all of this according to his unfathomable wisdom, and he has shown it to his prophets in visions for many generations. Submit yourselves to God's will, for "that which is fated must happen."[163] Now is the time of his anger.[164] Cling to his anger in silence!
>
> At the same time, however, consider that you are also even now in God's hands. Not one of all these things happens in opposition to God. Even the tyrant and his horrible regime are ordained by God.
>
> And hear, then, the consolation as well. This is the appointed time. When this time is over, Greece will vanish and the villain will be overturned. And then the dominion of the world will come — to you!

The prediction distinctive to this chapter is, accordingly, that the world dominion of the Jews will follow upon the Antiochene persecution, after the completion of a brief period of time, a period of time which is still ongoing. Of course, the only reader who would be capable of understanding this prediction would be one who was able to perceive that the account of the eleventh horn is actually related to the "current" situation.

In order to make this understanding more definite, the apocalyptist has explicitly presented an interpretation of certain features in the second part of the chapter. The four beasts are the four empires which the author enumerates from Babylon to *Yāwān*.[165] The ten horns are the ten kings of *Yāwān*.[166] Thereby the main point cannot be missed: that the *eleventh* horn stands for Antiochus Epiphanes. A whole series of details bear witness to him. After "the ten" comes an "eleventh" horn, the *eleventh* ruler. Three of the earlier horns, i.e., three of Antiochus's predecessors,[167] are destroyed before him. The actions of that horn take the form of religious persecution. After the empire of the eleventh horn's time has run its course, then the holy ones come to power. The son of man, therefore, represents the nation of the holy ones.[168]

Only some of the features are interpreted thereby. It is to be expected, of course, that all remaining features will likewise be made clear in the interpretation of the text. The practical value of the prophecy would be even greater if more details had been prophesied.[169] And for one who had the interpretive key, — so we surmise — the hidden meaning of all these things must immediately have popped into his mind.

This surmise will, however, be only partially fulfilled in the present. If we accept the fact that we do not correctly understand much of what the apocalyptic writer sought to convey, e.g., by the three ribs (which probably represent the three original provinces of the second kingdom), by the four heads (which probably represent the four Persian kings); and, moreover, if we also consider the details in light of the possibility of textual corruption. . . . If we consider all these things, then it cannot be denied that some details in the vision are not fully handled in the interpretation.

- Why do the animals come from the sea? In reality, only *Yāwān* (Greece) came from the sea. The remaining kingdoms came from the land.
- How should the four winds who make the sea "labor" be interpreted?
- What does it mean that the first beast receives the bearing and the comprehension of a human being?
- Why are the kingdoms symbolized by these animals specifically: a lion, an eagle, a bear, and a panther? How is it to be explained that the fourth kingdom does not correspond to any specific animal?
- Though it is clear that "the son of man" should, according to the reasoning of the apocalyptist, be an image of Israel, this is actually a very remarkable depiction for an earthly people, i.e., a son of man coming *with the clouds of heaven!?!*[170]
- Finally, the main point of the chapter, the secret number three and a half, is totally unexplained from the context!

The impression which these arguments leave with the reader may be summarized as follows: Daniel 7 is not an allegory devised by the writer. Rather, it is a body of material taken over and allegorized by him. In line with the comments made up to this point, the answer to the question of which materials lie behind Daniel 7 cannot be in doubt! Beasts which ascend from the sea and which symbolize kingdoms in opposition to God are well known to us from passages we have examined above. Daniel 7 is closely related[171] to Isa 27:1; 30:7; Ezek 29:32; Pss 68:31; 74; 87:4; *Psalms of Solomon* 2.[172] It should, therefore, be treated in the same way as those texts. Now it has been shown above that these texts preserve the Babylonian myth of chaos which has been transformed into a prediction and which tradition would have referred to a political enemy. The same, therefore, also holds true for Daniel 7. It follows, then, that Daniel 7 goes back, in the last analysis, to the Babylonian myth of *Ti'āmat*. One notes that among these related texts a good number belong to a very late period. Isa 27:1 and Ps 68:31 fall somewhat earlier. *Psalms of Solomon* 2 falls even later than Daniel. Psalm 74 falls at about the same time. We can conclude that this material was especially popular in the later periods of early Judaism.

Daniel 7 agrees in detail with the remaining recensions of the myth in the following ways:

- There are "beasts" [חיון [Aram. *ḥêwān*], as in Ps 68:31, חיות [Heb. *ḥayyôt*]; *4 Ezra* 6:49f., *animae*; *2 Apoc. Bar.* 29:4; *1 Enoch* 60:7, κήτη [*kētē*]].
- which "ascend" [סלקן [Aram. *sālqān*], Dan 7:3, as in *2 Apoc. Bar.* 29:4 ("Leviathan ascendet de mari"); cf. *4 Ezra* 11:1 (13:3, Syr.)].
- from "the great sea" [(ימא רבא [Aram. *yammā' rabbā'*], as in Isa 51:10, תהום רבה [Heb. *tĕhôm rabbāh*, "great deep"]; Ps 74:13f.; Job 3:8; 7:12, ים [*yām* — cf. above, pp. 54f.]; Hab 3:15; Ps 8:17; Add Esth 1:9, מים רבים [*mayim rabbîm*, "many waters"]].
- Before their "ascent" the winds (רוחי [*rûḥê*]) of the heavens make the sea whirl around (Dan 7:2). In Genesis 1, the spirit (רוח [*rûaḥ*]) hangs brooding over the waters. Here a primal feature is, therefore, truly preserved. The word גיח [*gîaḥ*, "bubbling spring"] is found in similar contexts at Ezek 32:2 and Job 38:8.
- The beasts, although they belong to the water, rule over the land. This is also a primal motif which echoes in *Pss. Sol.* 2:33.
- Their hegemony is a rule of horrors. The beasts are enemies of God and of humanity. The same is true at Isa 27:1; Ezekiel 29 and 32; Pss 68:31; 74; *Psalms of Solomon* 2; cf. Ezek 32:32; Pss 74:3, 10, 18, and 23; 89:11; *Pss. Sol.* 2:1, 25, etc.
- The existence of beasts in opposition to God is depicted more clearly in the fourth beast. It "tramples" with its feet what it has not eaten (Dan 7:7). The term רפס [*rāpas*, "to tread, to trample"] occurs again in some other contexts, Ezek 32:2 and Ps 68:31.
- The eleventh horn reviles God. This is also a standard feature of the chaos myth; cf. Ps 74:18; *Pss. Sol.* 2:32f.; Ezek 29:3, etc. It conducts a war against the holy ones and defeats them, Pss 68:31; 74; *Psalms of Solomon* 2.

- Finally, however, God will remember his own. He will vanquish the evil, hostile forces, and he will raise up his kingdom in the world. This is also the standard conclusion of the eschatological chaos tradition; cf. above, pp. 55ff.

With this, the material adopted by the author has still by no means been exhausted. Rather, the chapter also includes a whole range of features which — as we have already seen — cannot have originated with the author. The exclusion of these features is not very simple since, besides the features which have been taken over, there are certainly others which are the mental property of the author. The methodology by which such a distinction is to be made has already been treated several times in the foregoing materials.[173] This method will be set forth in detail in the following discussions of Revelation 13 and 17. There is sufficient indication in these texts that we are correct in holding these features to be pieces of a tradition, pieces which are attested in recensions of the myth, or which, by their nature, clearly belong to the mythic materials, or which, at the least, cannot very easily be held as inventions of the author. These features are to be held as *additions* by the author, additions which bear the mark of *his* contemporary history on their brow, and which, at the same time, stand out peculiarly from the material which has simply been adopted from the tradition. I stress here that, for the time being, we can come to only tentative conclusions of greater or lesser probability. Or perhaps we can actually only come to questions! I also stress, however, that such conclusions will become more certain when they receive confirmation from another sphere, perhaps through similar reconstructions.

The number *three and a half* is not to be interpreted "contemporaneously."[174] It is a part of the religion and is therefore not the invention of the author. Accordingly, it belongs to the tradition. In the myth, the hegemony of chaos would have lasted just that long.[175]

The beasts will be cast into the blazing fire. This stands in opposition to the elements in which these beings are most at home. The fact that marine animals will be cast into fire implies their complete annihilation. Until now we have not found this feature in the tradition. The ancient tradition was content either to speak of a wilderness in which the beasts must perish (cf. above, pp. 56f.), or to report that the chaos beast is not dead but only shut up in the abyss (cf. Prayer of Manasseh 3).[176]

The "son of man who comes upon the clouds of the heavens," so mysterious in the context of Daniel, also belongs to the tradition. It is difficult to say how the author, on his own, could have come into possession of exactly this depiction of Israel, especially since Israel has already been mentioned in the vision using the designation "the holy ones." In the myth "son of man" would have been the title of the divine conqueror.[177]

The mythologically reminiscent description of the throne of God, especially of the "river of fire" which goes forth from it, is also a piece of the tradition.

Most difficult of all is what is left out of the description of the beasts. The axial basis of this description must, by its very nature, belong to the tradition. On the other hand, we should expect from the very beginning that the author would have introduced contemporary history here, in these descriptions, if anywhere at all.

Let us begin, then, by dealing with these latter points. The fact that the eleventh horn has haughty eyes and a monumentally boastful mouth should be illustrative of the blasphemous arrogance of the eleventh king. It is, therefore, clearly intended to be taken contemporaneously. All the same, this feature does lie quite far from the actual concept of a horn, which has neither mouth nor eyes. It is, therefore, the work of the author, who understood the material as an allegory and who, hence, developed it in his own way.[178]

I do not advance the same view with as much certainty in regard to the three horns which are plucked up by the roots (Dan 7:8). To be sure, this element has been interpreted contemporaneously, but it is, on the other hand, also to be considered as a mythic fragment: the beast could indeed (perhaps in a battle) have lost three horns. A judgment concerning the exact number of horns is also not very easy. The eleven horns are understood by the author as eleven kings. Accordingly, because of a desire to specify the number of the kings, the horns appear to be material which has found its way into the more original tradition. On the other hand, however, the depiction of kings specifically by horns is not a very obvious one! In addition, there is the fact that the Babylonian tradition also attributes horns to *Ti'āmat*.[179] One further notes the extraordinary fact that the basic description of the same beast ascribes to it only *ten* horns, and that the *eleventh* horn is added only later. There is, finally, the *tenfold* nature of the kings. This can be attained in chapter 11 only by adding together the more important kings of the Seleucid and the Ptolemaic lineages, and by omitting the insignificant rulers. This can hardly be the invention of the author, a fact to which the round number *ten* attests! We shall, therefore, venture the hypothesis that the original tradition already knew of the *ten* horns of the beast,[180] and that the author, in order to make an allusion to Antiochus, has added to this number (already well-established even before his appropriation of it) an *eleventh* horn.

The question of how to consider the origin of the fourfold nature of the beasts is an especially difficult one. This number belongs, as far as we can tell, not to the original chaos tradition, which speaks, rather, of a single beast to which a second is added, and whom many others are made to serve.[181] Accordingly, this feature appears to have entered the picture only at a later time. The single chaos beast — so may I surmise — has been split into four since it was of four empires that the author knew . . . four empires which therefore would be depicted as four beasts. In this regard the analogy of Isa 27:1 comes to mind. It is an analogy where, in much the same way that we have considered to be possible here, the number of beasts is altered according to the number of the kingdoms they are meant to represent.[182] Certain features in the book of Daniel itself also point to this hypothesis. The actions which are ascribed to the chaos-being in the myth, its horrible rule, its rebellion, its slanderous words . . . we find these again in the four beasts of Daniel. On the other hand, the image of *Ti'āmat* appears most visibly in the first of the Danielic beasts, while the image of the fourth beast is not generally described.

Thus we conclude that the tradition which lies behind Daniel 7 originally had known of only one chaos beast which combined all the features of Daniel's four beasts within itself. Accordingly, it bore the image of a lion, an eagle, a bear, and a panther.[183] Such a mixed image would certainly be in conformity with Babylonian tastes. The idea that the author himself has taken on this differentiation must, however, be held as improbable.[184]

Finally, one must also refer to chapter 8, which represents, in many ways, a parallel to chapter 7, and where the same material appears to be operating in a different recension. Here as well there is the mysterious number *three and a half*. Here as well — though in another interpretation — there is the fourfold nature of the thing which is represented by horns symbolizing the empires, and by an additional horn which symbolizes the tyrant Antiochus. There is a mythological resonance in the form of the casting down of the "hosts of heaven" (the stars) by the horn. In this mythic scene, the author has portrayed the designs of Antiochus against the heathen gods (Dan 8:10f. ‖ Dan 11:36). Is this an echo of a more ancient myth which was able to speak of the chaos dragon's battles against the astral deities? And — now the question should at least be permitted — is the ram originally the second chaos beast?

We are at this point in a position to clarify for ourselves the attitude of the author in regard to the tradition. He was not the first to embrace the chaos myth as a prediction. Many generations had preceded him in this. The author had already received the myth in this form. By and large it is not at all clear that he even knew the original significance of it! An ancient prophecy had circulated around that time: At the end of days a dreadful time will come when the powers of darkness will rule upon earth. They will oppress God's people and will blaspheme horribly against the Most High. But on that day of wrath the time will come, after God's deliberation, when the "son of man," coming on the clouds of heaven, will overcome this regime!

For a long time the Jews had undoubtedly understood this prophecy to refer to themselves: "We are the oppressed ones and therefore we are those who are *coming to power*. The evil powers are the peoples who rule over us." It was not at all unusual to call this vision to mind in times of political need and to regard the adversary of the moment as "the foe" of whom the visionary saying spoke. Traces of this use of the myth are found in Daniel 7 itself. Even before Daniel — so it appears — this tradition came together with another one, a tradition which spoke of four great cosmic ages. Thereafter the chaos prophecy was comprehended as a compendium of world history, the horns actually being interpreted as kings.

These observations are critical for a correct assessment of the apocalyptist. The author of Daniel has not invented this prophecy *ex eventu*, and has not boldly deposited his own capricious fabrications into the mouths of the ancient prophets. How could he then himself have believed in it? Rather, he has taken it over from the tradition, and he has, thereby, acted under the very appropriate impression that the tradition was ancient. It must have been revealed by God to a prophet of ancient times![185]

His spiritual distinctiveness is, however, that he has applied this ancient material to his own time. In a time when affliction was actively real, affliction the likes of which had never befallen Judaism before, . . . in such a time the apocalyptic writer of Daniel has undertaken a new interpretation of the ancient prophetic vision. The predicted oppression is the oppression which has befallen "us." So it follows that the assistance of God draws near. For the "son of man" whom the prophet has seen is none other than Israel. Blessed be the one who perseveres and who makes it to the time when his world dominion must come, the "three-and-a-half" times!

This man [the author of Daniel] is, however, no prophet. He is not able, as Isaiah or even Ezekiel had been able, to fashion a new thing from that which he has received. He is an undistinguished successor who venerates the old even when he does not understand it. He stands in awe before these ancient mysterious visions. The old prophet himself who originally saw these things could have received them only with reverent horror.[186] He himself, a devout person, could not have understood them totally, even though they were partially explained to him. He could not have understood them totally since he did not, himself, actually know that to which they referred.[187] Even now, when the vision is fulfilled, these great and enigmatic mysteries will become comprehensible, but only to those in the know.[188] So the author has treated the tradition with honor, as an infinitely deep mystery. It can be understood why he did not attempt to change it. He didn't want to change it. It would have lost all value if he did. With it, though, he has accepted many features with which he himself is hardly able to connect any meaning. And what he could add were only interpretive comments. In a way which is typical of the decadent spirit of the time, there are no additions by which, even in a small way, he has attempted to come to the assistance of the words of the pious one. This is the apocalyptic spirit, a spirit which we have already come close to seeing in Isa 27:1.[189]

An investigation of what the theme of Revelation 12 is cannot ultimately ignore chapters 13 and 17. The close relationship of these three chapters is obvious. Chapter 12 speaks of a great dragon with seven heads and ten horns. On the heads are seven diadems. Its natural element is water (the abyss, Rev 20:3).[190] It has power on earth and wages war against the brethren of the Christ, until it is finally overthrown by the Christ (Rev 19:11ff.).

In the same way, Revelation 13 tells of a terrifying monster with ten horns and seven heads. On its horns are ten diadems. It comes up out of the sea (Rev 17:1). On earth it has power over all peoples (Rev 17:1). It wages war with the holy ones until it is cast into the sea of fire (Rev 19:20).

In Revelation 17 we hear of a woman who sits on "the great waters," on a monster. This beast also has seven heads and ten horns (Rev 17:3). It has come up from the abyss (Rev 17:8). The woman has dominion over all the kings of the earth (Rev 17:18). She is drunk with the blood of the holy ones (Rev 17:6). Her downfall is described in chapters 18 and 19:1-10.

Each of these monsters represents the Roman empire!

The chapters up to this point have been understood as products of their writer. Accordingly, the relationship of chapters 17 and 13[191] is comprehended as a merely literary one. Either chapter 17 — so it is said — is an imitation of chapter 12,[192] or chapter 13 is dependent on chapter 17,[193] or, perhaps, a redactor has only later inserted the common features from the one into the other,[194] or perhaps the same author has written both chapters.[195]

In regard to all of these statements the question to be considered, not simply as a possibility, is whether a common tradition exists here. Had this possibility actually been considered, these literary-critical hypotheses would not even have been put forward! But these chapters are, at the same time, quite characteristically distinct from one another — chapter 13 even speaks of a second beast, of which the other chapters say absolutely nothing. The woman who sits on the beast in chapter 17 has no counterpart in chapters 12 and 13, etc. This fact totally refutes the theory that it was copied from one of the other chapters. Add to this the fact that in a fourth passage, Rev 11:7, mention is made of "the beast which arises from the abyss," without a description or even an explanatory remark (unless there was an allusion to it somewhere previously). The fact that mention of "the beast" is made only once implies that "the beast" was a well-known thing! It is, therefore, to be concluded that we have before us in Revelation 11, 12, 13, and 17 four *different* traditions, all of which report on the *same* monster!

Among these traditions that of chapter 11 is, in terms of its material, a good bit disconnected from the others. Even literarily it has no close relationship to that which follows. No internal connection leads from chapter 11 to chapter 12. Nothing in the following chapters even brings the idea to mind that "the beast who came from the abyss" has ever been mentioned previously.

Among the remaining, substantially more closely related traditions, chapter 17 stands out from the other two literarily. The description of the woman on the beast begins as something new and makes no mention of that which precedes it.[196] Likewise, the interpretation of Rev 17:9ff. begins right at the beginning and does not presume that this thing has ever appeared even once before! Chapter 17 and its sequel, chapters 18 and 19:1-10, the fall of Babylon, announced, bemoaned, and celebrated, as well as the counterpart of the great harlot . . . i.e., the holy bride[197] . . . these are, altogether, a vision which is self-contained and independent.[198]

The relationship of chapter 13 to chapter 12 is a bit more complex. In the present literary context, chapter 13 appears as a continuation of chapter 12. In addition to the dragon, two other beasts appear. To the first of them the dragon gives "his power, his throne, and his great authority" (Rev 13:2b). For the sake of this beast the dragon lets him be worshiped (Rev 13:4a). In what follows, then, the preparations of the three beasts for the impending war with Christ are described together (Rev 16:13, 14, 16). In the same way, the conquering of them is drawn together into a single image: the revealed Christ (Rev 19:11-16) overcomes first the two beasts and the assembled "kings of the earth" (Rev 19:17-21), and finally the dragon itself (Rev 20:1-3).

Now if the dragon and the first beast — as we have seen — are duplicates, then this literary context cannot be original. The secondary nature of this combination may be demonstrated in detail. Chapter 12 has, with v. 17, arrived at a temporary stopping point. The Christ has been concealed safely in heaven. He will come again when the time is fulfilled. Presently, however, the dragon rules on earth and employs his power to battle the innocent brethren of the Christ. Thus the situation is described which will endure until the appearance of Christ. We now anticipate some indication of the dragon's preparations for war. Then we anticipate the concluding segment of the narrative, his being conquered definitively. Rev 12:17 thus represents a preliminary conclusion to the narrative. Rev 12:18–13:1 is also the beginning of a new vision. The seer walks on the seashore. He comprehends the beast which ascends from the waters.[199]

The linking of Revelation 12 with Revelation 13 may have been conceived thus: the dragon, for "the persecution of those who remain" (Rev 12:17), calls in an agent, to whom he transfers his power (Rev 13:26), and who then, in his service, "persecutes the holy ones" (Rev 13:7). This linkage, however, will not be totally smooth for the two chapters themselves. If, finally, the beast does nothing more against the holy ones than that which the dragon himself has previously done — this even being reported in the same words[200] — the question does arise as to why the dragon even had to call in a confederate! There is no longer a unified, clearly progressing plot, but rather there are two variant versions of the same story, two variant versions improvisationally placed in a "unity" which appeared to be suitable only to the redactor.

Furthermore, in the context which we presently possess, the dragon and the beast are so different that the former must have symbolized the devil and the latter the Roman empire. The devil gave Rome its power (Rev 13:2). The symbols which characterized the dragon itself as the embodiment of Rome (Rev 12:3)[201] . . . these symbols persisted, however.[202] It is apparent, therefore, that chapters 12 and 13 had a literary existence before they were brought together, but that the redactor also has interpreted the preexistent materials he received into the form which now exists.

Within chapter 13 two small traces of the redactor's activity are to be seen. Rev 13:2b and 13:4a are the only two passages in chapter 13 in which the dragon appears. Both are identifiable as later additions. In v. 2b it is reported that the dragon had given dominion (ἐξουσία [exousia]) to the beast. This verse is ultimately identical to v. 7, according to which the beast received hegemony (ἐξουσία [exousia]) over the peoples. One of these verses is, therefore, contextually superfluous. V. 2b interrupts the description of the beast. Previously in vv. 1-2a, and subsequently in v. 3, the authorial wording of the vision has been maintained. Only v. 2b, with its totally invisible larger tale, falls away from the context of the things being examined. — V. 4a, the adoration of the dragon, who has granted dominon to the beasts, stands and falls along with v. 2b. — The basic motive for all this is, however, to be taken from the whole context. One can certainly speak of a context, but only in the narrowest sense, from v. 5 on, where each sentence also represents a unit of its own. Nevertheless, it is possible to perceive a thread along which the details are strung. The beast has received an extreme wound on one of its heads, but the wound has been healed. The whole world is amazed by this and prostrates itself before him: "Who is like the beast, and who can fight against him?" (Rev 13:4b). While the whole world submits itself to the amazingly healed monster, it acts disdainfully. It opens its mouth to blaspheme against heaven (Rev 13:5f.). And it then begins to have dominion over the whole world, over Israel (Rev 13:7a) and over the heathen (Rev 13:7b). — The context thus describes how the beast, despite, yes, precisely because of his mortal wound, has come to power! The healing of that wound is a splendid confirmation of his wonderful might, so much so that by that might the whole world is brought down to a state of submissive resignation. The beast itself, however, aware of its own indomitability, at this point lays claim upon the empire. — Rev 13:2b and 4a break into the context, speaking (too early) of the beast's power, which, according to the flow of the narrative, will be reported only at Rev 13:7b. Rev 13:2b speaks of its power even before it speaks of its mortal wound! Moreover, Rev 13:4a separates the amazement of the world *at* (Rev 13:3b) and the voluntary subordination of the world *to* (Rev 13:4b) the healed beast, . . . it separates these features when they actually belong together! Thus the two passages of chapter 13 which speak of the dragon are shown to be later additions, . . . later additions which seek to establish a connection between chapters 12 and 13.

In the continuation as well, both traditions can, here and there, be distinguished. The word δράκων [*drakōn*] (Rev 16:3 and 20:2) serves as a clue to the first of these.[203]

Revelation 12, 13, and 17 (with their continuations) are, therefore, related passages, according to content, but are from different points in the actual flow of history! Before their insertion into our book of Revelation they existed as literally independent pieces of the tradition. Accordingly, the purpose, meaning, and origin of the traditions of chapters 13 and 17 arose in order to establish and enable referential linkages back to chapter 12.

Traditional exegesis explains the chapter as allegorical forms composed by the author, according to the example of David, for the representation of contemporary situations. This understanding is clearly dismissed by the observation that the chapter contains traditional materials. The totality of these individual passages does not permit us to conclude that an individual writer could have fabricated it as the image of a specific political situation. On the other hand, it is unquestionable that the apocalyptists did see, in the traditions handed down by them, images of the empire of their own time. The possibility exists that through the respective contemporary interpretations of the tradition certain contemporaneous features did indeed find their way into the material.[204] We must investigate whether and to what degree this is the case.

Let me begin with the features which were most certainly intended contemporaneously, i.e., the seven heads and the ten horns. In chapter 12 the dragon wears seven diadems on the seven horns. This is the case because seven kings would rule over the empire.[205] In chapter 13 the beast has ten horns with ten diadems. Whoever wrote this statement had to have been able to count out ten kings![206] Additionally, there is found in chapter 13 still another calculation. This one must indicate, like the wounded head of Rev 13:3 — as is commonly conceded — the fate of a particular Caesar. In this verse the seven heads thus represent kings, and accordingly they designate seven kings.

The second of the two royal calculi is internally linked to the context of the chapter itself. The enumeration of ten kings [κέρατα δέκα [*kerata deka*], "ten horns"] in v. 1 has, therefore, been added later.

Matters in chapter 17 are even more problematic! The description of the beast mentions no diadems. It appears generally to attempt a renunciation of the enumeration of the kings. This impression is confirmed by v. 9, where the seven heads are linked to the seven hills of Rome. With this, then, an explanation on the basis of kings and the calculation of seven kings is excluded as a truly viable option.

Rev 17:10 adds a second interpretation of the seven heads: they are seven kings! The author says in a slightly mysterious, though completely lucid manner that he himself lived under the sixth king. The most apparent assumption is, naturally, that the verse was an addition by a later hand.

The situation is a bit more secure for Rev 17:11.[207] Here an eighth figure will be mentioned in dark words, an eighth figure who (now finally!) shall be the last figure. The author endeavors to make this eighth figure compatible with the preceding heptad. He has devised two ways to make the impossible possible. He contends that (a) the eighth is one of the seven; and, at the same time, (b) the eighth is himself the beast. He probably means that the eighth is one of the Caesars who is already deceased, who comes again, and is also the incarnation of Roman power in the world. Such desperate images arise only in times of great need. Whoever wrote these verses lived under an eighth Caesar, and stood under the necessity of bringing this eighth one, who now was an undeniable reality, into line with the earlier teaching about "the seven."[208] Rev 17:10, which was written under the eighth Caesar, thus stems from a different time and is by a different hand.

Rev 17:12-14 and 17:16-17 give two interpretations of the ten horns. They do not forget that they represent actual kings. Since, however, actual kings of the empire could not be designated, they are interpreted as kings who are in the service of the universal monarchy. Their work may be considered differently: either these ten are those who in the final days will take the field against the Christ (cf. Rev 16:12-13f.) — so vv. 12-14 are to be explained; or they will help to execute the judgment upon Rome by means of a great rebellion of the kingdom against the capital.[209]

How is the great diversity of these varied regnal calculations to be explained? It was considered possible to obtain information from the form of the beast about the "number" of the Caesar and, thereby, to obtain information about the proximity of the end. When such calculations had, after a certain period of time, turned out to be in error, the attempt was made, by means of a new interpretation, as well as by means of a slight variation in the form itself, to bring together oracle and reality. The diversity of interpretive materials in Revelation 12, 13, and 17 demonstrates that the authors from whose hands the calculations came, were spread out over several decades. If it is noted that the interpreted material, despite all the differences of time and interpretive modality, has remained — the seven heads and the ten horns abide — then a vivid impression comes to the fore, an impression of the constancy of this tradition! The contemporaneous appropriation has left the traditional material at these most exposed points undamaged by tendentious alteration.[210]

We now turn to the investigation of the degree to which other features of the chapter belong to the tradition, or have been imported by the authors as they interpreted the tradition in terms of their own contemporary situations. In regard to this, there is, first of all, the question as to which features the authors understood in terms of their own times (i.e., contemporaneously). This question is not commonly raised at all by the usual modern exegesis. Because the chapter is considered to be a coherently designed allegory, it is looked upon as self-evident that these features are indicative of a *systematic* (i.e., total, or at least consistent in terms of all main points) . . . indicative of a *systematic* interpretive explication.[211] This supposition, however, is incorrect! In actuality we are dealing here with a tradition which only later has been applied to the contemporary situation of the moment, and with which even an ingenious allegorical interpretation could only partially deal! Moreover, we see in chapter 12[212] how a Jewish author was quite easily satisfied when he had comprehended only certain details of the tradition which he had received, and even then, only really understood them allegorically. In the same way, the contemporaneous interpretations which are appended to the vision[213] in Rev 17:9-18[214] touch upon only a portion of that which was actually perceived. We, therefore, have to distinguish, as carefully as possible, first, the materials which clearly are contemporaneously interpreted, then those which the author just barely understood, and finally those probably not contemporaneously understood by him at all. In the first two groups, those things which are to be regarded as tradition are those features which have parallels in the three related chapters, or those features of which the contemporaneous interpretations are so forced that they could not originally have been intended allegorically!

Let me first of all compile a list of those points in chapter 17 which probably belong to the tradition.

- The "many waters" on which the whore sits (Rev 17:1) have been linked to the peoples and the nations by the author (Rev 17:15).[215] This feature, however, has not been contrived, since it does have its parallels: Rev 11:7; 12:15; 13:1; 17:8; 20:3; Dan 7:2f.; *4 Ezra* 11:1; 13:2 (Syr. 13:52).[216]
- The seven heads are said to signify the seven hills of Rome (Rev 17:9). But

this form is so unnatural! — Who would come to this understanding without an explicit interpretation thereof? — And the other explanation, that there were seven kings (Rev 12:3, 13:3, and 17:10), lies so much closer to a good explanation that the understanding based on the seven hills is to be regarded as, at best, a secondary possibility.

- Likewise, the exegesis of the ten horns as supra-Roman kings is an unnatural one! Should the beast be the empire and should kings be depicted as horns, then it is obvious that the horns of the beast are the *KINGS* of the *EMPIRE!* This latter explanation is found, moreover, in the parallel passages of Rev 13:1 and Dan 7:7 and 24. At the same time, of the two interpretations expounded in chapter 17, the first (Rev 17:12-14), that they are kings allied with Rome, is still tolerable so some degree. The second interpretation (Rev 17:16ff.), that they are kings opposed to Rome, . . . this interpretation, according to which the correlated beast and woman would be separated . . . this interpretation is *completely unnatural!*
- The woman bears a name on her brow (Rev 17:5). The author adds that this name is "Babylon the great." But since the beast is also full of blasphemous names (Rev 17:3), and since in Revelation 13 the first beast bears blasphemous names on its heads (Rev 13:1)[217] . . . since this is the case, these pieces of information about the names would have to be considered as a tradition, all the more so since it cannot be said what the authors of Revelation 13 and 17 would themselves have understood by these names of the beast.[218]

Along with these clearly interpreted features come others which are implicitly understood contemporaneously.

- The author has comprehended the purple and scarlet robes in which the woman is clad as the exquisite garb of the empress (Rev 17:4; cf. 18:16).[219] But the feature has its parallels in the scarlet color of the beast (Rev 17:3) and the fiery-red color of the dragon (Rev 12:3), indications which certainly do not intend to point to the royal hegemony of these beings!
- The goblet which the woman holds in her hand (Rev 17:4) has, by analogy with Jer 51:7, been brought by the author into a relationship with the "wine" of her lasciviousness, a "wine" on which the kings of the world become drunk (Rev 17:2). Yet since Rev 17:8 also speaks of drunkenness, and certainly that drunkenness of the woman from the blood of the holy ones, the woman and the goblet of drunkenness appear already to have belonged together in the tradition.
- The wilderness in which the woman sits (Rev 17:3) cannot easily refer to

Rome.[220] It appears as if the author has adopted this feature without even knowing the first little thing about it!

- Finally, the "astonishment" of the seer who has seen the beast (Rev 17:6) is also a tradition. The feature appears again in Rev 17:8 and 12:3. In these passages, the whole world "is amazed" about the beast!

Consequently, at many points chapter 17 contains traditional material, material which certainly is, for the most part, interpreted contemporaneously but not essentially altered! Even those few features about which the same thing cannot be clearly established:

- the woman as an image of the city of Rome (Rev 17:18) in distinction from the empire; and
- her names, "the great whore" (Rev 17:1), "the mother of whores[221] and abominations of the earth" (Rev 17:5),[222] are not, therefore, to be understood as fabrications of the author.

Chapter 13 is the bulwark of the contemporaneous exegesis of the book of Revelation. Let me begin with the second beast, who rises from the earth. He has two horns of a lamb, "speaks like a dragon," and, by all kinds of miraculous signs — it makes fire fall from heaven and it makes an image of the first beast speak — it seduces humanity into the adoration of the first beast and of his image. It finally goes so far that the whole world accepts a signet marking on their foreheads and right hands, without which nobody can purchase or sell anything! This signet marking is the name or numeral of the first beast,

There are certainly enough interpretations of what this second beast is. It is either a particular historical personage, thus

- Vespasian;[223]
- Paul;[224]
- Josephus;[225]
- Alexander of Abonuteichos;[226]
- Herodes Atticus, governor of Asia Minor under Hadrian;[227]
- A Roman governor under Domitian;[228]
- Simon Magus;[229]
- "Some con-man from Ephesus, an adherent of Nero, perhaps, or the false Nero, or maybe even of Nero himself."[230]

Or it is the personification of a major group, e.g., astrologers, mathematicians, or entertainers of that time.[231] Or it is "the Caesarean representatives" in the provinces[232] — for example, the provincial parliament of Asia; above all, the Asiarchs themselves.

Each of these historical forms stands at quite a distance from the apocalyptic model. The designated individuals are much too insignificant to be a counterpart of the beast. But the Asiarchs had probably encouraged the Caesar cultus, even though they neither caused fire to fall from the heavens nor made the image of the Caesar a living reality; nor did they force the people into the acceptance of such a Caesar temple, nor were they — and please excuse me, for this sounds just a little bit crude — terribly horny![233] Or might the two lamb's horns, according to Matt 7:15, be an attempt to symbolize the seductive power of this being?[234] The false prophets in the gospel, however, wear a lambskin, a lambskin with which they conceal their wolfish pelt, which lies beneath! Lambs' horns, of course, conceal nothing. They are, accordingly, not a symbol for the seducer![235] Even if we wanted to retain a contemporaneous explication, we must explain this and other features as imaginative creations.[236] We have seen often enough in the materials above[237] that through this acceptance of an extremely imaginative enhancement of the contemporaneous *realia,* the whole contemporaneous interpretation becomes questionable. When one assumes, for example, that the Asiarchs were actually meant by the author, one then must ask: "Is this 'imaginative' description in chapter 13 of such a kind that the first reader, who certainly had to read the text without a contemporary commentary, . . . that that first reader would have been able, generally, to discover what it meant?"

The ultimate reason for the striking, yet also just a bit discouraging, fact that modern commentators who utilize the same methodology are, nevertheless, able to vacillate between the Asiarchs and Simon Magus . . . the ultimate reason for that fact is their common assumption that here, in any case, an historical portrayal must stand in the background! If secure results are to be obtained, however, we must go to work much more carefully! Since the author himself has appended no interpretation, a contemporaneous explanation of the whole picture, or of individual elements thereof, is permissible, but only if it arises naturally. Only the worship of the first beast fulfills this condition. Nothing other than the Caesar cultus can be understood behind that worship.[238] In the remaining materials the description of the second beast bears a great many features the natures of which have not come down to the present day. It contains so many of these features that it has been seen as an important depiction of the future.

Is this, perhaps, a product of the apocalyptic imagination?[239] This eventuality could be conceived as possible only if the description of the beast is internally unified. Now the second beast is designated in what follows (Rev 16:13;

19:20; 20:10) as a "false prophet," a designation consistent with Rev 13:12-17. To this designation, however, the first descriptive words of Rev 13:11, namely, the words about "the lamb's horns," have no relationship. One now observes that the peculiarly delineated features stand at the beginning and that the designation "false prophet" does not appear in the basic description[240] of the being in chapter 13, but rather appears only occasionally in that which follows, Rev 16:13, 19:20, and 20:10. One concludes, therefore, that we are dealing here with an appropriated tradition. The traditional material has been explained by the idea that the second beast was the "false prophet," i.e., the one who shall seduce the whole world into its final greatest sin — into the idolization of human beings.[241]

The words of v. 11 certainly do belong to the old tradition. There is the fact that the second beast comes from the earth,[242] and that the first one comes from the sea, just like Leviathan and Behemoth (Job 40:19; 41:23ff.; *4 Ezra* 6:49-52; *2 Bar.* 29:4; *1 Enoch* 60:7f.). Furthermore, there are the lamb's horns which the second figure (after the terrible beast) of Daniel 8 has. Finally, there is the "speaking like a dragon" (Rev 13:11),[243] which is totally incomprehensible in the present text.[244] For the remaining features which are consistent with the designation "false prophet" nothing is really certain.[245]

While in the matter of the false prophet interpretations diverge greatly, unanimity does almost occur in regard to the matter of the contemporaneous explanation of the first beast. In the case of the beast itself, the apocalyptist naturally had Rome in mind.[246]

Furthermore, the next thing is for contemporaneous interpretation to imagine "the leader as put to death." The question is which Caesar — for we must be dealing with a Caesar — which Caesar could the leader possibly have been intended to represent according to the understanding of the apocalyptist? Traditionally this question is answered on the basis of three different details of the Apocalypse concerning the leader, which are then combined:

- The healing of the mortal wound of the beast (Rev 13:3, 12, and 14).
- The existence, the nonexistence, and then the coming again of the beast (Rev 17:8).
- The mysterious number six-hundred-sixty-six (Rev 13:18).

Concerning these three details the following is then asserted: The wounded head and the beast which has been and now is no more, are symbolic representations of the same person, the deceased Nero. Likewise, the healing of the mortal wound and the return of the beast from the abyss imply the same thing: Nero would come again — a belief which, after Nero's death, did indeed circle widely. This exegesis is given "the seal of approval" by means of a numerological calculation of the number *six-hundred-sixty-six* — נרון קסר [*nirôn qēsār*].[247]

Very strong objections may be raised to this interpretation. The number *six-hundred-sixty-six* is the number of the beast, not that of one of his heads! The beast is to be understood allegorically so that it is actually the number of the empire and not the number of a Caesar.[248] Therefore, the explanation of the numerical enigma as stemming from נרון קסר [*nirôn qēsār*] is false!

Now it can indeed be said that in chapter 17 the worst Caesar is also equated with the beast itself. However, it is methodologically unsound to bring an interpretation from chapter 17 to bear facilely on chapter 13 as well.[249] And even in chapter 17, this identification does not occur in the foundational materials of the chapter, but rather in a very late, rather contrived, explanatory gloss (Rev 17:11), a gloss which had been written, during the distress, in order to reconcile the *eighth* Caesar of real time with the *seventh* Caesar of the dogmatic view.[250] The texts, however, which are drawn from chapter 13 for this equation, are quite different: one of the heads will be "wounded," but the wound of the beast will be healed (Rev 17:3, 12) and the beast "remains alive" (Rev 17:14).[251] This is not an analogizing of beast and head. Rather, it is to be understood quite plainly and naturally: a beast of whom a head is wounded has himself a mortal wound.

It would also be incorrect to read something like the second coming of Nero out of chapter 13. The reference to Rev 17:8, according to which the beast comes forth again from the abyss, is again methodologically reprehensible. Once again, the passage speaks of the beast, i.e., of the empire, not of an individual Caesar! Chapter 13 itself, however, does say (probably of the beast) that it has remained among the living despite its mortal wound, since that would had been healed again! This would mean, if an allegorical interpretation is believed to be recorded here, that one of the Caesars has been killed — by a sword (Rev 13:14) — and that the kingdom has, through this murder, become unstable. But the kingdom does continue to exist. That the deceased Caesar again comes to life is not said! Such a great and, by its nature, overwhelmingly unexpected miracle must naturally, if it was to be considered at all, be explicitly described. Therefore, the relation of the wounded head to the "returning" Nero = six-hundred-sixty-six is to be rejected on several grounds.[252]

Who could the wounded head be, then, if that feature was generally intended to be understood in contemporaneous terms? A Caesar whose murder had placed the *imperium* in question. A Caesar, after whose death, however, the *imperium* had emerged built on a new foundation!

Among the first seven Caesars we have here to choose only between

Caesar himself and Nero![253] Against Nero is the fact that he fell by his own hand (suicide). This and other characteristic features of the image of this ruler would hardly have been overlooked by the apocalyptist if he had actually intended Nero. In Caesar's favor is the fact that the upheaval after this ruler's death was far deeper than after that of Nero, and the fact that the establishment of the kingdom after the death of the first ruler is itself characteristic of Rome! It is further noteworthy that there is mention of this wounded head right at the beginning of the whole context, while the power over all peoples is only reported at the end (Rev 17:7b, 8). On this basis, the death of the emperor is to be taken as the first great event of the history of the empire. This interpretation based on Caesar has been expressed by the apocalyptist himself, if Rev 17:3 is translated into Hebrew.[254]

On the basis of all this I believe it to be probable that the apocalyptist understood the murdered Caesar to lie behind the "wounded" head. An opinion must be formed, or at least a broader question should be raised, as to whether the apocalyptist already had found this feature in the tradition (even if he has interpreted it contemporaneously) or whether he did not find it there at all. When interpreted as an allusion to Caesar's (or even Nero's) death, it does not quite leave the impression of an allegory devised ad hoc. Form and content deviate rather strongly from one another. Reference to the subsequent greater Caesar, the one who established the *imperium* anew, is completely lacking. And the form itself has a feature which neither can nor may be applicable in reference to actual history. If the whole world, horrified about the healing of the beast, raises the question, "Who can do battle with the beast?" then it is assumed that the beast had suffered the wound in a battle. This battle is not to be assigned either to Caesar's or to Nero's time, since neither Caesar nor Nero fell in a Roman war. There is also the point that this war is not described. Rather, it is simply assumed, but quite obscurely.[255] This is not the style of a writer who actually fashions allegories. Rather, it is the style of a tradition which obscures by means of allegory. This is consistent with the fact that the main point of the context of chapter 13, the "astonishment" (v. 3), occurs twice more in chapter 17, at vv. 6f. and 8. The "astonishment" of the world concerning the beast (Rev 13:3; 17:8), since it belongs to the context of the history in chapter 13, is more original than the astonishment of the seer in Rev 17:7. Furthermore, the fact of the world dominion of the beast, despite his wound, has a counterpart in chapter 12, where the earthly reign of the dragon begins *after* his defeat by the heavenly host. Rev 11:7 also mentions a victorious battle of the monster. Daniel 7 also tells of the plucked-off horns of the fourth beast. The most striking parallel to Rev 13:3, however, is offered by Dan 8:8, where the first sovereign, whose death caused the kingdom to stagger, is represented by a horn, a horn which is, certainly, smashed to pieces . . . but a horn in whose place four new horns develop. Thus it follows that the "wounded head" also belongs to the tradition. And the enumeration of this head as the first among the heads may very well go back to the interpretive author.[256]

The remaining elements in the description of the beast are to be viewed in the same way. All the individual features are to be similarly established as well: the emergence from the water (cf. p. 219 above); the makeup of the beast (cf. Daniel 7); the forty-two months (cf. pp. 170-72 above); the blaspheming of the heavens (cf. Dan 7:8, 11, 25; 4 Ezra 11:43; 2 Apoc. Bar. 67:7); the war against the holy ones (cf. Dan 7:21; Rev 12:17); the adoration of the beast by all humanity (cf. pp. 141f.); the kings of the world as allies in the final struggle [Rev 19:9; cf. 17:12f.; 12:9 (πλανῶν τὴν οἰκουμένην [planōn tēn oikoumenēn]), 16:12-13]; the sea of fire as an abode of the overthrown (Rev 19:2; cf. Dan 7:11). Only a few of these features could the apocalyptist have seen in any way as fulfilled in contemporaneous phenomena. By the prediction of the blasphemy he raises the notion of Rome's insolent demeanor. By the adoration of the beast he raises the notion of the Caesar cultus. By "the war against the holy ones" he raises the specter of the oppression of the people of Israel since the time of Pompey. By doing this he might even reserve to himself the fact that the complete fulfillment of all these things will take place only in the future, in which the transgressions of Rome, currently still a μυστήριον [mystērion, "mystery"], will come to complete revelation and thereby to complete judgment. At any rate, the author of Revelation has not invented these features. He has, rather, only appropriated them, and, in part, has applied them as well as he could to Rome.[257]

Thus we find in chapters 17 and 13 a tradition which was essentially unchanged by contemporary exegesis. The question now is this: "Whence did this tradition stem?" Since Vischer what has been tossed up as the main issue in such cases is whether the text in question was written by a Jewish or a Christian author. The significance of such a literary-critical question for the matter, i.e., for religious history, must not be overestimated. Christian eschatology is, for the most part and, at any rate, in its fundamental points, of Jewish origin. Only at certain points has the Christian community produced in the eschatology anything new. So, it is not unusual, but rather in the case of our sources it is the rule, that ancient Jewish tradition have been imparted to us by a Christian quill. For theological examination, however, the important question is not whether we hear a sentence perchance from a Jew or from a Christian, but rather whether, according to its nature, that tradition belongs to the materials common to Jews and Christians or to the specifically Christian realm of ideas!

Now in chapters 13 and 17 of Revelation there is very little of the specifically Christian materials. Certain words in 13:8; 17:6; 17:14 (ἀρνίον [arnion, "lamb, sheep"]); 18:20; 21:14, are easily dropped, or, in any event, are unimportant for the whole passage. However one might feel about the literary question,[258] the tradition as such does not exhibit Christian characteristics.[259] The mood with which the empire is viewed — a fearful expectation, as the prophecies of the final terrifying transgression begin to be fulfilled within it, a simple anticipation of the final "ripening" of sin, and a rapid judgment thereafter — this mood may also have prevailed in many Christian circles. It certainly did arise in Judaism.[260]

The mythological material which we have encountered especially clearly in chapter 13 also extends beyond Judaism. Thus, for example, there is that which is presumed about the battle with the beast — we are reminded of the battle of Hercules with the Hydra of Lerna; the blasphemy against "the one who is encamped in heaven," and so on.

We come even further by means of a comparison of Revelation 13 and 17 with Daniel 7. They are closely related to Daniel 7. This relationship is traditionally explained in the following manner: the author was literally dependent on Daniel 7, a supposition which is plausible enough since Daniel is a part of the Bible and was the most popular prophet.[261] In addition, there are verbal connections: Rev 13:5; Dan 7:8; 13:7; and 7:21.[262] On the other hand, the chapters do have many original features [e.g., ch. 17 has the red color of the beast, the naming of the blasphemy, and the astonishment; and ch. 18 has the pseudo-prophet, the wounded head, and the allies], so that the assumption of literary dependence alone will not be sufficient. We find, therefore, that Revelation 13 and 17, in view of Daniel, contain, in part, independent traditions and are, in part, literarily dependent on Daniel. The boundaries of one in relation to the other are, in general, not securely distinguished. The dependence appears certain to me at Rev 13:5 and 13:7. One notes that the blasphemy of the beast is described twice, in the parallel verses 13:5a and 13:6. Of these, v. 5a is very similar to the Daniel passage in wording. On the other hand, the verse which deviates from Daniel in terms of its wording is also, in accordance with its peculiar mythological contents, highly original. Here tradition and materials acquired from Daniel may stand extremely close to one another![263]

The relation of the "beast composition" of Rev 13:2 to the four beasts of Daniel has been consistently explained, until the present, to the effect that the four beasts are drawn from Daniel and have been joined together into one composite being. The whole thing looks a lot different to us, however, on the one hand, when we find in Revelation a tradition at least partially independent of Daniel, and, on the other hand, when in our investigation of Daniel 7 we have found it to be just as possible that the four beasts of Daniel have arisen from a single beast through differentiation.[264] We must, consequently, judge that Revelation instead of Daniel has preserved here the original tradition.

The relationship of the seven heads and the ten horns of Revelation 12, 13, and 17 to the book of Daniel, where the fourth beast likewise has ten horns and where the four beasts altogether possess a total of seven heads, . . . the relationship between these two sets of features is more complicated than what we have just examined. The combination of seven heads and ten horns is, since it is comprehended only with difficulty, certainly not original. The diadems would originally have been on the seven heads and could have been transferred to the horns only from there, since diadems properly belong on heads! Moreover, the diadems by their very nature are not appropriate for the heads of a beast, but rather they are derived from an interpretation of the then-contemporary moment. Since in this we are looking into the historical points which were most commonly explicated contemporaneously,[265] it is therefore to be expected that we may not be able to decipher something that is so very complex.

Consequently, in their main points Revelation 13 and 17 are variants of the Daniel tradition. Now Daniel 7 is, itself, a link in a great chain, the tradition history of the Babylonian chaos myth. Through it Revelation 13 and 17 also find their way into a larger context. They are, hence, simply "cuttings" from the stem of the Babylonian chaos myth.

In Revelation we do hear of a monster who belongs to the abyss (Rev 17:8). It is called (Rev 11:7) "the beast,[266] which climbs up from the abyss." This is a name like that of Isa 27:1 and Ezek 32:2 (cf. Ezek 29:3), "the dragon in the sea." The designation τὸ ἀναβαῖνον ἐκ τῆς ἀβύσσου [to anabainon ek tēs abyssou, "the one who ascends from the abyss"] assumes that the actual abode of the beast was the depths of the abyss, in the very place whence it would arise in the last days; cf. Rev 17:8, καὶ μέλλει ἀναβαίνειν[267] ἐκ τῆς ἀβύσσου [kai mellei anabainein ek tēs abyssou, "and is about to ascend from the abyss"]. Ἄβυσσος [abyssos, "abyss"] is the Greek equivalent of תהום [tĕhôm, "the deep"], the Hebrew term for the primal sea, Babylonian Ti'āmat. 2 Apoc. Bar. 29:4 sees it in the same way: Leviathan ascends from the sea. ים [yām, "sea"] is exchanged here with תהום [tĕhôm, "the deep"], e.g. Pss 74:13; 89:10; Job 7:12; and with ἄβυσσος θάλασσα [abyssos thalassa, "the deep sea," i.e., "the primal sea"] in Rev 13:1. So, the ὕδατα πολλά [hydata polla, "many waters"] of Rev 17:1[268] are equivalent to המים הרבים [hammayim hā-rabbîm, "the many waters"] ‖ תהום [tĕhôm, "the deep"] of Ezek 26:19 and 31:15, in passages which stand more or less close to the myth, e.g., Hab 3:15; Ps 18:17; Add Esth 1:9, etc. (Cf. תהום רבה [tĕhôm rabbāh] in Gen 7:11; Isa 51:10; etc. as well as ימא רבא [yammā' rabbā', "great sea"] in Dan 7:2.)

The beast has seven heads (Rev 13:1 and 17:3). Leviathan is multi-headed (Ps 74:14). The Babylonian tradition also knows of a mythological "seven-headed great serpent," which is mentioned right next to the "great serpent of the sea."[269]

The description of the beast (Rev 13:2) rings Babylonian: *Ti'āmat* also has a lion's mouth, a Babylonian image which has been preserved for us.[270] The other parts, parts of a panther and a bear, like the twofold nature of the horns,[271] cannot at present be pursued beyond Daniel. We do, however, know from our admittedly small amount of material that the tradition concerning *Ti'āmat*'s form has fluctuated several times.[272]

This beast has taken charge from the abyss right out onto the earth, where it slanders the deity and oppresses humanity. Many Hebrew parallels assume the same thing: "blasphemy," particularly, is a constantly recurring feature (Dan 7:8; Ps 74:18; *Pss. Sol.* 2:32f.). This is so, similarly, in the Babylonian traditions. In this regard Rev 13:6, the blasphemous slandering of the "name" of God and "his tabernacle in the heavens," is also reminiscent of a polytheistic expression concerning primal times: the beast slanders the gods of the heavens (cf. Dan 11:36).[273]

A second being is linked to the beast, just as in the Old Testament [*Rahab* and *Tannîn* (Isa 51:9), Leviathan and Behemoth (Job 40f.), Leviathan and *hat-Tannîn* (Isa 27:1)], and just as in the Babylonian materials *Ti'āmat* and *Kingu* stand beside each other.

- The second beast exercises the power of the first "before him," i.e., in his name and out of service to him.[274] The redactor who linked Revelation 12 and 13 viewed the relationship of the dragon and the first beast according to this model: *Ti'āmat* had transferred her power to *Kingu*.
- The second beast comes from the earth, the first from the sea. The same situation pertains in the case of Behemoth and Leviathan (Job 40f.; 2 *Apoc. Bar.* 29:4; 4 *Ezra* 6:49-52; 1 *Enoch* 60:7-9). This is not dealt with in the Babylonian materials.
- The second beast causes fire to flash forth from the heavens. *Kingu* appears to be a fire god.[275]
- Dan 8:3 gives a parallel to the two lamb's horns. Berossus also tells of a chaos being who had the horns of a goat.[276]
- At the final battle the beast calls in allies (Rev 16:13f., 16; 19:19; and 17:12). In the older recensions of the tradition we hear, in much the same way, of the "helpers of Rahab" (cf. pp. 438f. and 75ff. above).

A new heaven and a new earth (Rev 21:1) follow the report about the beast. Here the apocalyptic tradition has retained the very ancient ideas since this originally was a creation account, . . . ideas which at times also resound through the Old Testament recensions.[277]

The continuation of the account in Revelation is extremely characteristic of the myth: "But the sea was no more." This comment can only be comprehended if "the sea" in the earlier world had been the principle opposed to God. We have here, therefore, a view of the sea which can be explained only out of the context of the chaos myth.

We have, therefore, attained the right to lay claim to a broader series of this chapter's features, features which are not covered in the other recension . . . to lay claim to those features *for the myth!*

Chapter 13 allows us to read between the lines about a battle, a battle which has taken place before the actual defeat of the beast. One head of the beast would have had to be wounded therein, yet the beast does remain alive. The world is astonished![278] The beast is jubilant! The gods are treated with scorn, all of them, because of the beast's invincibility.

Similar things are described in the Babylonian myth. *Anu* and *Ea* will be called upon for the fight against *Ti'āmat.* The battle, however, doesn't take place. We therefore have a variant which bears the primal shading. The phrase which the world cries out:

> "Who is like the beast?
>   Who can fight against it?"

could be a word-for-word translation from the Babylonian epic. In a Babylonian back-translation it would be one verse of four stressed syllables, which is the standard verse form of the Babylonian epic![279]

In the same way, the red color of the beast (Rev 17:3)[280] is certainly an ancient tradition, though until the present it has not been substantiated in the Babylonian materials. The meaning of these colors is, therefore, not presently clear to us.

After the conquest of the beast in both traditions Rev 21:2, 9 speak of the marriage of the divine conqueror. In v. 9 the woman appears to bear the designation "the bride."[281] This feature would fit the primal mythological tradition quite excellently: After the battle there is the hero's prize, "the bride." After the conquest of chaos and the reordering of the world, the deity establishes a new divine dynasty.

The "name of blasphemy" (Rev 17:3, 5; 13:1) should perhaps be comprehended as something which is parallel to the "tablets of Lordship."[282]

The woman is in a wilderness (Rev 17:3). We find repeatedly in the chaos narratives a juxtapositioning of water and wilderness (as in Berossus), as we do in Ps 74:14, Ezek 29:5, and Ezek 32:4-6. According to *1 Enoch* 60:7-9, Leviathan lives in the sea, Behemoth in the wilderness of *Dēndāin.* It is to be expected that a primal view of nature would be seen. In primal time, prior to the blessed deity creating the fruitful land, the world was water and wilderness!

The chaos being appears in chapter 17 as a woman sitting on the beast. Since *Ti'āmat* is a woman,[283] an old cultic portrayal could quite possibly lie behind this description. It is very common in the history of religion that more ancient religion represents the deities as animals, that a later time, however, prefers the higher, anthropomorphic depictions. The beast, which was handed down from the tradition, is placed in a certain relationship to the humanized form of God. Then the deity holds the beast in his hand, or he has it on his head or he has some of the symbols taken from the beast's body, or he stands or sits on the beast.[284] It is noteworthy that the goddess in the tradition of Revelation 17 has the same color as the beast on which she sits. The woman, at the same time, may have held something in her hand, something which is explained as a cup and stands in relationship to her drunken lewdness and her blood lust.

The woman bears the name, "The Great Whore!"[285] It should, perhaps, be recalled that in the Babylonian myth *Ti'āmat* chose as her husband her own son *Kingu*.[286] She is called, furthermore, the mother of whores[287] and the horror of the earth. According to Damascius,[288] this primal being is called "mother of the gods." It would not be inconceivable that the apocalyptic name might be a Jewish twist on the Babylonian idea. Or should it be thought that the terrifying chaos monsters are actually children of *Ti'āmat?*[289]

The signs of the two beasts (Rev 13:13-17)[290] have, as of right now, no Babylonian parallels. Since, however, neither Jewish dogmas nor contemporaneous allusions emerge here, it seems to me most probable that mythic features do lie in their background. They have, however, probably become quite Jewish since the time of their adoption.

One should not lose faith in the interpretation of this chapter which has just been presented. Faith in that interpretation should not be lost just because there is a whole series of points within the chapter which bear nothing from the Babylonian materials known to us at present, nor does that series of points have anything even remotely analogous to those materials.[291] We should not lose faith in the interpretation because of this. It simply demonstrates that the myth existed in a great number of variant forms across the millennia. Furthermore, it must remain undecided as to whether the traditions of Persia, though which the myth did, perhaps, pass . . . whether the traditions of Persia inserted any new features into it.

If, therefore, the whole complex and a wealth of individual points within the total complex of these chapters are in agreement with the Babylonian tradition concerning primal time, then the chapters also bear the Babylonian tradition's highly characteristic peculiarities. The main difference is that the Babylonian narrative is played out in *primal* time, while the descriptions of the revelatory visions of Revelation deal with *final* things. We have already detected this eschatological use of the chaos myth on several occasions, most recently at Daniel 7, 2 *Apoc. Bar.* 29:4, 4 *Ezra* 6:49-52, and 1 *Enoch* 60:24f.[292] Such relocation of a myth from primal time to eschatological time may appear strange to the modern person. To the Jews and to the earliest Christians, however, such an identification of the first and the last things is not at all an unusual thing. Just as in the ancient world, the first heaven and the first earth[293] were created at the beginning by God's word, so a new creation is expected for the final time,[294] בריאה חדשה [*bĕrî'āh ḥădāšāh*, "a new creation"],[295] καινὴ κτίσις [*kainē ktisis*, "a new creation"],[296] in which a new heaven and a new earth[297] arise. So an ἀποκατάστασις πάντων [*apokatastasis pantōn*, "restoration of all things"], through which the old passes away and everything will become new, stands in contrast to the creation of the beginning.

This second creation is generally conceptualized by analogy to the old creation. Just as the old world, for example, was preceded by silence, so it is said of the final time as well: "And the world will be turned back to primordial silence for seven days, as it was in the first beginnings, so that no one shall be left."[298] And just as one person [Adam], whose actions and sufferings determined the character of his descendants, stood at the very inception of the human world, so will the new humanity be inaugurated by a new form, the image of which it will bear.[299] Just as the sin and death of the old Adam, of the old humanity,[300] was decisive for the earlier epoch, so the righteousness and life of the new humanity, the second Adam, will be decisive for the next one. Just as the old serpent[301] had tempted the first humans, before Christ comes again, it will tempt humanity in much the same way.[302]

The "paradise" in which the earliest human couple dwelt will, at the end time, again become the dwelling place of humanity (4 *Ezra* 6:1; 7:53; and 8:52).[303] At that time they will receive a share in the Tree of Life, of which they did not receive a taste at the beginning (Rev 7:2; 21:2; 22:2, 14, 19; 1 *Enoch* 24f.; 4 *Ezra* 8:52).

Likewise, the Exodus from Egypt, the first redemption of Israel, and the appearance of the Messiah, the final redemption of Israel, are comparable things. The plagues that will precede the end time are considered in terms of an analogy to those plagues which were brought against the Egyptians. The second redeemer figure, called גואל אחרון [*gô'ēl 'aḥărôn*, "final redeemer"], the Christ, is considered by analogy to the former (הראשון [*hā-ri'šôn*, "the first, the former"]) redeemer, i.e., Moses.[304] In the same way, there are times when the great judgment of the flood and the judgment of the world at the end of time appear in parallel to one another. "As the days of Noah were, so shall the appearance of the Son of Man be,"[305] except that the old world was destroyed by water, while the present one is preserved for a judgment by fire.[306]

The common idea which lies at the base of these particular pieces, i.e., that the things of the end time will be similar to those of primal time, . . . this common idea is expressed with more conceptual clarity in a quotation from an unknown writing cited in *Barn.* 6:13: ἰδοὺ ποιῶ τὰ ἔσχατα ὡς τὰ πρῶτα [*idou poiō ta eschata hōs ta prōta*, "Behold, I make the last things like the first things"]. He, himself, the Ἄλφα [*Alpha*] and Ὠμέγα [*Ōmega*], the first and the last, forms the last things exactly as the first things had been.[307] If one wished to know how the end would be, one had to ask how the beginning had been. On the other hand, one is quite certain that all the final things have always been there. The heavenly Jerusalem, which comes down in the final days (Rev 21:2), was created together with paradise (*2 Bar.* 4:3). The church of the end time corresponds to the ἐκκλησία πρώτη [*ekklēsia prōtē*, "first church"], (*2 Clement* 14). Christ, the goal of all things, is at the same time their creator. The names of those whom the God of final salvation will acknowledge are, from the beginning, written by God in the Book of Life [Rev 13:8 (the number of predestined ones, *4 Ezra* 4:36)]. All good things of the coming aeons exist before the foundations of the world (Matt 35:34; Col 1:5; 2 Tim 1:9f.; 1 Pet 1:20; etc.).[308] This model of the equivalence of the first and the last things, therefore, applies to a great portion of New Testament speculations — the christology, the teachings on predestination, the teachings concerning the primal state of things, etc.[309]

The question as to whether the primal chaos myth is now understood eschatologically . . . that question is appropriate in this context. In the end time what had happened in primal time will be repeated. The new world order will be preceded by a new chaos. The monsters of primal time will appear on the earth a second time. Moreover, one form of the ancient myth has been taken on here. The old myth, which saw in the storm floods of the present, even if weakly, a repetition of the primal chaos,[310] had, here and there, said that the monster of the primal period was only "pacified," "bound" in the abyss, "shut up with bolts and a gate," and that, at times, it attempted to escape the divine power which contained it.[311] This picture is continued: the chaos beast, bound in the beginning by God in a deep abyss, will at the end free itself and "climb up" into the upper world.[312] But then, just as once before at the creation, he will be overcome anew by God. This time, however, there will be *definitive* eradication of chaos. In the new world that ancient battle shall not occur again.[313] The first time, "the sea" was only vanquished and brought into the divine order.[314] The second time, "the sea is no longer there" (Rev 21:1).[315] The first time, the monster was imprisoned in the abyss.[316] The second time, he will be cast into the sea of fire (Rev 19:20; cf. 20:10, 14 and Dan 7:11), where his existence will end — "it goes to destruction" (Rev 17:8).[317]

Given this, then, an eschatological shift has, in all probability, penetrated from the myth into Judaism.[318] At the very least, it is totally certain that the material, in order for it to refer to the empire, has been transferred into the end time. In *1 Enoch* 60:24f., *4 Ezra* 6:49-52, etc. this eschatological twist does exist, though without an allegorization of the empire being linked to it in those texts. Since the tradition is looked upon, even in Judaism, as a revelation, it is quite natural that at those points where we find it expressed it appears in the form either of an angelic speech (*1 Enoch* 60:5, 9ff.) or of a prophetic vision (Revelation 13 and 17).[319]

Judaism had appropriated this tradition, linking it to its eschatology. It either simply adopted the perspective of the myth so that the new creation is at the end of the world,[320] or it substituted for the major features of the ancient myth some aspects of its own particular beliefs. Thereby the divine conqueror, originally *Marduk,* has become the Christ. His bride has become Jerusalem. Chaos has become the world empire, i.e., Rome, in the era of Revelation.[321]

We linger over the most important, and, for the modern reader, the most obscure feature of the text, the equation of chaos with Rome. This equation came to be as follows. We hear of a terrible creature which shall precede the end. It had been customary for quite some time to interpret this creature as the current empire. During the time of Greek hegemony, יָוָן *(Yāwān)* was understood to lie behind it. Now a new time had come, however. יָוָן's *(Yāwān's)* hegemony had passed away. The great judgment and Israel's world dominion had not yet come. Instead, Rome's Caesars ruled the world. So the prophecy came alive anew, and the Jews perceived that time with both horror and joy. The prophesied beast, to them, was Rome, . . . Rome with its world dominion, with its deification of human beings, with its blasphemous arrogance, with its hatred of God's people. Even the little details of the myth have come to pass. The chopped-off head is the murdered first Caesar. God's prophecies, therefore, have come to fulfillment in "our time." The monster of the last days has already existed. — The tradition has been used so as to preserve sufficient information about the future[322] and to answer the old question, "How much time remains?" Though the end is near, however, it is still not there for the writer of Revelation. Much of this prophecy still has not been fulfilled in the present. The oracle spoke in dark words of a final enormous transgression in which the second creature, similar to the beast but in service to him, will ensnare the whole world by skillful lying. The beast shall become the god of humanity. Only then can the end come! This mystery of the final sin, however, is still not clear. Only the faint beginnings of it have taken place. In the future, therefore, redemption is seen as at the door. Before that door is opened, however, the rule of the wicked shall exist on earth, under which rule the faithful must endure many sorrows. That rule will wage war, so says the prophecy, against the holy ones.

What should be done in "these times?" It is not viewed as possible to escape the divine destiny by any action. The monster reigns and oppresses. It does do according to God's will until its time is over. Therefore do not oppose it. Do not lift up opposition! "Whoever takes captives will himself be captured. Whoever kills with the sword will himself be felled by the sword. The patience and the faith of the holy ones consists of this" (Rev 13:10). So Judaism — and after it primal Christianity — by this revelation nursed along the strength of those who had hope, as well as the strength of those who had given up hope.

Judaism viewed this tradition concerning the beast of the sea as an infinitely deep mystery (*1 Enoch* 60:10; *4 Ezra* 6:52).[323] The explication of the beast as Rome was only quietly whispered from mouth to ear. Chapter 17 regards it as a "mystery" (Rev 17:5), a "proverb" for the "knowledgeable ones" (Rev 17:9). Even the added explanation does not declare it directly, but rather refers to it only more or less clearly. Chapter 13 speaks of it even more obscurely. There is no word of explanation, but only a hint that deep things are concealed here. "Whoever has an ear, hear!" (Rev 13:9),[324] i.e., "Reader! Pay attention! This means something!" In order to comprehend this characteristic mystically detached attitude, one must recognize that it was necessary not to refer to the terror before Rome. That terror forbade more explicit speech.[325] That mystically detached attitude is the way one deals with such things. In this regard the revitalized Leviathan of *1 Enoch* 60:10 has already been discussed; cf. above, pp. 201-2.

From this atmosphere it is clear that Judaism, which was able to explain only a portion of the material, has handed down with that portion those things which were not understood; cf. above, pp. 170f. and 229f. This was certainly only part of the whole. Comparing our chapters 13 and 17 with the Babylonian myth itself, we can see that only a few fragments of the original features have been preserved in those chapters. Above all, the origin of this tradition from the ancient chaos narrative is very thoroughly obscured. The chapter could certainly have been read no differently in ancient times than it is in the present, without even suspecting the origin of the tradition. But should someone in Judaism or primal Christianity have known this original sense, he would have viewed the "wisdom" that Rome, the monster of the end time, was at the same time the monster of the primal period, as an inexpressibly deep mystery!

This is not improbable, however, since even in a much later time the equation chaos = Rome was put forward. *Midr. Gen. Rab.* 2.4.d will remark (at the passage "'Darkness was upon the *Těhôm*': this means the wicked empire [Rome], which is just as unsearchable (borderless?) as the abyss," זו מלכות הרשעה שאין לה חקר כמו התהום [*zû malkût̲ hā-rāš'āh še-'ên lāh ḥēqer kěmô hat-těhôm*].[326]

The μυστήριον [*mystērion*, "mystery"] of the beast in Revelation 17 is to be deciphered accordingly. As the seer perceives the monster, he is quite amazed. The angel, however, explains the great mystery to him: "This beast which you saw was, and is not, and shall ascend from the abyss and go forth to destruction" (Rev 17:8). Instead of giving the name of the beast, the angel gives the history of the same in ambiguous words. It is the solving of one enigma by means of a second enigma. The reason for such a remarkable phenomenon lies very close at hand: the words will make sense only to those *in the know*. Whoever *knows* of a person who fits this description should *know* that that person is the beast. But whoever is not initiated into these mysterious things, that person cannot infer the significance from the history which is transmitted to him.

Our exegesis has to originate from the single concrete feature within these words: "and shall ascend from the abyss." This saying is the characteristic attribute of the chaos monster (Rev 11:7; cf. Dan 7:3; Rev 13:1; 2 *Apoc. Bar.* 29:4). That the beast of chapter 17 is the chaos monster would be certain if the history of the beast could be understood as the history of the chaos being. The beast *was* — before the creation. In the present it *is no more* — the creator-God has bound it in the abyss. But it *shall ascend from the depths* — the end time shall see, to the consternation of all humanity, the one long unseen again appearing upon the earth. Then, however, it will go forth to ruin — at its second appearance it will definitively be exterminated!

Our demonstration, then, has succeeded. Since the empire is the new appearance of ancient chaos, it is the extremely horrible mystery about which the seer himself cannot be sufficiently astounded and to which he dares to allude only in very obscure words. Thus the author[327] of chapter 17 had still known of that original sense of the tradition and has brought into the vision in a mystery loaded way things understood only by an "expert" in the tradition, i.e., one who knows.

Accordingly, we can also venture on to the enigma of the numbers in Rev 13:18. Just like the author of chapter 17, the author of chapter 13 has appended an explanation (σοφία [*sophia*]). And just as in chapter 17, the haze is only partially lifted by these obscure words. The name of the beast is also not disclosed in chapter 13. Only his "number" is revealed, and even that number is addressed only to "those in the know." Whoever already knows the beast may work back and be convinced by that reasoning that he himself is in position of "the insight of the wise." Whoever does not know the beast, however, can gather next to nothing from "the number of the beast" alone.

Before a solution to the riddle is attempted, one has to figure out in which direction one should look. More often than not any old word has provided for the investigator a most intriguing fortuity which has a meaning in the context of the vision, and the number of which, incidentally, just happens to be six-hundred-sixty-six.

That is the number "of the name" of the beast. We, therefore, seek out not just any old name which might be, at least, appropriate for the beast. Rather, we look for a *terminus technicus*. This is in the very nature of the thing. The word can be determined only if the circle of possible words is a very limited one. Whoever is acquainted with the matter must also know the word.[328]

"The name" should be a designation for the world power. It is, therefore, certainly not a personal name. The fact that the number is an ἀριθμὸς ἀνθρώπου [*arithmos anthrōpou*, "human number"] is not a problem. This word does not represent a personal name, which would rather have to be designated ἀνθρώπου ἑνός [*anthrōpou henos*, "a certain person"] or ἀνθρώπου τινός [*anthrōpou tinos*, "some person"]. Instead it should be taken in the sense of a "communal number."[329]

There is a clue as to the content of the name in the parallel, Rev 17:8, where the "secret" of the beast is that it is the ancient chaos monster which will ascend out of the abyss. In which language would we have expected such a name to occur?[330] This tradition is of Jewish origin. Therefore, the tradition concerning the enumeration of the name, if ancient, is to be considered as Hebrew.[331] There is also the reality that in chapter 13 there occurs a series of very strongly Hebraized passages. The phrase ἀριθμὸς ἀνθρώπου [*arithmos anthrōpou*, "number of a person"] also can hardly be understood in Greek.[332] Zahn[333] leans toward the assumption that such numerical calculations are of Greek origin and penetrated into Rabbinic Judaism only in a later period.[334] The first point remains to be seen. Concluding the second point from our very late and only slightly fluent sources is just a bit too precarious. Besides, word-plays[335] and, quite probably, also applications of the art of גְּמַטְרִיָּה (*gîmaṭrîyāh*) are already found in the Old Testament.[336]

The designation תהום קדמונית [*tĕhôm qaḏmônît*], the primordial chaos, fits the requirements of the situation. תהום [*tĕhôm*] is a *terminus technicus* for "chaos."[337] It corresponds to the Greek term regularly appearing in such contexts, the term ἄβυσσος [*abyssos*] (Rev 11:7, and particularly 17:8). It is the word which is immediately expected. The byword קדמוני [*qaḏmônî*] is the usual attribute of the important features of the primal period, features which in the final time will either appear again themselves, or will have, at least, a corresponding feature. Thus we find:

אדם הקדמוני [*'āḏām haq-qaḏmônî*, "the ancient human"],
ὁ πρῶτος ἄνθρωπος [*ho prōtos anthrōpos*, "the first human"];

נחש הקדמוני [nāḥāš haq-qadmônî, "the ancient serpent"],
ὁ ὄφις ὁ ἀρχαῖος [ho ophis ho archaios, "the ancient serpent"]

antiquum silentium pristinum silentium ["ancient silence, early silence"]

ἡ πρώτη ἐκκλησία [hē prōtē ekklēsia, "the first assembly"]

ὁ πρῶτος οὐρανὸς καὶ ἡ πρώτη γῆ
[ho prōtos ouranos kai hē prōtē gē, "the first heaven and the first earth"]

הגאולה הראשונה גאל הראשון
[hag-gĕʾûlāh hā-riʾšônāh gōʾēl hā-riʾšôn
"The first redemption   the first redeemer"][338]

The attribute (קדמוני [qadmônî]) does not stand idly by, but rather explicitly indicates that the monster who appears in the time immediately before the end is the same one who once had existed in the primal era.[339]

The number of the letters תהום קדמונית [tĕhôm qadmônît, "ancient deep"] is six-hundred-sixty-six.[340] The text which the author himself makes possible for the reader is successful. By this calculation it can be recognized whether one knows the correct interpretation. We have here, consequently, insofar as it is really necessary, a final confirmation for the proposed interpretation.

The solution to the riddle posed in chapters 13 and 17 has finally become possible for us because we possess an undeniable basis for it in the other traditions. The earliest reader, however, who did not know about the history of the religion, could only comprehend these things if they were known to him from elsewhere. So, even at the end of this investigation, we see that there were Jewish circles in which our material was an orally transmitted, totally secret tradition. There would have been an extremely great concern in such circles to keep the secret secret! As the circles died out, the "wisdom" went to the grave with them.[341]

5. The Tradition of Revelation 12 Is of Babylonian Origin

We return now to the actual topic of our investigation, to Revelation 12. We have already found that this chapter contains an extra-Jewish tradition of a mythological type.[1] Now we are able to say with certainty from which mythology it stems. — The influence of Babylonian religion on apocalyptic thought, even on Revelation, has been detected finally in chapters 13 and 17. The tradition of these chapters, however — as we have seen[2] — is closely related to that of chapter 12. We thus conclude that the tradition of Revelation 12 is also of Babylonian origin.

A second proof of the same claim is to be obtained from a comparison of Revelation 12 with Daniel 7. Both chapters have the following parallel features:

- The beasts ascend "from the great sea" (Dan 7:2). The dragon belongs in the abyss.
- The fourth beast has ten horns, like the dragon. The four beasts, together, have seven heads. That is the number of the dragon's heads.
- The beasts exercise a rule on earth which is hostile to God and to humanity. Likewise the dragon.
- The fourth beast wages war against the holy ones; the dragon wages it against the brethren of Christ who adhere to the laws of God.
- The fixed duration of their [the beast's and the dragon's] hegemony is two times, a time, and half-a-time.[3]
- In place of the beast, a son of man who appears on the clouds of heaven finally receives the hegemony. The dragon is overthrown by the son of the "woman" who comes down from the heavens.

- Furthermore, in Dan 8:10 the small horn casts down the stars from the heavens. Revelation 12 has the dragon do the same thing with his tail.[4]

Judaism interprets the beasts as the empire. It hs applied the same interpretation to the dragon.[5] The son of man represents, according to Dan 7:27, the people of the holy ones, who come to power after the empires. The son of the woman will free the brethren from the rule of the dragon.

On the other hand, Revelation 12 is superior to Daniel in a great many characteristic elements. Because this is the case, it cannot in any way be understood as an imitation of Daniel 7.[6] It therefore follows that Revelation 12 and Daniel 7 are, in regard to the tradition, closely related. Since the Babylonian origin of Daniel 7 has now been demonstrated,[7] the same thing is to be maintained in regard to Revelation 12.

A third series of proofs arises when we compare chapter 12 with the Babylonian myth and its offshoots in the Old Testament, and in the later Near Eastern traditions. We thereby lay the natural foundation for the oldest form of the myth, a foundation which we can infer behind Revelation 12.[8]

The dragon was — as we have seen[9] — originally the monster of the dark water creatures, hostile to the light and to the land. With these things, the characteristic attributes of the Babylonian *Ti'āmat* are listed. Furthermore, in Rev 20:3 the word ἄβυσσος [*abyssos*, "abyss"] explicitly occurs. Ἄβυσσος [*abyssos*] is the locale in which the beast has his headquarters.[10] Ἄβυσσος [*abyssos*] is equivalent to תהום [*tĕhôm*] = *Ti'āmat.* The being bears the name δράκων [*drakōn*, "dragon"], which is one name of the chaos monster in the Hebrew tradition.[11] A seven-headed serpent, basically identical to *Ti'āmat,* is also known to the Babylonian tradition.[12] This serpent has a terrible tail with which it can strike things.[13] In the Persian tradition[14] the monster has the tail of a crocodile. In the Manichean tradition it has the tail of a fish.

This dragon has also arrogated authority for itself from the abyss outward onto the earth.[15] It is in battle with the powers of the heavens. They will not be successful in defeating their foe, however,[16] until the young hero arises, a hero who vanquishes the monster and frees the heavens and the earth. There are also the essential features of the Babylonian chaos myth: *Ti'āmat* is "outraged" against the "higher gods." *Anu* and *Ea* cannot defeat her. But *Marduk, Ea's* son, will be "avenger of the gods."[17] These essential features are retained in the Hebrew tradition, although in an obscured form.[18] They are quite clear in the late Near Eastern recensions.[19]

It is, moreover, characteristic that the victorious god is a relatively young deity. In Revelation 12 this is clearly presumed. The powers of the heavens and of the deep are already in existence and are already engaging in battle when he is born. Indeed, he himself is the youngest among his "brethren."[20] This youngest one is successful at what was impossible for the elders. The Babylonian narrative has the same feature. *Marduk,* although a late-born god, will, nevertheless, through his victory over *Ti'āmat* become king among "the gods his fathers." The same motifs have been recorded in the Mandaean tradition.[21]

Furthermore, it is characteristic for the chaos monster to get for himself "assistance" for the battle. In the Babylonian version this is the eleven monsters of *Ti'āmat.*[22] In the Old Testament it is the "helpers of Rāhab" (עזרי רהב [*'ozrê rāhab*]; Job 9:13).[23] In Revelation it is the kings of the whole world.[24]

Finally the dragon will be bound and be cast into the abyss, which closes over him and will be sealed (Rev 20:3, καὶ ἔβαλεν αὐτὸν εἰς τὴν ἄβυσσον καὶ ἔκκλεισε καὶ ἐσφράγισεν ἐπάνω αὐτοῦ [*kai ebalen auton eis tēn abysson kai ekkleise kai esphagisen epanō autou,* "and threw him into the abyss and locked and sealed it over him"]. With almost the same words the Prayer of Manasseh 3 will describe the shackling of the sea before the creation: ὁ πεδήσας τὴν θάλασσαν . . . , ὁ κλείσας τὴν ἄβυσσον καὶ σφραγισάμενος αὐτὴν τῷ φοβερῷ καὶ ἐνδόξῳ ὀνόματί σου [*ho pedēsas tēn thalassan . . . , ho kleisas tēn abysson kai sphagisamenos autēn tō phoberā kai endoxō onomati sou,* "who shackled the sea . . . , who confined the abyss and sealed it with your terrible and glorious name"]. Only as a result of this unexpected coincidence would one be able to reach the conclusion that the dragon was the being of the primal sea. Incidentally, in the Old Testament[25] and the Mandaean recensions of the myth[26] the shackling of the powers of the beast is spoken of numerous times.

This explanation of the dragon as the "primal dragon" is explicitly voiced in the statement added at Rev 12:9b, ὁ ὄφις ὁ ἀρχαῖος [*ho ophis ho archaios,* "the primeval serpent"]. It is certainly to be suspected because of the continuation — which, of course, doesn't really stand immediately adjacent to it — ὁ πλανῶν τὴν οἰκουμένην ὅλην [*ho planōn tēn oikoumenēn holēn,* "the one who deceives the whole world"] (Rev 12:9d) . . . because of this it is to be suspected that the one who added this statement[27] understood these as names of the serpent of paradise. So also is הנחש הראשון [*han-nāḥāš hā-rī'šôn,* "the primal serpent"] explicated in rabbinic tradition.[28]

Meanwhile, there is such a difference between the dragon of Revelation 12, that terrible monster which casts down the stars with his tail, and the cunningly seductive serpent of paradise . . . such a difference between these two that it may be assumed that the latter is a byform of the former. The primal serpent would originally have been described as a chaos serpent. It was only later, when the name was no longer correctly understood, that it became indicative of the serpent of paradise.

Therefore, Revelation 12 coincides with the Babylonian-Israelite tradition in terms of the common framework of the narrative, in terms of a series of active persons, and especially in terms of the conclusion of the report, i.e., the vanquishing of the dragon by the young hero. We have therefore won, through this comparative study, a new piece of evidence that Revelation 12 comes from a Babylonian tradition.

Now Revelation contains a wealth of features which appear either in the Babylonian myth known to us or in the derivative recension thereof, which have been pointed out by us. It does not deal with these as trivial things. Rather, they belong to the very core of Revelation 12, the history of the birth of the one who vanquishes the dragon. Accordingly, the whole structure of chapter 12 is characteristically different from all the traditions already discussed in detail up to this point.[29] While in those the divine victor first appears in the second part of the narrative in order to bring the matter to a resolution, in Revelation 12 he is the person right from the beginning upon whom everything turns. While there the theme of the myth is the origin of the world from chaos, here the theme is the divine victor, his birth, and his battle with the dragon. Therefore, the material of Revelation 12, if it is conceived as a Babylonian myth, must be regarded not as a new recension of the tradition familiar to us, but rather as a myth properly belonging to the cycle of the Babylonian creation narrative.[30]

However, even this characteristic feature of the chapter is not completely isolated in the overall chain of tradition which we have been highlighting. In both the Old and the New Testament recensions of the myth some echoes are found, echoes which reflect events around the birth of the god. We have also detected the casting down of the stars in Dan 8:10,[31] there in an earlier interpretation. Rev 12:7-9 tells us that a battle of the heavenly beings against the monster had taken place even before the victory of Christ. Rev 11:7 and 13:3 also speak of such a battle. In the original narrative of the flight of the woman, a juxtapositioning of the wilderness and the sea is presumed for a period before the creation of the world. This has also been attested elsewhere.[32] It is especially worthy of note that the number *three and a half,* closely linked to the context of our narrative, is quite familiar to the Jewish tradition.[33]

It follows, therefore, that even the original material in chapter 12 is to be assessed as nothing other than that which this chapter, along with the other recensions of the myth, had intended. Revelation 12 is, accordingly, a Babylonian myth. Of course there is certainly the possibility, which we have already pointed out repeatedly[34] in regard to analogous traditions, that elements from another mythology have flowed in. This cannot be excluded here either. Note the character of the tradition of Revelation 12, and consider that Palestinian Judaism of the later period had been open to religious influences, probably from the East even more than from the West.[35] So Persian mythology must be considered as well. In this case, the common evolution of the Babylonian and Persian views — according to the model of the Esther narrative — probably had taken place in Babylon.[36] The answer to this question lies at a distance for the biblical scholar. It can, however, be attained from the materials at my command. The Babylonian creation myth certainly had a great many recensions and episodes, of which we know just enough that the lack of a birth account in the Babylonian traditions known to us should not prove to be any problem at all for the origin of that part of our tradition in Babylon. There is a need to recognize the mixed tradition in our chapter, which, itself, appears to have a very uniform context.[37] This need has not existed before Revelation 12.

How have we now conceived of the material of Revelation 12 as a Babylonian myth? We can work out the answer to this question concerning the nature of the thing only after many suppositions and questions. I hope, however, that the Assyriologist will not imprudently spurn this assistance by the theologian.[38]

First there are the persons with which we have dealt.

- The dragon in the Babylonian tradition is *Ti'āmat*. It may be postulated that even in this tradition she was red. What does this color signify?
- The young god who brings the divine conflict to a resolution is *Marduk*.
- His father was, in the Babylonian account, named *Ea*. In Revelation he is not named. The father was not present at the birth. Why did he not protect the mother and the child? Perhaps he was not — in the modern sense of the word — the husband of the "woman."
- The mother is described as a heavenly goddess. The individual features are:
  - her garment is the sun;
  - her footstool is the moon;
  - a garland of the twelve stars of the zodiac is on her head.

These features appear to be drawn from a cultic image.[39] The name of the mother of *Marduk* is *Damkina*.[40] Here she is called "the woman." This designation does not appear to have taken shape first in Judaism, which wasn't really sure exactly what to do with it.[41] It refers to an interpretation which had already experienced the myth in pre-Jewish times.[42] What is the purpose of these speculations?

In addition to the father and the mother of *Marduk* there did exist a series of heavenly beings, the gods of the upper world. Among them — if this is not a Jewish addition — there was a higher one, an enthroned one.[43] In addition "the great eagle" was specifically mentioned. Was it the constellation of "the eagle" which soars in "mid-heaven" (Rev 8:13) with broadly spread wings (Rev 12:14)?

Why is it just the eagle who is helpful in *Marduk's* birth?[44] Was it perhaps the special animal of *Marduk?*

Ti'āmat has servants and allies in her struggle. Her servants at Rev 12:7 are superhuman beings (ἄγγελοι [*angeloi*, "angels"]). As her allies Rev 16:14 mentions "the kings of the whole world." Accordingly they are human, though this may be a Jewish interpretation of an earlier feature of the myth.[45] Along with these, *Ti'āmat* has froglike creatures for messengers.[46]

Aside from these beings of the heights and of the depths, there are still the "others of their seed." Either these beings dwell in heaven — they have abandoned the aggression of the dragon who has plummeted from heaven — or they belong to the abyss — they are enemies of the dragon. In power they are inferior to the gods and to the dragon. Are these beings human? Or are they, perhaps, the ancestors of the present human race? From which ancestor do they come? Why are they brothers of *Marduk?*

The narrative is set in a time when — apart from the abyss — only the heavens, together with the stars and the earth (as a wilderness) existed. The "creation," accordingly, actually consists only of the "ordering of the world." This is an outlook for which there is also evidence in the Old Testament.

Ti'āmat is an enemy of the gods.[47] A scene from the battle with them will be recalled. She has cast down a third of the stars from the heavens with her tail. This feature can be understood only as an aetiological myth.[48] The Babylonian contemplation of nature found a gap in the heavens, the origin of which was supposedly explained by this myth. One day stars had stood there, but the chaos beast had cast them down. Is this gap, perhaps, the Milky Way which could well be regarded as the third part of the heavens?

Marduk's birth takes place under special circumstances the reasons for which are not apparent to us. *Ti'āmat* knows — probably through a spoken oracle — about the destiny of the child. The heavenly beings, however, have not been able to protect the mother before the attacks of the dragon. So *Ti'āmat* stands before the woman in order to devour the newborn infant. A heavenly being, however — the eagle? . . . In the talmudic parallel recension[49] of the tradition it is the "winds" — snatches the child into the heavens at just the right moment. *Tiâmat* is after him. To protect the child a heavenly army attacks her, and she is cast down. So *Ti'āmat's* fate is decided. She is not able to apprehend the child. The oracle will be fulfilled in its time. The monster is all the more furious against the innocent *Damkina,* who is rescued from before it by the compassion of the earth and by the great eagle who carries her off to "her place" — my phraseology of "her place," i.e., the place of *Damkina,* should be understood as the holy place where she is later worshiped and where the myth would be told. — So *Ti'āmat* stands at a distance from her and contends now — as is not said

— with her other sons, until finally the verdict comes. When *Marduk* grows up, he comes on a white horse. He is crowned with a diadem. He has a secret name, which he bears on his robe and on his thigh. He comes at the head of a heavenly army. He overthrows *Ti'āmat*[50] and binds her in *Tartarus*.

The myth contains *Marduk's* birth as content. I do not believe that all, or even just many, myths can be understood on the basis of meteorological phenomena. There are some, however, that must be explained in that way. Since the creation myth has definitely come forth from the experience of the sun's "victory" over the night and the spring's "victory" over the winter, the same thing is to be maintained as well for the myth of the birth of the god. Until the spring comes down from heaven to the earth, the winter has its ferocious dominion over the earth. Humanity languishes under its rule and looks to the heavens when the deliverer does not come. The myth is told in order to provide the consoling thought that the god of the spring, the one who will indeed vanquish the winter, . . . the god of the spring has already been born. The deity of the winter, who knows his fate, is the god of the spring's enemy and may gobble him up like a favorite dish. The winter, currently in power, is also stronger than the feeble little child. His attempt to get rid of his foe, however, is unavailing. Will he then realize why he is so enraged? His power has already been shattered even though he himself is not yet aware of it! The year has already been turned over to the spring.[51] The child grows up in heaven. The days become longer. The light of the sun becomes stronger. When it is first awakened, it comes down and overcomes the ancient enemy. "Just trust, undaunted, in God. Spring must then come!"

Here the theme of the myth, that the birth of the god and the beginning of the hegemony of *Ti'āmat* occur on the very same day,[52] . . . that theme is, certainly, to be interpreted. It is the day of the winter solstice, when the sun appears in the constellation of Aquarius,[53] the beginning of winter. It is, at the same time, the day on which the sun turns in the direction of the constellation of spring, Taurus.[54]

Since this day is dealt with in a myth, it may be postulated that the birthday of *Marduk* might have been a feast and that the myth which belonged to that feast depicted a legend in much the same way as the feast of the New Year and the creation myth did, as the feast of Purim and the Esther account did, and, in ancient Israel, as the feast of Passover and the Exodus narrative did. All these feasts and legends belong together.[55] Likewise, it is also probable that *Ti'āmat's* defeat was celebrated on a feast day. We therefore arrive at two Babylonian feasts, a winter feast commemorating *Marduk's* birth and a spring feast commemorating his victory.

Now the three-and-a-half times are to be deciphered as the "measure of *Marduk's* maturity," together with the time of the rule of *Ti'āmat*, i.e., the time of winter together with the time of the lengthening of the day, from Christmas to Easter. It is the three months טֵבֵת [*Ṭēḇēṭ*], שְׁבָט [*Šěḇāṭ*], and אֲדָר [*'Ăḏār*].[56] Just how the "half-month" emerged in terms of the calendar must, for the time being, remain uncertain. Was the birthday of *Marduk* perhaps celebrated on the fifteenth of כִּסְלֵו (*Kislēw* — the ninth month of the Jewish calendar)? Or is the half-month a "leap month" of ten days inserted, just as it was into the Babylonian calendar, at the end of the year [according to the Jewish calculation, it would be the אֲדָר בַּתְרָא (*'ăḏār baṯrā'* = the final *'Ăḏār*, the thirteenth "month" added to the Jewish leap year)]?

It is pleasing to see that we can also make out the mood of the Babylonian "Christmas" festival. "Christmas" was even then the feast of hope which was not to be violated, and the feast of faith which, on the very day in which winter, chaos, and evil appear victorious, celebrates the birth of spring, of world order, and of good things.

Placed in this context, the myth has a positive meaning. According to the standards which we laid out for Old Babylonian myths, it is powerful poetry.

Revelation 12, if it had arisen on Jewish or Christian grounds, would have contained nothing more than a chaotic, desolate, and — it should probably be said right now — half-crazy phantasmagoria. It is, if it is understood correctly, a wonderful myth which speaks to us from ancient times, . . . speaks to us both of the eternal pain and of the eternal faith of humanity!

This myth has found its way into Judaism. We discover it once in a Talmudic passage[57] which represents a very obscure parallel recension of Revelation 12. Then it appears in some later works: in the expression "messianic woes" used for the sorrows of the end time; in the secret name of the Christ, "son of a woman"; in the calculations and speculations concerning the number *three and a half*, i.e., the καιροὶ ἐθνῶν [*kairoi ethnōn*, "measure of peoples"], as well as the μέτρον τῆς ἡλικίας τοῦ Χριστοῦ [*metron tēs hēlikias tou Christou*, "measure of the greatness of the Christ"];[58] in the form of the casting down of the stars as the terrible blasphemy which precedes the end;[59] finally, in Revelation 12, where the myth is quite thoroughly reported.

Which religious concepts and views has Judaism linked to this material? For the answer to this question the data offer additional interpretations in chapter 12 for most of the main points.[60] Then there is the Jewish adaptation of the material, the adaptation in which form it is included in the Talmudic tradition.[61] Finally, there are the "echoes," and the speculations, which have been linked to the "echoes." Moreover, one has to pay attention to the kind of Jewish interpretations and appropriations; at the same time, however, one must raise the question as to why Judaism had taken hold of exactly these particular features out of the whole tradition.[62]

Judaism had again discovered itself in the "remnants of its sources," and it had stipulated this by the gloss "which God's command established." There is a kind of humanity that is interested in nothing nearly as greatly as that which has to do with itself. Here we have, then, in general, the interpretive focal point from which we must orient ourselves as we gaze both forward and backward.

First, in what way did Judaism think of itself? The Jews, although they keep God's law, will, nevertheless, be innocently embattled by the Roman empire.[63]

The words thus move us ahead into the situation which is so well known to us from the writings of Judaism all the way from the Psalms of lamentation to the *Apocalypse of Ezra* [*4 Ezra*] and the *Apocalypse of Baruch* [*2 Baruch*]. We do know the thoughts of these people: "Why must we suffer innocently? Why does the savior hesitate so long and leave the pious ones in the hands of the heathen? When will God's kingdom finally come?"

Has Judaism drawn the comforting answer to these difficult questions from the myth? Its hope for Rome's fall and the victory of the Christ is found in the descriptions of the final chapters of Revelation, descriptions of the conquest of the dragon by the divine hero. It is possible to imagine with what feelings the Jews must read our tradition! First, they read in pain of the sorrows of the innocent and with anger against Rome. Then, however, with joyful elation they read of Rome's fall. Hope there may be, since God has promised that fall![64]

On the whole, the appropriation of our tradition coincides with that of chapters 13 and 17. It differs, however, by also interpreting certain events which had occurred before the persecution by Rome. There is, first of all, the birth and carrying away of the Christ.[65] Comprehension of the meaning of these explanations hangs on the fact that these events occurred before the Roman persecution. To the Judaism which, languishing under the authority of a foreign people, looks so longingly for the redeemer, the wonderful consolation will be given: the Christ, whom it desires to behold, has already been born! And he comes *most certainly!* The devil is able to do nothing to him. The little child has escaped to God!

In the Talmudic tradition as well it had clearly been recorded that the birth of the child took place on the same day that the persecution by the enemy began[66] — the day of the destruction of the Temple. So the faith which overcomes the world has found a lovely expression: "On the very day that our sufferings began, God also prepared the Christ, the one who shall deliver us from all our sorrows!"

In the same way, Judaism, through interpretation of the fall of the dragon, has strengthened its own faith! Here the dragon is the categorical group against whom the pious bring suit before God, and against whom God's rage has been inflamed. Now, however, the categorical group has been destroyed. God is no longer angry. So, "God will again allow the sun to bear his favor upon you."

Or, according to another interpretation, the dragon was, until now, powerful even in heaven. Now, however, he is defeated. Now God has attained the victory and the strength and the authority. And Christ has attained the power. The dragon's defeat in heaven will, therefore, be followed, sooner or later, by defeat on earth. "He has just a short time."

On the other hand, Judaism has retrospectively explicated its faith as well as its patience in this tradition. Sufferings *will* precede the end. The dragon, fallen from heaven, *does* have power on earth and *does* wage war against the pious! As a most extreme horror which must be expected in the final time, Daniel 8:10 has recorded the very casting down of the stars and has explained it as a blasphemy against the heavens by the worldly power. In such a way Judaism has attempted to establish from the tradition the bitter and personally very-difficult-to-accept idea of the necessity of suffering! The sorrows preceding the birth of Christ, which were — for some reason — already emphasized in the tradition, have here been referred to the hardships of the end time.[67] The train of thought of such an interpretation was as follows: "Just as the pregnant woman, who wishes to see the child, must make allowance for the *pains* of birth, so also must we, who are longing for the birth of Christ, make allowance for the *sufferings* of Christ."[68]

Another consideration has been linked to a feature of the myth which Revelation omits, the growing up of the child. The Christ is born and certainly arrives. But he is currently a youngster! He needs to mature. This time in which he cannot help at all must be patiently endured, for nothing helps like patience![69]

Revelation 12:12 presents another consolation. The verse refers to the reason for the horrible anger of the dragon. He is so very angry because he has only a little time. To whomever this reason for the dragon's anger is known, that person will also seek to endure that brief time! But how long might it actually run? How long a time will the καιροὶ ἐθνῶν [*kairoi ethnōn*, "measure of peoples"] endure?

Judaism knew something! It knew just how great a significance this question had at that time! All worldly considerations have to bear this question in mind! Even within our tradition attempts are made to figure out "a plan." It is characteristic that no feature of the entire myth recurs as often as this one. Even the redactor who cut off the fall of the dragon and who abbreviated the flight of the woman[70] has retained this one feature. The persecution lasts three-and-a-half times. Who knows how long a "time" is? Who can figure out how long Israel has to suffer at the hands of the world power?!? So, Judaism had confidence that the salvation was close at hand. At the same time, the acceptance of the fact that for just a brief time the Roman oppression would have to be tolerated . . . that acceptance was also powerful within the tradition. The correctness of this view is confirmed by the parallels of chapters 13 and 17,[71] in which Judaism has regained both its faith and its acceptance of historical circumstances.

In these interpretations it has been assumed that the conflict with the dragon actually lay in the present of the Jewish interpreter. This assumption is a "given" by the very nature of the thing. The consolation which such an interpretive tradition seeks to deliver is directed at the present. No religion pursues such a luxury simply because it is concerned about the ideas on which it might build its future. Every generation seeks and finds before God consolation for its own difficulties. Accordingly, the present literary context, in which the chapter follows the seventh trumpet,[72] is to be considered as a later addition.

If we have shown, then, the manner in which Judaism has appropriated the tradition, and if, at the same time, we have had an opportunity to look into the very heart of this unfortunate people, we should not be silent, for only a certain part of the material in these interpretations has been fully worked out. Judaism has left another portion misunderstood.

At two points secret Jewish designations have been disclosed. One of these is the name "woman's son," a designation used for the Messiah. The preference for such secretive designations may be comprehended from the fact that those "in the know" recognized them. Accordingly, the secret designation "Armageddon" (Rev 16:16) shows us Judaism from another side. The inquisitiveness which, as a rule, also emerges strongly in Revelation, wants to know, somewhat too readily, where the final battle of the whole world against the Christ will take place. It is very pleased to know the name Armageddon, of which there is, sure enough, just enough known to make a beginning! Whoever has heard of it can then see exactly where the place actually lies.

Another part of the mythological tradition, one which is not at all insignificant, is totally unexplained and unutilized. It is, nevertheless, transmitted along with the tradition.[73] In order to discern the significance of this detail, comparison should be made to the way the myth is utilized in the Old Testament. While the prophets and poets of the Old Testament have used the tradition for their own purposes with great spiritual freedom,[74] a totally different attitude in relation to the tradition appears here: the weighty atmosphere of the Jewish conventicle wafts up against us here, i.e., the conventicle where people sit tightly packed against one another so as to whisper deep secrets about the pondering of half-understood things, and so as to marvel even more at those totally incomprehensible things. This is the spirit which we already see in such passages as Isa 27:1[75] and in the book of Daniel,[76] and it is the spirit which has now been fully developed here.

This spirit may be a bit refreshing to us, especially if we compare it with the high and free prophets. It is, on the other hand, the reason why the myth is preserved in such amazing purity and clarity. In the Old Testament we have, precisely because of this great skill of appropriation, simply echoes of the Babylonian tradition. The more this skill has weakened, however, in amalgamating the foreign features into the Jewish tradition, the more purely has the Babylonian tradition emerged.

So a peculiarly dramatic idea is offered here. It is the idea that the tradition, preserved from a later time, has come to us in an even more pure form than previously. The myth in Daniel is transmitted more fully and completely than it is in the prophets. The myth in Revelation is truer and more complete than it is even in Daniel. This is a phenomena which shows most clearly that the Babylonian material has flowed anew into Judaism repeatedly.

There is not much to say about the Christian viewpoint on the material, a viewpoint which is expressed in so very few words. It is typical that both of the uniquely Christian pieces of Revelation 12, v. 11 and v. 17,[77] are additions to the Jewish additions. Here a small piece of a much bigger reality is indicated. In relation to this strange tradition, both Judaism and Christianity are closely related phenomena. The Christian interpretation has been attached to the Jewish interpretation of the material. In the Christian interpretation of the "remaining materials," there are, naturally, Christians who are forced to adopt the consolation presented in the tradition in the midst of their own persecution by Rome. The Christ who is born is Jesus, the "lamb" who was slain (Rev 12:11), "witness" to whom is the cause of their sufferings (Rev 12:17). But it is also the power of their victory (Rev 12:11). The fall of the dragon is understood as the triumph of the martyrs over Satan (Rev 12:11). The Christian interpretation is, therefore, just as eclectic and nonorganismic as the Jewish interpretation. From the Christian perspective there is also the fact that this tradition, of which so little is really understood, will nevertheless be transmitted further only because of holy awe before the deep mystery of this "revelation."

We have recognized, with the assistance of the Creation myth, how the Babylonian tradition has fructified the Israelite tradition at many different points. For the kinds of acquired materials and the appropriation thereof Genesis 1 and Revelation 12 are characteristic. It is basically the same materials which appear here two times, although in a different form. In the early periods it is a myth of primal times, a myth which made its way from Babylon to Israel. In the later period it is a prophecy about the end time. The mood and the needs of humanity had changed between the two periods, in Babylon no less than in Israel.

We have, therefore, traveled the full circle which was traced out for this investigation. Are there still other and perhaps more important things in Judeo-Christian eschatology which go back to Babylonian ideas? It is enough for the time being to have secured a single point!

APPENDICES

I. The Babylonian Creation Epic[1]

Tablet I

(1) • Once, when above,   the heavens were not named,
     • when below, the earth   bore no name,
     • when still the Ocean[2] primeval,   producer of both,
     • Mummu,[3] Ti'āmat,   who gave birth to both,
(5) • their waters into one   mixed together,
     • when no field was yet formed,   no reed was yet seen.
     • Once, when of the gods   not a single one was created,
     • not a name given,   not a destiny established,
     • then were created   the gods [. . . . .]
(10) • Luḫmu and Laḫamu[4]   arose [. . . . .]
     • Aeons[5] became mature   [. . . . .]
     • Anšar and Kišar[6]   were crea [ted. . . . .]
     • For a long time they lived   [. . . . .]
     • Anu [. . . . .]   [. . . . .]
(15) • Anšar [. . . . .]   [. . . . .]

[That which follows is broken off.]

[After a great lacuna of approximately 60-70 lines, two complementary fragments[7] are probably to be inserted, fragments which contain a conversation between Apsū, Ti'āmat, and apparently the son of Mummu.]

[4 mutilated lines]

(5)   • *Ap*[*su*], *his* [*mo*]*uth*   *he opened and spoke*
      • *to* [*Ti'āmat,*]   *the magni*[*ficent things he said,*]
      • "*So lo*[*ng*] *their*[8] *way*[9]   [. . . . .]
      • [. . . . .] [. . . . .]
      • *I will thwart their*[10] *plan*   [. . . . .]
(10) • *May lamentations ring out,*   *wail*[*ings.* . . . ."]
      • [*When Ti*]*'āmat*   [*heard*] *the same,*
      • [then she cried out] *wailing*   [. . . . .]
      • [. . . . .]   [. . . . .]
      • [a curse] *she uttered*   [. . . . .]
(15) • [*"Wh*]*y should we*   [. . . . .]
      • *to them*[11] *a way will be exhausting,* [. . . . .]
      • [*Thereupon*] *divine Mummu*[12]   *Apsū* [*his*] *fa*[*ther*]
        an[*swered*]
      • . . . . *compliant* *counsel.* . . . .
                                                      [. . . . .]
      • "[*It will thw*]*art his plan*   [. . . . .]
(20) • [*The light*] *will become dark.*   *Like the night may* [*it be!*]
      • *Apsū himself* [*heard it*],   *for* [*his*] *counte*[*nance*] *brightened.*
      • *They planned an evil thing*   *against the gods.* . . .

[There follow 4 corrupted lines]

[After a lacuna of probably at least 15-20 lines, there follows the description of the ragings of *Ti'āmat* repeated three times][13]

[4 mutilated lines]

      • *Ti'āmat, the mother of the gods,*   *raged against them,*
      • *assembling a mob*   *fuming angrily,*
      • *she turned to*   *the gods together.*
      • *The Aeons who were created*   *went to her side.*
(5)   • *Cursing the day*   *they followed Ti'āmat,*
      • *raging, planning disaster*   *ceaselessly day and night,*
      • *prepared for war*   *rampaging, raving,*
      • *they raged together!*   *They began the fight!*
      • *The mother of the depths,*[14]   *the creatrix of everything,*
(10) • *She took on weapons of victory,*   *creating enormous serpents,*
      • *with sharpened fangs,*   *ruthless in the attack.*

> • With poison as well as with blood
> she filled their bodies.
> • Adders wreaking havoc,
> clothed with terrors,
> • she filled them with horror.
> She let them be on high.

(15) • Their appearance might be. . . .
. . . .
> • their body swelled up
> because irresistible is their breast.
> • She created a viper,
> a raging serpent, a Laḫamu,[15]
> • a "great day,"[16] a wild dog,
> a scorpion-person,
> • "circling days,"[17] a fish-person
> and a ram,

(20) • bearing merciless weapons,
> unafraid of battle,
> • defiantly minded,
> insurmountable to the foe.
> • And then, having formed
> these eleven in such a way,
> • among the gods her sons
> she made them into an assembly.
> • She raised up Kingu
> made him great in their midst.

(25) • "You are to go at the head of the host,
> which is your duty.
> • You will command the raising of weaponry
> the departure to the battlefield."
> • To be first in battle,
> to be most supreme in victory,
> • she laid this in his hand,
> and she place him upon the throne.
> • "I have cast a spell for you.[18]
> I have raised you up among the gods!

(30) • I have given you dominion
> over the gods as a body.
> • Highly awesome shall you be.
> You are my only husband.
> • Your name shall be great
> over [the globe]!"
> • Next she gave him the tablets of destiny,[19]
> laid them on his breast.
> • "Your command is unchangeable!
> The word of your mouth is established!"

(35) • Since Kingu now was exalted
> heavenly divinity[20] had obtained,
> • she set this destiny
> for the gods, her sons:
> • "The opening of your mouths
> shall calm the fire.
> • The sublime beauty of Kidmuri[21]
> shall extinguish the embers."[22]

Tablet II

[Here, as emerges from that which follows, is the speech against *Ti'āmat* by *Anšar* which must have occurred beside the futile speeches of *Anu* and *Ea* against *Ti'āmat*. Then *Anšar* turns to *Marduk* once again, given a description of the outrage of *Ti'āmat*][23]

	• "Ti'āmat, our mother,	has become enraged against us,
	• assembled a mob,	raged furiously.
	• She turned to	the assembled gods.
	• The Æons, who were created,	she kicked aside.
(5)	• They cursed day.[24]	They followed Ti'āmat,
	• angry, planning disaster	ceaselessly day and night;
	• Ready for the battle,	raging, raving,
	• They ganged up together,	they began the dispute.
	• The mother of the deep,	the creatrix of the All,
(10)	• Added weapons of victory,	creating enormous serpents,
	• with sharpened fangs,	merciless in the attack.
	• With poison as well as with blood	she filled up their bodies.
	• Furious poison vipers	she clothed with horror!
	• She fitted them out with fearful things.	She made them. . . . .
(15)	• "Her appearance might. . . .	
	• her body swelled up!	Even her breast was not resistant!"
	• She created a viper,	a raging serpent, a Laḫamu,
	• a "great day," a wild dog,	a scorpion-person,
	• "circling days," a fish-person,	and a ram,
(20)	• bearing merciless weapons,	unafraid of battle,
	• defiantly minded,	insurmountable for the foe!
	• And then, having formed	these eleven in such a way,
	• among the gods, her sons,	she then made them into an assembly.
	• She raised up Kingu.	She made him great in their midst!
(25)	• "You are to go at the head of the host,	which is your duty.
	• You will command the raising of weaponry,	the departure to the battlefield."
	• To be first in battle,	to be most supreme in victory,
	• these things she laid in his hand,	and placed him on the throne.
	• "I have cast a spell for you!	I have raised you up among the gods!
(30)	• I have given you dominion	over the gods as a body!
	• Highly awesome shall you be.	You are my only husband!
	• Your name shall be great	over [the globe]!"
	• Next she gave him the tablets of destiny,	laid them upon his breast.
	• "Your command is unchangeable!	The word of your mouth is established!"
(35)	• Since Kingu now was exalted,	had obtained heavenly divinity,
	• She decided this destiny	for the gods, her sons:

- "The opening of your mouths   shall calm the fire.
- The sublime beauty of Kidmuri   shall extinguish the embers.
- [As Marduk heard this   his heart was] very greatly dismayed!
(40) • [. . . . .]   on his li[ps] he was biting.
- [. . . . .]   his mind became enraged,
- [. . . . .]   his shouting. . . . .
- [. . . . .]   [he thought about] battle.
- [Then he spoke to] his fa[ther:]   "Do not be sad!
(45) • [. . . . .]   of the Ocean[25] you shall be lord.
- [. . . . .]   of Ti'āmat I shall counter.
- [. . . . .]   . . . . of destiny.

(More signs are missing, but not very many. Where the text again is readable, the situation is still that of the conversation between *Anšar* and *Marduk*).

(What follow immediately are simply partially mutilated line endings).

- [. . . . .] . . of his heart.[26]
- [. . . . .] . . near you,
- [. . . . .]   calm your [heart]!
- [. . . . .]   of his father,
(5*) • [. . . . .] Anšar
- [. . . . .   of la]mentation was full!
- [. . . . .] was removed.
- [. . . . .   the wo]rd of your lips,
- [. . . . .] of your heart,
(10*) • [. . . . .   The wo]rd of your lips,
- [. . . . .] of your heart,
- [. . . . . will] lead you out.
- [. . . . .] . . . .
- [. . . . .] act magnificently
(15*) • [. . . . .] you
- [. . . . .] act magnificently
- [. . . . .] you
- [. . . . . know]ing meaning.
- [. . . . .] act magnificently
(20*) • [. . . . .] . . . .
- [. . . . .] later."
- Ma[rduk heard]   the words of his father.[27]
- In the longing of his heart   he spoke to his father:

• "O lord of the gods,	scion[28] of the great gods,
(25*) • If I shall really	be your avenger,
• conquering Ti'āmat,	saving you all,
• then prepare a meal.[29]	Make the liberation banquet substantial.
• Assemble in Ubšugina![30]	Act joyfully!
• With my mouth, just like you,	I will then decide!
(30*) • I will not alter	whatever I create.
• The word of my lips	shall not be cancelled nor invalidated!

(Conclusion of Tablet II)

Tablet III[31]

• After that Anšar	opened his mouth.
• [To GA-GA] his emissary	he addressed this word:
• "[O GA-GA, you em]issary	who pleases my heart,
• [to Luḫmu and Laḫ]amu	I will send you.
(5) • [To my heart's command]	you shall diligently listen!
• [. . . . . .] yours [. . . . .]	before you.
• [Invite to the feast]	the assembled gods!
• [May they be seated at the table.]	May they stuff themselves at the banquet!"
• [May they eat bread!]	May they mix wine!
(10) • [May they take] their [seats]	and decree the destiny!
• [So go, now, of GA-]GA,	get over in front of them!
• [The command which I] caused you to hear	announce to them:
• Anšar, your son	has sent me.
• His heartfelt command	he has caused me to hear:
(15) • 'Ti'āmat, our mother,	has become enraged against us,
• assembling a mob against us,	raging furiously!
• The gods together	turned to her.
• The Aeons, whom she created,	move on beside her.
• Cursing the day	they follow Ti'āmat!
(20) • Raging, planning disaster,	ceaselessly day and night,
• ready for battle,	raging, raving,
• they banded together.	They began the strife!
• The mother of the deep,	the creatrix of everything,
• added invincible weapons,	creating enormous serpents,

(25) • with razor-sharp fangs,   merciless in their attack!
• With poison, as if with blood,   she filled their bodies!
• Furious adders   she clothed with horrors!
• She provided them with terrors!   She made them high . . .'
• 'May their appearance   . . . .
(30) • May their bodies swell up,   so that their chests cannot be turned back!'

• She created a viper,   an angry serpent, a Laḫamu,
• a 'great day,'[32] a wild dog,   a scorpion-person,
• 'circling days,'[33] a fish-person   and a ram,
• bearing merciless weapons,   unafraid of battle,
(35) • abhorring sensibility,   irresistible to their foes!
• At the same time, however, since she formed   the eleven in such a way,[34]
• among the gods, her sons,   she called an assembly.
• She raised up Kingu,   made him great in their midst.
• ' Go first before the host,   that is your commission!
(40) • Command the raising of weapons, the outbreak of the battle!'
• To be the primus in battle   the chieftain in victory,
• this she placed within his hands, and she placed him on the throne!
• 'I have cast a spell for you.   I have raised you up among the gods.
• I have vested you with authority over the assembled gods.
(45) • You shall be highly elevated.   You shall be my only husband!
• Great shall be your name,   great above [the earth]!'
• Next she gave him the tablets of destiny!   She placed them on his chest!

• 'Your command shall be valid! The dictates of your mouth will stand fast!'
• Now that Kingu was exalted,   had obtained heavenly dominion,
(50) • Then she established the destiny of the gods, her sons:
• 'The opening of your mouths shall dampen the fire!
• The exaltation of Kidmuri   shall obliterate the embers!'
• I dispatched Anu,   but he would not battle her.
• Nugimmud was terrified   and he turned back!
(55) • Then I sent Marduk,   the advisor of the gods, your son,
• to counter Ti'āmat.   His heart drove him!
• He opened his mouth   and he spoke to me:
• 'If I really   am to be your avenger,
• to conquer Ti'āmat,   to rescue you all,
(60) • then prepare a meal!   Throw a wild banquet!
• Assembling in Ubšugina,   enter in joyfully!

259

- With my mouth, like yours, | will I then decide!
- Whatever I do | shall be changed!
- The word of my lips | shall not be cancelled, shall not be voided!'

(65)
- So the lot came round | and fell on him immediately,
- that he might go | and so meet your powerful foe!"
- Then GA-GA went, | completed his journey,
- until he came to Luḫmu and Laḫamu, | the gods, his elders.
- He fell down there. | He kissed the ground at their feet!

(70)
- He stood up, bowing low, | standing upright he said to them:
- "Anšar, your son, | has sent me.
- The command of his heart | he caused me to hear:
- 'Ti'āmat, our mother, | has become enraged against us,
- assembling a mob, | raging furiously.

(75)
- The gods together | turned to her.
- The Aeons, *whom she created* | moved on beside her.
- Cursing the day | they followed Ti'āmat,
- raging, planning disaster | ceaselessly *day and night*,
- ready for battle, | raging, raving,

(80)
- they banded together. | They began the strife.
- The mother of the deep, | the creatrix of everything,
- added invincible weapons, | creating enormous serpents
- with razor-sharp fangs, | ruthless in attack!
- With poison, as if with blood, | she filled their bodies!

(85)
- Furious adders | she clothed with horrors!
- She provided them with terrors! | She made them high. . . . .
- 'May their appearance. . . . . . | . . . .
- May their bodies swell up | so that their chests cannot be turned back!'

- She created a viper, | an angry serpent, a laḫamu,

(90)
- a 'great day,'[35] a wild dog, | a scorpion-person,
- 'circling days,'[36] a fish-person, | and a ram,
- bearing merciless weapons, | unafraid of battle,
- abhorring sensibility, | irresistible to their foes.
- At the same time, however, as she formed | the eleven in such a way,

(95)
- among the gods, her sons, | she called an assembly.
- She raised up Kingu, | made him great in their midst.
- 'Go first before the host, | that is your commission!
- Command the raising of weapons, | the outbreak of battle!'

- To be primus in battle,   the chieftain in victory,
(100) • this she placed in his hand   and placed him upon the throne!
- 'I have cast a spell for you.   I have raised you up among the gods.
- I have vested you with authority   over the assembled gods.
- You shall be highly elevated,   you, my only husband!
- Great shall be your name,   great above [the earth]!'
(105) • Next she gave him the Tablets of Destiny.   She placed them upon his chest.

- 'Your command shall be valid.   The dictates of your mouth shall stand fast.'

- Now that Kingu was exalted,   had obtained heavenly dominion,
- she fixed the fates   for the gods, her sons.
- 'The opening of your mouths   shall dampen the fire.
(110) • The exaltation of Kidmuri   shall obliterate the embers.'
- I sent forth Anu,   but he would not battle her.
- Nugimmud was terrified,   and he turned back.
- Then I sent Marduk,   the advisor of the gods, your son,
- to counter Ti'āmat!   His heart drove him!
(115) • He opened his mouth   and spoke to me:
- 'If I really   am to be your avenger,
- to conquer Ti'āmat,   to rescue you all,
- then prepare a meal!   Throw a wild banquet!
- Assembling in Ubšugina,   enter in joyfully!
(120) • With my mouth, like yours,   I will then decide!
- Whatever I create   shall not be changed!
- The word of my lips shall not be cancelled,   shall not be voided!'
- So the lot came round   and fell on him immediately,
- that he might go,   and meet your powerful foe!"
(125) • Luḫmu and Laḫamu heard this,   and they la[mented loudly.]
- The gods of heaven assembled,   sobbed pain [fully].
- "How senseless are the Aeons,   since they act for [nothing]!
- We cannot understand   what Ti'āmat [is doing]!
- Then they gathered together.   They went [.........]
(130) • The great gods, all of them,   they fixed [the fate].
- They went in before Anšar.   They filled up [the chamber].
- They pressed in[37]
- They sat at table.   [They stuffed themselves] at the meal.
- They ate bread.   They mixed [wine.]
(135) • With sweet new wine   they gorged [themselves.]
- They drank mead!   They strengthened [their] bo[dies]!

• *Very greatly.*	*They ascended their* [thrones]
• *to fix the fate*	*of Marduk, their avenger.*

(Conclusion of Tablet III)

Tablet IV[38]

	• *Next they set him*	*upon the royal throne.*
	• *In view of his fathers*	*he was established as sovereign.*
	• *"You are honored*	*among the great gods!*
	• *Your destiny is without equal!*	*Your name is 'Anu'!*
(5)	• *Marduk, you are honored*	*among the great gods!*
	• *Your destiny is without equal!*	*Your name is 'Anu'!*
	• *From now on*	*your command is valid!*
	• *Exaltation and debasement*	*lie in your hand!*
	• *Your word stands fast!*	*Your command is absolute!*
(10)	• *None of the gods*	*disparages your rule!*
	• *Decoration*	*fit for the temple of the gods*
	• *may they do without,*	*so that your place may be richer thereof.*[39]
	• *O Marduk, since*	*you will be our avenger,*
	• *we bestow the kingship upon you,*	*kingship over everything!*
(15)	• *You are in the council,*	*so your word stands at the top.*
	• *Your weapon will be victorious.*	*It shall strike the foe.*
	• *O Lord, whoever trusts in you,*	*that person's life will be saved.*
	• *But the god who plans evil,*	*that person's life will pour out!"*
	• *Then they placed in their midst*[40]	*a sort of garment.*
(20)	• *They spoke to Marduk,*	*their firstborn, thus:*
	• *"Your destiny, O Lord,*	*surpasses that of the gods.*
	• *Existence and non-existence —*	*order it and it happens!*
	• *At the opening of your mouth*	*let the garment disappear!*
	• *Command again,*	*let the garment be there again!"*
(25)	• *Then he commanded with his mouth,*	*and the garment disappeared.*
	• *He commanded again,*	*and the garment was there again.*
	• *When the gods, his fathers,*	*saw the power of his word,*
	• *they saluted him joyfully:*	*"Marduk is king!"*
	• *They gave him a scepter,*	*a throne, a ring.*
(30)	• *They gave him a weapon without equal,*	*to smite the foe.*

- "Okay now! Cut off the head of Ti'āmat!
- May the winds carry off her blood into hidden places!"
- So the gods, his fathers, determined the destiny of Bēl.[41]
- They enabled him to set forth on a path of salvation.

(35)
- He prepared a bow, designated it as a weapon.
- A scimitar he made ready. He fastened it . . .
- He took the divine weapon.[42] Held it in his right hand.
- Bow and quiver he hung at his side.
- He placed a lightning bolt before himself.

(40)
- His inner self he filled with blazing flames.
- He made a net to trap the monster Ti'āmat.
- He placed the four winds in such a way that she might not escape.

- He caused the south wind, the north wind, the east wind, the west wind,
- the gift of his father Anu, to carry the net.

(45)
- He created a cyclone,[43] a storm, a weather front,
- the four winds, the seven winds, a whirlwind, a hurricane.
- Then he loosed the winds which he created, all seven of them,
- to confuse Ti'āmat, to follow him.[44]
- Then Bēl took the "storm," his great weapon.

(50)
- He mounted the incomparable terrible chariot.
- A four-horse team appeared. He harnessed it to the chariot.
- [Horses], merciless, courageous, rapid in flight,
- [with pointed] teeth full of venom,
- [. . . . .]. . . . , they knew how to overcome.

(55)
- [on the right . . .] terrible in battle.
- On the left [. . . . .] garbed in terror.
- These horrors over[came] . . . .
- He went forth directly. He pursued his way.

(60)
- To the place where Ti'āmat [. . . . . .] he turned his countenance.
- With his lips [. . . . .] . . . . holding,
- a poison herb [. . . . .] grasping with his fingers.
- At that hour he was praised.[45] The gods praised him.
- The gods, his fathers, praised him. The gods praised him.

(65)
- Bēl drew nigh, reconnoitering for the battle with Ti'āmat,
- looking for the defeat of Kingu, her husband.

- As he beheld him,   his [Kingu's?] planning became confused,
- his understanding became befuddled,   his actions became ensnarled.
- As the gods, his helpers   who went at his side,

(70)
- saw their leader [confused],   their vision was bewildered.
- Then Ti'āmat stood her ground,   not turning away.
- With her lips. . . . .   recalcitrance. . . . .
- Have you taken upon yourself, O Bēl,   the battle of the gods,
- [so that whe]re they are gathered   right now is your place?

(75)
- Then Bēl [grabbed] the "Storm,"   his great weapon.
- As for Ti'āmat whom they had celebrated,   he reproved her in this way:
- "[Down below] your were [str]ong;   up above you were exalted.
- But your he[art became occupied]   with starting a conflict,
- [so that the Aeons] [fell away]   from their fathers to [you].

(80)
- [You rallied] them.   You roused them up aga[inst us].
- [You made King]u   to be yo[ur] husband.
- [You presented] to him   divine power.
- [. . . . .]   you are planning [evil].
- On the gods, my fathers,   you cast aspersions.

(85)
- [So, let] your troops be fettered,   your weapons bound.
- Let me oppose you!   Let you and I, alone, do battle with each other."

- Ti'āmat, as she   heard these things,
- fell into dismay,   lost all understanding.
- She shrieked,   rearing up vehemently!

(90)
- To the very depths, utterly,   her bones shuddered.
- She recited an incantation,   pronounced a formula.
- The gods of battle   rattled their weapons.
- Ti'āmat and Marduk,   the divine counselor, came together.
- They dashed into battle.   They drew near to combat.

(95)
- Then Bēl spread out   his net. He enclosed her <<in it>>.
- The cyclone, which stood behind him,   he loosed upon her.
- Just as Ti'āmat opened   her mouth . . . . ,
- he drove in the cyclone,   so she had to spread wide her jaws.
- with fierce winds   he filled up her belly.

(100)
- Because she lost consciousness,   she opened her mouth widely.

• *He, however, grabbed the scimitar.*	*He thrust it into her belly!*
• *He sliced up her entrails!*	*He split open her innards!*
• *He conquered her!*	*He put an end to her!*
• *He threw down her carcass!*	*He stood upon it!*
(105) • *So he had conquered*	*Ti'āmat, the autocrat.*
• *Her military force dispersed.*	*Her troops scattered.*
• *The gods, her helpers,*	*who marched at her side,*
• *quivered, were terrified!*	*They turned around!*
• *They tried to get away,*	*to save their lives!*
(110) • *But a crowd surrounded them.*	*It was inescapable!*
• *He <<Marduk>> took them captive.*	*He smashed their weapons.*
• *In the net they lay.*	*They set in the snare.*
• *They also filled*	*the cosmos with wailing.*
• *They bore his chastising,*	*being locked up in a prison. —*
(115) • *The twelve creatures*	*whom she <<Ti'āmat>> gruesomely formed,*
• *a horde of demonic beings*	*who went at her side,*
• *these he placed in chains.*	*He bound their hands.*
• *And as for their resistance,*	*he trampled it under foot! —*
• *And Kingu, who [was powerful]*	*[over] all of [them],*
(120) • *he mastered him*	*and made him like the other gods.*
• *He took away from him the Tablets of Destiny,*	*[which hung upon] his [ch]est.*
• *He sealed them with his seal.*	*He hung them on his own ch[est].*
• *After he had conquered his foes*	*and had overcome them thus,*
• *had brought the arrogant*	*antagonist unto disgrace,*
(125) • *had totally accomplished*	*Anšar's victory over the foe,*
• *had fulfilled Nugimmud's⁴⁶ plan,*	*then the valiant Marduk*
• *made his power secure*	*over the conquered deities,*
• *and he returned*	*to Ti'āmat, whom he had conquered.*
• *Bēl trampled down*	*the body of Ti'āmat;*
(130) • *with his merciless⁴⁷ weapon*	*he cleaved⁴⁸ her skull.*
• *He cut through*	*her blood-vessels,*
• *and let it <<her blood>> be taken*	*into obscure places by the north wind.*
• *His fathers saw this.*	*They were glad. They rejoiced.*
• *They caused peace-offerings*	*to be brought to him.*
(135) • *Then Bēl was at peace*	*as he gazed at her body.*
•	*To create artistic things.*
• *He cut her up like a. . . . .⁴⁹*	*into two pieces.*
• *He took one half*	*and made it into the heavenly dome.*
• *He stretched out a barrier before it.*	*He set up a guard.*

(140) • He ordered them   not to let its waters flow out.
 • In the same way as he did in *the heavens,*   he fortified the underworld.
 • He placed himself opposite the Ocean,   the dwelling of Nugimmud.[50]
 • Then Bēl measured out   the form of the ocean.[51]
 • A palace similar to it   he erected, Ešara.
(145) • In the palace Ešara,   which he erected in heaven,
 • he allowed Anu, Bēl, and Ea   to dwell as their hall.

(Conclusion of Tablet IV)

Tablet V[52]

 • He made the sites   for the great gods,
 • when he laid out stars   like them, the stars of the zodiac.[53]
 • He established the year.   He determined all the constellations.
 • Twelve months he appointed,   three stars for each.
(5) • When he denoted *the days of the* year   according to *the constellations,*
 • he established the position of Jupiter   to designate their limits.
 • That none[54] should fail to come,   nor should any get lost,
 • he established Bēl's and Ea's positions   along with it.[55]
 • Then he opened gates   on both sides.
(10) • He set up a lock,   on the left and on the right.
 • In the middle of the heavens   he placed the zenith.
 • He caused the moon to shine forth.[56]   He entrusted the heights to him.
 • For him he set aside objects of the night   so as to designate the time.
 • Once a month   he formed him as a full moon.
(15) • "At the beginning of the month,   when the evening begins,
 • sparkle with beams   so as to mark the heavens.
 • On the seventh day   make the disk [a ha]lf.
 • On the [sab]bath   stand perpendicular[57] to the first half.
 • When, at the [set]ting of the sun   you rise on the horizon,
(20) • stand opposite it [on the fourteenth],   in fullest brilliance.

- [*from the fifteenth*][58] *on, draw near*   *to the course of the sun.*
- [*on the twenty-first*][59] *stand per-*   *to the sun a second time.*
      pendicular
- [*From the twenty-second on . . .*]   . . . . *to seek out their way.*
- [*On the twenty-eighth*] *draw near*   *and render judgment!*
      [*to the sun*]

(25)
- [. . . . .]   [. . . . .] *to damage,*
- [. . . . .]   [. . . . .] *me.*

(What follows has been broken off. It presumably contained, first of all, a continuation of the creation of the heavenly bodies, then, probably, the creation of the mainland and of the sea.)

Tablet VI

- [. . . . .] . . . *the gods*   *as he heard.*[60]

Tablet VII (??)[61]

- *Once upon a time, the gods to-*   *formed* [the world],
      gether
- *created* [*the heavens*],   *esta*[*blished the earth*],
- *produced living*   [*be*]*ings. . . .*[. . . . .]
- *cattle of the field,* [*beasts*] *of the*   *and vermin* [*of the field.*]
      field

(5)
- [. . . . .] . .   *the living beings* [. . . . .]
- [. . . . .] . . .   *and with living creatures the city*
                                            [*they*] *fi*[*lled,*]
- [. . . . . *al*]*l living ones,*   *all creatures* [. . . . .]
- •   *in my whole family*
      [. . . . .   [. . . . .]
      . . . .]
- [*because*] *the god Nin-igi-azag*   *two sm*[*all. . . . .*]
      [*created*]

[There follow the remains of simply four lines]

Final (?) Tablet[62]

[Beginning is a bit fragmented]

- *God Zi* [. . . . . *name him*[63] *a second time . . .*]
- *"who established* [. . . . .]
- *his ways* [. . . . .]
- *will not be forgotten among humans* [. . . . .]

(5)
- *God Zi-azag*[64] *they named him a third time:* "Who brings about *purification,*
- *god of the gentle breeze,* *lord of contentment and grace,*
- *who brings forth. . . . an abundance,* *who creates profusion,*
- *who makes everything* *which is sufficient more numerous,*
- *whose gentle breeze we inhale* *when we toil greatly.*

(10)
- *May he be proclaimed, praised,* and professed!"
- *God Mir-azag, for the fourth time* *thus did the world praise him:*
- *"Lord of the pure incantation,* *who brings the dead to life,*
- *who showed mercy* *to the conquered deities,*
- *who removed the yoke* *imposed by the gods, his foes,*

(15)
- *who in their place* *created humanity,*
- *the compassionate one,* *who has the power to give life."*
- *May such words concerning him endure.* *May they not be forgotten*
- *In the mouths of the black-headed ones,* *who were created by his hands.*
- *God Tu-azag, a fifth time* *they sounded forth his magic word with their mouths:*

(20)
- *"Who through his pure incantation* *wipes out all evil!"*
- *God Ša-zu: "Who knows the heart of the gods,* *who looks into the inmost places,*
- *who does not allow* *the evil-doer to escape,*
- *who convenes the divine council,* *who delights his heart,*
- *who then bends down the dis[obedient. . . . .* . . . .]

(25)
- *who makes the right prevail* [. . . . .]
- *who the rebelliousness* [. . . . .]
- *God Zi-si: "Who makes the storm[wind* *go there . . . .]*
- *[who causes the dust-storm* *to rage therein. . . . .]*

• *God Šug-kur, six times:* "*Who eradicates the [foe,*
(30) • *who covenants her.* . . . . [. . . . .]
• *who dest[roy]ed [all] evil [things* . . . .]

(The continuation is broken off.)

(The reverse side of the fragment has some mutilated lines at the beginning)

• [. . . . .] *star,* [*which beams forth in the heavens*]
• *it is recorded.* . . . .
(5) • *Since he sp[lit] the monster* *Ti'āmat*[65] [*without hesitation,*]
• *may his name be Nibiru,* *who placed there the* [*midpoint.*]
• *For the stars of the heavens* [*he established*] *the course.*
• *Like sheep he tended* *all the gods!*
• *He conquered Ti'āmat.* *He besieged her and cut her life short.*
(10) • *For all future generations,* *for all later days,*
• *he put her away without.* . . . *Put her away for all time.*"
• *Because he created the earth,* *formed the dry land,*
• "*Lord of the lands,*" *as a name,* *the father gave him Bēl.*
• *He received all the names* *given him by the heavenly gods.*
(15) • *Ea heard this* *and his heart was joyful,*
• *that his son had been given* *such wonderful names.*
• "*He is like me, myself.* *He should be named Ea.*
• *Let him be delivered* *my binding laws, all of them.*
• *Let him be sent* *all of my commands!*"
(20) • *According to the fifty names* *of the great gods,*
• *he was given fifty names.* *His might increased.*
• *May the foregoing be understood* *and proclaimed in such a manner.*
• *May the wise, the skilled* *take it to heart in the same way.*
• *May the father tell it to the son.* *May he enjoin it upon him.*
(25) • *As for the shepherd and guardian,*[66] *may he open his ears,*
• *that he may rejoice about* *the lord of the gods, Marduk,*
• *that his land may be fruitful,* *that he himself may remain safe and well!*

• *His* [*Marduk's*] *word is reliable!* *His command is valid!*
• *His remark not even* *a god may alter!*
(30) • *He looks on evil things* *without turning his neck.*
• *He comes in anger and fury.* *No god is like him.*
• *The long-suffering.* . . . . [. . . . .]
• [*the*] *sin and crime* *before him* [. . . . .]

(The conclusion is broken off.)

II. The Second Babylonian Recension of the *Ti'āmat-Marduk* Battle[67]

• The cities sighed. Humanity [moaned].
• People raised up lamentation [and cried out].
• At their cry there was no [help for them].
• At their lamentation there was no [assistance for them].
(5) • "Who then is the [great] dragon?"
• "Ti'āmat is the [great] dragon!"
• Bēl has drawn [his form] upon the heavens.
• Fifty leagues is its length. One league [is its breadth].
• A half a rod wide is its mouth. One rod wide [is its. . . . . .].
(10) • Sixty rods around are the of the [great] dragon.
  twistings[68]
• Sixty-five rods of a bird. . . . . . [. . . . .]
• In the water nine yards are measured [. . . . .]
• There lay on his tail [. . . . .]
• The gods of the heavens altogether [. . . . .]
(15) • In heaven the gods throw themselves at the feet [of the
  god . . .]

• And [they grasped] most urgently at the thought of salvation.
• "He will go forth [to kill] the dragon,[69]
• to save the whole, wide world,
• and to take possession of the royal dominion!"
(20) • "Go, O god ŠUḪ! Ki[ll] the dragon!
• Save the whole, wide world, and take possession of the royal dominion!"

270

- "You have sent me   lord. . . . . . [. . . . .]
- I was not able   the dragon [. . . . .]
- [. . . . .]
- [. . . . .]   in the water [. . . . .]

[Approximately fifty lines are missing.]

- [. . . . .] his mouth   he opened to the god [. . . . .]
- "Cause clouds to descend,   cause a storm!
- Your seal of life   upon your star
- O lay!   [Sl]ay the dragon!"

(5)
- Then he caused clouds to descend.   He caused a storm!
- His seal of life   upon his star
- He laid!   [He slew] the dragon!
- Three years, three months,   day and night,
- the blood of the dragon   flowed for just that long!

(There follows the usual signature, which establishes the tablet
as belonging to the library of *Aššurbanipal*)

III. The Second Babylonian Recension of the Creation[70]

- *Even the holy[71] house of the gods*   *was not built on a holy[72] place.*
- *A reed had not yet sprung up.*   *A tree had not yet been created.*
- *No brick had been laid.*   *No brick building had been erected.*
- *No house had been put up.*   *No town had been built.*
(5)   • *No city had been raised.*   *No dwelling had been prepared.*
- *Nippur had not been constructed.*   *E-kur[73] had not been built.*
- *Erech had not been fashioned.*   *E-anna[74] had not been erected.*
- *The Ocean had not been created.*   *Eridu had not been produced.*
- *As for the holy house of the gods,*   *its building had not been put up!*
(10)   • *The whole of the land*   *was a sea!*
- *But then a movement*   *[arose] in the sea.*
- *Eridu was erected.*   *Esagil[75] was built,*
- *Esagil, where in the midst of the ocean*   *divine Lugal-dul-azagu dwelt.*
- *Babylon was erected.*   *Esagil was completed.*
(15)   • *The gods, the Anunnaki,[76]*   *were created at the same time.*
- *The holy city where they loved to dwell*   *they designated as quite splendid!*
- *Marduk fixed*   *a bed of reeds upon the water.*
- *He formed dust[77]*   *and piled it up beside the bed of reeds.*
- *So as to allow the gods*   *to dwell in a more delightful state,*
(20)   • *he created humanity!*
- *The goddess Araru created*   *the seed of humanity right along with him.*

      • *Beasts of the field,*   *living creatures of the land he created.*
      • *The Tigris and the Euphrates*   *he created in their places.*
      • *He gave them proper names.*
(25) • ....   *bulrush, reed, and forest he created.*
      • *The greens of the field he created.*
      • *The land, the bulrush, the reed.*
      • *The wild cow with her young, the*   *the ewe with her young, the lamb of*
            young wild bull,   *the fold,*
      • *orchards and forests.*
(30) • *The billy-goat.* ....
      • *Next Marduk filled up*   *a terrace to the shore of the sea,*
      • [......................]   *as he had not done previously.*
      • [......................]   *he caused to arise.*
      • [......................]   *trees he created.*
(35) • [*Bricks*]   *he created at their place.*
      • [.................]   *brick structures he created.*
      • [*Houses he erected*].   *Cities he built.*
      • [*Cities he erected*].   *Dwellings he established.*
      • [*Nippur he erected*].   *E-kur he built.*
(40) • [*Erech he erected.*   *E-ann*]*a he built.*

(Continuation is incoherent.)
(The conclusion of the tablet contains an incantation.)

IV. The Adapa Myth[78]

(There are faults at the beginnings of certain lines.)

- *The South Wind [blew and pushed him under,]*
- *into the house [of its lord] it lowered him down.*
- *"O South Wind, [you have] done to me all your tricks.*

(5)
- *I will break your wing!"*   *As soon as he spoke this with his mouth,*

- *The wing of the South Wind was broken.*   *For seven days*
- *the South Wind blew no more over the land.*   *Anu*
- *said to his herald Ilabrat,*
- *"Why has the South Wind blown no more over the land for seven days?"*

(10)
- *His herald Ilabrat answered him: "My Lord,*
- *Adapa, the son of Ea, has broken the wing of*
- *the South Wind!" When Anu heard this thing*

• *he cried out, "Help!"*   He sat down on his throne [. . . . . . .]
• *. . . . .] Ea, who in*
  heaven. . . . .
(15) • *. . . . . cause him to wear*
  mourning clothes. . . . . . .
• *. . . . . he put it on.*
• *[. . . . . "to Anu,] to*
  the king must you go!
• *[If you ascend] to heaven,*
• *[and draw near to the throne of*
  Anu,]
(20) • *at Anu's gate [Tammuz*   and GIŠ-ZI-DA will be]
• *standing. They will see*
  you. . . . .
  . . . .

• 'By whose will *do you look in this*   O Adapa, for whom
  way?
• *are you wearing a raiment of*   'From our land two gods have disap-
  mourning?'   peared!
• *For that reason do I act this way.'*   'Who are the two gods
(25) • *who have vanished from the land?'*   'Tammuz and GIŠ-ZI-DA.'
• *and they will lament.*   *Then they will look at one another*
• *a good word to Anu.*   *Then, however, they will speak*
• *to look at you pleasantly.*   *And they will cause Anu*
• *the food of death will be offered to*   *When you then go in before Anu*
  you!
(30) • *Do not eat from it!*   *The water of death will be offered to*
    you.
• *Do not drink of it!*   *A garment will be offered to you.*
• *Put it on! Oil will be offered to you.*   *Anoint yourself with it!*
• *As for the counsel which I give to*   *As for the word*
  you, do not ignore *it!*
• *which I speak to you, adhere to it!"*   *Then the messenger*
(35) • *came to Anu:*   "Adapa has broken the South
• *wind's wing.*   *Let him be brought before me!*
• *. . . . . of heaven let him*   *To heaven let him ascend!"*
  encamp.
• *When he got to heaven,*   *when he drew near the gate of Anu,*
• *Tammuz and GIŠ-ZI-DA were*
  standing at the door.

(40) • When they saw Adapa they cried
aloud, "Help!
• O lord! By whose will do you look
in this way? O Adapa,
• for whom are you wearing that
garment of mourning?"
• "From our land two gods have dis-   Because of this do I wear the garment
appeared!   of mourning!"
• "Who are the two gods   who have disappeared from your
land?"
(45) • "Tammuz and GIŠ-ZI-DA."   Then they looked at one another,
• and they lamented.   Then when Adapa drew near
• to Anu, the king, and Anu caught   then he [Anu] spoke to him:
sight of him,
• "O Adapa! Why have you broken
the wing of the South
• Wind?   Adapa answered Anu: "My lord!
(50) • For the house of my lord,   I was catching, in the midst of the sea,
• a fish.   The sea was like glass.
• Then the South Wind blew   and it pushed me under.
• Into the house of my lord he sub-   In the raging of my heart
merged me.
• . . . . [Tammuz]
(55) • and GIŠ-ZI-DA said a good word
to Anu.
• Then his angry heart turned and   He said:
became calm.
• "Why has Ea allowed   an impure human to look at
• the innermost things   of heaven and of earth?
• He has made him great!   He has bestowed a name upon him!
(60) • As for us, however, what can we be-   The food of life
stow on him?
• hold out for him that he might eat?   The food of life
• was held out for him, but he did   The water of life
not eat!
• was held out for him? But he did   A garment
not drink!
• was washed for him? He put it on.   Oil
(65) • was held out for him?   With it he anointed himself."
• Then Anu saw him.   He lamented over him:
• "O Adapa! Why did you not eat?   Not drink?

• *So, you would not have eternal life*
  either?

                                    [. . . . .]"
                                              "*Ea, my lord,*

• *has commanded me: 'Do not eat!   Do not drink!'*

(70) • [. . . . .] *him*
        [*return*]*ed to his land.*

(The concluding lines are broken.)

V. The Flood[79]

(8) • Çît-napištum[80] spoke to him, to Gilgamesh,[81] thus.
• "I will reveal to you, O Gilgamesh, a secret thing.
(10) • The decision of the gods I will announce to you.
• Šurrippak, a city well known to you,
• which on the bank of the Euphrates lies,
• that city was (already) old. The gods were in it —
• Their hearts drove the great gods to send a flood!
(15) • [There w]as their father Anu, their advisor, the war-hero Bēl,
• their herald Ninib, their leader Ennugi.
• The lord of wisdom, Ea, had spoken with them.
• He told of their speech to a house of reeds.
• "O house of reeds, O house of reeds! O wall, O wall!

(20) • O house of reeds here! O wall, take heed!
• O man of Šurippak, son of Uburatutu,
• Erect a shelter! Build a ship!
• Leave your property! Consider your life!
• Abandon your possessions! And save your life!
(25) • Bring seeds of life of every type onto the ship!
• As for the ship which you now shall build,
• its measurements should be carefully calculated.
• May its breadth and its length[82] correspond.
• Lower it down into the ocean!"[83]
(30) • I understood this truly. I spoke to Ea, my lord.

- ["The comma]nd, *my lord,*   *which you have just given,*
- *I shall obey*   *and shall carry out!*
- *But what shall I say to the city,*   *to the people, to the elders?"*
- *Ea opened*   *his mouth and spoke.*

(35)
- *He spoke about this*   *to me, his vassal.*
- *"Speak to them*   *in this way as* [an answ]er:
- *'Bēl has spurned me*   *and has hated me.*
- *For that reason I shall no longer dwell*   *in your city.*
- *I shall no longer turn my head*   *to the land of Bēl.*

(40)
- *I shall* [*go do*]*wn to the ocean.*   *With* [Ea], *my* [lo]*rd, I shall dwell.*
- *He will then cover* [*y*]*ou*   *with rich blessings:*
- [*a mass*] *of birds,*   *a* lo[a]d *of fish,*
- [. . . . .] *of harvest.*
- [*But Šamaš has set a time*   *when the lord*] *of the darkness*

(45)
- [*in the evening*] [*will cover y*]*ou*   *with pernicious rains."*

- *as soon as* [*the first*   *red of dawn*] *appeared*

(There follow some mutilated lines.)

- . . . . [. . . . .]   *brought over that which was necessary.*
- *On the fifth day*   *I drew up its form.*
- *All the way round its sides*   *were one hundred and twenty ells high.*
- *The breadth of its deck*   *was* approximately *one hundred and twenty ells.*

(60)
- *I designed.* . . . . ,   *I myself delineated it.*
- *I built in it six decks,*   *dividing it into seven (levels).*
- *Its interior I divided*   [*into*] *nine sections.*
- . . . . *-water*   *I emptied out from therein.*
- *I looked round for a rudder.*   *I added the necessities.*

(65)
- *Six šars*[84] *of pitch*   *I poured upon the outer hull.*
- *Three šars of asphalt*   [*I poured*] *upon the inside of the hull.*
- *Three šars of oil*   *people brought over,* . . . . . . *-porters*
- *I held back one šar of oil*   *to use for the sacrifice.*
- *Two šars of oil*   *the sailors saved.*

(70)
- *For the* Te[*mple of the gods*]   *I slaughtered oxen.*
- *I killed a ram*   *each day.*
- *Pitchers with sesame-wine,*[85]   *oil and grape wine,*
- *ski*[*ns with.* . . . .]   *like river water.*
- *A feast I held,*   *as on New Year's day.*

(75) • [. . . . .] ointment   I dipped my hand.

• [On the seventh day] . . . .   the ship was ready.

• [. . . . .]   was difficult.

• . . . . was taken   above and below.

• [. . . . .]   two thirds of it.

---

(80) • With everything which I had,   I loaded it.

• With everything which I had   in silver, I loaded it.

• With everything which I had   in gold, I loaded it.

• With everything which I had   of the seed of living creatures, I loaded it.

• I brought to the ship   my family and my servants.

(85) • Beasts of the fields, game of the fields,   master craftsmen of all types I brought to it.

• Šamaš had established   a specific time.

• "Lords of darkness will   send a deadly rain in the evening.

• So get into the ship,   and close the door."

• That time   came.

(90) • The lords of darkness sent in the evening   a deadly rain.

• I was afraid   of the dawning of the day.

• I had fear   of the appearance of the day.

• I went into the ship.   I bolted the door.

• For the steering of the ship,   to the boatman Puzur-Bēl

(95) • I handed over the ark,   together with its contents.

• As soon as the first   red of morning appeared,

• a black cloud   rose up from the horizon.

• Rammān thundered   within it.

• Nebo and Marduk   went before it.

(100) • The couriers advanced   over mountain and vale.

• Urugal pulled up   the anchor.

• Ninib went there.   He caused the tumult to follow along.

• The Anunnaki raised up   their torches.

• Through their brightness   they illuminated the land.

(105) • Rammān's whirlwind of dust   reached up to the heavens.

• Everything bright   was transformed into darkness.

• [. . . . . .] the land as [. . .   . . . .] he knocked down.

• A whole day   the sto[rm. . . . .].

• It blew rapidly.   The [water climbed] up the mountains.

(110) • Like a raging battle   it set upon humanity.

        • *One no longer*   saw the other.

        • *Humanity was no longer*   recognizable from the heavens.

        • *Even the gods were afraid*   in the face of the deluge.

        • *They fell back. They climbed up*   to the heaven of Anu.

(115) • *The gods, like house dogs,*   cowered on the. . . . .

        • *Ištar wailed*   like a woman in labor.

        • *The lady of the gods lamented*   with a loud voice.

        • *"Humanity has prematurely*   become earth[86] again,

        • *since in the council of the gods*   I voted for a bad thing,

(120) • *and since I, in the council of the gods*   voting for a bad thing

        • *leading to the extinction of my human race,*   voted for a great deluge.

        • *Will I ever again*   bring humanity back to the earth,

        • *if they now fill*   the sea like spawn of fish?"

        • *The gods of the Anunnaki*   wept with her.

(125) • *The gods sat,*   bending over, weeping,

        • *their lips grimacing*   [. . . . .] . . . .

        • *for six days and six nights.*

        • *The storm, the flood raged.*   The rain pelted the land.

        • *When the seventh day arrived,*

(130) • *The weather, the flood,*   the storm[87] subsided.

        • *They had done battle*   like an army.

        • *The stirred-up sea came to rest.*   The typhoon, the deluge ended.

        • *"I glanced at the sea.*   I cast the vote. —

        • *But all humanity*   was still on earth.

(135) • In place of dwellings   everything was a swamp.

        • *I opened the upward doors.*   The light fell upon my cheek.

        • *I bowed down my head.*   I sat weeping there.

        • *Upon my cheek*   my teardrops flowed.

        • *I gazed upon the world*   — nothing but sea!

(140) • *In twelve directions*   land rose up.

        • *Into the land of Niṣir*   the ship drifted.

        • *The mountain of the land Niṣir*   held the ship fast and did not let it go.

        • *The first day, the second day,*   Mount Niṣir held the ship fast and did not let it go.

        • *The third day, the fourth day,*   Mount Niṣir held the ship fast and did not let it go.

(145) • *The fifth day, the sixth day,*   Mount Niṣir held the ship fast and did not let it go."

	• When the seventh day arrived:	
	• Then I released a dove	and set it free.
	• The dove flew	hither and yon.
	• But since there was no resting place,	it then returned.
(150)	• I then released a swallow	and set it free.
	• The swallow flew	hither and yon,
	• but since there was no resting place	it then returned.
	• I then released a raven	and set it free.
	• The raven flew.	It saw the water subsiding.
(155)	• It drew near . . . . ing and cawing.	But it did not return!
	• Then I released (all of them) to the four winds.	I offered up a sacrifice.
	• I made an offering	on the peak of the mountain.
	• Seven basins	I erected.
	• Into them I threw calamus,	cedar chips, and frankincense.
(160)	• The gods smelled the fragrance.	
	• The gods smelled	the sweet aroma.
	• The gods gathered	like flies around the one making the offering.
	• When the "lofty one"⁸⁸	had arrived,
	• she lifted up the wonderful jewelry	which Anu had prepared at her desire.
(165)	• O you gods here!	By my necklace, I shall never forget!
	• As for these days, consider them!	They will never be forgotten!
	• May the gods draw near	to the offering!
	• But may Bēl not draw near	to the offering!
	• For he thoughtlessly	produced the deluge.
(170)	• And my human beings	he surrendered to destruction!"
	• Then, when Bēl	arrived,
	• as he caught sight of the ship,	he became furious.
	• He was filled with rage	against the gods, the Igigi!
	• "Who then has escaped with his life?	
(175)	• Not one human	should have escaped destruction!"
	• Then Ninib opened	his mouth and spoke.
	• He spoke	to the great warrior Bēl:
	• "Who can do such	things without Ea?
	• Ea alone knows	every noble thing!"
(180)	• Then Ea opened	his mouth and spoke.
	• He spoke	to the great warrior Bēl:

   • *"Oh you, who are wise*   *among the gods, you great warrior!*
   • *O how rash you were*   *to cause a deluge!*
   • *His own sin*   *lay upon the sinner!*
(185) • *His own crime*   *lay upon the evil-doer!*
   • *It was fortunate that (everything)*   *It was most auspicious that (every-*
    was not destroyed.   *thing)* [*was not* eliminated]*!*
   • *Instead of your producing a deluge,*
   • *lions could have come*   *and tidied up among humanity.*
   • *Instead of your producing a deluge,*
(190) • *leopards could have come*   *and tidied up among humanity.*
   • *Instead of your producing a deluge,*
   • *a famine could have arisen*   *and* [. . . . .] *the land!*
   • *Instead of your producing a deluge,*
   • *the god of pestilence could have*   *and slaughtered humanity!*
    come
(195) • *I have not disclosed*   *the deliberations of the great gods*
   • *to Atraḫasis.*[89] *I sent a dream,*   *so that he might hear of the way of the*
                gods."

   • *Then coming to a decision,*
   • *Bēl climbed up*   *onto the ship.*
   • *He grasped my hand*   *and led me up.*
(200) • *He led my wife up,*   *leaning on my side.*
   • *He put us opposite one another.*   *He walked between us. He blessed us.*
   • *"Formerly Cît-napištum was*   *only a man.*
   • *Now Cît-napištum and his wife*   *are like us gods.*
   • *Cît-napištum shall dwell*   *in the distant place, at the mouth of*
                the rivers!"

(205) • *Then they took me and in the dis-*   *at the mouth of the rivers they caused*
    tant place,   *me to dwell.*

Notes

Notes to the Foreword

1. For a list of English translations, see the bibliography in the recent translation of several of Gunkel's essays in Hermann Gunkel, *Water for a Thirsty Land: Israelite Literature and Religion*, ed. K. C. Hanson (Minneapolis: Fortress, 2001), 168-69. On pp. 170-71 is a helpful bibliography of Gunkel's major publications in their original German along with a selection of studies of his work. Other translations include modern Hebrew, for Gunkel's introduction to his Genesis commentary, and Spanish, for his *Einleitung in die Psalmen*.

2. Bernhard Anderson, ed., *Creation in the Old Testament* (Philadelphia: Fortress, 1984), 25-52.

3. George Smith, *The Chaldean Account of Genesis* (London: Low, Marston, Searle, and Rivington, 1875), revising and elaborating on earlier publications going back to 1872. In this volume as well, Smith presents portions of *Enuma Elish*. The fullest, even if not fully balanced, history of the early decades of Assyriology, that is, scholarship on Mesopotamia, remains E. A. Wallis Budge, *The Rise and Progress of Assyriology* (London: Martin Hopkinson, 1925).

4. Biographical details on Gunkel may be found, e.g., in Werner Klatt, *Hermann Gunkel: Zu seiner Theologie der Religionsgeschichte und zur Entstehung der formgeschichtlichen Methode* (Göttingen: Vandenhoeck & Ruprecht, 1969); Rudolf Smend, *Deutsche Alttestamentler in drei Jahrhunderten* (Göttingen: Vandenhoeck & Ruprecht, 1989), 160-72, 314-15; and Martin J. Buss, in Donald K. McKim, ed., *Historical Handbook of Major Biblical Interpreters* (Downers Grove, Ill.: InterVarsity Press, 1998), 487-91.

5. W. G. Lambert, "A New Look at the Babylonian Background of Genesis," *Journal of Theological Studies* n.s. 16 (1965) 287 and n. 5, 288 and n. 1.

6. P. 296, n. 1 in the present volume; other references to Barton are on p. 289, n. 4; p. 294, n. 38; and p. 379, n. 1 (the last from Heinrich Zimmern's translations). Gunkel also cites Cheyne, p. 305, n. 7; p. 305, nn. 97, 98, but these citations do not refer to the papers that discuss the Babylonian mythic texts.

7. John Day, *God's Conflict with the Dragon and the Sea: Echoes of a Canaanite Myth in the Old Testament* (Cambridge: Cambridge University Press, 1985), 2.

8. See Day, *God's Conflict*, 2.

9. Douglas A. Knight, *The Traditions of Israel* (Missoula, Mont.: Society of Biblical Literature, 1973), 21, 73 and n. 2.

10. See Klatt, *Hermann Gunkel* (above, n. 4), 70 and n. 1.

11. The letter was to church historian Adolf (von) Harnack, cited in Christhard Hoffmann, *Juden und Judentum im Werk deutscher Althistoriker des 19. und 20. Jahrhunderts* (Leiden: E. J. Brill, 1988), 160, n. 40.

12. Julius Wellhausen, "Zur apokalyptischen Literatur," in idem, *Skizzen und Vorarbeiten*, VI. Heft (Berlin: Georg Reimer, 1899), 225-34; Hermann Gunkel, "Aus Wellhausen's neuesten apokalyptischen Forschungen," *Zeitschrift für Wissenschaftliche Theologie* n.f. 7 (1899), 581-611. The first part of Wellhausen's essay and all of Gunkel's are reprinted in Klaus Koch and Johann Michael Schmidt, eds., *Apokalyptik* (Darmstadt: Wissenschaftliche Buchgesellschaft, 1982) 58-66, 67-90.

13. Klatt, *Hermann Gunkel* (above, n. 4), 71-74.

14. See Buss, in McKim, ed., *Historical Handbook* (above, n. 4), 487. Buss offers further reflections on Gunkel's difficulties in his *Biblical Form Criticism in Its Context* (Sheffield: Sheffield Academic Press, 1999), 218-19.

15. An excellent edition and translation of the Baʻal and Anat cycle is by Mark S. Smith in Simon B. Parker, ed., *Ugaritic Narrative Poetry* (Atlanta: Society of Biblical Literature/Scholars Press, 1997), 81-180. The Mari letter is published by J.-M. Durand, "Le mythologeme du combat entre le dieu de l'orage et la mer en Mesopotamie," *Mari* 7 (1993), 41-61.

16. One thorough and relatively recent study is Day, *God's Conflict* (above, n. 7).

Notes to the Translator's Preface

1. K. William Whitney Jr., "Two Strange Beasts: A Study of Traditions concerning Leviathan and Behemoth in Second Temple and Early Rabbinic Judaism" (Th.D. dissertation, Harvard University, 1992) (forthcoming as a Harvard Semitic Monograph).

2. Thorkild Jacobsen, "The Battle Between Marduk and Tiamat," *Journal of the American Oriental Society* 88 (1968) 104-8.

3. The German word *Gattung* is often translated into English using the word "form." Essentially that is a correct translation, but often that is taken to mean something much more structured, something much more rigid, than Gunkel's use of the term meant. The key to understanding the term in Gunkel's eyes was linked to the second word with which it is combined, i.e., *Geschichte*. In English we often translate this as "history." That is a correct translation as long as we understand "history" not as some set of carefully delineated "facts" and more as a "developmental progression" through which a particular *Gattung* came to be, and in which particular biblical expressions of that *Gattung* can be understood to exist dynamically. In other words, *Gattungsgeschichte* is that discipline which attempts to trace the way in which a particular "form" developed over time, often in dialogue with a great number of other developmental factors within the life of the various communities within which it developed.

4. Julius Wellhausen, *Israelitische und Jüdische Geschichte*, ed. R. Smend, 9th ed. (Berlin: de Gruyter, 1958), 65. This citation is drawn from Werner Klatt, *Hermann Gunkel: Zu seiner Theologie der Religionsgeschichte und zur Entstehung der formgeschichtlichen Methode* (Göttingen: Vandenhoeck und Ruprecht, 1969) [hereinafter: Klatt, *Gunkel*], 49.

5. Klatt, *Gunkel*, 50-51, presents a statement by R. Kittel, made in 1925, which expresses the situation of biblical scholarship at this time quite well. Klatt notes that concerning the archaeological findings at Tell el-Amarna, Kittel received a report

> ... of the enormous revolution which had taken place just that year in our knowledge of the ancient Near East and consequently of the Old Testament. No one could have suspected the practical consequence of these discoveries. . . . As it was long clear to me that the history of Israel required a totally new approach, I saw still other portrayals of the subject come to light in the new editions, partly in the first treatment . . . portrayals which allowed practically nothing to be perceived, since the world had revolved in the meantime and world history has acquired a new appearance. With complete rectitude an exacting expert concerning the differences of this period could say that the scholars of our subject, almost without exception, acquired positive knowledge from the material remains by allowing them to remain unresolved, since they did not fit properly into the "schema." In reality it would not be too early for people like Wellhausen and Stade and those who are sworn to them, to make *practical* use of these new discoveries.

[R. Kittel, in *Die Religionswissenschaft der Gegenwart in Selbstdarstellungen*, ed. E. Stange [hereafter: Stange, *Religionswissenschaft*] (Leipzig: F. Meiner, 1925-29), 1:124f.].

6. Kittel, in Stange, *Religionswissenschaft*, 1:125 (again cited in Klatt, *Gunkel*, 51).

7. The following biographical details are drawn from the comprehensive Gunkel biography, Klatt, *Gunkel*, 15ff.

8. *Die Pastoren der Landeskirchen Hannovers und Schaumburg-Lippes seit der Reformation*, ed. Philip Meyer (Göttingen: Vandenhoeck und Ruprecht, 1942), 2:44, 108, 115.

9. Cited by Klatt, *Gunkel*, 16, taken from the notes of Gunkel's dissertation review, 4IIb/ 84 in the University Archives of Göttingen.

10. See, in greater detail, the discussion of Klatt, *Gunkel*, 16-17.

11. Klatt, *Gunkel*, 19.

12. H. Gunkel, "Gedächtnisrede auf Wilhelm Bousset an 9. Mai 1920," *Evangelische Freiheit* 20 (1920) 142.

13. For some sense of the import of this circle of scholars see the brief references to their individual scholarly biographies in Klatt, *Gunkel*, 20-21, nn. 14-18.

14. H. Gunkel, "Was will die 'religionsgeschichtliche' Bewegung?" *Deutsche-Evangelisch* 5 (1914) 346f., cited in Klatt, *Gunkel*, 26, n. 41.

15. H. Gunkel, "Die Richtungen der alttestamentliche Forschung," *Christliche Welt* 36 (1922) 66, cited in Klatt, *Gunkel*, 27, n. 43.

16. Jacob Grimm and Wilhelm Grimm, *Kinder- und Hausmärchen: Gesammelt durch die Brüder Grimm*, 2 vols. (Berlin: Realschulbuchhandlung, 1812-13).

17. Jacob Grimm und Wilhelm Grimm, *Deutsche Sagen: Herausgegeben von den Brüdern Grimm*, 2 vols. (Berlin: Nicolaische Buchhandlung, 1816-18).

18. Cf. "Grimm Brothers' Home Page," compiler D. L. Ashliman, "Chronology of Their Life."

19. In 1838 the Grimms (along with five other Göttingen faculty) criticized a constitutional violation by Ernst August, then king of Hannover. "The Göttingen Seven" (as they came to be called) were dismissed from their positions. Soon thereafter, however, the Grimms did take up residence and teaching at the University of Berlin.

20. Klatt, *Gunkel*, 30.

21. Hermann Gunkel, *Schöpfung und Chaos in Urzeit und Endzeit: Eine religionsgeschicht-*

liche Untersuchung über Gen 1 und Ap Joh 12 (Göttingen: Vandenhoeck und Ruprecht, 1895) [hereafter: Gunkel, *Sch. & Ch.*], 15; my trans., p. 11.

22. "We thus recognize in Genesis 1 a series of mythologically resonant features. It follows from this that Genesis 1 is not the composition of an author, but rather the written deposit of a tradition; and at the same time, that this tradition stems from a period of high antiquity" (Gunkel, *Sch. & Ch.*, 14; my trans., p. 11). Gunkel goes on a few paragraphs later saying, "It now appears probable that this tradition would not have arisen in Israel. The parallels to Genesis 1 from the cosmogonies of other peoples lead to this conclusion."

23. Gunkel deals with the following in section 4 of the first half of the work: Exod 15:7; Isa 17:12-14; 27:1; 30:6f.; 50:2f.; 51:9f.; 59:15-20; Jer 5:22; 31:35; 51:34, 36, 42; Ezek 29:3-6; 32:2-8; Amos 9:2f.; Nah 1:4; Hab 3:8; Pss 18:16-18; 33:6; 40:5; 44:20; 68:31; 74:12-19; 77:17; 87:4; 89:10-15; 93:3f.; 104:5-9, 25f.; 106:9; Prov 8:22-31; Job 3:8; 7:12; 9:13; 26:12f.; 38:8-11; 40:19–41:26; *1 Enoch* 60:7-9; *4 Ezra* 6:49-52; *Pss. Sol.* 2:28-34; Sir 43:(25) 23; Prayer of Manasseh 2-4.

24. Gunkel, *Sch. & Ch.*, 15; my trans., p. 11.

25. For the significance of the term "olden" in reference to gods or goddesses see Frank Moore Cross Jr., "The Olden Gods in Ancient Near Eastern Creation Myths," in *Magnalia Dei, The Mighty Acts of God: Essays on the Bible and Archaeology in Memory of G. Ernest Wright*, ed. Frank Moore Cross Jr., P. D. Miller, and W. E. Lemke (New York: Doubleday, 1976), 329-38.

26. I have searched in vain for the word *Chaoskampf* itself in the original edition of *Schöpfung und Chaos*. The word is, however, common parlance today among scholars when dealing with the same myths and mythic themes as those with which Gunkel deals in *Schöpfung und Chaos*.

27. Gunkel, *Sch. & Ch.*, 121-22; my trans., pp. 82-84.

28. Gunkel, *Sch. & Ch.*, 132-34; my trans., pp. 89-91.

29. Gunkel, *Sch. & Ch.*, 124-32; my trans., pp. 85-90.

30. Gunkel, *Sch. & Ch.*, 136-38; my trans., pp. 93-94.

31. Gunkel, *Sch. & Ch.*, 138-39; my trans., pp. 93-94.

32. Gunkel, *Sch. & Ch.*, 139; my trans., p. 94.

33. Gunkel, *Sch. & Ch.*, 149; my trans., p. 98.

34. Gunkel, *Sch. & Ch.*, 87; my trans., p. 58.

35. Gunkel, *Sch. & Ch.*, 99; my trans., p. 66.

36. Isa 17:12-14 (Gunkel, *Sch. & Ch.*, 100-101; my trans., pp. 67-68); Habakkuk 3, Nahum 1, Psalm 18 (Gunkel, *Sch. & Ch.*, 102-106; my trans., pp. 68-71); Ps 93:3-4 (Gunkel, *Sch. & Ch.*, 106-10; my trans., pp. 71-74); Ps 77:17 (Gunkel, *Sch. & Ch.*, 107-8; my trans., pp. 72-73); Isa 59:15-20 (Gunkel, *Sch. & Ch.*, 108-9; my trans., p. 73).

37. Gunkel, *Sch. & Ch.*, 170; my trans., p. 111.

38. Gunkel, *Sch. & Ch.*, 201; my trans., p. 129. The reference is to E. Vischer, *Die Offenbarung des Johannis: Eine jüdische Apokalypse in christlicher Bearbeitung*, Text und Untersuchungen zur Geschichte der altchristlichen Literatur, Bd. 2, Heft 3 (Leipzig: J. C. Hinrichs, 1886). Vischer had argued that the Revelation of John was an originally Jewish document which had been adopted and reworked by a Christian writer.

39. Gunkel, *Sch. & Ch.*, 194; my trans., p. 126.

40. Gunkel, *Sch. & Ch.*, 195; my trans., pp. 126-27.

41. My thanks to Peter Machinist for his suggestion of *contemporaneous* as the word for best translating the German "zeitgeschichtliche," in order that the "textual now" may remain distinct from the "exegetical now" of the critics who are, relatively speaking, Gunkel's *contemporaries*.

42. Gunkel, *Sch. & Ch.*, 202-3; my trans., pp. 130-31.

43. Gunkel, *Sch. & Ch.*, 203; my trans., p. 131.

44. Gunkel, *Sch. & Ch.*, 205; my trans., p. 132.

45. Gunkel, *Sch. & Ch.*, 205; my trans., p. 132. In the following sentence Gunkel goes on quite pertinently, "Even names are not insignificant to scholarship, since they frequently perpetuate the misunderstandings of earlier generations."

46. Gunkel, *Sch. & Ch.*, 235; my trans., p. 150.

47. Gunkel, *Sch. & Ch.*, 237; my trans., p. 152.

48. Gunkel, *Sch. & Ch.*, 238-39; my trans., pp. 153-54.

49. Gunkel, *Sch. & Ch.*, 239; my trans., pp. 153-54.

50. Gunkel, *Sch. & Ch.*, 239-40; my trans., pp. 154-55. These questions are not *directly* quoted here.

51. Gunkel, *Sch. & Ch.*, 248; my trans., pp. 158-59.

52. Gunkel, *Sch. & Ch.*, 249; my trans., p. 159.

53. Gunkel, *Sch. & Ch.*, 249; my trans., p. 159.

54. Gunkel, *Sch. & Ch.*, 250; my trans., pp. 159-60.

55. Gunkel, *Sch. & Ch.*, 250-51; my trans., pp. 160-61.

56. Gunkel, *Sch. & Ch.*, 251; my trans., p. 161.

57. Gunkel, *Sch. & Ch.*, 251; my trans., p. 161.

58. Gunkel, *Sch. & Ch.*, 252; my trans., p. 161.

59. Gunkel, *Sch. & Ch.*, 253; my trans., p. 162.

60. Gunkel, *Sch. & Ch.*, 255; my trans., p. 163.

61. Gunkel, *Sch. & Ch.*, 256; my trans., pp. 163-64.

62. Gunkel, *Sch. & Ch.*, 281-82; my trans., pp. 179-80.

63. Gunkel, *Sch. & Ch.*, 283-378; my trans., pp. 181-238.

64. Gunkel, *Sch. & Ch.*, 283-335; my trans., pp. 181-213.

65. Gunkel, *Sch. & Ch.*, 336-78; my trans., pp. 213-38.

66. Gunkel, *Sch. & Ch.*, 367-71; my trans., pp. 232-34.

67. Gunkel, *Sch. & Ch.*, 371-74; my trans., pp. 234-36.

68. Gunkel, *Sch. & Ch.*, 374-38; my trans., pp. 236-40.

Notes to the Introduction

1. Heinrich Zimmern, "Ein vorläufiges Wort über babylonische Metrik," *Zeitschrift für Assyriologie* 8 (1893) 121f.

2. See below, p. 253, n. 4 (= p. 380, n. 4).

3. Translator's note: I have placed my own additions to Gunkel's work in square brackets as well.

4. See below, p. 244, n. 44 (= p. 377, n. 44).

5. See below, pp. 108ff.

6. See below, p. 37, n. 100 (= p. 306, n. 100).

7. Cf. [Albrecht] Dieterich, *Abraxas: [Studien zur Religionsgeschichte des späteren Altertums: Festschrift Hermann Usener zur Feier seiner 25 jährigen Lehrtätigkeit an der Bonner Universität* (Leipzig: B. G. Teubner, 1905)], 41.

Notes to Chapter 1

1. Friedrich Delitzsch, *Wo lag das Paradies? Eine biblisch-assyriologische Studie* (Leipzig: Heinrichs, 1881) [hereinafter: Delitzsch, *Paradies?*], 93f.; Ignac Goldziher, *Der Mythos bei den Hebräern und seine geschichtliche Entwickelung* (Leipzig: Brockhaus, 1867) [hereinafter: Goldziher, *Mythos*], 384f. This is also certainly the intent of Bernhard Stade, *Geschichte des Volkes Israel* (Berlin: Grote, 1888) [hereinafter: Stade, *Geschichte*], 2:144.

2. Abraham Kuenen, "Bijdagen tot de Critiek van Pentateuchen Josua," *Theologisch Tijdschrift* 18 (1884) 168: second half of the seventh century. W. H. Kosters, "De Bijbelsche zontvloedverhalen met de Babylonische vergeleken," *Theologische Tijdschrift* 19 (1885) 344: terminus a quo 704/3 (the legation of Merodach-Baladan). Karl Budde, *Die biblische Urgeschichte (Gen. 1–12,4) untersucht* (Giessen: J. Ricker, 1883) [hereinafter: Budde, *Urgeschichte*], 516: under King Ahaz.

3. Hermann Schultz, *Alttestamentliche Theologie: Die Offenbarungsreligion auf ihr vor Christlichen Entwickelungsstufe*, 4th ed. (Göttingen: Vandenhoeck und Ruprecht, 1889) [hereinafter: Schultz, *ATl Theologie*[4]], 96, 106.

4. George A. Barton, "Tiamat," *Journal of the American Oriental Society* 15 (1894) [hereinafter: Barton, "Tiamat"] 19.

5. George Smith, *Chaldäische Genesis: Keilinschriftlich Berichte über Schöpfung, Sudenfall, Sintfluth*, . . . (Leipzig: Heinrichs, 1876) [hereinafter: Smith, *Chaldäische Genesis*], 244; Franz Delitzsch, in the "Appendix" to Smith, *Chaldäische Genesis*, 306; Franz Delitzsch, *Neuer Commentar über die Genesis* (Leipzig: Dorffling und Franke, 1887) [hereinafter: Delitzsch, *Neuer Genesis*], 42; Fritz Hommel, "Inscriftliche Glossen und Exkurse zur Genesis und zu den Propheten — II," *Neue kirchliche Zeitschrift* [hereinafter: *NKZ*] 1 (1890) [hereinafter: Hommel, "Glossen u. Exkurse II"] 405; Fritz Hommel, "Eine neugefundene Weltschöpfungslegende," *Deutsche Rundschau* 17 (1891) [hereinafter: Hommel, "Neu Weltschöpfungslegende"] 113.

6. Eberhard Schrader, *Die Keilinschriften und das Alte Testament*, 2d ed. (Giessen: J. Ricker, 1883) [hereinafter: Schrader, *KAT*[2]], 609; Hugo Winckler, *Geschichte Babyloniae und Assyriologiae* [hereinafter: Winckler, *Gesch. Babyl. und Assyr.*], 74; H. Holzinger, *Einleitung in den Hexateuch* (Freiburg i. B.: Mohr, 1893) [hereinafter: Holzinger, *Hexateuch*], 443, all leave the question open.

7. Eduard Riehm, *Handwörterbuch des biblischen Altertums für gebildete Bibelleser* (Bielefeld, Leipzig: Velhagen und Klasing, 1884) [hereinafter: Riehm, *Hw*], 1415, and Eduard Riehm, *Der biblische Schöpfungsbericht* (Halle a. S.: E. Strien, 1881) [hereinafter: Riehm, *BSchöpf*], 17.

8. August Dillmann, "Über die griechische Übersetzung des Qoheleth," *Sitzungsberichte der Königlich Preussischen Akademie der Wissenschaften zu Berlin, Sitzung der philosophische-historische Klasse vom 7 Januar, 1882* (s.l.: s.n., 1882) [hereinafter: Dillmann, *Qoheleth*], 427ff. and August Dillmann, *Die Genesis*, 6th ed. (Leipzig: S. Hirzel, 1892) [hereinafter: Dillmann, *Genesis*[6]], 11.

9. Julius Wellhausen, *Prolegomena zur Geschichte Israel*, 3d ed. (Berlin: G. Reimer, 1886) [hereinafter: Wellhausen, *Prolegomena*[3]], 312.

Notes to Chapter 2

1. Wellhausen's observations are quoted by H. Holzinger, *Einleitung in den Hexateuch* (Freiburg i. B.: J. C. B. Mohr/Paul Siebeck, 1893) [hereinafter: Holzinger, *Hexateuch*], 363.

2. Wellhausen, *Prolegomena³*, 317.

3. Wellhausen, *Prolegomena³*, 312.

4. Wellhausen, *Prolegomena³*, 312.

5. Therefore, it is of no consequence for the above assertion whether the Priestly writer has created something from a source still preserved only in fragments (J2 according to Budde, *Urgeschichte*, 231ff.); it is enough that the Priestly tradition contains what we know only from the Priestly tradition.

6. I note the creation myths of other peoples in light of the clear discussion of Dillmann, *Genesis⁶*, s.v. Gen 6:4-10; the theme of chaos is found among the Hebrews and the Babylonians, as well as among the Indians, the Greeks, the Egyptians, and the Phoenicians.

7. Philo Byblius in Eusebius, *Preparatio Evangelica* [hereinafter: Eusebius, *Prep. Ev.*], 1.10.7; cf. Dillmann, *Genesis⁶*, 7.

8. Cf. Dillmann, *Genesis⁶*, 20. The statement of Wellhausen, that chaos was created by God in the beginning, is untenable since "heaven and earth" of Gen 1:1 is the organized world (cf. Dillmann, *Genesis⁶*, 16).

9. Ps 33:6 (the breath — רוח [*rûaḥ*] — of God's mouth, i.e., his word) and Ps 104:29f. (the life-giving spirit of God in living creatures) do not belong here, *contra* Dillmann, *Genesis⁶*, 16.

10. Cf. Dillmann, *Genesis⁶*, 20.

11. Cf. Dillmann, *Genesis⁶*, 20.

12. The "world egg" of the Indians, Egyptians, and the Phoenicians (cf. Dillmann, *Genesis⁶*, 20), the idea of the development of the world conveyed by this concept stems from the ovoid form of the heavens; the lower half of the egg forms the earth. The origin of the world is conceived according to the analogy of the origin of a bird in an egg. The deity is, therefore, understood as a brooding hen. The figure of the goddess had already become an abstraction, the רוח [*rûaḥ*] of Gen 1:1, at a very early time.

13. *Prolegomena³*, 311. — The idea that the world arose from the separation of the materials which previously existed in chaos, which Wellhausen considers to be a vestige of this immanent "development," does not necessarily belong to this circle of ideas but rather is just as conceivable in a "creation account." The "division" of "chaos" could just as well be the consequence of an immanent principle as the consequence of a word of the creator.

14. Cf. Dillmann, *Genesis⁶*, 21.

15. However, v. 20, "the waters teemed," and v. 24, "the earth brought forth," reverberate with similarities, although obscured by the juxtaposed "Thus God created . . ." in vv. 21 and 25.

16. Isa 40:26.

17. Num 24:7; Isa 14:12.

18. Job 38:33.

19. Deut 4:19.

20. Isa 14:13.

21. Isa 24:21, q.v. Psalm 82.

22. Job 38:7; Deut 4:19, q.v. Deut 32:8 [LXX בני־אל [*běnê-ʾēl*]; cf. the opposite corruption in Amos 5:6 and Hos 10:15 LXX].

23. *1 Enoch* 82 shows that the conception of the stars as rulers of the times of the year was a familiar one in later Judaism.

24. Dillmann, *Genesis*[6], 31, explains the "we" by reference to the fact "that for the Hebrews, who name God אלהים [*'ĕlōhîm*], God is the living personal concentration of the totality of forces and powers." This idea is unfortunately not in keeping with Old Testament thought. YHWH is always a very realistically conceived individual who never speaks of himself as anything other than "I." That in the Old Testament this individual is designated by the originally plural אלהים [*'ĕlōhîm*] is not to be explained by the theological reflection of Dillmann, but rather by a long development in which an original plural has become an abstract noun and, finally, has become a designation for YHWH.

25. Cf. Delitzsch, *Neuer Genesis*, 64.

26. Ps 89:8.

27. Ps 82:1.

28. Dillmann, *Genesis*[6], 31.

29. Dillmann, *Genesis*[6], 32.

30. By Greeks and by Romans, cf. Dillmann, *Genesis*[6], 33.

31. Wellhausen, *Prolegomena*[3], 321.

32. Parallel to Isa 65:25; Wellhausen, *Prolegomena*[3], 320.

33. Thus also August Dillmann, *Der Prophet Jesaia*, Kurzgefasstes exegetisches Handbuch zum Alten Testament (Leipzig: S. Hirzel, 1890) [hereinafter: Dillmann, *Jesaia*], 120; Franz Delitzsch, *Biblischer Commentar über der Prophet Jesaia*, 4th ed., Biblischer Commentar über das Alte Testament, vol. 3, prophetisch Bücher, 1 Bd. (Leipzig: Dorffling und Franke, 1889) [hereinafter: Delitzsch, *Jesaia*[4]], 194.

34. Dillmann, *Genesis*[6], 36.

35. Wellhausen's view [*Die Composition des Hexateuchs und der historischen Bücher des Alten Testaments*, 3d ed., *Skizzen und Vorarbeiten* 2 (Berlin: G. Reimer, 1889) [hereinafter: Wellhausen, *Composition*[2]], 188] that the present "six day" schema replaces an early "seven day" schema; that originally the creation of humanity occurred on the seventh day, is wrong! The narrative reports on the seven days generally only for this reason: that they, together with that which happens on the seventh day, provide the basis for the holiness of the Sabbath (2:3). This holiness of the day, however, would not be explained by the fact that humanity was created on that day!

36. Wellhausen, *Composition*[2], 187; Dillmann, *Genesis*[6], 15; and elsewhere.

37. Dillmann's views (*Genesis*[6], 22) appear much too complicated to me. The simplest explanation is this: In Gen 1:3-5 two different concepts come together, the creation of light, and the first day, which, by their nature, cannot sustain a unified form.

38. Budde, *Urgeschichte*, 494f., suggests that the language of Exod 20:11 does not bear the stamp of P.

39. Immanuel Benzinger, *Hebräische Archäologie: Grundriss der theologischen Wissenschaften*, 2 Reihe, 1 Band (Freiburg i. B.: Mohr, 1894) [hereinafter: Benzinger, *Archäologie*], 32.

40. Egypt, which, as everyone knows, is almost totally without rain, need not even be taken into consideration.

41. Benzinger, *Archäologie*, 199f.

42. [The German word *Sitz* has to do with the situation from which something arose. We are not dealing here with a single factor but a multiplicity of factors, communal, religious, social, cultural, etc. The word cannot be easily translated well into English, so I have used here the German word to impart a richer, deeper sense than that present in the simple English word "situation." — trans.]

Notes to Chapter 3

1. Damascius, *Quaestiones de primis principiis*, in *Damascii Phil. quaestiones de primis principiis*, ed. J. Kopp (Frankfort a. M.: H. L. Broenner, 1826) [hereinafter: Damascius, *Quaestiones*], col. 125, p. 384. For a translation, cf. George Smith, *George Smith's Chaldäische Genesis: Keilinschriftliche Berichte über Schöpfung, Sündenfall, Sintfluth, Thurmbau, und Nimrod. Nebst vielen anderen Fragmenten ältesten Babylonisch-Assyrischen Schriftthums, mit 27 Abbildungen*, trans. Hermann Delitzsch (Leipzig: J. C. Hinrichs, 1876) [hereinafter: G. Smith, *Chaldäische Genesis*], 49. For a commentary, cf. Peter Christian Albrecht Jensen, *Die Kosmologie der Babylonier: Studien und Materialen* (Strassburg: Trubner, 1890) [hereinafter: Jensen, *Kosmologie*], 270ff. — Damascius lived in the sixth century c.e. under Justinian.

2. In which Damascius believes.

3. In the cod. Δαχή, Δαχός, corr. by Smith, *Chaldäische Genesis*, 50.

4. A priest of Bel in Babylon, ca. 300 B.C.E.

5. Under Sulla.

6. Eusebius, *Eusebi Chronicorum libri duo*, ed. Alfred Schoene, 2 vols. (Berlin: Weidmann, 1875-76) [hereinafter: Eusebius, *Chronicorum*], 1:14-18. For a textual commentary, cf. the remarks of Gutschmid on Schoene; Budde, *Urgeschichte*, 476ff. For a translation, cf. Smith, *Chaldäische Genesis*, 40f. The rendering of Schrader, *KAT*², is extremely inaccurate.

7. "He" being Berossus, so called in an attached report on the wonderful fish-men of Oannes; cf. Budde, *Urgeschichte*, 477.

8. In the codex, the term is ὁμόρωκα; Joseph Juste Scaliger, ed., *Thesaurus temporum. Eusebii Pamphili Caesareae Palestinae Episcopi Chronicorum canonum omnimodae historiae libri duo, interprete Hieronymo, ex fide vetustissimorum codicum castigati. Item auctores omnes derelicta ab Eusebio, & Hieronymo coninuantes* (Leiden: T. Basson, 1605) [hereinafter: Scaliger, *Thesaurus*] has emended, according to the numerical value, to ὁμόρκα; the Armenian has *Marcaje*. — All manner of Assyriological explanations for this name have foundered (cf. Schrader, *KAT*², 13f.; Jensen, *Kosmologie*, 301f.). Had the Assyriologists examined the Greek text a little more carefully, they could have spared themselves the trouble of seeking a Babylonian equivalent, for the word itself, on the basis of the continuity of the text, is clearly *not* Babylonian. Berossus says the woman Ὀμόρκα [*omorka*] is called *Thamte* by the Chaldeans (cf. p. 223, n. 9). It follows from this that the name Ὀμόρκα is itself not Chaldean. If it is not Chaldean, however, then it can only belong to the Aramaic dialect spoken in Babylon in the time of Berossus. — Ὀμόρκα = אם ארקא [*'om 'arqā'*] = "Mother of the Animals," or, according to the Armenian tradition, [O]*marcaye* = אם ארקיא [*'om 'arqayyā'*] = "Mother of the Underworld Beings." The pronunciation אם = *'om* is not especially well attested, but is also not impossible. ארקא [*'arqā'*] occurs in Jer 10:11, in the Zincjirli inscriptions, in the *Targûmîm*, in the Zabishes repeatedly, in the Nineveh weights, as well as in Mandaic [cf. Theodor Nöldeke, *Mandäische Grammatik* (Halle: Buchhandlung des Waisenhauses, 1875) [hereinafter: Nöldeke, *Mandäische Grammatik*], 73]. Against this, the pronunciation *'orqā'* is totally unknown; cf., however, the Armenian [O]*marcaje*. — In the *Targûmîm* ארעאה [*'ar'āh*] and ארעיתא [*'ar'îtā'*] are technical terms for Tehom, Sheol, etc.; on תהומא ארעאה [*tĕhûmā' 'ar'āh*], "the lower ocean," מיא ארעאי [*mayyā' 'ar'ā'ê*], "the lowest waters," גוב ארעיתא [*gôḇ 'ar'îtā'*], שיול ארעיתא [*šĕyôl 'ar'îtā'*], ארע אריתא [*'ar'a' 'a'rîtā'*], "the underworld," ארעיתא [*'ar'îtā'*] as a substantive; ארעית גובא [*'ar'îṯ gôḇā'*], ארעית ימא [*'ar'îṯ yammā'*], תהומא ארעית [*'ar'îṯ tĕhômā'*]; cf. Jacob Levy, *Chaldäisches Wörterbuch über die Targumim; und einen grossen Theil des rabbinischen Schriftthums*, 2 vols. (Leipzig: Baumgartner, 1867-68) [hereinaf-

ter: Levy, *Wb. über die Targumim*], s.v. ארעאה and ארעיתא. — In the OT ארץ [*'ereṣ*] is "The Underworld" on more than one occasion. Thus at Exod 15:12, ארץ [*'ereṣ*] swallows them (speaking of those who drowned in the sea); לארץ [*lā-'ereṣ*] in Qoh 3:21; Isa 14:12 = "to the underworld," מארץ [*mē-'ereṣ*] = "from Sheol" ‖ מעפר (*mē-'apar*) (עפר [*'apar*] is a name for the underworld, not for "dust") in Isa 29:4 (place of the dead); תחתיות ארץ [*taḥăṭîyôt 'ereṣ*] = "depths of the underworld" in Pss 53:10; 139:15; Isa 44:23 = שאול [*šĕ'ôl*] [the expression בור ירכתי [*yarkĕṭê bôr*] in Isa 14:15; Ezek 32:23; ארץ תחתית [*'ereṣ taḥtiyôt*] and ארץ תחתיות [*'ereṣ taḥtîyôt*] in Lam 3:55; Ps 88:7], etc. Opposed to ארץ [*'ereṣ*] in this sense is ארץ חיים [*'ereṣ ḥayyîm*] "land of the living." — This double signification of ארעא [*'ar'ā*], and ארץ [*'ereṣ*], and ארקא [*'arqā*] is probably to be explained thus: the base meaning of the word is "ground," "that which is 'under'" (cf. Dan 6:25). The word is common in the Targums with this meaning. The opposite of heaven is the soil of the earth. In the perspective of the whole universe, it is שאול [*šĕ'ôl*] — [*Ti'āmat* is also called *ummu huber* (i.e., "Mother of the Under-world, of Orkus"), perhaps correctly, although this meaning of *huber* still does not appear certain to me. Nevertheless, it does appear to me that here we have the prototype of the Ara-maic *'Om 'Orqa*. Perhaps the "o" in *'Om* is to be explained from this Babylonian prototype. — Zimmern]

9. In the codex, θαλάττ [*thalatth*]; corr. by W. Robertson Smith, "Θαλάττ in Berossus," *ZA* 6 (1891) 339.

10. Omitted in Armenian; — Ὁμόρκα [*homorka*] = σελήνη [*selēnē*] = 301.

11. The βῆλος [*bēlos*] of Berossus and of Damascius is the Marduk of the cuneiform in-scriptions, whose alternative name *bêlu* means "lord."

12. In the codex, ἐν αὐτῇ σύν [*en autę̄ syn*], corr. by Alfred Freiherr von Gutschmid, *Untersuchungen über die syrische Epitome der eusebischen Canones* (Stuttgart: W. Kohlhammer, 1886) [hereinafter: Gutschmid, *Untersuchungen*], 23, 5.

13. Berossus — what follows is polemic against Berossus by Eusebius.

14. τοιῶνδε [*toiōnde*] by Gutschmid, *Untersuchungen*, 23, 5.

15. The text at this point has the final [bracketed] sentence; a transposition of Schoene according to Gutschmid. The confusion is not from Eusebius himself (so Gutschmid), accord-ing to Budde, *Urgeschichte*, 480, but rather it is the fault of the copyist.

16. This is the extent of the allegorical explanation. In what follows, the narrative of the myth continues.

17. Codices read καρποφόρον [*karpophoron*], but should read ἀκαρποφόρον [*akarpo-phoron*].

18. The following is a "scornful summing-up" of the words of Berossus by Eusebius; cf. Budde, *Urgeschichte*, 479ff.

19. [As it sounds, the German word *Tendenz* is related to the English word "tendency." Tendency is, in English, however a much more limited factor than the German concept of *Tendenz*. *Tendenz*, for the German, has more to do with the whole of that to which it relates, than simply a part or singular focus of that to which it relates. It is not one tendency among many. Rather, it has to do with the whole *being* of that to which it relates. It is the very focus of that being, the very reality of its existence. It has to do less with appearance and more with exis-tence, more with essence. In effect, the German *Tendenz* is the very modality by which a thing exists. — trans.]

20. "Berossus presumes to such nonsense." — Cf. Budde, *Urgeschichte*, 479ff.

21. In the Babylonian myth, the head is chopped off *Ti'āmat*, and the veins are cut open so that the blood flows forth (cf. pp. 17-18 below).

22. That of Berossus, not of Eusebius.

23. Cf. p. 19.

24. At the end of this book, the reader will find, among the appendices, a translation of the text, so far as it presently exists. The translation is by Heinrich Zimmern. In the same place there is also a list of the relevant literature. In the text above there follows a brief paraphrase of the myth which may, at the same time, give some clarification to the text.

25. For the Babylonians as well as for the Hebrews, the *name* belongs to the essential existence of the thing.

26. The Hebrew equivalent is תהום [těhôm]. The term is feminine in Hebrew as well. Βάαυ is a woman, according to Phoenician tradition; cf. Dillmann, *Genesis*[6], 7.

27. The giving of a name, i.e., the assignation of a destiny, established, for the gods, power and a sphere of influence.

28. The "Tablets of Lordship," which play a major role in the myth, are probably to be viewed as an amulet which bestows cosmic dominion upon the bearer.

29. An assembly of the gods where "destiny" is "established."

30. The name is written ideographically. The Semitic pronunciation is, unfortunately, unknown.

31. Cf. Gen 27:25f. (the blessing of Isaac).

32. Similar signs are found at Exod 4:1-5, 6-8 (Moses' staff and his hands) and Judg 6:36-40 (the fleece of Gideon). We have in this case a clear description of how the Babylonians conceived of creation *(banû)*, for here *Marduk* receives the power which he later exercises in the "creation" of the world. The concept of "creation" is: humanity may form with its hands, but the god brings forth by his word. Hebrew expresses this concept of the efficacy of the divine "word" by ברא [bārā']. The best definition for this is Ps 33:9: כי הוא אמר ויהי [kî hû' way-'āmar yehî]. ברא [bārā'] means to call into existence by the world.

33. The fact that Zeus wields the same weapon as that seen in the depictions of the battle of *Marduk* has already been noted by Alexander Conze, *Heroen- und götter-Gestalten der griechischen Kunst erlautert* (Vienna: s.n., 1874-75) [hereinafter: Conze, *Heroen*], 7 and Jensen, *Kosmologie*, 333. This fact is not unimportant for archaeologists since it is a clear example of the borrowing of a Babylonian divine symbol by the Greeks.

34. Cf. p. 15 above.

35. The account of the creation of the fixed stars and of the moon has been preserved for us. In both cases, evidence of the intention of using them for the marking off of time is included.

36. [Again, it is easier to keep the German phrase which Gunkel uses than it is to translate it. That to which he refers is the *historical-critical* approach to religion, such as that which he uses. — trans.]

37. This "echoing function" which has given rise to the mythic is overlooked by those who see in our myth only a poetic description of a constantly recurring situation.

38. Jensen, *Kosmologie*, 309. — G. A. Barton, "Tiamat," *Journal of the American Oriental Society* 15 (1894) 24ff. views *Marduk* as the god of the storm who vanquishes the unruly sea.

39. Jensen, *Kosmologie*, 308.

40. The parting of *Ti'āmat* in the myth thus is not connected, it seems to me, with the concept that *Marduk*, at his rising, passes over a great sea in the east, *contra* Jensen, *Kosmologie*, 308.

41. In this regard, it is uncertain whether, as F. Hommel, "Inschriftliche Glossen und Exkurse zur Genesis und zu den Propheten — II," *Neue Kirchliche Zeitschrift* [hereinafter: *NKZ*]

1 (1890) 398-99, wishes, the eleven monsters of *Ti'āmat* correspond to the eleven zodiacal forms (i.e., the whole zodiac excluding the Bull-*Marduk*), or whether (as Jensen, *Kosmologie*, 309-20 suggests), the eleven monsters find their counterpart only in the winter quarter of the zodiacal cycle.

42. Thus, it appears to me as a corollary that the imagination perceived the zodiacal forms as monsters in the heavens. — Jensen, *Kosmologie*, 89, 315ff. Likewise Heinrich Zimmern, *Das Assyriologie als Hülfwissenschaft für das Studium des Alten Testaments und des Klassischen Altertums* (Königsberg i. Pr.: W. Koch, 1889), 14ff. [hereinafter: Zimmern, *Assyriologie Hülfwissenschaft*], views the situation a bit differently. He begins with the view that the imagination did not see a bull or a lion in Taurus or Leo, but rather that speculation on the constellation in which the sun rose in the spring of the year has given it the name "Taurus" (Bull), since the bull is the symbol of *Marduk,* who is the "spring sun." This should hold true in the same fashion for the majority of the constellations of the zodiac. — I am inclined to believe that the Babylonian imagination is too overrated. It is certainly not impossible, however, that this imagination imposed the alignment by reasonable reflection.

43. Cf., e.g., the stele of Esarhaddon from Zinčjirli (published in the *Mittheilungen aus den orientalischen Sammlungen der Königliche Museen zu Berlin* [hereinafter: *MOS*], Heft 11 (1889), pl. 1.

44. Alfred Jeremias, *Izdubar-Nimrod* (Leipzig: B. G. Teubner, 1891) [hereinafter: Jeremias, *Izdubar-Nimrod*], 11, first noted this connection.

45. Cf. Winckler, *Gesch. Babyl. und Assyr.,* 29, 33f.

46. Cf. p. 295, n. 42 above.

47. Jensen gives a related form of this theory in "Ursprung und Geschichte des Tierkreises," *Deutsche Revue über das gesammte nationale Leben der Gegenwart* 15 (1891) 112ff.

48. *Cf.* p. 295, n. 42 above.

49. Eberhard Schrader, *Keilinschriftliche Bibliothek: Sammlung von Assyrischen und Babylonischen Texten in Umschrift und Übersetzung,* 6 vols. (Berlin: Reuther und Teichard, 1889-1915) [hereinafter: Schrader, *KB*], 3.1, 143.

50. Schrader, *KB* 3.1, 13.

51. Cf. Louis de Clercq, *Collection de Clercq: catalogue methodique et raisonne: antiquites assyriennes, cylindres orientaux, cachets, briques, bronzes, bas-reliefs,* etc., 7 vols. (Paris: E. Lerouz, 1888-), 1, nos. 315ff., passim.

52. The picture in, e.g., Smith, *Chaldäische Genesis,* 90/91; Austen Henry Layard, *The Monuments of Nineveh: First and Second Series* (London: Murray, 1849) [hereinafter: Layard, *Monuments of Nineveh* 1-2], ser. II, pl. 5 — In this picture *Ti'āmat* bears a peculiar, budlike top-knot on her head which also occurs in old Greek representations of the Griffin; cf. Wilhelm Heinrich Roscher, ed., *Ausfürhliches Lexikon der griechischen und römischen Mythologie* (Leipzig: B. J. Teubner, 1884-1937), 1:1747ff. (s.v. "Furtwängler") [hereinafter: Roscher, *Lexikon Mythologie*].

53. Schrader, *KB,* 3.1, 145.

54. Schrader, *KB,* 3.1, 13.

55. Schrader, *KB,* 3.1, 143.

56. Schrader, *KB,* 3.1, 143; 3.2, 21, 35, 73, etc.

57. Cf. the translation of variants by Heinrich Zimmern in the appendix.

58. [The reading is indeed probably *labbu* (Heb. לביא [*lābî'* = lion]); cf. the "lion head" of *Ti'āmat* in the iconography. Cf. also 2 Tim 4:17, 1 Pet 5:8f. — Zimmern]

59. The blood of *Ti'āmat* which flows for a certain time after her death is perhaps the water of the river, which begins to swell at the time of first fruits (cf. Sir 24:25).

60. Translations: *Journal of the Royal Asiatic Society* 23 (1891) 393ff.; by Fritz Hommel, "Eine Neugefundene Weltschöpfungslegende," *Deutscher Rundschau*, July 1891, 105ff.; and by H. Zimmern in the Appendix.

Notes to Chapter 4

1. Riehm, *Hw*, 1262 (906) noted (in 1884) Isa 51:9; Jer 30:7; Pss 74:13f.; 87:4; 89:10f.; Job 7:12; 9:13; 26:2f.; H. Zimmern, *Das Assyriologie als Hülfswissenschaft für das Studium des Alten Testaments und des Klassischen Altertums* (Königsberg i. Pr.: W. Koch, 1889)[hereinafter: Zimmern, *Assyriologie als Hülfswissenschaft*], 16, noted Job 9:13 (cf. also Dillmann, *Genesis*[6], 9). F. Hommel, "Inschriftliche Glossen und Excurse zur Genesis und zu den Propheten — I," *Neue Kirchliche Zeitschrift* 1 (1890) 406 looks at Amos 7:4* (the asterisk indicates that, in actuality, the text does not belong at this point), Isa 27:1; 51:9f.; Job 8:13; Barton, "Tiamat," 22ff. notes the serpent of Genesis 3*; Isa 27:1; 30:7; 51:9; Pss 40:4; 89:10; 74:13f.; 87:4; 90:10*; 104:25; Job 3:8; 9:13; 26:12f.; 41; Hugo Winckler, *Alttestamentliche Untersuchungen* (Leipzig: E. Pfeiffer, 1892), 153, notes Isa 27:1. — Significant insights are so closely joined with outlandish ideas in the above-named treatments of Hommel and Barton that it is understandable why Old Testament scholarship has paid no attention to such statements up to the present. The gratitude of theologians to the Assyriologist would undoubtedly be greater if the Assyriologist ordinarily observed the practice of expounding his views relating to the Old Testament — i.e., that which lies outside of his special field of expertise — *first* to the specialists, and *only then* to the greater public.

2. I will indicate, with each poetic fragment, the metrical structure of the bicola; elsewhere I will develop more fully the significance and reason for these statements. I distinguish bicola of four, five, and six beats, each of which is divided into two cola by a caesura, and is often combined with distichs, tristichs, and tetrastichs. Isa 51:9-10 are lines of five beats (*qînāh* lines). The first bicolon of v. 9 has four beats and a partial caesura; cf. p. 299, n. 21.

In the printed form the most important thing is that, aside from the ends of the bicola and possibly the distichs, the caesura must also be clearly delineated. Because of space, I have printed the second colon in the five- and six-footed bicola after the first colon; in the four-footed bicola an interruption in the text is inserted to indicate the division. Moreover, I have distinguished the distichs and the like by the insertion of spaces.

3. √חצב [√ḥṣb = "to hew"] with the גרזן [*garzen* = "axe"] out of צור [*ṣûr* = "rock"] means "to hew something out" (e.g., a well, a wine press, a grave, a building stone, ore). It is not used to describe the site of the digging. Hos 6:5 and Ps 29:7 are understood to be corrupt. At Hos 6:5 read מחצתי [*māḥaṣtî* <√מחץ/[√mḥṣ] = "to smite, to wound, to shatter"]:

For this reason I have shattered them by the prophets,
I have murdered them with the words of my mouth!

מחץ [*māḥaṣ* = "to smite, to wound, to shatter"] ‖ המית [*hēmît* = "to cause to die, to kill"] (Deut 32:39); מחץ [*māḥaṣ* = "to smite, to wound, to shatter"] is possible (cf. Isa 30:26; Job 5:18). Concerning this, cf. Isa 23:39. Ps 29:7 is corrupt. Isa 51:9 should read, following Job 26:12, המחצת [*ham-mōḥeṣet* = "the one who shattered"] [Charles F. Houbigant, *Notae criticae in universos Veteris Testamenti libros: cum Hebraice cum Graece scriptus, cum integris ejusdem prolegominis ad exemplar Parisiense denue recusae* (Frankfurt a. M.: Varrentrapp filium & Wenner, 1777), vol. 2, s.v. Isa 51:9]. Emphatic type indicates the uncertainty of the translation, or a conjecture. I do not, however, consider any variant reading base on vocalization or on *matres lectionis,* nor readings which are explained through the translations, to be conjectures.

4. The tradition has adopted here, and at Job 26:12, the form חוֹלֵל [*ḥôlēl* = "to pierce through"] instead of חָלֵל [*ḥillēl* = "to violate, to dishonor"]. At Isa 53:5 it has adopted חוֹלֵל [*ḥôlēl* = "to pierce through"]. Modern scholarship adds Ezek 28:9 and 32:23 [cf. Carl Gustav Adolf Siegfried and Bernhard Stade, *Hebräisches Wörterbuch zum Alten Testaments: Mit Zwei Anhängen: I. Lexidion zu den aramäischen Stücken des Alten Testaments. II. Deutsche-Hebräisches Wörterverzeichnis* (Leipzig: Heit, 1893) [hereinafter: Siegfried-Stade, *Wb*], s.v. חוֹלֵל 204-5]. The parallel חלל [*ḥālal* = "to bore, to pierce"] || דכא [*dikkā'* = "to crush"] at Isa 53:5 (concerning דכא; cf. p. 298, n. 10, above), and the epic variant at Ps 89:11, דכאת כחלל [*dikki'ṭā keḥālāl* = "you crushed . . . like a profaned one"] (cf. p. 23) indicates that here, as well as at Job 26:14 and Isa 53:5, חָלָל [*ḥillal* = "to be violated, to be dishonored"] is to be read. Thus also Ezek 28:9 and 32:26 (cf. the treatment of חָלָל, p. 298, n. 10). — Likewise, at *Pss. Sol.* 2:30 τὴν ὕβριν αὐτοῦ ἐκκεκεντημένον [*tēn hybrin autou ekkekentēmenon*] = גאונו מחלל [*gĕ'ônô mĕḥullāl* = "his pride was violated"]. Ps 77:11, חלותי [*ḥălôṭî* = "my suffering"] [Gustav Bickell, *Carmina Veteris Testamenti metrice: Notas criticas et dissertationem de re metrica Hebraeorum adject* (Innsbruck: Wagner, 1882), 52]; Ps 109:22, חלל [*holal* = "he writhes" — Kautzsch's translation in E. Kautzsch, *Die heilige Schrift des alten Testament* (Freiburg/Leipzig: Paul Siebeck, 1894), 73]. Therefore, √חלל ["*Q'al, Po'lēl, Po'lal* = 'to pierce through'"] should be stricken from the lexicon.

5. What comes next, v. 11 (= 35:10), very different in tone from the foregoing, is an addition (Dillmann, *Jesaiah,* 446, among others).

6. Likewise, the water in the wilderness of Isa 41:17-20 is, at the same time, both symbolically *and* actually water. It is, therefore, necessary to maintain that v. 10b is a later addition.

7. Thomas K. Cheyne, *The Prophecies of Isaiah: A New Translation with Commentary and Appendices* (London: Kegan Paul, 1880) [hereinafter: Cheyne, *Isaiah*], 2:31; and Bernhard Duhm, *Das Buch Jesaiah, übersetzt und erklärt,* Handkommentar zum Alten Testament, Abt. III, "Die Prophetischen Bücher," 1 Bd. (Göttingen: Vandenhoeck und Ruprecht, 1892) [hereinafter: Duhm, *Jesaia*], 357, also consider the possibility of a myth, without recalling the Babylonian ones.

8. The psalm is not unified. Ps 89:2-3, 6-18a is a song of praise to YHWH which proclaims his might, his fidelity, and his grace. The poem has the four-beat bicola usual for hymns. The bicola are linked in double stichs. An appendix (47-58) implores YHWH to have pity on his creatures, i.e., on Israel, in the present. This fragment, in the same meter, yet less skillful and less well crafted, probably stems from a second hand. The whole thing is edited by a third hand. In this recension YHWH's eternal fidelity is not understood in terms of the grace of creation, but rather points to the covenant with David. In order to express this understanding vv. 4, 5, and 18b-46 are inserted and vv. 47-54 are reworked. The insertions are written in common bicola of six feet.

9. בשוא [*bĕ-śô'*], probably = בשאות [*bi-š'ôṭ*]; cf. LXX, Pesh., *Q'al* infinitive of שאה + ב || *Q'al* infinitive of גאה + ב. The word is a term for the arrogant and destructive raging of the Sea and of stormy weather, for the racket of the subverted order, etc. The reading בשוא [*bĕ-śô'*] lays the foundation for the confusion of שאה [*š'h*] and נשא [*nś'*]; likewise Nah 1:5, ותשא הארץ [*wat-tiśśā' hā-'āreṣ*], "the earth cries out"; Hab 1:3, מדון ישא [*māḏôn yiśśā'*], "the contention is loud"; Job 41:17, משתו = מְשָׁאֵתוֹ [*mštw = mĕšō'āṭô*], "his [Leviathan's] destructive raging" (Ps 62:5).

אַךְ מִשֵּׂאֵתוֹ   יָעֹצוּ לְהַדִּיחַ יִרְצוּ

['ak miśśĕ'ētô ya'ṣôr   lĕhaddîaḥ yirṣû]

"Indeed, his destruction they have resolved!
    They rejoice to cast [him] down!"

(the image of a toppling wall — v. 4, a *qînāh* bicolon); Gen 49:3, שְׂאֵת יֶתֶר [*yeter šĕ'ōt*], "an abundance of raging fury" (cf. v. 4, כַמַּיִם [*kam-mayim*]; Job 13:11, the שְׂאֵת, 31:23, the מַשְׂאֵת of God || פַּחַד אֵיד = the terrible catastrophe proximity to which God brings; Hos 13:1 should be read נָשִׂיא, "Ephraim was *prince* in Israel"; Gen 4:7 and Hab 1:7 are corrupted; שִׂיא at Job 20:6 is very dubious. Because of this, the intransitive meaning of נשא (Siegfried-Stade, *Wb*, s.v. נשא, 6, 443) should be stricken from the lexicon.

10. דכאת כחלל: Hermann Hupfeld, *Die Psalmen übersetzt und ausgelegt*, 3d ed., ed. Wilhelm Nowack [hereinafter: Hupfeld-Nowack, *Psalmen*], 2:344: "You have shattered Rahab, like those who have been stabbed to death." Friedrich Baethgen, *Die Psalmen übersetzt und erklärt*, Handkommentar zum Alten Testament, 2 Abt., 2 Bd. (Göttingen: Vandenhoeck & Ruprecht, 1892) [hereinafter: Baethgen, *Psalmen*], 277: "You have crushed Rahab like one who has been pierced." — How does one crush one who has been pierced? — דכא, "to crush under the feet," Lam 3:34; "to tread down to the earth," Ps 143:3; "to mistreat frightfully," Ps 94:5; Job 19:2f.; "to humiliate," Isa 57:15; Pss 24:19; 41:19; thus LXX and Ps 89:11. — The adjective חָלָל [*ḥālāl*] does not belong — as is commonly believed — to the same root as חלל [*ḥll*], "to play a flute"; חלון [*ḥallôn*], "window," and hence does mean "to bore through," but rather it belongs to the root חלל [*ḥll*], "to desecrate"; חל [*ḥol*], "profane," etc., and means "profaned." Thus, clearly at Lev 21:7 (cf. 19:29) חָלָל [*ḥālāl*], "profaned," or, more accurately, "profaned by the sword," is the term for the corpses (on the battlefield) of the fallen (of the defeated army), who "were not mourned, not buried, and not entombed, but rather they became dung on the surface of the land," Jer 25:33; cf. Jer 8:23 ("unlamented"); 14:18; 51:47; Ezek 11:6; 30:11; 35:8 (lying about everywhere, in the field, the mountains and valleys, in the alleys of the city); Isa 34:3 (flung down, rotting, bloody) || פגר [*peger*] (as at Nah 3:3); Job 39:30 ("food for the vulture"). Such "profane things" also find no peace in death. נפש חללים תשוע [*nepeš ḥālālîm tĕšawwēa'*]: Job 24:12 ("the souls of those who have been profaned howl"). The opposite of this is the honorable burial of the victors, whose swords are buried under their heads and who are covered up with their shields. The "shame" of the former (Ezek 32:24) still must be born in death; to die "the death of a profaned one" (Ezek 28:8); the phrase מוֹתֵי עֲרֵלִים תָּמוּת [*môtê 'ărēlîm tāmût*], "to die the death of the uncircumcised," Ezek 28:10; עֲרֵלִים [*'ărēlîm*] || חללי חרב [*ḥalĕlê ḥereb*], 21:25ff.; Ezek 31:18; 32:19f. How the חָלָל [*ḥālāl*] might still further be "mishandled" is described by 1 Sam 31:8ff.: not only were his garments stripped off, but his head was chopped off as well, and his carcass was impaled, etc. Correspondingly, there is also the word חָלָל [*ḥālāl*], where it is used to mean the dead or the fallen; cf. p. 297, n. 4 above. It means "to make חָלָל" [*ḥālāl*] or "to treat חָלָל" [*ḥālāl*]. The above translation "carcass" is not really sufficient since English [like Gunkel's German — trans.] lacks a corresponding term. It is, however, understandable.

11. תבל [*tēbēl*] was originally the fruit-bearing Earth, "mother Earth" (> √יבל/[√*ybl*]); the opposite of it is מדבר [*midbār*], Isa 14:17. The word, because it regularly occurs without the article, is of ancient mythological origin. The traditional translation of "the round earth" is misleading — the fact that the earth is round had *absolutely* nothing to do with תבל [*tēbēl*] — and should never again be repeated.

12. עמך ['*immāk*] according to Syr. *Pesh*.

13. The pride of the arrogant is brought to shame in Isa 23:8; Ezek 28:7; *Pss. Sol.* 2:30, etc.

14. The Hebrew sensibility appears to have understood the name רהב [*rahab̠*] as an insolent explosion; whether the name actually meant this originally it is impossible to say.

15. Bicola of six feet, as is customary in Job.

16. רגע [*rgʿ*] *Hip̄ʿîl*, "to create or find peace"; *Nip̄ʿal*, "to be peaceful"; [*rāḡēaʿ*] "peaceful"; מרגוע [*margôaʿ*], "peace," etc. cannot simultaneously also mean the opposite, "to stir up." According to Ps 89:10, שבה [*šbh* — *Piʿēl*], and Job 26:12 LXX, κατέπαυσεν [*katepausen*] — other parallels in that which follows — it means, in the *Qʿal* and more especially in the *Hip̄ʿîl*, "to calm." Concerning Isa 51:15; Jer 31:35, רגעהים ויחמו גליו [*rōḡaʿ hay-yām way-yehĕmû gallâw*], cf. that which follows.

17. Hebrew text: "through his spirit [breath] heaven is a beautiful thing." August Dillmann, *Hiob*, 4th ed. (Leipzig: Hirzel, 1891) [hereinafter: Dillmann, *Hiob*[4]], 242, "by his breath there is joy," i.e., by his breath the heavens are joyful. The meaning "joy" is not substantiated. LXX κλεῖθρα δὲ οὐρανοῦ δεδοίκασιν αὐτόν *(kleithra de ouranou dedoikasin auton)* = בריחי שמים שערה [*bĕ-rêḥê šāmayim śiʿāruhu*].

18. בריח [*bārîaḥ*] as an attribute of the נחש [*nāḥāš*], both here and in Isa 27:1, reflects √ברח [√*brḥ*], "to flee." However, the meaning of "fugitive" does not fit this context. The Vulgate has *tortuosus*.

19. Thus also Dillmann, *Hiob*[4], 227. That "the bolt of heaven" is a probable Hebrew formation cannot be disputed since "the sluices of heaven" (Gen 7:11; 2 Kings 7:2, 19), "the doors of heaven" (Gen 28:17; Ps 78:23), and the heavenly "canals" through which the rain streams (Job 38:25) are all clearly attested.

20. There are no grounds for assuming a completely new myth here; cf. also the following.

21. Feet of six beats; the second colon has four beats; this expansion of a three-foot colon to a bicolon of four beats divided by a pseudo-*caesura* is very common; cf. p. 21; Isa 51:9a.

22. Dillmann, *Hiob*[4], 80-81, also compares Babylonian materials to Job 9:13, without giving any definitive judgement.

23. So also the Targum.

24. The division of the words of the Hebrew text, which Dillmann still defends (*Jesaia*, 271-72), i.e., "therefore I have called her (fem. sing.) 'Violence' who are (masc. pl.) a 'Place of Silence,'" is completely improbable. הַמָּשְׁבָּת [*ham-mošbāt̠* [*Hop̄ʿal* participle fem. sing. — trans.]] is to be read naturally [Christian Gotthilf Hensler, *Jesaias, neu übersetzt, mit Anmerkungen* (Hamburg and Kiel: Carl Ernst Bohn, 1788) [hereinafter: Hensler, *Jesaia*], according to Dillmann, *Jesaia*, 271]; on this meaning of השבת [*hošbat̠*], cf. the *Hip̄ʿîl* השבית [*hišbît*] at Isa 13:11 and Ezek 7:24, where bravado is brought to silence; and the *Qʿal* at Isa 14:4, where the two words מרהבה [*marhēb̠āh*] (LXX; cf. Dillmann, *Jesaia*, 271) and שבת [*šāb̠at*] are linked just as רהב [*rāhab̠*] and שבת [*šāb̠at*] are linked here. — Duhm, *Buch Jesaia*, 217, has doubts that the code-name stems from the early prophets, though Isaiah has, at other times, set forth his thoughts in such oracular words (cf. Isa 7:8); and Isa 20:8 assumes the short phrase which has just been announced a moment before, which Isaiah is to write down on a tablet for public notice, just as he has done at Isa 8:1, with מהר שלל חש בז [*mahēr šālāl ḥāš baz*].

25. Other parallels follow.

26. Feet of five stresses, distichs.

27. Cf. Siegfried-Stade, *Wb*, 581-82.

28. ושטי [*wĕ-śāṭê*] ‖ פנה [*pānāh*] is to be read ושטה [*wĕ-śāṭāh*]. Accordingly, the assumption of an otherwise unattested שוט [√*śwt*] is unnecessary.

29. Likewise, the form תהו [*tōhû*] is the "nothingness" on which one cannot depend (Isa

59:4); together with אפס [*'epes*] (Isa 40:7), a designation for heathen gods (1 Sam 12:21; Isa 41:29); "do not turn back to 'nothingness' (תהו [*tōhû*]); they bring no help or salvation, for they are 'nothingness' (תהו [*tōhû*])." In this saying the same thought is expressed which lies behind the use of the name רהבים [*rĕhābîm*].

30. Four-footed, double distich.

31. אתה [*'attāh*] should stand here, as at the beginning of vv. 13-17.

32. LXX, Syr. Pesh., and Vulg. read מלכנו [*malkēnû*]. The plural appears to be a correction; cf. v. 9.

33. The caesura and the sense prove that "in the water" belongs to "the dragon." The same is true at Isa 27:1 and Ezek 32:2.

34. "to the people, to the ציים" [*ṣiyyîm*] is hardly correct. The deletion of ל [*lĕ-*] is not advisable, for how could it have found its way into the text? Rather, the corruption is to be sought in לעם [*lĕ-'ām*]. לחם [*leḥem* = "food"] is to be read; cf. Ps 147:9, "food" of animals.

35. The exact meaning of the word ציים [*ṣiyyîm*] is unknown. The translation can give the sense only approximately.

36. LXX, Sym, and Targ read "Moon," probably סהר [*sahar*].

37. One does not expect "the boundaries of the Earth" in a context which speaks of the times of the day and the seasons of the year and the heavenly bodies which regulate them. גבורות [*gebûrōt* — "powers," "authorities"] is to be read; thus a good link between vv. 16 and 17 is established; concerning the concept, cf. pp. 10f. and Job 38:33; the "powers, authorities" are the stars which rule over the earth and determine its seasons.

38. LXX B has a double translation: (1) ταύτης [*tautēs*] = זאת [*zō't*] (thus א alone); (2) τῆς κτίσεως (or κτήσεως) σου [*tēs ktiseōs* (or *ktēseōs*) *sou*] = אהזתך [*'ăhuzzātkā* — "your possession"]. The "possession of God" is the world which he has ordered (cf. pp. 18ff.).

39. Omit יהוה. One does not expect the 3d masc. sing., but rather the 2d masc. sing.

40. The Hebrew text, "Do not surrender the life of your dove to the beast [or pl. "beasts"]" is very objectionable, since the water monster — with which the text must deal — does not engage in a hunt for a dove. According to LXX, ἐξομολογουμένην σοι [*exomologoumenēn soi* — Syr. Pesh., Vulg.] ‖ עניך ['*ăniyêkā*], תורך [*tôrekā*] is to be read; for לחית [*lĕ-ḥayyat*], I conjecture לתחת [*lĕ-taḥat*]; cf. Job 41:25; תחת [*taḥat*] is corrupted to יחת [*yēḥat*], cf. p. 304, n. 71.

41. The word "creation" is clearly pronounced in v. 20: הבט לבריתך[י]ך ימלאו [*habbēṭ lab-bĕrîtĕkā yimlĕ'û*], "look upon (i.e., trouble yourself about) your creations." The continuation of the verse is not to be translated up to the word חמס [*ḥāmās*]; מחשכי [currently *maḥăškî*] should be divided into two words.

42. נהרות איתן [*nahărôt 'ētān*] thus are not perennial streams here, but rather are the streams of the primordial sea.

43. H. C. Rawlinson, *The Cuneiform Inscriptions of Western Asia* (London: R. E. Bowler, 1861-64) [hereinafter: Rawlinson, *CIWA*], 2, 19.14b; cf. Riehm, *Hw*, 328.

44. [*Kingu* is designated as *limnum* ("foe") and *ayabum* (Heb. איב ['*oyēb*] — "enemy") of *Marduk* in 4:123f.] — Zimmern

45. [It is difficult to translate this word into English. Literally it has to do with that which is submitted, which is presented. Here, however, Gunkel uses it in a way which appears to carry more "shades" than its "normal" usage. It appears to include a contextual edge, and to signify the very social, theological, national contexts in which hymns such as this one arise. — trans.]

46. [Again, it is difficult to translate this word into English. The translation often found in a dictionary is "type" or "class." This is, I believe, too structurally limited in the modern

English-speaking mind-set. Biblical scholars often translate the world as "form," but again such a translation seems to imply structure and shape. Gunkel's use of the term transcends such "physical" limitations. What he seems to imply is not simply shape or structure, but background. Similarity of *Gattungen* (*-en* is a German plural ending), for Gunkel, implies not simply similarity of the physical dimensions of the literary piece. It also implies a certain similarity of tradition history which led to that physical similarity. A literary *Gattung*, for Gunkel, encompasses structurally similar traditional material which took its structural shape from a common attempt to address a particular type of situation in a traditional community's life. In this case, the *Gattung* of creation hymns, Gunkel believes, arose in response to Israel's attempts at various points in time to understand how God would (or perhaps could) bring creative order out of what appeared as chaos to those who were living in a given situation. — trans.]

47. Besides purely poetic and purely prosaic texts, there is also, in Hebrew literature, a middle-*Gattung* which has, in common with poetry, the logical relationship which prevails between the half-lines and the elevated diction of poetry but which drops the poetic counting of beats. This "rhythmic prose" is especially common in the prophets. I find this stylistic *Gattung* in Isa 27:1. It is not often easy to know whether a text under consideration was originally in the most rigorous sense "poetic," but is now corrupted by "additions," or whether it was conceived from the beginning as "rhythmic prose." The transition from these three stylistic *Gattungen* to poetry happens much more easily in Hebrew than in German — one notes, however, the Shakespearian dramas; because of this they [poetry and rhythmic prose] *can* alternate with each other in the same passage.

48. Jensen, *Kosmologie*, 25f.

49. Generally, אפס [*'epes*] designates nonexistence, just like the ancient designation of chaos as תהו (*tohû*), which originally meant wilderness, void, or nonexistence.

50. The word appears in this connection only in poetry, and is perceived as a plural; the latter is, perhaps, not original. The above etymology of אפס [*'epes*] is, according to Fritz Hommel, "Inschriftliche Glossen und Exkurse zur Genesis und zu den Propheten — II," *Neue Kirchliche Zeitschrift* [hereinafter: *NKZ*] 1 (1890) [hereinafter: Hommel, "Inschriftliche Glossen II"] 41l.

51. [In the legend of the *Ribbum*, the tail is near the mouth. Thus the description of the *limiti* of the serpent: coils? (the Assyrian *lamū, limētu* is equivalent to Hebrew לְוָה [*lēwāh*], לִוְיָה [*liwyāh*]).] — Zimmern

52. Subsequently I note that the idea of Leviathan who "encircled" the whole world is still present in the later literature. According to Ethiopic vocabulary, "Behemoth and Leviathan are serpents (monsters) on the edge of the ocean, who encircle the earth like a ring" (from Goldschmidt, *Henoch*, 83); and Rashi remarked concerning נחש עקלתון [*nāḥāš 'ăqallāṭôn*] in Isa 27:1 "that this entwined Leviathan surrounds the whole earth" [from M. Grünbaum, "Beiträge zur vergleichenden Mythologie aus der Hagada," *ZDMG* 31 (1877) [hereinafter: Grünbaum, "Beiträge"] 275].

53. Especially 24:4:

It withers,	the earth decays
it decays,	the world withers.
It withers [אמלל (*'umlal*)],	the heavens with the earth.

and 24:18b, 19

18 For the windows of the heavens are opened,
because the foundations of the earth tremble.

19   *The earth is brought to ruin,*
        the earth is split into fragments,
        the earth starts to totter and shake.

54. So clearly Job 41:7-9, 22 (the scales on the back and on the abdomen).

55. It is, of course, currently conceded by all Old Testament scholars that the Hebrew *textus receptus* is corrupted at many points. Nevertheless, the early aversion to textual emendation still holds true in the present. It is often still the goal of exegesis to impose sense upon the *existing text* no matter how good or how bad it may be. If one imposes rigorous standards on exegesis, i.e., if one believes that the author could speak Hebrew and had a reasonable mind, then a plethora of explanations which have been advanced and which are advocated even now, fall away without further ado. The polemic against the exegesis of this text, as it has been practiced up to the present, is summed up as briefly as possible in the treatment which follows. The improbability of the disputed explanations will indeed become clear without a great many words on my part — or so I hope!

56. According to Ferdinand Hitzig, *Das Buch Hiob, übersetzt und ausgelegt* (Leipzig: C. F. Winter, 1874) [hereinafter: Hitzig, *Hiob*], 302, אף [*'ap*] belongs to v. 25.

57. V. 25 describes the capture of Leviathan with "a hook" and (appropriately) with "a cord"; v. 26 describes how he then is preserved (Dillmann, *Hiob*[4], 348). — השקיע [*hišqîaʿ*], "to cause to drop down," is hardly acceptable in the context; LXX περιθήσεις [*perithēseis*], A συνδήσεις [*syndēseis*], Vulg. *ligabis*, etc.; Johann David Michaelis, *Supplementa ad Lexica hebraica, partes sex*, ed. G. Rosenmüller (Leipzig: Weidmann, 1793-96) [hereinafter: Michaelis, *Supplementa*], 3:2349 [on Samuel 17, cf. S. Bochart, *Hierozoicon, sive de animalibus S. Scripturae* (Leipzig: Weidman, 1793-96) [hereinafter: Bochart, *Hierozoicon*], 3:739, n. 1] recalls the meaning of the word in Samaritan: √שקע [√*šqʿ*] Lev 8:13 = Heb. √שחב [√*šḥb*].

58. אגמן [*'agmōn*]. The word is usually taken to mean a "cord of rushes," yet it would be expected that Leviathan would bite through such a cord, no matter how strong it is thought to be. The poet does not, however, wish to comment on the intrinsic improbability of the action. He wishes, rather, to say that that which is, in itself, possible (at least for God) is impossible for human beings; e.g., at v. 29, God can certainly play with Leviathan, but for a human being it is not possible, etc. Theodotion κρίνων [*krinōn*], Vulg. *circulum*, Tg. Onq. all, perhaps, read another word.

59. בפיו [*bě-pîw*]; Theodotion ἐν τῷ μυκτῆρι αὐτοῦ [*en tǭ myktēri autou*] is required by the context. אגמן [*'agmōn* = "rush, bulrush"] and חוח [*ḥôaḥ* = "briar, bramble, hook, ring, fetter"] [cf. חח, Johann Georg Ernst Hoffmann, *Hiob* (Kiel: C. F. Haesler, 1891) [hereinafter: Hoffmann, *Hiob*], 90] are different designations for the same thing, in this case the ring which is inserted through the mouth and emerges again from the cheek. באפו [*bě-'appô*] is incorrect. A ring does not go through the nose and the cheek at the same time. Only infrequently is an animal bound with both a nose ring and a cheek ring at the same time.

60. One notes the contradiction between the terrifying monster and the tender words. Such a contradiction is consistent with the fear of death.

61. לנערותיך [*lě-naʿărôtěḵā*]; that the person addressed by God should have a daughter is a peculiar conception [the noun is of the feminine grammatical gender — trans.]. LXX ὥσπερ στρουθίον παιδίῳ *(hosper strouthíon paidíō)* = כתור לנער [*kě-ṭôr lě-naʿar*]. Once again, a general tone! Cf. n. 60 immediately above.

62. Vv. 30-31 could possibly have been read:

Will seamen [חבלים [*ḥoḇlîm*]] *carry on trade with him?*
Will men of Phoenicia [בני כנענים [*běnê kěnaʿănîm*]] *divide him?*

Will they load his skin into longboats?

*His flesh [*שארו* [*šĕ'ērô*]] into fishing [*דיגים* [*dayāgîm*], cf. LXX] boats?*

LXX translates שכות [*śukkôt*] as a type of boat; this translation is confirmed by the context, and by Isa 2:16 שכות [*śukkôt*] ǁ אניות ['*ŏnîyôt*]. The same is true for צלצל [*ṣilṣal*]/πλοῖα [*ploia*], which is seen in LXX also at Isa 18:1.

For התמלא [*hitmālē'*] the context requires a 3d masc. pl. LXX probably read יובילו [*yôbîlû*]. The head of such a monster is hardly valuable in trade. שאר [*šĕ'ēr*] ǁ עור ['*ôr*] in Mic 3:22ff. I do not wish to inquire as to whether mythological references also stand in the background of these words.

63. Hoffmann, *Hiob,* 90, on vv. 27ff.

64. 1 Sam 11:2.

65. So the Ethiopic text; the image of an animal reined in by a bridle goes further. Dillmann's [in *Das Buch Henoch, übersetzt und erklärt* (Leipzig: Fr. Chr. Wilh. Vogel, 1853) [hereinafter: Dillmann, *Buch Henoch*], 31] translation of *"fortgestossen"* [Eng.: "drag on" — trans.] does not fit the context.

66. מצולה [*mĕṣûlāh*], "deep," from √צלל [√*ṣll*] (Exod 15:10), "to sink down," has nothing to do with צלל [*ṣālal*], "to resound, to clatter" [from which מְצִלָּה [*mĕṣillāh*], "to clatter, to resound" (from which מְצִלָּה [*mĕṣillāh*], "bell")]. One should not confuse the two, mistakenly translating צלל [*ṣālal*] (Exod 15:10) as "turmoil" and מצולה [*mĕṣûlāh*] as "spring."

67. This seems to mean: "like a cooking kettle of salve froths."

68. In the usual translation, "He draws a shining path behind himself, one imagines that the sea has grey hair" (Hoffmann, *Hiob,* 91), not only is a shift in subject — which can be dismissed by the vocalization of יֵהָשֵׁב [*yēhāšēb*] — unacceptable, but also the shining path could be seen only on the surface of the sea and not in the depths, in the תהום [*tĕhôm*]. LXX (v. 23b, reconstructed from θ):

τὸν δὲ τάρταρον τῆς ἀβύσσου ὥσπερ αἰχμάλωτον
ἐλογίσατο ἄβυσσον εἰς περίπατον
[*ton de tartaron tēs abyssou hōsper aichmalōton
elogisato abysson eis peripaton*]

goes back to:

אחרית יאור שביה   יחשב תהום לנתיב:
['*ahărît yĕ'ôr šibyāh   yahšōb tĕhôm lĕ-nātîb*]

behind which the following is to be read:

אחרית יאור נתיב[ו]   יחשב תהום לשביח:
['*ahărît yĕ'ôr nĕtîbŏ[ô]   yahšōb tĕhôm li-śbîah*]

אחרית יאור ['*ahărît yĕ'ôr*] is almost exactly like מצולות יאור [*mĕṣûlôt yĕ'ôr*] in Zech 10:11, אחרית ים ['*ahărît yom*] in Ps 139:9; probably also Ps 8:9, אחרית ימים ['*ahărît yammîm*]. For the expression יחשב לשביח [*yahšōb li-śbîah*] cf. Phil 2:6, ἁρπαγμὸν ἡγήσατο [*harpagmon ēgēsato*]; for נתיב [*nātîb*] is perhaps to be conjugated as a verb.

69. על־עפר ['*al-āpār*] does not mean "on the earth," where Leviathan does not live, but rather "in the underworld," as at Job 17:16; 20:11; 21:26 [ǁ שאול — [*šĕ'ôl*]]; cf. Ps 30:10, etc.

70. LXX probably read מְשָׁלוֹ [*mĕšālô*]. Adalbert Merx, *Das Gedicht von Hiob: Hebräischer Text, kritische bearbeit und übersetzt, nebst sachlicher und kritischer Einleitung* (Jena: Mauke, 1871) [hereinafter: Merx, *Gedicht von Hiob*], 210.

71. לבלי חת [liḇlî ḥāṯ], "as one without fear," is syntactically, as well as in terms of its content, peculiar. LXX's (as at 40:19) πεποιμένον ἐγκατεπεπαίζεσθαι ὑπὸ τῶν ἀγγέλων μου [pepoimenon enkatepepaizesthai hypo tōn angelōn mou] is a correction which follows Ps 104:26. It can have as its aim only the elimination of the mythological tone from the text. לבעל תחת [lĕ-baʿal taḥaṯ] is to be read instead, with the ע [ʿ] dropping out, and י [y] taking the place of ת [t]. With תחת [taḥaṯ] cf. תהום רבצת תחת [tĕhôm rōḇeṣeṯ tāḥaṯ] in Gen 49:25 and מים מתחת לארץ [mayim mittaḥaṯ lā-ʾāreṣ] Deut 4:19. בעל תחת [baʿal taḥaṯ] is similar to the late Babylonian אם ארקא [ʾēm ʾarqāʾ] — lit. "mother of the earth"); cf. p. 14, n. 9 on p. 293 above.

72. "He looks upon every height" should not be read, following 40:11, since it lacks the definitive statement "and thus casts it down" (i.e., by a simple glance). What is to be read is: אתו כל־גבה יראה [ʾōṯô kol-gāḇōah yirāʾēhû]; the emphatic אתו [ʾōṯô] corresponds to the parallel emphatic הוא [hûʾ], just as כל־גבה [kol-gāḇōah] corresponds to בני־שחץ [bĕnê-šāḥaṣ].

73. בני־שחץ [bĕnê-šāḥaṣ] here and in Job 28:8, LXX 28:8 υἱοὶ ἀλαζόνων [huioi alazonōn]; in Talmudic and Ethiopic √שחץ [√šḥṣ] means "arrogant, proud" (Dillmann, Hiob⁴, 241). בני שחץ [bĕnê-šāḥaṣ] is the name of a type of monster. At Job 28:28, "lion" is its parallel. One notes regarding this that כפיר ותנין ‖ שחל ופתן [šaḥal wĕ-peṯen ‖ kĕp̄îr wĕ-ṯannîn] appears at Ps 91:13. LXX πάντων τῶν ἐν τοῖς ὕδασιν [pantōn tōn en tois hydasin] and Targum בני כוריא [bĕnê ḵawrayyāʾ] ("children of the fish") still have this tradition that the בני שחץ [bĕnê-šāḥaṣ] are water monsters. Likewise, כל־גבה [kol-gōḇāh] must have been a name understood at that time.

Since שחץ [šāḥaṣ] is a doubly attested word, it is not possible to assume a textual corruption; yet one cannot help but think of שֶׁרֶץ [šereṣ]. In this case גב = גבא = גבה [gēḇ = geḇāʾ = gōḇāh], "pit" (as a name for the underworld), could be read.

74. One who is dying comes into "the depths of the waters" in Ps 69:2, into "mire" in Ps 69:15, into the "fount" [באר [bĕʾēr]] in Ps 69:16. All these are names of שאול [šĕʾôl]; cf. Ps 18:5; "waves of death," "streams of destruction," cf. Jonah 2:4, etc.

75. The reader should note that this word is, indeed, preserved in the Hebrew text, and thus is not to be construed as "subjective."

76. Cf. Ps 89:10, the remarks on Psalm 74 above (p. 55), and the comments on the "vanquished" at Isa 51:9, Ps 89:11, and Job 26:13.

77. Cf. pp. 29-30 above.

78. Konrad Kessler, Mani: Forschungen über die manichäische Religion: Ein Beitrag zur vergleichenden Religionsgeschichte des Orients (Berlin: G. Reimer, 1889) [hereinafter: Kessler, Mani], 1, xii.

79. Gustav Flügel, Mani, seine Lehre und seine Schriften: Ein Beitrag zur Geschichte des Manichäismus: aus dem Führis des Abû Jaʾḳub an-Nadim, im Text nebst Übersetzung. Commentar und Index zum ersten Mall herausgegeben (Leipzig: F. A. Brockhaus, 1862) [hereinafter: Flügel, Mani], 87.

80. Cf. pp. 23-24, 25-26, and further in what follows.

81. משתו [miśśēṯô] is interpreted as משאתו [mĕšāʾeṯô]. √שאה [√šʾh] is a terminus technicus for the "roaring" of torches; cf. at Ps 89:10, p. 297, n. 9.

82. אלים [ʾēlîm], "gods," is better attested than אילים [ʾêlîm], "heroes," and it seems much closer to this mythological text. Human beings could not fight with Leviathan (40:32–41:2). That they are terrified before him is self-evident. That, however, even gods tremble before him is something special.

83. The usual translation — "they are thrown into confusion" — is invented ad hoc. The phrase could mean "they scatter away." I conjecture יתחבאו [yiṯḥabbēʾû].

84. משברים [miššĕḇārîm], "in the face of confusion," is itself a productive designation. The phrase could mean "in the face of wonder." One could read בשמי מרום [bi-šmê mārôm]. This conjecture is designated above as uncertain by parentheses. I would be thankful for a better proposal.

85. זכר [√zkr] is the infinitive, dependent on the "consecutive" imperative (Pesh.).

86. The chapter division has divided up the original relationship between the two chapters by a corruption of the suffixes. The second person singular still remains in the Pesh.

87. יטל [√yṭl] *Hip'îl*, אל ['ēl], "god"; thus Σ (except with a reversal of the subject and the object, which is caused by a reversion to these mythological motifs): ἀλλὰ καὶ ὁ θεὸς τὴν ἰδέαν αὐτοῦ καταβαλεῖ [alla kai ho theos tēn idean autou katabalei]. מראיו [mar'âw] could otherwise also express מוראו [môrā'ô], "his fear."

88. A noun parallel to אל ['ēl] is to be expected, as is a verb on which "to awaken him" is dependent. The above insertion of מלאך זר [mal'āk zār] should be seen as simply a very modest proposal.

89. Here, and in the following verse, the misunderstanding of the scribe has altered the suffixes; and because of this, the whole text has been displaced. The correct form is still preserved in לפניו [lipnâw] of the mss. and Targums.

90. וישלם [way-yišlām]; LXX; Merx, *Hiob*, 204-5.

91. לא־הוא [lō'-hû'], Jer 5:12. The sense of the whole is: "Attempt to touch Leviathan, so you might note what you are able to do against him. Hey! Not a single one of the gods themselves comes out victorious over him. How then can a mere human stand against him?" In v. 2 there is a contrast: "Not once does he [a divine figure] venture to awaken him when he is sleeping. How then can *anyone* dare to stand up to him publicly when he is awake?"

92. Flügel, *Mani*, 87f.

93. Brandt, *Mandäische Schriften*, 181f.

94. Brandt, *Mandaische Religion*, 182f.

95. Six-footed verses in distichs.

96. "Creatures small and great" does not fit metrically; on the other hand, a half-verse is lacking in 24. Therefore, the words are placed in 24 (probably after 24a).

97. אניות ['oniyôṯ = ships], "the posting of ships in the midst of the animals of the sea has always been somewhat conspicuous" [J. Olshausen, *Die Psalmen*, Kurzgefasstes exegetisches Handbuch zum Alten Testament, 7 Lfg., 14 Lfg. (Leipzig: S. Hirzel, 1853) [hereinafter: Olshausen, *Psalmen*], 402]. Moreover, we are dealing in this text with God's words (v. 24). — That the invention of ships could be a work of the deity (Cheyne, *Psalms*, 284) is an idea which could conceivably have been possible in antiquity, but which seems quite remote from the present situation in which we are dealing with God's wondrous works as they appear in nature. Moreover, Isaiah 2 teaches us how ancient Israelite religion viewed ships. — v. 26b is still problematic: a ship entreating God for nourishment? — What is to be read is אימות ['•y•m•w•t] [this is either אֵמֹות ['êmôṯ] or אַימֹות ['ayûmôṯ]; cf. Hab 1:14 (רמש [remeś] ‖ דגי הים [dĕḡê hay-yām]); concerning the word הלך [√hlk = "to walk, to go"], cf. Ps 8:9; עבר [√'br = "to cross over, to go across"]]. The versions as well as the Hebrew text. — Through this emendation, the excision of vv. 25f. (Hupfeld-Nowack, *Psalmen*, 441) is unnecessary. Vv. 27ff. refer, then, to all the creations of the earth and the sea.

98. Hupfeld-Nowack, *Psalmen*, 441, and Franz Delitzsch, *Biblischer Commentar über die Psalmen*, Biblischer Commentar über das alte Testament (Leipzig: Dörffling und Franke, 1867) [hereinafter: Delitzsch, *Psalmen*], 608, still make the בו [bô] refer to the sea in which Leviathan plays. However, "it is not natural to connect בו [bô] with the distant word הים [hay-yam]"

(Cheyne, *Psalms*, 284, n. 2). Delitzsch, *Psalmen* (608) raises the objection that God playing with Leviathan is "keine gotteswürdige Vorstellung" ["not a worthy divine activity" — trans.]. "Criticism of this sort, however, would lead us toward a prosaic rationalism, and impair the simple charm of the biblical treatment of the supernatural" (Cheyne, *Psalms*, 284).

99. תסף [*tōsēp* = "to take away, to remove"], more commonly תאסף [*te'ĕsōp* = "to take away, to remove"], antonym שָׁלַח [*šillaḥ* = "to send away, to dismiss, to send off, to cast out"].

100. The theory of modern critics, that Psalm 104 has developed its view out of Job, cannot be substantiated. The world is not constituted only of people who write books and who copy them!! Modern criticism has, up to the present, often overlooked the significance of oral tradition, and is, all too often, inclined to conclude a *literary* dependence in the case of every point of tangency between two writings!!

101. The pronunciation יוֹם [*yôm*], "day," given by the vowel signs, according to which Leviathan is understood as the eclipse-dragon, is incorrect, since we are dealing here with the cursing of the night of Job's conception, at which those who curse the day would not be skilled. A student of theology from Hannover, Mr. Gottfried Schmidt, reminded me of the pronunciation יָם [*yom*], "sea." This pronunciation is confirmed from Ps 74:13f., יָם [*yom*] ‖ לִוְיָתָן [*liwyātān*]; Isa 27:1, לִוְיָתָן [*liwyātān*] ‖ התנין אשר בים [*hat-tannîn 'ăšer bay-yom*]; Job 41:23, ישים כמרחה [*yom yāśîm kam-merqāḥāh*]; Ps 104:25, יָם [*yom*], 26 לִוְיָתָן [*liwyātān*].

102. ארר ['*ārar*], "to curse," frequently with the sense that the "cursed one" should be stripped of his idiosyncratic power: the (previously fruitful) earth becomes unfruitful through a "curse" (Gen 3:17); the free man becomes a slave (Josh 9:23); the woman cannot bear (Num 5:18ff.); the basket and the bowl are never full (Deut 28:17); the mighty are powerless (Num 22:6). A human curse is nothing more than an idle wish (Prov 26:2), but a divine curse is real. Therefore, ארר ['*ārar*] used of God or of a divine being is the same as actually being "under the spell of" or "cursed." The same goes for the parallel word (cf. Deut 28:20; Mal 2:3; Ps 119:21)גער [*gā'ar*] "to chide, to forbid" (Jer 29:27; Ruth 2:16); but used of God it actually becomes "to prevent" (Zech 3:2; Mal 3:11).

103. The night of Job's conception.

104. The same word is used of stirring up the shades in Sheol (Isa 14:9).

105. עתיד ['*atîd*], "able," "prepared," "decided," "empowered"; cf. התעתד [*hit'attēd*], Job 15:28.

106. חשך על־פני תהום [*ḥōšek 'al-pĕnê tĕhôm*] (darkness upon [the] face of the deep), Gen 1:2.

107. Concluded from the antonym ממעל [*mim-ma'al* = "on top of, above"] at Job 3:4.

108. In concrete terms one should probably think of dark and dismal winter nights.

109. This is especially clear at v. 15, "He eats grass like an ox."

110. Cf. Dillmann, *Hiob*[4], 344.

111. For example, he eats grass; cf. further, p. 41.

112. This investigation is also made quite difficult by the condition of the text.

113. Behemoth belongs, accordingly, in a greater series. The same series contains: *the primordial human* (Job 15:7); *wisdom* [Prov 8:22 (verbally similar to Job 40:19 on Behemoth), and elsewhere]; *the law* [Prayer of Joseph; cf. Emil Schürer, *Geschichte des jüdischen Volkes im Zeitalter Jesu Christi*, 2d ed. (Leipzig: J. C. Hinrichs, 1886-90) [hereinafter: Schürer, *Geschichte*], 2:672]; *the "son of man"* = Christ (1 Enoch 48:4, and elsewhere). This list causes one to think.

114. העשו יגש חרבו [*h • ' • ś • w   y • g • š   ḥ • r • b • w*]: the usual interpretation, "His creator brings near his sword," is correctly described by Dillmann (*Hiob*[4], 346) as "peculiar."

Other interpretations are given by Dillmann (*Hiob*⁴, 345-46). הֶעָשׂוֹ יִגַּשׁ חַרְבּוֹ [*hā-ʿāśûy yiggōś ḥărābô*] should be read.

115. Because of an aversion in the face of mythology.

116. Cf. pp. 28-29 above.

117. The text of *1 Enoch* 60 exists only in an Ethiopic translation from the Greek. The Greek is, for its part, a translation from the Hebrew. One could, therefore, wonder whether numerous misunderstandings could have crept into the present text with which the original text does not need to be burdened.

118. κῆτως, var. [*kētōs*], "Lion."

119. The sense was, it appears, originally: *on that day* (i.e., on the day when these things will be revealed) *will be separated* (‖ "divorced," v. 9), etc.

120. [In the Babylonian accounts, the *naqbu*; cf. Jensen, *Kosmologie*, 243-53.] — Zimmern

121. Leviathan lies on the deepest foundations, where the "sources" of the sea are to be found.

122. Breast?!?!

123. [Perhaps the Babylonian *dannînu*, "the solid land," in contrast to the sea; cf. Jensen, *Kosmologie*, 161.] — Zimmern

124. The question concerning their "power" (= "commission") is answered at vv. 24f.

125. Corruption of "on that day"?

126. Cf. *4 Ezra* 6:49-52.

127. A misunderstanding from Ps 50:10; cf. p. 309, n. 152.

128. Regarding the tradition concerning Leviathan and Behemoth in Judaism, cf. in *2 Apoc. Bar.* 29:4, and in Dillmann, *Buch Henoch*, 183.

129. "Furthermore, according to the divergent concept of the Jerusalem Targum, Leviathan is the male of the two creatures" (Dillmann, *Henoch*, 184). According to another tradition, Leviathan נחש בריח [*nāḥāš bāriaḥ*] and Leviathan נחש עקלתון [*nāḥāš ʿăqallāṭôn*] are understood as husband and wife, Johann Andreas Eisenmenger, ed., *Entdecktes Judentum: Das ist, Wortgetreü verdeutschung der sonstigen, den christen zu einem grossen Teile noch ganz unbekannten hebräisch-rabbinischen litteratur, welche einen sicheren Einblick in die jüdische Religions- und Sittenlehre gewährhen* (Dresden: s.n., 1893) [hereinafter: Eisenmenger, *Entdecktes*], 2:402.

130. In v. 20a the predicate is clearly ישאו־לו [*yiśʾû-lô*], "to look upon him." In v. 20b the subject is "all the beasts of the field."

131. [ה]שמ [*šammā[h]*] does not appear to belong to v. 20.

132. The repetition of צאלים [*ṣeʾĕlîm*] is completely intolerable. LXX's δένδρα μεγάλα [*dendra megala*] perhaps read אלים [*ʾēlîm*].

133. צללו [*ṣilălô*] Piʿʿēl.

134. √עשק [√*ʿšq*], "to oppress," "to take advantage of," makes no sense. LXX's ἐὰν γένηται πλημμύρα [*ean genētai plēmmyra*] points in a more profitable direction. שקעה [*šoqʿāh*] at Amos 9:5 (8:8: נשקע [*nišqaʿ*]) [‖ עלה [*ʿālāh*]] is a term for the sinking of the Nile. The ebb of the Nile comes to the fore since it would drive Behemoth from his hiding place.

135. ירדן [*yardēn*] is often translated as "a Jordan," though the Jordan itself has no hippopotamuses. Besides, the construction "a Jordan" is not a proper way to speak, and the sense is very peculiar. Who would speak of the Jordan when the much greater Nile is actually meant? An animal of the Nile would not be afraid of the Jordan, which it doesn't even know. The ירד is to be understood as יאור [*yĕʾôr*] ‖ נהר [*nāhār*], as usual.

136. V. 24 is to be laid out in the following manner:

יקחנו במוקשים ינקב   דן אל פיהו בעיניו
[dān 'ēl pîhû bĕ-'ênâw   yiqqāḥenu bĕ-môqĕšîm yinqoḇ]

In this, אל ['ēl] is clearly "God"; יקחנו [yiqqāḥēnû], "he captured him"; במוקשים [bĕ-môqĕšîm], "with snares"; One could suppose that the word יקיפנו [yaqqîpenû] ("he surrounded him") lies behind the word ינקב [yinqāḇ].

137. In fact, the root √קנה [√qnh] recurs in the Babylonian myths.

138. Cf. p. 26; cf. also p. 299, n. 24.

139. This is the translation of Delitzsch, *Isaiah*[4]. נגב [negeḇ] is a popular apocalyptic name for Egypt (Dan 8:9; 11:5ff.). In the text of Isaiah מצרים [miṣrayim] stands for Egypt. The provenance of the superscription is, thus, established.

140. Four-foot bicola, double stichs. — Concerning the translations made up to the present, cf. the commentaries.

141. The sentence lacks a subject. The bicolon lacks an accent.

142. The Psalm is a small apocalypse. It describes the theophany of YHWH at the last judgment. The tense of such a description — one compares the related texts Nahum 1; Habakkuk 3; Psalms 76; 82; 118; etc. — is most commonly the perfect. So also Ps 68:8, 19, 23, 25-26.

143. חית [h · y · t] can be singular [ḥayyat] or plural [ḥayyōt]. The resolution of such questions is to be found only from the context. By reason of parallelism I prefer the plural.

144. אבירים ['abbîrîm], "gods, angels," as at Ps 78:25: לחם אבירים [leḥem 'abbîrîm], ἄρτος ἀγγέλων (*artos angelōn*). אביר ישראל ['abbîr yiśrā'ēl] ("the Mighty One of Israel") = ישראל קדוש [qĕḏôš yiśrā'ēl] ("the Holy One of Israel") = צור ישראל [ṣûr yiśrā'ēl] ("the Rock of Israel") = אלהי ישראל ['ĕlōhê yiśrā'ēl] ("the God of Israel"). — עדת אבירים ['aḏat 'abbîrîm] ("congregation of mighty ones") as well as the phrase סוד קדשים [sôḏ qĕḏōšîm] ("gathering of holy ones") (Ps 89:8), and עדת־אל ['ăḏat-'ēl] ("assembly of God") (Ps 82:1), where a reproachful saying against the "assembly of the gods" is also given.

145. The misunderstanding of the writer has placed בעגלי [bĕ-'eglê] ("with calves") beside אבירים ['abbîrîm] ("bulls"). What the resultant "calves of the people" could mean may be looked up in the works of the various exegetes who have treated the text as it now stands. What should be read, however, is בעלי [ba'ălê] ("lords, masters, rulers, baals"). Daniel called the angels of the peoples their שרים [śārîm], thus שר פרס [śar pāras] ("lord of Persia"), שר יון [śar yāwān] ("lord of Greece"), etc. The more ancient languages spoke, among others, of בעל פעור [ba'al pĕ'ôr] and בעל חרמון [ba'al ḥermôn].

146. מתרפס ביצי־כסף [miṭrappēs bêṣê-ḵesep]. "This line of the verse is very unclear. The text in its original form cannot be preserved very well" [Olshausen, *Psalmen*, s.v.]. רפס [rāpāś] Q'al, "to stir up water"; מרפש [marpēś], "the stirred-up water," opposite משקע [mišqā']in Ezek 34:18 is the "cleared-up water," which has been calmed; רפש [repeś] is the "dirt," which the sea stirs up in Isa 57:20: נרפש [nirpāś] Nip'al, "to be stirred up" by the spring; Hitpa"ēl, "to stir oneself up" (Prov 6:3, התרפס לך [lēḵ hitrappēs], according to LXX ἴσθη μὴ ἐκλυόμενος [histhē mē eklyomenos] = אל תתרפה ['ēl titrappeh] is not possible.

The participle lacks an appropriate substantive. A stress is missing from the verse. The missing word is present in עמים ['ammîm], which should be divided into עם ['ām] ("people") and ים [yām] ("sea").

147. ברצי כסף [bĕ-raṣṣê ḵesep], LXX τοὺς δεδοκιμασμένους τῷ ἀργυρίῳ (*tous dedokimasmenous tǭ argyriǭ*), Σ ὡς δοκιμὴν ἀργυρίου [hōs dokimen argyriou], Vulg. *qui probati sunt argento*, Targ. "more pure than silver" read the first three letters as צרף [ṣ · r · p]; according to the Targum צרף מכסף [ṣārūp mik-kesep].

148. Psalm 82; Isa 24:21ff.; cf. Job 21:22.

149. The word קנה [qāneh] occurs both times.

150. At Job 3:8 it stands in parallel with ארר ['ārar]; cf. p. 37, n. 10.

151. Cf. pp. 22f., 26f., 29f., and 31ff.

152. The *mythological* בהמות [běhēmôt] does not appear in Ps 50:10's בהמות בהררי אלף [běhēmôt bă-harĕrê 'olep]. According to the parallels אלף ['elep] | לי [lî] || ידעתי [yāḏa'tî] | עמדי ['immāḏî], אלף should be taken as a Q'al imperfect ("to learn, to have learned"). The imperfect יאלף [ye'ĕlap] is found at one other place, Prov 22:25. The incorrect translation of אלף as "thousand" has led to the correction of בהרים [bě-hārîm] to בהררי [ba-hărārê] (LXX κτήνη ἐν τοῖς ὄρεσιν καὶ βόες [ktēnē en tois oresin kai boes]); בהמות בהרים [běhēmôt běhārîm] | כל־חיתו יער [kol-ḥayĕtô yā'ar] || (LXX, Pesh., Targ. — according to Heinrich Graetz, *Emendationes in Plerusque Sacrae Scripturae Veteris Testamenti Libros* (Breslau: Schlesische Buchdruckerei, 1892) כל עוף [kol 'ôp] | זיז שדי מרום [zîz śāḏay mārôm]. Accordingly, the sentence should be translated: "I know the animals on the mountains."

153. So Dillmann, *Hiob*[4] (pp. 66-67), which deals with this text. One should not consider the model of the inundation of the Nile or the crocodile. "Rather, one expects a being here against whom God himself has set a watch."

154. Six-foot bicola.

155. The usual translation, "You have crushed us in the place of the jackals," is generally taken in the sense either that the early Israelites were banished to the wilderness, or that Palestine itself was a wilderness. "These explanations do not quite satisfy" (Olshausen, *Psalmen*, 402). — LXX ἐν τόπῳ κακώσεως [en top ō̜ kakōseōs], Vulg. *in loco afflictionis* certainly read the Heb. text as תנין [tannîn] and thought of a derivative of √ינה [√y · n · h]. Behind the reading of the Pesh., *k'tad' tenyanā',* lies the Heb. במקום תנין [bi-mqôm tannîn], which is vocalized here as תנין [tinyān]. תנין [tannîn] is also written mistakenly as תנים (tannîm — "jackals") at Ezek 29:3 and 32:2. The inverse is true at Lam 4:3. (The Heb. text is correct at Jer 14:6, *contra* Siegfried-Stade, *Wb*, 858) — Targ. ירודין (yĕrûḏîn), A σειπήψων [seipēpsōn] read תנין [tannîn] like the Hebrew text. *2 Apoc. Bar.* 10:8's *advocabo sireres di mari* mixes up the תנינים [tannînîm] who belong to the sea with the תנים [tannîm — "jackals"] who have singularly plaintive voices and here are summoned as co-plaintiffs. — במקום [bi-mqôm] at Ps 44:20 is equal to "instead of," following Hos 2:1. — Olshausen is on the right track to an understanding of the text. He just hasn't quite reached it yet.

156. The translation follows the edition of Cornill, *Ezechiel*. Departures from Cornill are noted. The texts Ezek 29:2-8 and 32:2-8 are not poetic in the strictest sense, but rather belong to the "middle *Gattung*" described on p. 301, n. 47.

157. תנין [tannîn]; cf. p. 309, n. 155. LXX τὸν δράκοντα [ton drakonta].

158. Cornill (*Ezechiel*, 364) reads יאר [yĕ'ōr], following Targ. and Pesh. Heb. יארי [y · ' · r · y] is to be taken as a plural, LXX οἱ ποταμοί [hoi potamoi]; likewise also at v. 9. It regularly stands in the plural in these contexts.

159. Verse 4a can hardly be disposed of as a half-verse. That translation here follows LXX A. The triple occurrence of דגת יאריך [děgaṯ yĕ'ōrêḵā] is certainly quite striking.

160. [The original text of Gunkel's work says Ezek 32:2-8. The material with which he deals, however, runs only through v. 7, and, hence, I have changed the heading suitably. — trans.].

161. The lamentation embraces only the three (metrical) verses of two (Cornill, *Ezechiel*, 381-82). The rest returns again to a rhythmic prose.

162. Cornill (*Ezechiel*, 381-82) has correctly seen that two words have fallen out of the

verse, but his proposal, "A young lion of the nations (will come) against you (עָלֶיךָ ['alêkā]);
how (אֵיךְ ['êk]) you are like him," is not satisfactory. In what follows a young lion of the nations
(Nebuchadnezzar) does not appear against Pharaoh, only YHWH himself. LXX's λέοντι ἐθνῶν
ὡμοιώθης [leonti ethnōn hōmoiōthēs] reads לִכְפִיר [li-kpîr] and perhaps דָּמִים [dāmîm]; instead
of גוֹיִם [gôyīm], we should read גוֹרִים [gûrîm]; concerning כפיר גורים [kĕpîr gûrîm], cf. כפיר
אֲרָיוֹת [kĕpîr 'ărāyôt] at Judg 14:5; כפיר [kĕpîr] || תנין [tannîn] in Ps 91:13.

163. תנין [tannîn]; LXX ὡς δράκων [hōs drakōn].

164. The common conjecture since Heinrich Ewald, *Die Propheten des Alten Bundes*
(Stuttgart: Adolph Krabe, 1840) [hereinafter: Ewald, *Propheten AB*], 2:331, בְּנַחֲרוֹתֶיךָ [bi-
nḥîrôtekā], "You spout with your nostrils," appears necessary only if one does not recognize the
identity of dragon and sea. Both cases are either נהרתיך [nahărōtayik] or נהרתם [nahărōtām].

165. Verse 4b should not be missed as a colon.

166. [This was notes 6 and 7 in the German edition — trans.] רמותך [rāmûtekā], Vulg.
sanie tua, Σ, Pesh. = תמתך [rimmātkā] ("your rottenness," i.e., your rotting corpse). — The deletion of this verse by Cornill (*Ezechiel*, 383) is unnecessary. The filling of the mountains and the
valleys is, in any case, "completely meaningless in the case of a crocodile," but in the case of the
"great dragon" of the sea it is to be considered acceptable.

167. "Heat," according to the LXX צאתך [ṣō'atĕkā], in this case the fluid which flows from
the corpse.

168. "At your extinction" — Does the dragon of the sea cease to exist? Perhaps בכלתך
[bĕ-kālātĕkā].

169. So, e.g., Smend, *Der Prophet Ezechiel*, 2d ed. (Leipzig: S. Hirzel, 1788) [hereinafter:
Smend, *Ezechiel*], who, likewise, on p. 255 recalls mythological features (the great dragon of the
sea and the constellation of the dragon) (cf. our p. 310, n. 175).

170. In these and similar comments, I accept Adolf Jülicher's masterful analysis of the
stylistic forms of the parable and the allegory; *and* I gratefully acknowledge that these remarks
would hardly have come into existence at all had not Adolf Jülicher published *Die Gleichnisreden Jesu* (Freiburg i. B.: Akademische Verlagsbuchhandlung von J. C. B. Mohr–Paul Siebeck,
1888), 2 vols.

171. Cf. p. 300, n. 43.

172. Pp. 32, 39, and 41.

173. Cf. on this distinctively Hebrew concept, Isaiah 2 and 37:22ff.

174. Rudolf Smend, *Lehrbuch der alttestamentlichen Religionsgeschichte*, Sammlung
theologischer Lehrbücher (Freiburg: J. C. B. Mohr, 1893) [hereinafter: Smend, *Lehrbuch*]).

175. The interpretation is linked to the word בכבתך [bĕ-kabbôtĕkā] (32:7), for here the
constellation of Draco should be considered, "which according to a widespread opinion is the
basis of the darkening of the sun and moon" (Smend, *Ezechiel*, 255-56). Yet if this light-killing
constellation is annihilated here, the remaining heavens must light themselves up even more. A
purely naturalistic view cannot thus be wrested from this material.

176. For the following (free) translation, cf. Wellhausen, *Pharisäer und Sadducäer*, 141. For
the interpretation, cf. H. E. Ryle and M. R. James, Ψαλμοι Σολομωντος: *Psalms of the Pharisees,
commonly called the Psalms of Solomon. The Text newly revised from all the Mss. Edited, with Introduction, English translation, notes, appendix, and indices* (Cambridge: Cambridge University
Press, 1891)[hereinafter: Ryle and James, *Psalms of the Pharisees*] — insofar as the original form
can still be recognized within the Greek translation of a Hebrew text, 28b-33b are four-foot
verses. Then follow three-foot (or six-foot) verses.

177. τοῦ εἰπεῖν [*tou eipein*] למר [*lāmir*], להמיר [*lĕ-hāmîr*] is intended (Hos 4:7)]. Understood as לאמר [*lēʾmôr*] by Wellhausen, *Pharisäer und Sadducäer*, 133.

178. τοῦ δράκοντες [*tou drakontes*]. δράκων [*drakōn*] can be a translation of לויתן [*liwyāṯān*], נחש [*nāḥāš*], or תנין [*tannîn*]; תנין [*tannîn*] is to be preferred because of the text's connection with Ezekiel 29 and 32.

179. καὶ οὐκ ἐχπόνισα [*kai ouk echponisa*], codd.; ἐχρόνισεν [*echronisen*]. Adolf Hilgenfeld, *Messias Judaeorum: Libris corum Paulo ante et Paulo post Christum natum conscriptis illustratis* (Leipzig: Fuesiano-Reisland, 1869) [hereinafter: Hilgenfeld, *Messias Judaeorum*], 5 (cf. also 27-28), among others; 30ff. is a response to the prayers of 28ff.

180. τήν ὕβριν αὐτοῦ ἐκκεκεντημένον [*tēn hybrin autou ekkekentēmenon*], מחלל [*mĕḥallēl*], Isa 23:9; Ezek 28:7; cf. also Isa 51:9f., p. 297, n. 4.

181. ἐπὶ τῶν ὀρέων Αἰγύπτου [*epi tōn horeōn Aigyptou*]. The alternative of Hilgenfeld, *Messias Judaeorum*, 5, ὀρίων (*horiōn*) is not necessary (following Ezek 32:5f.).

182. ὑπὲρ ἐλαχίστου [*hyper elachistou*], "abused." Wellhausen, *Phar. und Sadd.*, 141, holds that a participial prefix has been misinterpreted as מן [*min*]; מָשְׁפָּל [*māšpāl*].

183. Cf. Ezek 28:1, 2; Ryle and James, *Psalms of the Pharisees*, 26.

184. Cf. Schürer, *Gesch. des jüd. Volkes*, 2:589.

185. Rhythmic prose.

186. Concerning the meaning of חתר [*ḥāṯar*], cf. what I have said about Ezek. 8:8 below.

187. Cf. p. 28, n. 4.

188. In the middle of the second section.

189. Cf. that which follows.

190. The relationship to Egypt exists at Job 40f., in which Leviathan and Behemoth bear traits of Egyptian animals. This is also the case with the dragon of Ezekiel 29 and 32. Rahab refers to Egypt in Isa 30:7; Rahab is a name for Egypt in Ps 87:4; Rahab is linked to the account of the Exodus in Isa 51:9f.; in Ezekiel 29 and 32 the dragon refers to Pharaoh; in Ps 68:31 the "reed animals" are linked to Egypt and Ethiopia; and *Psalms of Solomon* 2 relates the myth to a specific Egyptian event (the death of Pompey).

191. Cf. Smend, *Ezekiel*, 229.

192. It is not my place to investigate whether this Egyptian myth itself already went back to Babylonian influences. Professor Ed. Meyer has kindly made me aware of the fact that Egyptian art since, perhaps, the fifteenth century B.C.E. was influenced by Babylonian art. Among the materials discussed above are found representations of mixed- and flying-beings. — We possess examples of the migration of Near Eastern myths into Egypt from ancient times, in the form of the Tell el-Amarna discoveries (cf. in the following). Another example from Roman times is found in Roscher, *Lexicon der griech. und röm. Mythologie* (s.v. "Horos," by H. W. Stoll, 2740-50), which contains an illustration of an Egyptian relief from Roman times currently found in the Louvre. It is a relief in which the hawk-headed Egyptian god Horus, high on a steed, in the raiment of a Roman general, strikes down a crocodile (Seth?) with the lance. The illustration contains much that is non-Egyptian: the costume of the god and his depiction on a horse. The depiction of Seth as a crocodile is also not proven to be Egyptian. "It is clear at first glance that this figure served as the prototype for the Christian 'dragon killer,' St. George" (Stoll, "Horos," 2748).

193. Six foot bicola, distichs.

194. יסד [*yōsēḏ*], as in vv. 2-4, 10, etc.

195. מכוניה [*mĕḵônêhâ*]. Singular suffix, LXX, Targ., Vulg. The plural does not appear elsewhere.

196. כסיתו [*kissîṯô*] has long been perceived as a *crux*. תהום [*tĕhôm*] and ארץ [*ʾereṣ*] are

feminine. Here A and Θ read *operuisti eam*, according to which Heinrich Graetz, *Kritischer Commentar zu den Psalmen nebst Text und Übersetzung* (Breslau: Schottlaender, 1882-83), 226 and Bickell, *Carmina VT*, 73 read כסיתה [*kissîṯāh*]; LXX כסותו [*kĕsûṯô*] περιβόλαιον αὐτοῦ [*peribolaion autou*], כסתה [*kissāṯāh*] || לכסות הארץ [*lĕ-kassôṯ hā-ʾāreṣ*] should be read. — Baethgen's (*Psalmen*, 315) suggestion to add עליה [*ʿălêhā*], according to Ezek 31:15, is contrary to the sense of the verse and is prosaic. Besides, one will do just fine by dealing carefully with the feminines, which at one or two places are constructed as masculines.

197. Often also perceived as a difficulty. In vv. 6b, 7, and again in v. 9, thus also in v. 8b, the subject is מים [*mayîm*]; hence in v. 8a as well. V. 8a, however, cannot possibly be a parenthetical comment, in which the להם [*lā-hem*] of v. 8b must refer beyond the הרים [*hārîm*] and בקעות [*bĕ-qāʿôṯ*] to the מים [*mayîm*] of v. 6. It is even less likely that it is an extraneous insertion, since it is an indispensable colon. What should be read is the following: מעל־הרים [*mēʿal-hārîm*] || על־הרים [*ʿal-hārîm*]. י [*y*] and מ [*m*] are mixed up. The sentence then is interpreted according to Ps 107:26.

198. מן־גערתך [*min-gaʿărāṯĕkā*] carries two accents, just as at Ps 18:16.

199. Graetz, *Psalmen*, 226: יעדת (*yāʿadtā*); the same confusion of ס [*s*] and ע [*ʿ*] is seen at Ps 2:2: from נועדו [*nôʿdû*]; LXX; Graetz, *Psalmen*, 226.

200. Six-foot bicola, distichs.

201. The repetition of the ideas of vv. 8a and 10f., and of the word דלתים [*dĕlāṯayim*] is striking. Because v. 9 conceives of the "debouching" sea as a child which YHWH carefully wrapped in diapers (Ezek 16:4), it is thus probable that v. 8a describes something that happens at the birth (v. 8b) of a child. It is possible to understand בדלתים [*biḏ-lāṯāyim*] as a corruption of a word like לדת [*leḏeṯ*]; cf. Ezek 16:4: ביום הולדת [*bĕ-yôm hûlledeṯ*]. In the case of the verb ויסך [*way-yāsek*], then, one should expect something like that which Ezek 16:4 describes: the initial attention given to the child (cutting of the umbilical cord, washing, rubbing with salt, etc.). In line with this, I theorize the following:

ויסכן ביום הולדת ים [*way-yiskōn bĕ-yôm hûlledeṯ yām*]
". . . and did the service of an attendant at the birth of the sea";

סכנת [*sōkeneṯ*], "nurse" (1 Kings 1:2, 4), for David who has become childlike; ביום הולדת [*bĕ-yôm hûlledeṯ*] (Ezek 16:4f.; cf. Gen 40:20); the use of √ילד [√*y • l • d*] for "creation" (Ps 90:2) is an achaizing expression. ויסכן [*way-yiskōn*] should be understood as a continuation of מי ירה [*mî yārāh*] in v. 6 (Dillmann, *Hiob*[4], 324). The corruption arose from the loss of the ן [*n*] in ויסכן [*way-yiskōn*] and from the transposition of the consonants of ביום הולדת [*bĕ-yôm hûlledeṯ*]. It is necessary that v. 9, which is otherwise somewhat abrupt and the imagery of which is far from clear, be made fully understandable by these alterations. The idea that YHWH played the rule of an attendant at the birth of this child may sound remarkable to modern ears, but it is only a shortened form of the description at v. 10. As for the rest, such a conjecture cannot lay claim to certainty, but only to a certain level of probability. — Later I shall take notice of the Mandaic parallels [Wilhelm Brandt, *Mandäische Schriften, übersetzt und erläutert* (Göttingen: Vandenhoeck & Ruprecht, 1893) [hereinafter: Brandt, *Mand. Schriften*], 171f.] where Hibil-Jawar's activity at the birth of Ur, the "Lord of Darkness," is described: Hibil-Jawar takes care, both before and after the birth of the child, that his power over the "black waters" will not emerge, and to this end he surrounds him with seven golden walls.

202. Totally realistic: a newborn child is naked and needs clothing, diapers.

203. אשבר [*ʾešbōr*], Vulg. *circumdedi*, should probably read אסכר [*ʾăsakkēr*] or אסגר [*ʾesgōr*] (Hoffmann, *Hiob*, 84); cf. Gen 8:2.

204. ". . . and no further" is proven by the verse to be a gloss. It is worth noting that the verse with this gloss has become a household idiom. Without the gloss this would hardly have occurred. The same thing has taken place at Prov 1:10, where the phrase "so do not follow them" is a gloss (according to line-length). This, however, concerns the career of the *maxims,* and not the materials with which we are *actually* dealing here!

205. פֹּה [*pōh*] can, as an adverb, be neither subject (Dillmann, *Hiob*[4], 325) nor object (Hitzig, *Hiob*, 279). — ישית [*yāšît*], LXX συντριβήσεται [*syntribēsetai*] (ישבר [*yiššābēr*]) (Merx, *Gedicht von Hiob,* 176); concerning גאון [*gā'ôn*] (Lev 26:19; Prov 16:18); the Hebrew text lies closer to ישבת [*yōšēbet*] (Bickell, *Carmina VT,* 181); concerning גאון [*gā'ôn*] cf. Ezek 7:24 and 30:18. — LXX ἀλλ' ἐν σεαυτῇ συντριβήσεται σου τὰ κύματα [*all' en seautē syntribēsetai sou ta kymata*] read ובך [*ûbkā*]= ובכה [*ûbkāh*], "and here" (cf. 1 Kings 22:20).

206. Six-foot bicola; distichs (Bickell, *Carmina VT,* 128).

207. דרכיו (*dĕrākāw*), LXX, Σ, Vulg., Job 40:19 (Hitzig, *Hiob,* 300).

208. In vv. 23-25 the origin of "wisdom" is described. נסכתי [*nissaktî*] (cf. Job 10:11, תשככתי [*tĕsōkkēnî*] (√שכך [√*s • k • k*]), and Ps 139:12, תסכני בבטן אמי [*tĕsūkēnî bĕbeten 'immî*] (√סכך [√*s • k • k*] or √נסך [√*n • s • k*]) is the activity of the child in the body of the mother; חוללתי [*ḥôlāltî*] (first occurrence) in v. 24 is "labor"; for חוללתי [*ḥôlāltî*] (second occurrence) in v. 24, the Vulg., Pesh., and Targ. read another word, which, according to the context, must describe the birth itself. In v. 27 wisdom is in the world, but it is still a playful child who needs care.

209. A word is missing, probably a parallel to נסכתי [*nissaktî*], which LXX, Vulg., and Pesh. perhaps still read. Otherwise מקדמי [*miq-qadmê*] could be either a preposition or — like קדמת [*qadmat*] in Ps 129:6 — a conjunction.

210. נכבדי [*nikbadê*] is hardly correct. Perhaps read נבכי [*nibkê*].

211. Cf. n. 208 directly above.

212. The verse is quite remarkable and is certainly corrupt. I propose reading: עד לא עשתה ארץ הציר ['*ad lō' 'āśtāh 'ereṣ ḥāṣîr*]; for ראש [*rō'š*] one could propose דשא [*deše'*] (Gen 1:11).

213. All refer to an action of God with an initial ב [*bĕ-*] at the beginning of vv. 27, 28a, 29a, and 29b. Accordingly, בעזזו [*be-ʿzūzô*] (Bickell, *Carmina VT,* 128); thus the versions.

214. Vv. 29c and 30b are additions (Bickell, *Carmina VT,* 128).

215. אמון ['*ĕmûn*], A τιθηνουμένη [*tithēnoumenē*]. Wisdom, at this point a child, is affectionately tended by God and plays with the creations of God as a normal toddler does. What the play of wisdom signifies is not clear from the context. It can hardly be believed that the feature is derived simply from the imagination. The origin and sense of this concept is, however, presently unknown. — The understanding of the strange אמון as '*āmôn* already appears in Wis 7:21 (τεχνῖτης [*technitēs*]). This is an understanding which certainly lies quite apart from the context in which God creates the world at a time when "Wisdom" is only a child.

216. The expression is remarkable. Perhaps בני אדם ‖ ביבולי ארצו [*bĕnê 'ādām ‖ bîbûlê 'arṣô*], "the products of his earth," should be read. Perhaps one should read כי יבולי הרים [*kî yĕbûlê hārîm*] at Job 40:20 instead of חית השדה ‖ כי בול הרים [*ḥayyat haś-śādeh ‖ kî bûl hārîm*].

217. Four-foot bicola, arranged in distichs.

218. That the loose sand, cast around by every wind, nevertheless forms the impenetrable boundary of the mighty sea is one of the greatest wonders of God.

219. LXX and Pesh. have the singular, quite correctly for a reference to יָם [*yām* = "sea"].

220. The centerpiece of the verse consists of a four-foot bicola.

221. The following line has one beat too many. Given the context, חקות [*ḥuqqōt*] is pecu-

liar. The moon and stars, not the ordinances of the moon and the stars, light the night. חקות [ḥuqqôṯ] is omitted in the LXX.

222. According to the Targ. and Pesh. (cf. also LXX), גער בים [gāʿar bay-yām] should be read here; ויהמו [way-yēhammû] is a Nipʿal of the root √המם [√hmm] meaning (in the Nipʿal) "to be bewildered" (cf. Ps 18:15 and Ps 144:6). The Hebrew text contains a confusion of רגע [rāgaʿ] and גער [gāʿar]. The punctuation recalls, falsely, המה [hāmāh] which is often applied to the sea elsewhere. Here it is, however, unacceptable.

223. Six-footed lines.

224. Concerning this word cf. Exod 15:8.

225. Five-foot lines, distichs.

226. The LXX has a variant in the expression: Β ὕδωρ [hydōr], א κῦτος [kytos] ‖ ἤχους [ēchous], Vulg. profundum ‖ sonum, A ἦχον [ēchon] ‖ θόρυβον [thorybon].

227. Six-foot lines.

228. ἄβυσσος [abyssos] = תהום [tĕhôm].

229. καὶ ἐφύτευσεν αὐτὴν Ιησοῦς [kai ephyteusen autēn Iēsous]; Old Latin in illa dominus insulas = ἐν αὐτῇ νήσους [en autẹ̄ nēsous) [Otto Fridolin Fritzsche, Kurzgefasstes Exegetisches Handbuch zu den Apokryphen des Alten Testamentes, 1 Lfrng. (Leipzig: Weidmann, 1851) [hereinafter: Fritzsche, KEHApok], 256].

230. As it appears, five-foot verses.

231. κόσμος [kosmos] = צבא [ṣāḇāʾ] (Gen 2:1; Deut 4:19, etc.).

232. καὶ ἐνδόξῳ [kai endoxọ̄] is an addition to the line.

233. ὅν [hon] = אשר [ʾašer] is to be taken together with ἀπὸ προσώπου [מלפני] δυνίμεως αὐτοῦ [apo prosōpou (mil-lipnê) dynimeōs autou].

234. Six-footed lines.

235. תיבש [tîḇāš], ξηπανθήσονται [xēpanthēsontai] (Lowth).

236. The sequence "they decay [they dry up], they die" is not the natural one. I propose ובהמתם [û-ḇhemtām]; צמא [ṣāmē̄ʾ] should be understood as at Isa 44:3 (‖ יבשה [yabbāšāh], perhaps at both places צמאה [ṣimʾāh]).

237. Duhm, Jesaia, 350f.

238. It is characteristic of hymnic style for the participle to appear at the beginning of the sentence. The hymn begins with an appeal to God, whom the poet wishes to praise: "Bless YHWH, O my soul," "Sing to YHWH a new song," etc. Then follow the attributes of the deeds of YHWH which the poet praises, usually in participles. Compare Psalms 103, 104, 136, and 147. Hence the prophetic fragments which the hymns pick up and continue may be recognized by their participial style; cf. Jer 31:35; Amos 4:12; 5:8f.; 9:4, frequently in Deutero-Isaiah 40:22f., 26, 28f.; 42:15f.; 44:24ff.; 45:18, etc. Instead of the hymnic introduction "Give thanks to YHWH, you . . . ," the introduction used by the prophets is "Thus spoke YHWH, who . . ."

239. I do not present the text, for, because of its severe corruption, I can venture no reconstruction of the individual verses.

240. Six-footed line, distichs; v. 14b appears to be four-footed.

241. The parallelism and meter of this text are assisted by כבירים [kab-bîrîm]; so also LXX's ἐθνῶν πολλῶν [ethnōn pollōn].

242. לאמים כשאון מים רבים ישאון [lĕ-ʾummîm kišʾôn mayim rabbîm yiššāʾôn] is, naturally, a variant.

243. A colon is lacking (three beats). The subject for גער בו [gāʿar bî] is also lacking.

244. In Hermann Gunkel, "Nahum 1," ZAW 13 (1893) 233ff. I have attempted to demonstrate that this chapter, by its nature, is not an ancient prophecy, but rather a versified apoca-

lypse. There is also an attempt in that article to reconstruct the badly corrupted text. In this connection, Bickell, "Beiträge zur Semitischen Metrik," in *Sitzungsberichte der Akademie der Wissenschaften in Wien*, Philosoph.-histor. Klasse, Bd. 131, §V, pp. 1ff., has published a reconstruction of the text which I must reject as a whole, but from which I have learned something in regard to individual points. I believe that I am not able to put forward a restoration of the כ- [*n-*] and the פ- [*q-*] lines, something of which I still despaired in 1893. I refer to the following suggestions made when I remarked upon the lines in 1893.

8bc   כ *He dispatched his opponents,*
         his enemies he thrust into darkness.

9cb   ל *He took vengeance upon his oppressors without hesitation,*
         at the proper time he dispatched them.

It would probably be better to read מפעם [*mip-pa'am*], "before the time," in the ל-line. In the second half-line we should read כפעם [*kĕ-pa'am*] (Bickell, "Beiträge zur Semitischen Metrik," in *Sitzungsberichte der Akad. der Wissenschaften in Wien*, Philosoph.-histor. Klasse, vol. 131, §V, pp. 1ff.) — Now this is the application of common concepts to the particular case.

9a = 11   מ *Your time is at hand, for which you schemed schemes against YHWH!*
         You, O scoundrel, who planned mischief!

12   נ *The days are up, for I have reproved!*
         The hour has flown! It is past!

ממך [*mimmekkā*] is from מן [*min*] (Ps 68:24), "the portions," here the "allotted time" — הרע [*he-ra'*], "you scoundrel." משל מים רבים [*mōšēl mayim rabbîm*] LXX, with the necessary exchange of the מ [*m*] and the נ [*n*], should read משלמו ימי ריבי [*mĕšallĕmô yĕmê rîbî*]. The vowels have no binding authority for us here, as elsewhere. As is well known, the ם- [*-m*] of the plural belongs to later tradition. — כֵן [*kēn*], "that which is established" — נגזו [*nāgōzzû*] (cf. Ps 90:10a) — The psalm announces triumphantly that the time which God has appointed for tyranny is now past. The quarrel of God with Israel is over. Now comes the time of the judgment upon "the impious ones."

This judgment is described in lines ס [*s*] through פ [*q*]. The "impious one" is addressed throughout (as well as in v. 10) in the second person singular. The פ- [*q-*] line gives the conclusion of the description. V. 14e forms the first part of this line. The second part, through a scribal error, occurs after the נ- [*n-*] line at v. 12:

14e   פ *I made your grave into a dunghill;*

12d   *I so disgraced you that I will never need to disgrace you again!*

קברך אישים קיקלות [*qibrekā 'iššîm qîqālôṯ*] (according to Bickell: קיקלתא [*qîqaltā'*] in Syriac and Targumic Aramaic; the verse is lacking at 9b — פסל ומסכה [*pesel û-massēkāh*]). The ת- [*t-*] word I read as תך [*tōk* < √תכך [√*tkk*]], "oppression" || בליעל [*bĕlîya'al*]. I withdraw the conjecture of לעבר [*la-'ăbār*] and likewise the difficulty at בקקים [*bōqĕqîm*] (3). — In this reconstruction of the whole text only two glosses are accepted: the כה אמר יהוה [*kōh 'āmar YHWH*] at v. 12 and the two glosses in vv. 2b and 3a, the aim of which is clear. The major corruption has occurred by transposition. These restorations are commended, so I believe, by the solid contextualization which issues from them. I leave it to the reader to compare these and those proposed by Bickell.

245. Six-foot lines, distichs.

246. 2 Sam 22[:16]: ים [*yām*]; Ps 18[:16]: מים [*mayim*] (Baethgen, *Psalmen*, 52).

247. מגערתך [*mig-ga'ărāṯĕkā*] [Ps 18:16] — for metrical reasons — should be preferred

to the reading of 2 Samuel, בגערת [bĕga'ăraṯ]. Accordingly, אפך ['appeḵā] of Ps 18[:16] is better than אפו ['appî] of 2 Sam [22:16].

248. In 2 Sam 22[:18] and Ps 18[:18] מאיבי עז [mē-'ōybê 'oz] is singular, and in Ps 18[:18] LXX מאיבי עזים [mē-'ōybê 'ăzîm] is plural. (The following word — משנאי [miš-šōn'ay] in 2 Sam 22[:18] — begins with מ [m].)

249. The "Sinai" of the Old Testament is not the present mountain named "Sinai," but rather lay in Seir, in the mountains of Paran (Deut 33:2); cf. Rudolf Smend, *Lehrbuch der alttestamentlichen Religionsgeschichte*, Sammlung theologischer Lehrbucher (Freiburg: J. C. B. Mohr, 1893), 30, n. 2 [hereinafter: Smend, *Alttest. Religionsgesch.*].

250. Cf. my reconstruction of Nahum 1 in *ZAW* (1892) 223ff.

251. Six-foot lines, distichs.

252. הבנהרים הרה אפך אם־בים יהוה עברתך [hăḇinhārîm hārāh 'appeḵā 'im-bay-yām YHWH 'eḇrāṯeḵā].

253. 8b כי תרכב על סוסיך מרכבתיך [kî ṯirkaḇ 'al sûsêḵā markĕḇōṯêḵā] is metrically incomplete. Likewise, in terms of its sense, the line lacks a main idea: "Are you then angry at the sea, that you ride with your chargers over the sea?" ישועה [yĕšû'āh] (read אשפה ['ašpāh]) belongs to the following:

קשתך שבעת מטות	אשפה עריה תער
['ašpāh 'eryāh tĕ'ar	qašteḵā šĕḇ'aṯ maṭṭōṯ]

"You empty the quiver totally,
Your bow is sated with arrows."

V. 15, strange in the present context (cf. Kautzsch, *Bibelübersetzung*), is a variant of v. 8b.

8b כי תרכב על־סוסיך
[8b, kî ṯirkaḇ 'al-sûsêḵā]

חמר מים רבים	15 דרכת בים סוסיך
[15, dăraḵtā bay-yām sûsêḵā	ḥomer mayim rabbîm]

V. 15 contains the missing words from v. 8b. A secure reconstruction is impossible. The plural מרכבתיך [markĕḇōṯêḵā] is absurd, for God rides on only one chariot. The text may perhaps have read:

מרכבתך בחמר מים	כי הדרכת בים סוסיך
[kî hiḏraḵtā bay-yām sûsêḵā	markĕḇaṯĕḵā bĕ-ḥomer mayim]

Vulg. and Targ. appear to have read בחמר [bĕ-ḥomer].

254. The psalm appears to consist of verses of nine beats with two caesurae

‖ / / / ‖ / / / / / ‖ / / /

(cf. Bickell, *Carmina VT*, 65), if there is no major corruption.

255. The meter forbids the linking of אדירים ['addîrîm] with what goes before.

256. The meter of vv. 17-20 is like that of Psalm 93. The lines are inserted by a later hand into Psalm 77, which is a poem of six-footed lines (Bickell, *Carmina VT*, 52).

257. Six-foot lines, distichs.

258. בעיניו [bĕ-'ênâw] belongs before the caesura, according to the versification. וירא [way-yēra'] without a close modifier is striking. One may assume that this was originally ידעו [yāḏĕ'û]. The corruption of this to וירא [way-yēra'] followed the transposition of this ידעו [yāḏĕ'û] with בעיניו [bĕ-'ênâw].

259. תלבשת [*tilbošet*] is a gloss [Robert Lowth, *Isaiah: A New Translation with a Preliminary Dissertation and Notes, Critical, Philological, and Explanatory*, 5th ed. (Edinburgh: George Caw, 1807), 2:346 [hereinafter: Lowth, *Isaiah*]]. No offense should be taken at the parallel "garment of vengeance" ‖ "helmet of salvation" [*contra* A. Klostermann, *Deuterojesaia Hebräisch und Deutsch mit Anmerkungen*, Sammlung hebräisch-deutscher Bibeltexte, vol. 1 (Munich: C. H. Beck, 1893)[hereinafter: Klostermann, *Deuterojesaia*], 84].

260. על ['*al*] "price level" (Klostermann, *Deuterojesaia*, 84), חמה [*ḥēmāh*], LXX ὄνειδος [*oneidos*]-חמס [*ḥāmas*]. Literally translated: "Like the price of abuse [גמול [*gĕmûl*], גמולה [*gĕmûlāh*] 'that which is clad in injustice'], so high is the price of retribution [שלם [*šillēm*], substantive, A, Vulg.; B. Duhm, *Jesaia*, 416-17]; violence for those who oppose him; abuse for his enemies." Concerning the concept that God requites violence with violence, cf. Ps 18:27.

261. 18 לאיים גמול ישלם [*lā-ʾiyîm gĕmûl yĕšallēm*] is proven metrically to be an addition; the last five words are lacking in the LXX (Duhm, *Jesaia*, 416-17; Kautzsch, *Heilige Schrift*, 486).

262. ויראו [*way-yir'û*] (Duhm, *Jesaia*, 417; Klostermann, *Deuterojesaiah*, 84).

263. The usual translation, "prompts" (e.g., Dillmann, *Jesaia*, 593) is incorrect. נוס [*nôs*] means "to flee," נסס [*nissēs*] means "to drive into flight." Correspondingly, the stream is not an image of YHWH, but of YHWH's foes.

264. LXX καὶ ἀποστρέψει ἀσεβείας ἀπὸ Ἰακώβ [*kai apostrepsei asebeias apo Iakōb*], להשיב [*lĕ-hēšîḇ*] (Duhm, *Jesaia*, 417).

265. Cf. pp. 18f. above.

266. Cf. pp. 12f. above.

Notes to Chapter 5

1. Cf. pp. 3-12 above.

2. Thus I presently consider it risky to maintain that the sequence of the events in both reports is "absolutely the same" (Jensen, *Kosmologie*, 306). Therefore, it is to be assumed that as soon as the missing pieces have been found, the similarity will also clearly stand out here. — [The probable sequence of the creative actions in the Babylonian myth is: heaven, heavenly bodies, (earth), (plants), animals, (human beings), though the items in parentheses are only inferred. In the Babylonian narrative the heavenly bodies come, differently than in Genesis 1, directly after heaven itself!] — Zimmern

3. Cf. Fritz Hommel, "Inschriftliche Glossen und Exkurse zur Genesis und zu den Propheten — II," *Neue Kirchliche Zeitschrift* 1 (1890) 408ff. [hereinafter: Hommel, "Inschriftliche Glossen II"].

4. The presentation of the "upper waters" is found in Gen 7:41; Pss 104:3; 148:35. Cf. 2 Kings 7:2, 19; Job 38:25. God's throne is established on the waters, hence the vitreous "sea" of Rev 4:6 and 15:2.

5. The creation of humanity from earth, not preserved in Genesis 1, perhaps taken out by P[c], however reported by Genesis 2, is to be reclaimed for Babylonian sources, according to Berossus and certain cuneiform references (cf. Jensen, *Kosmologie*, 293-95). — According to the usual biblical tradition, humanity is formed from dust or עפר ['*āpār*, Gen 2:7; 3:19; Ps 103:14; Job 34:15, etc.] [variants: דכא [*dakkā*', Ps 90:3] and חמר [*ḥōmer*, Job 4:19; 10:9; and 33:6]. In the cuneiform tradition known to us humanity is not created from עפר ['*epru*] but from טיט [*ṭîṭu*] (which, perhaps, corresponds to חמר [*ḥōmer*]).

6. Noted by Dillmann, *Genesis*[6], 27.

7. The Israelite creation hymns, which proclaim the "gracious and true" God and which praise the creation as a "saving deed" (Ps 74:89), are no different. The words of Genesis, "and God looked upon everything which he had made, and he saw it was all very good" is the essential sense of Ps 104:31, "God took pleasure in his creations."

8. Cf. above, pp. 3-12.

9. Cf. above, pp. 11ff.

10. Wellhausen, *Prolegomena*[3], 311f.

11. Wellhausen, *Prolegomena*[3], 311.

12. Wellhausen, *Prolegomena*[3], 311.

13. [The German word is *Herrschen*, a substantival adjective form (i.e., "those things which rule"), which I believe to be, in this case, the zodiacal signs. — trans.]

14. The views of modern scholars concerning this are found in Holzinger, *Hexateuch*, 442.

15. Cf. Benzinger, *Archäologie*, 82, 288, 199,and 201.

16. 2 Kings 17:29-31 enumerates the deities brought along by those who colonized the territory of the northern kingdom, among which were many of Babylonian origin.

17. Less distinctively from Ezekiel.

18. להחריד אתם [*lĕ-haḥărîd ʾōtām*] in 2:4 is senseless. LXX's τοῦ ὀξῦναι [*tou oxynai*] = להחד [*lĕ-hāḥēd*], אתם = אתּים [*ʾittîm*]; את [*ʾēt*] is an agricultural instrument with which one would strike, i.e., ‖ "sword" (Isa 2:4, etc).

19. The conjecture of Wellhausen, לארבע [*lā-ʾarbaʿ*], "who go out to the four winds," is quite unfortunate. To the question "Who are these?" the answer is, "They are the four winds." The form of the answer is a lot like that of 4:10b. The color of the horses — the text of chapters 6 and 1 is repeatedly corrupt — corresponds to the cardinal points.

20. [An איפה [*ʾēpāh*] is a grain measure, equivalent to one tenth of a חמר [*ḥōmer*], i.e., about two-thirds of a bushel. — trans.]

21. For the concept, cf. *1 Enoch* 18.

22. Qĕrē LXX, Pesh., Targ., Vulg.

23. גֻּלָּה (*gullāh*), LXX, Pesh., Wellhausen; גֹל [*gōl*] is to be stricken from the lexicon.

24. רֹות [*nerōt*] LXX, Pesh.

25. LXX omits שבעה [*šibʿāh*]; Wellhausen, "From the oil receptacle (גלה [*gullāh*]) the tubes (מוצקות [*mûṣāqōt*]), which feed the lamps go forth." Furthermore, Wellhausen: אשר על ראשה [*ʾăšer ʿal rōʾšāh*] is "inserted." "Only the oil receptacle, not the lamps, are considered over the top of the candelabra."

26. "For מימין הגלה [*mîmîn hag-gullāh*] read מימינה [*miy-yĕmînāh*], the suffix referring to המנורה [*ham-mĕnôrāh*], cf. 11, הגלה [*hag-gullāh*] is a false explication." — Wellhausen

27. "6b-10a interrupt the unified context and belong at the end of the piece." — Wellhausen

28. The answer of the angel has dropped out.

29. The Hebrew text is incomplete. LXX καὶ ἐπαναγόντων [*kai epanagontōn*] מעלים [*û-maʿălîm*] (Vollers) τὰς ἐπαρυσιτρίδας τὰς χρυσᾶς [*tas eparystridas tas chrysas*], Targ. ומריקין מנהון משהא לבוציני דהבא [*û-mrêqîn minhôn mašhāʾ lĕ-bôṣînê dahĕbāʾ*]. The text perhaps read:

המריקים מעליהם היצהר למוצקות הזהב
[*ham-mĕrîqîm mēʾālêhem hay-yiṣhār lĕ-mûṣāqōt haz-zāhāb*]

"from them" = "from the groves." The sense is: from the two olive groves go forth two conduits, which lead to the גלה [*gullāh*], whence then the oil flows through the shafts to the lamps.

30. As suspected by Rudolf Smend, *Lehrbuch der alttestamentlichen Religionsgeschichte* (Freiburg: J. C. B. Mohr, 1893) [hereinafter: Smend, *Alttest. Religionsgesch.*], 341, n. 1.

31. The text, which at 1:8 speaks of only three winds, is defective.

32. Targum to this text.

33. This lamp is described in Exod 25:31ff. In the Temple of Solomon were found ten lamps (1 Kings 7:49); in the Temple of Zerubbabel only one (Sir 26:17). Judas Maccabeus allowed it to be restored (1 Macc 45:29f.). It was stolen by the Romans and, as is well known, is portrayed on the Arch of Titus; cf. Riehm, *Hw*, s.v. "Leuchter."

34. Subsequently I see that this significance of the seven-branched lamp was still known in Josephus, *War* 5.5.5 (ἐνεφαινον δὲ οἱ μὲν ἑπτὰ λύχνοι τοὺς πλατήτας [*enephainon de hoi men hepta lychnoi tous platētas*]); *Ant.* 3.6.7, 7.7, and Philo, "*Quis rerum divinarum heres sit*" (ed. Mangey), 1.504.

35. I also find this significance of the middle lamp subsequently in Philo, "*Quis rerum divinarum heres sit*" (ed. Mangey), 1.504 (ὁ μέσος τῶν ἑπτα ἥλιος [*ho mēsos tōn hepta hēlios*]); cf. *De vita Mosis* (ed. Mangey), 1.150f.

36. Treelike candlesticks are similarly reported from Greco-Roman antiquity. On these the lamps were suspended like apples; cf. Pauly, *RE*, s.v. "*lucerna*," 5:1161ff.

37. Riehm, *HW*, s.v. "*Leuchter*," p. 901.

38. So Wellhausen on Zech 4:14.

39. For the concepts, cf. Isa 40:27; 49:14ff. For the forms, cf. Ezra 5:5 and Ps 33:18; 34:16.

40. According to Wellhausen on Zech 4:12. Wellhausen, perceiving this difficulty, has been helpful in that he explains v. 12 as not genuine, without claiming to know the reason for the gloss and without indicating a knowledge of why, exactly, king and high priest would be depicted as olive trees before an oil lamp. — Smend, *Lehrbuch*, 343, n. 1 has recognized that the context of oil lamp and olive trees signifies, rather, that by them the anointing of Joshua and Zerubabel (the olive trees) by the divine spiritual power (the oil of the lamps) is represented. Thus, the olive trees could will provide the candelabra with oil. Certainly this would not be, as Smend himself agrees, "especially skillful."

41. √פרח [√*prḥ*], the same word as the *terminus technicus* in regard to the candlestick in P^c (Exod 25:31, etc.).

41. √פרח [√*prḥ*], the same word as the *terminus technicus* in regard to the candlestick in P[c] (Exod 25:31, etc.).

42. Benzinger, *Archäologie*, 338-89. More about this in what follows.

43. Particularly, in later time, *KAT*[2] 20: the Sargon tablets have the series: the seven walls of Ecbatana take after the planetary colors. Among them the golden one, which represents the sun, is the innermost and the highest wall (cf. Herodotus, *History* 1.98).

44. The golden one (the sun) stands in the middle of the colors of the step-temple of Borsippa (cf. Hommel, "Astronomie der alten Chaldäer," *Ausland* 64 [1891] #12, 221-73; #13, 381-407; #14, 59-91, 101-6 [hereinafter: Hommel, "Astronomie"], 2:5] — I consider it important to state that I inferred the two successions of the planets among the Babylonians from the form of the seven-branched lampstand, and subsequently have obtained, as a result, confirmation by my Assyriologist friend. — I append, even now, that — as is mentioned above on p. 319, n. 33 — even Philo knew a similar enumeration of the planets. *Yalkut Reubeni* 4 (in Eisenmenger, *Entdecktes*, 2:8) places the sun in the middle.

45. [Concerning the fact that the word כרוב [*kĕrûb*] (contrary to earlier statements of François Lenormant, *La Origines de l'Histoire d'après les textes cunéiformes et les monuments de l'art asiatique*, 2d ed. (Paris: Maisonneuve, 1880) [hereinafter: Lenormant, *Origines de l'His-*

toire], 112ff.) has not been identified in Assyrian until now, cf. F. [*sic*], "כרוב," *Zeitschrift für Assyriologie* 1 (1886) 68f.] — Zimmern. On cherubim and the paradise narrative, cf. that which follows.

46. Hommel, *Geschichte Babyloniens und Assyriens* (Berlin: G. Grote, 1885-88) [hereinafter: Hommel, *Gesch. Bab.*], 254; Friedrich Delitzsch et al., *Biblisches Handwörterbuch illustriert*, 2nd ed. (Calwer, Stuttgart: Verlag der Vereinsbuchhandlung, 1893) [hereinafter: Delitzsch, *Calwer Bibellex²*], 532.

47. According to Schrader, *KAT²*, 160, a name for the bull constellation [i.e., Taurus].

48. Five-footed verse (קינה [*qînāh*]).

49. אֵיךְ [*'ēḵ*]. K. Budde, "Das hebräische Klagelied," *ZAW* 2 (1882) 14.

50. For אֶרֶץ [*'ereṣ*] as a name for שְׁאוֹל [*šĕ'ôl*], cf. pp. 292-93, n. 8.

51. The usual translation, "the people stricken down," cannot be proven. גוים [*gôyîm*] = גוי' [*gôy*] = גוית [*gĕwîyat*].

52. הַר־מוֹעֵד [*har-mô'ēḏ*], the mountain of the assembly, i.e., quite probably the place where the gods come together, lies at a great distance in the north. It is thought to be, according to the context, the earth's highest mountain, and it appears to have originally been the North Pole, around which the stars rotated. For Indian and Iranian parallels, cf. Dillmann, *Genesis⁶*, 48f. [Cf. also Jenson, *Kosmologie*, 23, who brings the concept of הַר־מוֹעֵד [*har-mô'ēḏ*] together with the dwelling place of the Babylonian high god of heaven, *Anu*, at the North Pole.]

53. בּוֹר [*bôr*] is neither here (Dillmann, *Jesaiah*, 137), nor elsewhere in the Old Testament, a name for a grave. One was not to be buried in cisterns. On the contrary, however, it designates שְׁאוֹל [*šĕ'ôl*], which would be like a cistern, i.e., less than roomy, more than tight (the "mouth" or בְּאֵר [*bĕ'ēr*] (Ps 69:16); שְׁאוֹל [*šĕ'ôl*] ‖ בּוֹר [*bôr*] (Isa 38:18; Pss 30:4; 88:4f.; Prov 1:12); cf. further Isa 14:19; Ezek 26:20; 31:14; 32:18; Ps 88:7, where אַבְנֵי בוֹר [*'aḇnê-ḇôr*] is corrupt, probably from אדני [*'aḏnê*], etc. בּאר [*bō'r*] has the same meaning (Pss 55:24; 69:76). Another name for שְׁאוֹל [*šĕ'ôl*] is שחת [*šaḥat*], "pitfall" (Jonah 2:7; Pss 16:10; 30:10; Job 17:13f.).

54. Cf. Roscher, *Lexikon der Griech. und Röm. Mythologie*, 1:1269. I ask the reader to observe that in the forgoing material the similarity of Phaeton-*Hêlal* has not been expressed.

55. [The Babylonian myth of the journey to the infernal regions by Ishtar (the morning and evening star) can be ruled out as a direct parallel; it is, at best, a remote one. The "Legend of the God *Zu*" (*Beiträge zur Assyriologie*, 2:408ff.) contains two similar motifs. It also, however, cannot be the direct prototype.] — Zimmern

56. The הר מועד [*har mô'ēḏ*] of Isaiah 14 surely does not lie in the underworld, in contrast to which it is certainly placed here [Regarding the most problematic "mountain of assembly" in Babylonian materials, cf. Jensen, *Kosmologie*, 203ff.] — Zimmern

57. In Ps 19:6 ("the sun comes forth as a bridegroom from the bedroom") there are also mythological echoes. The bride of the שמש [*šemeš* = "sun"], with whom the sun spends the night, was originally the goddess of the sea.

58. *Cf.* generally the detailed article "Sterne" by Friedrich Delitzsch in *Biblisches Handwörterbuch illustriert*, ed. Paul Zeller, 2d ed. (Calwer/Stuttgart: Vereinsbuchhandlung, 1893) [hereinafter: *Calwer Bibellex²*].

59. In these and similar words a polemic against Persian dualism may be found, before it was known from the Babylonian particulars. Yet it is very questionable whether Deutero-Isaiah at that time already had known of the Persian religion. On the contrary, the natural thing is to see here a settlement with the Babylonians in whose domain the prophet lived. Cf. Dillmann, *Jesaia*, 409. — The verse in Isa 45:7 is four-footed.

60. Five-footed verse.

61. Duhm, *Jesaia,* 320, even asserts that it has "nothing to do" with Gen 1:2!

62. Six-footed verse.

63. Six-footed verse.

64. Six-footed verse.

65. Four-footed verse.

66. ידות (Duhm, *Jesaia,* 273).

67. Six-footed verse.

68. καὶ ἰδοὺ οὐθέν [*kai idou outhen*] = והנה בהו [*wĕ-hinneh bōhû*]

69. After ראיתי [*rē'îtî*] stands the accusative at vv. 23a, 24, 25, and 26. Only at v. 23b does the Hebrew text have אל ['*ēl*] The sense demands the accusative. The prophet wishes to say what he has seen in the vision. So also the Targ. and perhaps also the Vulg.

70. The form has no place here. There is no parallel — *contra* Friedrich Giesebrecht, *Das Buch Jeremia, übersetzt und erklärt,* Handkommentar zum Alten Testament (Göttingen: Vandenhoeck & Ruprecht, 1890), 3.2.2, 27 [hereinafter: Giesebrecht, *Jeremia*].

71. יעריו [*ya'ărāw*] (Isa 9:17; Jer 21:24).

72. The חרון [*ḥārôn*] is not "thrown down," but rather "burned up."

73. After the verse one word is missing, probably חמת [*ḥammat*]. חמה [*ḥammāh*] together with נצת [*niṣṣat*] (2 Kings 22:13, 17; Nah 1:6). — The text is a bit "filled up" with sections, so it appears.

74. The establishment of these facts is not without value for the interpretation of the prophetic oracle. The historical interpretation of the prophets will *have* to treat the prehistory of the materials adopted by the prophets as a central exegetical task.

75. Budde, *Urgeschichte,* 515f., thinks of the reign of Ahaz. Abraham Kuenen, "Bijdragen tot de Critiek van Pentateuchen en Jozua," *Theologische Tijdskrift* 18 (1884) 167ff., recalls the reign of Manasseh. Willem Hendrik Kosters, "De Bijbelsche zontvloedverhalen met de Babylonische vergeleken," *Theologische Tijdskrift* 19 (1885) 344, thinks of Hezekiah (the legation of Merodach-Baladan).

76. Our historical sources do not mention the names, but only the types of Babylonian deities which were worshiped in Judah. They were Sun, Moon, Zodiac, and the whole remaining host of the heavens (1 Kings 23:5). Other allusions give names: *Sakkuth* (Heb. סכות [*sikkût*], Amos 5:26) (a byname for *Ninib* — Saturn, *KAT²*, 443); and *Kêwan* (Heb. כיון [*kîyûn*], Amos 5:26) (Saturn, *KAT²*, 443 = Assyrian *Kaimânu*) from earlier times (Amos 5:26); *Tammuz* (= *Damuzu, KAT²,* 425), Ezek 8:14; מלכת השמים [*mĕleket haš-šāmayīm*], Jer 44:17-19, 25 [interpreted by Stade as "mistress of the heavens" (Bernhard Stade, "Das vermeintliche Aramäisch-assyrische Aequivalent der מלכת השמים Jer 7.44," *ZAW* 6 [1886] 289-339; cf. his "Die vermeintliche 'Königin des Himmels,'" *ZAW* 6 [1886] 123-32) — but the name probably equals *malkat ša šamê,* a byname of *Ištar* [Eberhard Schrader, "Die Göttin Ištar als *malkatu* und *šarratu,*" *Zeitschrift für Assyriologie* 3 [1888] 353ff., and his "Nachtrag zu dem Aufsätze: 'Die Göttin Ištar als *malkatu* und *šarratu,*'" *Zeitschrift für Assyriologie* 4 [1889] 74ff.]. [Additionally there are the *mazzālôt* of 2 Kings 23:5 (Μεζουρώθ [*me-zou-rôt*] [LXX], *mazzārôt* [Job 38:32], according to the interpretation of 2 Kings 23:5). The word מזלות [*mazzālôt*] probably goes back to the Assyrian *mazzaltu* (for *mazzaztu⟩* √נזז [*nzz*]), "location," of the star on the heavens. — Zimmern]. Thus the first law (Deut 5:8 = Exod 20:4), which is to be understood neither as that which is in the water on the earth nor that which is in the water under the earth: in heaven are the stars, on earth are humanity, cattle, angels, serpents, etc. What is "in the water under the earth"? This is the "dragon," the "helper of Rahab," i.e., according to the Babylonian view, zodiacal forms. That forms of the constellations had existed in the Babylonian culture is clearly shown; cf. the above-

cited (pp. 19f.) royal inscriptions and the testimony of Berossus (pp. 13ff.). Numerous representations of such constellations are preserved on the Babylonian "boundary stones," e.g., *West. As. Inscr.*, 5:57. Cf. as well the comments of Hommel, "Die Astronomie der alten Chaldäer," *Aufs. und Abhandl.* 18. This prohibition (Deut 5:8 = Ex 20:4) stands in opposition to Babylonian idolatry. It stems, therefore, from a time when the Babylonian religion was the adversary; cf. Deut 17:3 (Babylonian idolatry was, at that point in time, star worship), i.e., from the seventh century B.C.E.

Ezek 8:7-12 has given a description of a remarkable cult where, when one "squeezes" oneself through a hole in the wall of the inner courtyard — [This, not "dig through," is the meaning of חתר [*ḥātar*]. The word is used for "squeezing" through the "mouth" of Sheol (Amos 9:2), for the ship (Jonah 1:13) which works its way through the waves, technically for the thief who squeezes himself into a house through some sort of hole or crack; מחתרת [*maḥteret*] = "breaking in, burglary." Thus we deal with the objection of Cornill as to why Ezekiel digs since there is already a hole in the wall] — when one "squeezes" oneself through a hole in the wall of the inner courtyard, one comes to a door from that place into a dark chamber, on the walls of which are mounted idolatrous reliefs. The cult, quite outlandish by analogy to what follows (*Tammuz, Šamaš*), is to be considered Babylonian. It goes together with the tradition of the carved figures of Ezek 23:14. Who are these idols? It is characteristic that they were worshiped "in the dark" someplace where "YHWH doesn't see" (v. 21); cf. Amos 9:3 [Ezek 8:12, עזב יהוה את־הארץ (*ʿāzab yhwh ʾet hā-ʾāreṣ*) is a false explicating gloss]. Thus they are forces of the darkness. The text calls it [i.e., רמש ובהמה [*remeš û-bhēmāh*], if LXX, perhaps a gloss — Carl Heinrich Cornill, *Das Buch des Propheten Ezechiel* (Leipzig: J. C. Hinrichs, 1886), 225] a שקץ [*šeqeṣ*], "unclean animal." An unclean animal, an entity of darkness, and Babylonian deities altogether are the "Chaos Beasts" = the מזלות [*mazzālôt* — "signs of the zodiac"].

Thus it is explained that any creature of the waters without scales and fins is an abomination (Deut 14:9f.; Lev 11:9-12). They are beings associated with the serpent (נחש [*nāḥās*]) of the seas (תנינים [*tannînîm*]). The other aquatic creatures, with scales and fins, are דגים (*dāgîm*). The same are permitted to be used as food.

Ezekiel 8 mentions, in the first place, "the image of jealousy" (vv. 3, 5), which has previously gone unmentioned. סמל [*sēmel*] designates not just a likeness, but the image, the form (Deut 4:16), as well. הקנאה [*haq-qinʾāh*] (vv. 3, 5) and המקנה [*ham-maqneh*] (v. 3) are variants, and LXX τοῦ κτεμένου [*tou ktemenou* — "of the buyer"] is equivalent to הקונה [*haq-qôneh* — "the one who buys"]. סמל הקנה [*sēmel haq-qôneh*], "the reed image" ‖ חית הקנה [*ḥayyat haq-qôneh*] ("the beast of the reeds") (Ps 68:31) could be read. In accordance with this, סמל הקנה [*sēmel haq-qôneh*] is a name for the Chaos Animals. Images of the Chaos Animals are attested for the Babylonians (cf. pp. 43f.). It is advisable to discern here the Chaos Animal, even more so since what follows deals with the zodiac. [Ezek 8:5 is to be read: "and I saw [that] north of the gate stood the altar (מזבח [*mizbēaḥ*]) of the reed-creatures."]

Some cultic rites are mentioned. The Babylonian cult took place on the roofs (2 Kings 23:12; Jer 19:13). The sun was a wagon with horses, arrayed like Santa's sleigh (2 Kings 23:11). [One is reminded of the wagon and horses of Phoebus, and similarly of *1 Enoch* 72:5 and 37; 75:3, 4, and 8, as well as of the Mandeans (Brandt, *Mand. Schriften*, 189)]. For prayer to the sun one turns eastward (Ezek 8:16). To honor the "heavenly queen" they are baking cakes, which bear their form (Jer 7:8; 44:19). They were especially revered by women (Jer 44:15ff.). The women weep for *Tammuz* (Ezek 8:14); cf. *Tammuz* lamentations by the mourning women at the end of the "Infernal Journey of Ištar." Concerning the secret functions of the constellations cf. above.

Ezek 8:17, "that they hold the faggot to their nose," is traditionally understood as a cultic practice and, seen as an allusion to Persian practice, it comes to be understood as the cut bouquet having been held up to the nose while praying. Such utilization of Persian ideas for the interpretation of a topic which was treated by Babylonian-Israelites, is certainly a little overmethodical. The relationship lies quite a bit closer. The chapter describes the Babylonian abomination, each instance more serious than the other (6, 13, 15). At the end is the most serious thing — that they turn their backs on YHWH's temple in order to worship the sun! This is the most impudent insult!!! Such utilization of Persian ideas for the explication of a topic which was discussed among Babylonian-Israelites is certainly a bit overly methodical. The relationship lies quite a bit closer, however. The chapter describes the Babylonian "abominations," each even more unpleasant than the others (vv. 6, 13, 15). At the end is the worst thing of all, that they [the Babylonians] turn their backs on YHWH's temple in order to worship the sun! This is an even more impudent insult! Isn't it enough for them that they commit all these "abominations" (as just mentioned), abominations which they commit *here* (in the *holy* place), "while they turn their back on me? So I also will no longer look upon them!" [v. 17, כי מלאו את הארץ חמס *(kî māl'û ĕt hā-'āreṣ ḥāmās)* is a false explicating gloss]. The LXX has καὶ ἰδοὺ αὐτοὶ ὡς μυκτηρίζοντες *(kai idou autoi hōs myktērizontes);* the Pesh. and the Targ. here, quite correctly, have understood this to be a gesture of scorn, i.e., a "thumbing of the nose!" The expression was so strong that the LXX did not even translate it literally! For הזמורה *[haz-zĕmôrāh]* the Targ. read a word which it only attempted to paraphrase by using בהתא *[bahătā'],* doubtless הזרמה *[haz-zirmāh]* (Ezek 23:20), here "snot." For על *['al],* מעל *[mē'al]* is to be read: "that they blew snot from their noses."

77. Building further on Wellhausen's source-critical analysis. The views of the modern scholar concerning these questions will be found by the reader in a discussion put together by Holzinger, *Hexateuch,* 138-60.

78. Budde, *Urgeschichte,* 515.

79. This proposition will probably, in principle, not be challenged by anyone. In practice, however, it will seldom go unnoticed. Cf. p. 324, n. 83, below.

80. The sevenfold ancestral list of J[1] (Genesis 4) is related to the tenfold list of P[c] (Genesis 5). This, it appears, is also the tradition of the ten ancestral kings of the Babylonians. Cf. further in that which follows.

81. Cf. the opposite assumption by Holzinger, *Hexateuch,* 154, who, according to literary-critical method, attributes the "complete alteration of the fantastically mythologizing Babylonian productions" [German: "totale Veränderung der abenteuerlichen mythologisierenden babylonischen Vorlagen"] to the viewpoint of the writers in question (J[2]).

82. A few things regarding the "Flood Account": It is conspicuous that, in PC, God first ordered the building of the Ark (6:14-16) and only then revealed the approaching flood (v. 17). J had the same sequence, and — as Budde, *Urgeschichte,* 256, ingeniously surmises — motivated Noah, probably through a text of faith: first Noah must build the ship, without knowledge of why; only then does he learn of the reward, that it is designated for the salvation of him and of his family. This is consistent with the Babylonian saga, where Ea generally discloses nothing to *Atraḥasis* about the flood. Rather, he commands only the building of the ship, the remainder of which task he relinquishes to the wisdom of his minions. This feature is motivated in the Babylonian account by the worry of Ea that he might betray the secrets of the gods to a human. — The Babylonian saga tells, at the end, of the sending out of three animals, a dove, a swallow, and a raven. In J we read of *four* animals, a raven and three doves (in the current text 8:8 lacks a designation of time: "after seven days"). Here two variants flow together, one of which speaks of the threefold dispatching of the dove, the other of which speaks of the dispatching of three dif-

ferent creatures; cf. Wellhausen, *Composition*, 15 and Friedrich Delitzsch, *Wo lag das Paradies?* (Leipzig: Henrichs, 1891) [hereinafter: Delitzsch, *Paradies?*], 157f. The purpose in regard to this? It is "so as to see whether the water had dispersed from the earth" (v. 8), which belongs, according to the nature of the thing, at the beginning of the episode. There is an intensification since the dove first returns immediately, then, in the second occurrence, returns only in the evening and with an olive branch, which is interrupted by the presupposed story of the raven, who, as at the beginning, returns no more. — Finally, there is the parallel of the Babylonian saga. — The whole episode should illustrate the intelligence of the "wise" Noah, who, without looking at the earth to know for certain, understands enough to see in this information concerning the earth. — The dove with the olive branch in its beak does indicate something which we do not perceive in *our* sources.

83. Modern researchers often deal with the saga-composers J and E as creators of their materials — one might consult, for example, the treatment of the account of Cain's murder of his brother as a "parenthesis" composed by the redactor (cf. Budde, *Urgeschichte*, 183ff.). — Modern researchers oscillate, therefore, between, on the one hand, the impression of the high antiquity of the sagas, and, on the other hand, the similarly apparent impression of the influencing of the composer by the prophets. An inadequate compromise is concluded between the two impressions, a compromise in which J (specifically J^1) is usually fixed around 850 B.C.E. (for the opinions regarding this, cf. Holzinger, *Hexateuch*, 165ff.). However, the majority of the traditions are much older and the written copy which has come to us, in which, for example, אשרות [*'ăšērôt*] are eliminated, must be significantly younger. If I, consequently, am inclined to place in the seventh century the conclusion of the composition which is received by us in J, I explicitly place beside it the assertion that the material itself, and also the multiple earlier writings which are previous to our collection of sages, are *much* older.

84. Cf. Deuteronomy 12.

85. [Gunkel does not note his source for this. I have, unfortunately, been unable to locate it. I do, however, thank Simon DeVries for his personal assistance in my search for it. Though unable to locate the exact quotation, with his help I found a significant treatment by Kuenen, translated into German, concerning the general topic of critical methodology: "Kritische Methode," in *Gesammelte Abhandlungen zum Biblischen Wissenschaft von Dr. Abraham Kuenen*, trans. K. Budde (Freiburg i. B. and Leipzig: Mohr-Siebeck, 1894), 3-46. Though it does not contain the quotation itself, it is *totally* consistent with it. — trans.]

86. George Smith, *George Smith's Chaldäische Genesis: Keilinschriftliche Berichte über Schöpfung, Sündenfall, Sintfluth, Thurmbau und Nimrod: Nebst vielen anderen Fragmenten ältesten Babylonisch-Assyrischen Schriftthums*, trans. Hermann Delitzsche, ed. Friedrich Delitzsch (Leipzig: Hinrichs, 1875) [hereinafter: Smith, *Chald. Gen.*], 150ff.; recently Alfred Jeremias, *Izdubar-Nimrod: Eine altbabylonische Heldensage nach den Keilschriftfragmenten* (Leipzig: Teubner, 1891) [hereinafter: Jeremias, *Izdubar-Nimrod*].

87. A proof of this equivalency is to be found in a Syrian Christian writing, "The Cave of Treasures," which otherwise also contains all sorts of mythic material — cf., e.g., the myth of *Ba'l-Šāmêm, Tammûz, and Baltin* [C. Bezold, ed., *Die Schatzhöhle* (Leipzig: Hinrichs, 1883-88) [hereinafter: Bezold, *Schatzhöhle*], 1:37] — and the things which are told about "Nimrod" which are not included in the biblical saga but which agree with the Babylonian Gilgamesh epic (Bezold, *Schatzhöhle*, 43).

88. Friedrich Delitzsch, *Paradies?*, 93. Recently, Immanuel Benzinger, *Hebräische Archäologie*, Grundriss der theologischen Wissenschaft, 2 Reihe, 1 Bd. (Freiburg i. B.: Mohr, 1894), 111, n. 1.

89. Dillmann, *Genesis*[6], 48f.

90. [The construction of a Babylonian paradise description, as Delitzsch, *Paradies?* has attempted it, must be considered to be unavailing. On the other hand, the utopian viewpoint by which a river of Paradise, which is divided into four rivers (Euphrates, Tigris, Nile, and the Persian Gulf), relies, quite certainly, on the Babylonian idea that the place of happiness (wherein, e.g., *Atraḫasis* was placed) lies at the "mouth of the rivers," i.e., the place where the Euphrates, the Tigris, and, further, Kercha and Karina, flow into the one viewed as a great river, the Persian Gulf; cf. Jensen, *Kosmologie*, 507ff.; Hommel, "Inschriftliche Glossen und Exkurse zur Genesis und zu den Propheten — II," *NKZ* (1891) 881-902; Paul Haupt, "The Rivers of Paradise," *American Oriental Society Proceedings*, March 1894, 103ff.] — Zimmern

91. Delitzsch, *Paradies?*, 150ff.

92. Cf. *KAT*[2], 28; Eberhard Schrader, "Semitismus und Babylonismus: Zur Frage nach dem Ursprung des Hebräismus," *Jahrbucher für protestantische Theologie* 1 (1875) 124ff.; Baudissin, *Stud.*, 2:189f.; Lenormant, *Origenes de l'Histoire*, 74f.; Delitzsch, *Paradies?*, 148f. There are also the oft-debated depictions from a cylinder seal; cf. Rhiem, *Hw*, 1406, s.v. "Schlangen," where two arrayed forms, of which one is horned, sit on seats next to the Tree of Life, one hand of each being outstretched toward it. Behind the unhorned figure a snake lies curled. This could, quite possibly, depict the Babylonian paradise account.

93. This conclusion corroborates the position that the name בבל [*bāḇēl*] evokes the Aramaic *bā'bel* more than the Hebrew root בלל [*bālal*].

94. In addition to these Babylonian materials, the primordial history also includes the primal genealogy, to which the ten earliest kings of Babylon would correspond; cf. François Lenormont, *Essai de commentaire des fragments cosmogoniques de Bérose d'après les textes cunéiformes et les monuments de l'art asiatique* (Paris: Maisonneuve, 1871) [hereinafter: Lenormant, *Comm. de Bérose*], 235ff. Lately, cf. Hommel, "The Ten Patriarchs of Berossus," *Proceedings of the Society of Biblical Archaeology*, March 1893, 243-46. There is naturally the question of whether the Babylonian material is exhausted with the minutiae in the first chapter of Genesis.

95. Cf. Hoffmann, *Hiob*, s.v. Job 15:8, on this point.

96. Light falls on Phil 2:6 in this regard.

97. [The Babylonian Adapa myth (cf. below, pp. 99ff.) is — as it appears — the presumed Babylonian prototype of the biblical narrative about primal humanity and that humanity's loss of the closely related immortality — The supposition that Adapa is the first representative of humanity to have comprehension receives support from a fragment (K8214), likewise dealing with Adapa, found in the library of Ashurbanipal, to which A. H. Sayce, "The Babylonian Legend of the Creation of Man," *The Academy* 1055, July 23, 1892, 77 has called attention, and which recently has been published by Arthur Strong, "Note on a Fragment of the Adapa Legend," *Proceedings of the Society of Biblical Archeology*, November 1894, 274-79.] — Zimmern

98. Cf. H. Zimmern, "Palästina um das Jahr 1400 v. Chr. nach neuen Quellen," *Zeitschrift der Deutsche Palästina Vereins* 13 (1091) 133-47; cf. H. Winckler, "Babyloniens Herrschaft in Mesopotamien und seine Eroberungen in Palästina in zweiten Jahrtausend," in his *Altorientalischen Forschungen* (Leipzig: Pfeiffer, 1893-95), 2:140-58.

99. Translated and discussed by E. T. Harper, "Die babylonischen Legenden von Etana, Zu, Adapa und Dibbara," *Beiträge zur Assyriologie* 2, 418-25.

100. Eduard Meyer, *Geschichte des Altertums* (Stuttgart: J. G. Cotta, 1884-1902) [hereinafter: Ed. Meyer, *Gesch. des Altertums*], 1:237ff., 252; Richard Pietschmann, *Geschichte der Phönizier*, Allgemeine Geschichte in Einzeldarstellungen 1 (Berlin: Grote, 1889) [hereinafter: Pietschmann, *Gesch. der Phönizier*], Hauptabt. 4 Theil, 2 Hälfte 144f.; Benzinger, *Archäologie*, 67.

101. Ed. Meyer, *Gesch. des Altertums*, 251f.

102. The Philistine *Dagon* has also been declared a Babylonian god, a presumption which, according to Jensen, *Kosmologie*, 449-56, is quite doubtful.

103. "Babylonian measure, weight, and money was already widespread in Syria in the sixteenth century B.C.E." "In regard to Hebrew dry measure, Babylon may securely be inferred as the homeland." "The Hebrew had also received the system of weights from the Babylonians by way of the Canaanites." Benzinger, *Archäologie*, 67, 181, 185; cf. also Wilhelm Nowack, *Lehrbuch der Hebräischen Archäologie*, Sammlung Theologischer Lehrbücher (Freiburg i. B.; Leipzig: J. C. Mohr [Paul Siebeck], 1894) [hereinafter: Nowack, *Hebr. Archäologie*], 1:205, 207.

104. קנה [*qāneh*] = Babylonian *qanū* (Benzinger, *Archäologie*, 181).

105. This is characteristically Babylonian according to Herodotus, *Historicus* [hereinafter: Herodotus, *Hist.*] 1.195; Strabo, *Geographus* [hereinafter: Strabo, *Geogr.*] 16.1, 20; cf. Nowack, *Hebr. Archäologie*, 1:129.

106. Benzinger, *Archäologie*, 258; Nowack, *Hebr. Archäologie*, 1:262.

107. Herodotus, *Hist.* 2.109.

108. Amos 3:12.

109. Cf., e.g., the marble relief entitled "Assurbanipal mit der Königen in der Weinlaube" ["Ashurbanipal with the Kings in the Vine-leaves" — trans.], reproduced by Hommel, *Gesch. Bab.*, 697.

110. Nowack, *Hebr. Archäologie*, 2:34.

111. This will be demonstrated by the fact that they bear names. Ordinary בות [*maṣṣēḇôt*], or even only technically necessary pillars, they most certainly are *not!*

112. W. H. Kosters, "De Cherubîm," *ThT* 13 (1879) 445ff.

113. The testimony of 2 Chron 4:6, that it had been a wash basin for the priests, is, according to the form, a late accounting for the ornamentation and for its designation as the "Sea." The "Sea" = the primordial sea; cf. Job 7:12; 38:8, etc.

114. Schrader, *KB* 3, Hälfte 1, p. 13, l. 143; cf. above, p. 19.

115. The understanding, given above (pp. 84-89), of the seven-branched candelabrum, as well as the expressed conjecture of its Babylonian origin, is corroborated anew by the parallel of the "Sea."

116. The bronze serpent which stood in the Temple and which represented a שרף (*śārāp*), had a counterpart in Babylon [Schrader, *KB* 3, 2, pp. 23, 35, and especially 73 (where the serpent forms are, similarly, of bronze)]. In Babylon such forms stand at the Temple gates. These serpents are, thus, guardians of the deity, similar, in a way, to the שְׂרָפִים [*śĕrāpîm*] of Isaiah 6.

117. אפסי הארץ [*'apsê hā-'āreṣ*); cf. above, pp. 33f.

118. תהום רבצת תחת [*tĕhôm rōḇeṣet tāḥat*] (Gen 49:25; cf. Amos 7:4).

119. [Cf. on the last point, Alfred Jeremias, *Die Babylonische-Assyrischen Vorstellungen vom Leben nach dem Tode, nach dem Quellen mit Berücksichtigung der Alttestamentlichen Parallelen* (Leipzig: Hinrichs, 1887) [hereinafter: Jeremias, *Leben nach Tode*], although (Jensen, *Kosmologie*, 215ff.) the name שאול [*šĕ'ôl*] for the world of the dead has not yet been recorded with any certainty in Assyrian.] — Zimmern

120. Descriptions of שאול [*šĕ'ôl*] are preserved for us chiefly in late writings. It by no means follows, however, that this concept came to be known in Israel only at a late date. A series of old passages speak of שאול [*šĕ'ôl*], e.g., Gen 37:35; 1 Samuel 28; 1 Kings 2:6; Isa 5:14; 7:11; 29:4; Amos 9:2; and Hab 2:5. And these occurrences coincide with those preserved from a later time, so that we do not have even the right to differentiate between "an older and a younger under-

standing of *šĕ'ōl*" (*contra* Smend, *Alttest. Religionsgesch.*, 504-5, and Duhm, *Jesaia*, 94f.). One should also be on guard here against an overestimation of literary criticism.

121. Cf. Wilhelm Lotz, *Quaestiones de historia sabbati: Libri duo. Commentatio historico-critica quam summa venerandi, theologorum ordinis* (Leipzig: J. C. Hinrichs, 1883), especially pp. 24-68; and P. Jensen, "The Supposed Babylonian Origin of the Week and the Sabbath," *The Sunday School Times* (Philadelphia), January 17, 1892, 35-36.

122. It really doesn't matter that the Babylonians calculated the week a little differently than the Hebrews. In Babylonia each month would be divided into four weeks of seven days. Among the Hebrews the Sabbath, independent of the beginning of a new month, went its own way. [In other words, the Sabbath was more determinative than the month — trans.]

123. *Šabattu* is interpreted as *ûm nuh libbi*, i.e., "day of the resting of the hearts (of the gods)." Though the Sabbath is a day of atonement among the Babylonians, among the Hebrews it is, in contrast, a day of rest. The original identity of the two is not disproved by this. Rather, a religio-historical relationship between these two can quite probably be understood. On which day the Babylonian Sabbath was is still uncertain. — However, if one wished to investigate Babylonian religious institutions which were adopted by Israel, one would have had the expectation, until now, that the concepts which are linked with the institution of the Sabbath would have been essentially different in each society.

124. Thus Stade, *Geschichte*, 2:3 traces it back to Deutero-Isaiah.

125. They are Amos 4:13; 5:8f.; 9:5f. (Duhm); Jer 5:22b (Bernhard Stade, "Weitere Bemerkungen zu Micha 4.5," *ZAW* 3 [1883] [hereinafter: Stade, "Micha 4.5"] 15f., demurs to vv. 20-22); however, v. 22a and with it 20f. as well, will be established by the contrast with 23ff. Concerning these glosses, cf. below, pp. 105f.); 10:12f.; 31:35-37; 32:17-23 (Stade).

126. Smend, *Alttest. Religionsgesch.*, 110.

127. A similar argumentation is found at Job 9:24.

128. Accordingly, the threat of the poor harvest, e.g., Isa 1:19f.

19If you are willing and follow good advice, you shall eat the good of the land.
20If you, however, are rebellious and you refuse, you shall get barrenness to eat.

Thus is it to be separated according to the קינה [*qînāh*] versification; שמע טוב [*šĕmāʿ ṭôb*], "listen to the good word," usually שמע עצה [*šĕmāʿ ʿēṣāh*] ["listen to the advice"]. "To eat the land"; cf. Gen 3:17; Isa 1:7; חרב [*ḥōreḇ*], "drought," "barrenness."

129. Jer 5:22b is a later gloss.

130. Based on Jer 27:5-11.

131. Cf. p. 106.

132. Six-footed poetry.

133. Reconstructed by Wellhausen according to the LXX.

134. [Greek ἄδυτος [*adytos*] = "innermost chamber, sanctuary" — trans.]

135. E.g., Gen 7:11b (P^c, though a more primordial, more poetic feature), Deut 28:12, and 2 Kings 7:2.

136. Amos 7:4 and Gen 49:25.

137. תהום רבצת תחת [*tĕhôm rōḇeṣet tāḥaṯ*] (Gen 49:25).

138. Cf. pp. 100f.

139. Cf. Schrader, *KB* 3, 1, p. 143.

140. One need only reflect on the "orientation" of our churches and graves, on the "rooster" on a steeple, and on many other things, the significance of which our modern Christian community simply does not understand.

141. "Sea" is the name of the World Ocean; cf. p. 54, etc.

142. Cf. Riehm, *Hw*, 902.

143. Riehm, *Hw*, 902.

144. Cf. 1 Kings 7:49.

145. Exod 25:31ff.

146. Josephus, *Flavii Iosephi opera, edidit et apparatu critico instruxit*, ed. Benedict Niese (Berlin: Weidmann, 1887-95), 3:6:7 §145 [hereinafter: Josephus, *Ant.*, ed. Niese].

147. The lack of these monsters in the descriptions of the lamps is quite comprehensible given the Jewish aversion to images.

148. Cf. Flügel, *Mani*, 86.

149. Cf. pp. 14f.

150. Cf. pp. 31f.

151. Cf. p. 301, n. 51.

152. Ezek 35:5, according to Cornill, *Ezechiel*, 375. Four-footed verse.

153. Benzinger, *Archäologie*, 387.

154. So it *can* be cautiously concluded from this fact that this common form has nothing to do with Babylon.

155. Johannes A. Overbeck, *Pompeji in seinen gebauden, altertumern und kunstwerken dargestellt*, ed. August Mau, 4th ed. (Leipzig: W. Engelmann, 1884), 575.

156. It is not necessary for the historian to establish that the descriptions of the religion of the patriarchs in the Genesis sagas do not render the religion of the primordial times in which the sagas take place, but rather that of a later time in which the sagas were narrated.

157. The hypothesis that Genesis 1 goes back to a primal revelation which, in other respects, will be expressed wordlessly in Genesis 1 itself . . . this hypothesis has been refuted on pp. 79ff., especially pp. 80f.

158. "Wisdom" was, in ancient understanding, also the skill of forming cultic utensils out of bronze or gold.

Notes to Chapter 6

1. Eberhard Vischer, *Offenbarung Johannis: Eine jüdische Apokalypse in christlicher Bearbeitung . . . mit einen Nachwort von Adolf Harnack* (Leipzig: Hinrichs, 1886), 19ff.

2. [Gunkel consistently uses "Apocalypse of John," or simply "Apocalypse," to refer to the final book of the New Testament. This book has a great variety of designations among modern English speakers — the Society of Biblical Literature, for example, has, in its list of acceptable abbreviations, rendered it as "Apocalypse of John . . . Rev," indicating its preference for the common English title: "Revelation." Throughout this book we will follow the SBL's conventions and use "Revelation." — trans.]

3. Especially Otto Pfeiderer, *Das Urchristentum, seine Schriften und Lehren in geschichtlichen Zusammenhang* (Berlin: G. Reimer, 1887), 331ff. [hereinafter: Pfeiderer, *Urchristentum*]; Friedrich Spitta, *Das Offenbarung des Johannes* (Halle: Waisenhaus, 1889), 125ff. [hereinafter: Spitta, *Offenbarung*].

4. Especially Daniel Völter, *Die Offenbarung Johannis: Keine Ursprüngliche Judische Apokalypse: Eine Streitschrift gegende Herren Harnack und Vischer* (Tübingen: J. J. Heckenhauer, 1886), 9ff. [hereinafter: Völter, *Offenbarung Johannes (Streitschrift)*]; Willibald Beyschlag, "Die Apokalypse: Gegen die jüngste kritische Hypothese in Schultz genommen," *Theologische*

Studien und Kritiken: Eine Zeitschrift für das gesammte Gebiet der Theologie 61 (1888) 106ff.; Adolf Hilgenfeld, "Die Johannes-Apokalypse und die neueste Forschung," *Zeitschrift für Wissenschaftliche Theologie* [hereinafter: *ZWT*] 31 (1890) 441ff. [hereinafter: Hilgenfeld, "Joh.-Apok. n. Forschung"]; Carl Weizsäcker, *Die Apostolische Zeitalter der Christliche Kirche*, 2d ed. (Freiburg: Mohr, 1892) [hereinafter: Weizsäcker, *Apost. Zeitalter²*], 363f.

5. So, e.g., Frederick Bleek, *Vorlesungen über die Apokalypse*, ed. T. Hossbach (Berlin: Reimer, 1862) [hereinafter: Bleek, *Vorlesungen*], 275; W. M. L. de Wette, *Kurze Erklärung der Offenbarung Johannis*, 2d ed. (Leipzig: Hirzel, 1854) [hereinafter: de Wette, *Commentar²*], 119f.; E. W. Hengstenberg, *Die Offenbarung des heiligen Johannes; für solche die in der Schrift forschen* (Berlin: Ludwig Oehmigke, 1849-50) [hereinafter: Hengstenberg, *Offenbarung des heiligen Johannes*], 1:607f.; August Ebrard, ed., *Biblischer Commentar über sämmtliche Schriften des Neuen Testaments zunächst für Prädiger und Studirende* (Königsberg: A. W. Unzer, 1862) [hereinafter: Ebrard, *Bibl. Commentar*], 360; Bernhard Weiss, *Lehrbuch der biblischen Theologie des Neuen Testaments*, 5th ed. (Berlin: W. Hertz, 1888) [hereinafter: Weiss, *Biblische Theologie⁵*], 557; Völter, *Offenbarung Johannis (Streitschrift)*, 13; Daniel Völter, *Die Entstehung der Apokalypse*, 2d ed. (Freiburg i. B.: J. C. B. Mohr, 1885) [hereinafter: Völter, *Entstehung der Apokalypse²*], 63; Adolf Hilgenfeld, "Joh.-Apok.," 446; and many others.

Theodor F. D. Kliefoth, *Die Offenbarung des Johannes*, 3 vols. in 1 (Leipzig: Dorffling und Franke, 1874) [hereinafter: Kliefoth, *Offenbarung des Johannes*], 9ff., gives another explanation which understands what the chapter portrays as a Christian depiction of the end time: out of the "Christian community of the end" will Christ, the judge of the world, be born. His birth is "his development into the royal judge over the world which is opposed to God, his accession to the throne in the eschatological sense" (p. 24). He will "be born" from the community of the end, which means: "this development of the liberator into the final judge of the world is dependent upon the fact that the Christian Church will turn into the pure and holy community of the end time" (p. 25). "The 'rapture' should represent how, if the Lord will arise as the judge of the world and will come forward as the power of the world, it will be quite impossible for the Satan to prevent it" (p. 27). — This explanation runs aground on the fact that the Christian community can, in no sense, be considered as the mother of Christ. The allegorical explanations of the birth as the carrying off of the Christ are invented quite arbitrarily. — Heinrich Ewald, *Die Johannischen Schriften, übersetzt und erklärt*, vol. 2: "Johannes' Apokalypse" (Göttingen: Dieterischen Buchhandlung, 1862) [hereinafter: Ewald, "Johannes' Apokalypse"], 239, offers a similar explanation: the seer hopes that the Christian community (of his time) will give birth to the Messiah of splendor from its painful struggles and wars. This interpretation is to be dismissed for the same reasons.

Friederich H. C. Düsterdieck, *Kritisch exegetisches Handbuch über die Offenbarung Johannes*, 4th ed. (Göttingen: Vandenhoeck und Ruprecht, 1887) [hereinafter: Düsterdieck, *Handbuch Offenbarung⁴*], 495f., recognizes that the actual history of Jesus is not laid out. The seer does not wish to portray history, but rather to illustrate an idea. This idea would be "the deadly hatred of Satan against the Lord and, in addition, the inviolability of the Lord." The persecution by the dragon and the carrying off of the children are expressions of this idea, to which no historical data correspond. — It is, nevertheless, a peculiar thing that this idea, which could be a reality, would be produced by a contrived history. On the contrary, the seer must, if he wishes to illustrate Jesus' inviolability, produce examples from the actual life of Jesus for that purpose. Invented examples prove nothing. Düsterdieck calls the special technique of the apocalyptist an "ideal" representation. It would be more correct to call it an inconceivably fantastic representation!

Daniel Völter, earlier a definite champion of the orthodox interpretation — "We find the death and resurrection of Jesus in this pictorial representation depicted as clearly as possible" [Völter, *Offenbarung Johannes (Streitschrift)*, 13] — has now satisfied himself concerning the "insurmountable difficulties" of this interpretation [Daniel Völter, *Das Problem der Apokalypse nach seinem gegenwärtigen Stande* (Freiburg i. B.: J. C. B. Mohr, 1893) [hereinafter: Völter, *Problem der Apokalypse*], 154]. At present he explains chapter 12 from the teaching of Cerinthus, according to which the Christ had descended from above onto Jesus at the baptism, in the form of a dove, in order to forsake him again before Jesus' passion. The "great and remarkable" agreement between Revelation 12 and the opinion of Cerinthus exists, according to Völter, because in both cases the Christ comes from above, is on earth only a very short time, and the dangers which threaten him are taken away by assimilation into the heavens (cf. Völter, *Problem der Apokalypse*, 156f.). Völter thinks, according to these and similar conformities, that the composition of the piece 12:1-10 by Cerinthus is probable (Völter, *Problem der Apokalypse*, 164). But the text says not a word about the Christ coming into union with a human being, not a word about baptism and a dove, not a word about the sufferings of the human whom the Christ had abandoned. Not once does it say that the Christ comes to earth (cf. n. 6 immediately below). It is clear that Revelation 12 contains not a trace of the christology of Cerinthus. Hey! Do I have any *real* need to refute such a perilously weird hypothesis!?!

6. Some of this argument has already been made regarding Methodius, "Convic X. Virg," *Orat.* 8:4, by Vischer, *Offenbarung* (Adolf Harnack, "Nachwort"), 113f. The improbability of the traditional interpretation had been perceived most clearly, among the modern interpreters before Vischer, by Kliefoth, *Offenbarung des Johannes*.

7. Karl Erbes, *Die Offenbarung Johannis: Kritische Untersucht* (Gotha: Perthes, 1891) [hereinafter: Erbes, *Offenbarung Johannis*], 6; Völter, *Entstehung der Apokalypse*, 62. Völter, *Problem der Apokalypse*, 151f., having finally satisfied himself that the issue here is "heavenly" events, now, however, attempts to arrive at the sense that, at the very least, the Messiah "right after his birth" *had* been on earth: "the one who was designated as begotten for the earth should come therein by birth, and since the birth takes place unhindered by location, he will also have come to the earth in the same way" (p. 152). This argumentation violates the text: its assumption, that the Messiah should come into the world by birth, is contrived and is false since, according to the context, the Messiah comes to earth not through his birth, but rather through his παρουσία (parousia) [= "arrival, advent"] (19:11ff.). Indeed, how should it be presented that the Messiah, who will be born in heaven, comes to earth by birth?!? And finally, if the writer wishes to say that the Messiah, after his birth in heaven, will be, for a short time, on earth, he would have had to say that much more clearly!

8. The flight of the woman into the wilderness is to be treated separately, since the wilderness is, to be sure, not a heavenly locus (*contra* Völter, *Problem der Apokalypse*, 151). This verse is, however, problematic for other reasons; cf. that which follows.

9. [By "*in* the heavens" Gunkel refers to the divine sphere. By "*on* the heavens" he refers to the visible sky, i.e., to stars, constellations, etc. The relationship between the two exists in the fact that realities "*in* the heavens" are reflected "*on* the heavens." — trans.]

10. Pfeiderer, *Urchristentum*, 331, has seen this correctly; accordingly Spitta, *Offenbarung*, 127.

11. Adolf Hilgenfeld, "Ein französischer Apologet des Johannes Evangeliums," *Zeitschrift für wissenchaftliche Theologie* [hereinafter: *ZWT*] 32 (1889) 144, recognizes that Revelation 12 speaks of the superterrestrial birth of the Messiah. He appears, however, not to have seen that this event could, then, have taken place, in the Christian formulation of the chapter, only pri-

mordially, at the beginning of the creation. Christ is, then, truly "the beginning of the Creation" (3:14). It is quite clear, however, that Revelation does not seek to describe a *primordial* event here.

12. Erbes, *Offenbarung Johannis,* 4f.

13. Weizsäcker, *Apost. Zeitalter*², 363; thus says de Wette, *Kommentar*², 119f.: "Christ's 'death,' since it clearly has to do with the body, and, furthermore, his resurrection from the dead, will be considered as nothing." [German: "Christi 'Tod' da derselbe blos den Leib betraf, und er noch dazu mit diesem auferstand, wird für nichts gerechnet."]

14. Weizsäcker, *Apost. Zeitalter*², 363; Völter, *Offenbarung Johannis (Streitschrift),* 13.

15. Vischer, *Offenbarung,* 23; Kliefoth, *Offenbarung des Johannes,* 3:22.

16. As is claimed, e.g., by Hengstenberg, *Offenbarung des heiligen Johannes,* 1:607: before the following: "and her child was taken away," this is intentionally added: "and the dragon continues its persecution," just as that "persecution" actually took place, according to the evangelistic accounts, from the temptation up to the death on the cross."

17. Vischer, *Offenbarung,* 23.

18. This feature, essentially to complete the context, has, as far as I can see, not been noticed until now (e.g., Völter, *Problem der Apokalypse,* 147).

19. Thus Völter, *Offenbarung Johannis (Streitschrift)* 13; Völter, *Entstehung der Apokalypse*², 63; cf. Beyschlag, "Apokalypse," 106ff.; Weizsäcker, Review of Fr. Spitta, *Die Offenbarung des Johannes,* in *Theologische Literaturzeitung* 15, no. 19 (20 September 1890), col. 470; Adolf Hilgenfeld, ed., *Messias Judaeorum,* 446. Hilgenfeld calls the deliverance of the Christ child a "heavenly Ur Form of the ascension of Jesus." However, by introducing the idea of the "Ur Form" at this point, he introduces a not insignificant complication. Things which have a "heavenly Ur Form" exist doubly, in the heavens *and* on the earth. Is Christ, therefore, doubly born and doubly saved from the Dragon? — I mention, only out of curiosity, that Erbes, *Offenbarung Johannis,* 6, also notes, in regard to the representation of the Messiah as a child, that it is "similar to, for example, the Roman Caesar, who, even if he was already quite old, was called, according to the Egyptian terminology, 'the lovely lad.'"

20. I do not, therefore, investigate whether the failure to complete the messianic task might be a generally possible concept in the New Testament; cf., however, John 17:4 and 19:30.

21. John 12:31; Eph 1:20f.; Col 2:15; Heb 2:14. The argument is that made by Kliefoth, *Offenbarung des Johannes,* 3:26.

22. Cf. pp. 116-17 above.

23. On this interpretation almost all modern interpreters are in agreement. The question is simply whether beneath it the Israel of the Old Testament, or the Christian church, or a combination of the two is to be perceived. Concerning the different understandings refer to Kliefoth, *Offenbarung des Johannes,* 3:14ff.; Düsterdieck, *Handbuch Offenbarung*⁴, 414ff.; Heinrich Julius Holtzmann, R. A. Lipsius, P. W. Schmiedel, and H. von Soden, eds., *Hand-commentar zum Neuen Testament* (Freiburg i. Br.: J. C. B. Mohr, 1889-91) [hereinafter: Holtzmann et al., *Hand-commentar*], 3:39.

24. Bleek, *Vorlesungen Apok.,* 275f.; de Wette, *Kommentar*², 120; Ewald, *Johannes' Apokalypse,* 243; Hengstenberg, *Offenbarung des heiligen Johannes,* 2:609f.; Adolf Hilgenfeld, *Historisch-kritische Einleitung in das Neue Testament* (Leipzig: Fues, 1875) [hereinafter: Hilgenfeld, *Einleitung in das NT*], 433; Weiss, *Biblische Theologie*⁵, 540, n. 4; Weizsäcker, *Apost. Zeitalter*², 363; Erbes, *Offenbarung Johannis,* 7, etc. understand the vision in terms of a persecution of Christians (usually in terms of the persecution of the primordial church).

25. So Weiss, *Biblische Theologie*⁵, 540, n. 4, and our p. 331, n. 23.

26. This is the argument of Kliefoth, *Offenbarung des Johannes,* 3:14.

27. Kliefoth, *Offenbarung des Johannes,* 3:17.

28. The correct judgment, that "those who remain" stands in contrast to the Messiah, has been seen by F. J. Züllig, *Die Offenbarung Johannis* (Stuttgart: Schwizerbarts, 1834), 2:215, and by Düsterdieck, *Handbuch Offenbarung*[4], 416.

29. Bleek, *Vorlesungen Apok.,* 282; de Wette, *Kommentar*[2], 124; Willibald Beyschlag, "Die Offenbarung Johannis," in *Zur deutsch-christlichen Bildung popular-theologische Vortrage* (Halle a. S.: Eugen Strien, 1888) [hereinafter: Beyschlag, "Offenbarung"], 190; Kliefoth, *Offenbarung des Johannes,* 3:57.

30. Düsterdieck, *Handbuch Offenbarung*[4], 417; Ewald, *Johannes Apokalypse,* 247; Bernhard Weiss, *Lehrbuch der Einleitung in das Neue Testament,* 2d ed. (Berlin: W. Hertz, 1889) [hereinafter: Weiss, *Einleitung*[2]], 378; Ebrard, *Bibl. Commentar,* 372.

31. Hilgenfeld, *Einleitung in das NT,* 433. Erbes, *Offenbarung Johannis,* 7-10, for whom the flight of the woman indicates the persecution of Stephen, understands "those who remain" as the Jews "who up to now have not believed"! They had been informed of the testimony of Jesus. They had heard it. Such an exegesis is certainly quite possible. — According to Völter, *Problem der Apokalypse,* 160, 164f., the flight of the woman represents the fall of Jerusalem in the year 70 C.E. — Cf., on the contrary, pp. 120ff. above. — "Those who remain should then be the Christians" (Völter, *Problem der Apokalypse,* 165ff.). It is an otherwise remarkable way to describe the siege of Jerusalem allegorically.

32. Johann Gottfried Herder, "Μαραν αθα," *Herders Sammtliche Werke,* ed. Bernhard Suphan (Berlin: Weidmann, 1877-), 9:174; Ernst Renan, *L'Antechrist,* 2d ed., Histoire des origines des Christianisme, vol. 4 (Paris: Michel Levy frères, 1873) [hereinafter: Renan, *L' Antechrist*], 325; Adolf Hilgenfeld, *Die jüdische Apokalyptik in ihrer geschichtlichen Entwickelung: Ein Beitrag zur Vorgeschichte des Christentums, nebst einem Anhange über das gnostische System das Basilides* (Jena: Mauke, 1857) [hereinafter: Hilgenfeld, *Jüdische Apokalyptik*], 433; Heinrich Julius Holtzmann, *Lehrbuch der historisch-kritischen Einleitung in das Neue Testament,* 3d ed. (Freiburg i. B.: J. C. B. Mohr, 1892) [hereinafter: Holtzmann, *Einleitung*[3]], 415; Weiss, *Einleitung*[2], 378; Weizsäcker, *Apost. Zeitalter*[2], 364; etc. — In addition, still one more explanation exists among modern interpreters, an explanation which does not see an allegory here at all, but rather sees an unadulterated "model," i.e., a fantastic representation: Bleek, *Vorlesungen Apok.,* 280; de Wette, *Commentar*[2], 120f.; Düsterdieck, *Handbuch Offenbarung*[4], 412. — This interpretation will be discussed in what follows. Concerning Erbes, *Offenbarung Johannis,* and Völter, *Problem der Apokalypse,* cf. our n. 31 immediately above.

33. Concerning this event reported by Eusebius, *Hist. Eccl.* 3.5; cf. Schürer, *Geschichte*[2], 1:519f.

34. E.g., by אִישְׁבַעַל [*'Išba'al*] (2 Sam 2:8), David (2 Sam 17:22), יִשְׁמָעֵאל בֶּן נְתַנְיָהוּ [*Yišmā''ēl ben Nĕtanyāhû*] (Jer 41:9ff.), and 1 Macc 5:24: "And Judah Maccabee and his brother Jonathan went across the Jordan and went three days' march into the wilderness."

35. It is, of course, not permissible to think, additionally perhaps, about "a horrible peril which pushed the fleeing mother community to the Jordan," a peril which is certainly not reported to us, as Ewald, *Johannes Apokalypse,* 247, and Renan, *L'Antechrist,* 326 think. Then, the allegedly unknown thing would be *explained by* an unknown thing!

36. Cf. our n. 31 above.

37. Züllig, *Offenbarung Johannis,* 2:216.

38. Völter, *Entstehung der Apokalypse*[2], 64.

39. Völter, *Entstehung der Apokalypse*[2], 83.

40. As examples, cf. *1 Enoch* 85–90, and *4 Ezra* 11f.

41. E.g., *1 Enoch* 86: Stars fall from the heavens and feed among the cattle. Cows get pregnant by the stars and bear elephants, camels, and asses. The artist wishes to portray thereby the account of Genesis 6, that the angels engender giants with the daughters of humanity. Or, e.g., *1 Enoch* 89:10: Cattle produce wild animals and birds; which means, without allegory, Noah's descendants produced the peoples of the world, etc.

42. So Herder, Ewald, etc.

43. E.g., Völter, *Problem der Apokalypse,* 160.

44. So Bleek, de Wette, Düsterdieck, etc.

45. Cf. our p. 332, nn. 31 and 32. Weizsäcker, *Apost. Zeitalter²,* 364, sees here an invitation to the flight into the wilderness for the primal communities.

46. Examples are Dan 2:31ff.; 7; 8; 11f.; *1 Enoch* 85–90; 91–93; *4 Ezra* 11f.; *Ascension of Moses* 2ff.; *Second Apocalypse of Baruch* 3, 9f., 53, 56–74.

47. On this often overlooked intention (e.g., Hilgenfeld, *Einleitung in das NT,* 422 and the most recent commentaries on Daniel by J. Meinhold [J. Meinhold, "Das Buch Daniel," in J. Meinhold and Samuel Oettli, eds., *Die Geschichtlichen hagiographen (Chronike, Esra, Nehemia, Ruth, Esther, und das Buch Daniel),* Kurzgefasster Kommentar zu den heiligen Schriften Alten und Neuen Testamentes, so wie zu den Apokryphen, A. "Altes Testament," 8 Abt. (Nordlingen: C. H. Beck, 1889), 255-339] and Georg Behrmann [Georg Behrmann, *Das Buch Daniel, übersetzt und erklärt,* Handkommentar zum Alten Testament, 3 Abt., *Die Prophetischen Bücher,* 3 Bd., T. 2 (Göttingen: Vandenhoeck und Ruprecht, 1874)]), . . . [On the often overlooked] intention of such descriptions, cf. Schürer, *Geschichte²,* 2:610.

48. Daniel 4.

49. *1 Enoch* 85.

50. Hilgenfeld, "Joh. Apok," 444, notes this. Cf. also Erbes, *Offenbarung Johannis,* 4.

51. Dan 4:7-9.

52. Dan 2:32.

53. The contents of a similar vision, *2 Apocalypse of Baruch* 53, will so indicate. 56:2: *indicans indicavit tibi fortis rationes temporum* (= world periods).

54. Daniel 7.

55. *1 Enoch* 85–88. The historical vision in *2 Apoc. Bar.* 5:3 is to be viewed somewhat differently. In it quite a bit of the past is contained, a past which does not speak of individual events since careful measurement lays all value on the division of the periods, *not* on the individual events. Here, therefore, it is not the generally well-known past, but rather the divine secret of the twenty-four world periods which is revealed. — On the other hand, the historical God has revealed the primordial time (3:8-19). This "primordial era" is, for the Sibyl, the period from world-creation through to Noah (Gen 1:5–9:20), which is, therefore, a time from which the present generation can be distinguished only through divine revelation. I believe, in the above, *1 Enoch* 85–88 has been properly viewed; however, I do not credit this to the Sibyl's remarks.

56. This is the answer to the question posed by Spitta, *Offenbarung,* 249: "Why are historical events which have already occurred not allowed to appear once again in visionary experiences in new, meaningful relationships?"

57. Such as, e.g., Isaiah in the *Ascension of Isaiah* [August Dillmann, ed., *Ascensio Isaiae, aethiopice et latine: cum prolegomenis, adnotationibus criticis et exegeticis, additis versionum latinarum reliquiis* (Leipzig: F. A. Brockhaus, 1877) [hereinafter: Dillmann, *Asc. Isa.*]], chs. 3f.

58. In this regard it is quite insignificant whether the name of John is pseudonymous or not.

59. Cf. the examples in chapter 12. For the former possibility, "the testimony of Jesus" (v. 17). For the latter possibility, "the blood of the Lamb" (v. 11).

60. Revelation 12 can be compared with the "period" vision of 2 *Baruch* 53 (cf. p. 338, n. 53 above). There is no point to the periodization of universal time in our chapter. Our chapter also has nothing in common with the Sibylline retrospectives on the primordial era. Jesus' birth and death, or perhaps the flight from Pella, are not "revelations," as is the case in the narrative of the creation and the flood.

61. Spitta, *Offenbarung*, 131. Vischer, *Offenbarung*, 61, excludes in v. 11 only Ἰησοῦ [*Iēsou*]. About this probably not very important question I have no opinion.

62. *Offenbarung*, 28f. De Wette, *Kommentar²*, dubbed the verse an anomaly. The same observation and exclusion of the verses is found also in Völter, *Entstehung der Apokalypse²*, 68, and in Völter, *Problem der Apokalypse*, 146. Cf. also Spitta, *Offenbarung*, 130.

63. The word is used by de Wette, *Kommentar²*, 121.

64. [Original German: "verrät aufs augenscheinlichste nicht bloss die Verschiedenheit der Varfasser, sondern auch die principielle Verschiedenheith ihrer religiösen Standpunkte." — trans.] — Pfleiderer, *Urchristentum*, 332.

65. A summary of Völter, *Problem der Apokalypse*, 133-45.

66. The former opinion, naturally the traditional one, is championed among the source critics by Vischer, *Offenbarung*, 19f.; Spitta, *Offenbarung*, 122ff.; Paul W. Schmidt, *Anmerkungen über die Komposition der Offenbarung Johannis* (Freiburg i. B.: J. C. B. Mohr, 1891) [hereinafter: Schmidt, *Anmerkungen*], 13f. The latter opinion is championed by Weizsäcker, *Apost. Zeitalter²*, 490-92; Völter, *Entstehung der Apokalypse²*, 61f.; Völter, *Problem der Apokalypse*, 133f.; and Erbes, *Offenbarung Johannis*, 84f., etc.

67. Cf. Weizsäcker, *Apost. Zeitalter²*, 488ff., and Friedrich Schleiermacher, *Einleitung ins Neue Testament, aus Schleiermacher's handschriften Nachlasse und nachgeschriebenen Vorgesungen; mit einer Vorrede von Friedrich Lücke*, ed. Georg Wolde, Friedrich Schleiermacher's *Sammtliche Werke*, 1 Abt., 2 Bd. (Berlin: G. Reimer, 1845) [hereinafter: Schleiermacher, *Einleitung NT*], 462: "If all of these (the many disparities in Revelation) are considered, then hardly any other conclusion is attainable except that a number of individual visions are put together here which were probably not originally considered to be a unity." [Original German: "Wenn man dies alles (die vielen Ungleichheiten in der Apokalypse) erwägt, so giebt es doch schwerlich einen andern Schlüssel dazu, als dass hier eine Menge einzelner Visionen zusammenestellt ist, die gar nicht ursprünglich als Eins gedacht sint." — trans.]

68. Cf. Weizsäcker, *Apost. Zeitalter³*, 489ff. Weizsäcker's observations, which are related to certain parts of Revelation, may be extended to the rest. So, in the vision of the seven seals, there is an internal connection only among the first four seals, which portray a unified image "of the four horsemen." The fifth seal presents a totally new picture, the martyrs under the altar. The new persecution will bring them into view, and we expect a description of them in what follows. That doesn't happen, however. On the contrary, the *sixth* seal once again presents something totally new, the signs on the heavens. Though the stars fall from the heavens (6:13), the trumpet vision presumes that they still stand *on* the heavens (8:12). The sealing of the righteous (7:1-8) in the sixth seal presumes that up to this point no plagues have come upon the earth. This stands in contradiction to the first four seals, and so on.

69. No literary-critical theory has been promulgated concerning this since the possibility that the individual vision could have existed in oral tradition before the written copy, . . . this possibility has to be considered. Surely every scientific (in terms of its nature) source-critical hypothesis which would be correct must emanate from the above-mentioned fundamental ob-

servations. Only then, when the distinction between the literary and the objective context is maintained, and when primary emphasis is placed on the latter of the two, . . . only then can we hope to emerge successfully from the entanglement into which the results achieved almost exclusively from literary contexts, as well as from highly doubtful chronological assessments, i.e., the results of investigative source criticism, have continued to place Revelation.

70. It is, consequently, a methodological error for Vischer to proceed in the opposite direction: "It is possible to understand the meaning of this vision only when one perceives the place which this chapter occupies in the construction of the writing" [original German: "Es ist nur dann möglich, die Bedeutung dieser Vision richtig zu verstehen, wenn mann erkennt, welchen Platz dies Capitel in der Anlage der Schrift einnimt." — trans.] (Vischer, *Offenbarung,* 19). Likewise, it is highly questionable methodologically to separate, perhaps, the flight of the woman (vv. 13-17) from the preceding materials; so Weizsäcker, *Apost. Zeitalter²,* 364; Völter, *Problem der Apokalypse,* 146ff.; Pfleiderer, *Urchristentum,* 332f. That would mean that the organic whole would encounter the scalpel in a piecemeal fashion.

71. Further details in that which follows.

72. Spitta, *Offenbarung,* 123, has, even further, sought to find a connection between chapter 12 and 11:19 in the appearance of the Ark of the Covenant, since, according to rabbinic tradition *haec arca futuro tempori advente Messia nostra manifestibur* (Abravenel on 1 Sam 4:4) ["This ark, in future time, will manifest the approach of Messiah." — trans.]. This use of the rabbinic text, however, is based on its wording and not on its sense. The appearance of the Ark has nothing to do with the Messiah. The text seeks only to say that which will happen in the final days. It could just as well say: "When God gathers his people and is gracious to them again" (2 Macc 2:1). If, then, these coincidences are not really accidental — which I am inclined to believe — it is, however, only a very superficial relationship. Nevertheless, the use of the number three at 12:4 ‖ 8:7, 8f., 10, 12, etc. (Spitta, *Offenbarung,* 124) is a very loose association. Our conjecture will not be bothered by these observations, since chapter 12 has the material anew.

73. Bleek, *Vorlesungen Apok.,* 116, and de Wette, *Kommentar²,* 116f., have noted the new beginning in chapter 12.

74. Cf. further concerning this at the conclusion of these investigations.

75. Völter, *Offenbarung Johannes (Streitschrift),* 12f.; Völter *Problem der Apokalypse,* 154; Hilgenfeld, "Joh. Apok.," 445; and Erbes, *Offenbarung Johannis,* 5.

76. Even if the birth of the Christ in Revelation 12 took place on earth, few would thereby in any way rebuke the Jewish origin of the chapter. Even then a "twofold" appearance would not be the issue here. Beneath an "appearance" of Christ is naturally to be understood his appearance *as* Christ, i.e., as a revelation of divine power. Christianity speaks of two "appearances" of the Christ: a provisional one, where he has revealed much of his divine power; and a definitive one, where he will totally reveal himself before the whole world. — On the other hand, Christ in the tradition of chapter 12 appears only once in chapter 19, after he had been previously born on earth, but without, at that time, "being revealed." It gives no grounds for declaring these concepts as non-Jewish. At any rate, it is not completely identical with the Christian outlook.

77. According to Spitta, *Offenbarung,* 127.

78. Carl Weizsäcker, "Review of *Omwerkings — en Compilatie — Hypothesen toegepast of de Apokalypse van Johannes* by G. J. Weyland; of *Apocalyptische Studiën* by M. A. N. Rovers, and of *Die Offenbarung des Johannes* by Fr. Spitta," *Theologische Literaturzeitung* 15, no. 19 (September 20, 1890) 470.

79. Schürer, *Geschichte,* 2:447f.

80. Cf. the Latin translation of Lightfoot, *Horae Hebraicae et Talmudicae* (Oxford: Oxford University Press, 1859), s.v. Matt 2:1.

81. This is the"actual basis" for the linking of the Messiah's birth and the destruction of the Temple, *contra* W. Baldensberger, "Die neuern kritischen Forschungen über die Apokalypse Johannis," *Zeitschrift für Theologie und Kirche* [hereinafter: *ZTK*] 4 (1895) [hereinafter: Baldensberger, "Neuern Forschungen"], 246, n. 1.

82. Völter, in *Offenbarung Johannes (Streitschrift)*, 16, and in *Problem der Apokalypse*, 170f., even explains the Talmudic text as a "derision" of Revelation 12: the original purpose of the legend was to show that the Christian messianic faith was "an empty wind"! — A refutation is simply unnecessary!

83. Traces of an originally Hebrew (Aramaic?) composition in chapter 12 are: (1) the construction of ὠδίνουσα καὶ βασανιζομένη τεκεῖν [*ōdinousa kai basanizomene tekein*] (2) is quite Hebraic; cf. 1 Sam 4:19 הרה ללדת [*hārāh lĕ-leḏeṯ*] (cf. Siegfried-Stade, *Wb*). — The expression υἱοῦ ἄρσενα [*huiou arsena*] (5), extraordinary in Greek, is explicable as a literal translation of בן זכר [*ben zāḵār*] (Jer 20:15). In Hebrew בן [*ben*] means "child." זכר [*zāḵār*] is, therefore, not superfluous. — In ὅπου ἔχει ἐκεῖ τόπον ἡτοιμασμένον (6, 14) [*hopou echei ekei topon hētoimasmenon*], ὅπου ... ἐκεῖ [*hopou ... ekei*] is an imitation of a Hebrew phrase שם ... אשר [*'ašer ... šam*]. — The beginning of v. 7, καὶ ἐγένετο πόλεμος ἐν τῷ οὐρανῷ, ὁ Μιχαὴλ καὶ οἱ ἄγγελοι αὐτοῦ, τοῦ πολεμῆσαι μετὰ τοῦ δράκοντος [*kai egeneto polemos en tǭ ouranǭ, ho Michaēl kai hoi angeloi autou, tou polemēsai meta tou drakontos*], has given the exegetes very great difficulties. The solution is barely comprehensible to the exegetes who approach it from the Old Testament and in line with traditional "restorations." ὁ Μιχαὴλ καὶ οἱ ἄγγελοι αὐτοῦ [*ho Michaēl kai hoi angeloi autou*] is an inserted subject. We will be dealing with the object of this insertion in what follows. That which remains,

καὶ ἐγένετο πόλεμος ἐν τῷ οὐρανῷ, τοῦ πολεμῆσαι μετὰ τοῦ δράκοντος
[*kai egeneto polemos en tǭ ouranǭ, tou polemēsai meta tou drakontos*]
is considered totally Hebraic,
ותהי מלחמה בשמים להלחם בתנין
[*wa-tĕhî milḥamāh baš-šāmayim lĕ-hillāḥēm bat-tannîn*]
"Then there was a war in the heavens which was fought with the Dragon."

In v. 8, καὶ οὐκ ἴσχυσεν [*kai ouk ischysen*] = ולא יכל [*wĕ-lō' yāḵōl*], "but he did not attain victory" (cf. Düsterdieck, *Handbuch Offenbarung*[4], 399) is a stronger Hebraism. — In v. 10 ἄρτι ἐγένετο ἡ σωτηρία καὶ ἡ δύναμις καὶ ἡ βασιλεία τοῦ θεοῦ ἡμῶν καὶ ἡ ἐξουσία τοῦ Χριστοῦ αὐτοῦ [*arti egeneto hē sōtēria kai hē dynamis kai hē basileia tou theou hēmōn kai hē exousia tou Christou autou*], the word σωτηρία [*sōtēria*] is very troublesome (de Wette, *Kommentar*[2], 122). The sentence seeks to say: By the overthrow of the Dragon Christ has received the dominion, God the power and the kingdom. How peculiar σωτηρία [*sōtēria*] is in this context!?! — The *soaring* explanation of Düsterdieck, *Handbuch Offenbarung*[4], 402 may be examined. Of course, σωτηρία [*sōtēria*] is a translation of the Hebrew תשועה/ישועה [*tĕšû'āh/yĕšû'āh*], "salvation, victory" (so Ewald, *Johannes Apokalypse*, 245). Likewise in the parallels — κατέβη [*katebē*] (v. 12) ‖ ἐβλήθη [*eblēthē*] (vv. 9, 13) is explicated from a Hebrew ירד [*yāraḏ*] (Aramaic נחת [*nĕḥēṯ*]), which would also be required by an involuntary degradation (Ewald, *Johannes Apokalypse*, 245). — καιρὸν καὶ καιροὺς καὶ ἥμισυ καιροῦ [*kairon kai kairous kai hēmisy kairou*] (v. 14) must, according to the context and according to calculation, mean "three and a half times." How does the plural come to mean "two times?" The same phrase is a translation at Dan 7:25 of the Aramaic עדן ועדנין ופלג עדן [*'iddān wĕ-'dnyn* [*'id-dā-nîn* (in MT)] *û-plag 'iddān*], at Dan 12:7 of the

Hebrew מוֹעֵד מוֹעֲדִים וָחֵצִי [*mô'ēḏ mw'dym* [*mô-'ă-dîm* (in MT)] *wā-ḥēṣî*]. In both of these texts עִדָּנִין ['*dnyn* ['*id-dā-nîn* (in MT)]] and מוֹעֲדִים [*mw'dym* [*mô-'ă-dîm* (in MT)]] are considered to be dual terms, which, for all that, cannot be distinguished from the plural in consonantal writing. Therefore, LXX, Θ, and even the Masoretic pointing have misinterpreted the dual as a plural. This error lies even closer in Dan 7:25 since the dual has become absolute in later Aramaic. In what follows I will show that Revelation 12 contains an independent tradition vis-à-vis Daniel. The καιρούς [*kairous*] from Revelation 12 does not, therefore, go back to Daniel, but instead goes back to a translation error paralleling the misunderstanding in Daniel. — From the strong Hebraization, it appears that a person of a Jewish mind-set wrote the chapter, and that it was originally composed in Hebrew (because of the translation errors).

Notes to Chapter 7

1. [My thanks go to Professor Peter Machinist for his suggestion of this terminology to translate what can only be described as a difficult technical term which Gunkel uses from this point forward in his work. That term is "'zeitsgeschichtlichen' Exegese." It applies to the effort to understand the text in the context in which it was written, as opposed to attempting to understand it in terms of some sort of "real meaning." In this respect Professor Machinist suggested "contemporaneous" versus the more usual translation of *zeitsgeschichtlich,* which is "contemporary." The latter translation would tend to focus the reader on the type of exegetical methodology which existed at the moment of Gunkel's writing, of which he is, indeed, critical in what immediately follows, but which is not really the referent of the word as he uses it. — trans.]

2. Völter, *Entstehung der Apokalypse*², 1; Baldensperger, "Neuern Forschungen," 245.

3. The name since Karl August Auberlen, *Der Prophet Daniel und die Offenbarung Johannis, in ihrem gegenseitigen Verhältnis betrachtet und in ihren Hauptstellen erklärt . . . mit einer Beilage . . .* (Basel: Dahnmaier/Detloff, 1857), 390.

4. Holtzmann et al., *Hand-commentar*², 4:288.

5. More about this chapter in section 4, below.

6. Cf. the example on p. 120 above.

7. Cf. in the following, pp. 136f.

8. Weizsäcker, *Apost. Zeitalter*², 495, warns expressly against extending the "contemporaneous" interpretation to material which in reality was descended from mythological fantasy or from Old Testament prophecy.

9. Friederich Lücke, *Versuch einer vollständigen Einleitung in die Offenbarung des Johannes: Oder, allgemeine Untersuchungen über die apokalyptische Litteratur, überhaupt und die Apokalypse des Johannes insbesondere,* 2d ed., Commentar über die Schriften des Evang. Johannes, Bd. 1 (Bonn: E. Weber, 1852) [hereinafter: Lücke, *Einleitung*], 825: "We find well-defined chronological indications only at 11:1ff., 13:3, and 17:10-11." [Original German: "Bestimmte chronologische Andeutungen finden wir nur xi,1ff., xiii,3, xvii,10. 11." — trans.]

10. Holtzmann et al., *Hand-commentar,* vol. 4, "contemporaneously" understands — disregarding chapters 13 and 17 — the first five trumpets, which precede the conquest of Jerusalem (ch. 11), the flight of the woman (12:6, 14), and the march of the Parthians (16:12).

11. Weiss, *Einleitung*², 380ff.

12. Jülicher, *Einleitung,* 178ff.

13. Cf. pp. 130f. above.

14. Regarding this definition cf., e.g., Ewald, *Johannes Apokalypse*, 2; Düsterdieck, *Handbuch Offenbarung*[4], 50f.; Schmiedel, *Hand-commentar*, 2:1, n. 2 and 2:39.

15. The issue here, then, is not whether the second and third explanations provide a useful methodology. That is certainly self-evident for the third. The second shall be briefly discussed in what follows. All three explanations are found side-by-side in Holtzmann, *Einleitung*[2], 414.

16. There is, for example, the perpetuation of confusion when, at present, the eschatological hope of the prophets is still called "messianic hope," even after it has long since been acknowledged that the king of Israel was for that hope an element of significance not to be underestimated, though surely *NOT* the central element thereof.

17. Holtzmann et al., *Hand-commentar*[2], 4:292.

18. Weiss, *Einleitung*[2], 376.

19. So, e.g., Völter, *Problem der Apocalypse*, 460, assumes a literary relationship between Rev 6:9-14 and *4 Ezra* 4:34f., even though a linkage does not exist in the text, and the sense of neither of the two texts is shown clearly to be dependent on the other; cf. Spitta, *Offenbarung*, 298.

20. Spitta, *Offenbarung*, 301.

21. For example, the vision of the sealing of the servants of God (7:1-8) was originally attached to a continuation in which the four winds, which, until the "sealing," had been "bound," now, after these things take place, will be set free upon the earth. This indispensable sequel does not currently follow. The subsequent plagues come not from the four winds, but rather from seven "trumpeting" angels. The sealing of the servants of God is, therefore, an individual piece taken out of a greater context and picked up here, a piece which clearly, in this current isolation, is no longer completely comprehensible (Spitta, *Offenbarung*, 315f.). — The millennium of world dominion of the faithful (20:4ff.) was originally linked, as is well known, with a world era of seven thousand years. Revelation had not, however, established this connection. Rather, it transmitted the enumeration "a millennium" as an adumbrated and misunderstood note. — For other examples, cf. Spitta, *Offenbarung*, 319, 321, 333, and 434. Cf. also above, p. 334, n. 68, and that which follows.

22. Spitta, *Offenbarung*, 315, 434.

23. Spitta, *Offenbarung*, 466.

24. Cf. the examples cited above, n. 21 immediately above.

25. This possibility — as far as I can see — has not even been taken into account: not even by Spitta (*Offenbarung*), who, even at the end, knows only an apocalyptic tradition "from writing to writing" (Spitta, *Offenbarung*, 301).

26. The title of Völter's most recent publication [as of 1895 — trans.].

27. Such literary-critical works naturally have their splendid claims, but their results will generally be certain only when they, as is done by Wellhausen's examination of the age of "P[c]," are placed into the framework of a religio-historical investigation. Nevertheless, all literary criticism may be viewed only as the preliminary work. It has real value only when it contributes to the historical understanding of the text in question and thereby, on its part, advances the real purpose of all biblical investigation, i.e., the apprehension of their history of religion. So it has to be considered at what point the "source-critical investigation" into Genesis has come to a positive end since, thereby, only the preliminary work for the purpose of the examination of Genesis, i.e., the history of the origin and tradition of the patriarchal sagas, has been accomplished.

28. Thus Ewald, *Johannes Apokalypse*, has dealt with apocalyptic totally according to the manner of an Old Testament prophet.

29. Hilgenfeld, "Joh. Apok. n. Forschung," 427.

30. Erbes, *Offenbarung Johannis*, 60f.

31. So the current explanation.

32. Weizsäcker, *Einleitung*², 364.

33. Spitta, *Offenbarung*, 338ff.

34. Erbes, *Offenbarung Johannis*, 61.

35. Spitta, *Offenbarung*, 338ff.

36. Erbes, *Offenbarung Johannis*, 44.

37. Theodor Mommsen, *Römische Geschichte*, 8th ed. (Berlin: Weidmann, 1888-89) [hereinafter: Mommsen, *Röm. Gesch.*], 5:520f.

38. Gustav Volkmar, *Commentar zur Offenbarung Johannes* (Zurich: Drell, Fussli, 1862) [hereinafter: Volkmar, *Comm. Offenbarung Joh.*]; Thomas Haweis, *The Evangelical Expositor, or A Commentary on the Holy Bible. Wherein the Sacred Text of the Old and New Testament Is Inserted at Times* (London: s.n., 1765-66) [hereinafter: Haweis, *Evangel. Expos.*]; and Spitta, *Offenbarung*, are all cited by Holtzmann et al., *Hand-commentar*², 4:355.

39. The general view of, e.g., de Wette, *Kommentar*², 77; Renan, *L'Antechrist*, 308; Holtzmann et al., *Hand-commentar*², 4:330; Weizsäcker, *Einleitung*², 338.

40. Spitta, *Offenbarung*, 300.

41. Völter, *Problem der Apokalypse*, 58.

42. Spitta, *Offenbarung*, 300.

43. The common view.

44. Erbes, *Offenbarung Johannis*, 42f.

45. Gerard Johann Weyland, *Omwerkings — en Compilatie — Hypothesen toegepast of de Apokalypse van Johannes* (Gröningen: J. P. Wolters, 1888) [hereinafter: Weyland, *Omwerkings Apok. Johannes*], 82.

46. The common view.

47. According to Renan, *Antechrist*, 322 this pair is Jacob or John the Baptist and Jesus.

48. Völter, *Entstehung der Apokalypse*², 58f.; Völter, *Problem der Apokalypse*, 122; Pfleiderer, *Urchristentum*, 329; likewise, certainly, Johann Jakob Wettstein, *Prolegomena ad Novum Testamentum: Notas adiecit atque appendicem de vetustioribus latinis recensionibus quae in variis codicibus supersunt Ioh. Sal. Semler. Cum quibusdam characterum graecorum et latinorum in libris manuscriptis exemplis* (Halae Magdeburgicae: Rangeriana, 1764) [hereinafter: Wettstein, *Prolegomena NT*]; Johann Gottfried Eichhorn, *Commentarius in Apocalypsin Joannis* (Göttingen: Dieterich, 1791)[hereinafter: Eichhorn, *Comm. Apoc. Joannis*]; Johann Gottfried Herder (all cited by Holtzmann et al., *Hand-commentar*², 4:38).

49. Hence Weizsäcker's (*Apost. Zeitalter*², 360f.) attempt to see here the views of the Judeo-Christian community shortly before the exodus from Jerusalem is to be considered as having foundered.

50. Erbes, *Offenbarung Johannis*, 61; cf. also Holtzmann et al., *Hand-commentar*², 4:334.

51. Erbes, *Offenbarung Johannis*, 61, names, e.g., a pit near Seleucia. Why not that one, or the Solfatara near Pazzuoli, which Renan, *L'Antechrist* has in mind, or, for that matter, just about any other pit?

52. שאול [šĕʾôl] ‖ בור [bôr], cf. above, p. 320, n. 53; באר [bĕʾēr], LXX φρέαρ [phrear], Pss 55:24; 69:16. In the later periods בור [bôr] and באר [bĕʾēr] are names for hell (b. ʿErûb. 19a, according to Eisenmenger, *Entdecktes*, 2:24). Concerning the identification of the Old Testament

שאול [šĕ'ôl] and the apocalyptic ἄβυσσος [abyssos] cf. the name Abaddon (Rev 9:11, one name of which is, in the Old Testament, שאול [šĕ'ôl], which, in Revelation, is a name of the angel of the abyss. The idea of the hell hole is also seen at 4 Ezra 6:4 [Robert L. Bensley, *The Missing Fragment of the Latin Translation of the Fourth Book of Ezra* (Cambridge: Cambridge University Press, 1875) [hereinafter: Bensley, *Frag. 4 Ezra*], "et apparebit λάκκος [lakkos] tormenti" ("and a pit of torment appeared"). The image is parallel to κλίβανος [klibanos] ("oven"), 4 Ezra 6:1: "clibanus geennae ostendetur" ("an oven of Gehinnom will appear"); cf. also 1 Enoch 18:11. Therefore, the idea is that of the "keys of death and of Hades" (Rev 1:18), of the "keys of the abyss" (Rev 9:1) [cf. Ferdinand Wilhelm Weber, *System der Altsynagogalen Palästinischen Theologie: Aus Targum, Midrasch und Talmud*, ed. Franz Delitzsch und Georg Schmedermann (Leipzig: Dorffling und Franke, 1880) [hereinafter: Weber, *Altsyn. Theol.*], 333]. Concerning the "pit of hell" from which Samael, with his devils, sometimes emerge, cf. Eisenmenger, *Entdecktes*, 2:336f.

53. Eisenmenger, *Entdecktes*, 2:348.

54. "ein Stich auf den Kleinasian viel verehrten Apollo" ["a jab at Apollo, very revered in Asia Minor" — trans.]. Erbes, *Offenbarung Johannis*, 60f.

55. Erbes, *Offenbarung Johannis*, 179.

56. The second question as to why this name should appear on a white stone I do not intend even to attempt to answer. At present this image lacks a parallel. A parallel, nevertheless, should be sought in the spheres of religious imagination and ritual.

57. Holtzmann et al., *Hand-commentar*², 4:335.

58. A monster having a serpentine tail appears on a Babylonian bronze; cf. Georges Perrot and Charles Chipiez, *Histoire de l'Art dans l'Antiquite* (Paris: Hatchett et Cie, 1882) [hereinafter: Perrot, *Histoire de l'Art*], 2:363.

59. Pfleiderer, *Urchristentum*, 329, in regard to the appearance of the two witnesses: "Ich weiss hier keines Rat als anzunehmen, dass dem Seher geschichtliche Vorfälle und ideale Vorstellungen in wirren Ducheinender sich vermischten." ["I know of no reason to assume here that the seer blended historical events and ideal images into a mixed-up mess." — trans.]

60. The vision, considered by de Wette, *Kommentar*², 94; by Bleek, *Vorlesungen Apok.*, 112; by Beyschlag, *Offenbarung Johannis*, 187, etc. is more purely fantastic! This is an understanding, however, which is not very different from the "contemporaneous" interpretation since even according to the latter, the majority of the features should stem from the fantasy of the seer. Both explanations agree since they regard the vision as a product of the writer in question without even considering as possible an adoption from the tradition!

61. Spitta, *Offenbarung*, 336ff.

62. A rejection of the "contemporaneous" explanation by de Wette, *Kommentar*², 97; Bleek, *Vorlesungen Apok.*, 112; etc., even here, however, without recourse to a tradition.

63. Spitta, *Offenbarung*, 400f.

64. Cf., in addition, pp. 107f. above.

65. Cf. p. 136 above.

66. For example, Joel 3:5.

67. The common opinion of Lücke, *Einleitung in die Offenbarung des Johannes*, 825ff.; Renan, *L'Antechrist*, 379; Hilgenfeld, *Einleitung in das NT*, 447; Weiss, *Einleitung*², 384; Völter, *Entstehung der Apokalypse*², 58; Pfeiderer, *Urchristentum*, 328; Jülicher, *Einleitung*, 179, etc.

68. So Erbes, *Offenbarung Johannis*, 82.

69. Spitta, *Offenbarung*, 422f.

70. Weizsäcker, *Apost. Zeitalter*², 359.

71. "The affliction" . . . "ἀνάγκη" [ananke] (1 Enoch 1:1).

72. Dan 11:36.

73. Cf. also 3 Maccabees 1, *Psalms of Solomon* 1.

74. Cf. Schürer, *Geschichte³*, 2:448.

75. Schmiedel's argumentation (*Hand-commentar*, 2, 1²:39): The text should be understood, *vis-à-vis* Daniel, in many autonomous, thus contemporaneous, ways.

76. Cf. Schürer, *Geschichte²*, 2:444f.

77. 1 John 2:18, 22; 4:3; 2 John 7.

78. Revelation 13 speaks of two beings, the two other texts of one. 1 John has the name ὁ ἀντίχριστος [*ho antichristos*], 2 Thessalonians the names ὁ ἄνθρωπος τῆς ἀνομίας [*ho anthrōpos tēs anomias*], ὁ υἱὸς τῆς ἀπωλείας [*ho huios tēs apōleias*], ὁ ἄνομος [*ho anomos*], etc.

79. Spitta, *Offenbarung*, 497ff.; Theodor Zahn, "Apokalyptische Studien II," *Zeitschrift für kirchliche Wissenschaft und kirchliches Leben* [hereinafter: *ZKW*] 6 (1885) 572.

80. Schürer, *Geschichte³*, 1:421ff.

81. Schmiedel, *Hand-commentar*, 41ff. In παρουσία [*parousia*] (v. 8) there is no innate hint, as Schmiedel wishes, of a "return." Παρουσία [*parousia*] is only a reappearance, if the context (somewhat as at Rev 17:8) was from an earlier occurrence of the reading. That is, however, not the case here.

82. Such as the contemporaneous interpretation at Schmiedel, *Hand-commentar*, 38ff.

83. Albrecht Dieterich, *Abraxas: Studien zur Religionsgeschichte des spätern Altertums: Festschrift Hermann Usener zur Feier seiner 25 jährigen Lehrtätigkeit an der Bonner Universität* (Leipzig: B. G. Teubner, 1891) [hereinafter: Dieterich, *Abraxas*], 113.

84. 2 Pet 3:9; Weber, *Altsyn. Theol.*, 335; Eisenmenger, *Entdecktes*, 2:677ff.

85. Of course, in this regard, only the manner in which one should think of κατέχων [*katechōn*] is explained. The origin of this concept is not explicated at all. The concept probably, in the last analysis, comes from mythology.

86. Spitta, *Offenbarung*, 499.

87. Schmiedel, *Hand-commentar*, 42f.

88. Schmiedel, *Hand-commentar*, 39.

89. Schmiedel, *Hand-commentar*, 10; Spitta, *Offenbarung*, 500.

90. Renan, *L'Antechrist*, 307f.; Erbes, *Offenbarung Johannis*, 39ff.; Völter, *Entstehung der Apokalypse²*, 55ff., *Problem der Apokalypse*, 94; Holtzmann et al., *Hand-commentar²*, 4:328f.

91. Opinions about the first rider are varied. A methodical investigation of that rider would have to start from the fact that he brings, according to the context, the first plague upon earth, a plague which is to be considered a natural analogy to that which follows; and the fact that he, likewise, represents, like the remaining riders (the angel of war, and of famine, and of death, and of Hades), not a historical thing, but rather a heavenly one. If from this point on no clear interpretation of all features of the image can be obtained, the possibility has to be considered as to whether the present text is no longer quite so simple, but rather obtained its present complicated form through some sort of history.

92. Zech 1:8ff.; 6:1ff.

93. Jer 21:7, 14:2, etc.

94. The "contemporaneous" explanation is rejected by de Wette, *Kommentar²*, 70ff.; Bleek, *Vorlesungen Apok.*, 112; Ewald, "Johannes Apokalypse," 170f.; and Pfleiderer, *Urchristentum*, 325.

95. Spitta, *Offenbarung*, 294ff.

96. The common view.

97. Völter, *Entstehung der Apokalypse²*, 42ff.

98. Völter, *Entstehung der Apokalypse²*, 55ff.

99. Renan, *L'Antechrist*, 308.

100. Erbes, *Offenbarung Johannis*, 40.

101. Erbes, *Offenbarung Johannis*, 41.

102. Völter, *Entstehung der Apokalypse²*, 55ff.

103. Spitta, *Offenbarung*, 294ff.

104. Renan, *L'Antechrist*, 307.

105. Erbes, *Offenbarung Johannis*, 39ff.

106. Völter, *Entstehung der Apokalypse²*, 55ff.

107. Erbes, *Offenbarung Johannis*, 41.

108. Especially arbitrary is the "contemporaneous" significance of the wild animals, which, according to the prophetic models, are, of course, considered to be scourges.

109. Erbes, *Offenbarung Johannis*, 179.

110. Pp. 121-25.

111. Holtzmann et al., *Hand-commentar²*, 4:295; Holtzmann, *Einleitung³*, 414; Völter, *Entstehung der Apokalypse²*, 2, etc.

112. According to Luke 21:31 and Matt 24:33.

113. Cf., however, pp. 150f. as well.

114. Beyschlag, "Apokalypse," 133. [Nero was declared a public enemy by the Roman Senate in 68 C.E. and, shortly thereafter, killed himself, marking the end of the Julio-Claudian line of emperors . . . the end of his reign was followed by a year of great political and social turbulence in the empire (including the beginnings of the great Jewish revolt). That period of turbulence ended in 69 C.E. with the ascension of General Vespasian to the throne. — trans.]

115. If modern exegetes understand the angel of the famine, of the war, etc. as "allegorical figures" (Düsterdieck, *Handbuch Offenbarung⁴*, 250), they simply reveal that they no longer understand the Judeo-Christian belief that such plagues would be caused by an angel. In reality, the angel of war is an "allegorical figure" just as little as the angel of the abyss (9:11), the angel of the fire (14:18), etc.,

116. Cf. above, pp. 145-46.

117. Völter, *Entstehung der Apokalypse²*, 55; Völter, *Problem der Apokalypse*, 92; Erbes, *Offenbarung Johannis*, 38f.; Holtzmann et al., *Hand-commentar²*, 4:329. Cf. above, p. 341, n. 91. [Vologases I was the Parthian ruler ca. 63 C.E. — trans.]

118. Dan 7:2; cf. *4 Ezra* 11:1.

119. Völter, *Entstehung der Apokalypse²*, 72f. In the first edition of his work, p. 23, Völter found in this passage an allusion to Antoninus Pius, who, as Caesar, bore the name Hadrian. Now, in *Problem der Apokalypse*, Völter explains the Beast as Domitian. He has also assigned the allusion to the Adriatic.

120. Spitta, *Offenbarung*, 368.

121. Schmidt, *Anmerkungen*, 47.

122. Cf. the summaries of Holtzmann, *Einleitung³*, 416; Holtzmann et al., *Hand-commentar²*, 4:299f., 303; and in what follows.

Notes to Chapter 8

1. Cf. pp. 127f.

2. Cf. pp. 115-19.

3. Wherever, then, the inadequacy of a tradition has been noted, the problem, acknowl-

edged by everyone, at least in theory, but not always mentally formulated in actual practice, . . . the problem is that of establishing a more proper thing in place of the tradition and of once again placing the newly perceived reality into the historical context to which it belongs. Whoever, for example, would take the narratives of Genesis to be legends, or even just to be legendary, has to attend to the origin of the legends or of the legendary themes. If criticism, i.e., the examination of the tradition, has not customarily occupied itself with challenging the tradition, it should not extend to itself the designation "negative criticism," at least not correctly.

4. Vischer, *Offenbarung*, 30.

5. Pfleiderer, *Urchristentum*, 332.

6. Pfleiderer, *Urchristentum*, 331: "simply ideal forms without an historical basis" [German: "nur ideale Bilder ohne geschichtlichen Grund" — trans.]; cf. Spitta, *Offenbarung*, 361.

7. Kliefoth, *Offenbarung des Johannes*, and Hengstenberg, *Offenbarung des heiligen Johannes*, do not interpret, in this context, significantly differently than de Wette *Kommentar*[3]; Düsterdieck, *Handbuch Offenbarung*[4]; or Holtzmann et al., *Hand-commentar*[2], vol. 4. Cf. the examples cited below.

8. Dillmann has interpreted *1 Enoch* according to the same methodology. Dillmann is convinced "that all 'the teachings of wisdom' which he [Enoch] gives in his book are based on exegetical inquiries into the biblical books" [actual German: "dass alle 'die Lehren der Weisheit,' welche er [Henoch] in seinem Buche giebt, auf exegetischen Forschungen in den Bibelbüchern ruhen" — trans.]. Dillmann, *Buch Henoch*, p. xiv, cf. p. xv.

9. Cf. that which follows herein.

10. The current common use of the word in New Testament theology is dangerous since it produces superficiality in terms of compliance. Accordingly, at best, it should be totally abandoned.

11. How superficially one is often taken up with the allusions is shown by Völter's example. His *Entstehung*[2], 109ff., 138f., 160f., and 176, designates Old Testament passages which are "employed" in Revelation (p. 161); in the "additions and emendations," however, he admits that in these he has picked up merely a whiff of the assemblage of texts on which Revelation is dependent, but that also, in the same way, he has discerned that an indefinite similarity to Revelation is to be asserted. This confusion of "points of contact" and "parallels" is found, not uncommonly, in the commentaries on Revelation.

12. Spitta, *Offenbarung*, 352.

13. [German: "Ahnlehnung an den Ausdruck Micha 4:10" — trans.]; Mic 4:9, "Now why do you cry so loudly? . . . Have labor pains overcome you as in the case of one giving birth? 10Writhe and groan, O daughter of Zion, like one giving birth."

14. As is already argued by Hengstenberg, *Offenbarung des heiligen Johannes*, 1:598; Völter, *Entstehung der Apokalypse*[2], 149f.; Holtzmann et al., *Hand-commentar*[2], 4:339; Erbes, *Offenbarung Johannes*, 4.

15. As already noted by Düsterdieck, *Handbuch Offenbarung*, 416.

16. Gal 4:26.

17. Spitta cites a third passage from the *Zohar* to Exod 21:22, "where the pregnant woman *is* interpreted, the man (who strikes the woman so that her foetus goes away) signifies Sammael, and the foetus the exilic community" (*Offenbarung*, 352). [German: "wo das schwangere Weib auf Israel gedeutet wird, der Mann, welcher das Weib stösst, so dass ihre Frucht abgeht, auf Sammael und die abgegangene Frucht auf die Gemeinde des Exils" — trans.]. This allegory, however, speaks not of the Messiah and is, therefore, not a parallel to Revelation 12.

18. Düsterdieck, *Handbuch Offenbarung*[4], 416; Völter, *Problem der Apokalypse,* 480; Holtzmann et al., *Hand-commentar*[2], 4:339; Erbes, *Offenbarung Johannis,* 4.

19. Düsterdieck, *Handbuch Offenbarung*[4], 416.

20. Völter, *Problem der Apokalypse,* 480.

21. Hengstenberg, *Offenbarung des heiligen Johannes,* 1:598.

22. Hengstenberg, *Offenbarung des heiligen Johannes,* 1:598; Holtzmann et al., *Hand-commentar*[2], 4:339; Völter, *Problem der Apokalypse,* 480.

23. Völter, *Problem der Apokalypse,* 150.

24. *There* a heavenly woman, *here* the ancestress of humanity; *there* enmity of the dragon against the child, *here* a battle between the offspring of the serpent and the offspring of the woman; the dragon is a monster of the deep, the נחש [*naḥaš*], on the other hand, is, in the present report, the ancestor of the serpent species; etc., etc.

25. Cf. pp. 120f., 131f., 138f.

26. The piling up of such "points of contact" is generally characteristic of the whole methodology. It would not, however, be the preferred all-around procedure for a great many passages, if one instead sought out by a stronger methodology not certain parallels, but rather the "base passage" which sufficiently explains the matter. Völter, *Entstehung der Apokalypse*[2], explained the chapter by means of Old Testament echoes and a bit of contemporary history, without any flaw in his hypothesis seeming (at least for him) to remain. In his latest publication (*Problem der Apokalypse*) he includes the christology of Cerinthus. Furthermore, he has become aware, since the earlier work, through Dieterich, of the similar Apollo myth, which he now adds to all the other "impartial" explanations, without perceiving that they rule out one another. In such circumstances, quantity really does not matter!

27. Spitta, *Offenbarung,* 302.

28. [In German: ". . . Herabwerfen der Sterne vom Himmel vielleicht seinen nächsten Anlass in Dan 8:10 habe, wo das kleine Horn bis an den Himmel wächst und Sterne herabstösst." — trans.]; so also Bleek, *Vorlesungen Apok.,* 274; Ewald, *Johannes Apokalypse,* 243; Züllig, *Offenbarung Johannis,* 2:209; Hengstenberg, *Offenbarung des heiligen Johannes,* 1:604; Holtzmann et al., *Hand-commentar*[2], 4:340. Völter, *Problem der Apokalypse,* 480, even adds Isa 14:13f.

29. This type of examination may, to a certain extent, sound heretical to the literary critic. Revelation is, however, so much younger literarily than Daniel. If it is related, is it in any way dependent on Daniel? The question will be answered in that which follows.

30. Züllig, *Offenbarung Johannis,* 2:194, 210, notes additionally Isa 51:9; Jer 51:34; Ezek 29:3, 5. Hengstenberg, *Offenbarung des heiligen Johannes,* 1:602, cites Isa 27:1; Jer 51:34; Ezek 29:3f.; Ps 74:13f. Others note other references as well.

31. That Leviathan at Job 3:8 has nothing to do with the "solar eclipse" has been shown above, p. 306, n. 101.

32. Spitta, *Offenbarung,* 353, lines 9-11 from the bottom of the page.

33. One should not, with Spitta, *Offenbarung,* 354, 169 (who attempts to make the dragon's struggle *against* the stars comprehensible), equate "the lords in heaven" (who accompany the Christ during his *parousia,* 19:14) with the stars, and then, on the basis of that equation, view the description as an emulation of Judg 5:20. The heavenly warriors of 19:14, on white chargers, have, at least for the writer of the Revelation, nothing in common with stars.

34. So Düsterdieck, *Handbuch Offenbarung*[4], 393, finds in the text, not a "clearly related prophetic concept" [German: "bestimmt bezüglichen prophetischen Gedanken" — trans.] but rather "only the striking characteristic of a poetic presentation" [German: "nur den sprechenden

344

Zug eines poetischen Gemäldes" — trans.]. One should not, however, believe every question to have been resolved by the word "poetic."

35. Vischer, *Offenbarung*, 26.

36. Cf. above, pp. 116f.

37. Cf. below, pp. 118-19.

38. Spitta, *Offenbarung*, 358f., in accordance with Holtzmann et al., *Hand-commentar*², 4:340.

39. E.g., *Sib. Or.* 3:804: ἐν νεφελῇ δ' ὄψεσθε μάχην πεζῶν τε καὶ ἱππέων [*en nephelę d' opsesthe machēn pezōn te kai hippeōn*] — "in the clouds you will see a battle of infantry and cavalry" — [note that this is *Sib. Or.* 3:805 in most treatments of the latter part of the twentieth century — trans.].

40. deWette, *Kommentar*², 121.

41. Ewald, *Johannes Apokalypse*, 244.

42. Züllig, *Offenbarung Johannis*, 2:211, combines Dan 12:1 and Zechariah 3; Völter, *Problem der Apokalypse*, 480f., adds to the two passages those of 1 Enoch 40:7 and 54:6. — However, the remarkable words of Luke 10:18, which are cited by Ewald, *Johannes Apokalypse*, 244, and Hengstenberg, *Offenbarung des heiligen Johannes*, 1:620, are actually closely connected to the apocalyptic interpretation, although certainly the nature of the relationship should be clearer.

43. Düsterdieck, *Handbuch Offenbarung*⁴, 401.

44. Spitta, *Offenbarung*, 361.

45. [German: "die offenbar der Errettung Israels aus Ägypten entnommen sind" — trans.]; so most of the modern exegetes — e.g., Kliefoth, *Offenbarung*, 2:47; Düsterdieck, *Handbuch Offenbarung*⁴, 410; Züllig, *Offenbarung Johannis*, 2:210. Bleek, *Vorlesungen Apok.*, 276, recalls the wilderness wanderings of Israel and attaches the Elijah narrative of 1 Kings 17:5ff., as well as the flight of the mother of the Lord to Egypt. de Wette, *Kommentar*², 120, accepts all three explanations and produces more in his turn. It would not be totally unsuitable to consider seclusion from the world and renunciation of the world; or to consider inner solitude and peace of mind; or to consider pilgrimage through the wilderness of life. Hengstenberg, *Offenbarung des heiligen Johannes*, 1:609f., cites the Exodus and the Elijah narratives, as above, in addition to prophetic sayings of Jer 31:1-2, Ezek 20:34-38, and Hos 2:14, as well as the "wilderness journey" of Jesus (with the temptation narrative), and, finally, even the flight of the parents of Jesus to Egypt. The "contemporaneous" critics, like Ewald, *Johannes Apokalypse*, 246, also assume that the details of the passages dealt with here are Old Testamental echoes; cf. p. 120.

46. So almost all modern exegetes, certain of whom even refer to Ps 36:8 (Kliefoth, *Offenbarung*, 2:47; Düsterdieck, *Handbuch Offenbarung*⁴, 409), Isa 40:31 (Holtzmann et al., *Hand-commentar*², 4:321), or Ezek 17:37 (Hengstenberg, *Offenbarung des heiligen Johannes*, 1:637).

47. So, especially, Bleek, *Vorlesungen Apok.*, 281, who, however — obviously by literary criticism — infers a form employed in an earlier writing.

48. So also Holtzmann et al., *Hand-commentar*², 4:340.

49. Spitta, *Offenbarung*, 361; so also Bleek, *Vorlesungen Apok.*, 280; Ewald, *Johannes Apokalypse*, 246, and deWette, *Kommentar*², 124. — Those who object to the passage through the Red Sea (Düsterdieck, *Handbuch Offenbarung*⁴, 412; Kliefoth, *Offenbarung des Johannes*, 2:54) or, at least — as almost all do — somehow or other "restore," thinking, in turn, of Hos 5:10, where the floods of water represent the divine rage (Holtzmann et al., *Hand-commentar*², 341); or texts the likes of Pss 18:5, 17; 32:6; 42:8; 124:4, where the floods of water represent surging dangers (Düsterdieck, *Offenbarung*⁴, 412). Kliefoth, *Offenbarung des Johannes*, 2:54, recalls the flood

stream arising suddenly from the thunderstorms in the wilderness, which, however, will be quickly soaked up again by the dry ground. Züllig, *Offenbarung Johannis*, 2:215, suggests that "the poet by this his fabrication" [German: "der Dichter by dieser seiner Erfindung" — trans.] may have had the spouting of the whale in mind. J. T. Beck, *Einleitung in das System der christliche Lehre, oder Propadeutische Entwicklung der christliche Lehr-Wissenschaft: Ein Versuch* (Stuttgart: C. Belser, 1838) [hereinafter: Beck, *Einleitung*], 221, thinks of the sea serpent which often gushes forth a great amount of water onto passing ships. Or the representation of Leviathan as a water monster (Ezek 29:3ff.; 32:2ff.; Ps 74:14) is raised (so Spitta, *Offenbarung*, 361; Holtzmann et al., *Hand-commentar*[2], 4:361; and Völter, *Problem der Apokalypse*, 494), or that of Isa 43:1f. (de Wette, *Kommentar*[2], 124; Züllig, *Offenbarung Johannis*, 2:215). — For the opening of the mouth of the earth, Gen 4:11 (Züllig, *Offenbarung Johannis*, 2:214f.), or Num 16:31f. (Ewald, *Johannes Apokalypse*, 246; Düsterdieck, *Handbuch Offenbarung*[4], 411; Holtzmann et al., *Hand-commentar*[2], 4:341), or Isa 5:13 (Ewald, *Johannes Apokalypse*, 246), etc., are cited. — It is clear that the apocalyptist had at least one of the designated texts or concepts in mind, there being no shortage or, perhaps even better, no lack of strong proof thereof.

50. Likewise, in view of the contemporaneous explanation, cf. pp. 138f. The "stronger" methodology has been sketched out above, pp. 153f.

51. [German: "die Herrlichkeit der unvergänglichen Theokratie sei zwar für kurze Zeit verschwunden, aber doch nur verborgen, um bald wie der zur siegreichen Erscheinung zu kommen." — trans.]; Pfleiderer, *Urchristentum*, 331f., "The preservation of the Church under the Cross" [German: "Die Erhaltung der Kirche unter dem Kreuze" — trans.]; Hengstenberg, *Offenbarung des heiligen Johannes*, 1:609; similarly Bleek, *Vorlesungen Apok.*, 280, etc.

52. This is explicitly acknowledged by Bleek, *Vorlesungen Apok.*, 28: the details in this account should not "be explicitly put forward as separate concepts" [German: "als besondere Gedanken ausdrückend zu urgieren" — trans.].

53. Bleek, *Vorlesungen Apok.*, 107.

54. [German quotation: "als Ankündigung von einzelnen Ereignissen gemeint, welche sich in dieser Reihenfolge begeben würden, sondern nur mehr als allgemeine Bilder zur Bezeichnung der schwersten Zeiten für die Welt" — trans.]

55. Beyschlag, "Apokalypse," iii. Similarly, Düsterdieck, *Handbuch Offenbarung*[4], 400: "Victory over the Satan through Christ" [German: "Überwindung des Satans durch Christum" — trans.].

56. [German: ". . . siegesmacht der ewigen Liebe, wie sie sich im Blute Christi offenbart hat." — trans.]

57. Above, it has been expressed that those scholars who are compelled to allow the imagination of the apocalyptic writer such a broad latitude must more consistently abandon such "fantastic images" to a *reasonable* exegesis (Holtzmann et al., *Hand-commentar*[2], 4:343). Cf. pp. 107ff., 138f., etc.

58. Beyschlag, "Apokalypse," 117; Züllig, *Offenbarung Johannis*, 2:211.

59. Ewald, *Johannes Apokalypse*, 24.

60. Schmidt, *Anmerkungen*, 22.

61. Holtzmann et al., *Hand-commentar*[2], 4:294.

62. Beyschlag, "Offenbarung," 195.

63. Beyschlag, "Offenbarung," 196.

64. Beyschlag, "Offenbarung," 197.

65. [German: "schönen Spiele seiner geheiligten Phantasie" — trans.]; Düsterdieck, *Handbuch Offenbarung*[4], 327; likewise Beyschlag, "Offenbarung," 181.

66. [In German this is n. 10 — trans.]; de Wette, *Kommentar²*, 11.

67. [In German this is n. 9 — trans.]; Bleek, *Vorlesungen Apok.*, 276.

68. Bleek, *Vorlesungen Apok,* 107.

69. [German: "als wirklich zu erfüllende Weissagungen" — trans.]; Düsterdieck, *Handbuch Offenbarung⁴*, 412, cf. 327.

70. [German: "reine Gebilde der poetischen Phantasie" — trans.]; de Wette, *Kommentar²*, 11.

71. [German: "in freier Phantastik" — trans.]; Beyschlag, "Offenbarung," 187.

72. de Wette, *Kommentar²*, 11. Even a theologian like Hengstenberg, *Offenbarung des heiligen Johannes,* 1:441, has not flinched from crediting the apocalyptic writer with a choice, according to which he could give the archangels of 8:2 either the number 7, or perhaps the number 10, whichever suited him. He perceived seven angels before God's throne, since he required them for the subsequent seven trumpets. "Had ten trumpets been necessary, then there would, without a doubt, also have been ten angels standing before God." [German: "Wären zehn Posaunen erforderlich, so würde ohne Zweifel der zehn Engel gedacht werden, welche vor Gott stehen." — trans.] (Hengstenberg, *Offenbarung des heiligen Johannes,* 1:441). How this might be compatible with the allegation of Hengstenberg, the allegation that Revelation reproduces an actual vision, I cannot say!

73. ὁ μάρτυς ὁ πιστός [*ho martys ho pistos* — "the faithful witness" — trans.]; Rev 1:5; 14:9; 21:5; 22:6.

74. [German: "visionäre Phantasmagorieen" — trans.]; Holtzmann et al., *Handcommentar²*, 4:343.

75. [German: "Spiel der Phantasie"— trans.]; Düsterdieck, *Handbuch Offenbarung⁴*, 327.

76. In the historical visions, for example, there is the allegorical "fitting out" of generally independent additional materials of the apocalyptist. On the other hand, there is the delineation of the past through the *historical* tradition, a delineation which presents the future by means of the *eschatological* tradition.

77. E.g., Bleek, *Vorlesungen Apok.*, 142; Beyschlag, "Offenbarung," 182; and often in other commentators.

78. Cf. pp. 135f. above.

79. Just as infrequently, perhaps, as the Psalms, which, although they are poems, nevertheless do contain fact and fiction right next to one another.

80. Kliefoth, *Offenbarung des Johannes,* 1:137.

81. Weizsäcker, *Apos. Zeitalter²*, 488.

82. Cf. pp. 152f. above.

83. These things have already been examined in the foregoing materials at pp. 6f. The treatment of Genesis 1 on pp. 6-11 similarly serve as an example of the methodology explicated herein.

84. Cf. above, pp. 97f.

85. Analogous to that seen in 1 Sam 6:2-9.

86. There is also the remarkable relationship which the statements about the woman at the beginning and at the end of the chapter have with one another. At the beginning the woman appears in the heavens adorned with stellar insignia. In the second unit she flees beyond the earth. The passage does not explain how she came to earth. It is also not possible to imagine how that flight into the wilderness could have taken place in solar garments. The first problem is alleviated only by the assumption of a lacuna. The solution to the second would have to be

sought in the original recital of the tale, which, as imputed from the description of 12:1, arose as a cultic form (cf. pp. 174f., following).

87. Cf. above, p. 341, n. 83.

88. de Wette, *Kommentar*[2], 118; Bleek, *Vorlesungen Apok.*, 273; Holtzmann et al., *Hand-commentar*[2], 4:339; etc.

89. Spitta, *Offenbarung*, 352f.; de Wette, *Kommentar*[2], 118.

90. Volkmar, *Comm. Offenbarung Joh.*, 187, as well as the treatment by Holtzmann et al., *Hand-commentar*[2], 4:340.

91. Ebrard, *Bibl. Commentar*, 356.

92. The relation of this feature to our tradition is unclear. Cf. what follows.

93. The sense here is that the name appears both (a) on his robe, and (b) on his hip, not, perhaps, "on the robe, that is, on the spot where the hip is" [German: "auf dem Gewande und zwar an der Stelle, wo die Hülfte ist" — trans.], "thus clearly on the cincture" [German: "also wol am Gürtel" — trans.](!); Düsterdieck, *Handbuch Offenbarung*[4]; Holtzmann et al., *Hand-commentar*[2], 4:354. A similar modern shading of the text is, when the red coloration of the beast (17:3) refers less to the beast itself than clearly to the covering which may lie upon the beast (Holtzmann et al., *Hand-commentar*[2], 4:349; Züllig, *Offenbarung Johannis*, 2:315; de Wette, *Kommentar*[2], 152; Spitta, *Offenbarung*, 447).

94. This is the common interpretation since Beza. Another interpretation, עָר מְגִדּוֹ [*'îr mĕgiddô*], "city of Megiddo," is represented by Hilgenfeld, *Einleitung in das NT*, 440. Against this the reasoning is also fleshed out in the following manner: spiritual relationship cannot be proven between the city of Megiddo and the final battle! — The conjecture expressed by D. R., "Die hebräische Grundlage der Apokalypse," *ZAW* 7 (1887) 170, n. 1, that καὶ συνήγαγεν αὐτοὺς εἰς . . . Ἀρμαγεδών [*kai synēgagen autous eis . . . harmagedōn*] may be a translation of the phrase וַיְכַנְּסֵם אֶל הַר מְגִדּוֹ [*way-yĕkanĕsēm 'el har mĕgiddô*], "and he will gather on his precious mountains (= Canaan)," . . . this conjecture runs aground on the fact that our tradition understands Ἀρμαγεδών [*harmagedōn*] as a name. We clearly have no reason to have doubts about this tradition. — Even more compelling is the hypothesis of Ewald, *Johannes Apokalypse*, 294, that ארמגדון = 304 = רומה הגדופה [*'rmgdwn* = 304 = *rwmh hgdwph* [*'armagĕdôn* = *rômāh hag-gĕdûpāh*], "the reviled Rome"]. — The apocalyptic writer clearly considered his reader as a "good thinker and a mathematician"! — Hommel's derivation from הַר מוֹעֵד [*har môʿēd*, "appointed mountain"] in Hommel, "Glossen u. Exkursen, II," 406, n. 3, is linguistically untenable, etc.

95. Spitta, *Offenbarung*, 403, attempts a "contemporaneous" explication even here: Under Caligula the combination of three Roman legions could be expected at a particular moment; cf. above, pp. 140f. But such armies called together by frogs certainly did not consist of Roman soldiers. — According to Spitta the following things come together for the explication of Armageddon: (1) that situation (i.e., the combining of the legions under Caligula); (2) the memory of the Song of Deborah; (3) passages such as Ezek 38:8, 21; 39:2, 4, 17. For the assessment of such an accumulation of explanations cf. above, p. 344, n. 26.

96. Other apocalyptic "code names" are Taxo (*As. Mos.* 9:1); Arzareth (ארץ אחרת [*'ereṣ 'aḥeret*, "another land"]; Schürer, *Geschichte*[3], 2:452), (*4 Ezra* 13:45); Esau (*4 Ezra* 6:8), Edom, or Babel for Rome; ארמילוס [*'armîlûs*] [= "Romulus"; Theodor Nöldeke, "Über Mommsen's Darstellung der römischen Herrschaft und römischen Politik im Orient," *ZDMG* 39 (1885) [hereinafter: Nöldeke, "Ueber Mommsen's Darstellung"], 343] as a name for the Antichrist (Schürer, *Geschichte*[3], 2:448, etc.). Elements even in the Old Testament, e.g., "Rahab," "Leviathan" (cf., in the preceding, pp. 25ff. and 39ff.), the אתבש [*'aṭbaš*]-idiom, etc. A great many code

names are found in *1 Enoch*, e.g., the creation word *bēqā* (*1 Enoch* 69:13) (variant: *'akā'e/ 'akā'e;* *1 Enoch* 69:15). One secret tradition, which was certainly no better understood in New Testament times, is the βδέλυγμα τῆς ἐρημώσεως [*bdelygma tēs erēmōseōs*, "desolating sacrilege"] (Mark 13:14, etc.).

97. Dan 7:25; 9:27; 12:7; cf. 8:14 and 12:11f.

98. The "holiness" of the number lies primarily not in itself, but usually in the fact that it is characteristic of a specific sacred phenomenon. *Seven* was, therefore, originally holy because the planets, which were venerated as gods, were *seven* in number; *twelve* because the zodiac consists of *twelve* "stars," etc. These numbers, then, in the course of a long history, have been assigned to other objects as well, especially to those things which could be well designated by them in accordance with their nature — things such as the *seven* days of the week, the *twelve* months of the year. Finally, then, the origin of the numbers' "mysterious" significance was forgotten and the numbers themselves became holy. Thus was determined the origin of the significance of the number "three and a half." The feature for which that number is characteristic is that which must, therefore, be sought out!

99. A summary of the explication given by Johannes Meinhold, *Die Composition des Buches Daniel* (Griefswald: Julius Abel, 1884) [hereinafter: Meinhold, *Daniel*], 304; as well as the calculations of Carl Heinrich Cornill, "Die siebzig Jahrwochen Daniels," *Theologische Studien und Skizzen aus Ostpreussen*, ed. Albert Klöpper et al. (Königsberg: Hartungsche Verlagsdruckerei, 1887-89) [hereinafter: Cornill, "Seibzig Jahrwoche"], 2:26ff.; and Georg Behrmann, *Das Buch Daniel, übersetzt und erklärt*, Handkommentar zum Alten Testament, Abt. 3, Bd. 3 (Göttingen: Vandenhoeck und Ruprecht, 1894) [hereinafter: Behrmann, *Daniel*], 50 and 55. J. Meinhold, ed., "Das Buch Daniel," in *Die Geschichtlichen Hagiographen (Chronika, Esra, Nehemia, Ruth, Esther) und des Buch Daniel*, Kurzgefasster Kommentar zu den heiligen Schriften Alten und Neuen Testaments, so wie zu den Apokryphen, 8 Abt. (Nordlingen: C. H. Beck, 1889) [hereinafter: Meinhold, "Daniel"], 304, concludes with *"non liquet,"* but without investigating the origin of the computational problem.

100. The number is also found in passages other than in Daniel, e.g., the trampling down of Jerusalem (Rev 11:2 — forty-two months [= three-and-a-half years]); the prophesying of the two witnesses (Rev 11:3 — one thousand two hundred and sixty days [= three-and-a-half years]; for the duration of the period of mourning for those witnesses (Rev 11:9 — three-and-a-half days); for the reign of the beast (Rev 13:5 — forty-two months [= three-and-a-half years]); for the duration of the famine at the time of Elijah (Luke 4:25; Jas 5:17 — three years, six months). *4 Ezra* 4:11f. [the numbers differ in vv. 11 and 12; v. 12 appears, according to the Ethiopic, more reliable: *superant eius duae prae* (*praeter* is to be read) *medium decimae partis* (Am Sg)] gives an appraisal of the world according to which three-and-a-half world ages are still immanent. The three-and-a-half days until the resurrection (Rev 11:9) recall the three days of Jonah 2:1 and the resurrection "after three days" in the Gospel tradition. To this material belongs, finally, also the καιροὶ ἐθνῶν [*kairoi ethnōn*] (Luke 21:24) and the μέτρον ἡλικίας τοῦ Χριστοῦ [*metron hēlikias tou Christou*] (on this cf. what follows) (Eph 4:13). In most of these cases the number, as in Daniel, designates the horrifying reign of the wicked, the καιροὶ ἐθνῶν [*kairoi ethnōn*]. How it happens that the same number would be applicable, at the same time, to the preaching of the witnesses *and* to the time remaining until their resurrection . . . this is not apparent from our tradition. — In the Old Testament history of Elijah the number does not originally occur. The famine, which Elijah announces, came to an end, according to the Old Testament report, in the third year (1 Kings 18:1). The number "three-and-a-half" has then come into the "historical" account from the eschatological tradition by way of addition. The basis of such a transferal is to be

sought in the fact of the appearance of Elijah in final times. This is because the model of his effectiveness under Ahab has been called to mind. On that basis the narrative of Elijah is modeled inversely onto the eschatological traditions. Accordingly, we obtain, by inference from Luke 4:25, an apocalyptic tradition to the effect that Elijah would return in the future eschaton and would preach for three-and-a-half days. It is a tradition which is related to that of Rev 11:3.

101. The tradition has understood "the times" in terms of "world periods," or as years or as days. The "three-and-a-half years" is also assessed in a variety of ways. Rev 11:3; 12:6 understand it as one thousand, two hundred, and sixty days. Three calculations exist in Daniel: one thousand, one hundred, and fifty days (Dan 8:14); one thousand, two hundred, and ninety days (Dan 12:11); one thousand, three hundred, and thirty-five days (Dan 12:12). The fact that there actually could be different calculations for the number is based on the mutability of the Jewish calendar. Some things just don't "fit" here since the calendar actually laid them out according to different eschatological calculations based on different situations. — The three calculations in Daniel accordingly stem from different times. Chapters 11 and 12 are from different hands. Within these glosses is deposited a whole history: Time distorted the fulfillment, but the faith did not falter. One concludes that, in reality, there must have been another computation of the portentous number. A new "*terminus*" is designated according to a new calculation, a new "*terminus*" in which now, surely, "the judgment" *must* finally come. These two glosses are a relic of the disappointment and of the unshakable faith of the Maccabean period. One can see not only emotion ("How abrupt endings are!"), but emotion in the midst of which at the same time one dared to hope for the end! Since originally the "days" would have been actual days, only a later time may have explained the days in a new way, in order to obtain a greater period of time.

102. Cf. above, pp. 164-65.

103. P. 156.

104. For example, Leto bears an astral cloak (Dieterich, *Abraxas*, 120, n. 4).

105. Perhaps — and I implore you not to blink at this very unassuming "perhaps" — perhaps alongside the tradition being investigated by us there also existed a tradition which attributed a fiancée to the Christ, a fiancée who would be brought to him after the defeat of the dragon (Rev 21:2; cf. 21:9). The "names" could have linked up with the "thigh" at the same time. — It is certain that the "divine conqueror," although the ruler of the world, appears in the tradition as a late-born god!

106. In addition to the heavenly beings, against whom the dragon struggles (v. 7), three further spheres reveal themselves. The original tradition designated divine beings. Judaism originally omitted them. Later, however, the specifically Jewish figures of "Michael and his angels" came into play. The older, truer tradition *omits* objectionable features. A later, less-faithful tradition *brings in* specifically Jewish features.

107. This is the correct way to say it. Dieterich, *Abraxas*, 118, n. 2, says that "vv. 6 and 14 are a doublet" [German: "vv. 6 und 14 Doppelgänger"]. This is not incorrect, but it is insufficient. — Spitta, *Offenbarung*, 133, would emend by the omission of v. 6 without, however, an explanation which adequately indicates the reason why this verse was inserted. Weizsäcker, *Apost. Zeitalter*², 490; Pfleiderer, *Urchristentum*, 332f.; and Völter, *Problem des Apocalypse*, 146f., would emend by elimination of the whole second portion (vv. 13ff. or vv. 11ff.), while they regard the fall of the dragon as the final or penultimate scene of the whole thing. By doing this, they overlook, however, that the fall of the dragon to the earth, without the assistance of Christ, is still *not* the actual overcoming of the dragon since a further account is necessary. After the narrative of the birth of the Christ, an account of his definitive victory over the dragon must finally come since the sequence of child, mother, and those who remain represents a carefully prepared

heightening of the narrative tension. — Dieterich, *Abraxas,* 118, proceeds even more forcefully in that he produces from the "mystical disorder" [German: "mystischen Wirrwarr"] "of this intentionally obscure revelation" [German: "dieser geflissentlich unklaren Offenbarung"] — following the model of the Apollo myth — the following as an original narrative sequence: vv. 1-4, 14-16, 5 (6, 7, 12b?), 7-12a. This reconstruction succumbs to the same misgivings as the critical attempts of Weizsäcker, Pfleiderer, and Völter. Furthermore, the change of place of vv. 14-16, the persecution of v. 4, and the rescue of the child in v. 5 are separated from each other. Dieterich, *Abraxas,* would not have found time for such textual dislocation if he had not so hastily remodeled Revelation 12 according to the example of the Greek myth, and further, if he *had* considered the possibility of "corruption" by tradition, and — this is a point which may not quite be concealed — if he would have approached the book of Revelation with somewhat greater respect. And investigation which traces the disorder of the chapter back to the "conceptual errors" of the apocalyptist, errors "which skewed the otherwise intelligible piece of work" . . . such an investigation may thereby be spared the necessity of giving sufficient account of the bases of the "corruption" (Dieterich, *Abraxas,* p. 120, n. 3). Such an investigation must, at the same time, also *give up on* the explication of such a passage!

108. Cf. pp. 164-69 above.

109. From Isa 63:1-3. — In the description of Rev 19:11ff. there is the acquired material and the appended Jewish materials. They cannot be clearly distinguished one from the other. In addition, still one other mythological tradition, one related to the first, has come in here. Concerning this cf. that which follows.

110. Cf. Dan 7:6, and then look at Dan 11:2.

111. Cf. Dan 7:7, and then look at Dan 7:24 and Rev 13:1.

112. For variations note, for example, Rev 5:6, where the lamb has two horns but no crowns on them; or Rev 19:12, where Christ wears "many diadems" — the feature could indicate that he is "King of kings" (v. 16) — but the number of diadems is not indicated. Cf., regarding this, that which follows.

113. For more about these symbols see the examination of Rev 13:17 (pp. 170ff.).

114. [The verb found in the German text, "berabkommen" is, apparently, a typographical error. It should read "herabkommen," a reading reflected in the translation. — trans.]

115. In the original myth it would have been the god himself.

116. A "personified idea" [German: "personificierte Idee"]; Pfleiderer, *Urchristentum,* 331.

117. The Christian συζυγία [*syzygia,* "a yoked pair"] of Χριστός [*Christos,* "Christ"] and ἐκκλησία [*ekklēsia,* "assembly, gathering, church"], i.e., the combination of a divine person and an entity conceived — originally — as an allegory, is no argument against the above discussion. Rather, the combination came into being in a very comparable way.

118. In his concluding remarks to Vischer, *Offenbarung,* 134.

119. Cf. above, pp. 119ff.

120. Hence there are some improbable interpretations here and there. Vischer, *Offenbarung,* 30, explains the woman and those who remain as the whole of Israel and the individual Jews (*contra* pp. 119ff. above). According to Spitta, *Offenbarung,* 129f., the flight of the woman describes the fate of the heavenly people of God; the persecution of those who remain describes the fate of earthly Israel, although the statements about the woman flying through the air to freedom become a phantasmal image with neither meaning nor function. Pfleiderer, *Urchristentum,* helps out by separating the two parts of the chapter; cf. above, pp. 350-51, n. 107. By doing this, however, that which belongs together in terms of content is, unfortunately, riven asunder!

121. On methodology see 46ff. and that which now follows.

122. Cf. pp. 326-27, n. 83.

123. Cf. pp. 176f. above.

124. One recalls the Jewish belief in angels as "national princes" (Dan 10:13, etc.), and one notes, especially, Ps 68:31 (cf. above, pp. 42ff.) and the dual significance of Rahab: "Egypt" (Isa 30:7) and "pagan deity" (Ps 40:5; cf. above, pp. 27ff.). Eisenmenger, *Entdecktes*, 2:805, cites Jewish traditions (*Yalqut Ḥadaš*, fol. 80, col. 4, no. 20), according to which Sammael (the devil) is, at the same time, the "sovereign" (שׂר [śar]) of Edom, i.e., he (i.e., Rome) is described as the הרשעה מלכות [malkût hā-rišʿāh, "the evil power"].

125. Düsterdieck, *Handbuch Offenbarung*⁴, has seen that the overwhelmed opponent is designated by the appellation κατήγωρ [katēgōr, "accuser"], "a new appellation, not even mentioned in vv. 3ff., and thus a designation also indicative of a totally new dimension" [German: "von einer neuen, in v 3ff. gar nicht berührten und jener Darstellung auch ganz fremdartigen Seite"]. Düsterdieck has noted this without, however, investigating the basis for such a remarkable situation!

126. One notes that the Jewish interpreter says κατήγωρ, διάβολος, or σατανάς [katēgōr, "accuser"; diabolos, "devil," or satanas, "Satan"], Rev 12:9, 10, 12; and 20:2), while the tradition speaks of the δράκων [drakōn, "dragon"] or of the ὄφις [ophis, "serpent"]. On this basis we have a linguistic proof of the fact that the thousand-year kingdom and Gog and Magog (cf. Rev 20:7, 10) no longer belong to one tradition.

127. Take a look at the various commentaries!

128. It is characteristic of the eclectic technique of the Jewish interpreter that the reference to the devil occurs first at Rev 12:9, then is repeated at Rev 20:2. If the interpretation were to be systematic, this reference would certainly already have been given at Rev 12:3. But the author interprets only that which interests him!

Notes to Chapter 9

1. Dieterich, *Abraxas*, 117ff.; Albrecht Dieterich, *Nekyia: Beitrage zur Erklarung der neuentdeckten Petrusapokalypse* (Leipzig: Teubner, 1893) [hereinafter: Dieterich, *Nekyia*], 217, n. 3.

2. Hygin fab. 140 in Dieterich, *Abraxas*, 117.

3. Dieterich, *Abraxas*, 118.

4. Dieterich, *Abraxas*, 122, n. 2, to his own detriment, has assessed the hypothesis of Vischer, *Offenbarung*, as significant!

5. Dieterich, *Nekyia*, 218ff. Cf. p. 352, n. 14 below.

6. Even in Hellenistic Judaism only those cases are known to us where the gods are viewed as human beings, and their stories are interpreted as human stories. So Kronos, Titan, and Iapetus appear as "kings" of the humans (*Sib. Or.* 2:110ff.). According to Artapanus, "Hermes" is a byname of Moses. The Hercules saga is united by Malchus with the story of Abraham; etc. Cf. Schürer, *Geschichte*³, 2:735-38.

7. This argument counts against Dieterich's view, even in this case, that Revelation 12 — as he believes — stems from a Hellenist.

8. Dieterich, *Nekyia*, 217, n. 3.

9. ["ein 'wildes Verfahren,'" lit. "a 'wild scheme'" — trans.]

10. ["'mystischen Wirrwarr'" — trans.]

11. Cf. above, pp. 350-51, n. 107.

12. At Rev 12:9 he asserts: "εἰς τὴν γῆν has no meaning" (*Abraxas*, 120, n. 1), and therefore he omits the phrase [εἰς τὴν γῆν [*eis tēn gēn*]].

13. He identifies the rescued child and Michael (who confronts the dragon) in this way (*Abraxas*, 119, n. 2).

14. The situation is quite similar to another one. Dieterich, *Nekyia*, has compared the primitive Christian concepts of hell and paradise to the Greek Orphic-Pythagorean concepts of the same. In this regard he has identified a whole series of extremely peculiar and astonishing parallels. If one abandons oneself to the ideas of the parallels advanced by Dieterich, and the ideas of the many other parallels which can be drawn from the materials assembled by him and from Judeo-Christian eschatology, . . . if one abandons oneself to such ideas one can hardly doubt that an historical context also exists here. On the other hand, however, Dieterich's conclusion that the early Christian conceptions of paradise and of hell were strongly influenced by Greek views . . . this conclusion appears to me to be quite doubtful. At the very least, in the case of Judaism, I believe Dieterich's investigation to be totally useless. The rivers of the kingdom of death (*1 Enoch* 17:6) which Dieterich, *Nekyia*, 218f., considers to be of Greek origin, are already found in the book of Psalms; cf. נחלי בליעל [*naḥălê bĕlîyaʿal*, "rivers of perdition"] (Ps 18:5). Perrot, *Histoire de l'Art*, 2:364, furnishes a Babylonian picture of the rivers of Hades. The punishment of the stars, who will be held in prison at the appointed time (*1 Enoch* 18:12-16; 21:1-10), is not an imitation of a Greek idea. The same thing has already been seen at Isa 24:21f. What *1 Enoch* 9:9 and *1 Enoch* 15 tell us about the giants (τιτάνες [*titanes*], *1 Enoch* 9:9; γίγαντες [*gigantes*], *1 Enoch* 15:6) is not Hellenistic, It is, rather, the continuation of Genesis 6. "Titans," "Giants," are the Greek equivalents of the Hebrew גבורים [*gibbôrîm*] and נפלים [*nĕpilîm*] of Gen 6:4 (cf. *1 Enoch* 15:11, νεφελάς [*nephelas*], a corrupted transcription of נפלים [*nĕpilîm*]). The parallels pointed out by Dieterich persist, but explanation is to be sought by other means.

15. Those "others" are chapters 13 and 17. I deal with both at some length in what follows.

16. Dillmann, *Buch Henoch*; cf. above, p. 343, n. 8.

17. For details Dillmann has already attributed *1 Enoch* 15 to tradition.

18. Read, perhaps, *1 Enoch* 42 or the cosmological *1 Enoch* 17ff. Pay attention to the many names and technical terms, to the diverse variant forms in which the same material is transmitted in *1 Enoch*, etc.

19. So the band of bronze and iron "in the grass of the field" (Dan 4:15) is not encountered in the allegory of Dan 4:12.

20. Cf. above, pp. 128-37.

21. How far these observations either apply to the other so-called "apocalypses," or whether real apocalyptic things are blended in them with a different kind of material . . . these issues do not belong here, where only the main features should be given.

22. I therefore pursue the history of the material, insofar as this has not already been done in the preceding materials. I do not pursue it back into prophecy, where it is found definitely only at a few points and not in any broader degree. And I do not examine what significance the "apocalyptic reality" had for the rest of the New Testament. I believe that only one thing is required: to establish that the thinking of the Gospels is generally quite far removed from these materials, and that, as far as I can see, only a single sphere of thought is held in common between the two. There are individual pieces of the eschatology, above all the belief in the resurrection, and in "paradise" and "hell," which reflect this common sphere.

23. Belief in the resurrection originated neither from prophetic eschatology nor from the piety of the psalmist. The prophets preach a hope in regard to the *people*, not in regard to the *individual*. The psalmists believe in a God who can be praised only "in the land of the living." We

do not see the resurrection faith either in the Old Testament or in postcanonical Judaism. We do observe it, however, at those places which are open to it and which are appropriate for it. It definitely did not come from "premonition," since faith does not generally arise in that way. It is also certain that it is not derived from religious reflection. This is clearly shown by a concept like that of "hell," a concept which is not produced by rational reflection, but rather is of a totally different origin. This belief, however, is not a very difficult puzzle for the Old Testament scholar. The solution has been suggested above. A more adequate explanation, however, I will postpone until later!

24. Cf. above, pp. 173ff.

25. Cf. above, pp. 83ff.

26. Cf. the passages cited by Dillmann, *Buch Henoch*, xv.

27. I am thinking, specifically, of the theories concerning the origin of the Essenes. The most immediate one is the fact that this sect, not to be explained from the Old Testament, had arisen through oriental influence, an influence which — as we have seen — had a quite powerful effect on the Judaism of that period. The fact that, meanwhile, *we* cannot trace the foreign factor does not demonstrate according to the foregoing that such a factor did not actually exist!

28. [In this view Gunkel foreshadows the important work of Paul D. Hanson, *The Dawn of Apocalyptic* (Philadelphia: Fortress, 1975) — trans.]

29. Concerning the (very complicated) criticism of the *Avesta*, cf. Ed. Meyer, *Gesch. des Altertums*, 1:504-9. [Our knowledge of Babylonian religion is based mainly on the treasures preserved for us in the library of Aššurbanipal and, therefore, refers largely to the Old Babylonian period. The evolution of Babylonian religion in the later period is, at present, almost totally a *terra incognita*.] — Zimmern

30. I accordingly dismiss the Persian origin for other parts of the apocalyptic materials, as I have stressed explicitly.

31. Dieterich, *Nekyia*, 219 [German: "Ist den überhaupt möglich dass babylonische Schriften und babylonische Kultur damals so stark eingedrungen wären?"].

32. Dieterich, *Abraxas*, 43f.; Kessler, *Mani*, 1:xii; Brandt, *Die Mandäische Religion: Ihre Entwicklung und geschichtliche Bedeutung, erforscht, dargestellt, und beleuchtet* (Leipzig: Hinrichs, 1889) [hereinafter: Brandt, *Mandäische Religion*], 182ff.

33. This idea has been expressed, in regard to the seven angels, most clearly by Hengstenberg, *Offenbarung des heiligen Johannes*, 1:441.

34. So Bleek, *Vorlesungen Apok.*, 151f.; Renan, *L'Antechrist*, 304; Spitta, *Offenbarung*, 238f.; Holtzmann et al., *Hand-commentar²*, 4:317.

35. According to the three obligations of rulers: judgment (1 Kings 3:12, illustrated in vv. 16-28), war (Isa 36:5), and service of God.

36. Dillmann, *Jesaiah*, 117.

37. It is incomprehensible to me how Spitta, *Offenbarung*, 239, and Holtzmann, *Hand-commentar²*, 4:317, can render the number *seven*, with no skill, as possibly invoking an "original" of seven spirits.

38. So Hengstenberg, *Offenbarung des heiligen Johannes*, 1:89; and Düsterdieck, *Handbuch Offenbarung⁴*, 113.

39. Bleek, *Vorlesungen Apok.*, 162; Spitta, *Offenbarung*, 34; and Holtzmann, *Hand-commentar²*, 4:319.

40. Tob 12:15: "the seven holy angels, which convey the prayers of the holy ones and have access to the splender of the Holy One" (cf. Luke 1:19, 26 = ἀρχάγγελοι [*archangeloi*]; 1 Thess

4:16; Jude 9 = (in Hebrew) שָׂרִים הָרִאשֹׁנִים [*śārîm hā-rī'šōnîm*]; Dan 10:13). Concerning the names of these angels there are a series of different traditions; cf. Weber, *Altsyn. Theol.*, 164. Perhaps there already existed, at Ezek 9:2ff. , a first allusion to the teaching of the seven archangels. According to the following, Ezekiel 9 is not to be considered as a "seed" for this teaching; *contra* Smend, *Ezekiel*, 56.

41. The contention of Spitta, *Offenbarung*, 32, depends on similar examples. His argument is that Rev 1:20 was an addition by a redactor. That is a literary-critical thesis which is refuted by Rev 2:5; a literary-critical thesis for which one should not mistake the understanding which I have put together above.

42. Note that the description (Tob 12:15; Luke 1:19; Rev 1:4; 4:5; 8:2) recurs with great regularity.

43. Cf. Tob 12:15.

44. Weber, *Altsyn. Theol.*, 164.

45. If, in chapter 4, apart from the torches, the twenty-four elders and the twenty-four [*sic*] animals stand before God's throne, this means that here traditions not originally related to each other have come together.

46. The designation "spirits" for superhuman beings in heaven and on earth is particularly common in *1 Enoch*. — On the other hand, the objection should not be raised that the angels, in the linguistic usage of Revelation, never hold the title of "spirits" (Hengstenberg, *Offenbarung des heiligen Johannes*, 1:92). It is methodologically preposterous in the case of a writing like Revelation, which brings together many different traditions, to recover, through separation of the individual expressions from each other, a general perception of the whole writing. The use of this faulty methodology has hindered a correct understanding of the "seven spirits" up to the present time; cf. also Bleek, *Vorlesungen Apok.*, 151f.; Düsterdieck, *Handbuch Offenbarung*[4], 113; Kliefoth, *Offenbarung des Johannes*, 1:120f.; and Hengstenberg, *Offenbarung des heiligen Johannes*, 1:88-92.

47. This — and nothing more — is the significance of the word μυστήριον [*mystērion*, "mystery"], cf. Eph 5:32; Rev 17:5; *contra* Düsterdieck, *Handbuch Offenbarung*[4], 133; Hengstenberg, *Offenbarung des heiliges Johannes*, 1:148; Holtzmann et al., *Hand-commentar*[2], 4:319.

48. Cf. above, p. 85.

49. Eisenmenger, *Entdecktes*, 2:384ff.

50. Since, consequently, a feature in the likeness of the "lamb" can be identified, with great probability, as having a mythological origin, a further question may be raised as to whether this figure of the "lamb" has already had a prehistory prior to its coming to Christianity.

51. This understanding is particularly appropriate in the context of the vision of chapter 1, a vision in which Christ purely and simply receives the attribute of his power and authority; cf. Spitta, *Offenbarung*, 32. Spitta's own interpretation (p. 35 — Jesus holds the stars in order to illuminate the night with them, in relation to which the number of stars is insignificant) . . . this interpretation is quite inadequate.

52. Dieterich, *Abraxas*, 44f.; *KAT*[2], 21; Brandt, *Mand. Schriften*, 19.

53. Precisely *Rō'š haš-šānah*, *Běrē'šît Rabbāh*, c. 48 (Franz Delitzsch, "Engel," in Riehm, *HW*, 381).

54. Cf. above, pp. 85ff.

55. Noted by Weber, *Altsyn. Theol.*, 164.

56. Šamaš	the sun	Sunday	Raphael
Sin	the moon	Monday	Gabriel
Nirgal	Mars	Mardi (= Tuesday)	Sammael
Nabu	Mercury	Mercredi (Wednesday)	Michael
Marduk	Jupiter	Thursday	Izidkiel
Ištar	Venus	Friday	Hannael
Ninib	Saturn	Saturday	Kephariel

57. Judeo-Babylonian magical texts, for awareness of which I thank Dr. Stübe, speak of "the seven angels which move orbitally around heaven, and earth, and stars, and constellations, and moon, and sea." The Kabbalah knows of seven angels over the planets, etc. [Cf. Rudolf Heinrich Karl Stübe, *Jüdisch-babylonische Zaubertexte, herausgegeben und erklärt* (Halle a. S: J. Krause, 1895), a brief (30 pp.) treatment of his work on these texts, work which he, presumably, shared orally with Gunkel. — trans.]

58. Moreover, the possibility remains open that the Babylonian concepts and symbols had come to the Jews via Persian mediation. Persian religion also knew of seven high spirits (*Amneša-Spenta*). These have long been compared to the seven archangels [cf. Alexander Kohut, *Über die jüdische Angelologie und Daemonologie in ihrer Abhängigkeit vom Parsismus*, Abhandlungen der Deutschen Morgenländischen Gesellschaft, vol. 4, no. 3 (Leipzig: F. A. Brockhaus, 1866) [hereinafter: Kohut, *Angel. u. Daemon.*], 24ff.], which, however, are not themselves definitively independent from the seven planetary deities of the Babylonians.

59. Spitta, *Offenbarung*, 277.

60. 1 Kings 22:19; Jer 23:18; Ps 89:8; Job 1:6ff.; 2:1ff.; 15:8. Cf. the use of the plural in Gen 1:26; 11:7; Isa 6:8. Also cf. 1 *Enoch* 14:22; 47:3, etc.

61. Dan 7:10; cf. Dan 4:4 — those who are "sitting [first] in the royal power" [i.e., the Hebrew phrase: היושבים ראשנה במלכות [*hay-yōšěbîm rî'šōnāh bam-malkût*] — Esth 1:14; cf. Zech. 3:8.

62. Weber, *Altsyn. Theol.*, 170f. The commonly cited passages from Christian Schöttgen, *Horae Hebraicae et Talmudicae in universum Novum Testamentum* (Dresden, Leipzig: Christoph Hekelii b. fillium, 1733-42) [hereinafter: Schöttgen, *Horae Hebraicae*], 1107, mention a false interpretation of Isa 24:23 and do not belong here.

63. This is, e.g., the sense of Matt 5:3.

64. עירין ['*îrîn*, "watchers"] and קדישין [*qědîšîn*, "holy ones"] (Dan 4:14).

65. "There the moon blushes, there the sun is shamed, for YHWH Ṣěbā'ôt has become king on Mount Zion and in Jerusalem, and before the elders is [his] splendor." [German: "Da errötet der Mond, da schämt sich die Sonne, denn Jahve Zebaoth ist König geworden auf dem Berge Zion und in Jerusalem, und vor seinen Ältesten ist Herrlichkeit."] The sense of this is: Instead of the powers which have heretofore arrogated dominion for themselves, now they come to the authority and the glorification to which they are properly entitled. Prior to this they were lords of moon and sun. Now YHWH is king, and *his* "elders" are exalted." The context does not, therefore, allow the "elders" to be considered as human beings, nor even as divine advocates of Israel. — The usual assumption, that Revelation 4 is literally dependent on this passage, . . . this assumption has not been established.

66. According to the witness of the LXX of the Pentateuch, the זקנים [*zěqēnîm*] frequently are rendered by γερουσία [*gerousia*, "council of elders, Senate"]. Cf. also LXX Prov 31:23, γέροντες συνέδριον [*gerontes synedrion*, "council of elders"], etc.

67. Cf., e.g., 1 Kings 22:19.

68. Cf., e.g., 1 Sam 22:6.

69. This had been the official title of the "great king" since the Assyrians.

70. So the seven flaming torches (Rev 4:5).

71. So the four "living creatures," who surely originally were neither priests (Rev 5:8) nor magicians (Rev 6:1), etc.

72. [German: "Verdoppelung der Zwölfzahl, der Signatur des Volkes Gottes"]; Kliefoth, *Offenbarung des Johannes,* 2:13f.

73. Bleek, *Vorlesungen Apok.,* 205; de Wette, *Kommentar²,* 61; Weizsäcker, *Apost. Zeitalter²,* 617.

74. Hengstenberg, *Offenbarung des heiligen Johannes,* 1:267; Düsterdieck, *Handbuch Offenbarung⁴,* 220f.

75. Compare, e.g., Rev 7:9ff. and the explicit explanation of it at Rev 7:13ff.

76. Cf. Hengstenberg, *Offenbarung des heiligen Johannes,* 1:269.

77. Hilgenfeld, *Einleitung in das NT,* 425; Renan, *L'Antechrist,* 303; Ewald, *Johannes Apokalypse,* 159; Züllig, *Offenbarung Johannis,* 2:24; Spitta, *Offenbarung,* 275; and Erbes; *Offenbarung Johannis,* 49. — Holtzmann et al., *Hand-commentar²,* 4:326, allows for free choice among the standing explications.

78. The transformation of this assembly into a בית דין [*bêt dîn* — "courtroom"] by the rabbis appears to have been an interpretation of the idea on the basis of the Palestinian situation. According to this understanding, the crowns are omitted and the royal throne is transformed into a judgment seat.

79. Cf. above, pp. 89 and 96.

80. The stages of this process should be pursued in detail: the Assyrian king is called "king of kings" (Ezek 26:7), "the great king, the mighty king" (Akkadian: *šarru rabû šar kiššati* = Greek: ὁ βασιλεὺς ὁ μέγας ὁ κύριος πάσης τῆς γῆς [*ho basileus ho megas ho kyrios pasēs tēs gēs*] (Jdt 2:5); Mardûk *(Ašur),* "Lord of lords, king of the gods," "the great lord'"; YHWH, "God of gods, Lord of lords, the great, mighty, and terrifying God" (Deut 10:17; cf. Ps 136:2f.)," a great King over the whole earth" (Ps 47:3); God (Christ), King of kings, Lord of lords (1 Tim 6:15; Rev 17:14 and 19:16); cf. Rev 1:5. — In addition, I add the Babylonian "king of the gods," the Old Testament's "YHWH, a great king above all gods" (Ps 95:3), and the New Testament's "King of the ages" (1 Tim 1:17).

81. *Diodori Siculi Bibliotheca historica,* ed. Immanuel Bekker (Leipzig: B. G. Teubner, 1853-54), 2:31: μετὰ δὲ τὸν ζῳδιακὸν κύκλον εἴκοσιν καὶ τέτταρας ἀφορίζυσιν ἀστέρας, ὧν τοὺς μὲν ἡμίσεις ἐν τοῖς βορείοις μέρεσι, τοὺς δ' ἡμίσεις ἐν τοῖς νοτίοις τετάχθαι φασί, καὶ τούτων τοὺς μὲν ὁρωμένους τῶν ζώντων εἶναι καταριθμοῦσι, τοὺς δ' ἀφανεῖς τοῖς τετελευτηκόσι προσωρίσθαι νομίζουσιν, οὓς δικαστὰς τῶν ὅλων προσαγορεύουσιν [*meta de ton zōdiakon kyklon eikosin kai tettaras aphorizysin asteras, hōn tous men hēmiseis en tois boreiois meresi, tous d' hēmiseis en tois notiois tetachthai phasi, kai toutōn tous men horōmenous tōn zōntōn einai katarithmousi, tous d' aphaneis tois teleutēkosi prosōristhai nomizousin, hous dikastas tōn holōn prosagoreuousin*] — see translation above.

82. Which stars it was among the Babylonians, and how they came to the status of "judge" . . . this does not belong here. Fritz Hommel, "Über den Ursprung und das Alter der arabischen Sternnamen und insbesondere der Mondstationen," *ZDMG* 45 (1891) 599ff., believes it to be the lunar stations.

83. Eisenmenger, *Entdecktes,* 2:328ff.

84. The seven *viae* will, in the tradition transmitted by *4 Ezra,* be described in such peculiarly abstract terms that they can be understood only as faded images of originally more con-

crete concepts. The basic idea must be that of seven hells. Tantamount to the corresponding theory of the seven *viae* of torment, the reward for the righteous (*4 Ezra* 6:64ff.) is developed from the idea of the seven heavens.

85. Brandt, *Mandäische Religion,* 182.

86. D. Feuchtwang, "Die Höllenvorstellung bei den Hebräern," *ZA* 4 (1889) 42ff.; Jensen, *Kosmologie,* 233.

87. Paul de Lagarde, *Purim: Ein Beitrag zur Geschichte der Religion,* Abhandlungen der Königlichen Gesellschaft der Wissenchaften zu Göttingen 34 (Göttingen: Dieterich, 1887) [hereinafter: Lagarde, *Purim*].

88. Heinrich Zimmern, "Zur Frage nach der Ursprung der Purim-festes," *ZAW* 11 (1891) 157ff.

89. The latter identification I believe to be unavailing. Babylonian *puḫru* would mean "assembly, feast." פור [*pûr*], however, means "lot," according to Esth 3:7. The Babylonian New Year's feast fell at the beginning of Nisan. The feast of Purim falls on the 15th of Adar. Cf. below.

90. Peter Christian Albrecht Jensen, "Elamitische Eigennamen: Ein Beitrag zur Erklärung der semitische Inschriften" [hereinafter: Jensen, "Elam. Eigennamen"], *Wiener Zeitschrift für die Kunde des Morgenlandes* 6 (1893) 47ff., 209ff.

91. מרדכי [*mordĕkay*], Μαρδοχαιος [*mardochaios*] = "belonging to מרדך [Heb. *mĕrōdak;* Akkadian *marduk*]."

92. The Babylonian goddess *Ištar,* with the Palestinian עשתרת ['*aštōret*], the deity of love and the "star" Venus, called by the Mandaeans עסתרא ['*istrā*'] (cf. Brandt, *Mand. Schriften,* 45, n. 6); in the targums called אסתהר ['*istehar*] or אסתירא ['*istîrā*'] (cf. Levy, *Wb über die Targumim,* s.v. אסתהר or אסתירא); among the Sabeans אסתרא ['*str*'] [Wilhelm Gesenius, *Thesaurus philologicus* (Leipzig: F. C. G. Vogelii, 1829-53) [hereinafter: Gesenius, *Thesaurus*], 1:134]; on Judeo-Babylonian incantation bowls, the plural occurs, איסתרתא ['*istrātā*'] (according to a communication of Dr. Stübe — see above, p. 356, n. 57). Therefore, אסתר ['*estēr*] in the book of Esther turns out to be a later orthography for *Ištar* "vocatum est nomen eius Esther a nomine stellae Veneris," Targum II to Esth 2:7, noted by Gesenius, *Thesaurus,* loc. cit.

93. The foregoing foundational observations are expressed by Jensen in a letter cited by Nowack, *Hebr. Archaeologie,* 2:200.

94. Even if the contention of Jensen, "Elam. Eigennamen," that the original single-day feast of Purim had become a two-day feast through unification with the days of ניקנור [*nî-qā-nôr*] . . . this contention is improbable. Purim takes place on אדר ['*Ăḏar*] 14/15. The ניקנור [*nî-qā-nôr*] feast falls on 13 אדר ['*Ăḏar*]. Cf. Nowack, *Hebr. Archäologie,* 2:195.

95. Jensen, "Elam. Eigennamen," assumes that the human king has taken the place of a god. In line with the points noted above, this is not really necessary. Why this god must have been *Šamaš* I do not know. Nothing in the Esther legend points to a solar deity. — What still might be Persian eludes me!

96. In the legend, Mordecai is a cousin of Esther (2:7). [The same relation exists, according to a Babylonian tradition, between *Marduk* and *Ištar. Marduk* is the son of *Ea.* According to one tradition, *Ištar* is the daughter of *Anu* (according to another, the daughter of *Sin*). *Ea* and *Anu* are brothers. Cf. above, pp. 13ff.] — Zimmern

97. [Translator's note: For *Haman* as an Elamite deity, cf. Jensen, *Elam. Eigenname I,* 56-61.]

98. This nationalistic element has certainly — insofar as inferences from the Esther legend are permissible — . . . certainly not, as Jensen so ardently desires, been mixed together with the myth, but rather is the actual content of the myth!

99. The "enemy," Esth 7:6; "the enemy of the Jews," Esth 3:10; 8:11; 9:19.

100. Cf. pp. 63f. above.

101. Cf. pp. 33f. above.

102. Cf. p. 59 above.

103. For *Psalms of Solomon* 2, cf. pp. 51f. above.

104. This text has been presented above, pp. 40ff.

105. ["And you will keep them until they are consumed by whomever and whenever you wish." — trans.]

106. The text of *1 Enoch* 60:7-9 is presented above (pp. 40f.). The continuation of the text I now give in that which follows.

107. Should probably be understood: "about the purpose."

108. [Gunkel gives the quotation in Latin, even though *Second Apocalypse of Baruch* is preserved in Syriac. The following is the Latin which he presents: "et revelabitur Behemoth ex loco suo, et Leviathan ascendet de mari, duo ceta (κῆτη) magna, quae creavi die quinto creationis, et reservavi eos usque ad illud tempus; et tunc erunt in escam omnibus qui residui fuerint." — trans.]

109. Mark 13:14.

110. In that which follows (*2 Apoc. Bar.* 29:5ff.), there is the description of that which those who remain drink — the well-known passage about a grapevine that produces abundantly — and then about the fragrances which revive the blessed ones, and the manna which they will eat instead of bread!

111. This question and provisional answer (*1 Enoch* 60:9f.) and the definitive answer (*1 Enoch* 60:24f.) have been divided from each other by the insertion of vv. 11-23.

112. The phrase inserted between v. 25a and 25b, "so that the punishment of the Lord of Spirits does not come upon them for nothing," is meaningless in v. 25. It appears to be a variant of v. 24b.

113. This is the sense of the Ethiopic word, as Professor Prätorius [usually spelled "Praetorius" in English-speaking libraries — trans.] has most kindly communicated to me.

114. Not, as Dillmann, *Buch Henoch*, 183, desires, the time of the great flood!

115. Cf. above, p. 40, n. 3.

116. [*En mystēriǭ* "in mystery," i.e., "in mysterious speech" — trans.]

117. [עוֹלָם הַבָּא ['ôlām hab-bo'], "the world to come" — trans.]

118. Cf. Weber, *Altsyn. Theol.*, 195, 370, 384; Grünbaum, "Beiträge," 277ff.; and Eisenmenger, *Entdecktes*, 2:872ff.

119. Cf. above, p. 58.

120. Cf. above, pp. 40f.

121. P. 31, n. 51.

122. Cf. pp. 35f.

123. Cf. p. 36.

124. The fact that Judaism knew of pagan images of dragons on vessels and signet rings is expressly attested in the Babylonian Talmud. The passages are noted by C. J. Ball, "III. Bel and the Dragon," *The Holy Bible, according to the Authorized Version (A.D. 1611), with an explanatory and critical commentary and a revision of the translation: Apocrypha*, ed. Henry Wace (London: J. Murray, 1888) [hereinafter: Wace, *Apocrypha*], 2:348 [hereinafter: Ball, "Bel and the Dragon"].

125. The translation follows the text of Swete (B). Exceptions have been indicated.

126. καὶ [*kai*], א︮ᶜ ᵃ, A, etc. Fritzsche, *KEHApok*.

127. ἐβόησαν πρὸς τὸν θεὸν ἀπὸ δὲ τῆς βοῆς αυτῶν [eboēsan pros ton theon apo de tēs boēs autōn] is "chosen," says Fritzsche.

128. καὶ φῶς [kai phōs], A, a second subject for ἐγένετο [egeneto]; cf. Esth 10:3.

129. The customary text reads ταπεινοί [tapeinoi, "low places"]. Lucian reads ποταμοί [potamoi, "rivers"], which fits excellently. This recension contains, especially for Additions to Esther, a subsequently edited text. However, since Lucian at the interpretation of the river (10:5) has inserted at the reading ποταμοί [potamoi, "rivers"] an inappropriate text, this reading must have been the one which he encountered. ναπεινοί [napeinoi, "glens"] has arisen from the opposite ἐνδόξους [endoxous, "notable things"] in accordance with Ezek 21:31.

130. Gen 7:20, 24.

131. Heb. Esth 11:29, Fritzsche.

132. So the original sense. It was already misunderstood by those who transcribed it. Hence the additions, in the customary text οὗτος ἐστιν Ἰσραήλ [houtos estin Israēl, "those/they are Israel"], in Lucian ποταμός [potamos, "river"].

133. It has already been understood as mythological by Hugo Grotius (Egyptian) and by J. M. Fuller (Persian) (J. M. Fuller, "The Rest of the Chapters of the Book of Esther, which are found neither in the Hebrew, nor in the Chaldee" [hereinafter: Fuller, "Rest of Esther"] in Wace, Apocrypha, 1:370, 376f.).

134. In Lucian Ἀδὰρ Νισάν [adar nisan], where Νισάν [nisan] is to be taken as a correction of the original Ἀδάρ [adar].

135. Joel 2:2; Zeph 1:15; cf. Rom 2:9.

136. The motif appears in the dream of Mandane [the father of Cyrus]; cf. Wace, Apocrypha, 1:376f.

137. Chisianus δράκων [drakōn], Θ δράκων μέγας [drakōn megas].

138. καὶ φαγὼν διερράγη [kai phagōn dierragē].

139. Cf. above, pp. 14f., 19f., and 321-22, n. 76. Cf. also Diodorus Siculus, Bibl. hist. 2.9.

140. Eberhard Schrader, "Drache," in Riehm, Hw, 327-28; Ball, "Bel and Dragon," in Wace, Apocrypha, 2:348f.; Brandt, Mandäische Religion, 182, n. 5, and Brandt, Mand. Schriften, 150, n. 3.

141. Cf. above, pp. 17f.

142. Job 41:19 [English version 41:27]. Cf. the whole description of Job 41:7-9, 18-21 [English version 41:15-17, 26-29] and Ezek 29:4 [scales of the תנין [tannîn, "great dragon"]].

143. In the Babylonian myth he causes a furious wind to travel into her mouth, and he follows with the sword (cf. above, pp. 17f.). The celebrated image of Layard, Monuments of Nineveh, vol. 3, plate 5.

144. Laid out by Ball in Wace, Apocrypha, 2:345f., 357; the first is from Midrash Genesis Rabbah 68, the second from Jossipon ben Gorion. Two other recensions of the same legend are mentioned by Nöldeke, from the Alexander Romance, in his "Beiträge zur Geschichte des Alexanderromans," in Denkschriften der Kaiserlichen Akademie der Wissenschaften, Philosophisch-Historische Klasse, Bd. 38, Abhandlung 5 (1890), p. 22. The death of a dragon under similar circumstances to that told by the Alexander Romance concerning Alexander is narrated by y. Ned. 3:12 regarding King Sapor II. The voracious nature of the dragon is, in the first legend, depicted as a camel pelt, into which straw and charcoal have been stuffed; in the second legend, it is depicted as an animal skin stuffed with plaster, pitch, lead, and sulfur. The latter legend is, according to Nöldeke (p. 25), not of Jewish but of heathen origin. Concerning such examples one also recognizes that we are dealing with ethnic traditions.

145. "This may represent an older, as it certainly is more reasonable, form of the story" (Ball, "Bell and Dragon," 357). Accordingly, there is the presumption of Brandt, Mand. Schriften,

150 n. 3, that this feature of the apocryphal legend has arisen from a misunderstood Babylonian carving. Brandt's view is wrong!

146. Brandt, *Mand. Schriften* 150.

147. The book of Jonah may be viewed in much the same way that we here view the material in regard to the Δράκων [*drakōn*]. There as well it is totally certain that the mythic sphere stands in the background. The very idea that a person could be devoured by a "fish," linger for three days in its belly, only then to be vomited out alive again . . . that very idea belongs, according to its nature, within mythology. Here also, then, there is a prophetic legend within which a mythic sphere echoes strongly!

148. [Gunkel is apparently arguing here that Daniel is, in effect, taking over the role of Marduk in slaying the dragon, i.e., *Ti'āmat.* — trans.]

149. Cf. above, pp. 27f., regarding Ps 40:5, and pp. 42ff., regarding Ps 68:31.

150. Cf. above, pp. 19f., and in the appendices.

151. Cf. above, pp. 58f.

152. The legend has endured in the peculiarly imaginative style in which such Jewish legends are written. In our case, the power of the imagination has been evoked especially strongly by the shifting of the dragon account from an ancient primordial era to an actual historical time! This sort of pseudo-historical legend is certainly not something which is admirable. On the other hand, Otto Zöckler's opinions concerning this narrative being "childish" or "senseless" [German: "läppisch," "sinnlos"] [Otto Zöckler, *Die Apokryphen des Alten Testaments: Nebst einem Anhang über die Pseudepigraphenliteratur,* Kurzgefasster Kommentar zu den heiligen Schriften Alten und Neuen Testamentes so wie zu den Apokryphen, Altes Testament, 9 Abt. (München: Beck, 1891) [hereinafter: Zöckler, *Apokryphen*], 215 and 221] are incorrect!

153. In the following I assume, in all its essentials, the translation given by Georg Behrmann in his Daniel commentary (Behrmann, *Daniel,* s.l.).

154. This would be the meaning of the difficult מגיחן [*měğîḥān*]. Cf. the Hebrew גיח [*gîaḥ,* "to burst forth"] (Mic 4:10).

155. The text says that its wings "were plucked off"; cf. below.

156. The text of v. 11a, which must have contained the judgment upon the eleventh horn, has been mutilated.

157. Cf. Dan 7:12.

158. יציבא [*yaṣîbā'*] (Dan. 7:16).

159. This is the sense even if the text of Dan 7:17, מלכין [*malkîn,* Aramaic "kings"] should be correct. Cf., however, LXX Θ.

160. The dual form, intended by the writer, has been misunderstood by those who inserted the pointing, which treats it as plural; cf. p. 336, n. 83.

161. Certainly the opposition to this view has *still* not died away and will, for the time being, probably not be put to rest.

162. Dan 12:1.

163. Dan 11:36.

164. Dan 8:19.

165. How he calculates them is of little consequence for our purposes. That he had in mind four individual and, for him and his readers, well-known kingdoms (he could indeed have given names to the second and the third) should not be doubted, *contra* Behrmann, *Daniel,* on Dan 7:5. Behrmann asks: "For what reason would the author and the original circle of readers of the book have had to make an allusion to an event of the *distant* past?" [German: "Welchen Zweck hätte es für den Verfasser und den ursprünglichen Leserkreis des Buches gehabt hier eine

Anspielung auf ferne Vergangenheit zu machen?"]. The answer is given above on pp. 121f. Certainly the more definitely positive, already fulfilled predictions have been given by the prophet, the more he will be believed to be a "true witness." [Translator's note: The Hebrew word יון [Yāwān] appears to be linked to the ancient name of the predominately Greek area of Asia Minor, i.e., Ionia, and is hence a Hebrew designation meaning "Greeks."]

166. It is quite certain here as well that the author speaks of ten distinct kings, *contra* Behrmann, *Daniel,* on 7:8 [p. 46]. How the author came up with this number I will not examine here. The solution to this question can be discerned only in connection with chapter 11, where the author has pointed to specific kings of *Yāwān,* and thereby reveals to us his knowledge and his view of Diadochene history. [The διάδοχοι [*diadochoi*] is the designation given to the twelve leaders who divided Alexander's empire among themselves after his death. — trans.]

167. These are also certainly actual kings, *contra* Behrmann, *Daniel,* on 7:8 (p. 46).

168. This is expressed in a totally clear way in the author's own interpretation, *contra* Behrmann, *Daniel,* on 7:14 (p. 48).

169. Cf. above, pp. 121ff. Thus the detailed prophecies of chapter 11. The most recent Daniel commentaries of Meinhold ("Daniel") and Behrmann *(Daniel)* have not understood this significance. — The fact that these exegetes have been correct so very little in this and similar apocalyptic cases is based on their aversion to taking a firm position and consequently a critical standpoint in relation to the material. The motto "pone ... haec dice de Antiocho quid nocet religioni nostrae?" ["Assuming that these things do refer to Antiochus, what harm does that do to *our* religion?"] [cf. Jerome, "Commentariorum in Danielem libri III (IV)," in *Corpus Christianorum,* Series Latina (Turnholt: Brepols, 1964), 75:4, 11, 44/45, ll. 407-9 (p. 932)] ... this motto is certainly comprehensible out of the present situation of the author, but it is also totally inadequate. Criticism should not only do no harm. It should produce benefit. It should create a positive picture. It should bring about understanding. It produces a benefit, however, only if it is resolutely pursued!

170. This explains why the son of man is usually described as a "Messiah"; so, again, Behrmann, *Daniel,* 47.

171. This relationship has also been regularly acknowledged by the exegetes of Daniel. A more distant relationship exists between Daniel 7 and Isa 17:12-14; 59:19f.; Jer 4:23-26; Hab 3:8; Ps 46 (cf. above, pp. 67-74, 93). Cf. also Add Esth 1:4-10 (cf. above, pp. 202ff.).

172. Cf. above, p. 58.

173. Cf. above, pp. 29f., 51f.

174. Cf. above, pp. 171ff.

175. There will be proof of this later. At the same time I will also deal with the meaning of this particular feature.

176. More about this later as well.

177. Parallels of this will be given in the following pages.

178. Concerning the characteristic modality of such Jewish allegories cf. p. 120 above.

179. The chaos figure has a horn in Babylonian and in Persian images; cf. Riehm, *Hw* 1171, 1262. Other representations show instead a peculiar topknot on the brow of the beast. [Serpents with horns (Akk. *qarnu* = Heb. קרן [*qeren*]) are often the objects of the Babylonian omen texts. Cf. also the frequent reference to horns in the text which concern themselves with the description of the types of gods [Carl Bezold, "Über keilinschriftliche Beschreibungen babylonisch-assyrischer Göttertypen" [hereinafter: Bezold, "Göttertypen"], *ZA* 9 (1894) 116f.] and the horned caps which *Agumkakrime* caused to be prepared for *Mardūk* and *Sarpānītu* (*KB,* 3:141). — Zimmern]

180. In that which follows in our discussion there will, again, be confirmation of this statement.

181. [Translator's note: Gunkel appears to be referring to the Babylonian creation myth, where *Ti'āmat* is the original chaos beast, and *Kingu*, her appointed general, is "the second one ... added." The demonic figures who provided the army of these two deities are the "many others who are made to serve."]

182. Cf. above, pp. 31f.

183. In what follows there is, again, a confirmation of this.

184. It is quite certain that the author has not invented the number of *four* world empires. We find the material numerous times in Judaism. In Daniel we find it in the parallel of chapter 2. Dan 8:8 gives yet another calculation (based on the four kingdoms of the *Diadochoi*). The four empires represented by the four horns are also presented at Zech 2:15. That the tradition of Daniel 2, which represents the four empires by four metals, concurs with Greek (cf. Hesiod's four world ages) and with Iranian traditions is certainly not a coincidence; *contra* Behrmann, *Daniel*, on Dan 2:39 (p. 15).

185. In *1 Enoch* such traditions will be dated to even more ancient times. This is by no means as foolish as it seems. In actuality it (i.e., the chaos tradition) is indeed older than *1 Enoch* itself.

186. Cf., especially, Daniel 10.

187. Cf. Dan 8:27 [A. A. Bevan, *A Short Commentary on the Book of Daniel for the Use of Students* (Cambridge: Cambridge University Press, 1882) [hereinafter: Bevan, *Daniel*], s.v. Dan 8:27].

188. Dan 12:10.

189. Cf. above, pp. 160ff.

190. Cf. pp. 164ff.

191. That chapters 12 and 13 are parallel to each other is not noteworthy. Chapter 13 is commonly considered to be a natural continuation of chapter 12, or at least the concluding section of chapter 12; cf. Weyland, *Omwerkings — en Compilatie — Hypothesen*, 160; Spitta, *Offenbarung*, 134ff.; Schmidt, *Anmerkungen*, 14f.; Erbes, *Offenbarung Johannis*, 10; Völter, *Problem der Apokalypse*, 192ff.

192. Weizsäcker, *Apost. Zeitalter*[2], 500; Weyland, *Omwerkings — en Compilatie — Hypothesen*, 109f.; Auguste Sabatier, *Les origines Litteraires et la Composition de l'Apocalypse de Saint Jean* (Paris: Librairie Fischbacher, 1888) [hereinafter: Sabatier, *Origine Apocalypse*], 119; Erbes, *Offenbarung Johannis*, 14f., 98ff.

193. Völter, *Problem der Apokalypse*, 201, 291.

194. From chapter 13 into chapter 17, Spitta, *Offenbarung*, 182f.; for details, Schmidt, *Anmerkungen*, 36; and Erbes, *Offenbarung Johannis*, 19.

195. Pfleiderer, *Urchristentum*, 351.

196. The fact that chapter 13ff. and chapter 17 are by different authors and from different times is recognized by Weizsäcker, *Apost. Zeitalter*[2], 496; Weyland, *Omwerkings — en Compilatie — Hypothesen*, 107f.; Henri Schoen, *L'origine de l'Apocalypse de Saint Jean* (Paris: Librairie Fischbacher, 1887), 119; Spitta, *Offenbarung*, 182ff.; Schmidt, *Anmerkungen*, 16; Erbes, *Offenbarung Johannis*, 11; Völter, *Entstehung der Apokalypse*[2], 65ff.

197. Thus in essential agreement with Spitta, *Offenbarung*, 176ff.; Erbes, *Offenbarung Johannis*, 184; and Völter, *Problem der Apokalypse*, 301.

198. The precise settlement of these literary questions I intentionally keep at a distance

from this theological investigation, and I postpone it until another more appropriate time and setting.

199. The reading ἐστάθην [estathēn] makes good sense in connection with that which follows; cf. Gen 41:1f.; 17f.; Dan 8:2f. The better-attested reading is certainly ἐστάθη [estathē]. What is the fact that the dragon walks on the sea supposed to mean, however (Bleek, *Vorlesungen Apok.*, 282f.; de Wette, *Kommentar*², 125; Ewald, *Johannes Apokalypse*, 250; Hengstenberg, *Offenbarung des Heiligen Johannes*, 2:4; Spitta, *Offenbarung*, 362f.)? In line with all this, ἐστάθην [estathēn] is the original reading; ἐστάθη [estathē] would improve the loose connection between chapters 12 and 13, but without helping our comprehension very much (*contra* Bernhard Weiss, "Die Johannes Apokalypse: Text-kritische Untersuchungen und Text-herstellung," *Texte und Untersuchungen zur Geschichte der Altchristlichen Literatur*, Bd. 7, Hft. 1 (Leipzig: J. C. Hinrichs, 1891) [hereinafter: Weiss, "Joh.-Apok."], 5.

200. ποιῆσαι πόλεμον μετὰ τῶν ἁγίων [poiēsai polemon meta tōn hagiōn, "to make war with the holy ones"] (Rev 13:7); ποιῆσαι πόλεμον μετὰ τῶν λοιπῶν [poiēsai polemon meta tōn loipōn, "to make war with those who remain"] (Rev 12:17).

201. Cf. above, pp. 176-77.

202. Explication of the symbols of the empire, symbols worn by the devil (Rev 12:3), has given the exegetes no small amount of difficulty! This is especially so since these symbols were consistent with those of the beasts of chapter 13, and yet, at the same time, they characteristically deviate from them. Very general explanations will simply have to do: the horns are a symbol of power; the heads are a symbol of intelligence; the numbers *seven* and *ten*, however, still lack a definite explanation (de Wette, *Kommentar*², 118); or the seven heads represent seven evil angels (Ewald, *Johannes Apokalypse*, 242; Erbes, *Offenbarung Johannis*, 12f.); or this symbol may only describe the dreadfulness of the dragon (Spitta, *Offenbarung*, 366). The difference, however, between the beast and the dragon (the basis of which cannot be successfully examined) is explained, somewhat, by the fact that they would have had to be distinguished somehow (Hilgenfeld, "Joh. Apok. n. Forschung," 434; Erbes, *Offenbarung Johannis*, 13). Or a skillful harmony between the attributes of the dragon and of the beast may be established, attributes which are actually distinctively different (Düsterdieck, *Handbuch Offenbarung*⁴, 389ff.). The judgment expressed above rescues us from these innumerable vicissitudes.

203. The binding of the dragon (Rev 20:1ff.) belongs naturally to chapter 12. The conquering of the two beasts and the kings of the earth (Rev 19:17-21) appears to be consistent with (and therefore to belong to) chapter 13. The report of Christ's appearance (Rev 19:11-16) has been compounded from both traditions. In regard to this, for example, Rev 19:15a, καὶ ἐκ τοῦ στόματος αὐτοῦ κτλ. [kai ek tou stomatos autou, etc.], is to be considered along with Rev 19:21; 19:15b, καὶ αὐτὸς ποιμανεῖ αὐτοὺς κτλ. [kai autos poimanei autous, etc.], is to be considered along with Rev 12:5. Accordingly, Rev 13:15a is linked to the tradition of chapter 13, and Rev 13:15b is linked to that of chapter 12. Both of the sources may have spoken of the armaments; cf. Rev 19:19ff. 16:13, 14, and 16, as they have survived for us, probably stem from the "dragon tradition." — In the discussion which follows I will depend predominately on chapter 13 for the "beast tradition." That is where this tradition is preserved in its most unadulterated form. Those passages which have a closer or a more distant literary relationship to chapter 13, without belonging to the contextual setting of the tradition (Rev 14:6-20 and Revelation 16), will not be dealt with in this investigation. I will deal, however, with the continuation of chapter 17. As to methodology, cf. above, pp. 126ff.

204. Cf. the remarks concerning Daniel 7 on pp. 209-13.

205. Cf. above, pp. 171f. and 202 immediately above.

206. Thus with Düsterdieck, *Handbuch Offenbarung*[4], 424ff., and Völter, *Problem der Apokalypse*, 202ff., works which take the seven heads of the chapter — correctly — as kings. Despite this, however, they then attempt a harmonization of the numbers *seven* and *ten!* The common exegesis of the ten kingdoms of the beast (Ewald, *Johannes Apokalypse*, 251; Renan, *L'Antechrist*, 328; Erbes, *Offenbarung Johannis*, 13; Holtzmann et al., *Hand-commentar*[2], 4:341; Weizsäcker, *Apost. Zeitalter*[2], 499) is that they encompass the ten provinces of Roman rule. This would be indicated if, for instance, the single head of the beast wore ten crowns, as at 19:12.

207. Harnack, "Nachwort," 135.

208. It is quite similar when Daniel 7, as is probably the case, adds the "eleventh" to the traditional "ten" kings. Cf. pp. 211ff.

209. Which of the chronological results of these calculations actually came to pass is not a problem which we will consider here!

210. An instructive parallel to this whole process is the history of the interpretation of the number *three and a half;* cf. above, pp. 349-50, n. 100.

211. Though Weizsäcker, *Apost. Zeitalter*[2], 495, also certainly warns of interpreting the "imaginative images" [German: "Pantasiebilder"] of the author contemporaneously.

212. Cf. above, pp. 176-80 and at Dan 7 (pp. 207ff.).

213. The vision itself covers Rev 17:3-6.

214. V. 8, the interpretation of the beast, is not a contemporaneous interpretation; cf. in that which follows.

215. *4 Ezra* 13:52 offers an explanation of the feature. The visions of the eschaton come from the sea, i.e., out of concealment.

216. The wording τῆς καθημένης ἐπὶ ὑδάτων πολλῶν [*tēs katēmenēs epi hydatōn pollōn* — "the one who sits upon many waters"], in fact, does show some close kinship to Jer 51:3, שכנתי על־מים רבים [*šōḵantî ʿal-mayim rabbîm* — "you sit upon many waters"]. The passage from Jeremiah may thus have influenced the wording of Revelation. It cannot, however, because of the parallels mentioned above, be the original thing since in this context waters are mentioned generally. For more about this, cf. below, pp. 228ff.

217. In the book of Revelation I follow, here and elsewhere, the text edited by B. Weiss.

218. The common explanation (Ewald, *Johannes Apokalypse*, 251; Renan, *L'Antechrist*, 329; Hilgenfeld, "Joh. Apok. n. Forschung," 434; Holtzmann et al., *Hand-commentar*[2], 4:341f.; Jülicher, *Einleitung*, 179) that it is the name Σεβαστός [*sebastos*, "Augustus"] is suitable only for Rev 13:1, but not for Rev 17:3. Moreover, it cannot be substantiated. Such explanations would undoubtedly be ingenious if the modern investigator had the assignment of interpreting the chapter on its own allegorically. They are methodologically misguided, however, since the modern investigator in actuality has the assignment of determining which allegorical explanation the ancient author had in his mind!

219. This feature is to be understood from the fact that next to purple and scarlet materials (we would say: velvet and silk) are placed gold, jewels, and pearls (Spitta, *Offenbarung*, 183). The explanation that the purple material suggested *royal* purple (Bleek, *Vorlesungen Apok.*, 322; Ewald, *Johannes Apokalypse*, 300; Düsterdieck, *Handbuch Offenbarung*[4], 499) is, therefore, too concrete. Of course, it is also the vesture of prostitutes (Renan, *L'Antechrist*, 342). It is even less likely that the scarlet coloration of the beast or of the woman has anything to do with blood shed by martyrs (Düsterdieck, *Handbuch Offenbarung*[4], 499) or with the mantle of Roman soldiery (Holtzmann et al., *Hand-commentar*[2], 4:349).

220. It is not natural to see in the wilderness an indication of the impending fate of Rome (Rev 17:16, ἠρημωμένην [*erēmōmenēn*, "that which is made barren"] — Bleek, *Vorlesungen Apok.*,

321; de Wette, *Kommentar²*, 151; Ewald, *Johannes Apokalypse*, 299; Düsterdieck, *Handbuch Offenbarung⁴*, 498; Holtzmann et al., *Hand-commentar²*, 4:349). The woman whom the seer beholds is Rome in Caesarean splendor. It thus has still not been destroyed!

221. The parallel of "the whores" ‖ "the abominations" is peculiar. Perhaps some corruption exists.

222. By these names the author implies the well-known Old Testament image of the metropolis as a whore, on whom all peoples or all kings of the earth call (Rev 17:2; 18:9; cf. Isa 23:15-18; Jer 51:7f.; Nah 3:4f.).

223. Auguste Hildebrandt, "Antichristentum," *ZWT* 17 (1874) 57f.

224. Volkmar, *Comm. Offenbarung Joh.*, 197; cited by Hilgenfeld, *Einleitung in das NT*, 436.

225. Max Krenkel, *Der Apostel Johannes* (Berlin: F. Henschel, 1874) [hereinafter: Krenkel, *Apost. Joh.*], 179f.; cited by Hilgenfeld, *Einleitung in das NT*, 436.

226. Völter, *Entstehung der Apokalypse¹*, 23. [For information regarding Alexander of Abonuteichos, cf. Lucian of Samosata, "Ἀλεξάνδρος ἡ Ψευδόμαντις," in *Lucian with an English Translation*, ed. and trans. A. M. Harmon, Loeb Classical Library (New York: G. P. Putnam's Sons, 1925), 4:173-233; W. J. Rose, "Alexander of Abonuteichos," *The Oxford Classical Dictionary* (Oxford: Clarendon, 1949), 35; A. D. Nock, "Alexander of Abunoteichos," *The Classical Quarterly*, 22 (1928) 160-62. — trans.]

227. Völter, *Entstehung der Apokalypse²*, 78f.

228. Völter, *Problem der Apokalypse*, 209.

229. Spitta, *Offenbarung*, 382ff., who in addition considers both the Egyptian Helicon and Apelles of Ashkelon; Erbes, *Offenbarung Johannis*, 25f., who also considers Petronius, governor of Syria under Caligula, and Apelles, the advisor of the same Caesar.

230. [German: "Irgend ein Betrüger aus Ephesus, ein Anhänger des falschen Nero oder gar dieser selbst." — trans.]; Renan, *L'Antechrist*, 334, who also brings under consideration an Asian high priest, Simon Magus, and Balbillus of Ephesus.

231. de Wette, *Kommentar²*, 133; Hilgenfeld, "Joh. Apok.," 436, n. 1; Beyschlag, "Offenbarung," 190.

232. Mommsen, *Röm. Gesch.*, 5:522.

233. But if the fire is actually fire, the image of Caesar an actual image of Caesar, why should the lamb's horns not be actual, but rather allegorical, lamb's horns?!?

234. Bleek, *Vorlesungen Apok.*, 228; Düsterdieck, *Handbuch Offenbarung⁴*, 443; Weizsäcker, *Apost. Zeitalter²*, 497; Holtzmann et al., *Hand-commentar²*, 4:343; Spitta, *Offenbarung*, 139. According to Spitta, *Offenbarung*, 383, the lamb's horns describe "in an absolutely accurate manner" [German: "in durchaus zutreffender Weise"] the Samaritan origin of Simon Magus. He is a lamb, i.e., similar to an Israelite. He will not easily be named as such, however!

235. It is even less acceptable to see in the words "horns similar to a lamb" a play on "the Lamb" of Rev 5:6 (Ewald, *Johannes Apokalypse*, 257; Völter, *Problem der Apokalypse*, 210). In the case of Rev 5:6, the definite article must be used, i.e., "*THE* Lamb."

236. Holtzmann et al., *Hand-commentar²*, 4:343.

237. Cf. above, pp. 119 and 137ff.

238. The seal impressions on hand and brow may, according to Holtzmann et al., *Hand-commentar²*, 4:343f., be a comparison to the image of the Caesar on coins. This is possible, but a definitive assertion of this cannot actually be formulated.

239. Bleek, *Vorlesungen Apok.*, 101f.; Weizsäcker, *Apost. Zeitalter²*, 498.

240. Regarding the methodology here, cf. pp. 193f. and 210f.

241. Whether the idea of the false prophet existed formerly, or whether it was only constructed ad hoc as the explanation of the second beast cannot be said. Evidence for the former does not exist.

242. This feature has given a great many headaches to contemporary exegetes. It has, generally, no symbolic significance (Bleek, *Vorlesungen Apok.,* 287), or "the earth" means Asia (Ewald, *Johannes Apokalypse,* 255f.), or "Palestine" (Spitta, *Offenbarung,* 377), or both (Renan, *L'Antechrist,* 335). Or the beast comes from the earth because it will make an impression on the earth (Düsterdieck, *Handbuch Offenbarung⁴,* 442), or because it existed in relationship to the first beast who ascended from the sea onto the earth, a relationship of susceptibility and servitude (de Wette, *Kommentar²,* 132), etc.

243. The speech which it makes characterizes the beast, according to Holtzmann et al., *Hand-commentar²,* 4:343, as standing in the service of the dragon. But is the "servant" recognized by the fact that he speaks in the same way as his master. Usually the phrase ἐλάλει ὡς δράκων [*elalei hōs drakōn*] is explicated: "just as mischievous and cunning as is necessary in order to seduce humanity," like the serpent of Eden (Bleek, *Vorlesungen Apok.,* 288; de Wette, *Kommentar²,* 128; Ewald, *Johannes Apokalypse,* 257; Düsterdieck, *Handbuch Offenbarung⁴,* 443; Beyschlag, "Apokalypse," 190). One overlooks thereby, however, the fact that δράκων [*drakōn*] lacks the article. Furthermore, the serpent of Eden was, to be sure, cunning. Usually, however, power and formidability, but not cunning, are the characteristic features of the dragon!

244. It might be attributed to a translation error: perhaps a Hebrew ותאמר [*wat-tō'mar*], "and she said" — Hebrew חיה [*ḥayyāh*] / Greek θηρίον [*thērion*], meaning "beast," are both also feminine nouns, hence the "she" was misread for ותאר [*wĕ-tō'ar*], "and a form" (therefore: "he had horns like a lamb and a form like a dragon"). Concerning a Hebrew composition of Revelation 13, cf. below, p. 227, n. 259.

245. The parallel traditions say nothing. Contemporary explications are not reliable. Biblical allusions are only relevant to details (the fire from the heavens as in the case of Elijah, the speaking idol similar to Bel in Babylon). At the same time the words are highly peculiar. I might even suspect an acquired tradition here!

246. That the beast represented the world power, or the world-dominating people, is confirmed by his specific attributes in Rev 13:1(-3a), and is made certain especially by the parallels (Daniel 7; *4 Ezra* 11; Revelation 17). This is almost universally recognized. If the beast is to be taken as an individual person (Spitta, *Offenbarung,* 364ff.; Erbes, *Offenbarung Johannis,* 19), then the heads and horns of Rev 13:1 must be understood as thoughtless and insignificant appropriations from Daniel 7, and the injured head of Rev 13:3 must be removed from the text arbitrarily. According to Völter, *Problem der Apokalypse,* 202f., the beast is a Caesar, which doesn't prevent him from declaring the injured head to be a Caesar! — Spitta, *Offenbarung,* 364f., raises as an objection to this view the fact that Rev 16:13; 19:19f., etc. will speak of the first beast generally as it would speak of a person, so that it therefore does not represent the world power generally but rather an individual Caesar. This reservation is completely resolved, however, if there exists here a feature allegorized only lately, a feature in which the beast originally existed only as an individual and only later came to be a personification of the world power! In the same way, Daniel speaks of the fourth beast. Rev 19:2 = Dan 7:11. — The shift from the masculine grammatical gender to the neuter grammatical gender at Rev 13:8 provides just as little proof that the θηρίον was a particular person (Spitta, *Offenbarung,* 374f.; Erbes, *Offenbarung Johannis,* 17). This is a simple slip of the tongue like Rev 11:15, φωναὶ λέγοντες [*phōnai legontes*]; 14:19, τὴν ληνὸν τὸν μέγαν [*tēn lēnon ton megan*], etc. For other examples, cf. Schmidt, *Anmerkungen,* 25.

247. So according to F. Benary ["Offene Erklärung gegen Dr. Ferd. Hitzig," *Haller*

Allgemeine Literaturzeitung Intelligenzblat, August 1837, p. 428; and "Erklärung der Zahl 666 (χξσ′) in der Apocalypse (13, 18) und ihrere Variante 616 (χισ′)," *Zeitschrift für spekulative Theologie* 1 (1836); F. Hitzig [*Ostern und Pfingsten in zweiten Dekalog: Sendschreiben an Kirchenrath und Professor Alexander Schweizer in Riesbach* (Heidelberg: C. F. Winter, 1838), 3]; Eduard Reuss ["Vermischte Anzeigen," *Haller Allgemeine Literatur-Zeitung Intelligenzblat*, September 1837, p. 520]; O. F. Fritzsche ["Über die Zahl 666 in der Apokalypse, eine Abhandlung über Apocal. 13, 16-18," *Annalen der gesammten theologischen Literatur und der christlichen Kirche Überhaupt*, 3 Bd., 1 Heft, 42-64] (all cited by Holtzmann et al., *Hand-commentar*[2], 4:297); Ewald, *Johannes Apokalypse*, 14:292; Hilgenfeld, "Joh. Apok. n. Forschung," 434f., 441; Renan, *L'Antechrist*, 330ff., 344; Beyschlag, "Offenbarung," 182f., 190; Mommsen, *Röm. Gesch.*, 5:296, 521; Pfleiderer, *Urchristentum*, 334; P. Schmidt, *Anmerkungen*, 42f., 47f.; Holtzmann et al., *Hand-commentar*[2], 4:296f.; Jülicher, *Einleitung*, 180. — Bleek, *Vorlesungen Apok.*, 293; de Wette, *Kommentar*[2], 131, 155f.; Lücke, *Einleitung in die Offenbarung Johannes*, 382ff., dispute the opinion that "666" = נרון קסר [*nirôn qēsār*]. They are otherwise in agreement with the preceding ideas, however. Düsterdieck, *Handbuch Offenbarung*[4], 436 and Weiss, *Einleitung*[2], 382f., both oppose even the identity of the wounded head (Rev 13:3) and the returning beast (Rev 17:8), and thus they oppose the assumption of a *Nero redivivus*. They do, however, recognize in the wounded head the fall of Nero. D. Völter, F. Spitta, and K. Erbes diverge from the traditional explication of the chapter (Völter, *Entstehung der Apokalypse*[1], argues that v. 28 points to Antoninus Pius; Völter, *Entstehung der Apokalypse*[2], 72ff., points to Hadrian, טיריון אדרינוס [*ṭîryôn ᾿aḏrîyānôs*]; Völter, *Problem der Apokalypse*, 200ff., points to Domitian; Erbes, *Offenbarung Johannis*, 19ff., and Spitta, *Offenbarung*, 135ff., both point to Γάιος Καῖσαρ [*gaios kaisar*] = 616, in agreement with the majority of the exegetes, in that they combine the wounded head in the present text with the returning beast of 17:8 and, thereby, point to *Nero redivivus*; cf. Völter, *Problem der Apokalypse*, 203; Erbes, *Offenbarung Johannis*, 11, 17f., 31, 169; Spitta, *Offenbarung*, 134ff., 184). Against this connection to Nero, however, Charles Bruston, *Les Origene de l'Apocalypse* (Paris: Librairie Fischbacker, 1888) [hereinafter: Bruston, *Apocalypse*], 5ff., has raised an objection. For his part he links the injured head to Caesar. To a large degree I concur with Bruston in the positive and negative points. The valuable contributions of Theodor Zahn, "Apokalyptische Studien III," *Zeitschrift für kirchliche Wissenschaft* [hereinafter: ZKW] 7 (1886) [hereinafter: Zahn, "Apok. Stud. III"] 337ff., to the history of the Nero saga are, of course, not really important to the struggle against the usual exegesis of chapter 13. This exegesis, I believe, can be refuted by many more ordinary methods.

248. Thereupon both the calculation which is based on the Greek Γάιος Καῖσαρ [*Gaios Kaisar*] and the calculation based on the Hebrew/Aramaic טיריון אדרינוס [*ṭîryôn ᾿aḏrîyānôs*] fail. Whether the orthography קפר [*q · p · r*] is possible for the more common קיסר [*q · y · s · r*] must remain undiscussed!

249. On the methodology, cf. pp. 126ff. It is comprehensible that those exegetes who assume the unity of the book of Revelation see a unified contemporaneous background for the different images, and thereby, for example, employ elements from chapter 17 for the exegesis of chapter 13. It is hardly pardonable, however, if this same exegesis goes on into areas where the distinctive origins of the individual chapters have been distinguished, for example, by Erbes, *Offenbarung Johannes*, by Spitta, *Offenbarung*, and by Völter, *Problem der Apokalypse*.

250. Cf. above, pp. 217ff.

251. ἔζησεν [*ezēsen*; Heb. ותחי *û-ṯḥî*] means this: "and he will again be sound"; cf. Gen 20:7; Josh 5:8; 2 Kings 1:2; Isa 38:21 (in the last two passages LXX has ζῆν [*zēn*]). From ἔζησεν

[*ezēsen*] it does not, therefore, follow that the beast would actually have been killed before; *contra* Spitta, *Offenbarung*, 138. Concerning the Hebrew origin of chapter 13, cf. below, p. 227, n. 259.

252. Researchers are also misled here by the "contemporaneous" explanation. It is believed that something from the contemporary period, something which the author himself experienced, . . . that something must be found. But this is in no way actually necessary. Compare the facts reported by Daniel 17, facts which extend back over many decades. It is certain only that the event reported here was characteristic of the whole world and of Rome. It has been told so that the significance of the beast to that event might be recognized. — I am not investigating at this point whether it is to be concluded from this that Revelation 13 was originally written under an ancient pseudonym. That *is* to be claimed for Antiochus 17, however, because of οὐκ ἔστιν [*ouk estin*] at 17:18 (cf. in what follows).

253. The ancient authors began the series of Roman "Caesars" with Caesar himself, or with Augustus. With Caesar, e.g., Suetonius, Josephus, *Chronicon Paschal*. Cf. Lücke, *Einleitung in die Offenbarung des Johannes*, 389, n. 2.

254. καὶ μίαν ἐκ τῶν κεφαλῶν αὐτοῦ (sc. θηρίου) [*kai mian ek tōn kephalōn autou (thērion)*] = (sc. חיה) ואחד מראשיה (*wĕ-'eḥad mē-rō'šêhā* [sc. *hāyāh*]), "the first of the heads." The usage of cardinal number words is very frequent in Hebrew in the case of the enumeration of days of the month and of the year [*Wilhelm Gesenius' Hebräische Grammatik*, ed. E. Kautzsch, 25th ed. (Leipzig: F. C. W. Vogel, 1889) [hereinafter: Kautzsch, *Gesenius' Gram.*^{25}], §134, n. 4). In the New Testament, the case of the numbering of the weekdays (μία τῶν σαββάτων [*mia tōn sabbatōn*]) was established by Georg Bendikt Winer, *Grammatik des neutestamentlichen Sprachidioms als sichere Grundlage der neutestamentliche Exegese*, 2d ed. (Leipzig: F. C. W. Vogel, 1825), §30.1 (p. 100); cf. below, p. 227, n. 259.

255. This observation is also made by Spitta (*Offenbarung*, 139), who immediately scissors out the difficulty and totally excises v. 4b.

256. Dan 8:2 certainly gets one thinking!

257. It is not established that a definite individual situation is in evidence here, not even the time of Caligula (Spitta, *Offenbarung*; Erbes, *Offenbarung Johannis*). The intention of the Caesar to set up his image in the Temple of Jerusalem, though adverted without words, is still comprehensibly suggested in some way or another. The question as to which common political situation the chapter refers does not belong in this investigation!

258. More details concerning this at another place.

259. The style of chapter 13 lies close to the basic tenets of Hebrew composition. The following are to be considered as Hebraic: v. 3, καὶ μίαν ἐκ τῶν κεφαλῶν αὐτοῦ [*kai mian ek tōn kephalōn autou*], in Hebrew ואחד מראשיה [*wĕ-'eḥad mē-rō'šêh*], "the first of the heads"; cf. p. 369, n. 253b; v. 3, ἡ πληγὴ τοῦ θανάτου αὐτοῦ [*hē plēgē tou thanatou autou*], in Hebrew מכת מותה [*makat māwĕtōh*], "his mortal wound" (Kautzsch, *Gesenius' Gram.*^{25}, §128, 2i); vv. 12, 14; 19:20, ἐνώπιον αὐτοῦ [*enōpion autou*], in Hebrew לפניה [*lipnêhū*], "under his oversight" (cf. Siegfried-Stade, *Wb*, s.v. פנים); v. 14, καὶ ἔζησε [*kai ezēse*], in Hebrew ותחי [*wat-tĕḥî*], "and remain alive" (cf. pp. 217f. above); v. 18, ἀριθμὸς ἀνθρώπου [*arithmos anthrōpou*], like חרט אנוש [*ḥeret 'ĕnôš*], γραφὶς ἀνθρώπου [*graphis anthrōpou*], Isa 8:1; cf. μέτρον ἀνθρώπου [*metron anthrōpou*] (Rev 21:17, "common reckoning"). The following are perhaps reading errors: v. 11, καὶ ἐλάλει [*kai elalei*], reading, in Hebrew, ותאמר [*wat-to'mar*] for an original ותאר [*wĕ-tō'ar*] (cf. p. 368, n. 244 above); and v. 3, ἐθαυμάσθη ὀπίσω τοῦ θηρίου [*ethaumasthē opisō tou thēriou*], reading, in Hebrew, ותתמה מאחרי החיה [*wat-titmāh mē-'aḥărê hā-ḥayyāh*], where the מאחרי [*mē-'aḥărê*] was read, incorrectly, for the word מאחרית [*mē-'aḥărît*], "the whole world is horrified about the final fate of the beast" (namely, that it remains alive). The construction

θαυμάζεσθαι ὀπίσω [thaumazesthai opisō] is supported neither in the Greek nor in the Hebrew, as far as I know. אחרית [ʾaḥărît] speaks of the final end of a (critical) thing, the ultimate fate of a person.

260. Vischer, Offenbarung, 85.

261. Cf. Behrmann, Daniel, xxxix.

262. Rev 13:5, στόμα λαλοῦν μεγάλα [stoma laloun megala, "a mouth uttering big things"] is equivalent to Dan 7:8, ופם ממלל רברבן [û-pūm mĕmallīl raḇrĕḇān, "and a mouth speaking great things"]; LXX Θ, στόμα λαλοῦν μεγάλα [stoma laloun megala]. Rev 13:7, ποιῆσαι πόλεμον μετὰ τῶν ἁγίων καὶ νικῆσαι αὐτούς [poiēsai polemon meta tōn hagiōn kai nikēsai autous, "to make war with the holy ones and to conquer them"] is equivalent to Dan 7:21, עבדא קרב עם־קדישׁין ויכלה להם [ʾāḇdā' qĕrāḇ ʿim-qaddîšîn wĕ-yāḵlāh lĕ-hem, "he made war on the holy ones and prevailed against them"].

263. The indication of the end time in Rev 13:56 is, in any event, not literally taken from Daniel. Whether it is an independent tradition I cannot say.

264. Cf. above, pp. 212f.

265. (Ptolemaic) kings numbered seven as well (Sib. Or. 3.192, 318, 608); the ten horns are recognized to be Seleucids (Sib. Or. 3.397).

266. For the expression "beast," cf. Ps 68:31 and Dan 7:3, and cf. above, pp. 209ff.

267. For the expression ἀναβαίνειν [anabainein, "to arise"], cf. Rev 13:1; Dan 7:3; 4 Ezra 11:1; 13:3; and 2 Apoc. Bar. 29:4.

268. Cf. above, p. 220, n. 216.

269. Cf. above, pp. 228f. [Friedrich Delitzsch, Paradies?, 148, and Bernhard Schrader, "Drache, Drache zu Babel," in Riehm, Hw², 1:328f., have already connected the beast of Revelation with this seven-headed Babylonian serpent.] — Zimmern

270. In 2 Tim 4:17 one name for the devil is "the lion"; cf. 1 Pet 5:8.

271. That the Babylonian tradition knew of a horned Ti'āmat has already been shown above, p. 211.

272. Manî (Flügel, Mani, 86) describes the form of the being of darkness as follows: Head of a lion, body of a dragon, wings of a bird (Brandt, Mandäische Schriften, 194: more specifically, wings of an eagle), tail of a fish, four feet of a reptile. Among the Mandaeans, Ur, the "king of the darkness," has a lion's head, a dragon's body, eagle's wings, the flanks of a tortoise, and the hands and feet of the demon (לאטאבא [la'ṭa'ba']), and is doubly evil. "In the breath of its mouth iron boils" (Brandt, Mandäische Religion, 43; Brandt, Mandäische Schriften, 226).

273. In regard to the expression (Rev 13:6) τοὺς ἐν τῷ οὐρανῷ σκηνοῦντας [tous en tō ouranō skēnountas, "those who dwell in heaven"] (cf. Rev 12:12), it should perhaps be recalled that the houses in which the stars live are, in the Babylonian representations, similar to reed huts. [Cf., e.g., Rawl, 5:57.] — Zimmern

274. Cf. above, pp. 369-70, n. 259.

275. [Cf., in this regard, Edward J. Harper, "Die babylonischen Legenden von Etana, Zu, Adapa und Dibarra," Beiträge zur Assyriologie und vergleichende Semitischen Sprachwissenschaft 2 (1894) 434, n.] — Zimmern

276. Cf. above, pp. 13f. [and the materials cited in Bezold, "Göttertypen," 116f.] — Zimmern

277. Cf. above, pp. 55f. and 209f.

278. One notes that the domination of Behemoth over the beasts of the field (Job 40:20) — in an uncertain text, of course — is described with a similar phrase, ישׁאו־לו [yaśśi'û-lô]

"seeing him, they marvel at him." [Gunkel appears to be reading the verbal stem as √נשא II [√nš] and to understand the present word as a Hebrew *Hip'îl* imperfect 3d pl. form — trans.]

279. In a Mandaean source (cf. Brandt, *Mandäische Schriften*, 231f.) the high spirit of *Ur* is described quite similarly. He says, "Is there anyone greater them I am? Is there anyone who has developed as far as me? . . . Or is there anyone who is stronger than I am? Therefore *I* will stand up! *I* will fight with him! *I* will stand up! *I* will fight with him!" "*I* will climb up to this brilliant land and *I* will wage war with its king. *I* will take his crown, and *I* will put it on *my* head, and *I* will be king of the high place and of the deep!" (Cf. *Pss. Sol.* 2:33.) — Job 41 too appears to be alluding to such a struggle of Leviathan against the gods; cf. pp. 35ff. above.

280. The great beast, which is found in Hermas, *Vision* 4, is in any case related to the apocalyptic beasts. It comes forth out of the dust, which darkens the sun (Rev 9:2). It looks like a whale or κῆτος [*kētos*] (1 Enoch 60:7). From its mouth come forth fiery locusts (Rev 9:2ff., 7ff.; 16:13). It has a head like a tortoise shell (cf. above, p. 370, n. 272). As Hermas, through his faith and through the protection of the angel Θεγρί [*Thegri*] (who is placed over the beast), gets past the beast, a young woman encounters him, dressed as if coming from a bridal chamber, veiled all in white raiment (cf. Rev 21:2, 9). "This beast is the 'type' of the coming great privation." It has four colors on its head: black, fire/blood red, golden, and white, which chapter 3 will then allegorize as the world, the persecution, the trials and testings, and the coming aeon. According to Adolph Harnack, *Patrum apostolicorum opera: texta ad fidem codicum et graecorum et latinorum adhibitis praestantissimis editionibus recensuerunt commentario exegetico et historico illustraverunt apparatu critico versione latina passim correcta prolegomenis indicibus instruxerunt,* editio post Dresselianam alterum tertia (Leipzig: Hinrichs, 1876-78) [hereinafter: Harnack, *Patr. Apost.*], 3:lxxv, Revelation had not known Hermas. — In the case of the red beast, Spitta, *Offenbarung,* even after he has dealt with the horns and the heads (p. 183), thinks of an ass (p. 447).

281. 4 Ezra 7:26 is not speaking of the "bride." Lat. Syr. "et apparebit sponsa ['et' om Maz] apparescens civitas"; ἡ νύμφη φαινομένη [*hē nymphē phainomenē*]. It is made better by ἡ νῦν μὴ φαινομένη [*hē nyn mē phainomenē*]; Arm., Aram., Eth. 5:27, "manifestabitur urbs quae nunc non apparet"; "et ostendetur quae nunc subducitur terra," is parallel.

282. In regard to this cf. pp. 16f. above. In the Mandaic narrative of the battle of *Hibil-Ziwâ* with *Krûn,* the firstborn king of the darkness, a narrative which Brandt, *Mandäische Schriften,* 150f., compares with the myth of *Tiâmat* . . . in that narrative there is mention of a "deed," i.e., of a signet ring, "on which is written and inscribed the name of the great darkness, a ring which was concealed, and which had not been seen since the day when it was set." [German: "auf welchem geschrieben und gemalt war der Name der grossen Finsternis, der verborgen war, den er nicht gesehen hatte von dem Tage, da er gepflanzt worden, an."] This "deed" *Krûn,* having been defeated by *Hibil-Ziwâ,* must hand over to him from his treasure trove. By means of this "deed," which all beings respect, the divine hero wins the return of the upper world.

283. Berossus, γυναῖκα [*gynaika*]; cf. above, pp. 14ff.

284. Compare the depictions in Eberhard Schrader, "Dagan," in Riehm, *Hw,* p. 250; Eberhard Schrader, "Assyrien, Assur," in Riehm, *HW,* p. 108; Constantin Schlottmann, "Astarte und Aschera," in Riehm, *HW,* p. 113; and Constantin Schlottmann, "Baal," in Riehm, *HW,* p. 129; more in Roscher, *Lexikon Mythologie,* 194, the form of Jupiter from Dolich with a thunderbolt and an axe, on the bull (cf., in addition, the illustration of Schlottmann, "Baal," in Riehm, *Hw,* 129), and especially the form of Phoenician *'Anat,* who sits on a lion (Schlottmann, "Astarte und Aschera," in Riehm, *Hw,* 114). — The style of placing the deities on animals stems, according to

Ed. Meyer (in Roscher's *Lexikon Mythologie*, 1191), from Babylon and had made its way from there to Syria and Cilicia. This style will even be ridiculed as characteristically Babylonian by Deutero-Isaiah (Isa 46:1, 2):

1 *Bēl* collapsed   Nebo fell.

     . . . .

     Their images were placed on beasts.

       Their (cast images) were loaded on cattle

         A burden for those exhausted and weary.

2 They collapse.   They fall down together

     The burdens remain unsaved.

       They are shattered!

[For נשאתיכם [*nĕśu'ōṯêkem*, "your things borne"], perhaps מסכותיהם [*massēḵôṯêhem*, "their molten images"] should be read. The second masculine plural is surely incorrect. LXX has a parallel word before עיפה ['*ăyēpāh*, "faint, weary"]. For בשבי [*baš-šĕbî*, "into captivity"] we should read בשבר [*bĕ-šeber*, "in pieces"].] The prophet thinks the beasts have carried their gods long enough and now, being tired, they will let their burdens drop. Beasts and gods thereby come to shame. YHWH is compared to this, YHWH who is not carried, but who carries himself, and endures forever and ever.

285. As to how the Jewish tradition explained this name cf. p. 366, n. 221.

286. Likewise in Mandaic tradition, cf. Brandt, *Mand. Schriften*, 187f.

287. Cf. p. 366, n. 222.

288. Cf. above, pp. 13f.

289. As in the Babylonian-Aramaic tradition (according to the Armenian tradition), the woman is called *Om orqaye*, "Mother of the underground ones" (cf. above, pp. 14f.); or as in the Mandaic tradition, she is called *Qin*, "Mother of the darkness" (Brandt, *Mand. Schriften*, 146).

290. Cf. above, p. 367, n. 245.

291. I draw the attention of Assyriologists to this point.

292. Cf. above, pp. 200ff., 208ff.

293. Rev 21:1.

294. *1 Enoch* 72:1.

295. Weber, *Altsyn. Theol.*, 382.

296. 2 Cor 5:17; Gal 6:15 = δεύτερα πλάσις [*deutera plasis*, "second creation"]; *Barn*. 6:13. — The expression "new creation" originally focused on the macro-cosmos, and then was transferred to the human beings of the final days, and finally to the individual human beings in whom "everything" will become "new."

297. Isa 65:17; 66:22; *1 Enoch* 91:16; cf. *4 Ezra* 7:31.

298. [Latin: "et convertetur saeculum in antiquam silentium diebus VII sicut in prioribus initiis, ita ut hemo derelinquatur"]; *4 Ezra* 7:30. Cf. *2 Apoc. Bar.* 3:7, "et saeculum redibit ad silentium pristinum" [translation: "and the world return to pristine silence"]. This primordial "silence" at *4 Ezra* 7:30 (cf. *4 Ezra* 6:39) refers to the silence before a human voice was heard, therefore to the seven days — the days before human speech (Gen 2:19). Originally it was probably the σιγή [*sigē*, "silence"] of God which preceded the λόγος [*logos*, "word"]; Wis 18:14f.; Ignatius of Antioch, *Epistle to the Magnesians* 8:2.

299. This is the schema of Judeo-Christian Adam speculation.

300. אדם הקדמוני אדם הראשון ['*āḏām haq-qaḏmônî, 'āḏām hā-rī'šôn*, "the primitive

Adam, the first Adam"] [cf. Jacob Levy, *Neuhebräisches und Chaldäisches Wörterbuch über die Talmudim und Midraschim* (Leipzig: F. A. Brockhaus, 1876-89) [hereinafter: Levy, *Neuhebr.*], s.v. אדם and קדמוני]; ὁ πρῶτος Ἀδάμ ὁ ἔσχατος Ἀδάμ [*ho prōtos Adam, ho eschatos Adam,* "the first Adam, the last Adam"], 1 Cor 15:45; ὁ πρῶτος ἄνθρωπος ὁ δεύτερος ἄνθρωπος [*ho prōtos anthrōpos, ho deuteros anthrōpos,* "the first human, the second human"], 1 Cor 15:47; ὁ παλαιὸς ἄνθρωπος ὁ νέος (καινὸς) ἄνθρωπος [*ho palaios anthrōpos, ho neos (kainos) anthrōpos,* "the old person, the new (new) person"], Col 3:9f. (Eph 4:22ff.; Eph 2:15). The "new human being" is originally a divine form ἐξ οὐρανοῦ [*ex ouranou,* "from heaven"] (1 Cor 15:47). Then it became the embodiment of an ideal.

301. ὁ ὄφις ὁ ἀρχαῖος [*ho ophis ho archaios,* "the ancient serpent"], Rev 12:9; נחש קדמוני [*nāḥaš qadmônî,* "the ancient serpent"], Weber, *Altsyn. Theol.,* 211; הנחש הראשון [*han-nāḥaš hā-ri'šôn,* "the first serpent"], Levy, *Neuhebr.,* s.v. נחש [*nāḥaš*].

302. πλανᾶν [*planan,* "he deceives"], Rev 12:9; 20:10, etc.

303. *1 Enoch* 85–90 depicts the same idea: the earliest humanity is allegorically depicted as knowing cattle, from which all kinds of wild animals, lions and tigers and dogs and wolves, etc., have been generated. This must depict the depravation of humanity. Even the earliest Israelites appear as knowing sheep At the end, however, all animals of the field shall be transformed again, and all will become knowing creatures. So the end returns to the beginning.

304. Weber, *Altsyn. Theol.,* 344, 348, 350, 355; cf. the late Jewish tradition in Eisenmenger, *Entdecktes,* 2:808, "the future redemption will be like the first, כראשונה [*kā-ri'šônāh,* "like the first"]. [Original German: "die künftige Erlösung wird wie die erste כראשונה sein."]

305. Matt 24:37, which is applied to the sudden ruin which descends upon the unsuspecting children of the world.

306. 2 Pet 3:6f.

307. How this principle originated and what basis it actually had I cannot say. It is highly improbable that the primal myths were first related eschatologically in Israel. Rather, we may postulate, with greater certainty, that this shift had already taken place in Babylonian tradition; cf. above, pp. 58ff. and 202ff. In Israel we can establish this eschatological use of the myth from the time of Jeremiah or later; cf. above, pp. 58ff.

308. The reader should note that only the form, not the religious interest, of the concept of "preexistence" will be treated here.

309. The drawing together of "the first and the last things," e.g., *1 Enoch* 60:11; *Sib. Or.* 3:819f., 827, is seen here as the major part of the "revelation" of the great secret knowledge of God.

310. Cf. above, pp. 31f., 61ff., etc.

311. Cf. above, pp. 24, 26f., 33f., 39f., 56f., 61f.

312. This is the sense of the term ἀναβαίνειν [*anabainein*]; cf. pp. 228f.

313. Parallel to this is the following: the old heaven and the old earth were transitory, but the new heaven and the new earth exist eternally before God (Isa 66:22; *1 Enoch* 72:1; 91:16f.).

314. Cf. above, pp. 61-63.

315. This addition, "but the sea is no longer there," shows that the eschatological twist of the myth occurred at a time when the original depiction of the sea as a divinely opposed principle was still comprehended.

316. Cf. above, pp. 58f.

317. Later apocalyptic, in which all sorts of different traditions are gathered together in one image, speaks of a double assault of the heathen against the people of God, hence also a double appearance of the monster in the end time. If everything is taken into account, three ap-

pearances of the "devil" therefore occur. At the same time, the relation of the second to the third appearance is conceived by means of an analogy to the relation of the second to the first appearance. The vanquished dragon will be "shut up" in the abyss (Rev 20:2f.). It escapes again, however, a thousand years later. Then it once again will be overpowered and — and this is, finally, the *definitive* situation — it will be cast into the sea of fire and destroyed (Rev 10:10).

318. Cf. p. 373, n. 307.

319. The form of the vision is better realized in chapter 17 than it is in chapter 13. Certainly even in chapter 17 it is suffused with many inscrutabilities, the whore's cupful of abomination, her drunkenness from the blood of the saints.

320. This dogma is found first in Isa 65:17.

321. Other major features are added by the very dark tradition of Revelation 11, traditions which certainly originally also dealt with the chaos dragon, and which hence belong to the same mythic circle as the traditions of chapters 13 and 17.

322. Cf. the calculation of the number *three and a half*, pp. 217-19; and the heads or horns of the beast, pp. 171-73.

323. Cf. above, pp. 200-201 and 213f.

324. The word *ear* occurs here within a larger context. There are "hearing" ears (Matt 11:15f.), the likes of which can "accept" (Matt 11:14). [The term οὖς [*ous*, "ear"] is, therefore, parallel to νοῦς [*nous*, "mind, thought"] (Rev 17:9) or σοφία [*sophia*, "wisdom, insight"] (Rev 13:8 and 17:9)]. The sentence "Whoever has ears hear!" is, therefore, related to the other phrase, "Let the reader consider" (Mark 13:14). It points to a situation when secret knowledge is communicated, which seeks to make the reader attentive without, however, explicating it to him explicitly. This is also the way the phrase is used in Matt 11:15, often after a parable, since it is interpreted as an allegory and is understood to be secret knowledge [Matt 13:9; cf. Matt 13:15f., 43; Mark 7:16; etc. — cf. Adolf Jülicher, *Die Gleichnisreden Jesu* (Freiburg: J. C. B. Mohr-Paul Siebeck, 1888) [hereinafter: Jülicher, *Gleich. Jesu*], 121ff.]. Finally, the phrase has been used in a hackneyed sense at Rev 2:11 and 17. The phrase is, according to its nature, very much at home in apocalyptic literature. Accordingly, since it also occurs in the Gospels, it is not necessary to consider it to be of Christian origin and therefore to remove it from chapter 13 (Vischer, *Offenbarung*, 140f.). If Rev 13:9f. is stricken, then the very heart of the chapter, its practical application, is lost (cf. Erbes, *Offenbarung Johannis*, 23).

325. Völter, *Entstehung der Apokalypse*², 76; Erbes, *Offenbarung Johannis*, 32f.; etc.

326. From Levy, *Neuhebr.*, s.v. תהום. Here, therefore, the equation תהום [*těhôm*] = Rome is certainly acknowledged. Its original reason, that the monster of the end time was at the same time the monster of the beginning . . . that reason has been forgotten. Another reason has been invented to explain this remarkable equation [תהום [*těhôm*] = Rome]. — Eisenmenger, *Entdecktes*, 2:678f., cites from *b. Sanhedrin* 97b: "In year 4291 after world creation, the war of the dragons, תנינים [*tannînîm*], and the war of God and Magog will belong, and in the (then still) remaining time will the day of the Messiah be" [German: "nach 4291 Jahren von der Erschaffung der Welt werden die Kriege der Drachen תנינים und die Kriege des Gogs und Magogs aufhören, und in der (dann noch) übrigen Zeit werden die Tage des Messias sein"]. According to the exegesis of Isaac Abravanel [a medieval Jewish exegete], the "dragons" are the kings of the earth who fight with each other and against Israel. — Such tradition had persisted just that long!

327. This is certainly in reference only to the first author of the chapter. Whether the later authors actually saw through the mystery has escaped our comprehension.

328. The orthography of the word must also be communal. It should not make comprehension more difficult for those "in the know." Rather it should, perhaps, make it easier.

329. Cf. pp. 369-70, n. 259. Therefore, the אנוש מספר [*mispar 'ěnôš*, "number of a human"] is to be calculated in a totally different way. We do not really know one from the other. This translation of ἀριθμὸς ἀνθρώπου [*arithmos anthrōpou*] is that of Bleek, *Vorlesungen Apok.*, 291; Ewald, *Johannes Apokalypse*, 260; Holtzmann et al., *Hand-commentar²*, 4:344; Düsterdieck, *Handbuch Offenbarung⁴*; etc.

330. Concerning this there is considerable scholarly discussion!

331. According to the very nature of the thing, the number does not belong to the actual foundation of the tradition. This is demonstrated by the placing of the notation at the end of the whole chapter, not immediately after the description of the first beast.

332. Cf. above, pp. 369-70, n. 259. Even if the chapter may originally have been written in Greek, Hebrew, the sacred language of the Jews, was more fitting for such calculations than the "secular" language of Greek.

333. Theodor Zahn, "Apokalyptische Studien II," *ZKW* 6 (1885) [hereinafter: Zahn, "Apok. Stud. II"] 564ff.

334. Ewald's assumption (*Johannes Apokalypse*, 261f.). That *gîmaṭrîyāh* stems from the Old Babylonian sphere has since been proven incorrect. The Old Babylonian did not have an alphabetic writing, but rather had a syllabic one. In later times, of course, Aramaic was the language spoken and written in Babylon.

335. Like the אתבש [*'atbaš*] style of speech and the alphabetic poetry. אתבש [*'atbaš*] is a writing method which exchanges the letters of the Hebrew alphabet in reverse order, i.e., the first letter (א, *'ālep*, ') is replaced with the last letter (ת, *tāw*, *t*); the second letter (ב, *bêt*, *b*) is replaced by the second to the last letter (שׁ, *šîn*, *š*); etc.

336. Gen 14:14, the three-hundred-eighteen servants of Abraham. Three-hundred-eighteen = אליעזר [*'ělî'ezer*, "Eliezer"]. So also *Midrash Genesis Rabbah* 43f.

337. Cf. pp. 227f. above.

338. Cf. pp. 231ff.

339. Grammatically it is to be noted that תהום [*těhôm*] is feminine (since it was originally a personal name, there is no article); קדמוניה [*qaḏmônîyāh*] is also without an article (just as in the case of תהום רבה [*těhôm rabbāh*, "great deep"] of Gen 7:11; Ps 36:7, etc.). — Naturally the author also wondered about the three sixes. — The Old Testamental tradition is undecided about spellings with or without the letter ו [*wāw* or *wāw̄*] (six times *plēne*, four times defective). Levy, *Neuhebr.*, has only the *scriptio plena*.

340. ת = 400, ה = 5, ו = 6, מ (ם) = 40, total = 451; ק = 100, ד = 4, מ = 40, ו = 6, נ = 50, י = 10, ה = 5, total = 215. Grand total = 666. 666 is the reading established best by Irenaeus and the codices. The other reading, 616, has, of course, another solution in mind. The number was changed because nothing was known to be explained by 666, while, on the other hand, it was believed that a suitable name could be gained by using the number *616* (according to Zahn, "Apoc. Stud. II," 569-71, this name is Γάιος Καῖσαρ [*Gaios Kaisar*, "Gaios Caesar"]. This solution is definitely problematic. It directly equates the beast and Caesar (precision by the original writer, precision like that we would like to have, may not, of course, been required of a later writer, one who was satisfied if he could find a word which was not too far removed, and, in terms of its meaning, was at least a little bit suitable here.) This reading appears then to stem from the time of Caligula. At that time our chapter, therefore, already existed in Greek. Not a trace of broader intrusions inserted by the Caligulan interpreter are to be found in the present text, however.

341. Irenaeus (*Contra Haeresis* 5.30.3) did not know the solution to the numerical riddle. He knew, only guessing, of Λατεῖνος [*Lateinos*, "Latinos — the almost deified Roman ancestral figure, whom tradition made the founder of the Latin tribe] or of Τειτάν [*Teitan*, "Titan"].

Zahn, "Apok. Stud. II," 575, explicitly states that it clearly follows that the apocalyptist himself did not know the solution since the Spirit did not inform him of it (p. 576). Other investigators would appear to have the correct conclusions, that at the time of Irenaeus the tradition concerning the number 666 was already lost.

Whether the enigmatic word is Greek or Hebrew will not bear any weight in regard to the authority of Irenaeus and his tradition from John (*contra* Zahn, "Apok. Stud. II," 562). For, if he did not have a tradition about the word itself, Irenaeus most definitely did not possess anything concerning the language of this word. One notes, incidentally, that Irenaeus, *Contra Haeresis* 5.30.1, explicitly referred to the tradition of those persons whom John had known face-to-face. This is not at all unimportant for the illumination of this "tradition."

Notes to Chapter 10

1. Cf. above, pp. 176ff.

2. Cf. above, pp. 214f.

3. Cf. above, pp. 171-73.

4. Cf. above, pp. 156ff., 173f.

5. Cf. above, p. 170.

6. This has already been shown for the three-and-a-half times and for the casting down of the stars; pp. 172ff.

7. Cf. above, pp. 208f.

8. Cf. the observations of pp. 163-69.

9. Cf. above, p. 165.

10. Cf. above, p. 165.

11. δράκων [*drakōn*]: *Pss. Sol.* 2:29; Add Esth 1:5; "dragon" at Babylon, תנין [*tannîn*], Isa 51:9; Job 12, etc.; cf. above, pp. 52ff.; ὁ δράκων ὁ μέγας [*ho drakon ho megas*]: Rev 12:9; cf. Rev 12:3, which = התנין הגדול [*hat-tannîn hag-gāḏôl*], Ezek 29:3. Rev 12:15 names the monster ὁ ὄφις [*ho ophis*]; cf. Rev 12:9, ὁ ὄφις ὁ ἀρχαῖος [*ho ophis ho archaios*] = Heb. הנחש [*han-nāḥāš*], Isa 27:1; Amos 9:3; Job 26:13.

12. Cf. p. 228, n. 269; concerning the horns, cf. p. 229, n. 271.

13. In the most well-known Babylonian depiction, *Ti'āmat* has a harmless bird's tail. In another, instead of the tail, there is a sort a forearm with a hand; cf. Riehm, *HW,* 1262. Note, by the way, the particular emphasis on the "tail" in the "variants" of the Babylonian creation epic.

14. Cf. the depiction in Riehm, *HW,* 1171.

15. Cf. above, p. 165.

16. Cf. above, p. 165.

17. Cf. above, p. 16.

18. Cf. above, pp. 55f.

19. This is so in the case of Mani (cf. Flügel, *Mani,* 86ff.) and of the Mandaeans (cf. Brandt, *Mand. Schriften,* 128ff., 138ff., 178, and 181f.).

20. They already existed before his birth; *Enuma Elish,* tablet 12, line 17.

21. *Hibil-Ziwâ,* son of the *Mandâ d' Hayyê,* will be sent out by his "fathers" for the conquest of the powers of the deep; Brandt, *Mand. Schriften,* 137ff.

22. Cf. above, p. 16.

23. Cf. above, pp. 52ff.

24. The fact that frogs emerge from the mouth of the dragon has a parallel in Hermas, *Vis.* 4[:6, where it is not frogs, but locusts that emerge. — trans.].

25. Cf. above, pp. 56f., in reference to *Rahab* and Leviathan, etc. In reference to the sea, cf. above, pp. 61ff.

26. Brandt, *Mand. Schriften,* 131, 153, 154, 155, 161, 162, 172, 182f.

27. Cf. above, p. 232.

28. Cf. Levy, *Neuhebr.,* s.v. נחש.

29. Compare the Babylonian recension as well as Daniel 7 and Revelation 13 and 17.

30. The same judgment applies to the obscure traditions of Revelation 11.

31. Cf. above, p. 156 and pp. 173f.

32. Cf. above, pp. 53f.

33. Cf. above, p. 177, n. 100.

34. Cf. above, p 187, n. 30; p. 193, n. 58; p. 198. In earlier times Egyptian ideas flowed into the tradition as well; cf. pp. 60f. above.

35. Cf. above, pp. 182f.

36. Cf. above, p. 198.

37. Cf. above, pp. 164f. and p. 176.

38. This explication assumes the "reconstructions" presented above on pp. 164-76.

39. [Cf., e.g., the not identical, but similar representation on a small engraved metal plate of the Berlin Museum (*MOS*, vol. 11, 1893), 43, where a deity *(Ištar?)* appears clothed in the sun. Over her are the moon and seven stars. — Similar representations are also often found on the Babylonian cylinder seals, e.g., de Clercq, *Collection,* vol. 1, nos. 308, 326 *(ter),* 327, and 332. For a representation of the moon under the feet of the deity cf., e.g., de Clercq, *Collection,* vol. 2, no. 41.] — Zimmern. The twelve stars of the zodiac form a circle on the heavens and can, therefore, according to their very nature be depicted as a crown.

40. According to Damascius, Δαύκη [*daukē*]; cf. pp. 13f. above.

41. [The name *Damkina* means "woman of the earth."] — Zimmern

42. In what we have just gone over I have pointed to the broad similarities. *Marduk* = Son of Man. *Ṣarpanītu* = bride. It depends on drawing the broader parallels together and on explaining their history.

43. Cf. the god *Anšar* in the Babylonian epic.

44. There is a similar motif in the *Etana* legend.

45. Originally these beings may have been monsters of the dry land, so that the sense would be that all beings of the water and the land conclude a treaty against the powers of the heavens, until the god overcomes them. Cf. the parallels to *Ti'āmat* and *Kingu* in chapter 13.

46. That the messengers of *Ti'āmat* are actually frogs is not as remarkable as it appears. *Tiâmat's* place is in the watery deep. She sends floods upon the earth. She also utilizes beings who live in the water and on the land at the same time. Frogs are amphibians. These frogs must have represented a certain greatness.

47. [What follows is Gunkel's reading of Revelation 12 as a retelling of the Babylonian *Marduk* myth. — trans.]

48. Cf. above, pp. 17f.

49. Cf. pp. 129f. above.

50. *Ti'āmat* assembles her army, and the deciding battle takes at Ἁρμαγεδών [*harmagedōn*]. We will not venture to give a secure explanation for the name. We do, however, point out the parallels. The fallen angels of Genesis 6 are assembled on Mount Hermon in *1 Enoch* 6:6. According to *Manî,* the "primal human being" sees the devil at the battle on the border of the

land of light and the land of darkness, on the so-called "battlefield" (Flügel, *Mani*, 87). Among the Mandaeans the "angels of the imperfection" are assembled "on the top of the heavens and the earth, on the mountains for destruction" (Brandt, *Mand. Schriften*, 89). [The second part of the word, μαγεδών [*magedōn*], is probably, as Jensen suspects, identical with μιγαδών [*migadōn*] in the divine name Ύεσμιγαδών [*yesmigadōn*] [cf. Ernst Kuhnert, "Feuerzauber," *Rheinisches Museum für Philologie* 49 (1894) 49], the husband of the Babylonian goddess of the underworld Ἐρεσχιγαλ (= Akkadian *Ereškigal*).] — Zimmern

51. The flight of the woman cannot be explained from the experience of natural events. Perhaps in an older recension of the myth it had its place before the birth of the god. — In the Temple of *Bêl* in Babylonia there were, according to Diodorus Siculus, [*Bibliotheca historica*] 2.9, statues of Zeus, of Hera, and of Rhea. These were, so it appears, the images depicted in our tradition: son of a woman, a woman, a bride, and the serpents. Was our tradition, therefore, localized in the Temple of *Bêl* at Babylon?

52. "Day" in the broadest sense, since perhaps the god will be born on a "consecrated night."

53. The heavenly signs "Aquarius" and "Taurus" were the signs of winter and of spring in old Babylonian times.

54. It is the same day which the Christian church, even now, celebrates as Christmas. [In German the word for Christmas, *Weihnacht*, means, literally, "consecrated night." — trans.]

55. [Note J. Epping and J. N. Strassmaier, "Neue babylonische Planteten-Tafeln, III," *ZA* 6 (1891) 222, according to which the Temple of *Marduk*, *Esagil*, in Babylon is the "house of day," for which reason the "daughters of *Ezida*" on the winter solstice are drawn to *Esagil* in order "to lengthen the days," while inversely at the summer solstice the daughters are drawn from *Esagil* to *Ezida*, "the house of the night," in order "to lengthen the night." Accordingly, the shortest day was celebrated in the cult of *Marduk*.] — Zimmern. The day of *Marduk*, which I have inferred from Revelation 12, is therefore attested by the documents. At the same time, two clues (cf. p. 378, n. 51) point to the same shrine, the Temple of *Marduk* at Babylon. Then "the wilderness" of the myth would be the great wilderness which borders upon Babylon. The river is the Euphrates.

56. [These are the tenth through the twelfth months of the Jewish calendar. — trans.]

57. Cf. above, pp. 128ff.

58. Cf. above, pp. 172ff.

59. Cf. above, pp. 239 and 212.

60. Discussed on pp. 177-80 above.

61. Cf. above, pp. 128f.

62. I repeat, from the remarks on pp. 177f. above, that the task is not to interpret the material from the standpoint of Judaism as successfully as possible. Rather, it is to establish how Judaism actually has itself appropriated the material.

63. Even here I raise the chronological question as to which "war" this may be. And, furthermore, I refer to the fact that the expression ποιῆσαι πόλεμον [*poiēsai polemon*, "to make war"] was probably already given by the tradition. It therefore is not referring to a particular king.

64. A rabbinic tradition says that the future redemption will take place in the month of Nisan (Eisenmenger, *Entdecktes*, 2:807). This calendrical estimation is probably to be explained as deriving from the counterpart of the redemption of the Hebrews from the Egyptians in the book of Exodus. Cf., however, Add Esth 1:1, and above, pp. 203f.

65. Both also are seen in the Talmudic tradition.

66. The juxtapositioning of the two themes lies in the background of Revelation 12, but there it is not explicitly explained.

67. Thereby, the birth of the god — other than in Revelation 12 — is understood allegorically as the appearance of Christ.

68. For a similar train of thought in a very similar form cf. *4 Ezra* 5:46ff.

69. We find these speculations, then, continued in Christianity. "How?" does not belong here.

70. Cf. above, pp. 175ff.

71. Cf. above, pp. 237f.

72. Cf. above, pp. 127f.

73. Cf. the remarks on Ἁρμαγεδών [*armagedōn*] on pp. 169f.

74. Cf. above, p. 60.

75. Cf. above, pp. 60f.

76. Cf. above, p. 213.

77. Cf. above, p. 125.

Notes to Appendix I

1. From older literature concerning the interpretation of the text [cf. additionally, Carl Bezold, *Kurzgefasster Überblick über die babylonisch-assyrische Literatur, nebst einem chronologischen Excurs, zwei Registern und einem Index zu 1700 Thontafeln des British-Museums,* (Leipzig: O. Schulze, 1886) [hereinafter: Bezold, *Literature*], 174, the catalogue of the same, *sub* KK5419c, 3473, 3437, 3567, 8522] the following are chiefly to be mentioned: Smith-Delitzsch, *Chald. Gen.,* 62ff.; Jules Oppert in Eugène Ledrain, *Histoire d'Israel* (Paris: A. Lemerre, 1871) [hereinafter: Ledrain, *Histoire*], 1:411ff.; Lenormant, *Origines de l'histoire,* 494ff.; Schrader, *KAT²*, 1ff.; A. H. Sayce, *Lectures on the Origins and Growth of Religion as Illustrated by the Religion of the Ancient Babylonians,* Hibbert Lectures, 1887 [hereinafter: Sayce, *Hibbert Lecs. 1887*], (London: Williams and Norgate, 1887), 384ff.; A. H. Sayce, ed., *Records of the Past: being English Translations of the Ancient Monuments of Egypt and Western Asia* [hereinafter: Sayce: *Records Past*], New Series (London: S. Bagster, 1888), 1:133ff. From recent years there is the comprehensive treatment of Jensen in his *Kosmologie,* 261-364. Cf. further Theophilus Pinches, "A Babylonian Duplicate of Tablets I and II of the Creation Series," *The Babylonian and Oriental Record* 4 (1880) 25-33; Hommel, "Glossen u. Exkurse II," 393ff., and "Inschriftliche Glossen und Exkurse zur Genesis und zu den Propheten x2013 — VI," *NKZ,* 89ff.; Rudolf Zehnpfund, "Altbabylonische Götter- und Heldensagen, Teil 4: Der babylonische Weltschöpfungsbericht," *Beilage zur Allgemeine Zeitung* (München) 65, 18 March 1891, 2-3; Hugo Winckler, ed., *Keilinschriftliche Textbuch zum Alten Testament* (Leipzig: E. Pfeiffer, 1892) [hereinafter: Winckler, *Keilinschr. Txtbch.*], 88ff.; Barton, "Tiamat," 1-27; Franz Lukas, *Die Grundbegriffe in den Kosmologonien der alten Völker* (Leipzig: W. Friedrich, 1893) [hereinafter: Lukas, *Grundbegriffe Kosmologonien*], 1-46 (with contributions by Jensen). — The meter is that which is most common in Assyro-Babylonian poetry: a strophe consisting of two verses. Each verse is in two half-verses. Each half-verse is in two stressed syllables. The half-versification is, at least at times, always present in the original. This is the case in the exemplar 82-9-18, 3737 found in the fourth tablet. (The fact, by the way, that the Babylonians became aware of some-verses which had been divided not only into two half-verses, but also further into four quarter verses, can now be shown by the London tablet Sp. II, 265a, in which, in an acrostic hymn, there is a division into four half-verses by verti-

cal lines, while the duplicates exhibit continuous non-metrical writing). — Square brackets in the following indicate "originally broken off." Non-italicized script indicates "translation uncertain."

2. *apsū.*

3. Meaning still uncertain, perhaps "primal ground" or the like.

4. Cf. on this oldest pair of gods, Tablet III, 4, 68 and 125.

5. *a-di,* variant *a-di-i;* cf. Tablet III, 18, 123, and Hebrew עַד (*'ad* = "perpetuity").

6. Personifications of the upper and lower universe.

7. K3938 obv. and 81-7-27, 80 obv. First made accessible to me by Jensen, to whom, for his part, Bezold had made his copies of the tablets available. Recently this material has been seen by me personally in the original form.

8. Third plural suffix.

9. Lit. "way," here in the figurative sense, as in the Hebrew דרכי יהוה (*darkê YHWH* — "ways/plans of the LORD").

10. Here then, if the quite mutilated and badly preserved original text is interpreted, is the proper name of the son of *Apsū* and *Ti'āmat,* in accordance with the Μωΰμις of Damascius, [Ἀπορίαι καὶ Λύσεις περὶ τῶν πρώτων ἀρχῶν, *Aporiai kai Lyseis peri tōn prōtōn archōn,* "problems and solutions concerning the first leader," §125a (cf. Damascius, *Quaestiones*)].

11. The following 38 lines are given under the very probable assumption that the raging of *Ti'āmat* in Tablet I was described with the same words with which it later, in Tablets II and III, is told about other gods. In lines 1 and 4 the text must naturally here read somewhat differently than in Tablet III. Thence my amendment thereof. — It is quite possible that this first description of *Ti'āmat's* raging (probably forming the end of Tablet I) is extant from line (14) on at 81,7-27,80 and from line (20) on at 82,7-14,402.

12. *Ummu ḫubur,* probably the prototype of Ὁμόρκα [*homorka*], cf. above, p. 14, n. 8.

13. The *Laḫamu*-deity here enumerated as a monster in the retinue of *Ti'āmat,* actually has only a *name* in common with the *Laḫamu* of the first generation of gods (Tablet 1, l. 10).

14. The "great day" (cf. Jensen, *Kosmologie,* 487ff.) is usually also viewed as a personified monster. Franz Delitzsch, *Assyrisches Handwörterbuch,* 33, thinks differently.

15. [Translator's note: The Akkadian word which Zimmern here translates as "day[s]" is *ūmu.* The word can mean "day" (as Zimmern translates it). It can, however, also mean both "storm" and a mythical "lion" figure. Today the last of these is generally accepted as most fitting in this context.]

16. The immediately preceding words are to be understood as words by which *Ti'āmat* fixed *Kingu's* "destiny", i.e., his sphere of power.

17. Cf. above, p. 16, n. 8.

18. Actually *"Anu-hood."*

19. Probably a byname for *Kingu.*

20. The sense of these redemptive words appears to be that the gods who stand at *Ti'āmat's* side, the element of whom is darkness, will be given power over the light which they hate.

21. From line 22 on, the text is preserved in K4823 [Samuel Alden Smith, *Miscellaneous Texts of the British Museum, with Textual Notes* (Leipzig: Edward Pfeiffer, 1887) [hereinafter: Smith, *Misc. Texts*], 8f.].

22. [Again the Akkadian word *ūmu.* Cf. p. 380, n. 15 above. — trans.]

23. *apsū.*

24. K 4832 obv. (S. A. Smith, *Misc. Texts,* 9).

25. Here begins K 292. P. 380, n. 7 above makes remarks about the use of this tablet.

26. Or "fate"(?), in the sense of "the one who determines the fate of."

27. *puḫru;* cf. Zimmern, "Purim-festes," 163.

28. A name for the assembly room in which the gods come together at the beginning of the year to determine destiny. Cf. Jensen, *Kosmologie,* 239-43, and Zimmern, "Purim-festes," 161.

29. K 3473, etc. (Smith, *Misc. Texts,* 1ff.). Additionally there is the duplicate mentioned in Carl Bezold, *Catalogue of the Cuneiform Tablets in the Kouyounjik Collection of the British Museum* (London: Trustees of the British Museum, 1889) [hereinafter: Bezold, *Catalogue*], under K 3473, concerning my use of which p. 380, n. 7 above makes remarks.

30. [Again the word *ūmu;* cf. p. 380, n. 15 above. — trans.]

31. [There is a problem in the Babylonian text here. — trans.]

32. [Again the word *ūmu;* cf. p. 380, n. 15 above — trans.]

33. Similar to *innišku aḫu u aḫi;* cf. Ezek 3:13; Ps 85:11.

34. Cf. Bezold, *Catalogue,* K 3437.

35. Cf. in regard to the translation of these two difficult lines, Belser, in *BSS* 2, 155.

36. Originally *i-na bi-ri-šu-nu.*

37. Here, as repeatedly in what follows, *Marduk* is designated by the name *Bēl,* "lord." Later it will be used as a proper name for him. Likewise in Berossus it is always βῆλος *(bilos).*

38. I.e., according to the epigraphic figures, probably a double-headed trident.

39. *šaru limnu,* "wicked wind," is just a gloss on *imḫullu.*

40. Probably applies to *Marduk.*

41. Or "to look at" instead of "to praise."

42. I.e., *Ea's.*

43. Original *pa-di-e.*

44. Cf. the military inscriptions of *Aššurbanipal,* series I, no. 7, section ix, where, in light of the foregoing passage, *muhhašu unatti* is also certainly to be read. Furthermore, series IV², no. 56, l. 3a reads: *paṭnu* [*ša qaq*]*qadu inattū,* "a dagger, with which the head is split." Cf. perhaps the Hebrew נתח [*nittaḫ,* "to divide, to cut in pieces"]. On *muḫḫu,* "sense," cf. Bruno Meissner, "Lexicographische Studien," *ZA* 8 (1893) 76, n. 2.

45. Probably the name of a weapon with a following adjective. Or is it to be read *ṣalmê,* "the twins" (in the heavens)? On this cf. Jensen, *Kosmologie,* 65.

46. I.e., *Ea.*

47. What is to be read is *bi-nu-tu-uš-šu.* The *bi-* of this edition does not stand after *apsū* in the preceding lines in the original.

48. Cf. Bezold, *Catalogue,* sub K 3567.

49. Not identical to the signs of the zodiac, but in proximity to them. Cf. concerning this Jensen, *Kosmologie,* 47ff.

50. Namely, "none" of the days.

51. Namely, along with the position of Jupiter.

52. Or: "he created"?

53. In reference to the earth, rather than the sun, i.e., at the meridian, where the moon does not stand at sunset in the first and last quarter.

54. Originally *-kan,* not *-tar.*

55. Preserved as a "catchword" on the reverse side of the fragment. That reverse side contains the beginning of the fifth tablet presented above.

56. The relation of this fragment, DT 41 [published by Friedrich Delitzsch, *Assyrische Lesestücker: Nach den originalen Theils revidirt Theils zum ersten Male herausgegeben: nebst Paradigmen, Schrifttafel, Textanalyse, und kleinen Wörterbuch zum selbst unterrecht wie zum*

akademischen gebrauch, 3d ed. (Leipzig: J. C. Hinrichs, 1885) [hereinafter: Delitzsch, *Assyr. Lesest.*³], 94f.] to the creation account of the redaction "at one time as shown above" is, in any event, not certain, and does not even appear probable.

57. Published by Delitzsch, *Assyr. Lesest.*³, 95f. Cf. Bezold, *Catalogue,* sub K 8522. The relation to the creation account of the redaction "at one time as shown above" is not absolutely certain.

58. Namely, *Marduk.*

59. The meaning of this and the following honorific names of *Marduk* will probably be given in the verses which follow.

60. Actually reads *"the middle of Tiʾāmat."*

61. I.e., as for the king.

62. RM 282 (likewise from the library of *Aššurbanipal),* published by Friedrich Delitzsch, *Assyrisches Wörterbuch zur gesammten bisher veroffentlichten Keilschriftliteratur: Unter Berücksichtigung Zahlreicher unveroffentlicher Texts,* Assyriologische Bibliothek 7 (Leipzig: J. C. Hinrichs, 1887) [hereinafter: Delitzsch, *Assyr. WB*], 390. — The metrical form is less uniform than in the preceding sections. Verses of six (perhaps nine) beats alternate with verses of four beats.

63. *limāti* √*lamū* = [Hebrew] √לוה [III]. Cf. לִוְיָתָן [*liwyātān,* "Leviathan"]. Cf. above, p. 31, n. 51.

64. Here, and repeatedly in what follows, the monster will be designated by a word which because of the polyphonous characters of the Assyrian script can be read as *kalbu* ("dog"), *labbu* ("lion"), as well as *rebbu* (for *rahbu),* the Assyrian equivalent of רַהַב (*rahab,* Rahab).

65. London Tablet 82-5-22 1048, published and translated by T. G. Pinches, "Creation Story," 393-408. Cf. T. G. Pinches, "The New Version of the Creation Story," *Transactions of the Ninth International Congress of Orientalists* 2 (1893) 190-98 [hereinafter: Pinches, "New Creation"], and Hommel, "Neu Weltschöpfungslegende," 105-14. — Mostly in standard Babylonian meter: the verse has four beats, though with many variations in detail. The strophic structure does not appear clearly consistent here.

66. Literally "pure."

Notes to Appendix II

67. The Temple of *Bēl* at Nippur.

68. The Temple of *Ištar* at Erech.

69. Usually, as in line 14, the great *Marduk* Temple in Babylon. Here, however, it is probably a designation for a temple in Eridu on the Persian Gulf. Hence also the greater specificity in line 13.

Notes to Appendix III

70. Secondary divine beings.

71. *epiru* = Hebrew עָפָר [*ʿāpār*].

72. On a clay tablet found with the Tell el-Amarna letters, thus stemming from the middle of the second millennium B.C.E. Published by Hugo Winckler, *Die Thontafeln von Tel el-Amarna,* Keilinschriftliche Bibliothek 5 (Berlin: Reuter and Reichard, forthcoming [1896]), 166. Translated in Harper, "Babylonischen Legenden," 420ff. Cf. also H. Zimmern, "An Old Babylonian Legend from Egypt," *Sunday School Times* (Philadelphia), June 18, 1892. — The translation

given here, in regard to the line divisions, reflects the nonmetrically written original. Nevertheless, the rhythm at many places is unmistakable. It seemed to me, however, that it would be even more risky to depart from the prosaic style of the original, especially since at many places the text is not totally undamaged.

73. From the numerous writings about the Babylonian reports concerning the flood (cf. concerning this Bezold, *Literatur*, 172f., and Bezold, *Catalogue*, sub K 2252), the treatments of Paul Haupt in Schrader, *KAT*, [2] and of Jensen, *Kosmologie*, 367f., are to be particularly noted. Recently there must be added to the preceding, in a generally limited relationship to those works, the translation of Jeremias, *Izdubar-Nimrod*, 71ff.; W. Muss-Arnolt, "The Chaldean Account of the Deluge," *The Biblical World* 3 (1891) 109-18; Winckler, *Keilinschriftliche Textbuch*, 71ff. — The metrical format of the Babylonian flood narrative, as is the case generally in the whole Gilgamesh epic (of which it forms a part), has not been pursued as strongly as, e.g., that in the creation epic. At any rate, in far-and-away the majority of cases it is possible to make out with ease the common Babylonian strophe (consisting of two verses, each with two half-verses of two stressed syllables each). There do, however, also occur among them strophes with three verses (e.g., ll. 146ff.) and other anomalies.

74. The reading concerning the first component of the name is still not completely certain. Hommel, "Patriarchs Berosus," 243, recently read *Nuḥ- (napištim)* = נח, which is, however, still quite problematic. [The use of *C* by Gunkel is actually not the accepted vocalization today. — trans.]

75. This is the current epigraphically attested reading of the hero's name, which earlier was conventionally read *Izdubar* or *Gišdubar*. This does not exclude the possibility, however, that a Semitic name, e.g., *Namrudu*, could also have been common in addition to this clearly non-Semitic expression of the name.

76. Probably to be understood thus: the transverse lines of the ship should form a square.

77. Lines 19-29 form the content of the dream which *Ea* sends to *Cît-napištum* in a reed hut.

Notes to Appendix IV

78. [A *šar* was a Babylonian measure of volume equal to about 8,000 gallons — i.e., 29,680 liters. What is being suggested here is, therefore, that 48,000 gallons/18,080 liters of pitch were used to seal the hull. Wow! — trans.]

Notes to Appendix V

79. [In German *Sesamwein*. But cf. A. Poebel, "Sumerische Untersuchungen IV," *ZA* 39 (1929) 148-49, who notes that a better translation would be (in English) "must" (i.e., "unfermented grape or other fruit juice"). — trans.]

80. Lit., "clay, loam."

81. In the original, ll. 129-30 form a single line.

82. I.e., *Ištar*.

83. I.e., "the very clever one" [according to Paul Haupt, "The Book of Ecclesiastes," in *Oriental Studies: A Selection of Papers Read before the Oriental Club of Philadelphia 1888-1894* (Boston: Ginn, 1894), 270, n. 26, it is, instead "the very devout one"], an epithet of *Cît-napištum*. In its reverse form *Ḫasîs-atra*, it is probably the prototype for the Greek Εἰσουθρος [*Xisouthros*].

Bibliography

American Oriental Society Proceedings — *AOSP*

Auberlen, Karl August. *Der Prophet Daniel und die Offenbarung Johannis, in ihrem gegenseitigen Verhältnis betrachtet und in ihren Hauptstellen erklärt . . . mit einer Beilage . . .* Basel: Dahnmaier (Detloff), 1857. — Auberlen, *Daniel und Offenbarung Johannis*

Baethgen, Friedrich. *Die Psalmen übersetzt und erklärt.* Handkommentar zum Alten Testament, part 2, vol. 2. Göttingen: Vandenhoeck & Ruprecht, 1892. — Baethgen, *Psalmen*

Baldensperger, W. "Die neuern kritischen Forschungen über die Apokalypse Johannis." *Zeitschrift für Theologie und Kirche* 4 (1895) 232-50. — Baldensperger, "Neuern Forschungen"

Ball, C. J. "III. Bel and the Dragon." Pp. 344-60 in vol. 2 of *The Holy Bible, according to the Authorized Version (A.D. 1611), with an explanatory Commentary and a revision of the translation: Apocrypha.* Ed. Henry Wace. London: J. Murray, 1888. — Ball, "Bel and Dragon"

Barton, George A. "Tiamat." *JAOS* 15 (1894) 1-27. — Barton, "Tiamat"

Baudissin, Wolf Wilhelm Graf von. *Studien zur Semitischen Religionsgeschichte.* 2 vols. Leipzig: Fr. Wilh. Grunow, 1876-79. — Baudissin, *Stud.*

Beck, Johann Tobias. *Einleitung in das System der christliche Lehre, oder, Propaedeutische Entwicklung der christliche Lehrwissenschaft: Ein Versuch.* 2d expanded ed. Stuttgart: J. F. Steinkopf, 1870.

Beck, *Einleitung*

Behrmann, Georg. *Das Buch Daniel, übersetzt und erklärt.* Handkommentar zum Alten Testament, part 3, vol. 3, sub-vol. 2. Göttingen: Vandenhoeck & Ruprecht, 1894.

Behrmann, *Daniel*

Benary, Ferdinand. "Offene Erklärung gegen Dr. Ferd. Hitzig." *Haller Allgemeine Literaturzeitung Intelligenzblatt,* August 1837, 428.

Benary, "Erklärung"

———. "Erklärung der Zahl 666 (χξϛ′) in der Apokalypse (13, 18) und ihrere Variante 616 (χιϛ′)." *Zeitschrift für spekulative Theologie* 1 (1836) 205-6.

Benary, "Zahl 666"

Bensley, Robert Lubbock. *The Missing Fragment of the Latin Translation of the Fourth Book of Ezra.* Cambridge: Cambridge University Press, 1875.

Bensley, *Frag. 4 Ezra*

Benzinger, Immanuel. *Hebräische Archäologie: Grundriss der theologischen Wissenschaften,* Series 2, vol. 1. Freiburg i. B.: Mohr, 1894.

Benzinger, *Archäologie*

Bevan, A. A. *A Short Commentary on the Book of Daniel for the Use of Students.* Cambridge: Cambridge University Press, 1882.

Bevan, *Daniel.*

Beyschlag, Willibald. "Die Apokalypse: Gegen die jüngste kritische Hypothese in Schultz genommen." *Theologische Studien und Kritiken* 61 (1888) 102-38.

Beyschlag, "Apokalypse"

———. "Die Offenbarung Johannis." In *Zur deutsch-christlichen Bildung popular-theologische Vortrage.* Halle a. S.: Eugen Strien, 1888.

Beyschlag, "Offenbarung"

Bezold, Carl. *Catalogue of the Cuneiform Texts in the Kouyounjik Collection of the British Museum.* London: Trustees of the British Museum, 1889.

Bezold, *Catalogue*

———. *Kurzgefasster Überblick über die babylonische-assyrische Literatur, nebst einem chronologischen Excurs, zwei Registern und einem Index zur 1700 Thontafeln des British-Museums.* Leipzig: O. Schulze, 1886.

Bezold, *Literatur*

———. *Die Schatzhöhle.* 2 vols. Leipzig: Hinrichs, 1883-88.

Bezold, *Schatzhöhle*

————. "Über keilinschriftliche Beschreibungen babylonisch-assyrischer Göttertypen." *ZA* 9 (1894) 114-25.

Bickell, Gustav. "Beiträge zur Semitischen Metrik." *Sitzungsberichte der Akademie der Wissenschaften in Wien, Philosoph.-histor. Klasse*, vol. 131, V, 1ff.

————. *Carmina Veteris Testamenti metrice: Notas criticas et dissertationem de re metrica Hebraeorum adjecit.* Innsbruck: Wagner, 1882.

Bleek, Frederick. *Vorlesungen über die Apokalypse.* Ed. Th. Hossbach. Berlin: Reimer, 1862.

Bochart, S. *Hierozoicon, sive de animalibus S. Scripturae.* Leipzig: Weidmann, 1783-96.

Brandt, Wilhelm. *Die Mandäische Religion: Ihre Entwicklung und geschichtliche Bedeutung, erforscht, dargestellt, und beleuchtet.* Leipzig: H. C. Hinrichs, 1889.

————. *Mandäische Schriften, übersetzt und erläutert.* Göttingen: Vandenhoeck & Ruprecht, 1893.

Budde, Karl. *Die biblische Urgeschichte (Gen. 1–12,4) untersucht.* Giessen: J. Ricker, 1883.

————. "Ein althebräisches Klageleid." *ZAW* 3 (1882) 299-306.

Cheyne, Thomas K. *The Prophecies of Isaiah: A new translation with commentary and appendices.* London: Kegan Paul, 1880.

Clercq, Louis de. *Collection de Clercq: catalogue methodique et raisonne: antiquites assyriennes, cylindres orientaux, cachets, briques, bronzes, bas-reliefs,* etc. 8 vols. Paris: E. Lerouz, 1888-1912.

Conze, Alexander. *Heroen- und götter-Gestalten der griechischen Kunst erlautert.* Vienna: s.n., 1874-75.

Cornill, Carl Heinrich. *Das Buch des Propheten Ezechiel.* Leipzig: J. C. Hinrichs, 1886.

————. "Die siebzig Jahrwochen Daniels." Pp. 1-32 of vol. 2 of *Theologische Studien und Skizzen aus Ostpreussen.* Eds. Albert Klöpper, Carl Cornill, Friedrich Zimmer, and Franklin Arnold. Königsberg: Hartungsche Verlagsdruckerei, 1887-89.

Bezold, "Göttertypen"

Bickell, "Metrik"

Bickell, *Carmina VT*

Bleek, *Vorlesungen Apok.*

Bochart, *Hierozoicon*

Brandt, *Mandäische Religion*

Brandt, *Mandäische Schriften*

Budde, *Urgeschichte*

Budde, "Klagelied"

Cheyne, *Isaiah*

de Clercq, *Collection*

Conze, *Heroen*

Cornill, *Ezechiel*

Cornill, "Siebzig Jahrwochen"

Damascius. *Quaestiones de primis principiis,* in *Damascii Phil. quaestiones de primis principiis,* ed. J. Kopp. Frankfurt a. M.: H. L. Broenner, 1826.

Damascius, *Quaestiones*

Delitzsch, Franz. *Biblischer Commentar über der Prophet Jesaia.* 4th ed., vol. 1 of part 3 ("prophetische Bücher") of Biblischer Commentar über das Alte Testament. Leipzig: Dörffling und Franke, 1889.

Delitzsch, *Jesaia*[4]

————. *Biblischer Commentar über der Psalmen.* Vol. 1 of part 4 ("poetische Bücher") of Biblischer Commentar über das Alte Testament. Leipzig: Dörffling und Franke, 1867.

Delitzsch, *Psalmen*

————. "Engel." Pp. 379-82 of vol. 1 of Riehm, *HW.*

Delitzsch, "Engel"

Delitzsch, Friedrich. *Assyrische Lesestücker: Nach den originalen Theils revidirt Theils zum ersten Male herausgegeben: nebst Paradigmen, Schriftafel, Textanalyse, und kleinen Wörterbuch zum selbst unterrecht wie zum akademischen gebrauch.* 3d ed., Leipzig: J. Hinrichs, 1885.

Delitzsch, *Assyr. Lesest.*[3]

————. *Assyrisches Wörterbuch zur gesammten bisher veroffentlichen Keilinschriftliteratur: Unter Berücksichtigung Zahlreicher unveroffentlicher Texts.* Assyriologische Bibliothek 7. Leipzig: J. C. Hinrichs, 1887.

Delitzsch, *Assyr. WB*

———— et al. *Biblisches Handwörterbuch illustriert.* 2d ed., Calwer/Stuttgart: Verlag des Veriensbuchhandlung, 1893.

Delitzsch, *Calwer Biblex*[2]

————. *Wo lag das Paradies? Eine biblisch-assyriologische Studie, mit zahlreichen assyriologischen Beiträgen zur biblischen Länder- und Völkerkunde.* Leipzig: Hinrichs, 1881.

Delitzsch, *Paradies?*

Dieterich, Albrecht. *Abraxas: Studien zur Religionsgeschichte des spätern Altertums: Festschrift Hermann Usener zur Feier seiner 25 jährigen Lehrtätigkeit an der Bonner Universität.* Leipzig: B. G. Teubner, 1891.

Dieterich, *Abraxas*

————. *Nekyia: Beitrage zur Erklarung der neuentdeckten Petrusapokalypse.* Leipzig: B. G. Teubner, 1893.

Dieterich, *Nekyia*

Dillmann, August. *Ascencio Isaiae, aethiopice et latine: cum prolegominis, adnotationibus criticis et exegeticis, additis versionum latinarum reliquiis.* Leipzig: F. A. Brockhaus, 1877.

Dillmann, *Asc. Isa.*

————. *Das Buch Henoch, übersetzt und erklärt.* Leipzig: Fr. Chr. Wilh. Vogel, 1853.

Dillmann, *Buch Henoch*

————. *Die Genesis.* 6th ed. Leipzig: S. Hirzel, 1892.

Dillmann, *Genesis*[6]

————. *Hiob.* 4th ed. Leipzig: S. Hirzel, 1891.

Dillmann, *Hiob*[4]

————. *Der Prophet Jesaia.* Kurzgefasstes exegetisches Handbuch zum Alten Testament. Leipzig: S. Hirzel, 1890.

Dillmann, *Jesaia*

————. "Über die griechische Übersetzung des Qoheleth." *Sitzungsberichte der Königlich Preussischen Akademie der Wissenschaften zu Berlin, Sitzung der philosophische-historischen Klasse vom 7 Januar, 1882.* S.l.: s.n., 1882, 3-15.

Dillmann, "Qoheleth"

Diodorus Siculus. *Diodori Siculi Bibliotheca historica.* Ed. Immanuel Bakker. 4 vols. Leipzig: B. G. Teubner, 1853-54.

Diodorus, *Biblioth. hist.*

Duhm, Bernhard. *Das Buch Jesaiah, übersetzt und erklärt.* Vol. 1 of Section III ("Die Prophetischen Bücher") of Handkommentar zum Alten Testament. Göttingen: Vandenhoeck & Ruprecht, 1862.

Duhm, *Jesaia*

Düsterdieck, Friederich H. C. *Kritisch exegetisches Handbuch über die Offenbarung Johannes.* 4th ed. Göttingen: Vandenhoeck & Ruprecht, 1887.

Düsterdieck, *Handbuch Offenbarung*[4]

Ebrard, August, ed. *Biblischer Commentar über sämmtliche Schriften des Neuen Testaments zunächst für Prädiger und Studirende.* Königsberg: A. W. Unzer, 1862.

Ebrard, *Bibl. Commentar*

Eichhorn, Johann Gottfried. *Commentarius in Apocalypsin Joannis.* Göttingen: Dieterich, 1791.

Eichhorn, *Comm. Apoc. Joannis*

Eisenmenger, Johann Andreas. *Entdecktes Judentum: Das ist, Wortgetreü verdeutschung der sonstigen, den Christen zu einem grossen Teile noch ganz unbekannten hebräisch-rabbinischen litteratur, welche einem sicheren Einblick in die jüdische Religions- und Sittenlehre gewähren.* Dresden: s.n., 1893.

Eisenmenger, *Entdecktes*

Epping, J., and J. N. Strassmaier. "Neue babylonische Planeten-Tafeln, III." *ZA* 6 (1891) 217-44.

Epping und Strassmaier, "Planeten-Tafeln III"

Erbes, Karl. *Die Offenbarung Johannis: Kritische Untersucht.* Gotha: Perthes, 1891.

Erbes, *Offenbarung Johannis*

Eusebius, *Eusebi Chronicorum libri duo.* Ed. Alfred Schoene. 2 vols. Berlin: Weidmann, 1875-76.

Eusebius, *Chronicorum*

———. *Preparatio Evangelica.*

Eusebius, *Prep. Ev.*

Ewald, Heinrich. *Die Johannischen Schriften, übersetzt und erklärt.* 2 vols. vol. 2: *Johannes Apokalypse.* Göttingen: Dieterischen Buchhandlung, 1862.

Ewald, *Johannes Apokalypse*

———. *Die Propheten des Alten Bundes.* 2 vols. Stuttgart: Adolph Krabbe, 1840.

Ewald, *Propheten AB*

F. "Zu כרוב." *ZA* 1 (1886) 68-69.

F., "Zu כרוב"

Feuchtwang, D. "Die Höllenvorstellung bei den Hebräern." *ZA* 4 (1889) 41-45.

Feuchtwang, "Höllenvorstellung"

Flügel, Gustav. *Mani, seine Lehre und seine Schriften: Ein Beitrag zur Geschichte des Manichäismus: Aus dem Führis des Abû Ja'ḳub an-Nadim, im Text nebst Übersetzung. Commentar und Index zum ersten Mall herausgegeben.* Leipzig: F. A. Brockhaus, 1862.

Flügel, *Mani*

Fritzsche, Otto Fridolin. *Kurzgefasstes Exegetisches Handbuch zu den Apokryphen des Alten Testamentes.* Leipzig: Weidmann, 1851.

Fritzsche, *KEH Apok*

———. "Über die Zahl 666 in der Apokalypse, eine Abhandlung über Apocal. 13, 16-18." *Annalen der gesammten theologischen Literatur und der christlichen Kirche Überhaupt,* vol. 3 (1833), issue 1, 42-64.

Fritzsche, "Zahl 666"

Fuller, J. M. "The Rest of the Chapters of the Book of Esther, which are found neither in the Hebrew nor in the Chaldee." Pp. 361-402 in vol. 1 of *The Holy Bible, according to the Authorized Version (A.D. 1611), with an explanatory Commentary and a revision of the translation: Apocrypha.* Ed. Henry Wace. London: J. Murray, 1888.

Fuller, "Rest of Esther"

Gesenius, Wilhelm. *Thesaurus philologicus.* 6 vols. Leipzig: F. C. G. Vogelii, 1829-53.

Gesenius, *Thesaurus*

———. *Wilhelm Gesenius' Hebräische Grammatik.* Ed. E. Kautzsch, 25th ed. Leipzig: F. C. W. Vogel, 1889.

Kautzsch, *Gesenius' Gram.*

Giesebrecht, Friedrich. *Das Buch Jeremia, übersetzt und*   Giesebrecht,
    erklärt. Handkommentar zum Alten Testament, Sec-   *Jeremia*
    tion 3: "Die Prophetischen Bücher," vol. 2, sub-vol. 2.
    Göttingen: Vandenhoeck & Ruprecht, 1890.

Goldziher, Ignac. *Der Mythos bei den Hebräern und seine*   Goldziher, *Mythos*
    geschichtliche Entwicklung: Untersuchungen zur
    Mythologie und Religionswissenschaft. Leipzig:
    Brockhaus, 1876.

Graetz, Heinrich. *Emendationes in Plerusque Sacrae*   Graetz, *Emend.*
    Scripturae Veteris Testamenti Libros. Fasc. 1. Breslau:
    Schlesische Buchdruckerei, 1892.

———. *Kritischer Commentar zu den Psalmen nebst Text*   Graetz, *Psalmen*
    und Übersetzung. Breslau: Schottlænder, 1882-83.

Grünbaum, M. "Beiträge zur vergleichenden Mythologie   Grünbaum,
    aus der Hagada." *ZDMG* 31 (1877), ca. 275.   "Beiträge"

Gunkel, Hermann. "Nahum 1." *ZAW* 13 (1893) 223-44.   Gunkel, "Nahum"

Gutschmid, Alfred Freiherr von. *Untersuchungen über die*   Gutschmid,
    syrische Epitome der eusebischen Canones. Stuttgart: *Untersuchungen*
    W. Kohlhammer, 1886.

Harnack, Adolph. "Nachwort." In Vischer, *Offenbarung*.   Harnack,
     "Nachwort"

———. *Patrem apostolicorum opera: texta ad fidem codicum*   Harnack, *Patr.*
    et graecorum et latinorum adhibitis praestantissimis   *Apost.*
    editionibus recensuerunt commentario exegetico et
    historico illustraverunt apparatu critico versione latina
    passim correcta prolegominis indicibus instruxerunt. 3
    vols. Edition post Dresselianam alterum tertia. Leip-
    zig: Hinrichs, 1876-78.

Harper, E. T. "Die babylonischen Legenden von Etana, Zu,   Harper,
    Adapa und Dibbara." *Beiträge zur Assyriologie* 2 (1894)   "Babylonischen
    390-521.   Legenden"

Haupt, Paul. "The Book of Ecclesiastes." *Oriental Studies: A*   Haupt, "Ecclesias-
    Selection of Papers read before the Oriental Club of   tes"
    Philadelphia 1888-1894. Boston: Ginn, 1894, 258-77.

———. "7. — Transitive and Intransitive Verbs in Semitic."   Haupt, "Trans. —
    American Oriental Society Proceedings, March 1894, ci-   Intrans. Verbs"
    cii.

———. "8. — The Origin of the Pentateuch." *American*   Haupt, "Pent.
    Oriental Society Proceedings, March 1894, cii-ciii.   Orig."

————. "9. — The Rivers of Paradise." *American Oriental Society Proceedings,* March 1894, civ-cxi.

Haupt, "Rivers of Paradise"

Haweis, Thomas. *The Evangelical Expositor, or, A Commentary on the Holy Bible. Wherein the Sacred Text of the Old and New Testament Is Inserted at Times.* 2 vols. London: s.n., 1765-66.

Haweis, *Evangel. Expos.*

Hensler, Christian Gotthilf. *Jesaias, neu übersetzt mit Anmerkungen.* Hamburg und Kiel: Earl Ernst Bohn, 1788.

Hensler, *Jesaias*

Hengstenberg, E. W. *Die Offenbarung des heiligen Johannes; für solche die in der Schrift forschen.* 2 vols. Berlin: Ludwig Oehmigke, 1849-50.

Hengstenberg, *Offenbarung des heiligen Johannes*

Herder, Johann Gottfried. "Μαραν αθα." Page 174 in vol. 9 of *Herders Sammtliche Werke.* Ed. Bernhard Suphan. Berlin: Weidmann, 1877.

Herder, "Μαρανα θα"

Herodotus, *Historicus*

Herodotus, *Hist.*

Hildebrandt, Auguste. "Antichristum." *Zeitschrift für wissenschaftliche Theologie* 17 (1874) 57-58.

Hildebrandt, "Antichristum"

Hilgenfeld, Adolf. "Ein französischer Apologet des Johannes Evangeliums." *Zeitschrift für wissenschaftliche Theologie* 32 (1889) 129-47.

Hilgenfeld, "Apologet"

————. *Historisch-kritische Einleitung in das Neue Testament.* Leipzig: Fues, 1875.

Hilgenfeld, *Einleitung in das NT*

————. "Die Johannes-Apokalypse und die neueste Forschung." *Zeitschrift für Wissenschaftliche Theologie* 33 (1890) 385-467.

Hilgenfeld, "Joh. Apok. n. Forschung"

————. *Die jüdische Apokalyptik in ihrer geschichtlichen Entwickelung: Ein Beitrag zur Vorgeschichte des Christentums, nebst einem Angange über das gnostische System das Basilides.* Jena: Mauke, 1857.

Hilgenfeld, *Jüdische Apokalyptik*

————, ed. *Messias Judaeorum: Libris corum Paulo ante et Paulo post Christum natum conscriptis illustratis.* Leipzig: Fusiana-Reisland, 1869.

Hilgenfeld, *Messias Judaeorum*

Hitzig, Ferdinand. *Das Buch Hiob, übersetzt und ausgelegt.* Leipzig: C. F. Winter, 1874.

Hitzig, *Hiob*

————. *Ostern und Pfingsten in zweiten Dekalog: Sendschreiben an Kirchenrath und Professor Alexander Schweizer in Riesbach.* Heidelberg: C. F. Winter, 1838.

Hitzig, *Zweiten Dekalog*

Hoffmann, Johann Georg Ernst. *Hiob*. Kiel: C. F. Haesler, 1891. — Hoffmann, *Hiob*

Holtzmann, Heinrich Julius. *Lehrbuch der historisch-kritischen Einleitung in das Neue Testament*. 3rd ed. Freiburg i. B.: J. C. B. Mohr, 1892. — Holtzmann, *Einleitung*³

————, R. A. Lipsius, P. W. Schmiedel, and H. von Soden. *Hand-commentar zum Neuen Testament*. 2d ed. 4 vols. Freiburg i. B.: J. C. B. Mohr, 1892-93. — Holtzmann, et al., *Hand-commentar*²

    V. 1: Holtzmann, H. J. "Die Synoptiker — Die Apostelgeschichte."

    V. 2.1: Schmiedel, P. W. "Die Briefe an die Thessalonicher und die Korinther."

    V. 2.2: Lipsius, R. A. "Briefe an die Galater, Romer, Philipper."

    V. 3.1: Soden, H. von. "Briefe an die Kolosser, Epheser, Philemon, der Pastoral-briefe."

    V. 3.2: Soden, H. von. "Der Hebräerbrief, die Briefe des Petrus, Jakobus, Judas."

    V. 4: Holtzmann, H. J. "Evangelius, Briefe, und Offenbarung des Johannes."

Note that when the reference is to Holtzmann's treatment of Revelation, it is cited as the above, with volume and page numbers following.

Holzinger, H. *Einleitung in den Hexateuch*. Freiburg i. B.: J. C. B. Mohr, 1893. — Holzinger, *Hexateuch*

Hommel, Fritz. "Astronomie der alten Chaldäer." *Ausland* 64 (1981), #12, 221-73; #13, 381-407; #14, 59-91, 101-6. — Hommel, "Astronomie"

————. *Geschichte Babyloniens und Assyriens*. Algemeine Geschichte in Einzeldarstellung, vol. 1, part 2. Berlin: G. Grote, 1885-[88]. — Hommel, *Gesch. Bab.*

————. "Inschriftliche Glossen und Exkurse zur Genesis und zu den Propheten — I." *NKZ* 1 (1890) 60-70. — Hommel, "Glossen u. Exkurse I"

————. "Inschriftliche Glossen und Exkurse zur Genesis und zu den Propheten — II." *NKZ* 1 (1890) 393-412. — Hommel, "Glossen u. Exkurse II"

————. "Inschriftliche Glossen und Exkurse zur Genesis und zu den Propheten — IV." *NKZ* 2 (1891) 881-902. — Hommel, "Glossen u. Exkurse IV"

———. "Eine neugefundene Weltschöpfungslegende." *Deutsche Rundschau* 68 (1891) 105-14.

Hommel, "Neu Weltschöpfungs-legende"

———. "The Ten Patriarchs of Berosus." *Proceedings of the Society of Biblical Archaeology,* March 1893, 243-46.

Hommel, "Patri-archs Berosus"

———. "Über den Ursprung und das Alter der arabischen Sternnamen und insbesondere der Mondstationen." *ZDMG* 45 (1891) 692-19.

Hommel, "Sternnamen"

Houbigant, Charles F. *Notae criticae in universos Veteris Testamenti libros: Cum Hebraice cum Graece scriptus, cum integris ejusdem prolegominis ad exemplar Parisiense denue recusae.* Frankfurt a. M.: Varrentrapp filium & Wenner, 1777.

Houbigant, *Notae criticae*

Hupfeld, Hermann. *Die Psalmen übersetzt und ausgelegt.* 3d ed. Ed. Wilhelm Nowack. 2 vols. Gotha: F. A. Perles, 1888.

Hupfeld-Nowack, *Psalmen*

Jahrbücher für protestantische Theologie.

JPT

Jensen, Peter Christian Albrecht. "Elamitische Eisennamen: Ein Beitrag zur Erklärung der semitischen Inscriften." *Wiener Zeitschrift für die Kunde des Morgenlandes* 6 (1893) 47ff. , 209ff.

Jensen, "Elam. Eisennamen"

———. *Die Kosmologie der Babylonier: Studien und Materialen.* Strassburg: Trubner, 1890.

Jensen, *Kosmologie*

———. "Ursprung und Geschichte des Tierkreises." *Deut-sche Revue über das gesammte nationale Leben der Gegenwart* 15 (1891) 112-16.

Jensen, "Tierkreises"

———. "The Supposed Babylonian Origin of the Week and the Sabbath." *Sunday School Times* (Philadelphia), January 17, 1892, 35-36.

Jensen, "Babyl. Week"

Jeremias, Alfred. *Izdubar-Nimrod.* Leipzig: B. G. Teubner, 1891.

Jeremias, *Izdubar-Nimrod*

———. *Die Babylonische-Assyrischen Vorstellungen vom Leben nach dem Tode, nach dem Quellen mit Berücksichtigung der Alttestamentlichen Parallelen.* Leipzig: Hinrichs, 1887.

Jeremias, *Leben nach Tode*

Josephus, *Flavii Iosephi opera, edidit et apparatu critico instruxit.* Ed. Benedict Niese. Berlin: Weidmann, 1887-1895.
Vols. 1-4: *Antiquitatum iudaicarum.*

Vol. 5: *De iudaeorum vetustate, sive Contra Apionem, libri I.*
Vol. 6: *De bello iudaico, libros VII*
Vol. 7: Index   Josephus, *Ant.*
                                                                     Josephus, *Bel.*
                                                                     Jud.

Journal of the Royal Asiatic Society.   *JRAS*

Jülicher, Adolf. *Einleitung in das Neue Testament.* Grundriss   Jülicher,
der Theologischen Wissenschaften, Series 1, vol. 2,   *Einleitung*
sub-vol. 1. Freiburg i. B./Leipzig: Mohr, 1894.

————. *Die Gleichnisreden Jesu.* Freiburg i. B.: Akademische   Jülicher, *Gleich.*
Verlagsbuchhandlung von J. C. B. Mohr–Paul Siebeck,   *Jesu*
1888.

Kautzsch, E. *Die heilige Schrift des Alten Testament.*   Kautzsch, *Heilige*
Freiburg/Leipzig: Paul Siebeck, 1894.   *Schrift*

Kessler, Konrad. *Mani: Forschungen über die manichäische*   Kessler, *Mani*
Religion: Ein Beitrag zur vergleichenden
Religionsgeschichte des Orients. Berlin: G. Reimer,
1889.

Kliefoth, Theodor F. D. *Die Offenbarung des Johannes.* 3   Kliefoth,
vols. in 1 vol. Leipzig: Dorffling und Franke, 1874.   *Offenbarung des*
                                                                     Johannes

Klostermann, A. *Deuterojesaia Hebräisch und Deutsche mit*   Klostermann,
Anmerkungen. Sammlung hebräisch-deutscher   *Deuterojesaia*
Bibeltexte 1. Munich: V. H. Beck, 1893.

Kohut, Alexander. *Über die jüdische Angelologie und*   Kohut, *Jüd. Angel.*
Daemonologie in ihrer Abhängigkeit vom Parsismus.   *u. Daemon.*
Abhandlungen der Deutschen Morganländischen
Gesellschaft 4, no. 3. Leipzig: F. A. Brockhaus, 1866.

Kosters, W. H. "De Bijbelsche zontvloedsverhalen met de   Kosters, "Babyl.
Babylonische vergeleken." *ThT* 19 (1885), ca. 344.   vergel."

————. "De Cherubîm," *ThT* 13 (1879) ca. 445.   Kosters,
                                                                     "Cherubîm"

Krenkel, Max. *Die Apostel Johannes.* Berlin: F. Henschel,   Krenkel, *Apost.*
1874.   *Joh.*

Kuenen, Abraham. "Bijdragen tot de Critiek van Pentateuch   Kuenen, "Critiek
en Josua." *ThT* 18 (1884) ca. 168.   P-J"

Kuhnert, Ernst. "Feuerzauber." *Rheinisches Museum für*   Kuhnert,
Philologie 49 (1894) 49.   "Feuerzauber"

Lagarde, Paul de. *Purim: Ein Beitrag zur Geschichte der Religion.* Abhandlungen der Königlichen Gesellschaft der Wissenschaften zu Göttingen 34. Göttingen: Dieterich, 1887.

Lagarde, *Purim*

Layard, Austen Henry. *The Monuments of Nineveh. First and Second Series.* London: Murray, 1849.

Layard, *Monuments of Nineveh*

Ledrain, Eugène. *Histoire d'Israel.* Paris: A. Lemerre, 1871.

Ledrain, *Histoire*

Lenormant, François. *La Origines de l'Histoire d'après et les Traditions de Peuples Orientaux.* Paris: Maisonneuve, 1871.

Lenormant, *Origines de l'Histoire*

————. *Essai de commentaire des fragments cosmogoniques de Bérose d'après la Bible les textes cunéiformes et les monuments de l'art asiatique.* Paris: Maisonneuve, 1880.

Lenormant, *Comm. de Bérose*

Levy, Jacob. *Chaldäisches Wörterbuch über die Targumim; und einen grossen Theil des rabbinischen schrifttums.* 2 vols. Leipzig: Baumgartner, 1867-68.

Levi, *Wb über die Targumim*

————. *Neuhebräisches und Chaldäisches Wörterbuch über die Talmudim und Midraschim.* Leipzig: F. A. Brockhaus, 1876-89.

Levi, *Neuhebr.*

Lightfoot, John. *Horae Hebraicae et Talmudicae in quatuor Evangelistas: Cum tractibus chorographicis, singulis suo Evangelistae praemissis.* Leipzig: Fr. Lancksii, 1675.

Lightfoot, *Horae*

Lotz, Wilhelm. *Quaestiones de historia sabbat: Libri duo. Commentatio historico-critica quam summa venerandi, theologorum ordinis. Publice defendet Guillimus Lotz.* Leipzig: J. C. Hinrichs, 1883.

Lotz, *Quaestionum*

Lowth, Robert. *Isaiah: A New Translation with a Preliminary Dissertation and Notes, critical, philological, and explanatory.* 5th ed. Edinburgh: George Caw, 1807.

Lowth, *Isaiah*

Lücke, Friederich. *Versuch einer vollständigen Einleitung in die Offenbarung des Johannes: Oder, allgemeine Untersuchungen über die apokalyptische Litteratur, überhaupt und die Apokalypse des Johannes insbesondere.* 2d ed. 2 vols. Commentar über die Schriften des Evang. Johannes, vol. 4, part 1. Bonn: E. Weber, 1852.

Lücke, *Einleitung*

Lukas, Franz. *Die Grundbegriffe in den Kosmologien der alten Völker.* Leipzig: W. Friedrich, 1893.

Lukas, *Grundbegriffe Kosmologonien*

Meinhold, J. "Das Buch Daniel," Pp. 255-339 of *Die Geschichtlichen Hagiographen (Chronika, Esra, Nehemia, Ruth, Esther) und das Buch Daniel*. Eds. Samuel Oettli and J. Mainhold. Kurzgefasster Kommentar zu den heiligen Schriften Alten und Neuen Testaments, so wie zu den Apokryphen, part 8. Nordlingen: C. H. Beck, 1889.

Meissner, Bruno. "Lexicographische Studien," *Zeitschrift für Assyriologie* 8 (1893) 276ff.

Merx, Adalbert. *Das Gedicht von Hiob: Hebräischer Text, kritische bearbeit und übersetzt, nebst sachlicher und kritischer Einleitung*. Jena: Mauke, 1871.

Meyer, Eduard. *Geschichte des Altertums*. 5 vols. Stuttgart: J. G. Cotta, 1884-1902.

Michaelis, Johann David. *Supplementa ad Lexica hebraica partes sex*. Ed. G. Rosenmüller. Leipzig: Weidmann, 1793-96.

Mitteilungen aus den orientalischen Sammlungen der Königliche Museen zu Berlin

Mommsen, Theodor. *Römische Geschichte*. 8th ed. 4 vols. (vols. 1, 2, 3, 5). Berlin: Weidmann, 1888-89.

Muss-Arnolt, W. "The Chaldean Account of the Deluge." *The Biblical World* 3 (1801) 1009-18.

Neue kirchliche Zeitschrift.

Nöldeke, Theodor. *Mandäische Grammatik*. Halle: Buchhandlung des Waisenhauses, 1875.

————. "Über Mommsen's Darstellung der römischen Herrschaft und römischen Politik im Orient." *ZDMG* 39 (1885) 331-51.

Nowack, Wilhelm. *Lehrbuch der Hebräischen Archäologie*. Sammlung Theologischer Lehrbücher. 2 vols. in 1 vol. Freiburg i. B./Leipzig: J. C. Mohr (Paul Siebeck), 1894.

Olshausen, Justus. *Die Psalmen*. Kurzgefasstes exegetisches Handbuch zum Alten Testament. Fasc. 7 of 14 fascicles. Leipzig: S. Hirzel, 1853.

Overbeck, Johannes A. *Pompeji in seinen gebauden, altertumern und kunstwerken dargestellt*. 4th ed. Ed. August Mau. Leipzig: W. Engelmann, 1884.

Meinhold, "Daniel"

Meissner, "Lexicog. Stud."

Merx, *Gedicht von Hiob*

Ed. Meyer, *Gesch. des Altertums*

Michaelis, *Supplementa*

MOS

Mommsen, *Röm. Gesch.*

Muss-Arnolt, "Deluge"

NKZ

Nöldeke, *Mandäische Grammatik*

Nöldeke, "Ueber Mommsen's Darstellung"

Nowack, *Hebr. Archäologie*

Olshausen, *Psalmen*

Overbeck-Mau, *Pompeji*

Pauly, August Friedrich von. *Pauly's Real-encyclopädie der Classischen Altertumswissenschaft in Alphabetischer Ordnung.* 2d ed. Stuttgart: Metzler, 1864.

    Pauly, *RE*

Perrot, Georges, and Charles Chipiez. *Histoire de l'Art dans l'Antiquite.* Paris: Hatchette et Cie, 1882- [10 vols. by the time its publication was completed].

    Perrot, *Histoire de l'Art*

Pfleiderer, Otto. *Das Urchristentum, seine Schriften und Lehren in geschichtlichen Zusammenhang.* Berlin: G. Reimer, 1887.

    Pfleiderer, *Urchristentum*

Philo of Alexandria, "*Quis red. div. haer.,*" Pp. 1-141 of vol. 4 of *Philonis Iudaei opera omnia — graece et latine.* Ed. Thomas Mangey. Erlangae: Heyderiana, 1820.

    Philo, "*Quis rerum divinarum heres sit*" (ed. Mangey)

Pietschmann, Richard. *Geschichte der Phönizier.* Allgemeine Geschichte in Einzeldarstellungen, Division 1, section 4, part 2. Berlin: Grote, 1889.

    Pietschmann, *Gesch. der Phönizier*

Pinches, Theophilus G. "A Babylonian Duplicate of Tablets I and II of the Creation Series." *The Babylonian and Oriental Record* 4 (1880) 25-33.

    Pinches, "Creation Series"

————. "A New Version of the Creation Story." *Journal of the Royal Asiatic Society of Great Britain and Ireland* 1891, 393-408, plus two plates.

    Pinches, "Creation Story"

Proceedings of the Society of Biblical Archaeology.

    PSBA

R., D. "Die hebräische Grundlage der Apokalypse." *ZAW* 7 (1887) 167-76.

    D.R., "Hebräische Grundlage"

Rawlinson, H., ed. *The Cuneiform Inscriptions of Western Asia.* 5 vols. London: R. E. Bowler, 1861-84.

    Rawlinson, *CIWA*

Renan, Ernst. *L'Antechrist.* 2nd ed. Histoire des origines des Christianisme, 4. Paris: Michel Levy frères, 1873.

    Renan, *L'Antechrist*

Reuss, Eduard. "Vermischte Anzeigen." *Haller Allgemeine Literatur-Zeitung Intelligenzblat.* September 1837, 520.

    Reuss, "Anzeigen"

Riehm, Eduard. *Handwörterbuch des biblischen Altertums.* 2 vols. Leipzig: Vielhagen & Klasing, 1884.

    Riehm, *Hw*

————. *Die biblische Schöpfungsbericht.* Halle a. S.: E. Strien, 1881.

    Riehm, *Bschöpf*

Roscher, Wilhelm Heinrich, ed. *Ausführliches Lexikon der griechischen und römischen Mythologie.* Leipzig: B. J. Teubner, 1884-1937.

    Roscher, *Lexikon Mythologie*

Ryle, H. E., and M. R. James. *Ψαλμοι Σολομωντος: Psalms of the Pharisees, commonly called the Psalms of Solomon. The text newly revised from all the Mss. Edited, with introduction, English translation, notes, appendix, and indices.* Cambridge: Cambridge University Press, 1891.
    Ryle and James, *Psalms of the Pharisees*

Sabatier, Auguste. *Les origines Litteraires et la Composition de l'Apocalypse de Saint Jean.* Paris: Librairie Fischbacher, 1888.
    Sabatier, *Composition Apocalypse*

Sayce, Archibald Henry, ed. *Lectures on the Origins and Growth of Religion as Illustrated by the Religion of the Ancient Babylonians.* Hibbert Lectures, 1887. London: Williams and Norgate, 1887.
    Sayce, *Hibbert Lecs. 1871*

————. *Records of the Past: Being English Translations of the Ancient Monuments of Egypt and Western Asia.* New Series. London: S. Bagster, 1888.
    Sayce, *Records Past*

Sayce, Francis. "The Babylonian Legend of the Creation of Man." *The Academy,* no. 1055 (23 July, 1892), 77.
    Sayce, "Babyl. Creation Man"

Scaliger, Joseph Juste, ed. *Thesaurus temporum. Eusebii Pamphili Caesareae Palestinae Episcopi Chronicorum canonum omnimodae historiae libri duo, interprete Hieronymo, ex fide vetustissimorum codicum castigati. Item auctores omnes derelicta ab Eusebio, & Hieronymo continuantes.* Leiden: T. Basson, 1605.
    Scaliger, *Thesaurus*

Schleiermacher, Friedrich. *Einleitung ins Neue Testament, aus Schleiermacher's handschriften Nachlasse und nachgeschriebenen Vorgesungen; mit einer Vorrede von Friedrich Lücke.* Ed. Georg Wolde. Part 1, vol. 2 of Schliermacher's Sammtliche Werke. Berlin: G. Reimer, 1845.
    Schliermacher, *Einleitung NT*

Schlottmann, Constantin. "Astarte und Aschera." Pp. 111-15 in vol. 1 of Riehm, *HW.*
    Schlottmann, "Astarte und Aschera"

Schmidt, Paul Wilhelm. *Anmerkungen über die Komposition der Offenbarung Johannis.* Freiburg i. B.: J. C. B. Mohr, 1891.
    Schmidt, *Anmerkungen*

Schmiedel, P. W., H. H. Holtzmann, R. A. Lipsius, and H. von Soden, eds. *Hand-commentar zum Neuen Testament.* 4 vols. Freiburg i. B.: J. C. B. Mohr, 1889-91.
    Schmiedel, *Hand-commentar*

Schoen, Henri. *L'origine de l'Apocalypse de Saint Jean.* Paris: Librairie Fischbacher, 1887.
    Schoene, *Origine Apocalypse*

Schöttgen, Christian. *Horae Hebraicae et Talmudicae in universum Novum Testamentum.* Dresden/Leipzig: Christoph Hekelii b. filium, 1733-42.

    Schöttgen, *Horae Hebraicae*

Schrader, Eberhard. "Assyrien, Assur." Pp. 99-111 of vol. 1 of Riehm, *Hw.*

    Schrader, "Assyrien, Assur"

———. "Dagon." Pp. 250-51 of vol. 1 of Riehm, *Hw.*

    Schrader, "Dagon"

———. "Drache." Pp. 327-28 of vol. 1 of Riehm, *Hw.*

    Schrader, "Drache"

———. "Drache zu Babel." Pp. 328-29 of vol. 1 of Riehm, *Hw.*

    Schrader, "Drache z. Babel"

———. "Die Göttin Ištar als *malkatu* und *šarratu.*" ZA 3 (1888) ca. 353.

    Schrader, "Itar 1"

———. "Die Göttin Ištar als *malkatu* und *šarratu.*" ZA 4 (1889) ca. 74.

    Schrader, "Itar 2"

———. *Die Keilinschriften und das Alte Testament,* 2nd ed. Giessen: J. Ricker, 1883.

    KAT[2]

———. *Keilinschriftliche Bibliothek: Sammlung von Assyrischen und Babylonischen Texten in Umschrift und Übersetzung,* 6 vols. Berlin: Reuther und Teichard, 1889-1915.

    KB

———. "Semitismus und Babylonismus: Zur Frage nach dem Ursprung des Hebraismus." *Jahrbucher für protestantische Theologie* 1 (1875) 117-33.

    Schrader, "Semitismus und Babylonismus"

Schultz, Hermann. *Alttestamentliche Theologie: Die Offenbarungsreligion auf ihr vor Christlichen Entwickelungsstufe.* 4th ed. Göttingen: Vandenhoeck & Ruprecht, 1889.

    Schultz, *ATl Theologie*[4]

Schürer, Emil. *Geschichte des jüdischen Volkes im Zeitalter Jesus Christi,* 2nd ed. Leipzig: J. C. Hinrichs, 1886-90.

    Schürer, *Geschichte*[3]

Siegfried, Carl Gustav Adolf, and Bernhard Stade. *Hebräisches Wörterbuch zum Alten Testament. Mit Zwei Anhängen: I. Lexidion zu den aramäischen Stücken des Alten Testaments. II. Deutsche-Hebräisches Wörterverzeichnis.* Leipzig: Heit, 1893.

    Siegfried-Stade, *WB*

Smend, Rudolf. *Lehrbuch der alttestamentlichen Religionsgeschichte.* Sammlung theologischer Lehrbücher. Freiburg: J. C. B. Mohr, 1893.

    Smend, *Alttest. Religionsgesch.*

————. *Der Prophet Ezechiel.* 2nd ed. Kurzgefasstes exegetisches Handbuch zum Alten Testament, 8. Leipzig: S. Hirzel, 1880.

Smith, *Ezechiel*

Smith, George. *George Smith's Chaldäische Genesis: Keilinschriftlich Berichte über Schöpfung, Sündenfall, Sintfluth, Thurmbau und Nimrod: Nebst vielen anderen Fragmenten ältesten Babylonisch-Assyrischen Schriftthums.* In Hermann Delitzsch, trans. Friedrich Delitzsch, *Nachwort.* Leipzig: Hinrichs, 1876.

Smith-Delitzsch, *Chaldäische Genesis*

Smith, Samuel Alden. *Miscellaneous Texts of the British Museum, with Textual Notes.* Leipzig: Edward Pfeiffer, 1887.

Smith, *Misc. Texts.*

Smith, W. Robertson. "Θαλάτθ in Berossus." *ZA* 6 (1891) 339.

Smith, "Θαλάτθ"

Spitta, Friederich. *Das Offenbarung des Johannes.* Halle: Waisenhaus, 1889.

Spitta, *Offenbarung*

Stade, Bernhard. *Geschichte des Volkes Israel.* Berlin: Grote, 1888.

Stade, *Geschichte*

————. "Das vermeintliche Aramäisch-assyrische Aequivalent der מלכת השמים Jer 7.44." *Zeitschrift für Alttestamentliche Wissenschaft* 6 (1886) 289-339.

Stade, "מלכת השמים"

————. "Weitere bemerkungen zu Micha 4.5." *Zeitschrift für Alttestamentliche Wissenschaft* 3 (1883) 123-32.

Stade, "Micha 4.5"

————. "13. Die vermeintliche 'Königin des Himmels.'" *Zeitschrift für Alttestamentliche Wissenschaft* 6 (1886) 123-32.

Stade, "Königen des Himmels"

Stoll, H. W. "Horos," cols. 2744-2749 of vol. 1 of *Ausführliches Lexikon der Griechischen und Römischen Mythologie.* Ed. W. H. Roscher. Leipzig: Teubner, 1884-90.

Stoll, "Horos"

Strabo, *Geographus.*

Strabo, *Geogr.*

Strong, S. Arthur. "Note on a Fragment of the Adapa Legend." *PSBA,* November 1894, 274-79.

Strong, "Adapa"

Stübe, Rudolf Heinrich Karl. *Jüdisch-babylonische Zaubertexte, herausgegeben und erklärt.* Halle a. S.: J. Krause, 1895.

Stübe, *Zaubertexte*

Sitzungsberichte der Berliner Akademie der Wissenchaften [Sometimes: Sitzungsberichte der Deutschen Akademie der Wissenschaften zu Berlin]

SBAW

Theologische Literaturzeitung.   *ThLitztg*

Theologisch Tijdschrift [Titled: *Teylers Theologisch*   *ThT*
Tijdschrift, published from 1903 to 1911; then became
Nieuw Theologische Tijdschrift from 1912-].

Vischer, Eberhard. *Offenbarung Johannis: Eine jüdische*   Vischer,
Apokalypse in christlicher Bearbeitung . . . mit einen   *Offenbarung*
Nachwort von Adolf Harnack. Texte und
Untersuchungen zur Geschichte der altchristlichen
Literatur, 2.3. Leipzig: J. C. Hinrichs, 1886.

Vita Mosis in Thomas Mangey, ed. *Philonis Iudaei opera*   *Vita Mosis* (ed.
omnia, 2d ed. Erlangen: Libraria Heyderiana, 1820.   Mangey)

Volkmar, Gustav. *Commentar zur Offenbarung Johannes.* Zu-   Volkmar, *Comm.*
rich: Drell, Fussli, 1862.   *Offenbarung Joh.*

Völter, Daniel. *Die Entstehung der Apokalypse.* 2d ed.   Völter, *Entstehung*
Freiburg i. B.: J. C. B. Mohr, 1885.   *der Apokalypse*[2]

———. *Die Offenbarung Johannis: Keine Ursprüngliche*   Völter,
Jüdische Apokalypse: Eine Streitschrift gegende Herrn   *Offenbarung*
Harnack und Vischer. Tübingen: J. J. Heckenhauer,   *Johannes*
1886.   *(Streitschrift)*

———. *Das Problem der Apokalypse nach seinem*   Völter, *Problem*
gegenwärtigen Stande. Freiburg i. B.: J. C. B. Mohr,   *der Apokalypse*
1893.

Wace, Henry, ed. *The Holy Bible according to the Authorized*   Wace, *Apocrypha*
Version (A.D. 1611) with an explanatory and critical
commentary and a revision of the translation: Apocry-
pha. 2 vols. London: J. Murray, 1888.

Weber, Ferdinand Wilhelm. *System der Altsynagogalen*   Weber, *Altsyn.*
Palästinischen Theologie: Aus Targum, Midrasch und   *Theol.*
Talmud. Leipzig: Dörffling & Franke, 1880.

Weiss, Bernhard. *Lehrbuch der biblischen Theologie des*   Weiss, *Biblische.*
Neuen Testaments. 5th ed. Berlin: W. Hertz, 1888.   *Theologie*[5]

———. *Lehrbuch der Einleitung in das Neue Testament.* 2d   Weiss, *Einleitung*[2]
ed. Berlin: W. Hertz, 1889.

Weizsäcker, Carl. *Die Apostolische Zeitalter der Christliche*   Weizsäcker, *Apost.*
Kirche. 2d ed. Freiburg: Mohr, 1892.   *Zeitalter*[2]

————. Reviews of: "1. Weyland, G. J., *Omwerkings — en Compilatie — Hypothesen toegepast of de Apokalypse van Johannes.* Gröningen: Wolters, 1888 (182 S. gr. 8), *Fl.* 1, 50.; 2. Rovers, D. M. A. N., *Apocalypse Studiën.* Leiden: van Doesburgh, 1888 (VII, 126 S. gr. 8); 3. Spitta, Fr., *Die Offenbarung des Johannes.* Halle: Buchh. d. Waisenhauses, 1889 (XII, 587 S., gr. 8) M. 12. — " [sic], *Theologisches Literaturzeitung* 15.19 (20. September 1890), cols. 465-71. — Weizsäcker, "Reviews 1890"

Wellhausen, Julius. *Die Composition des Hexateuchs und der historischen Bücher des Alten Testaments.* 3d ed. Skizzen und Vorarbeiten 2. Berlin: G. Reimer, 1889. — Wellhausen, *Composition*[3]

————. *Pharisäer und die Sadducäer: Eine Untersuchung zur Inneren Jüdischen Geschichte.* Griefswald: L. Bamberg, 1874. — Wellhausen, *Phar. und Sadd.*

————. *Prolegomena zur Geschichte Israel.* 3d ed. Berlin: G. Reimer, 1886. — Wellhausen, *Prolegomena*[3]

Wette, W. M. L. de. *Kurze Erklärung der Offenbarung Johannis.* 2d ed. Leipzig: Hirzel, 1854. — de Wette, *Commentar*[2]

Wettstein, Johann Jakob. *Prolegomena ad Novum Testamentum: Notas adiechit atque appendicem de vetustioribus latinis recensionibus quae in variis codicibus supersunt Ioh. Sal. Semler. Cum quibusdam characterum graecorum et latinorum in libris manuscriptis exemplis.* Halae Magdeburgae: Rangeriana, 1764. — Wettstein, *Prolegomena NT*

Weyland, Gerard Johann. *Omwerkings — en Compilatie — Hypothesen toegepast of de Apokalypse van Johannes.* Gröningen: J. P. Wolters, 1888. — Weyland, *Omwerkings — en Compilatie — Hypothesen*

Wiener Zeitschrift für die Kunde des Morgenlandes — WZKM

Winckler, Hugo. *Alttestamentliche Untersuchungen.* Leipzig: E. Pfeiffer, 1892. — Winckler, *AT Untersuchungen*

————. "Babyloniens Herrschaft in Mesopotamien und seine Eroberungen in Palästina in zweiten Jahrtausend." Pp. 140-58 in vol. 2 of his *Altorientalischen Forschungen,* 3 vols. in 1 vol. Leipzig: E. Pfeiffer, 1893-1895. — Winckler, *Babylonische Herrschaft*

————. *Geschichte Babyloniens und Assyriologiens.* Völker und Staaten des Alten Orients 1. Leipzig: E. Pfeiffer, 1822.

Winckler, *Gesch. Babyl. und Assyr.*

————, ed. *Keilinschriftliche Textbuch zum Alten Testament.* Leipzig: E. Pfeiffer, 1892.

Winckler, *Keilinschr. Txtbch.*

————. *Die Thontafeln von Tel el-Amarna.* Keilinschriftliche Bibliothek 5. Berlin: Reuter und Reichard, 1896.

Winckler, *Thontafeln*

Winer, Georg Benedikt. *Grammatik des neutestamentlichen Sprachidioms als sichere Grundlage der neutestamentliche Exegese.* 2d ed. Leipzig: F. C. W. Vogel, 1825.

Winer, *Grammatik*

Zahn, Theodor. "Apokalyptische Studien II." *Zeitschrift für kirchliche Wissenschaft* 6 (1885) 572.

Zahn, "Apok. Stud. II"

————. "Apokalyptische Studien III." *Zeitschrift für kirchliche Wissenschaft* 7 (1886) 337ff.

Zahn, "Apok. Stud. III"

Zehnpfund, Rudolf. "Altbabylonische Götter- und Heldensagen, Teil 4: Der Babylonische Weltschöpfungsbericht." *Beilage zur Allgemeine Zeitung* (München) 65, 18 März 1891, 2-3.

Zehnpfund, "Babyl. Welt- schöpf"

Zeitschrift für Assyriologie [und verwandte Gebiete]

ZA

Zeitschrift für Alttestamentliche Wissenschaften.

ZAW

Zeitschrift der Deutschen Morgenländischen Gesellschaft.

ZDMG

Zeitschrift für kirchliche Wissenschaft und kirchliches Leben (10 vols. published, 1880-89)

ZKW

Zeitschrift für Theologie und Kirche.

ZTK

Zeitschrift für wissenschaftliche Theologie.

ZWT

Zimmern, Heinrich. *Das Assyriologie als Hülfwissenschaft für das Studium des Alten Testaments und des Klassischen Altertums.* Königsberg i. Pr.: W. Koch, 1889.

Zimmern, *Assyriologie Hülfwissenschaft*

————. "Ein vorläufiges Wort über babylonische Metrik." *ZA* 8 (1893) 121-24.

Zimmern, "Metrik"

————. "An Old Babylonian Legend from Egypt." *Sunday School Times* (Philadelphia), June 18, 1892, 2-5.

Zimmern, "Bab. Leg. Egypt"

————. "Palästina um das Jahr 1400 v. Chr. nach neuen Quellen." *Zeitschrift der Deutsche Palästina Vereins* 13 (1891) 133-47.

Zimmern, "Jahr 1400"

————. "Zur Frage nach dem Ursprung des Purim-festes." *ZAW* 11 (1891) 157-69.

Zimmern, "Purim-festes"

Zöckler, Otto. *Die Apokryphen des Alten Testaments: Nebst einem Anhang über die Pseudepigraphenliteratur.* Vol. 9 of Kurzgefasster Kommentar zu den heiligen Schriften Alten und Neuen Testamentes so wie zu den Apokryphen, Altes Testament. Munich: Beck, 1891.

Zöckler, *Apokryphen*

Züllig, Friedrich Jakob. *Die Offenbarung Johannis.* 3 vols. Stuttgart: Schwizerbarts, 1834.

Züllig, *Offenbarung Johannis*

Later Works Cited in This Translation

Hanson, Paul D. *The Dawn of Apocalyptic.* Philadelphia: Fortress Press, 1975.

Hanson, *Dawn*

Jerome, "Commentariorum in Danielem libri III (IV)." Vol. 75 of *Corpus Christianorum,* Series Latina. Turnholt: Brepolis, 1964.

Jerome, "Comm. Dan."

Kuenen, Abraham. *Gesammelte Abhandlungen zum Biblischen Wissenschaft von Abraham Kuenen.* Trans. K. Budde. Freiburg i. B. und Leipzig: Mohr-Siebeck, 1894.

Lucian of Samosata, "Ἀλεξάνδρος ἡ Ψευδόμαντις." Pp. 173-233 of vol. 4 of *Lucian with an English Translation.* Ed. and trans. A. M. Harmon, Loeb Classical Library. New York: G. P. Putnam's Sons, 1925.

Lucian, "Ἀλεξάνδρος"

Nock, Arthur Darby. "Alexander of Abonuteichos." *The Classical Quarterly* 22 (1928) 160-62.

Nock, "Abonuteichos"

Poebel, A. "Sumerische Untersuchungen IV." *ZA* 39 (1929) 145-64.

Rose, W. J. "Alexander of Abonuteichos." *The Oxford Classical Dictionary.* Oxford: Clarendon, 1949.

Rose, "Abonuteichos"

Index of Persons Cited

General/Topical Index

Index of Ancient Documents Cited

CPSIA information can be obtained
at www.ICGtesting.com
Printed in the USA
LVHW042352100723
752016LV00001B/30

9 780802 828040